BIB 21130
BAR 227055

N350/ZUC

LORD CHANCELLOR'S
DEPARTMENT
10 FEB 1998
HEADQUARTERS
LIBRARY

# Reform of Civil Procedure

# *Reform of Civil Procedure*

## Essays on 'Access to Justice'

Edited by

A. A. S. ZUCKERMAN

ROSS CRANSTON

CLARENDON PRESS · OXFORD
1995

*Oxford University Press, Walton Street, Oxford* OX2 6DP
*Oxford New York*
*Athens Auckland Bangkok Bombay*
*Calcutta Cape Town Dar es Salaam Delhi*
*Florence Hong Kong Istanbul Karachi*
*Kuala Lumpur Madras Madrid Melbourne*
*Mexico City Nairobi Paris Singapore*
*Taipei Tokyo Toronto*
*and associated companies in*
*Berlin Ibadan*

*Oxford is a trade mark of Oxford University Press*

*Published in the United States*
*by Oxford University Press Inc., New York*

© *The Several Contributors and, in this collection,*
*Adrian Zuckerman & Ross Cranston 1995*

*All rights reserved. No part of this publication may be reproduced, stored in a retrieval system, or transmitted, in any form or by any means, without the prior permission in writing of Oxford University Press. Within the UK, exceptions are allowed in respect of any fair dealing for the purpose of research or private study, or criticism or review, as permitted under the Copyright, Designs and Patents Act, 1988, or in the case of reprographic reproduction in accordance with the terms of the licences issued by the Copyright Licensing Agency. Enquiries concerning reproduction outside these terms and in other countries should be sent to the Rights Department, Oxford University Press, at the address above*

*This book is sold subject to the condition that it shall not, by way of trade or otherwise, be lent, re-sold, hired out or otherwise circulated without the publisher's prior consent in any form of binding or cover other than that in which it is published and without a similar condition including this condition being imposed on the subsequent purchaser*

*British Library Cataloguing in Publication Data*
*Data available*

*Library of Congress Cataloging in Publication Data*
*The reform of civil procedure: essays on 'Access to justice' / edited by A.A.S. Zuckerman, Ross Cranston.*
*p. cm.*
*1. Civil procedure—Great Britain. 2. Justice, Administration of Great Britain. 3. Law reform—Great Britain.*
*I. Zuckerman, A.A.S. II. Cranston, Ross.*
*KD7325.R44 1995 347.41905—dc20 [344.1075] 95-44805*
*ISBN 0–19–826093–8*
*ISBN 0–19–826092–X*

1 3 5 7 9 10 8 6 4 2

*Typeset by Hope Services (Abingdon) Ltd.*
*Printed in Great Britain*
*on acid-free paper by*
*Bookcraft Ltd., Midsomer Norton, Avon*

# *Preface*

The administration of civil justice has been a subject of deep and widespread public concern for many years. Civil litigation is protracted and expensive. The process may be complex and subject to serious delay. The high cost of seeking civil remedies has placed litigation beyond the reach of the very rich and those supported by legal aid. The Treasury has found it progressively harder to meet the ever increasing demands for legal aid funding. Repeated reductions in eligibility for legal aid, designed to save money, have gravely restricted access to justice.

These phenomena are by no means new, nor are they peculiar to the English system of civil justice. But their cumulative effects have grown in seriousness over the last decade or so. In 1985 the Lord Chancellor appointed the Review Body on Civil Justice to seek improvements in the machinery of civil justice. *The Civil Justice Review*, published in 1988, was followed by a good deal of public debate and by some legislation. But the reform process has lost steam.

In 1994 the Lord Chancellor appointed Lord Woolf to consider the system of civil procedure in order:

- to improve access to justice and reduce the cost of litigation;
- to reduce the complexity of the rules and modernize terminology;
- to remove unnecessary distinctions of practice and procedure.

In June 1995, Lord Woolf published his Interim Report to the Lord Chancellor on the civil justice system in England and Wales, under the title *Access to Justice*. The aim of this collection of essays is to discuss this report and to address the wider aspects of reform.

The collection is divided into three parts. The first consists of essays dealing with the strategy adopted by Lord Woolf and the recommendations that he puts forward. The second part aims to provide a wider perspective. The first two essays deal with the way in which similar concerns have been addressed in the United States, while the third contrasts the German method of legal fees with our own. The essays in the third part deal with social and economic aspects of the administration of civil justice.

Accordingly, while the Woolf Report provides the platform for much of the discussion, the object of this collection is more far-reaching. It is to advance the exploration of the various facets of the reform of civil justice.

The book has had to be produced under a strict time constraint, motivated by a desire to bring it out close to the report's publication. The success in doing so is due to the contributors, who produced their essays within two months of the Report's publication, and to the commitment of the

Oxford University Press and, especially, of Richard Hart and Margaret Shade to this project. Lord Woolf has taken a close interest in the enterprise, despite the critical tone of some of the essays, and we are grateful to him for taking the trouble to write the foreword.

AASZ, RC.

*October 1995*

# Foreword

I am now well past the half-way stage of the Inquiry into Access to Justice I am conducting at the request of the Lord Chancellor. An Interim Report was published in July 1995 and it is hoped that during the summer of 1996, the Final Report and the new unified Rules of Procedure will be published. In the intervening period the process of consultation is continuing and a programme for implementing the recommendations which are contained in the Interim Report has started.

During the first stage of the Inquiry I was astonished by the breadth and degree of interest it attracted. This was reflected by the extent of the coverage which the media gave to the Inquiry, the many representations which the Inquiry received and the numbers attending the various public 'road shows' which were held in conjunction with it. The central feature of both the Bar's and the Law Society's 1995 conferences was the Interim Report's recommendations. This demonstrated the importance which the legal profession attached to the Interim Report. The other striking feature of the Inquiry has been the degree of unanimity among the contributors. There has been broad agreement with the conclusions of the Interim Report that there is need for fundamental reform to the civil justice system. There is also agreement that reform should follow the lines recommended in the Report. This is not entirely surprising as the Interim Report had built on the recommendations of both sides of the profession contained in the Heilbron/Hodge report which in its turn had been generally welcomed. The welcome was not only by the profession. It also came from users of the system (including consumers) and the judiciary.

This favourable response to the Interim Report could have lulled the Inquiry into a sense of complacency as to the extent of the work which remained for the second stage of the Inquiry. If this was a danger, it will be removed by the publication of this book. Its two editors, Mr Zuckerman and Professor Cranston, who are to be warmly congratulated on collating the book, have been closely involved in the Inquiry. Professor Cranston is the academic consultant to the Inquiry and Mr Zuckerman provided an insight into an alternative approach to civil litigation founded as to costs on the system in Germany. The editors have drawn together a remarkable collection of essays from distinguished authoritative commentators from this country and abroad. The essays subject a number of the recommendations in the Interim Report to a critical examination. This can only be beneficial for the future of the Inquiry.

The examination is primarily from an academic perspective. It includes three especially valuable contributions from overseas academics. Professor Marcus from the University of California, Professor Issacharoff from the University of Texas and Professor Leipold from the University of Freiburg. The American contributors wisely counsel caution in assuming that case management will provide a universal panacea. This caution is based upon the experience of case management in the U.S. going back 30 years. Professor Leipold gives a more detailed account of the German approach to limiting costs than was possible in the Interim Report.

The other contributors fall into one or more of a number of different categories. There are those who take advantage of the length of this publication (over 450 pages, twice the length of the Interim Report) to provide more information as to the background to the Interim Report. Here the contributions of Professor Cranston and District Judge Greenslade are important. Throughout the Inquiry, I have been concerned as to the lack of research and empirical evidence as to the working of our civil justice system. Professor Cranston gives a detailed account in his essay of the material to which I did have access, largely thanks to his own efforts. District Judge Greenslade describes the approach to the new unified Rules. He is in the ideal position to do this as he is one of my assessors and is personally involved in the preparation of the new Rules.

Professor Hazel Genn, who was also involved in the preparation of the Interim Report, falls within a different category. Her involvement with the Inquiry, which continues, is to direct a survey of costs in the Supreme Court Taxing Office, the preliminary findings of which were published in the Interim Report. In this book she contributes two essays. The first essay gives an insight into the difficulties created by actions based on allegations of medical negligence. The second essay (a joint exercise with Roy Sainsbury) draws attention to the lessons for civil justice which can be drawn from the way individual cases are conducted before administrative tribunals. The contribution on medical negligence litigation is timely since the special problems to which it gives rise will be a subject on which the Inquiry will focus during stage two. The essay on tribunals helpfully draws attention to what can be achieved by the more informal approach by a specialist body. The need to focus on a specialist area is the subject of the essay by Professor Harlow. The area is judicial review. Like many public lawyers Professor Harlow criticizes the procedural exclusivity to which judicial review is subjected at the present time. She invites me not to miss the opportunity of considering during the second stage of the Inquiry the problems which this creates. I am pleased to be able to say that I have accepted this invitation. For this purpose I am assisted by a sub-committee of distinguished members chaired by Mr Justice Brooke, the Chairman of the Law Commission.

A subject which is not examined in detail in the Interim Report, and is the subject of two essays in this book, is legal expenses insurance. I have no doubt that legal expenses insurance is capable of making a contribution to improving access to justice. However, unless we can achieve greater certainty within the system than exists at present, the contribution of legal expenses insurance is likely to remain peripheral.

Section 3 of the book, in addition to the essays of Hazel Genn and Roy Sainsbury and those on legal expenses insurance, contains four other essays which deal with the socio-economic dimensions of civil justice reform in a manner which complements the Interim Report. It is, however, the remaining category of contributions to which I have not yet referred which removes any risk of complacency. These are the contributions which contain express criticisms of the Interim Report.

Many of the essays make the fair comment that if the 60 previous reports to which I refer in the Interim Report have not succeeded what hope is there of my doing better? Is mine a mission impossible? I do not think so. I will of course bear fully in mind the contents of these essays, particularly the critical comments, but despite these comments I am confident that if the whole package which I have recommended is implemented, we will have a civil justice system that offers a much better service to litigants than they have at present.

This is not the place in which to answer in detail the criticisms which I regard as being ill-founded. It is however important that, what I hope will be the many, readers of this book see these criticisms in context. They need to bear in mind that many of the recommendations I make are not commented upon adversely in any of the essays. The greater procedural flexibility, the single set of Rules applying to all courts, the creation of the office of Head of Civil Justice, and the Civil Justice Council, the redeployment of the judiciary and the increased deployment of technology are either not the subject of criticism or are welcomed. It is primarily my expectations of the benefits of case management about which there are reservations. Professor Scott strikes a cautionary note, suggesting that being a recent convert to case flow management, I may be overzealous in its pursuit. However, under my recommendation the vast majority of cases will be dealt with without resorting to hands-on judicial case management. This will only be a part of the multi-track. The vast majority of cases will be dealt with *either* within the small claims jurisdiction (to be increased to £3,000 but not to include personal injury cases), *or* on the fast track. The cases which will be subject to case flow management on the multi-track will be a small minority. Here the case flow management I am recommending is a natural extension to what is already occurring in the parts of the civil justice system which are at present the subject of the least criticism. Users of the Official Referees Court and the Commercial Court are happy with the case management to which they are already subject and they would like to see more case management not less. Appropriate case management is essential if there is to be control over what in the majority of cases is excessive discovery.

As to small claims Professor Baldwin, to whose views I attach particular importance, is worried as to whether the system will be able to cope with the greater demands which the increased jurisdiction will place upon district judges. This is undoubtedly an area which will have to be monitored carefully. However I have had a favourable response to my Report from the Association of District Judges and there is now every likelihood that they will receive increased training and guidance. This will help them to cope with the increased scale of their jurisdictions.

There remains the strong criticism of Professor Zander. Professor Zander and I have agreed to disagree. Readers will have to make their own minds up about his approach. Is Professor Zander grossly underestimating the scale of the problems? Rightly or wrongly, I cannot accept that the views expressed by the Cantley Committee on Personal Injury Litigation in 1979 reflect the standard which would be appropriate either now or in the next century. The Committee took the view that it was reasonable in personal injury litigation for cases to be disposed of within 12 to 24 months after issue of the writ. I do not agree that this should be the standard. Nor do I agree that, because the majority of cases settle, nothing should be done about them so that, for example, they can settle at the door of the court when the maximum expense and delay have occurred. Professor Zander regrets that the Cantley suggestion for a new rule was not implemented. This rule would have required that 'where a case had not been set down for trial 18 months after issue of the proceedings, the plaintiff's solicitors should be required to report on the progress of the case to the court'. This is a rudimentary form of case management. It therefore appears that Professor Zander's objections to my case management proposals are more about the method than the principle. While there is no rule of this sort in the High Court there is a rule already of a rather more draconian effect in the County Court. I refer to Order 17 Rule 11(9) which provides for automatic striking out of proceeding if there is no request for a hearing date within 15 months from the close of pleadings. This rule has been far from popular. I have no doubt that active case management from an early stage is greatly to be preferred to this crude method of control.

I regard it as essential that this book should be read by anyone interested in the reform of civil justice. It is an unprecedented contribution to the subject. I am deeply indebted to the editors and the contributors for this. I will try to ensure that Stage Two of the Inquiry benefits as fully as possible from the contents of this book.

Lord Woolf

*October 1995*

# *Contents*

## I—Procedure



## II—Foreign Perspectives

# 1

# *Caseflow Management in the Trial Court*

I. R. SCOTT*

## A. INTRODUCTION

It is sometimes said that converts are more zealous than those brought up in the faith. Zealots cause alarm, even in the breasts of the devout. They disturb believers by forcing them to re-examine the depths of their own faith; further, they are not easily distinguished from misguided fanatics. It is not disrespectful to say that Lord Woolf is a convert to caseflow management (CFM). His zeal for CFM, exhibited in every chapter of his Interim Report, is strikingly apparent. Indeed, without exaggeration it can be said that CFM is the linch-pin of the whole of the Report. Court control of case progress is the basic principle of CFM. Of all the many proposals put forward none is more important than the recommendation that there should be 'a fundamental transfer in the responsibility for the management of civil litigation from litigants and their legal advisers to the courts'.[1] The author can claim to be one of the faithful, having spent most of his professional life engaged in missionary work, that is, in extolling the virtues of CFM to unbelievers, principally in the form of English and Australian judges, lawyers and court administrators (on the whole, an agreeable bunch of heathens).[2] It is to be expected, therefore, that he should welcome Lord Woolf's commitment to CFM.[3] However, as will become clear in what is said below, the author believes that the implementation of

* Barber Professor of Law, Institute of Judicial Administration, Faculty of Law, University of Birmingham.

[1] *Access to Justice : Interim Report to the Lord Chancellor on the civil justice system in England and Wales (June 1995)* p. 52, hereinafter 'Interim Report'.

[2] It should be said at the outset that throughout his report Lord Woolf routinely uses the expression 'case management' and only speaks of 'caseflow management' very occasionally, e.g. on p. 91. In the judicial administration literature these two expressions are not always used interchangeably.

[3] See e.g. Scott, 'Problems in Court Structures and Processes' 1991 Current Legal Problems 15. In the *Report of the Personal Injuries Litigation Procedure Working Party (Cmnd. 7476, 1979)* (the Cantley Committee) and in the *Report of the Review Body on Civil Justice (Cm 394, 1988)* (at para. 223 et seq.) recommendations concerning case management were made. For an explanation of these and other English sources, see Plotnikoff, 'The Quiet Revolution: English Civil Court Reform and the Introduction of Case Management' 13 J.S.J. 202 (1989).

the ambitious CFM recommendations contained in the Interim Report is likely to prove very difficult indeed and in the event may fall well short of achieving the intended objectives unless certain underlying structural issues are tackled and dealt with properly.

## B. THE ORIGINS OF CASEFLOW MANAGEMENT (CFM)

### 1. Congestion and delay

The origins of the expression 'caseflow management' in the context of the administration of justice can be traced to the American legal scene of the early 1970s. In the previous decade, much was said of the need to find remedies for, on the one hand, court 'congestion' and, on the other, court 'delay', particularly in trial courts.[4] The doctrine of judicial responsibility for 'congestion', rather than for 'delay', was perhaps first publicly advocated in the 1950s by the Pretrial Committee of the Judicial Conference of the United States. The idea was not readily accepted.[5] The mood began to change with the alarming revelations about the state of America's criminal courts arising from the investigations conducted by President Johnson's Commission on Law Enforcement and Adminstration of Justice (appointed in 1965). These revelations threatened the integrity of the judiciary as a whole and it was no longer possible for judges to distance themselves from the organisation and management of the institutions in which they served.[6]

### 2. Master and individual calendars

The active promotion of the doctrine of judicial responsibility for 'congestion' focused attention on the two principal methods of case assignment then extant in U.S. courts; first, the master calendar (or central assignment system) under which cases, as they progressed, were assigned to available judges from time to time according to need, and, secondly, the individual calendar (or individual assignment system) under which cases were assigned

[4] The word 'congestion' was used to describe court backlogs that were avoidable in the sense that it lay in the hands of the court to take remedial action to deal with them. It implied court mismanagement. The word 'delay' was used to describe court backlogs that, from the court's point of view, were unavoidable and it was always understood that a certain amount of delay was necessary and that the reasons for the conditions that cause delay could be either justifiable or unjustifiable.

[5] Friesen, 'Cures for Court Congestion: The State of the Art of Court Delay Reduction' 23 The Judges' Journal No. 1 p. 5 (1984).

[6] The major findings of the Commission were embodied in a general report, *The Challenge of Crime in a Free Society (1967)*. In a section headed 'Court Scheduling, Management and Organisation' it was recommended that courts should 'establish standards for the completion of the various stages of criminal cases'.

to a judge when commenced with that judge retaining the case for all purposes until final disposition.[7] At a federal level, individual judicial calendar control was actively promoted by the Federal Judicial Center (established in 1968) and was accepted in 1969. At a state level, progress was slower despite the persistent advocacy of judicial control by the National Judicial College (established in 1963) but a shift towards individual calendars became noticeable in the early 1970s when it appeared that delays in the federal courts were being reduced whilst, in the state courts, they remained static or increased.

3. The 1973 standards

In America, the expression 'caseflow management' became firmly established in 1973. In that year, the National Advisory Commission on Criminal Justice Standards and Goals published its *Report on Courts*[8] and a study by Maureen Solomon, entitled *Caseflow Management in the Trial Court*, was published as a supporting study with the Report of the American Bar Association Commission on *Standards of Judicial Administration*.[9] According to Solomon, CFM is a goal orientated process and the 'basic principle' is control by the court of the progress of cases. CFM is defined as 'management of the continuum of processes and resources necessary to move a case from filing to disposition'.[10] The emphasis on the management of resources makes this definition of CFM almost indistinguishable from 'court management' in the round. Obviously, 'control by the court' requires the continuous monitoring of the court's caseload and the continual monitoring of the progress of individual cases. According to Solomon, CFM is 'strictly a management process'. It works against a background of existing jurisdictional and procedural rules. However, decisions made within the CFM system can affect the adjudicative and quasi-adjudicative functions of the court. Indeed, the enhancement of the quality of adjudication is a 'realistic and important result of effective caseflow management'.

[7] In the 1960s and early 1970s an enormous amount of ink was spilt on the respective and relative merits of the two systems. It was at this stage that the word 'management' crept in with some authors writing of 'calendar management'. The proponents of judicial responsibility for caseflow tended to favour individual calendar systems because they created a continuing link between a judge and 'his' cases.

[8] Standard 9.4 dealt with caseflow management and began with the statement that 'ultimate responsibility for the management and movement of cases should rest with the judges of the trial court'.

[9] Solomon, *Caseflow Management in the Trial Court, Supporting Studies 2, American Bar Association Commission on Standards of Judicial Administration (1973)*. This study was brought up to date in Solomon & Somerlot, *Case Management in the Trial Court, Now and in the Future (1987)* see further text at n. 23 below. In the mid-1970s, the Federal Judicial Center's District Court Project sought to identify and evaluate (amongst other things) the procedures and techniques for 'case management and processing', see Flanders & Sager, 'Case Management Methods and Delay in Federal District Courts' in *Judicial Administration: Text and Readings (Wheeler & Whitcomb eds., 1977)* p.226.

[10] Clearly, CFM is much broader than, in English legal parlance, 'listing'.

## 4. The NCSC Studies

The striking feature of CFM as described by Solomon is that it envisages judge controlled systems that tackle not only court 'congestion' but also court 'delay'. The importance of the adopting of the broader focus was demonstrated by the results of a number of empirical studies undertaken by the National Centre for State Courts from 1978 onwards.[11]

Much of what was said in the years before the 1980s about the problem of reducing delay was based on the notion that the real difficulty was the lack of court-based resources; lack of judge-power and court-room space was stressed and most of the solutions proposed focused on changes in jurisdiction and procedural reforms designed to improve efficiency. The cures proposed, by what Thomas Church called, the 'old conventional wisdom', were directed 'at the resources, organisation and formal procedures of courts because [it was] . . . assumed that these rule- and court-orientated elements controlled the pace of litigation'.[12] Practising lawyers did much to promote these ideas; the temptation to blame the courts for delays for which they were no more than partly responsible proved irresistible. The NCSC research cast doubt on the postulated link between delay and court resources. It was discovered that it was not uncommon to find that courts with widely differing paces of litigation did not differ markedly in their resource dimensions.[13] It appeared that courts could be relatively speedy despite burdensome caseloads, high trial rates, limited judicial settlement activity and the absence of speedy-trial rules. Conversely, slower courts were frequently found among those with comparatively light caseloads, low trial rates, high judicial settlement activity and the presence of speedy trial rules.

These research results demonstrated that the link between formal procedural rules and lawyer behaviour is weak and drew attention to the importance of studying the informal relationships between all characters involved in the processing of cases and research efforts were directed away from those things that are easily counted (volume of cases, varieties of case-types, numbers of judges and court-rooms) and towards these relationships.[14] In short, attention was shifted from 'the court' to 'the court in its environment'. The ways in which lawyers and others involved in case processing accommodate one another to the detriment of case progress, the ways in

[11] The key NCSC publications of the period were, *Pretrial Delay—A Review and Bibliography (1978)*, *Justice Delayed—The Pace of Litigation in Urban Trial Courts (1978)* and *Managing to Reduce Delay (1980)*. The reports contained an up-beat message: trial court delay is not inevitable. They were enormously influential.

[12] Church, 'The 'Old' and the 'New' Conventional Wisdom of Court Delay' 7 J.S.J 395 (1982).

[13] The same phenomenon was observed in English courts, see Scott, 'Crown Court Productivity' [1980] Crim.L.R. 293.

[14] The phrase 'local legal culture' entered the language of academic judicial administration discourse.

which lawyers determine the priority they should give to cases on their desks, the ways in which lawyers' expectations of what will happen in the development of a case affects their perceptions of what ought to happen (and, therefore, of what is normal, right and just), all became matters for study. This shift in focus had important implications for CFM. It indicated that the distinction between 'congestion' and 'delay' was of limited use and that success in delay reduction did not boil down to a simple choice of individual over master calendaring systems. It added credibility to an enlarged concept of caseflow management and, in particular, to the idea that court 'monitoring' or court 'control' measures, designed for the purpose of regulating dilatory practices, should always be built into CFM systems.

5. Procedural uniformity and caseload diversity 

In the early days, there was a tendency to assume that the principles of CFM could be operationalized in a uniform manner to all cases, regardless of type. This was understandable, for three reasons. First, the discipline was in its infancy and, therefore, prone to oversimplification. Secondly, initially CFM concepts were designed with the problems of superior criminal courts primarily in mind. Thirdly, CFM developed against a background of assumptions about the virtues of uniformity in procedural law.[15]

Court systems are bureaucracies (in the classical sense) and as they grow they acquire bureaucratic characteristics. This is shown, for example, by the way in which work is separated into functional categories.[16] The handling of criminal work is regarded as a separate specialization from the handling of civil work. Further, within civil work, family law work is readily identified as a specialisation and often hived off to separate fora.[17] Early on, within the great bulk of general civil business, American courts distinguished 'complex' and 'routine' cases for the purpose of applying a level of case management appropriate to each. Here we have the origins of what are sometimes called differentiated case management systems (DCM) and the introduction of the word 'tracks' (seized on by Lord Woolf) to distinguish the different procedural routes (or 'routines') through which cases may be channelled.[18]

[15] In America, on the civil side, the throwing off of the shackles of the 'forms of action' and the adoption of the unitary action and uniform rules to be applied to all cases regardless of the relief sought were regarded as important and necessary advances. In England, significant progress towards similar goals was made by less dramatic means.

[16] Friesen, Gallas & Gallas, Managing the Courts (1971) at p. 156.

[17] The extent to which this 'task' specialisation should be mirrored by 'people' specialisation, is one of the perennial judicial administration issues. Roscoe Pound favoured 'generalist' courts consisting of 'specialist' judges.

[18] It may be thought that this grand title over-dignifies a rather obvious concept. In Planet et al, 'Screening and Tracking Civil Cases: Managing Diverse Caseloads in the District of Columbia' 8 J.S.J 338 (1983), the authors report on a differentiated case management system

## 6. The later years

By the time the National Conference of State Trial Judges published their Standards Relating to Court Delay Reduction in 1984 (replacing the 1976 ABA Standards relating to Trial Courts) CFM principles as outlined by Solomon ten years earlier and, in particular, the principle of judicial responsibility for caseflow, were clearly established.[19] In subsequent years, the progress of CFM in the U.S. was rapid. It reached its apotheosis in 1990 with the enactment of legislation requiring improved caseflow management programmes in federal courts.[20] CFM ideas were 'exported', notably to the Canadian and Australian jurisdictions.[21] In England, in recent times, some limited case management schemes have been introduced in individual courts and specialist jurisdictions but there has been no full-blooded commitment to CFM. Now, thanks to Lord Woolf, that is about to change.[22]

During the 20 years that have elapsed since 1973, the principles of CFM, particularly the principle of control by the court, have proved remarkably resilient. In 1987, Solomon and a co-author re-stated the fundamental elements of CFM in the light of experience in the intervening years. They said

put in place in 1978. DCM systems seek to classify proceedings for case management purposes according to sets of criteria that go beyond the mere nature of the cause of action and the more obvious characteristics relevant to case 'weight', see Baake and Solomon, 'Case Differentiation: An Approach to Individualized Case Management' 73 Judicature No. 1 p. 17 (1989).

[19] In these Standards the 'general principle' of caseflow management and delay reduction was stated as follows: 'From the commencement of litigation to its resolution, whether by trial or settlement, any elapsed time other than reasonably required for pleadings, discovery and court events, is unacceptable and should be eliminated. To enable just and efficient resolution of cases, the court, not the lawyers or litigants, should control the pace of litigation. A strong judicial commitment is essential to reducing delay and, once achieved, maintaining a current docket.'

[20] See Plotnikoff, 'Case Control as Social Policy: Civil Case Management Legislation in the United States' 10 C.J.Q. 230 (1991) and Aspen, 'Procedural Reform in United States Courts' 14 C.J.Q. 107 (1995).

[21] In Australia, CFM made its first appearance at the Inaugural Seminar of the Australian Institute of Judicial Administration held in Sydney on August 14, 1982, see Scott, 'Is Court Control the Key to Reduction in Delays?' 57 A.L.J 16 (1983). The adoption of CFM principles was first recommended in that country in the Report of the Victorian Civil Justice Committee (1984) pp. 75–87. For an account of subsequent developments, see Cairns, 'Managing Civil Litigation: An Australian Adaption of an American Experience' 13 C.J.Q. 50 (1994). The application of CFM principles to the work of the Family Court of Australia is extensively discussed in the *Report of the Working Party on the Review of the Family Court (1990)* Chp. 12. Lord Woolf appears to have been strongly influenced by several recent North American and Australian reports including, Access to Justice Advisory Committee, *Access to Justice : An Action Plan (1994)* Chp. 17 (Australia), *Ontario Civil Justice Review (1995)* (Canada) and *Manual for Complex Litigation (3rd ed 1994, FJC)* (America).

[22] In a recent report, published shortly before Lord Woolf's Interim Report, the Law Commission has considered the problem of delays in the handling of applications for judicial review and discussed 'principles relevant to case-load issues', see *Administrative Law: Judicial and Statutory Appeals (Law Com. No. 226, 1994)* para. 2.28 et seq. and Appendix C.

these elements are: (1) judicial commitment and leadership, (2) court consultation with the legal profession, (3) court supervision of case progress, (4) the use of standards and goals, (5) a monitoring information system, (6) listing for credible dates, and (7) strict control of adjournments.[23]

In the judicial administration literature on CFM (which is now vast) and in the documentation supporting the many CFM systems now in place in America and elsewhere these 'fundamental elements', or versions of them, are stated over and over again. They have become the conventional wisdom. Empirical research into the operation of CFM systems has been patchy but, on the whole, the results of research projects have not seriously challenged the validity of the received CFM principles.[24]

## C. 'CASEFLOW' AS 'WORKFLOW'

Writers on management speak of the 'workflow' of organisations; 'case flow' is the judicial administration version of workflow. Courts are seen a formal organisations with an input which is turned into output by processes. Cases form the input, the procedures of the court (including the trial) constitute the processes, and the conclusion of cases by trial or other disposition forms the output. At three key points the 'passive' court has no control.

First, it has no control over 'input demand'. If a party wishes to commence a case the court cannot prevent him from doing so.[25] If a case 'epidemic' develops the court has to grin and bear it.[26] If an interlocutory 'cottage industry' emerges the court has to deal with is as best it can (for example, applications to strike out for want of prosecution, applications to reinstate actions automatically struck out by rule, etc.). Secondly, the court has no control over 'case survival'. Some cases, even those that look fiendishly complicated at the outset, may settle quite quickly. Others will not and will survive for varying and unpredictable periods. Some of these will go to trial and a proportion will settle 'on the steps of the court'. Thirdly, the court has no control, or at best very limited control, over the

[23] See Solomon & Somerlot, *Caseflow Management in the Trial Court: Now and for the Future (1987)*, a study prepared for the ABA, at p. 7.

[24] See Interim Report p. 33.

[25] Very little is known a about 'civil case formulation'. Why is it that, in relation to some civil disputes, but not the majority, one or other of the parties will resort to issuing legal process thereby invoking the jurisdiction of the court? We know that in many cases it is purely a tactical manoeuvre to pressure the opposing party into agreeing a settlement. Sometimes the principal purpose is to gain access to the coercive aspects of the pre-trial process, usually those aspects that force the opponent to make disclosures. Often the purpose is to avoid the effect of limitation statutes.

[26] In England, the courts have made special arrangements for the handling of 'group actions' or 'multi-party actions', for example, the industrial deafness cases, and the Lloyd's litigation. On the whole, such ad hoc arrangements have proved quite successful.

length of trial. As the parties are in control of the case, the number of issues they wish to develop and the number of witnesses the wish to call are matters for them.

When a 'passive' court decides to become an 'active' court and seeks to 'tame' its environment by taking control of its cases through a CFM system it will attempt to gain control over the three key points mentioned above. The prospect of gaining control over input demand is remote.[27] Progress can be made in controlling the length of trials. The ultimate form of control is a rule which restricts the time available for trial hearings to a specific number of hours and minutes. Such a rule has the effect of ensuring that cases are handled on an 'appointments' basis.[28] In many CFM systems, much of the detail goes into attempting to affect the 'survival' rate of cases. The principal objectives are to improve the settlement ratio[29] and to improve the capacity of the court to predict with accuracy case 'fall-out'. The court gains if these objectives can be met. If, in the process, average delays are reduced, that is a bonus.

### D. TRANSPLANTING CFM

Much law reform in common law countries consists of following, at a respectful distance, American innovations. Legal 'transplants' are always tricky. CFM systems that are effective in one jurisdiction may not 'work' in another. (This has been shown to be true even within the U.S.) When foreign proceduralists and judicial administrators look to American CFM systems for inspiration (as Lord Woolf has done) there are a number of points they should bear in mind.

It should be remembered, as has been mentioned already, that CFM systems were initially introduced in America for the purpose of dealing with backlogs in superior criminal courts (felony courts). The management of civil caseloads gives rise to problems that do not exist on the criminal

[27] To an extent the ability to regulate court fees may be used to control input but the effect is likely to be marginal only. Changes in substantive law can increase input demand significantly. Ideally, reforms likely to have this effect should not be implemented until their 'judicial impact' is assessed.

[28] This is quite easily done in appellate courts but is less easily accomplished in trial courts. But on its own it does not completely prevent 'steps of the court' settlements.

[29] The only certain thing that can be said about settlements is that they are highly likely to occur when the parties are confronted with an imminent hearing which will be dispositive of the case. In those circumstances, two conditions are present. First, anxiety caused by the inability to predict with certainty the likely outcome of the case is at its highest; secondly, for the first time both parties know as much about the case as they have ever done and, more to the point, they are in this state of knowledge *simultaneously* (whereas previously, when one side was 'up' on the case the other was not or, at least, was not as well prepared). CFM techniques designed to encourage earlier settlements seek to advance the second of these conditions. This is not easily achieved in jurisdictions where the legal profession is divided.

side.[30] It can be argued that, in designing CFM systems for civil courts, one should be wary in adopting concepts, principles and techniques originally designed for reducing delays in criminal cases. It is not unfair to say that, in America (at least in the early days of CFM) the particular problems involved in managing civil cases and, indeed, in managing misdemeanour courts, were not adequately understood.

A further point to remember is that, when CFM came to the fore in America, the use of pre-trial conferences for the purpose of encouraging settlement of civil cases, though far from universal, was already quite widespread. They were a recognised part of the procedural landscape and judges and lawyers were experienced in working with them. CFM systems could be designed on the assumption that active judicial involvement in the settlement of cases would remain a common procedural activity. But, of course, direct judicial involvement in settlement is not a necessary element of CFM.

Also, the structure of American law as to limitation of actions is significantly different to that found in England and in those jurisdictions that have followed English reforms in this area of the law. CFM systems have to operate against a limitation background. Limitation periods and CFM systems attempt to achieve similar goals and can get in the way of one another. In particular, the efficacy of sanctions within a CFM system can be affected by limitation rules. In American jurisdictions it is not unusual to find that actions have to be brought within a two year limitation period, even personal injury actions can fall into this category, and sometimes one year periods are imposed for particular proceedings (for example, defamation actions). On the other hand, American limitation statutes usually contain 'tolling' provisions which have the effect of suspending the further running of the relevant limitation period from the time when the proceedings are commenced until the proceedings, for one reason or another, cease to be on foot. Possible counterclaims can receive a similar dispensation. Such provisions can have the useful effect of differentiating clearly the impacts of limitation sanctions and CFM sanctions.

It is important to note that, in America, judicial recruitment is very broadly based. Lawyers joining the bench are often thoroughly familiar with managerial systems and technology designed to facilitate work flow in large private law offices, in public law offices, or in government agencies. This familiarity breeds a sympathy for CFM systems and an awareness of

[30] Criminal cases are simpler to manage in the sense that the number of actors and agencies requiring control is quite limited, possibly only (in addition to defendants) the local offices of the District Attorney and the Public Defender, and a small number of private practitioners undertaking criminal defence work. Further, in the great bulk of cases multiple interlocutory proceedings will be rare. In the designing of a CFM system, the incidence of jury trials is an important consideration. A significant feature of the English civil justice system is that jury trials are highly exceptional.

the beneficial and harmful effects of management techniques on professional work that is useful to them in the discharging of the judicial managerial role. Further, it gives an understanding of the ways in which professionals, on the one hand, and administrative and support staff on the other, can work together in fruitful partnership in formal organisations. In other jurisdictions, certainly in England, the level of 'management literacy' of judicial recruits is very low indeed and likely to remain so.

Further, there are some important differences concerning the legal profession. In American jurisdictions the profession is not divided. (It can be argued that the English distinction between barristers and solicitors is an advantage for CFM because it should make it easier to schedule cases.) The 'indemnity' costs rule does not apply and the basis upon which lawyers are remunerated is different. These differences are important because CFM systems have to be alert to the impact of the economics of litigation practice on the way lawyers handle cases. Further, in many American jurisdictions, courts play a limited regulatory and disciplinary role in relation to the legal profession. This bench and bar connection can be used to advantage in obtaining support for, and compliance with, CFM systems.

Finally, it is very important to note that, in America, CFM has grown out of concepts, principles and techniques found, not in the law, but in the world of organisation and management. In particular, courts have been seen, not only constitutionally but also from an organisation and management point of view, as formal organisations which are independent from other branches of government and which administer themselves. In America, judicial administration is judiciary-based and not, as in England, executive-based. Consequently, the judges are in control, not only of the design, implementation and operation of CFM systems, but also of other identifiable court administration functions. In jurisdictions where courts are administered by executive branch officials and staff confusion arises as to what is meant by 'the court' and this creates problems when efforts are made to introduce CFM systems based on American concepts.

## E. LORD WOOLF'S CFM PROPOSALS

Lord Woolf's CFM proposals are part of a package of measures designed to reduce costs and delay in the processing of civil cases. They have to be seen in the context of the mischiefs he identifies and the importance he places upon dealing with each of them.

### 1. Emphasis on 'lawyer induced' delay

It is sometimes said that there is a broad distinction between 'lawyer' induced delay and 'court' induced delay. What is meant by this is that overall delays are the sum of delays which are the fault of the lawyers and their clients and delays which arise from the court's inability to respond promptly to the parties' requests for their services ('court response time'). Figures drawing the distinction are not routinely available in England. However, Lord Woolf does make use of some limited information concerning the delays, on the one hand, between issue and setting down and, on the other, between setting down and trial for cases going to trial in 1994. These figures showed that the average overall delay was 163 weeks for High Court cases in London and 189 weeks for cases proceeding in district registries. The equivalent county court figures were around 80 weeks. Between 75% and 78% of the overall delay consisted of delay before setting down. Lord Woolf comments that these figures 'are unacceptable in relation to the great generality of cases'.[31] In his lordship's view, in the majority of cases the reasons for delay arise from failure to progress the case efficiently, wasting time on peripheral issues or 'procedural skirmishing' to wear down an opponent or to excuse failure to get on with the case.[32]

Lord Woolf is quite blunt about what, in queuing theory terms, would be called the 'capacitation' problems of lawyers who practise in litigation. He says delay is of more benefit to legal advisers than to parties because it allows litigators 'to carry excessive caseloads in which the minimum possible action occurs over the maximum possible timescale'.[33]

### 2. The key recommendation: judicial case management

Lord Woolf states categorically that 'unmanaged adversarial procedure has led to an unacceptable situation'.[34] His lordship recommends that there should be 'a fundamental transfer in the responsibility for the management of civil litigation from litigants and their legal advisers to the courts'.[35] This

[31] Interim Report p. 13.

[32] Ibid. The seriousness of the problem of 'lawyer induced' delay was referred to in the *Final Report of the Royal Commission on Legal Services (Cmnd. 7468, 1979)* in terms that did not bring out the specific criticisms now made by Lord Woolf. The Commission said (para. 22.21): 'One side or the other may have a vested interest in delay and if the conduct of proceedings is left to the parties . . . many opportunities arise to slow them down. Even if there is the will to make progress, it may require considerable drive and determination in some proceedings to achieve the desired pace. Moreover, speed itself is not a criterion of quality. A lawyer's duty is to secure enough time to develop and present his case in the way that is most advantageous to his client.'

[33] Interim Report p. 12. Nowadays, more than ever, lawyers (particularly solicitors) are very conscious of the costs involved in running their practices and in profit margins. As in all other businesses, there is a trade off between volume and price.

[34] Interim Report p. 28.

[35] Interim Report p. 52. Lord Woolf is critical of the Lord Chancellor's failure to implement the court control proposals put forward in 1988 in the *Report of the Review Body on Civil Justice (Cm 394, 1988)* (at para. 223 et seq.). The scheme outlined in that report was broadly similar to that proposed in the *Report of the Personal Injuries Litigation Procedure Working Party (Cmnd. 7476, 1979)* (the Cantley Committee). His lordship believes that this failure has prejudiced the effective working of procedural reforms recommended by the

is a clear acceptance of the 'basic principle' of CFM. He says the introduction of 'judicial case management' is crucial to the programme of change which he recommends. It is necessary (a) for the purposes of achieving his inquiry's 'overall aim' (that is, 'to improve access to justice by reducing inequalities, cost, delay and complexity of civil litigation and to introduce greater certainty as to timescales and costs'[36]), (b) as the means by which many of the 'working objectives' of his 'new approach' to the administration of civil justice through the courts will be achieved,[37] and (c) as the means for achieving his 'specific objectives'.[38]

It is submitted that the key to Lord Woolf's thinking is his view that procedures should be 'substance sensitive'. He says the current system 'applies the same procedures to all cases regardless of financial weight, complexity or importance'. His proposals involve 'the allocation of cases to appropriate tracks for case management and trial by the appropriate level of judge'.[39] It is not necessary here to elaborate on the several 'tracks' proposed (they are explained in Chapters 7 and 8 of the Interim Report) or the types of cases appropriate for each. However, it may be commented that in his 'fast track' proposals Lord Woolf is, in effect, attempting to devise a form of 'summary' as distinct from 'formal' procedure for civil cases. Cases proceeding on this track would be subjected to 'limited' procedures as to the development of the parties' contentions; further, the court time available for trial would be confined to not more than three hours and the costs payable by parties would be restricted to a scale of standard fixed costs.[40]

Review Body and subsequently implemented (see pp. 28–29). It may be noted that, in the Government's response to the recommendations of the Review Body (given on April 6, 1989 in the form of a written answer by the Lord Chancellor to a question by Lord Colwyn), it was stated that the Government intended to give the courts 'a more active role in the management of case progress' but it was also said that 'a full system of court control will take some years to achieve.'

[36] Interim Report p. 26.

[37] Listed on pp. 19–21 of the Interim Report.

[38] Listed on p. 26 of the Interim Report. Lord Woolf picks up lists of 'aims' and 'objectives' and 'principles' (general and specific) rather as a magpie picks up bright objects. In addition to those already mentioned, it may be noted that on p. 28 the objectives stated by the Civil Justice Review Body are listed (for the purpose of making the point that they have not been achieved) and on pp. 2–3 one finds set out the 'basic principles' which should be met by a civil justice system 'so as that it ensures access to justice'. The specific objectives of case management are listed on p. 30, see further below.

[39] Interim Report p. 21.

[40] Interim Report pp. 42–43 & 45. The idea that legal systems should offer at least two forms of adjudicatory procedures for dealing with cases is well-entrenched in both civilian and common law jurisdictions. The 'formal' system is expected to be the paradigm (the best practical system that legal and political thinking can devise and which can be sustained) and the 'summary' system is in derogation of it in significant respects. The departures from the paradigm are justified on the basis that the utilisation of the summary procedure is restricted to the less serious cases (though parties may consent to them). The difficulty arises in devising acceptable derogations from the paradigm, not only in the form of trial, but also in the manner in which the parties are permitted or required to develop their contentions and evidence. English lawyers are familiar with summary judgment and with the summary small

Lord Woolf summarises 'what case management involves' as follows:[41]

Case management for the purposes of this report involves the court taking the ultimate responsibility for progressing litigation along a chosen track for a predetermined period during which it is subjected to selected procedures which culminate in an appropriate form of resolution before a suitably experienced judge. Its overall purpose is to encourage settlement of disputes at the earliest appropriate stage; and, where trial is unavoidable, to ensure that cases proceed as quickly as possible to a final hearing which is itself of strictly limited duration.

According to his lordship, the specific objectives of case management are: (a) achieving an early settlement of the case or issues in the case where this is practical; (b) the diversion of cases to alternative methods for the resolution of the dispute where this is likely to be beneficial; (c) the encouragement of a spirit of co-operation between the parties and the avoidance of unnecessary combativeness which is productive of unnecessary additional expense and delay; (d) the identification and reduction of issues as a basis for appropriate case preparation; and (e) when settlement cannot be achieved by negotiation, progressing cases to trial as speedily and at as little cost as is appropriate.[42]

Lord Woolf says that in his consultations it had appeared that the majority accepted that the courts needed to take a more active role in case management (this was also the experience of the Civil Justice Review Body). However, a minority raised one or more of the following objections: (a) that case management by the courts will increase the cost of litigation, not reduce it; (b) that it is premature to make further changes until the effect of those that have been recently made can be properly assessed; and (c) that there is a lack of reliable research evidence on the effectiveness of case management by the courts. His lordship briefly rebuts these objections.[43]

claims procedure. However, by a process of 'procedural compaction' the separate procedural regimes of the High Court, on the one hand, and the county courts on the other, insofar as they apply to general civil business, have long since ceased to be, respectively, 'formal' and 'summary'. This process was encouraged by the demise of civil juries and the consequence became inevitable as more and more High Court work, previously regarded as not suitable for the county courts, was loaded on to the lower courts.

[41] Interim Report p. 29.

[42] Interim Report p. 30. It is clear that, for Lord Woolf, the principal advantage of CFM is that 'it will facilitate and encourage earlier settlement through earlier identification and determination of issues and tighter timetables' (p. 22). Other measures to encourage settlements include the introduction of plaintiff's offers and a requirements to report on costs at key stages. Lord Woolf does not appear to have been impressed by the arguments put forward by writers who do not believe that courts have a role to play in encouraging parties to settle litigation, e.g. Fiss, 'Against Settlement' 93 Yale L.J. 1073 (1984). However, his lordship does not recommend that judges should be directly involved in 'settlement conferences'. His view is rather that the court controlled CFM system should be designed so that the opportunities for the parties to settle their differences are enhanced.

[43] Interim Report pp. 32–33. Lord Woolf's answer to (a) is that his case management proposals have been designed in such a way 'as to avoid additional expense to the parties unless that expense can be justified by the benefits its produces' (p. 32).

3. 'Courts', 'tiers', 'tracks' and 'management'

Section II of Lord Woolf's interim report is entitled 'Case Management'. The first two chapters in this section, Chapters 5 and 6, are entitled respectively, 'The Need for Case Management'[44] and 'The Approach to Case Management'.[45] In these chapters Lord Woolf sets out in more detail the system of case management proposed and the procedural changes which he believes 'are required to facilitate the effective preparation of cases'. Earlier on in his report, in outlining his major reform proposals[46], Lord Woolf says cases will be managed by 'procedural judges', who will generally be Masters or district judges working in teams with High Court and Circuit judges.[47] For the heavier cases, that is, those 'requiring full hands-on judicial control', the procedural judge may be a High Court or Circuit judge.[48] In all cases where a defence is received the procedural judge will: (a) conduct the initial scrutiny of all cases to allocate them 'to the appropriate management track', (b) conduct the 'case management conference' (a mandatory feature of the multi-track procedure), (c) generally monitor the progress of the case and investigate if parties are failing to comply with timetables or directions, and (d) draw the existence of ADR to parties' attention where this is appropriate or desirable.[49]

It was explained above that Lord Woolf believes that procedures should be 'substance sensitive' and to this end proposes a three-tier system. Rather confusingly, he does not distinguish clearly, on the one hand, matters of jurisdiction and procedure from, on the other, matters pertaining to case management. For his lordship, case management is all. Thus, Chapter 6, which is devoted to the details of his proposed management scheme, begins with a substantial explanation of, and justification for, the three-tier approach[50] and with an account of his proposals relating to 'entry to the court system' and, surprisingly, 'summary judgment'.[51] The allocation of a particular case to a particular 'tier' or 'track' by the procedural judge is, for Lord Woolf, the allocation of the case to and 'appropriate form of management'.[52] In describing each 'track' Lord Woolf gives details of (a) the mechanisms for allocating cases to appropriate tracks (which are, essentially, rules of jurisdiction),[53] (b) the procedures appropriate for cases proceeding in each, and (c) the case management techniques to be used. However, in the exposition of these matters, isues dealt with under (a) and

[44] Interim Report p. 26 et seq.

[45] Interim Report p. 34 et seq.

[46] See Chp. 4.

[47] For further information on 'judicial teams' see Chp. 11 at p. 66 et seq.

[48] Interim Report p. 22.

[49] Ibid an p. 38.

[50] See Interim Report pp. 34–37; much of this is repeated in Chps. 7 & 8.

[51] Interim Report pp. 37–38.

[52] Interim Report p. 38.

[53] For the extent of the fast track and allocation of cases to it, see pp. 41–42, and for comparable information about the multi-track, see p. 48.

(b), on the one hand, are not routinely distinguished from those explained under (c), on the other, with the result that jurisdictional and procedural differentia are presented as mere variations in the case management techniques thought appropriate for identifiably different blocks of litigation. Court systems have always used jurisdictional and procedural rules for allocating cases to different procedural regimes (both within courts and across court boundaries). Lord Woolf has invented some new procedural regimes (the most significant of which is the summary 'fast track' procedure mentioned above) and made the procedural judges, in effect, the gatekeepers and the recruiting sergeants for those regimes.

For Lord Woolf, case management begins with the allocation, by the procedural judge, of a case to an appropriate track (or tier) in accordance with jurisdictional rules. It seems that, to a significant extent, the allocation will be determined by rules in legislative form. However, 'the court' has the ultimate responsibility for the allocation of a case to the appropriate track.[54] The allocation is not necessarily permanent and for good reason it can be subsequently changed. The essence of the tracking system is that it should provide flexible handling for cases which turn out to be more complex than they may initially appear, or which require judicial management at one stage but not at others. Where a case is allocated to the multi-track the procedural judge will have to take a decision as to whether the case requires full hands-on judicial control, more limited judicial case management, or whether it can be dealt with by standard directions on a standard timetable.[55]

Lord Woolf says that in determining what is 'the appropriate form of management' for a case proceeding in a particular track, it is necessary to have regard to: (a) what is needed in order to achieve a just result; (b) the need to achieve that result in a time and at a cost which is reasonable having regard to the nature of the issues involved and the means of the parties; (c) the desirability of the parties being able to conduct the litigation, so far as possible, on fair and equal terms; (d) the wishes of the parties to the litigation; and (e) the need to prevent any one case being conducted in a way that interferes with the resolution of other disputes and wastes the resources of the court.[56]

After considering the papers, the procedural judge will: (a) issue appropriate directions including a timetable appropriate to meet the needs of the particular case; (b) fix a case management conference; (c) if necessary, transfer the action to the appropriate court; and (d) in specialised and complex cases, arrange for the papers to be considered by a judge of the appropriate seniority.[57] As would be expected, the arrangements for the management of cases proceeding in the multi-track are rather more detailed and sophisticated than those that are to apply to cases proceeding in the

[54] Interim Report p. 39. [55] Interim Report p. 38.
[56] Interim Report p. 38–39.

fast track (which is meant to be, after all, a summary procedure).[58] It could be said, that in the endeavour to reduce the costs and the delays in cases allocated to the fast track Lord Woolf is putting his trust primarily in the impact that the limited procedures on offer in that summary procedural regime can be expected to have on the way parties conduct cases (particularly the proposed rules as to fixed costs) with case management techniques such as the monitoring of compliance with timetables and the issuing of any necessary special (as distinct from standard and automatic) directions playing a supporting role. On the other hand, for cases proceeding in the multi-track case management techniques may prove to be the principal engine for reducing delay and costs (particularly the costs associated with delays). In cases allocated to the multi-track the procedural judge will be required to take a decision as to whether the case requires full hands-on judicial control, more limited judicial case management, or whether it can be dealt with by standard directions on a standard timetable.[59]

It is clear that effective judicial case management requires continuity of management. Lord Woolf says that, case by case, management and trial should be by judges of an appropriate level, but who are no more senior than is necessary. Continuity might best be served if cases were assigned to one judge, or perhaps to a judge and a 'paired' procedural judge (as is done in some foreign jurisdictions). However his lordship believes that this would render inflexible and inefficient the 'traditional system of judicial deployment' and would be very difficult to introduce except for specialist lists.[60] In an effort to accommodate the respective claims of continuity and flexibility he recommends that in the larger court centres judges engaged on the management and trial of civil proceedings should work in teams, and that normally a case should be handled only by members of the same team.[61]

Lord Woolf is aware that sophisticated management and information systems are crucial to successful CFM systems. He sees information technology as playing a vital role in this respect.[62] He admits that the intro-

[57] Interim Report p. 39. The detailed arrangements for this are set out in the chapters on the fast track and the multi-track, viz., Chps. 7 & 8.

[58] Lord Woolf says (see pp. 48–51) that, on the multi-track, cases will always be proceeding to a fixed timetable and, initially, to an approximate and subsequently to a fixed date of trial. Case management will usually be provided through at least two 'interlocutory management hearings'. The first will be a case management conference (usually conducted by the procedural judge), to be attended by a counsel or solicitor with responsibility for the conduct of the ease and to be held shortly after the defence is received. The second will be a pre-trial review (normally conducted by the trial judge) at which counsel or solicitor instructed to attend the trial must appear. The lay client, or someone fully authorised to act on his behalf, will be required to attend both hearings. Among the information to be made available on each occasion will be estimates of the amount of costs already incurred by each party and of the costs which will be incurred if the case proceeds to trial.

[59] Interim Report p. 22.

[60] Interim Report p. 40.

[61] As noted above, the subject of 'judicial teams' is dealt with in detail in Chp. 11.

[62] See Interim Report p. 82.

duction of the systems necessary to support CFM and the other court administration reforms he recommends 'will be a very major technical undertaking and will take several years to specify, design, develop and deliver'.[63]

## F. TEN CONCERNS

Lord Woolf's CFM proposals are ambitious, indeed, they may be regarded as 'state of the art'. In England, the notion that the court has a legitimate interest in the control of cases coming before it has gradually taken hold in recent years.[64] However, the idea that the court should be involved in each contested case from beginning to end strikes many as heavy-handed and as an unnecessary interference with 'party control'. Some would prefer a CFM system under which, as a Canadian Report put it, 'the court becomes involved in the general picture of the movement of cases through the court and intervenes in individual cases when delays have reached unacceptable levels or procedural complexities require untangling in order to permit the case to proceed'.[65] Under the former 'comprehensive' approach there is the risk that judicial officers will waste their time 'eye-balling' many cases that would proceed quite satisfactorily without any court intervention at all. Under the latter 'selective' approach (which sees the court as a sheep-dog gently prodding the case 'mob' along) there is the risk that too many cases will slip through the net. Lord Woolf adopts the 'comprehensive' approach but when one looks at the detail of his proposals it is clear that he has tried to recommend a CFM scheme which keeps intervention by the court to a minimum. If the scheme is fully implemented it is likely that it will be operated in a heavy-handed manner initially but, as experience is gained and as the behaviour or judicial officers, court staff and lawyers adjust, a certain amount of streamlining should occur leading to greater efficiency.

In the course of this article several issues relevant to the design and implementation of CFM systems have been raised, at least in passing. The reader will have gathered that the author is enthusiastic about CFM

[63] Interim Report p. 91.

[64] In a flurry of activity, shortly before the appearance of Lord Woolf's Interim Report the heads of the several Divisions of the High Court have issued Practice Directions indicating that the judges now intend to take greater control over case progress; see *Practice Direction (Civil Litigation : Case Management)* [1995] 1 W.L.R. 508, *Practice Direction (Chancery Division : Procedure and Case Management)* [1995] 1 W.L.R. 364, *Practice Direction (Family Proceedings : Case Management)* [1995] 1 W.L.R. 332, and note also *Practice Direction (Jury List : Setting Down)* [1995] 1 W.L.R. 364. Support for 'judicial intervention' was given in *'Civil Justice on Trial—The Case for Change'* Report by the Independent Working Party set up jointly by the General Council of the Bar and the Law Society (Hilary Heilbron Q.C. Chairman) (1993) at paras. 4.8, 4.31–33, 6.2 & 6.13–14.

[65] *Report of the Ontario Courts Inquiry (1987)* (the Zuber Report) para. 7.39.

systems, but not uncritically so. In what follows, ten particular concerns are briefly explained. The author believes that they can all be accommodated within Lord Woolf's scheme provided care is taken in the implementation of his detailed proposals and provided, above all, it is made clear that the judges, and not court administrators under the direct or indirect control of the executive branch of government, are in charge of CFM.

1. Resources

CFM emerged in America at a time when there was great confidence that social problems could be solved (President Johnson's 'Great Society' and all that.) The assumptions were that, once new delivery systems were identified and designed (according to proven organisation and management principles and techniques), the necessary investment in resources would be forthcoming. The fact that the manner is which American courts were funded was being overhauled added to the feeling of economic well-being. The picture is very different today. Nowadays, every effort is made by government to reduce public expenditure. Greater 'value for money' is demanded. In all aspects of the administration of government 'efficiency gains' are expected. 'More' has to be done with 'less'. The reality is that 'justice is rationed'.

In the administration of justice, CFM systems will expose courts that are over-resourced in the sense that they are not using their resources to maximum advantage. In these situations an investment in CFM pays off in the long run. However, CFM systems also expose those courts that are severely under-resourced. Where the resources are insufficient the goals of any CFM system introduced will not be achieved. CFM systems create much additional work for judges and court staff. Extra judge power and administrative support is required. Lord Woolf's CFM proposals appear to have been designed without any serious concern for their resource implications. His terms of reference provided no restraint. There are no serious costings. Despite the fact that his recommendations have received an initial warm response in government circles, there must be serious doubts whether the resources necessary to implement them will be forthcoming.[66]

2. The implementation of CFM

Lord Woolf's proposals contain detail that other jurisdictions with a long-standing commitment to CFM have moved towards over the years in the light of experience. Going from virtually nowhere to a 'state of the art' system is a mighty leap. Lord Woolf does not ignore the fact that the imple-

[66] It is submitted that it would be unwise to place to much confidence in the prospects of the administration of civil justice becoming largely self-financing.

mentation of his recommendations generally, and his CFM proposals in particular, will present great difficulties. Two aspects of this are worth noting; one relates to systems, the other to people.

A comprehensive and reliable management information system (MIS) lies at the heart of successful CFM. The development of such a system is going to take a lot of time and effort. Further, it is going to require expertise which is in very short supply in England, if it exists at all. The risk that serious mistakes will be made, either through ignorance or through the temptation to cut corners, is great. For a 'full blown' CFM system of the type recommended by Lord Woolf, the MIS must be capable of collecting and recording accurate information concerning thousands of cases. It must be able to retrieve and report on individual cases providing judges, court administrators and lawyers with the information they need for the purposes of case management. It must be capable also of giving the court accurate and up-to-date reports on each court's 'case inventory'. Such reports should show at a glance whether the court is meeting its own system management standards (current disposal rates for all classes of business, incidence of adjournments granted, etc.) and they should also offer an analysis of the inventory indicating the 'age' of pending cases and trends in backlogs.[67]

The successful implementation of CFM requires the education of judges, court administrators and court staff, legal practitioners and major court users. In the recent past, the implementation of important changes in the administration of civil justice has been poor. In particular, no real effort was made to alert the legal profession to the effects of the reforms recommended by the Civil Justice Review Body. The result has been increased work for the courts in the form of a torrent of applications for extensions of time for complying with certain court rules. (The implementation of the Children Act 1989 reforms were managed rather better.) The implementation of the CFM reforms proposed by Lord Woolf will place great demands on the agencies that undertake training for judges and court staff. The need to provide CFM education for legal practitioners will have to be taken seriously by the professional bodies.

### 3. The credibility of the court's response

Usually, CFM systems are justified on the ground that they concentrate the minds of parties and bring discipline to legal representatives. However, an equally important justification is that such systems impose discipline on the courts. CFM systems can be seen as agreed and promulgated bargains between, on the one hand, parties and their legal advisers and, on the other,

[67] It should be said in passing that a court's backlog does not consist of all waiting cases but only of those cases which the MIS predicts will not be disposed of within the court's 'proper' delay norms and which, therefore, require prompt remedial action.

judges (of all levels), court administrators and court staff. It is important that the courts should be able to keep their part of the bargain. The courts must have the capacity to respond to the demands made for their services in accordance with the standards and goals of the CFM system. In coming to such a bargain the most important thing the court has to offer is firm dates for hearings (it may be a time-limited hearing, but that is another matter). This puts the court in a powerful 'trading' position because lawyers will be prepared to offer a lot by way of modifications to their own behaviour in return for that facility.

If the courts are not capable of keeping their side of the bargain the CFM system will fall into disrepute. A CFM system will create expectations. It is important that hearings (whether interlocutory or final) should take place when they are scheduled to happen and that they have their intended effect so that 'case churning' is avoided. It is also important that reasonable notice should be given as to where hearings are to be held and that parties and lawyers should not be put to great inconvenience by changes of venue at the eleventh hour.

It is clear that English practitioners are extremely sceptical of the ability of the courts to deliver a quality service within the context of an elaborate CFM system. The experience of family law practitioners with the Children Act time standards is not good. Judges also have their doubts.

### 4. Court consultation with the legal profession

In the CFM literature, the need for the legal profession to be involved in the setting of CFM norms and standards is consistently listed among the fundamental elements. In the past, the relationship between the branches of the legal profession and the court administration division of the Lord Chancellor's Department (now altered to agency status) has been poor, particularly at local level. Recently, court users committees have sprung up and this has brought some improvement (but one hears the criticism that they are merely 'talking shops').[68] However, it is still the case that many members of the legal profession feel that the only way to influence the court service is to throw rocks at it from a safe distance.

If a CFM system is to be regarded as legitimate in the eyes of lawyers they have to feel that they can influence its design and evolution. If it is to be successful the legal practitioners have to be locked into its objectives. This is particularly important in relation to the setting of timescales and system norms and goals. It is important that these should not be simply

[68] The Beeching Commission recommended that Advisory Committees should be established at a circuit level to provide a bridge between the court service and court users of all varieties but this scheme, although provided for by legislation (see Courts Act 1971 s. 30), did not prosper.

plucked out of the air but that they should bear some resemblance to what can be reasonably expected as possible in the short term on a court by court basis and that they should be set in the expectation that they will be improved in the medium term. In short, the judges and the court service on the one hand and the legal profession on the other need to be frank with one another as to what each can expect to deliver. If the judges are in control of CFM there is a real prospect that at court centre level the windows of the court service will be thrown open. If they are not the prospects for the successful implementation of Lord Woolf's CFM are remote. The evidence is that legal practitioners can learn to love CFM and to appreciate the advantages it brings for them. Every effort should be made to encourage this change of heart.

CFM systems are presented as being beneficial to the administration of justice. The support of the practising profession is crucial to the success of CFM. Such support will be readily given in crisis situations, particularly where lawyers face enormous delays before they can get their cases on.[69] But, generally, support will not be immediately forthcoming and the lawyers will have to be won over. On the whole, the judges command the respect of the profession. However, from the profession's point of view, the court service lacks credibility.[70]

## 5. Flexibility and certainty

When one contrasts the administration of justice in England with the legal systems of America, Canada and Australia, one is immediately aware of vast differences in geography and demography. These differences have implications for CFM. Ideally, CFM systems should take account of local conditions and the resource dimensions of the court (for example, the number of judges and extent of other resources, significant caseload characteristics, fluctuations in caseloads, the capacity of the local legal profession, etc.). This means that, within the same jurisdiction, for very good reasons different courts may have CFM systems that differ significantly in their detail. (This

[69] In America, some of the most important procedural innovations have come about in such circumstances (notably, the introduction of court-annexed arbitration systems). In England, lawyers have accepted, almost without demur, radical changes in the procedures and practices of the Commercial Court designed to reduce delays. In fact, they had no real choice. If the Court did not adapt much of the business would have gone elsewhere because the Court has no jurisdictional monopoly.

[70] In the author's view, one of the principal reasons for this is that the service is an integral part of the executive branch of government. Rightly or wrongly, it is seen as being (1) over-bureaucratic and secretive, (2) obsessed with hierarchy and with the need to stay in line with directions 'from above', (3) at a senior level, overly pre-occupied with keeping 'their' Ministers in good order with Parliament, (4) almost wholly concerned with economy and efficiency, (5) inclined to treat judicial officers as problems to be managed rather than as professionals to be served, and (6) insufficiently aware of the importance of identifying and maximising 'justice values'.

has the additional advantage of enabling a certain amount of experimentation.) In jurisdictions where the several courts serve very substantial regional catchment areas which are quite distinct and largely self-contained these differences can be easily tolerated. However, in England, the position is quite different. This is a small, densely populated country with very good communications. Court centres, large and small, exist in close proximity one to another. Lawyers, particularly those practising out of London, and major court users may find themselves dealing routinely with a number of centres. Further, judges, both whole-time and part-time, may find themselves sitting at a number of centres. This will create a demand for standardisation of CFM systems, not only in their operational detail, but also in the way in which they are operated in practice, particularly in the way discretions are exercised. (It may be noted that, already, there is considerable opposition from lawyers to 'local' practice directions.) Consequently, in the implementation of Lord Woolf's proposals tensions are likely to arise between the demand for certainty through standardisation and the operational need for flexibility (for example, to take corrective action to reduce an emerging case backlog at a particular court centre) and innovation. These tensions will create considerable management challenges.

### 6. Cost to parties

Where sophisticated CFM systems are in place, lawyers are required to do work that they did not have to do previously. Further, they have to be ready to work to much shorter deadlines than those to which they were previously accustomed and their capacity to vary deadlines for their own convenience is much restricted. The short point is that successful delay reduction costs money. It is for this reason that delay reductions do not always yield significant reductions in costs. Lawyers who run highly efficient practices and are capable of making these adjustments under CFM will flourish, those who do not and cannot will not. Some law firms may find that certain types of litigation work (particularly work channelled to the 'fast track' under Lord Woolf's proposals and subjected to standard fixed costs) becomes, for them, unprofitable and may be prepared to see it go 'down market'.

It has to be accepted that CFM systems do increase costs unless the system offers trade-offs. Lord Woolf's proposals for the streamlining of procedures (particularly for cases proceeding in the 'fast track') are intended as trade-offs. His lordship also places great faith in the hope that his proposals overall will increase the incidence of early settlements very significantly with a consequent marked reduction in the costs of many cases. Whether or not his proposals have this effect may prove crucial to the success of his whole CFM plan.

7. Sanctions

Looked at in the round, a CFM system may be a 'command' system or a 'consensus' system, or something in between. A command system will tend to be dictatorial and to be larded with sanctions directed at parties and their lawyers and designed to secure compliance with the system. A consensus system will look like a compact between bench and lawyers put together on the basis of 'look, we are all in this together, let's do the best we can'. It will rely heavily on exhortation reinforced through court user group consultation.

Obviously, sanctions are required. But a CFM system that has to rely too much on sanctions is an unhealthy system. In England, procedural sanctions are likely to consist principally of orders for costs and the charging of additional court fees, but sometimes more Draconian measures will be appropriate. Sanctions have to be clear. They have to be effective. They have to be credible. They have to be fair and applied consistently. They have to be proportionate to the transgression. Care has to be taken to ensure that sanctions that may attach to 'bespoke' directions given in a particular case (perhaps by a 'procedural' judge) are congruent with those found in formal court rules (including 'automatic' directions). Sensible distinctions have to be drawn between sanctions imposing penalties to be borne by practitioners personally and those penalising parties, and it has to be remembered that, in a given case, the real party at interest (for example, an insurer) may not be a party on the record. It is important that sanctions can be made to work without creating further work for the courts (through applications to set aside, appeals and reviews etc.). In England, the track record of the courts in enforcing court rules and in granting and enforcing 'unless' orders, 'wasted' costs orders, interlocutory costs orders payable forthwith and other orders affecting case progress is uneven. Further, the response of the courts to applications to strike out for want of prosecution has been erratic and highly technical. On the whole practitioners have been treated tenderly. Furthermore, the long shadow cast by the Limitation Acts has had a distorting effect.[71] Also, the distinction between 'mandatory' and 'directory' rules has become largely a matter of judicial taste.

Lord Woolf and others have spoken of the need to 'change the culture' of lawyering. It is said that litigators should be 'more cooperative' in seeking to settle cases and less 'adversarial' in their attitudes towards one

[71] The Court of Appeal has expressed concern about the number of appeals from the granting or refusing of applications to strike out for want of prosecution, see *Manama Holdings S.A. v. Marubeni Corporation*, June 24, 1994, C.A., unrep. and *Sparrow v. Sovereign Chicken Ltd.*, June 8, 1994, C.A., unrep. In the Sparrow case Sir Thomas Bingham M.R. expressed the hope that the House of Lords might review the relevant authorities. In the Heilbron Report, op cit n. 64, it is recommended that limitation periods should be re-examined for the purposes of reducing delay, see para. 4.7.

another. It is said that a new spirit of cooperation between lawyers will assist in reducing 'interlocutory warfare' and will facilitate greater use of mediation and conciliation as means for dispute resolution.[72] This is an attractive point of view. However, the truth is that the role of the legal representative in litigation is ambivalent and likely to remain so.[73] There is plenty of evidence which suggests that parties are becoming more 'rights assertive' and lawyers more partisan and aggressive in serving their clients. On both sides of the Atlantic there is increasing concern about excessive combative behaviour of litigation lawyers leading, in extreme instances, to serious breakdowns of professional standards and etiquette.[74] It has to be assumed that this trend will not be quickly reversed.

This hardening of professional attitudes strengthens the case for CFM and it shows that careful attention has to be given to the sanctions that should be introduced for the purpose of securing compliance. There is a further point to note. It has to be admitted that, because CFM systems put lawyers under new and increasing pressures, they can add to the level of conflict between lawyers and lead to an increase in the incidence of aggressive 'adversarial' tactics and 'incivility'.[75] The sanction arrangements in a CFM system have to anticipate these consequences and have to be robust enough to deal with them effectively.

## 8. Collapsing procedure into management

Although CFM systems are seen, at least initially, as existing for the purpose of encouraging the proper functioning of settled processes (in the form of procedural rules and court practices), in time such systems have the effect of altering the processes themselves. For example, commonly the implementation of a CFM system exposes a need for 'standardisation' of rules with the result that certain procedures are dropped in favour of others. Also, in the interest of achieving CFM goals, well-known pre-trial procedures are amended in significant ways; for example, discovery is limited

[72] Interim Report p. 30. In the Child & Co. Lecture delivered on March 15, 1995, Lord Alexander Q.C. (former chairman of the Bar Council) raised the question whether lawyers should see themselves as 'healers' or as 'hired guns'.

[73] This is well explained in Simon, 'The Ideology of Advocacy: Procedural Justice and Professional Ethics' 1978 Wis. L. Rev. 29.

[74] For an account of the American response to lawyer 'incivility', see Aspen, 'Procedural Reform in United States Courts' 14 C.J.Q. 107 (1995). In *ZYX Music GmbH v. King* [1995] 3 All E.R. 1 at pp. 11 & 15, Lightman J. expressed concern about the role of solicitors in preparing witness statements subsequently standing as evidence in chief at trial.

[75] It is convenient to note here that CFM systems reduce the control that parties have over their dispute partly for the purpose of disciplining lawyers who represent them. (It also reduces the control that lawyers have customarily had in the handling of cases.) It is said that one of the weaknesses of court-based adjudication, when contrasted with ADR as a dispute resolution mechanism, is that it reduces the control of the parties over 'their' dispute. CFM systems, by further restricting party control, can aggravate this weakness.

(or made wider), pleadings are abolished (or introduced), interrogatories are abolished (or introduced), settlement conferences are introduced or (if they existed already) modified. Further, CFM systems give rise to a tendency to reduce aspects of procedural law to 'mere matters of administration'. Procedures that were previously dealt with in primary legislation or rules of court are handled instead through practice directions, guidelines, or even administrative instructions issued by the court administrator's office.[76] The short point to note is that CFM systems are not benign, they threaten the integrity of procedural law.

Many of the reforms that have been made in procedural law over the years have had as their objectives the reduction of costs and delays. To that extent, procedural reform and the objectives of CFM have been congruent. However, it is submitted that procedure is important and should not be regarded as merely an adjunct to case management.[77] Procedural law should reflect the 'process values', 'procedural rights', and 'principles of natural justice' that form the fulcrum of justice. It is to be expected that judges and court administrators responsible for the effective operation of CFM system will from time to time be frustrated by the ways in which procedural rules can impede case progress. However, it must be appreciated that procedural law is not concerned only with case progress. It has its proper role to play, for example, in facilitating the orderly and deliberate development of the respective contentions of the parties and in revealing the merits of the case and in preserving the subject-matter in dispute.[78] It is an important role and should not be weakened. It needs to be protected from the predatory instincts inherent in CFM systems.

It was explained above, that Lord Woolf adopts a very broad definition of CFM.[79] This is in accordance with the modern trend in CFM thinking which proposes that cases should be channelled into 'tracks' where they will be handled in accordance with the appropriate 'procedural menu' on offer. This approach does encourage the encroachment of CFM techniques on to the preserve of procedural law. It is to be hoped that, in implementing Lord Woolf's proposals, this risk is borne in mind.

76 Such relegation is often justified on the ground that it gives needed flexibility. It has to be expected that court administrators, in the pursuit of CFM goals, will encourage such 'watering down' of procedural rules that impinge on case progress.

77 See Scott, 'Procedural Law and Judicial Administration' 12 J.S.J. 67 (1987). Unfortunately, in England many judges and lawyers tend to regard procedure as nothing more than a mass of technical rules devoid of principle. Some revel in the technicalities, others are impatient with them. Neither fully appreciates the importance of procedure to the proper administration of justice. The fault lies in a failure in formal legal education.

78 Obviously, if procedural rules are not achieving agreed policy objectives they should be reformed. But such corrective action should be taken by amendment to the relevant procedural rules and not by fiddling with the operational details of the CFM system.

79 See text at nn. 41 and 45 above.

## 9. Managerial judging risks

In the U.S., the concept that judges should manage their caseloads has not gone unchallenged. The principal concern has been that there is a risk that the role of judges as impartial adjudicators is likely to be weakened when they are required to participate in CFM systems and to act as 'managerial judges'. This concern has been expressed by judges, practitioners and academic writers.[80] Those who have raised objections have not argued that judges should not be directly involved in the design and operation of CFM systems. The argument has been that such systems should be designed in a manner that preserves the capacity of judges to perform the adjudication function.

On the whole the contention that the overall benefits brought by CFM outweigh any disadvantages in this respect has prevailed. However, it is submitted that the particular objections that have been made to 'managerial judges' should not be lightly dismissed. There is some evidence that, in making his proposals, Lord Woolf has been aware of these objections but perhaps they have not been given the weight they deserve.

One particular concern which has been expressed is that CFM systems require judges to make decisions on important issues before all of the facts are known. Such issues may be relevant, not merely to case progress, but also to the ultimate outcome of the case. One author has argued that, 'to help judges remain impartial' when making such decisions, CFM systems should incorporate rules designed to 'limit the flow of untested information to them'.[81] Obviously, if a judge is heavily involved in the pre-trial development of a case under a CFM system there is a risk that he will receive and act upon information that is not 'filtered by the rules of evidence'; further he may receive information on ex parte hearings.

It has also been argued that CFM systems, by requiring judges to make many decisions in the course of the progress of cases which are better described as 'administrative' or 'managerial', rather than as 'judicial' or 'quasi-judicial', judges are invited to make decisions (mostly in the form of the exercise of discretions) without having to make recourse to established norms or standards and, generally, without being required to give detailed reasons. It is submitted that although this concern is not without significance and must constantly be borne in mind, it is possible to over state it. It is a criticism that could be made of much interlocutory work cur-

[80] See notably, Resnik, 'Managerial Judges' 96 Harv. L.R. 374 (1982) and Elliott, 'Managerial Judging and the Evolution of Procedure' 53 U. of Chic. L. Rev. 306 (1986). The main lines of argument have been summarised in a source readily available to English readers, see Sallmann, 'Observations on Judicial Participation in Caseflow Management' 8 C.J.Q. 129 (1989) at pp. 139–144.

[81] Resnik, 'Managerial Judges and Court Delay: The Unproven Assumptions' 23 The Judges' Journal vol. 23 no. 1 p. 9 (1984) at p. 55.

rently done by judges. Further, by instinct judges (unlike non-judicial administrators) tend to give reasons appropriate to the importance of the decisions being made and there is no reason to believe that this predisposition will desert them when they become more involved in case management. Obviously, some decisions made by the court for case management purposes may be rather more important than others. Under Lord Woolf's proposals, from the point of view of the parties, the initial decision made by a procedural judge to assign a case to a particular 'track' will be crucial and it is important that it should be made in accordance with clear norms and standards relating to the characteristics of the case itself and that factors solely relevant to the convenience of the court should not be determinative.[82]

Another concern which has been expressed is that, through his pre-trial involvement as 'case manager', a judge may develop a bias towards a party or towards his lawyer. It is generally accepted that care has to be taken to ensure that a case is not tried by a judge who previously has learned of matters that ought not to be known to a trial judge.[83] Further, it is also accepted that a party ought to be able to request that a judge should disqualify himself if there is a risk of bias arising for other reasons. This particular concern is directed at the risk that circumstance may arise in which it would be unfair on one party if the pre-trial management of the case continued to lie in the hands of the same judicial officer. Obviously, if judges are expected to have close contact with the pre-trial development of cases under a CFM system the risks of such unfairness arising are increased.

It is also argued that a CFM system will alter judicial behaviour detrimentally because it will cause judges to become overly concerned with meeting the standards and goals of the system and with meeting the timetables laid down either generally or specially for the disposal of cases. Doctors and health service workers, and teachers at all levels of education, can attest to the fact that the introduction of 'performance indicators' affects professional behaviour both for good and for ill. Members of the court service are familiar with the pressures that 'circuit objectives' can impose. It is submitted that this is a very real risk. Its existence provides one of the main reasons for insisting that CFM systems remain under the control of the judges rather than under the control of administrators.

[82] It may be noted that, under existing law, the criteria to be applied by the High Court and the county courts for determining whether a case should be transferred from one level of court at another include 'whether transfer is likely to result in a more speedy trial of the action' but it is specifically provided that no transfer shall be made on the ground of this criterion alone, see High Court and County Courts Jurisdiction Order 1991 art. 7(5)(d).

[83] English procedural rules require that the trial judge should not know of payments into court or of various other matters.

10. What is 'the court'?

It was explained above that Lord Woolf is of the view that there should be a fundamental transfer in the responsibility for management of civil litigation 'from litigants and their legal advisers to the courts'.[84] Accordingly, his lordship has recommended an elaborate and sophisticated CFM scheme. In his Interim Report Lord Woolf uses such expressions as 'court management', 'judicial case management', 'case management' and 'caseflow management' as if they are interchangeable. These expressions are used to convey the intention that 'the court' should administer the CFM system. It is submitted that if it is the case that 'the court' should design, implement and operate a CFM system, with all that that involves, it is important to be clear about what is meant by 'the court' in this context.

In England, the Royal Commission on Assizes and Quarter Sessions was established in 1966 and reported in 1969.[85] In retrospect, the timing was unfortunate. The Commission made some effort to learn from the American experience. However, at that time, CFM principles had not entered upon the American judicial administration scene; consequently, the yield was meagre. The Commission took the view that the judges (particularly the senior ones) should be relieved of such responsibilities as they had for 'running the courts' and that the courts should be administered by the executive branch of government, that is to say, by the Lord Chancellor's Department. It was recommended that key administrative officers in the court service should exercise 'firm managerial control' over all matters affecting the smooth running of the courts other than those that have 'a direct bearing upon the discharge of judicial functions'.[86] The presiding judge system was invented in an attempt to ensure that judicial independence was not eroded by court administration emanating from within the executive branch of government. After 1971, the 'listing' of cases was regarded primarily, if not exclusively, as an administrative function and therefore the responsibility of the civil servants working in the court service and not of the judiciary. Subsequently, as a practical matter there was some retreat from this view, at least in some courts. As a result, doubts remain as to the proper apportionment of responsibility for this aspect of case management.

In other places the author has argued that the Beeching constitutional settlement was misguided and that, as a result, judicial administration in England has foundered. These views, and those of others who happen to agree with the author to a great or lesser extent, need not be repeated here.[87]

[84] See text at n. 27 supra.

[85] Report of the *Royal Commission on Assizes and Quarter5Sessions (Cmnd. 4153, 1969)*.

[86] Ibid para. 256.

[87] See Browne-Wilkinson, 'The Independence of the Judiciary in the 1980s' [1988] P.L. 44 and Scott, 'The Council of Judges in the Supreme Court of England and Rules' [1989] P.L. 379, and sources referred to therein.

However, it is appropriate to point out that the Beeching view of court administration has become a real impediment to progress towards the implementation in England of modern CFM systems. The key to CFM is judicial commitment and control. This concept is not likely to find favour within an executive-based court service (even one with 'next steps' agency status). Lord Woolf does appear to be aware of the problem and it is clear that his recommendations do envisage the judges taking control of CFM. His proposals concerning the role of the 'procedural judge' and of the judicial 'Head of Civil Justice'[88] are important in this respect. It is submitted that it is not sensible to think of one 'side' or the other, the judiciary or the executive, having control. What is needed is a partnership based upon a mutual agreement to get the job done. However, the judges must remain in overall control and they must take their responsibilities seriously in this respect and discharge them properly. The commitment of the senior judges to CFM is crucial to the success of Lord Woolf's proposals.

## G. CONCLUSION

This article began with religion, it ends with politics (not an unknown progression).

The link between disputes and processes for resolving them is not mechanical. It is dynamic. That is to say, an alteration in the processes for handling a dispute can have the effect of altering the dispute itself. The failure to anticipate that the relationship between disputes and processes is dynamic helps to explain why it is that so many procedural reforms do not have their intended effects, or at least have unexpected (and sometimes unwelcome) effects. In his CFM and other proposals, Lord Woolf is recommending wholesale changes in the processes that English courts use. The impact that they will have on the way civil cases develop cannot be accurately predicted. Further, the ways in which parties, and more particularly, litigation lawyers will adjust to this remains to be seen. Their resourcefulness and their capacity, for good reasons and bad, to undermine the best laid plans should not be underestimated.

The aims and objectives of the civil justice system are contradictory in some respects. Attitudes towards the adminstration of civil justice through the courts cluster around two broad views as to the nature of civil proceedings. According to one view, disputes are essentially private matters in which the law and the mechanisms provided by the state for supporting the enforcement or application of law are reluctantly engaged.[89] Dissatisfaction

[88] As to the role of the Head of Civil Justice, see Interim Report p. 58.

[89] This approach was well described, and its virtues fairly expressed, in the *Report of the Personal Injuries Litigation Procedure Working Party (Cmnd. 7476, 1979)* (the Cantley Committee).

with aspects of the practical consequences of this view leads to disapproving caricature designed to highlight its weaknesses for the purpose of emphasising that, although the 'party control' approach to litigation has its merits, the civil justice system should also aim to bring an adjudication to a final conclusion with reasonable promptness and within reasonable limits of cost.[90]

The other view, sometimes regarded as a Continental invention, in its modern form can be traced to the highly influential publications and draft statutes produced at the turn of the century by the Austrian jurist Franz Klein.[91] These works reflected his views on the social function of court proceedings and in particular his idea that every court action constitutes a 'social emergency' which must be ended rapidly by the activity of the judge. He believed that the powers of the judge, like other organs of the state, 'should be placed in the service of the law, the common weal and social peace'. Klein said:[92]

> Court proceedings will become rational and consonant with the modern conception of the state only when legal protection is indeed the provision of government assistance, not just with effect from the passing of judgment, but from the first step in the proceedings onwards.

It is no exaggeration to say that the two broad views spring from different political and legal conceptions (1) of the nature of law (one seeing law as a private enabling and empowering resource and the other as the 'language of the state'), (2) of the role of law in society and, indeed, (3) of the nature of the state itself. These are deep and muddy waters for the judge who believes that his job is to get on with the business of faithfully adjudicating according to law and for the practising lawyer who is seeking to understand caseflow management whilst endeavouring to make a living out of exercising the difficult and socially useful skills of the litigator.

[90] Thus, for example, in *Towli v. Fourth River Property Co. The Times* November 23, 1976, C.A., Templeman L.J. spoke disapprovingly of the view that 'litigation was a game which litigants or their advisers were at liberty to play at their own pace and that the only duty of a judge was to decide a proportion of those few cases which survived to the last round'.

[91] The following is derived from Baur, 'The Active Judge' 15 Law and State 31 (1976).

[92] Quoted in Baur ibid at p. 35.

# 2

# 'The Rational Study of Law': Social Research and Access to Justice

ROSS CRANSTON*

## INTRODUCTION

In an ideal world of making public policy, problems and objectives would be clearly defined, options rigorously canvassed and calculated choices made. In the real world this is a counsel of perfection; rationality must be pursued under severe constraints. Not only does one never start with a blank sheet but resources are limited (time being one of the most important); the problem as opposed to its symptoms may not be immediately identifiable; there are opposing interests which close off certain lines of inquiry and outcome; and values might be contested and a trade off necessary. For these reasons it has been popular to conceptualize public policy making as 'the science of muddling through' rather than as a completely rational process.[1] In this interpretation large policy changes ('big bang') are not typical; rather there is a public policy cycle in which incremental changes are adopted, these giving rise to further demands, this in turn producing more adjustments.[2]

A decade from now it may be possible to analyse whether the Woolf Interim Report, and the changes it brings about to civil procedure, fit a big bang or incremental model of public policy making. Some contemporary commentators see the proposals, in particular for case management, as constituting a radical break with the adversary nature of English civil procedure. Although we will only be in a position to make this judgment sometime in the future, this view does not seem to accord with either long standing procedures (e.g. summary judgment) or procedural developments

* Cassel Professor of Commercial Law, London School of Economics.

[1] C. Lindblom, 'The science of "muddling through" ' (1959) 19 *Public Admin R.* 79.

[2] *ibid.*, p.86. See also C. Lindblom, *The Policy-Making Process*, 2nd ed., Prentice-Hall, Englewood Cliffs, N.J., 1980; *The Intelligence of Democracy*, New York, Free Press, 1965; H. Redner (ed.), *An Heretical Heir of the Enlightenment. Politics and Science in the Work of Charles E. Lindblom*, Boulder, Westview, 1993; M. Bayes, *Incrementalism and Public Policy*, New York, Longman, 1992.

during the more recent past (e.g. case management in the commercial court/by the official referees; the small claims procedure). Nor with its conservative connotations does it do justice to the sense of crisis and need for significant change felt by leading judges, practitioners and court administrators.[3] Moreover, the commentators seem to have overlooked Lord Woolf's own advice that his recommendations be implemented in stages and that the effect of changes be carefully monitored (p.33). Most importantly the critics do not on the whole seem to have any positive proposals, save perhaps pouring more resources into the present system, to overcome the very real problems of cost and delay affecting the administration of civil justice.

One dimension to the formulation and implementation of public policy is the role of social research. However one might conceptualize the process to what extent do the findings of social research feed into policy making? If so do they broaden or limit the range of choices? Is social research taken seriously by policy makers and are their recommendations consistent with it? Are policy changes monitored by social researchers for unintended consequences so that adjustments to redress these can be made? Is social research less necessary with incremental change since knowledge is acquired in doing and large scale change never made by definition?

Almost a hundred years ago Holmes took the view that social research is necessary for the rational study of law.[4] Indeed, it can be argued that in legal policy making social research is especially important because it highlights the run of the mill, rather than the vivid, individual case which lawyers typically use in argument to identify problems and suggest solutions. Yet there is still an uneasy relationship between law and social research. Judicial decision-making in England is largely untouched by social research and even the Law Commission makes only occasional use of it. While the former is perhaps excusable given its focus, the style of reasoning and how information enters the process, the latter is at first glance difficult to fathom.[5] Perhaps one explanation is that the law schools have proved remarkably resistant to using social research and this affects law reform generally. Most forms of legal scholarship are unsociological or

[3] For one of the most elegant: Sir Thomas Bingham, 'The price of justice' (1993–94) 16 *Holdsworth L.R.* 4.

[4] Oliver Wendell Holmes, 'The path of the law' (1897) 10 *Harv.L.R.* 457, 469. ('For the rational study of law the black-letter man may be the man of the present, but the man of the future is the man of statistics and the man of economics').

[5] One recent valuable inquiry, sponsored by the Law Commission, is H. Genn, *Personal Injury Compensation: How much is Enough?*, Law Com. No. 225, 1994. See J. Tanford, 'Law reform by courts, legislatures, and commissions following empirical research on jury instructions' (1991) 25 *Law & Soc.R.* 155.

[6] W. Twining, *Blackstone's Tower: The English Law School*, London, Sweet & Maxwell, 1994, pp.144–5. See also L. Friedman, 'The law and society movement' (1986) 38 *Stan.L.R.* 763.

antisociological.[6] The tone is set by the fashions in contemporary legal theory, which largely eschew social research as a source of understanding and as a guide to law.

In his consideration of 'access to justice', Lord Woolf followed the practice he had used for his prisons inquiry of appointing assessors with a practical knowledge of the field and an academic consultant.[7] As the academic consultant one of my tasks was to assemble the existing body of social research relevant to the Inquiry. Unfortunately civil justice has been a cinderella subject and not a great deal of social research has been done. Recently in the United States four directors of leading research institutions into civil justice called for a systematic collection of data so that reasoned and effective policy could be made.[8] How much worse the position is in this country, although the Civil Justice Review did commission some important studies, and there is some other relevant social research as we shall see.[9] During the course of the Inquiry some limited research was also conducted: in particular reference will be made in this essay to the surveys of clients carried out by two large City law firms (referred to as 'the Client Surveys').[10]

This essay refers to some of the social research which was available to Lord Woolf as he formulated his recommendations. Given the limitations of space it is inevitably selective.[11] It demonstrates that the recommendations of the Inquiry are broadly consistent with the existing social research, such as it is. Another point the essay makes is that Lord Woolf proceeded on a number of fronts and that although case management comprises a central component of his reform package there are other important dimensions to it as well. In addition to what has been described as managerial judging, the essay discusses some other broad themes of the Inquiry—procedural change, simplification and alternative dispute resolution. Let us begin with the first of these.

[7] *Prison Disturbances. Report of an Inquiry by the Rt. Hon. Lord Justice Woolf*, Cm. 1456, 1991.

[8] M. Galanter, B. Garth, D. Hansler & F. Zemans, 'How to improve civil justice policy' (1994) 77 *Judicature* 185.

[9] Civil Justice Review, *Report of the Review Body on Civil Justice*, Cm. 394, 1988, para.349 (hereafter *Civil Justice Review*).

[10] Herbert Smith, *Reform of the Civil Justice System. The Views of UK Corporations*, London, 1995 (41 industrial companies and 20 financial organisations interviewed, sampled from top 400 companies in Times Top 1000); Simmons & Simmons, *A Paper on Lord Woolf's Proposals for the Reform of the Civil Justice System*, London, 1995 (40 clients and contacts, typically in-house lawyers with large organisations).

[11] It is based on chapters 4, 7, 8 and 9 of my *Access to Justice. A Background Report*, unpublished, 1995.

## PROCEDURAL CHANGE

Procedural rules loom large in discussion by lawyers about the cost and efficiency of litigation. Changes in the rules of court are regularly proposed as solutions to these problems. Procedural solutions are sometimes radical, as with Zuckerman's argument for a more truncated form of procedure along the lines of summary judgment.[12] While it cannot be denied that procedural rules have an effect on cost and efficiency, they are part of the equation, a point almost universally acknowledged. Unfortunately we are hampered by the lack of empirical data. For example, there is no systematic evidence that the enhancement to the central philosophy of 'cards on the table' as a result of implementation of the recommendations of the Civil Justice Review has improved the rate of settlement. As Lord Hoffman has said:

> The result of the witness statement rule is that although it may shorten the trial, it increases very considerably the costs which must be incurred before trial and advances the time at which the bulk of those costs must be incurred. In a long trial which goes all the way to judgment, there may be an overall saving in costs. In a case which settles at the door of the court, the costs will have been much higher than if there had been no witness statement rule. It may be that in macro terms, this disadvantage is outweighed by the increase in settlements, but I know of no way to establish whether this is true or not . . . I am not sure that sufficient account has been taken of the cost to the system, both in expense and potential injustice. These are questions which cannot be decided on principle: *they require some empirical research which could confirm the wisdom of the changes but might instead produce some surprising results*[13] (my emphasis).

Responding to a chorus of criticism about the rule for the exchange of witness statements, mentioned by Lord Hoffman, the Interim Report contains recommendations for its modification (chapter 22).

Procedural reform is central to the Woolf Inquiry. The Final Report will contain draft rules for the high court and county court—a new procedural code—as well as recommendations on matters such as the handling of multiparty actions. The Interim Report sets out Lord Woolf's philosophy for the new procedural code (chapter 26) and his recommendations on pleadings and offers to settle (chapters 20, 24). An aspect of procedure which attracts attention in Lord Woolf's Interim Report is discovery (chapter 21). Let me use this to illustrate the interaction in the area of procedural change of empirical evidence and the Inquiry's recommendations.

[12] A. Zuckerman, 'A reform of civil procedure—rationing procedure rather than access to justice' (1995) 22 *J.Law & Soc.* 155.

[13] Sir Leonard Hoffman, 'Changing perspectives on civil litigation' (1993) 56 *MLR* 297, 306.

Traditionally discovery was justified in our system over the civil law jurisdictions which do not permit it on the ground that it enables parties to make a more accurate evaluation of the strengths and weaknesses of a case, with the result that issues are narrowed or cases settled, thereby saving time and costs. Surprise at trial is also supposed to be reduced in that discovery exposes false or misleading evidence. But the arguments about the deleterious effect of modern discovery are well known: it is increasingly common for there to be a lack of cooperation, with parties adopting an adversarial and obstructive manner. It is not uncommon in major cases for the documentation to be enormous; much is unnecessary and irrelevant. The adverse consequences are said to be complicated pleadings, more witnesses and experts, obfuscation of issues, proceedings becoming more labour intensive, and if a settlement is achieved it tends to be after the costs have mounted up.[14] But if these are common arguments it is also said that the problem is not so much discovery as the complexity of modern commercial litigation, modern technology (i.e. the photocopier) and the adversarial system which is not always conducive to a spirit of cooperation.

Unfortunately there is virtually no empirical evidence about discovery in England. It intensive discovery common, or is that a feature of only a small number of cases? How costly is it—not neglecting, of course, indirect costs such as the disruption to a party's business when documents relating to the matter are being rooted out? What of abuse? In making his recommendations, Lord Woolf was obliged to resort to a number of United States studies of the cost of discovery and its effects on delay. (Discovery in some of these studies encompasses oral interrogatories.)

Perhaps the earliest was an empirical study of federal discovery in the early 1960s, based on interviews with lawyers, which found that its supposed benefits did not seem to occur. Lawyers were not less likely to be surprised if they discovered and were surprised more often if their adversaries discovered. The study suggested that while discovery might reduce surprise due to evidence, it increased it due to the new ideas inspired by the discovered facts. As to the supposed benefit of providing evidence for trial, the study found that while discovery did lead lawyers to new witnesses, evidence and issues, there was no indication that this was presented at trial more efficiently and effectively than evidence first found at the trial itself. Finally, the study did not find any positive evidence that discovery led to a narrowing of issues, more concessions or more settlements.[15]

More recently, the Federal Judicial Center conducted two major studies

[14] e.g. Report by the Independent Working Party set up jointly by the General Council of the Bar and the Law Society, *Civil Justice on Trial—The Case for Change*, June 1993, paras.5.1–5.3 [hereafter Heilbron-Hodge Report].

[15] W.A. Glaser, *Pretrial Discovery and the Adversary System*, New York, Russell Sage, 1968.

of discovery in the federal courts. The first involved an analysis of discovery in 3000 terminated cases in six federal district courts. In more than half the cases there was no discovery at all, and in fewer than 5 per cent of the cases were there more than ten requests for discovery. If 'abuse' is defined as attempting to swamp an opponent with discovery requests, there seemed little evidence of abuse. However, the report cautioned that it was possible for a single discovery request to be abusive, as it was possible for many requests to be appropriate, relevant, and facilitative in the just disposition of a particular case. Another finding of the report was that where courts exercised tight control over discovery by imposing time limits, this shortened overall disposition time without impairing discovery rights.[16]

The second study by the Federal Judicial Center involved the detailed examination of 23 instances of 'abuse' of discovery rules, which interviews with a large number of lawyers had uncovered. Over-discovery problems seemed to be inherent in certain types of substantive claims, those which were large and complex (e.g. medical malpractice, antitrust cases). The report cautioned against the view that a change of the rules could solve all discovery problems, because rules cannot prevent factors such as different lawyer styles, relative law firm size, acrimony, motives for litigation and the relative resources of the parties. Nonetheless, it thought that the best short-term solution to discovery problems lay in greater judicial control, as appropriate to the case, by means of an early directions hearing.[17]

An influential study funded by the American Bar Foundation conducted with a sample of Chicago lawyers argues that the world of discovery is not monolithic.[18] In smaller cases discovery was not a consumer of time, but was straightforward and not greatly encumbered by friction or evasion.[19]

[16] P. Connolly, E. Holleman & M. Kuhlman, *Judicial Controls and the Civil Litigative Process: Discovery*, Washington, Federal Judicial Center, 1978. In a Californian experiment time limits for discovery were not as effective in reducing overall times as eliminating interrogatories: S. Weller, J. Ruhnka & J. Martin, 'American experiments for reducing civil trial costs and delays' (1982) 1 *Civil Justice Quarterly* 151.

[17] J. Ebersole & B. Burke, *Discovery Problems in Civil Cases*, Washington, Federal Judicial Center, 1980. The influential Brookings Institution Report, *Justice for All*, was not based directly on research. It overwhelmingly favoured increasing the role of judges as case managers to monitor and limit discovery. The task force recommended that guidelines be set for the completion of discovery—the deadlines might be for simple cases, 50–100 days; for standard cases, 100–200 days; and for complex cases, 6–18 months (possibly phased for different stages of discovery): see R. Litan, et al., *Justice for All: Reducing Costs and Delay in Civil Litigation*, 1989.

[18] W. D. Brazil, 'Views from the front lines: observations by Chicago lawyers about the system of civil discovery' [1980] *A.B.F.Res.J.* 217; *ibid.*, 'Civil Discovery: lawyers' views of its effectiveness, its principal problems and abuses' [1980] *A.B.F.Res.J.* 787; *ibid.*, 'Improving judicial controls over the pretrial development of civil actions' [1981] *A.B.F.Res.J.* 875. For an Australian study replicating this research: B. Cairns, *The Use of Discovery and Interrogatories in Civil Litigation*, Australian Institute of Judicial Administration, 1990.

[19] The very large Wisconsin Civil Litigation Project, funded by the US Department of Justice, found that there was no discovery at all in 37% of the cases it sampled. In the major-

With larger cases, however, there were many problems in the views of the lawyers interviewed. Delay was used as a tactic and there was over discovery and over production. Many lawyers believed that the expense was often disproportionate to the benefits. Indeed in fifty per cent of the large cases at least one party believed at the end of the day that it still knew something of significance which the other party didn't. Accusations were also made of abuse. The problem with discovery in larger cases was attributed to lawyers failing to think through a case before entering discovery and because judges were inhospitable or superficial in handling discovery disputes.

As evidenced by the Heilbron-Hodge Report, and confirmed by submissions to the Inquiry, there is a widespread view in the profession in England that discovery is over-used, costly and leads to delay. But while the United States research lends some support for these views, it is only in particular cases: discovery is not a problem in the great majority of small and average cases. Too often in England the issue is looked at through the lens of the larger, commercial case. The recommendations of numerous reports in the United States—not all backed by empirical study—are based on the premise that discovery needs control. These recommendations include beginning discovery early, imposing judicial controls on the amount of discovery, establishing separate discovery 'tracks' for cases of different complexity, and imposing judicial sanctions to enforce orders and to control discovery abuses. 'Discovery events' have been limited in several federal judicial districts in the United States.

With all this as background Lord Woolf decided that reform was in order, although not for certain classes of cases where discovery was not perceived of as a problem (e.g. running down cases). For the fast track cases, discovery will be limited. This is consistent with the evidence that in these cases discovery is (a) limited at present and; (b) in the main not a problem. With larger cases discovery is to be under the control of the procedural judge, who in any particular case is to conduct a cost-benefit analysis of the value of going beyond limited to detailed discovery. This is consistent with the rather sceptical light which some of the American research throws on the value of discovery, while recognising that because of the cultural belief that discovery contributes to just outcomes it cannot be abolished altogether.[20] It is also consistent with the Client Surveys, which found a majority opinion that discovery is too burdensome.[21] If

ity of cases where there was discovery it took less than 20% of the time spent on the case: D. Trubek et al., *Civil Litigation Research Project Final Report*, University of Wisconsin Madison Law School, Part B (1983), pp.III 358–60, Part C (1987), pp.119, 132–134, 321–322.

[20] A recent US study suggests that in medical negligence cases discovery is conducive to just results: it examined internal hospital record data on thirteen years of medical malpractice cases against one hospital: H. Farber & M White, 'Medical malpractice: an empirical examination of the litigation process' (1991) 22 *RAND J.Econ.* 199.

[21] Herbert Smith, pp.25–28; Simmons & Simmons, pp.5–6.

greater judicial control is one solution to the problems associated with discovery, another lies in the hands of practitioners and their clients. Whether as Lord Woolf desires the culture will change is another matter.

## MANAGERIAL JUDGING

At the outset of his Interim Report, Lord Woolf develops his ideas for greater court control of litigation. The courts through new mechanisms and the work of the procedural judges will decide what procedure is suitable for each case, set realistic timetables and ensure compliance. The objective will be to define the issues and to encourage the settlement of cases at the earliest stage. A less combative approach will be required of the parties and those who do not behave reasonably will be penalised. If settlement is not achieved court control will ensure that a case is tried as quickly and economically as can be.[22]

This aspect of the Interim Report conforms in its broad thrust to the modern trend in judicial administration, towards greater court control as the way to reduce delay and possibly costs. There is also the widely held assumption that court control relates to greater access to justice.[23] The key element is said to be early and continuous judicial control of cases by contrast with the traditional laissez-faire approach of the adversarial system. The belief is that although a court should be prepared to reach a reasonable accommodation with lawyers, they should be wary about allowing lawyers to breach orders made. In other words, the court should create among lawyers the expectation that events will occur as ordered and when scheduled. Essential for greater court control is the routine collection of statistics and the constant monitoring of case progress.

Court control as envisaged in the modern judicial administration literature already exists in a form in the Commercial Court, in business before the Official Referees, and with multi-party actions.[24] Outside these three areas attempts at court control in England seem to have floundered. The Evershed Committee advocated court intervention by means of a 'robust' summons for directions whereby the Master would consider the state of the pleadings, any outstanding orders that were required, and then give directions to enable the case to be set down for trial.[25] The scheme was a failure:

[22] These are of course the bare bones of the case management approach: see *Interim Report*, section II.

[23] e.g. Access to Justice Advisory Committee, *Access to Justice*, Commonwealth of Australia, 1994, para.17.6

[24] N. Armstrong, *A Question of Priorities: Court Management of Civil Litigation in England and Wales*, Ph.D. thesis, Nottingham Trent University 1995, ch 1.

[25] *Final Report of the Committee on Supreme Court Practice and Procedure*, Cmnd. 8878, 1953, pp.70–83.

Without any serious commitment to provide the considerable amount of sub-judicial time required to make it effective, and lacking the sanctions needed to persuade the parties to complete their preparations at an earlier stage, the summons remained a perfunctory effort. It usually involved a few minutes hearing time attended by junior clerks, with no real knowledge of the case, and whose only interest lay in obtaining a few stock directions, often including an Order for discovery which had not previously taken place, and permission to set down the case for trial. Thereafter the proceedings would often go to sleep for a considerable time before the case entered the Warned List and the parties began to negotiate frantically to achieve a settlement forced on them by lack of previous preparation.[26]

Despite past failures there is now a strong head wind in favour of greater court control. In one study about 140, mainly barristers, responded to questionnaires about their experience with the Commercial Court, the Official Referees or in multi-party actions. 98% of respondents agreed that timetables reduced delay with the use of fixed dates for trial being particularly useful. Over 90% thought that timetables should be formulated as early as possible, and the need for strict enforcement of timetables was mentioned by many. However, a majority thought that the best method of devising a timetable was by party agreement, followed by court scrutiny. Importantly, respondents were divided as to whether 'contact time' with the court would be reduced by the use of timetabling. Almost three quarters of respondents thought that the court could play a useful role in defining the issues.[27] Similarly, the Client Surveys found widespread support for court control. Giving control of the timetable to specially appointed procedural judges and taking it away from parties and their lawyers was an especially popular reform in the Herbert Smith survey.[28] Many respondents in the Simmons & Simmons study supported greater control although some cautioned that the reformed system should not operate to the detriment of justice in the larger or more complex cases.[29]

The philosophy of greater court control through involvement in the interlocutory stages of civil cases is not an uncontroversial matter. The proponents argue that civil litigation can no longer be regarded as a private matter between parties who can conduct it at their own pace. Since the courts are blamed for overall delay in the system, it is said, they must take action to reduce it. Thus the philosophy of court control is said to represent the public interest by improving efficiency. In its most developed form it involves having for each case someone in the court who has responsibility for moving it expeditiously to completion. There must always be a scheduled next date by which certain specified tasks are to be completed,

[26] C. Glasser, 'Civil procedure and the lawyers—the adversary system and the decline of the orality principle' (1993) 56 *MLR* 307, 313. On the summons for directions see also *Civil Justice Review*, para.238–254.

[27] N. Armstrong, 'Perspectives on court management' *New L.J.*, Jan.28, 1994, p.131.

[28] *op.cit.*, p.46.

[29] *op.cit.*, p.12.

and that next date must always be quite short in relation to what the lawyers think is desirable or possible. Efficient court management is an integral part of attacking court delay involving measures such as classifying cases for handling in ways depending on their particular type, and using information to monitor the progress of cases through the pre-trial process. There are other justifications apart from delay reduction which are now being developed: thus proponents of court control are thinking of ways of assessing the improved quality of justice which some argue results.

One of the most powerful critiques of court control is by Professor Judith Resnik in the *Harvard Law Review*.[30] Apart from questioning the empirical basis and arguing that issues of quality are neglected—we return to both these matters below—she argues that court control results in judges having a broad, and uncontrolled discretion since pre-trial conferences are not recorded and the institutional constraints which ordinarily operate, such as appeal, are removed. Parties might capitulate and comply with judicial pressure to settle. Moreover, Professor Resnik contends that no explicit norms guide judges in their decisions about what to demand of litigants; there is consequently a threat to judicial impartiality, especially where judges later try cases which they have attempted to settle.

> In the debate over appropriate responses to the increasingly heavy workload of the federal courts, I am concerned about preserving the uniqueness of the judicial function. . . . Among all of our official decisionmakers, judges—and judges alone—are required to provide reasoned explanations for their decisions. Judges alone are supposed to rule without concern for the interests of particular constituencies. Judges alone are required to act with deliberation—a steady, slow, unhurried task.[31]

These views have not passed unchallenged. Apart from the arguments in favour of court control which have been mentioned, some proponents argue that judges are representatives of litigants and the public and need to act as a check on the practice of lawyers. In fact, it is contended that court control has actually enhanced accountability, not least because it has also generated more management information in the courts.

Various strands of court management can be identified in its home, the United States. The first, case management, is conveniently summarised for the federal judiciary in a document published by the Federal Judicial Center, the education and research arm of the federal judiciary.[32] First is the pre-trial conference, held under Rule 16 of the Federal Rules. The central principle underlying Rule 16 is that a judge or magistrate judge must take charge of a case early on and establish a programme for its resolution.

[30] J. Resnik, 'Managerial Judges' (1982) 96 *Harv.L.R.* 374. It should be noted that Professor Resnik is addressing, in part, the very special US public law litigation where judges have overseen prison reform, busing schemes etc.

[31] *ibid.*, at p.445.

[32] Federal Judicial Center, *The Elements of Case Management*, 1991.

Preferably, that judicial officer will be the judge to whom the case is assigned, although in some courts magistrate judges supervise the pretrial process. (For the latter to work well, it is said, the magistrate judge needs the assigned judge's backing, a point taken on board by Lord Woolf with his notion that judges, including procedural judges, should work in teams.[33]) A conference should be scheduled before the lawyers become bogged down in discovery or motions. The lawyers should be there (not clerks); clients might in some cases appropriately attend. Some conferences are held by telephone to save time and money. Secondly, judges should facilitate early settlement where practical, and thirdly, discovery must be controlled. Fourthly, at the final pretrial conference judges should enquire again about settlement, but in any event ascertain in advance what issues have to be tried and what evidence is necessary.

Differential case management is a second strand of court control. It was given a definite boost by the Brookings Institution study which recommended that it be adopted in all courts. Cases of different complexity are placed on different time tracks of discovery and trial.[34] The Brookings study suggested three tracks: track one to apply to 'simple' or expedited cases, which require little or no judicial intervention prior to trial and can be resolved in fairness to all parties relatively quickly; track two, which applies to complex cases[35] which are characterised by the need for early and intense judicial involvement; and track three which applies to standard cases, which do not fall into the other two categories. This early categorisation of cases is designed to facilitate individual case management so that a case can be moved to disposition with appropriate efficiency. The National Center for State Courts in one of its studies examined differential case management in six demonstration sites for the Department of Justice (only two were civil courts).[36] Unfortunately it was not possible to evaluate on the civil side whether it produced cost savings or benefits which exceeded its costs. Certainly in one of the sites differential case management

[33] *Interim Report*, pp.66–69.

[34] *Justice for All: Reducing Costs and Delay in Civil Litigation*, Brookings Institution, 1989. See also H. Bakke & M. Solomon, 'Case differentiation: an approach to individualized case management' (1989) 73 *Judicature* 18.

[35] At the IXth World Conference on Procedure Law, held in Portugal in 1991, the following were identified as complex cases: major disasters (for example train/plane crashes) or the distribution of defective products resulting in injury to large numbers of people; environmental law disputes regarding major projected or existing projects; insolvency cases involving large numbers of litigants, which are potentially complex; possibly expropriation proceedings; large corporate and commercial disputes in particular instances—for example major corporate crashes, corporate takeovers, shareholder suits: H. Lindblom & G. Watson, 'Complex litigation—a comparative perspective' (1993) 12 *Civil J.Q.* 33.

[36] T. Henderson et al., *Differentiated Case Management. Final Report*, National Center for State Courts, 1990. Differential case management has emigrated from the US; for example, it has been introduced in the New South Wales Supreme Court, the largest of the state jurisdictions in Australia: Practice Note 81 (1994) 32 NSWLR 243.

reduced delay by early disposition of easily disposable cases. At no site was it possible to develop quantitative data on whether it improved use of judge and lawyer time. Regarding participant satisfaction the study found little outright opposition. The presiding judge in the superior court study was able to overcome major problems of compliance by informal contact although compliance is not, as the report notes, approval.

A third strand of court control is the use of case processing time standards. The most well known are those of the American Bar Association: for general civil cases 90% should be disposed of within a year of filing and the remainder within two years (unless there are exceptional circumstances).[37] California, for example, has adopted case processing time standards modelled on the ABA standards pursuant to its Trial Court Delay Reduction Act of 1986. The ABA has also promulgated *Trial Management Standards* (1992) for trials; one aspect is the setting of reasonable time limits (after consultation with counsel) and maintaining momentum once the trial has begun.

What of the empirical point raised by Professor Resnik, that research on its impact means the case for greater court control is empirically unsupported? In summarising the quite considerable body of research I think it can be said that there is *some* evidence that court control expedites cases; its impact on the private cost of litigation is, however, speculation. An early study by the Federal Judicial Center of federal district courts suggested that the success or otherwise of strong case management turned on its appropriateness. While most of the courts it investigated were characterised by strong case management, the differences lay in the relative effectiveness of alternative forms. Moreover, the courts which enforced a comprehensive pretrial order were not necessarily the speediest or the most efficient.[38] The National Center for State Courts has conducted three major research projects into the impact of court management on efficiency. The National Centre for State Courts is, as a body, dedicated to the concept. In the classic study, *Justice Delayed*,[39] the authors found that structural, case load and procedural factors were not associated with the pace of litigation and they advanced their well known theory that the pace of litigation is most strongly associated with the 'local legal culture'. A subsequent study, *Changing Time in Trial Courts*, examined the case processing times in 18 general jurisdiction trial courts located in urban areas. The study found that based only on qualitative observation courts with relatively fast case processing times tended to exhibit some common characteristics, including

[37] American Bar Association, *Standards Relating to Trial Courts*, 1992 edition. See also H. Schwartz & L. Ratliff, 'Delay in state courts: are time standards an answer?' (1986) 70 *Judicature* 124.

[38] S. Flanders, *Case Management and Court Management in United States District Courts*, Federal Judicial Center, 1977.

[39] T. Church et al., *Justice Delayed*, National Center for State Courts, 1978.

leadership, commitment to achieving time goals, and effective communication with the local Bar. In relation to case flow management procedures, the authors write that managing cases 'is clearly much more an art than a science at the present time.'[40]

The most recent study by the National Center for State Courts, *Examining Court Delay*,[41]and its follow-up, [42] analysed data from 39 urban trial courts. The former concluded that two case management characteristics, strict time disposition goals and early court control, were generally associated with courts that featured a faster pace of litigation. The latter also found that case management, especially early court intervention in scheduling case events, was correlated with a faster case processing time. In the latter, more extensive, study, however, stricter time goals displayed only a moderate correlation with a speedier pace of litigation for cases reaching the trial calendar. Yet even the finding about early case control was heavily qualified by the authors, since further analysis found that in relation to the 'typical' civil case, case management had no effect, although it did have an impact on the oldest cases. Moreover, the number of pending cases per judge displayed a stronger association with the pace of contested cases than did the point of court control. The authors conceded that it may have been because early court control was implemented in courts with smaller pending case loads per judge that produced the correlation between early court control and the quicker pace of litigation.[43]

There is also an important study by the American Bar Association, which used 'experimentation' in various jurisdictions to examine how litigation could be expedited.[44] They selected three models: simplification of the pretrial phase, i.e. court control; shortening the time consumed by appeals; and using telephone conferencing in lieu of court appearances whenever feasible. For court control the primary test site was in Kentucky, where combined judicial control and simplified rules were put into effect in late 1980. The study found that as a result of the new procedures, the average time from filing to disposition was reduced from sixteen months to five months, cases involved less discovery and fewer motions, and attorneys spent less time on each case. The study looked at variations of this basic programme

[40] B. Mahoney et al., *Changing Times in Trial Courts*, National Center for State Courts, 1988, p.120. See also W. Hewitt et al., *Courts That Succeed*, National Center for State Courts, 1991.

[41] J. Goerdt et al., *Examining Court Delay*, National Center for State Courts, 1989.

[42] J. Goerdt, et al., *Reexamining the Pace of Litigation in 39 Urban Trial Courts*, National Center for State Courts, 1991.

[43] *ibid*, pp.59, 68. These studies focused mainly on overall disposition times, but a separate study of 1500 trials in nine courts found that court control reduced actual hearing times: D. Sipes, 'The lengths courts go to try a case—and possible remedies' (1988) 12 *State Court Journal* 4.

[44] *Attacking Litigation Costs and Delay. Final Report of the Action Commission to Reduce Court Costs and Delay*, American Bar Association, 1984.

in Vermont, Colorado, and California and found that without both judicial control *and* procedural simplification, programmes did not accomplish as dramatic results. Indeed, judicial control alone could even increase discovery and motion activity. Simplification alone did not reduce delay. Interviews with lawyers and judges found no perceptions that the quality of the litigation process had been adversely affected. In relation to court control the study concluded that the key was a cooperative bench-bar mechanism to locate the points of delay and design programmes. Significantly the ABA study noted the obvious point that reductions in delay through savings in attorney time will not result in a reduction of litigants' costs unless those savings are translated into lower lawyers' fees.

Court management techniques are not confined to the United States. Canadian jurisdictions have adopted them and have conducted some evaluation. A report of the Courts Administration Division of the Ministry of the Attorney General, Ontario, examined the pace of litigation in four pilot courts using case management techniques.[45] In the Windsor and Sault Ste. Marie courts it found a substantial reduction in the pace of litigation after case management was introduced, but there was no strict control group of non-case managed cases. In the Toronto court there was a control group and although the statistics did not provide a sufficiently large base for comparison it seemed that the rate of disposition of the managed cases was significantly higher. The report had no direct evidence as to the impact of case management on clients' costs. However, the report concluded that the cost per file to the court of administering case managed cases was lower than for others. This did not take into account the capital costs and the operating costs of case management, where the report notes that operating the projects necessitated some significant expenditures.

## FACILITATING SETTLEMENT

The movement for greater court control often runs in parallel with that to facilitate more settlements. The first of the ten basic principles of reform set out in the Heilbron-Hodge Report was that the philosophy of litigation should be primarily to encourage early settlement of disputes.[46] Lord Woolf conceives of his proposals for case management as encouraging settlements at the earliest possible stage.[47] And settlement is of course pivotal to the smooth functioning of the legal process. The courts could not cope if there was not a substantial attrition of cases as they passed through the

[45] *Case Flow Management. An Assessment of the Ontario Pilot Projects in the Ontario Court of Justice*, Ministry of the Attorney General, Ontario, 1993, p.4.

[46] *Heilbron-Hodge Report*, para.1.8.

[47] *Interim Report*, p.30.

different stages of litigation.[48] But it would be wrong to draw too strict a line between settlement on the one hand and adjudication on the other. Although a case might not be tried to completion, judicial resources might have been involved. Decisions on interlocutory points might lead the parties to settle and cases might also settle during trial. Settlements also occur, as the American literature puts it, in the shadow of the law. A decision in a particular case might lead to the settlement of a tranche of similar cases.

Recognising its importance, the law facilitates settlement in various ways, such as the protection given to 'without prejudice' communications. The way interest rates are calculated on judgment might also provide an incentive to settle, although much depends on the comparison between that and market rates of interest. Then there are the rules about payment into court, which are designed to facilitate settlement by providing for a costs penalty if plaintiffs obtain less than the amount the defendant pays in. There is a little evidence on the effect of this rule in the Inbucon Report, commissioned by the Civil Justice Review.[49] That costs follow the event in our system is also said to facilitate settlement, possibly unfairly, compared with the American rule that in general each party bears his or her own costs.[50] In fact if a litigant were confident of winning the rule might encourage the pursuit of smaller cases which otherwise it would not be economical to litigate.[51]

Settlement practices vary with a range of factors including the parties involved, the type of case and the attitudes and reputation of the legal representatives. Some cases are more difficult to settle than normal, for example they are test cases. In personal injury litigation a plaintiff's solicitors experienced in the field would generally regard defendants' first offers as too low and expect to initiate litigation before any settlement will be close to what they think a case is worth. Generally, solicitors might not rush into settlement negotiations for fear of giving the impression that their case is shaky. Clients might sometimes determine the pace of settlement. In some areas solicitors might delay matters deliberately in the interests of clients, for example if they are representing a defendant debtor or a person who

[48] Unfortunately there is a lack of data on the number of settlements. Even after cases are initiated it is difficult to identify precisely those which are settled as opposed to withdrawn or otherwise disposed of. Of those cases set down in Queen's Bench it is possible to be more exact: *Judicial Statistics Annual Report*, Cm.2623, 1994, pp.30–31. The Legal Aid Board keeps figures on settlements in the cases it has funded; it notes an increase in settlements in recent years: *Legal Aid Board Annual Report 1993–1994*, HC 435, 1994, pp.56–58.

[49] J. Garrett et al., *Civil Justice Review Study on Personal Injury Litigation*, Inbucon, London, 1986, pp.25–26.

[50] C. Glasser, 'Civil procedure and the lawyers—the adversary system and the decline of the orality principle' (1993) 56 *M.L.R.* 307, 309.

[51] H. Kritzer, *Fee Arrangements and Fee Shifting: Lessons from the Experience in Ontario*, Disputes Processing Research Program, University of Wisconsin-Madison, Working Paper 1983–3. See also N. Rickman, 'The economics of cost shifting rules', in this volume.

wishes a particular contact arrangement with children to continue. The practices of institutional litigants regarding settlement are clearly important. It is said that insurance companies now generally follow a policy of settling cases early, possibly because of the economic advantages of doing so.[52] One complaint is that settlements occur too late in the present process. The criticism is that there are unnecessary delays and that costs are unnecessarily incurred. Moreover, 'when this happens the litigant has to make within minutes a decision which may affect his or her whole life'.[53] The contrary view of late settlements is that if lawyers are to perform their duties to their clients then they must wait until realistic offers are made.[54]

The issue that arises is whether courts should intervene more to promote earlier settlements, and possibly also to facilitate more settlements. There is quite a powerful literature which gives an emphatic no to this question. Its argument is that courts should have nothing to do with settlement because settlement is a negation of the judicial process. This view can be traced back at least 150 years to Bentham. He abhorred compromise as a denial of justice. However equal the parties, he argued, compromise involves a sacrifice of results. In discussing Bentham's views, Professor William Twining says that it seems likely that he 'would have looked with deep suspicion on modern efforts to promote mediation, negotiation or arbitration (especially in private) . . .'.[55] The most notable modern critic is a leading Yale professor, Owen Fiss. In his 'Against Settlement'[56] Fiss attacks what he calls the dispute perspective. Equating this with adjudication is based on a fundamental misunderstanding of the nature of law as well as of judicial institutions. Fiss argues that advocates of the dispute perspective 'act as though courts arose to resolve quarrels between neighbours who had reached an impasse and turned to a stranger for help'.[57] This 'trivialises' adjudication by which courts possess 'power that has been defined and conferred by public law not by private agreement'.[58] Fiss' argument is that the job of courts is not to maximise the ends of private parties but to give force to the public values embodied in law. In the judicial administration perspective, he would argue, the opportunity to articulate legal values gives way to an overemphasis on efficiency and technique, which diminishes the value of law.

The implications of Fiss' argument cannot go unchallenged. Quite apart from anything else there are the practicalities that without settlement the

[52] KPMG Peat Marwick, *Study on Causes of Delay in the High Court and County Courts. Final Report*, London, 1994, p.26.

[53] *Royal Commission on Legal Services*, Cmnd. 7648, 1979, p.300.

[54] It may be that the explanation for settlements at the door of the court is because of the late briefing of barristers, or because plaintiffs at this point might for the first time appreciate what a court hearing involves.

[55] W. Twining, 'Alternative to what? Theories of litigation, procedure and dispute settlement in Anglo-American jurisprudence: some neglected classics' (1993) 67 *M.L.R.* 380.

[56] (1984) 93 *Yale L.J.* 1073.

[57] at p.1082.

[58] *ibid.*, at p.1085.

courts would not be able to handle their case load. Moreover, Fiss' arguments turn partly on the more prominent role which United States courts take in enunciating and applying general public policy and to that extent do not have the same relevance in this country. Professor Menkel-Meadow attempts a balance between Fiss and his critics. After finding wanting the efficiency arguments for settlement, she observes that:

> What settlement offers is a substantive justice that may be more responsive to the parties' needs than adjudication. Settlement can be particularised to the needs of the parties, they can avoid win/lose, binary results, provide richer remedies than the commodification or monetarization of all claims and achieve legitimacy through consent. In addition, settlement offers a different substantive process by allowing participation by the parties as well as the lawyers. Settlement fosters a communication process that can be more direct and less stylised than litigation, and affords greater flexibility of procedure and remedy.[59]

To an extent the issue resolves into an empirical question about the quality of settlements compared with what could be obtained by vindicating rights in a court. Are parties pressured into accepting redress less than their full entitlement? In particular, do the delays associated with formal litigation compel parties to settle and to abandon valid claims and defences? Professor Hazel Genn's *Hard Bargaining* found that hard bargaining did achieve better results. In many cases, however, she found that solicitors were not achieving the best they could for their clients. She attributes this partly to inequalities in power, for example that plaintiffs' solicitors felt that they had to cooperate when they were in a disadvantageous position with insurance company representatives. But partly also it was because of solicitors inexperienced in personal injury work and their approach to negotiations and the preparation of the particular case they were presenting.[60] A similar conclusion derives from ESRC-sponsored research, which thoroughly analysed 80 financial relief cases. The authors say that the system is characterised by settlement but not necessarily by purposeful settlement-seeking, one reason being inactivity on the part of solicitors.[61] The authors are especially critical of the 'settlement culture' among practitioners, necessary they concede because of the huge case-load the latter carry. Settlements in the authors' view are too often the product of fatigue and domination rather than the triumph of a strategic and effective approach.[62]

The Winn Committee considered the idea of formal settlement conferences conducted by the courts. It rejected it on empirical grounds, that the

[59] H.C. Menkel-Meadow, 'For and against settlement: uses and abuses of the mandatory settlement conference' (1985) 33 *UCLA Law Review* 485, 504–505.

[60] H. Genn, *Hard Bargaining*, Clarendon, Oxford, 1987.

[61] G. Davis, S. Cretney & J. Collins, *Simple Quarrels*, Clarendon, Oxford, 1994, p.257.

[62] Echoing Fiss they also say that the courts too have developed methods which ensure that very few trials are held: *ibid.*, p.167.

American evidence did not show clearly that it led to a higher level of settlements, but also because it would delay and increase the cost of litigation as well as putting undesirable pressure on the parties to settle.[63] Likewise the Civil Justice Review, which concluded that its proposals for early exchange of witness statements would increase opportunities for settlement and that pre-trial intervention by judges should be reserved to a pre-trial hearing in the more substantial cases.[64] Yet the idea of settlement conferences has swept important parts of the common law world and they are now an accepted feature in the United States and in some Canadian and Australian jurisdictions. In the United States settlement conferences are part of a whole managerial philosophy, that judges should be actively involved in promoting settlement. (That settlement philosophy is not present to anything like the same degree in Canada and Australia.[65]) The assumption is that more settlements result and in some quarters that settlements produce superior results to trial. Even if cases do not settle, settlement conferences may shorten any hearing by narrowing the issues, eliciting admissions and eliminating non-contested matters. The settlement efforts of judges in the United States are sustained and various, although it would be wrong to think it is intensive in all, or even a majority of cases.[66] Opponents of settlement conferences see any advantages more than counterbalanced by the way in which they might coerce parties into unwanted settlements and generally undermine the adversary system. It is also said by opponents that parties do not receive the same fair hearing which they would otherwise and that cases are resolved away from public view. Settlement conferences are said by the opponents to take time and to involve costs and if judges are involved their impartiality and dignity might be undermined.

Which side of the argument does the empirical evidence about settlement conferences support? Comparing the quality of settlement with adjudication is fraught with difficulties and it should not be surprising that there do not seem to be any studies attempting it. As far as efficiency is concerned, an early study over a six month period of personal injury motor vehicle

[63] *Report of the Committee on Personal Injuries Litigation*, Cmnd. 3691, 1968, para.355.

[64] *Civil Justice Review*, para.259.

[65] For a somewhat dated account of settlement conferences in New South Wales: R. Cranston, P. Hayes, J. Pullen, I Scott, *Delays and Efficiency in Civil Litigation*, Australian Institute of Judicial Administration, 1985, chapter 19.

[66] 'The settlement techniques vary from judge to judge, and, with any given judge, from case to case. Sometimes a judge places a value on the case and tries to bring the two parties into agreement over it. In other cases, the judge will only point out to each side the strength of the opposition's case and the weaknesses of its own. But the key feature of the conference is informality and the atmosphere of compromise generated by the judge or other third parties.': P. Ebener, *Court Efforts to Reduce Pretrial Delay*, Rand Corp., Santa Monica, 1981, pp.70–71. See also the handbook, D.M. Provine, *Settlement Strategies for Federal District Judges*, Federal Judicial Center, 1986.

claims in New Jersey concluded that in all likelihood settlement conferences did not lead to fewer cases reaching trial. More definitely it concluded that mandatory settlement conferences achieved neither a higher settlement rate nor shorter trials than where the parties had a choice about the matter. However, it did find a gain in the fairly definite improvement in the quality of trials in an appreciable fraction of cases which had been to a settlement conference but not settled.[67] The classic study of delay for the National Center for State Courts found that those courts exerting more effort in settling cases did not necessarily dispose of more cases per judge than those where less was expended.[68] Similarly, the important study by the Federal Judicial Center reported that the courts with the strongest settlement activity had the fewest civil terminations per judge, while the court with the least settlement involvement had the second most civil terminations.[69] So none of this is very encouraging. One consistent finding of a variety of studies is that the use of settlement conferences does not increase disposition times; indeed it might actually increase delays.[70] The puzzle is then why many United States judges are enamoured of the settlement role, in particular in settlement conferences.[71] In the light of this evidence it is not surprising that, while Lord Woolf assumes that case management will facilitate settlement, he eschews the idea that judges should formally promote settlements.

[67] M. Rosenberg, *The Pretrial Conference and Effective Justice*, Columbia U.P., New York, 1964, pp.29–41, 45–53. As a result of the study, New Jersey promptly made settlement conferences in personal injury vehicle claims optional rather than mandatory.

[68] T. Church, et al, *Justice Delayed*, *op.cit.*, p.33.

[69] S. Flanders, 'Case management in federal courts' (1978) 4 *Justice System J.* 147, 161. See also S. Flanders, *Case Management and Court Management in United States District Courts*, Federal Judicial Center, 1977, pp.37–39.

[70] But there may be greater predictability and hence more efficient listing: C. Baar, *The Reduction and Control of Civil Case Backlog in Ontario*, Advocates' Society, Toronto, 1994, p.4.

[71] Professor Marc Galanter offers a number of reasons, which are certainly suggestive.

'1. Resource savings: imposed decisions require the decision maker to employ elaborate procedures and to supply elaborate justifications.

2. Avoidance of supervisions: settlements are largely unreviewable and their occurrence increases the autonomy of the forum from its hierarchic superiors.

3. Minimisation of enforcement problems: imposed decisions are less likely to be complied with than decisions that are consented to.

4. Vertical credibility: imposition endangers credibility since at least one party is agreed with the forum. Settlement enables avoidance of untoward results which would attract attacks on the forum.

5. Sense of accomplishment: participation in settlements induces a feeling of accomplishment and control.

6. Fun: finally, participation in settlements may strike a judge an engaging activity that enables him to employ beneficially his talents as a negotiator.'

M. Galanter, 'A settlement judge, not a trial judge: judicial mediation in the United States', in S. Shetreet (ed.), *The Role of Courts in Society*, Martinus Nijhoff, Dordrecht, 1988, pp.310–311 (footnotes omitted).

## SIMPLIFICATION

Simplification is a theme running through the Interim Report. It is a reaction to the complexity which Lord Woolf sees in the procedures and the substantive law. Complexity in Lord Woolf's view facilitates the aggressive tactics of lawyers which he deprecates, and indeed 'is considered by many to require it'.[72] Simplification is the goal for the new rules for the high court and county courts.[73] Pleadings (the 'statement of case') are to be less complicated, discovery is to be reduced in many instances ('standard discovery'), and the new fast track is to provide a simplified procedure, fixed timetable and fixed costs for cases up to £10,000.[74]

The small claims procedure has for some twenty five years offered a simplified method of resolving disputes. In *Afzal v. Ford Motor Co. Ltd.*[75] the Court of Appeal drew attention to the main aims of the small claims procedure—furthering access to justice, dealing with matters in an inexpensive, informal manner and getting directly to the real issues in dispute. The Civil Justice Review concluded, on the basis of research by Touche Ross,[76] that the small claims procedure had fulfilled these aims, although it was concerned with inconsistencies between courts (timescales, the award of costs etc.) and recommended an interventionalist approach by judges, more training and certain procedural changes.[77] The small claims procedure now disposes of the majority of cases which go to a hearing in the County Court—in 1994, 24,219 cases were disposed of by trial, while the number of arbitrations (i.e. small claims) was 87,885.[78] As Lord Woolf himself says: 'I see the small claims scheme as the primary way of increasing access to justice for ordinary people.'[79]

In other jurisdictions small claims courts are separate from the ordinary courts. In the past the issue has been raised whether this should happen in England and Wales so as to symbolise and foster a completely new, and simpler, approach. In some fairly extensive but dated research into small claims, the National Consumer Council contacted a range of institutions which dealt with small claims and others with experience of the system.[80] It found that the image and approachability of the courts achieved a universally poor rating. There were considerable variations of practice and attitude. In some areas litigants in person were treated unsympathetically by court personnel. When arbitrations were held, conventional court attitudes and procedures survived. Yet the NCC recommended against an

[72] *Interim Report*, p.7.
[73] Chapter 26.
[74] Chapters 20, 21, 7 respectively.
[75] [1994] 4 All E.R. 720 at p.747.
[76] This has some serious methodological flaws: C. Whelan, 'The role of research in civil justice reform: small claims in the county court' [1987] *C.J.Q.* 237.
[77] paras.505, 510, R68.
[78] Judicial Statistics, 1993, Cm. 2891, p.42.
[79] *Interim Report*, p.100.
[80] National Consumer Council, *Simple Justice*, 1979.

entirely separate system of small claims courts to break these habits. However, it did suggest that each county court should have a separate 'Small Claims Division' clearly labelled and recognised as such, intended to promote the creation of a distinctive new identity for small claims. It also recommended a separate, simplified procedural code, although this was rejected by the County Court Rules Committee (without it seems adequate reasons).[81] More recently the Scottish Office has commissioned detailed research into the small claims procedure there. Significantly no-one claimed to have used the rules as a source of information 'and most advisers considered they were too complex for the average member of the public to comprehend'.[82] The Touche Ross research for the Civil Justice Review found—rather disturbingly, given that the procedure is supposedly straightforward—that the most frequently used source of help was solicitors.[83]

Unfortunately the cause of simplicity has not been assisted by the Court of Appeal view that small claims procedure ought not to be fundamentally different form the ordinary adversary process. In *Chilton* v. *Saga Holidays plc*[84] the registrar (district judge) had quite sensibly ruled that where one side was unrepresented he did not allow cross-examination and questions had to be put through him. Yet the Court of Appeal upheld an appeal—it was fundamental that each party should be able to probe the accuracy and completeness of the evidence of the other side. The decision is unfortunate to say the least. Many unrepresented individual litigants are generally not capable of framing questions so there is an immediate advantage given to the represented or sophisticated. In 1989 the National Consumer Council recommended that all questions to witnesses should be put through arbitrators, whether or not the parties were represented, and the Civil Justice Review endorsed this.[85] Again unfortunately in the *Afzal* case the Court of Appeal has opined that 'the process is adversarial . . .'.[86] Lord Woolf has made it quite clear that he sees the process as interventionist.[87]

The National Consumer Council prepared a 'Model Code of Procedure for Small Claims', with forms, in 1980. To some extent this has been overtaken by new small claims rules, introduced in 1992. Those changes were accompanied by a new series of forms and by new simplified leaflets (they have the crystal mark for clarity in plain English). But a completely separate and simplified 'code' would contribute to sweeping away the residual

[81] Very early research by Applebey had also spoken of the complexity of the small claims procedures: G. Applebey, *Small Claims in England and Wales*, Institute of Judicial Administration, *Birmingham, 1978.*

[82] H. Jones et al., *Small Claims in the Sheriff Court in Scotland*, Scottish Office Central Research Unit, 1991, pp.105–6.

[83] Touche Ross, *Civil Justice Review: Study of the Small Claims Procedure*, 1986, Table 18.

[84] [1986] 1 All E.R. 841.

[85] Ordinary Justice, *op.cit.*, p.303; Civil Justice Review, R.68.

[86] at p.733.

[87] *Interim Report*, pp.100, 108.

view that anything less than the adversary system is somehow inadequate. Coupled with a separation of 'small claims' matters within the County Court—touched on in the recommendations of the Civil Justice Review—this would serve to provide an important psychological break from the traditional procedures in the county court. Lord Woolf's approach to small claims procedure in the new procedural code is yet to be enunciated.

A key recommendation of the Interim Report is that the small claims jurisdiction be increased from £1,000 to £3,000, with consideration being given to a possible further increase to £5,000. Many consumer representatives favoured an expansion—albeit with the qualification that more assistance etc. be available for individual litigants—as a way of furthering access to justice. Yet powerful voices were raised against expanding the small claims jurisdiction, especially for personal injuries. They have been accommodated in the Report's recommendations by a more flexible test for removing matters from the small claims jurisdiction and by locating personal injuries in the new fast track. The strongest empirical point would seem to be that elsewhere many small claims courts exceed the £1000 limit in England. Victoria and Queensland have a $A5000 limit; New South Wales and Western Australia have a $A6000 limit (£1 = approx $A2), and British Columbia increased its jurisdiction to $C10,000 in 1991 (£1 = approx $C2). An evaluation of the latter concluded that the increase provided access to a way of resolving disputes which did not exist before. New cases seemed to be entirely in the range from $3000 (the old limit) to $10,000. Moreover, the new cases came 'out of the woodwork'—previously they were neither litigated in the small claims court or the superior courts. However, the evaluation observed that whereas some 70% of cases involved lay claimants *and* lay defendants (both before and after the change), for claims over $3000 this dropped to 55%. (The likelihood of the claimant only being represented remained high, regardless of the amount of the claim). Moreover, at the time of the research, timely access was at risk because of the sheer volume of claims, particularly those valued at over $3,000.[88]

A minority of North American and Australasian jurisdictions bar lawyers from small claims jurisdictions. The rationale is that lawyers mean longer, more costly and complex hearings and that they perpetuate inequalities if employed by one party only. Access to justice for individuals might be compromised since those who cannot afford lawyers will be deterred from suing. The National Consumer Council at one time wanted a ban on legal representation in the great majority of cases, although subsequently it has relented, on the philosophical basis of freedom of choice, and for the practical reason that there has been an expansion in lay representation (a

[88] Semmens & Adams, *Evaluation of the Small Claims Program*, Ministry of Attorney General, 1992, p.21.

doubtful proposition).[89] In the 109 cases observed by John Baldwin and his co-workers, legal representatives appeared in just under a quarter of them, three times as often for the plaintiff as the defendant. In only one case were both sides represented. Baldwin noted that in the majority of cases the district judges either side-lined legal representatives or preserved their interventionist role (with an accommodation to the lawyer's presence). Baldwin notes that his sample is very small, but says that despite this it could nevertheless be asserted of his cases that the benefits of legal representation in the small claims arena are unlikely to be great.[90] Of course this does not go to the important issue of preparation before the hearing. The Touche Ross research found that solicitors acted at hearings in 30 percent of cases for one party (in 12 percent for the plaintiff and in 27 percent for the defendant), and in 9 percent of cases for both parties. Solicitors were more likely the larger the claim and the larger the claimant.[91]

Research suggests, albeit not unequivocally, that a ban on legal representation might be unnecessary so long as other steps are taken to assist the unrepresented litigant. The focus is on outcome rather than complexity/simplicity *per se*. Thus the leading American research found, surprisingly, that a sizeable number of litigants sought legal advice for small claims, even if they were not represented at the hearing. It also found that the presence of a lawyer tended to increase significantly the time necessary for a hearing. As well as the obvious conclusion that more had to be done to assist the unrepresented, the study argued for careful control of legal representatives—'their participation should be limited to presenting additional legal or evidentiary points at the end of a case, and that questioning of witnesses should be conducted by the judge'.[92] The follow-up study by the National Center for State Courts found that representation at trial by a lawyer was not a statistically significant correlate of success at trial after controlling for other independent variables. It suggested that one explanation might be that if permitted, lawyers were usually not given the opportunity to dominate the unrepresented party.[93] The Scottish small claims research found that most sheriffs interviewed thought self-represented litigants did well, even when the other side was represented. Over half individual pursuers (plaintiffs) thought the procedure was easy enough to use without a solicitor, although as long as the matter was straightforward. On the basis of observing a very small number of hearings in Northern Ireland, the Consumer Council there did not think that unrepresented litigants were

[89] *Ordinary Justice*, 1989, p.

[90] Unpublished research report for the Lord Chancellor's Department and Office of Fair Trading, 1994, p.58.

[91] *op.cit.*, Table 12. See also C. Whelan, 'Small claims in England and Wales: redefining justice', in C. Whelan (ed.), *Small Claims Courts*, Oxford, 1990, p.119.

[92] J. Ruhnka & S. Weller, *Small Claims Courts*, National Center for State Courts, 1978.

[93] J. Goerdt, *Small Claims and Traffic Courts*, 1992, p.69.

at a disadvantage, even when facing a lawyer on the other side. Judges adopted an inquisitorial role and this helped redress any potential imbalance.[94]

For many years a more interventionist approach has been urged on those conducting small claims arbitrations (in practice, of course, district judges). Lord Woolf has given his official blessing to this. We have seen that it is essential for various reasons, including the simplicity of the proceedings. Earlier research threw up some disturbing findings about the registrars conducting small claims hearings—a dislike for the work, undue formality and an adherence to adversary modes.[95] While some of this might still exist the overwhelming approach is interventionist although John Baldwin cautions against complacency: '[A] judicial concern with ensuring that litigants understand what is happening at hearings and feel able to participate effectively in them needs to be recognised both in training and in practice.'[96] From his observations Baldwin found that there were considerable differences in judges' interpretation of what it means to be interventionist. However, he also found that there is now widespread acceptance of the desirability of the interventionalist role and that hearings are conducted in a pragmatic, down to earth manner.

The small claims procedure is designed, of course, to be informal. Critics have argued that informality leads to overlooking rights and subverting the goal of preserving public rules and standards of conduct. Empirical evidence tends to identify as the critical factor whether the procedure is perceived as fair and dignified.[97] Recent United States evidence confirms an overwhelmingly high degree of satisfaction among small claims litigants, even those who lost. Litigants who went through mediation tended to be more satisfied, while delay had adverse effects on defendants' perceptions. The more highly educated were more satisfied, perhaps because they were better able to understand the procedures. Treatment by the judge was the strongest correlate of litigant satisfaction along with both outcome and procedures.[98] Earlier research had shown that after outcome helpfulness of the court office was the most important influence on litigant satisfaction.[99] Litigant satisfaction in the Scottish research could not be explained entirely by whether they had won or not. The overwhelming majority of litigants praised the sheriffs for their fairness, irrespective of the outcome of cases.[100]

[94] General Consumer Council for Northern Ireland, *How to Make Small Beautiful*, p.33.

[95] e.g. Appelbey, *op.cit.*; O'Grady, cited in C. Whelan, *op.cit.*

[96] *op.cit.*, p.29. He identified four main approaches: going for the jugular; hearing the parties; passive, mediatory: see *Interim Report*, pp.107–8.

[97] E. Clark, 'Recent research on small claims courts and tribunals: implications for evaluators' (1992) 2 *J.Judicial Admin.*, 103, 117.

[98] J. Goerdt, *op.cit.*, pp.64, 68.

[99] S. Weller, et al., 'Litigant satisfaction with small claims court: does familiarity breed contempt?', *State Court Journal*, Spring 1979, p.5.

[100] H. Jones, et al., *op.cit.*, p.110.

In the Touche Ross research for the Civil Justice Review there was a high percentage of plaintiffs who said they were very likely to use the procedure again, although as the consultants themselves note, this 'may reflect the inclusion of business as well as private litigants in this sample'.[101] In terms of fairness, reactions varied with whether a party was successful, although nearly half of those who lost their cases thought the proceedings were fair. All these results accord with the current wisdom that the opportunity to give their grievance a good airing is perceived by litigants as important, if not more important for some, than outcome.[102] Simplicity, in other words, cannot be an end in itself.

## ALTERNATIVE DISPUTE RESOLUTION

Alternative dispute resolution (ADR) is the flavour of the month, if not the decade. The Interim Report is not immune to fashion. One way the new system of case management is to encourage settlement is by suggesting the use of ADR when this is likely to be beneficial. Judges are to be able to take into account a litigant's unreasonable refusal to attempt ADR. Certain forms of ADR are positively encouraged.[103] Yet it would be wrong to think that ADR has the wholly uncritical imprimatur of the Interim Report. The Report identifies the enormous variety of initiatives and cautions that claims of success are sometimes exaggerated. It points to the need for monitoring and evaluation with support for the most promising and successful schemes.[104]

An example of how the conclusions about ADR were shaped by the available empirical evidence is evident in the recommendations about court annexed arbitration. Sometimes called court administered arbitration, compulsory arbitration or mandatory arbitration, such programmes channel the less important civil litigation for a speedy hearing before a judicial officer (not a judge) or lawyer or panel of lawyers, whose order can then become an order of the court. If either party wishes to challenge the decision an appeal can be taken to the court and the matter heard *de novo*. Cases can be heard more quickly than before the courts, it is said, and the courts should be able to expedite the matters which remain because there are fewer of them. Although in broad terms similar to traditional arbitration, court annexed arbitration differs in its coverage and if it has a compulsory character.

[101] *op.cit.*, p.24.

[102] T. Tyler, 'What is procedural justice? Criteria used by citizens to assess the fairness of legal procedures' (1988) 22 *Law & Soc.R.* 104; W. O'Barr et al., 'Law expectations of the civil justice system' (1988) 22 *Law & Soc. R.* 131.

[103] *Interim Report*, pp.22, 136ff.

[104] *ibid.*, p.146.

The United States has led the way in court annexed arbitration, but it has also been introduced in some other common law jurisdictions such as New South Wales. Typically in the United States smaller civil cases are assigned to arbitration, automatically in some jurisdictions, after screening in others. Lawyers act as arbitrators for a small or nominal fee in most jurisdictions. Lawyers, the parties and any witnesses appear before the arbitrator for a private hearing where the rules of evidence are relaxed and matters expedited. The parties have a specified period in which to reject the award and request a trial *de novo*. As a disincentive to reject awards, most programmes include a monetary disincentive in the form of a penalty or costs if the party's position is not improved at trial. With some of the programmes fees must be paid before the *de novo* hearing so as to discourage frivolous requests.

An early evaluation by the Federal Judicial Center of court annexed arbitration in three federal district courts had produced strong evidence that it decreased time from filing to disposition in two of the three districts, attributable almost exclusively to settlement of cases prior to the arbitration hearing. In the third court no such effect was found, probably because of the court's procedures for the scheduling of arbitration hearings. However, in about 60% of arbitrated cases the arbitration award was voided by a demand for a trial *de novo*.[105] An evaluation of compulsory court annexed arbitration in Rochester, New York, found that the total disposition time for arbitration did not vary from the total time taken previously.[106] Another study of a court annexed arbitration programme in California found that the hearing time spent per personal injury case arbitrated averaged 2.5 hours, compared to 3.3 days for the average trial.[107] Research into civil claims in a county of Pennsylvania suggested that court annexed arbitration had made progress in limiting the length and number of protracted cases. Whether this had happened by chance or by a concerted effort to monitor cases to identify those most likely to be complex was not clear.[108] An evaluation of ten mandatory federal court schemes in 1990 found that from 5% to just over one quarter of the civil case load in the ten districts went to arbitration. Depending on the district, cases resolved by arbitration were disposed of from 2–18 months sooner than cases resolved by trial. However, less than one half of arbitration awards were accepted in 8 of the

[105] E. Lind & J. Shepard, *Evaluation of Court Annexed Arbitration in Three Federal District Courts*, Federal Judicial Center, 1981.

[106] S. Weller et al., 'American experiments for reducing civil judicial trial costs and delays' (1982) 1 *Civil J.Q.* 151, 161–4.

[107] E. Johnson et al., *Outside the Courts*, National Center for State Courts, Denver, 1977, p.46. However, this was at a time when the Californian programme was voluntary so there is no certainty that the cases going to arbitration were comparable with those going to trial.

[108] D. Steelman et al., *Case Processing in the York County Court of Common Pleas*, National Center for State Courts, Andover, 1979.

10 districts, with parties exercising their right to a *de novo* hearing in the ordinary way. One of the most important findings was that a majority of lawyers reported a saving in costs. As would be expected, no such savings were reported in cases going to a *de novo* hearing. Moreover, over two thirds of those participating in arbitration cases were corporations or business parties.[109]

Perhaps the most impressive study to date of court annexed arbitration is one by the Institute for Civil Justice of the Rand Corporation and the Duke School of Law Private Adjudication Center. It is distinguished in two ways from earlier research: first, it covered high value claims, whereas research previously had focused on smaller claims; secondly, and more importantly, it used a control group which was randomly removed from arbitration and dealt with by ordinary pre-trial processes. There were a number of important findings. One was that arbitration increased the likelihood that a case would receive some form of adjudication since one third of the arbitration cases, but only 15% of the control group, went to a hearing. Next, there was no significant difference in delay between the two groups of cases. Unfortunately the data on costs was not as good as that on other matters. But a cost difference was found for parties, although the lower cost of arbitration for parties was for defendants, not plaintiffs. Importantly, there was no difference in the public costs, i.e. to the courts. In interviews with litigants it was found that those whose cases went to a hearing were more frequently disposed of, and since a greater proportion of the arbitration group went to a hearing than those dealt with ordinarily, overall litigants in the arbitration group were more favourable in their ratings. The study concluded that court annexed arbitration increased access to justice: there was no evidence of increased case filings but in substituting arbitration hearings for bilateral settlement, it gave litigants something they wanted—an opportunity to have their cases adjudicated.[110]

There would therefore seem to be no savings of public expenditure with court annexed arbitration, although there is some (but not strong) evidence of cost advantages to litigants. Arbitrated cases are not necessarily processed quicker. One reason might be that lawyers carry the same workload whether their case is going to arbitration or the courts, so that in as much as delay can be attributed to lawyers' practices arbitration might not have a great impact. There is some evidence in the United States that parties welcome court annexed arbitration as an opportunity to have an official decision on their cases, but in a very high number of cases the parties are dissatisfied with the result since they request a *de novo* hearing. With this

[109] B. Meierhoefer, *Court-Annexed Arbitration in Ten District Courts*, Federal Judicial Center, Washington, 1990.

[110] E. Lind, *Arbitrating High-Stake Cases*, The Institute for Civil Justice, Rand Corporation, Santa Monica, 1990.

as background Lord Woolf concluded that it was not the appropriate time to introduce court annexed alternative dispute resolution, although he refers expressly to other reasons—the burden for the courts of adopting his other recommendations and the plethora of private ADR schemes. However, he did recommend for further investigation the use of retired lawyers and others as 'civil magistrates', who amongst other things could offer alternate means of resolving disputes such as arbitration, mediation and conciliation.[111]

## CONCLUSION

Making public policy is not an exact science. Quite apart from the difficulty in some instances of identifying how to reach a particular goal, there is the problem in foreseeing all the ramifications of reform. One such consequence is that individuals and organisations can adjust their behaviour to change and by so doing undermine its very purpose.[112] Part of the folklore in American judicial administration concerns the introduction of a speedy trial list in Baltimore. That list soon became so clogged that if lawyers wanted to delay matters they would ask for a speedy trial! This is not an argument for petty tinkering and against comprehensive change.[113] But in achieving comprehensive change incrementalism has the advantage that corrections can be more easily made as any undesirable consequences of a change in policy become manifest. In any event incrementalism is all that is possible in some instances because of resource constraints, a clash of interests and a lack of consensus on values.

In advance of policy changes it is desirable to bring to bear relevant social research. What really is the problem? how has it been dealt with successfully in the past, or in similar settings? what unintended side effects must be guarded against?—these are some obvious questions which social research might have addressed. Systematically monitoring change once it is introduced is also essential. Unfortunately social research and monitoring have not been prominent features of the civil justice system. By comparison with what has been achieved in criminology, research into civil justice is minimal. Significant changes in civil justice are constantly made without monitoring. This does not mean that social research is non-problematic. Research findings clearly turn on the questions asked. In order to reduce life's complexity researchers must structure their observations and highlight

[111] *Interim Report*, pp.143, 145.

[112] e.g. G. Priest, 'Private litigants and the court congestion problem' (1989) 69 *Boston U.L.R.* 527.

[113] The criticism of Roscoe Pound in his famous address in 1906. 'The causes of popular dissatisfaction with the administration of justice': see J. Jolowicz, 'Comparative law and the reform of civil procedure' (1988) 8 *Leg.Stud.* 1, 13.

the characteristics which they regard as important. Sometimes this misleads us into thinking that they have uncovered more than is actually known and evidence which is not persuasive is put forward as supporting the authors' own particular dispositions. This is clearly not helpful to the policy maker who is already under pressure to make decisions and take action quickly and on the basis of inadequate data.

This essay has set out some of the social research available to Lord Woolf for his Access to Justice inquiry. Although we know too little of the operation of the civil justice system in this country, by drawing also on the experience of other common law countries we have at least some findings bearing on the major issues which Lord Woolf has addressed in his Interim Report. They can hardly be said to be definitive or to reveal universal truths. Yet treated cautiously, and used alongside experience, they suggest that some avenues are more likely than others to accord with the principles and objectives for the civil justice system which Lord Woolf identifies in his Interim Report.

# 3

# *Reform in the Shadow of Lawyers' Interests*

A. A. S. ZUCKERMAN*

## INTRODUCTION

At the outset of his interim report, *Access to Justice*,[1] Lord Woolf stresses that procedure is essential to protecting individual rights and to the maintenance of civilised society. At the same time, he paints a gloomy picture of a system riven by high, disproportionate and unpredictable costs, by undue delays and by excessive complexity.

Lord Woolf considers the ills of cost, delay and complexity to be interrelated and to arise from the uncontrolled nature of the litigation process. He draws attention to the fact that a number of litigation processes have degenerated into expensive and wasteful devices. Discovery is sometimes pursued without any regard to efficiency and economy so that it may consume vast resources for little benefit. Expert evidence, instead of assisting the court, may cause unreasonable delay and confusion at great expense to the parties. Even the newly fashioned process of exchange of witness statements, Lord Woolf notes, has been stood on its head. Instead of expediting matters, it had proved fertile ground for the employment of 'the draftsman's skill often used to obscure the original words of the witness', not infrequently at enormous expense (Report, 8).

The problem of disproportionate costs, Lord Woolf has concluded, occurs throughout the system and is not confined to particular areas of litigation. He does not, however, see the source of these evils as lying in the nature of our procedural rules. True, he accepts, some of these rules are too cumbersome or complex, but this is not the root of the problem. Rather, the source of the problem is to be found in the proliferation of 'adversarial tactics' which have resulted in the procedural tools 'being subverted from their proper purpose' (Report, 7, 8). Left to their own devices, litigants may complicate and protract the litigation process without limit. It is this so called adversarial freedom which, in Lord Woolf's view, is the cause of complexity, cost and delay.

* Fellow of University College, Oxford.

[1] Interim Report to the Lord Chancellor on the civil justice system in England and Wales, 1995. Hereinafter referred to as 'Report'; references report are to page numbers.

Having diagnosed the problem Lord Woolf concludes that 'there is now no alternative to a fundamental shift in the responsibility for the management of civil litigation from litigants and their legal advisers to the courts' (Report, 18). The preeminent theme of this report is, accordingly, a cultural move towards court control of litigation practices. Under his proposals, it would be the courts, and not the parties, who would determine the pace of the litigation process and its intensity. It would be for the courts, and not for the parties, to ensure that the investment in legal process is in reasonable proportion to the importance and complexity of the issues in question.

The present paper is concerned with three main points. First, Lord Woolf is correct in his diagnosis that the cause of complexity, delay and cost is due not to the nature of our procedural devices but, rather, to the excessive and disproportionate use and abuse of the procedural tools. Secondly, it will be argued that judicial control on its own would be an ineffectual way of preventing disproportionate use of procedure. This is because judicial management would be pitched against a profession still dominated by incentives to complicate and protract the litigation process. Thirdly, and perhaps most importantly, it will be suggested that Lord Woolf points in the right direction when he proposes the fast-track procedure which combines proportionality in the employment of legal process with powerful incentives to lawyers and their litigants to economize in litigation expenditure.

## THE DIMENSION OF SELF-INTEREST

Although Lord Woolf has not systematically investigated the reasons for which parties tend to complicate and protract litigation, he draws attention to some of the principal causes. He points out that parties tend to exploit the rules of practice to their own advantage. It is not uncommon for the financially stronger or more experienced party to 'spin out proceedings and escalate costs, by litigating on technical points or peripheral issues instead of focusing on the real substance of the case. All too often, such tactics are used to intimidate the weaker party and produce a resolution of the case which is either unfair or is achieved at a grossly disproportionate cost or after unreasonable delay.' (Report, 27) There is considerable evidence, he says, that individual plaintiffs in personal injury cases are often forced to settle for inadequate compensation because of delaying tactics employed by insurance companies and their own financial inferiority.

Lord Woolf's observations—that, first, litigants will tend to exploit the procedure to their own advantage and, second, that there is at present a very considerable scope for doing so—are undoubtedly correct. But it is essential not to lose sight of the distinction between these two very different factors. The pursuit of self-interest is a fundamental human trait in any socio-economic context which it is neither possible nor desirable to change. It is therefore an immutable factor. By contrast, the scope for the pursuit of self interest in the conduct of litigation is largely a function of the system of rules governing the civil process.

It is natural that litigants should seek to exploit procedure to their advantage. Litigants do not resort to legal proceedings for altruistic disinterested motives. They go to law in order to advance their own interests. In so doing they will take whatever advantage the rules of court afford. Litigants want to win, and they can be hardly condemned for having such a desire or, indeed, for following the course which is most conducive to their objective.

A party to a dispute would wish to secure a favourable result at minimum cost and in the shortest time. It follows that the commencement of proceedings, the pre-trial process, trial and final judgment are all means to an end, rather than ends in themselves. The end is to secure interests: the remedy sought (such as a money payment) by the plaintiff; or the freedom of not having to make good the plaintiff's demand, in the defendant's case. Parties would much rather achieve their goals without having to take proceedings; having taken proceedings, without the need to go to trial, and so on. In other words, they desire to secure their interest with the minimum of effort and cost.

It is, therefore, normal for litigants to seek advantage from whatever superiority they possess, be it greater economic resources or wider experience or strong nerves. The degree to which one is able to sustain litigation and bear the consequence of an eventual loss has a direct bearing on one's prospects of recovering one's entitlement in a settlement. Defendants who know that their plaintiffs cannot afford even the initial cost of commencing proceedings, need hardly respond to claims made against them. Defendants who cannot make a show of being able to defend their case, must expect to pay in full the plaintiffs' demands. Quite plainly, the less one is able to commit resources to litigation and bear the risk of failure, the less one can expect in settlement; and vice versa: the more a litigant can sustain litigation, the greater the prospect of biting into the opponent's entitlement.[2] Where the plaintiff has only a limited ability to sustain litigation, the defendant is in a position to insist on a settlement that is tailored not to the plaintiff's prospects of winning but to his ability to finance litigation.

While no one can, or should, change the tendency of people to pursue their self-interest within the bounds allowed by the rules, it is legitimate to try and limit these bounds. Lord Woolf is therefore right to deal with the second of the factors mentioned above: the scope for procedural

[2] H. L. Ross, *Settled Out of Court: The Social Process of Insurance Claims Adjustment*, Aldine Pub. Co., New York, 2nd edn., 1980; H. Genn, *Hard Bargaining: Out of Court Settlement in Personal Injury Action*. Clarendon Press, Oxford, 1987.

manipulation. He is justified in seeking to restrict the extent to which litigants are free to use the process of the law regardless of the complexity of their cause or its importance. Indeed, it is imperative in the interests of justice to circumscribe the degree to which the litigants with deep pockets are able to use their financial advantage to undermine the entitlements of their poorer opponents. For where a decision to settle a claim or a defence is driven not by the strength of a party's case on its merits but by his poverty, the outcome cannot be considered just.[3]

The parties are not the only participants in the litigation process with an interest. Although lawyers are on the whole interested in the pursuit of justice, their professional activities are not wholly altruistic. They too have an interest at stake: professional remuneration. Just as it is natural that litigants should be keen to further their objectives so it is normal for lawyers to be concerned about their own financial interests. This is not to say that the legal profession is dominated by greed. On the contrary, the prevalent ethical standards in England are rather high. But it would be wholly unrealistic to suppose that the legal profession is unique amongst all professions in being indifferent to financial rewards.

We must therefore accept that, as in any other context, economic considerations do play a part in the development of professional practices. Accordingly, we need to consider the economic factors that may influence lawyers. Solicitors are commonly paid for their services on an hourly basis. Barristers have traditionally charged according to the complexity of the case and on the basis of days spent in court, though there seems to be an increasing trend for them too to seek an hourly return.[4] Whether charging is by the hour or in proportion to complexity, it seems obvious that lawyers have no direct incentive to economize in the provision of services. On the contrary, the more complex and protracted litigation becomes the more they earn.

Not only do lawyers have an interest in making litigation more complex and lengthy, but their clients' ability to resist costs is neutralised by the clients' lack of information about the legal process. Lay clients do not have independent means for making decisions about the cost efficiency of particular procedural moves. They must rely on their lawyers to judge whether this or that procedural step is necessary or cost efficient. Moreover, it is largely in the hands of lawyers to determine, by the custom of professional practice, the parameters of acceptable procedural deployment. It is in the

[3] The same may be said of a settlement dictated by urgent need. Those who have an urgent need for a remedy may feel constrained to forego some of their entitlements, even if they could afford litigation, for the sake of an early remedy.

[4] It is, however, not unknown nowadays for clients to demand certain services at a fixed cost and for solicitors to ask barristers to quote a flat fee.

nature of things that forensic practices should, without any self-conscious decision on the part of individuals, follow the most rewarding path.[5]

Self-interest finds expression not only in seeking maximal remuneration, but also in acquiring immunity from claims in negligence. In order to minimise liability for negligence lawyers would naturally tend to follow all procedural avenues open to their client. Since reasonable standards of litigation practice are determined by what practitioners normally do, it follows that here too we have a mechanism which continually expands the intensity of litigation.

Lord Woolf's views about the influence of the lawyers' financial interest on the cost of litigation are unclear. On the one hand, he says: 'there is a misconceived view that the entire problem is due to the scale of lawyers' charges. This is not so.' (Report, 199) On the other hand, however, he makes two points. First, that 'market forces, which in other contexts have acted as a restraint on prices, operate rather weakly in relation to the supply of professional services' (*id*). Secondly, he points out that hourly pay rates have 'an inflationary effect on costs' (Report, 200). Sadly, he does not consider any further the correlation between the hourly payment system and the intensity of use of procedural devices. Yet, given the scope for procedural manoeuvring and low client resistance, it would be a miracle if there were no substantial connection between lawyers' financial interests and litigation practices.

In fact, it is not difficult to find signs of this correlation, and witness statements provide a good illustration. Lord Woolf condemns the practice of drafting lengthy witness statements at exorbitant expense (Report, 175–7). But he believes that the reason for this is to be found in the rule that witness statements stand in place of examination in chief. The fear that witnesses would not be allowed to supplement their statements has lead, Lord Woolf suggests, to a practice whereby lawyers try to cover every possible angle of the dispute in their witness statements.

This explanation is, however, unconvincing. There is no substantial body of case law to encourage or justify such a fear. There are no reported decisions suggesting that litigants have suffered a reversal because something was missing from a witness statement, which they were not allowed to supplement during the trial. There is no hint in the *Chancery Guide*, 1995, which has been produced to help expedite litigation, that the problem with witness statements is due to the fact that they stand in place of evidence in chief. Although the *Chancery Guide* acknowledges that witness statements

[5] Research suggests that the hourly fee can lead lawyers to put in more hours than the client would wish; E. Johnson, 'Lawyer's Choice: A Theoretical Appraisal of Litigation Investment Decisions' (1981) Law and Society Rev 15; H. Kritzer et al, 'The Impact of Fee Arrangements on Lawyer Effort' (1985) 19 Law and Society Review 251; M. White, 'Legal Complexity and Lawyers' Benefits from Litigation' (1992) 12 International Review of Law and Economics 381.

have tended to be too elaborate and lengthy, the Chancery Division does not believe that it is necessary to alter the rule that witness statements will normally stand in place of evidence in chief.[6] Under the *Chancery Guide*, a party is allowed to supplement his witness statement, if he can persuade the judge of the need to do so.[7] Since this is already the position at present,[8] it seems clear that the source of trouble with witness statements must be found elsewhere.

The witness statement process, like most other procedural aspects, is strongly influenced by the prevalent professional culture. In this culture lawyers possess no incentive to exert an effort to produce concise witness statements which only reproduce the witness's words and which are narrowly confined to the issues on which the witness is called to testify. On the contrary, lawyers have an incentive to elaborate these statements, for the greater the elaboration the greater the lawyer's reward. It is not suggested that individual lawyers make conscious decisions to spin out the witness statement process for gain. But the supposed advantage that may be gained from embellishing and expanding witness statements has provided the excuse for the development of a practice which coincides with the financial interests of practitioners.

As this last point suggests, the professional incentive to complicate and protract the process does not operate in isolation. Its influence is most powerful when it combines with the litigant's self-interest. Where lawyers can show that by investing a little extra in procedure the client would thereby obtain some advantage, they can justify to themselves recommending that the client undertake the extra expenditure. Indeed, at times the pursuit of the extra advantage can lock both opponents in a competition of investment in procedure; each trying to undo the other by raising the procedural stakes.

The indemnity rule, whereby the loser in litigation has to pay the winner's costs, also makes a contribution here. Given that success brings with it not only the sum claimed but also the expenses laid out in securing judgment, a litigant who believes that an increase in the amount spent on litigation will increase his chances of success has a very good reason for progressively raising his stakes. Once one party has increased the stakes, the opponent would feel compelled to follow suit for fear that by using inferior procedural devices, be it a less celebrated lawyer or a less qualified expert, he would compromise his chances of success and run a greater risk of having to pay the other party's costs as well on losing the subject matter in dispute. Indeed, a point may come where the parties would have reason to

[6] *Chancery Guide*, paras 3.7(6), 6.9(2).

[7] Ibid. para 6.9(4). Supplemental witness statement are also allowed by leave: para 6.9(10). See also para 6.9(4).

[8] RSC Ord 38, r 2A(7).

persist with investment in litigation not so much for the sake of a favourable judgment on the merits, as for the purpose of recovering the money already expended in the dispute, which may well outstrip the value of the subject matter in issue. On their part, the parties' lawyers have of course no interest in breaking such a spiral of costs and persuading their clients to desist.

It is a serious omission in the Report that it does not address the mechanisms which help ratchet up the cost of litigation; that it does not draw attention to the economic aspects which explain why the legal profession has tended to resist any drive for economy and efficiency in procedure. This inattention to the incentives possessed by lawyers weakens Lord Woolf's proposals concerning court control of litigation.

## JUDICIAL MANAGEMENT V. LAWYERS' INTERESTS

Lord Woolf's proposals go a long way towards reducing the scope for complicating and protracting litigation. He pursues a twin policy of simplification of procedure and of judicial supervision of the conduct of litigation. Although this policy has the potential of rendering the civil process less susceptible to procedural manipulation and waste, it risks being thwarted by the adverse incentives that the legal profession will continue to enjoy.

Broadly speaking, our system lacks effective mechanisms for adjusting the intensity of procedural consumption to the real needs of the case. A litigant need only show an arguable case in order to have unimpeded access to the full panoply of procedural devices. Furthermore, while litigants are not obliged to take advantage of full access regardless of real need, there are benefits to be had from doing just that, because a litigant may thereby exhaust his opponent, or obtain a better settlement or improve his tactical position in some other way. Even litigants who would like to be thrifty are not always in a position to be so. In order to determine whether procedural economy is feasible, one has to have an overall view of the dispute. In an adversary system litigants can obtain such a view only at the end of an expensive and protracted pre-trial process. Moreover, this process could take on a life of its own and become a quagmire of applications and counter-applications, of appeals and counter-appeals which lead not so much to final judgment as to even more pre-trial proceedings. Under the present procedural arrangements, there is no sure way of gauging in advance how much procedural investment the case is likely to consume.

Lord Woolf is therefore correct in believing that the absence of enforceable standards of proportionality in litigation is a major contributory cause of the phenomenon of excessive use and abuse of procedure. He is also right in thinking that in order to affect a substantial change in the practice of litigation it is not enough to change the rules of procedure; rather, it is necessary to bring about a change in attitudes to the conduct of litigation. What is less clear is that court control on its own could produce the desired cultural change.

We have seen that it is in the nature of things that litigants should desire to win and that they would tend to use all legitimate means to that end. We have also seen that this natural attitude combines with the financial incentives that lawyers have to encourage ever increasing investment in procedure. If this powerful cost driving combination is left untouched, judicial control of litigation would be going against the grain of the interests of the participants in the civil process, lawyers and their clients.

A system in which the courts continually have to pitch themselves against the professional instincts of lawyers is bound to be inefficient. It can hardly be denied that the judicial task of controlling litigation is bound to be easier when its objective is shared by practitioners, and much harder when the court's aim runs counter to that of practitioners. Moreover, not only is the court's task likely to be more difficult to achieve in these circumstances, it risks being defeated altogether. This is because professional culture is as likely to influence judicial practices as the latter are likely to shape forensic practice. One should not overlook the fact that there is a two way traffic of influence between the courts and practitioners. It is plainly not the case that the courts can lay down standards of their own choosing which practitioners will observe as the courts envisage. The courts are as likely to be influenced by the professional standards as the profession is likely to observe standards laid down by the courts. This is especially true in a system such as ours, where judges are drawn from the ranks of the profession.

A few examples will illustrate how Lord Woolf's expectations from judicial control of litigation could be disappointed, even if his proposals are implemented.

Lord Woolf identifies a number of problems with pleadings (Report, 153–4). They often fail to set out the facts, they are too long, convoluted and attempt to keep open all possible arguments. Lord Woolf's solution to this is routine scrutiny by the court backed by the sanctions of striking out and costs. He says that '. . . the courts must take the responsibility for ensuring that claimants and defendants plainly state the factual ingredients of their case so that the true nature and scope of the dispute can be identified' (Report, 155). But it is hard to see how this can be done. A court must needs rely on the raw material provided by lawyers. If this input is obscure, ambivalent and complicated, the court would have to invest a great deal of effort in knocking the pleadings into shape. The court's efforts to clarify the issues would, naturally, involve the participation of lawyers, with the result that lawyer time will also have to be invested in the exercise. What interest, then, could lawyers have to invest effort in producing brief and clear pleadings?

This last point brings out an important consideration. Brevity in pleadings and, indeed, in legal argument generally, requires the investment of greater effort than the production of long and rambling pleadings or other forms of legal argument. It takes a great deal more time and ingenuity to produce pleadings which are brief, clear and comprehensive. It calls for discrimination between important and unimportant aspects of the case. It requires confident understanding of the law and it calls for refined drafting skills. It is much easier to put down indiscriminately and inelegantly all aspects that may possibly raise an issue and leave it to the court to work out the real issues. As things stand, lawyers have few incentives to develop the skill of brevity. It is much easier to justify a substantial charge for pleading running into many pages than for pleadings measured in a few sentences. There is little in the Woolf proposals to encourage the kind of forensic skills that effective brevity requires. Quite possibly the contrary is true, for lawyers would be tempted to leave more and more to the managerial judges to sort out.

There are two further aspects of the proposals for judicial case management which could be counterproductive, if faced with lack of co-operation from the profession. Lord Woolf proposes the use of case management conferences conducted by procedural judges. A major aim of such conferences would be to 'produce an agreed statement of the issues in dispute. This will be the responsibility of the parties . . . The statement of issues will effectively take over from the pleadings' (Report, 155–6). A heavy burden will therefore rest on the parties' lawyers to negotiate amongst themselves in an attempt to produce an agreed list of issues. When lawyers are paid on an hourly basis, there is a clear danger that the process of producing an agreement will itself become a source of great expense, just as witness statements proved to be expensive. Similar comments may be made about the proposals concerning discovery, which will be discussed presently. The need to co-operate in producing agreed discovery parameters will offer lawyers an opportunity to build up the number of their billable hours.

Lord Woolf has rightly identified the excess of discovery as one of the major contributory factors to the high cost of litigation. The process of discovery, it is widely acknowledged, can consume large resources and produce little if any benefits. Lord Woolf therefore proposes to limit the scope for discovery. As with pleadings, considerable reliance is placed on the need to change lawyers' approach to the process of discovery. 'Discovery is an area where culture has to change', Lord Woolf says, 'initially, the burdens upon procedural judges to make directions are likely to be heavy. However, once the parties appreciate the approach of the courts, I anticipate that it is only in a minority of situations that discovery will give rise to difficulty' (Report, 172). This is a very optimistic view. Much of the new approach depends on a distinction between documents which are adverse to a party's own case, and which would need to be discovered as a matter of course, and documents which are otherwise relevant (Report, 168). In the absence of an incentive to economize in discovery, practitioners are bound to play safe and press for maximal discovery.

They will almost certainly tend to assume that whatever relevant documents the opponent does not himself rely on, which must also be disclosed as a matter of course, must be adverse to the opponent's interest. Practitioners are therefore likely to blur the bounds between adverse documents and merely relevant documents. Determined lawyers would be tempted to argue that, although the opponent says that certain documents are not adverse to the opponent interests, they would be able to turn the documents to the advantage of their clients. Since, at that early stage, the court would possess limited knowledge of the case and since such knowledge would be derived from what the parties disclose, it would be difficult for the court to resist the pressure for discovery. Indeed, the time and argument that may be involved in determining the breadth of disclosure may outweigh any saving achieved in limiting its extent. Besides, a party's own lawyers would still have to examine every one of that party's documents, in order to determine whether they are adverse or not and whether they are covered by privilege, so that the cost of the new limited discovery would not be much lower than at present.

One more instance will suffice to expose the limitations of the court control strategy. We have already seen that Lord Woolf believes that the process of producing witness statements has become unnecessarily expensive because lawyers fear that they would be bound by the statements without being able to amplify them. His proposal for the multi-track system is as follows (Report, 175–80).[9] For the early case management conference, only the identity of witnesses and a brief note of the issues with which they deal will be prepared. At that stage the issues will be identified, thereby determining which witnesses will need to be called. Only statements from these witnesses would then have to be exchanged. At the subsequent pre-trial review it will be decided which witnesses should be actually called and the issues on which they would testify. At the trial itself the parties would be allowed to ask their witnesses to amplify their statement (but they will not be allowed to raise new points without leave).

Lord Woolf's scheme is admirable in a number of respects. It connects the initial process of identifying the issues to the available witness testimony. It enables the court to tailor the number of witnesses and their testimony to the real issues in the case and in proportion to other available

[9] The multi-track procedure is essentially the present procedure with one important difference. It will involve intensive court supervision and direction of the pre-trial process. For the purpose of this paper it is not necessary to go into the details of Lord Woolf's proposals in this regard.

evidence. Indeed, during the pre-trial preparation, the courts might be able to remove the need for some testimony by bringing the parties to agree on facts that appear to be uncontroversial or not worth challenging. These are very real advantages, but they may well be expensive to achieve. At present, witness statements obviate the need for examination in chief. Under the Woolf scheme this will not be the case, as parties would be free to call on witnesses to amplify their statements. Furthermore, both at the case management conference and the pre-trial review the courts and the parties' lawyers would have to devote considerable time to discussing witness statements. As a result it may well be the case that the processing of witness testimony would become even more laborious and costly than at present.

Perhaps conscious of this danger Lord Woolf warned that '. . . the solution to the present problem will depend on practitioners behaving in a sensible and co-operative way. . . . If they do not, the court must make it clear that they will bear the cost' (Report, 179). The sanction in costs is a general method adopted in the Report for implementing the proposals. There is a discretion to award costs against unreasonable conduct in relation to pleadings, discovery, witness statements and the like. Yet if applications for costs become a general feature, the scope for disputes concerning procedure is bound to increase and so would the expense of civil proceedings.

## THE STRENGTH OF THE REPORT'S MECHANISMS FOR HUSBANDING PROCEDURAL RESOURCES

Notwithstanding the problems just outlined, the Woolf report lays a sound foundation for an effective and flexible system of adjusting procedure to the requirements of the dispute in question.

His recommendations employ an ingenious combination of rule and discretion for economizing in procedure. Economy by rule consists in establishing different procedures for cases requiring different levels of procedural investment. He recommends three levels of procedure: small claims procedure, fast-track procedure and multi-track procedure (Report, chs 7, 8). Cases involving claims of up to £3,000 would be directed to the small claims procedure. The fast-track procedure is designed for cases with a subject matter value of between £3,000 and £10,000, while the multi-track process is reserved for cases exceeding the latter sum.

The Lord Chancellor has already agreed to raise the small claims jurisdictional limit from £1,000 to £3,000. The small claim procedure is well tried and while it has not been free from criticism,[10] it offers great advantages to litigants. A claim falling within this jurisdictional limit is

[10] See J. Baldwin, 'Raising the Small Claims Limit', 185, *infra*.

automatically transferred to arbitration by a district judge. The procedure is simple. It requires the plaintiff to state his claim in informal and simple terms and the defendant to respond in similar fashion. No further pre-trial preparation is involved. The hearing before the district judge is informal and litigants are encouraged to present their case in person. Most importantly, there is a 'no costs' regime. As the winner will not recover his costs from the loser, the employment of lawyers is thus greatly discouraged. The small claim jurisdiction offers therefore a simple and relatively expeditious process which is accessible to lay people without the need to employ lawyers. Judges retain a discretion of transferring a dispute out of the small claim jurisdiction in cases of complexity.

Two features of this process are particularly significant in the context of a policy of husbanding procedural resources. First, the small claims process is shorn of most, if not all, procedural complexity. It does not involve pleadings, discovery, witness statements and the like. In other words, the process is adjusted to the limited importance and relative simplicity of small claims. Second, the 'no costs' rule discourages the employment of legal representatives and therefore avoids complexity. Litigants are not forbidden to employ lawyers, but they have a powerful incentive for not doing so, because the legal fees may well wipe out their gains.

Lord Woolf has built on these two factors, proportionality and disincentive to cost, in his proposal for a fast-track procedure, designed, as we have seen, for claims valued between £3,000 and £10,000. It 'is intended to provide improved access to justice for litigants with modest cases by providing a strictly limited procedure designed to take cases to trial within . . . a reasonable time scale at a fixed cost that litigants can afford' (Report, 41). As with the small claims procedure, there would be a discretion to take out of the fast-track process cases which raise complex issues or which are of wide public importance (Report, 42).

The central features of the procedure are as follows (Report, 42 *et seq*). The fast-track process will be governed by a pre-determined time table, aiming to bring the case to trial in 20–30 weeks. The pre-trial process will be largely governed by standard directions. For instance, discovery will be limited to the documents on which each party relies and to those which are adverse to the interests of the discovering party. Similarly, witness statements will be confined to a summary of the evidence that it is proposed to adduce from the witness. On receipt of the defence, the district judge will consider whether any adjustments should be made to the standard directions. At that stage the judge could lay a timetable for the different procedural steps.

The fast-track procedure represents a significant shift of emphasis from orality to use of written materials. Trials will be confined to about three hours; the period being allocated equally between the parties. Given the limited scope for oral process, no oral expert evidence will be allowed. Other witnesses will be given only limited trial time, but the parties would be invited to supplement their testimony with written submissions and written evidence. The parties will be encouraged to produce their legal arguments in writing. Judgment will be given at the end of the hearing or shortly afterwards. Judges will not be required to provide detailed discussions of the legal arguments presented; an indication of their approach will suffice.

The crucial feature of this procedure is the embedded disincentive to spending disproportionately on procedure. Lord Woolf recommends that a rule of standard fixed costs should apply. Accordingly, the winning party will be able to recover only this fixed sum from the losing party. Lord Woolf does not recommend that lawyers be limited to claiming this amount from their own clients. Nonetheless, it is quite clear that if a litigant knows that he will not be able to recover more than a given sum, the litigant would be most reluctant to invest any more than that sum for fear of losing any potential gains in costs.

A fixed costs regime will provide lawyers with a powerful incentive to transact the litigation as economically and as efficiently as possible. This arrangement, it may be safely assumed, will do more than any court control and any judicially imposed sanction to maintain the efficiency of the fast-track procedure, and to ensure that it does not develop complication and delay. Professor Leipold's essay, which describes the German fixed fee system, provides support for this view.

## THE JUSTFICATION FOR RATIONING PROCEDURE AND FOR CURBING ADVERSARIAL EXCESSES

Lord Woolf's proposals for rationing procedure generally, and for the fast-track procedure have been criticised by some as diluting the commitment to the determination of truth and to giving litigants their due. It has been suggested that the fast-track procedure represents second rate justice.

Such criticism is misconceived for two reasons. The first reason is empirical. There is no factual ground for believing that the fast-track procedure would yield results of greatly inferior quality, as far as the ascertainment of law and fact is concerned. All we can tell with confidence about our present process, entailing as it does an involved pre-trial procedure, is that it probably lasts longer and costs more than do summary proceedings and than would the fast-track process. It cannot be stated with any confidence that the full pre-trial and trial process achieves a significantly higher degree of accuracy in decision.

However, there is a more fundamental retort to the criticism just mentioned. The objection to a dilution of procedural quality seem to rest on the assumption that the commitment to accuracy in judgments is unlimited or on the assumption that our present process represents the optimal level of accuracy achievable. Both these assumptions are simply false. A country can no more maintain an absolute commitment to reaching the truth in civil litigation than it can maintain an unlimited commitment to the best possible health system, regardless of cost, or to the most efficient transport system. The provision of adjudication, like the provision of any other amenity, must be subject to what the country can afford and necessitates compromises. A highly accurate system of adjudication would require intensive preparation and extensive judicial manpower, but it would be very expensive. By contrast, a very cheap system may produce a very low level of accuracy.

When a country cannot afford a limitless investment in the administration of justice, a sensible half way house, whereby the level of accuracy that the administration of justice would produce will reflect the level of support that the state can reasonably be expected to give to legal services, has to be found. Given that the administration of justice must operate within available resources, all procedures involve trade offs between the need to arrive at the truth, on the one hand, and the fact that resources are finite, on the other hand. In other words, the need to strike a balance between accuracy and cost is present in every legal system.[11] It follows that in devising a system of procedure the legislature has a considerable scope for choice between different ways of balancing accuracy against cost.

Since a compromise is inescapable, there is nothing wrong with a flexible compromise. That is, a compromise in which different levels of procedural resources are made available to different types of cases. It is reasonable to try and adjust procedure to the complexity or, indeed, importance of the dispute in question. After all, within our present system we already distinguish between small claims and other claims in the county court and we reserve the High Court jurisdiction for cases of general importance or for those requiring specialization. We also make compromises compared with other systems. In England, for example, default judgment is no more than an administrative rubber stamping of the plaintiff's claim, involving no judicial scrutiny of the claim. By contrast, in Germany the court must examine the validity of the plaintiff's claim even if the defendant does not appear.[12]

When we consider the reform of civil procedure, we must therefore not be deterred by arguments that the introduction of savings may lead to a deterioration in the accuracy of judgments. What matters is not any particular level of accuracy but the correct balance between accuracy of justice

[11] Zuckerman, 'Quality and Economy in Civil Procedure—The Case for Commuting Correct Judgment for Timely Judgments' (1994) 14 OJLS 353.

[12] Thomas and Putzo, *ZPO*, 18th edn., 1993, para 331, ann 5.

and affordability. There is nothing wrong with saying that when the subject matter of the dispute is below a certain level, the system can only afford limited procedural investment; any more than it is unjust to refer the bulk of civil litigation to county court judges rather than to their more senior (and presumably better qualified) High Court brethren.

Lord Woolf believes that 'the adversarial process is likely to encourage an adversarial culture' (Report, 7). By an adversarial culture he means a culture in which litigants tend to intensify the litigation process rather than economize; a culture in which pleadings become increasingly long and complex, in which discovery is ever more extensive, in which resort to expert witnesses is ever more frequent, in which witness statements grow in length and detail and the like. Lord Woolf's attack on this 'adversarial culture' has been seen by some as an attack on the adversarial tradition of English law. This is unfortunate since a clear distinction should be drawn between the idea of an adversarial system and the negative aspects that Lord Woolf has, perhaps unfortunately, termed as 'adversarial culture'.

In an adversarial system, as distinguished from non-adversarial systems, the responsibility for initiating the litigation, defining the issues in dispute, gathering the evidence and presenting it to the court rests upon the parties. In non-adversarial systems the courts shoulder a substantial portion of, though by no means all, the responsibility for these processes.[13] However, it is important to appreciate that there is no pure adversarial system any more than there is a pure inquisitorial system.

Even in an adversarial system, such as ours, the parties are not given complete freedom. The law imposes diverse limitations upon party freedom of choice of when and how to litigate. There are time limits upon the bringing of actions and upon performing the procedural steps involved in litigation. Actions must be brought within the limitation period, a defence must be served so many days after service of the statement of claim, discovery must take place so many days after the close of pleadings and so on. Similarly, litigants are not free to go to the court of their choice; it is the legislature which determines whether a dispute would go to the county court, to the High Court or, indeed, to a specialised tribunal. Yet no sensible person would argue that these provisions are clogs on the adversarial system. It is accepted that complete party freedom would lead to complete paralysis and to denial of justice and that some limits on litigant choice is inevitable.

Of special significance in this context is the summary judgment procedure. Litigants who have only a flimsy defence may not insist on having recourse to the normal pre-trial and trial procedures. All they can expect is a summary adjudication. Thus, plaintiffs who believe that their defendants

[13] Damaska, *The Faces of Justice and State Authority*, Yale University Press, 1986.

have no reasonable or credible defence, may apply for summary judgment under RSC Ord 14. Similarly, upon an application by one party, whether plaintiff or defendant, a court may strike out any pleading that 'discloses no reasonable cause of action or defence' in accordance with RSC Ord 18, r 19(1)(a). The object of these provisions is to prevent the use of the normal processes where the opponent's case does not deserve the normal procedural investment. Summary methods of adjudication are, therefore, concerned with proportionality. The full procedure is not waived because it is incapable of making a difference to the eventual outcome. A summary dismissal of a claim or of a defence may not be as precise and dependable as a dismissal after trial. The standard procedure is waived because, as the case stands at the time, it is unlikely to make a difference and it is therefore wasteful to employ it. Summary processes are accordingly illustrative of the notion of procedural proportionality, which holds that a dispute has to be sufficiently substantial to justify the use of the normal process.[14]

Lord Woolf's call for proportionality in procedure is not a challenge to the adversarial system any more than time limits or summary adjudication threaten the adversarial tradition. He has done no more than underscore the need for allocating the limited procedural resources available in the most economic and rational way. What he says is, essentially, that while a system of procedure must contain the facilities necessary for coping with complex and weighty disputes, it cannot afford to allow these facilities to be used regardless of the complexity or importance of the case in hand. Lord Woolf's view, that we must develop measures that would ensure that the process pursued for the resolution of a given dispute is appropriate and proportionate to that dispute, is more than just sensible. It is imperative, because in the absence of mechanisms for husbanding procedural resources some litigants will consume excessive resources while others will be left with nothing at all. Indeed, it is legitimate to ask whether it is really better to offer high quality justice to a few, rather than dispense justice, albeit of lesser quality, to a wider segment of society.

## CONCLUSION

In his interim Report Lord Woolf pursues two strategies for promoting speed and cost efficiency in litigation. The first is court management of the litigation process, while the second relies on an innovative fast-track procedure.

The employment of court control of the litigation process, backed by sanctions against wasteful procedural posturing, is bound to be ineffectual,

[14] See Zuckerman, 'A Reform of Civil Procedure—Rationing Procedure rather than Access to Justice', (1995) 22 J of Law and Society 155.

if the incentives for such behaviour are not removed at the same time. The forensic practices of the legal profession are, inevitably, bound up with the profession's financial interest in litigation. Accordingly, as long as practitioners are paid by the hour or by the day, they will continue to have an interest in expanding the litigation process.

The objectives of the court management policy are likely, therefore, to be obstructed by three related factors. First, court management will be working against the grain of professional instinct. While the courts will be pushing for paring down the process, the profession will be pressing for expanding it. Second, the courts do not act in a vacuum, their own perception of what is reasonable is bound to be affected by the customs and habits of the profession. The courts would be as likely to be influenced by the profession as would the profession by the courts. It is reasonable to expect that judges will end up reflecting the professional culture. Third, the court driven processes proposed by Lord Woolf make considerable room for procedural disputes. Even under the watchful gaze of procedural judges lawyers will have ample opportunity to dispute the extent of discovery or to protract the process of pleadings, to mention just two instances. Even the sanction of costs for procedural improprieties creates fertile ground for sterile procedural manoeuvring.

To affect the changes that Lord Woolf seeks, it is not enough to lay down norms of efficient litigation and ordain that they be observed by litigants and their lawyers, even if these norms are continually monitored by the courts and backed with sanctions. Litigants and lawyers who engage in procedural waste do not do so without reason. They usually respond to a real incentive. In the absence of measures directed to remove these incentives, judicial management will be battling against a strong socio-economic current.

The second of Lord Woolf's strategies is likely to be much more successful because it combines procedural efficiency with incentives to economize. The proposed fast-track procedure both offers a speedy and simplified process for claims of up to £10,000 and, at the same time, gives litigants and their lawyers a compelling reason to keep down expenditure on the process. For there will be a fixed costs regime in the fast-track process, whereby the winner will recover from the loser a fixed sum. This costs rule will ensure that parties do not exceed the fixed sum for fear that any extra expense will wipe out their gains.

A successful reform must surely be sought in this direction. For only if procedural efficiency can be combined with incentives for economies can we hope to break the pattern of undue complexity and unacceptable cost in the administration of civil justice.

# 4

# *Why Lord Woolf's Proposed Reforms of Civil Litigation should be Rejected*

MICHAEL ZANDER*

Lord Woolf, rightly regarded as one of the great legal figures of the day, has entitled his paper an 'Interim Report on Access to Justice in the civil justice system in England and Wales'. An official report commissioned by Ministers on this sort of subject would normally present some historical perspective on the issues, a rounded in-depth analysis of the problems, a weighing of options and a conclusion. This is not that kind of report. There is hardly any historical overview, no rounded analysis of the problem, and no weighing of options. But there is very definitely a conclusion. The report is in fact the working through, in carefully considered detail, of the conclusion. It is a powerful statement of one man's vision of what needs to be done 'To Put Matters Right'.

It was clear from the outset that Lord Woolf knew where he was heading. Lectures he gave before he was appointed, statements to the press shortly after he was appointed and frequent interviews he gave thereafter all indicated his basic thinking. Though he received many submissions, he did not put out a general invitation to present written evidence nor did he take oral evidence.[1] He wrote the Report himself. There was little of importance in the Report that could have come as a surprise to anyone who had followed the progress of the matter.

The Report[2] notes that the problem is not a new one. Since the mid-nineteenth century there have in fact been some 60 or so reports on aspects of civil procedure and organisation of the courts. In a brief introductory section to set the scene Lord Woolf mentions only the two most recent of these, the Civil Justice Review and the Bar Council-Law Society 'Heilbron-Hodge report'[3]. Having referred to these two reports and having cited Cyril

* Professor of Law, London School of Economics

[1] There were also a number of valuable seminars to address topics that Lord Woolf identified as important.

[2] p. 4, para 2.

[3] Report by the Independent Working Party of the Bar Council and the Law Society, 'Civil Justice on Trial—the Case for Change', June 1993.

Glasser's statement that civil litigation 'is in a state of crisis', the Report turns to 'The Problems and their Causes'.

The problems are what they have always been (and probably always will be)—excessive cost, excessive delay and excessive complexity. This is stated in paragraph 1 which then also offers the explanation. The problems are said to be interrelated and to stem from a single cause—'the uncontrolled nature of the litigation process'. In particular, it is stated, 'there is no clear judicial responsibility for managing individual cases or for the overall administration of the civil courts'(p. 7, para 1).

This proposition lies at the heart of the Report. It would not be difficult to identify dozens of causes that contribute to cost, delay and complexity in civil litigation. But in this Report only one explanation is ever considered. The Report simply states that the chief culprits are what it calls the uncontrolled nature of the litigation process and more especially the lack of judicial management.

The reason, it is said, is that without effective judicial control the adversarial process is 'likely to encourage an adversarial culture and to degenerate into an environment in which the litigation process is too often seen as a battlefield where no rules apply' (p. 7, para 4). The consequence is that expense is often excessive, disproportionate and unpredictable and delay is unreasonable. This is because the conduct, pace and extent of litigation are left almost completely to the parties. There is no effective control of their worst excesses. (p. 7, para 5).

The fact that alternative explanations for cost and delay are not considered clearly weakens the persuasiveness of the conclusion. But obviously that does not mean that the Report can simply be ignored. The Report is basically a call for judicial case management to cure the ills of the litigation process. Judicial case management was recommended in the Civil Justice Review and again by Heilbron-Hodge. Now Lord Woolf is putting all his authority behind the same concept. Considering the far-reaching and radical nature of the recommendations, his Report has been greeted with what seems to me a surprising amount of support from many important quarters.

I hold Lord Woolf in the highest professional and personal esteem but I find myself in the unhappy position of believing, for reasons explained below, that implementation of the Report will make the situation worse rather than better. I sense, however, that this Cassandra-like view is destined to be ignored. The mood of the times, both here and in other common law countries, is to follow the lead of the United States and embark on a period of reform under a banner called 'Judicial Case Management'. (The manifest failure of this reform movement to solve the problem in the United States is simply ignored.) There is a widely held belief that 'There is No Alternative'. Unless the Treasury intervenes for fear of the cost, it will probably be tried; it will be found 'not to work'; and in due course the cry will go up 'Something Needs to be Done'—and we will go back to the drawing board. But in the process something, perhaps much, of value will have been lost—and, if I am right, little of benefit will have been gained.

The issue is not a trivial one. Lord Woolf's Report calls for a 'fundamental shift in the responsibility for the management of civil litigation' (p. 18, para 2) and 'a radical change of culture for all concerned' (p. 18, para 4). He is playing for big stakes. (Whether his programme can be achieved is a different question to which I will return.) The matter is therefore one worthy of very careful consideration—which I fear it may not receive.

The first question is definition of the problem. That 'costs are too high', 'delays are too great' and that 'there is too much complexity' is a cliché. All three are regarded as bugbears in most, probably all, legal systems—though it should be noted in passing that at the same time their effect in curbing the pursuit of legal remedies is, up to a point, beneficial. One does not want the citizen to reach for his legal remedy like his six-shooter in the Wild West.

But, granted that they are a problem, the crucial question is how much of a problem. In what proportion of cases are they a factor? In all cases? In most cases? Or only in some cases—and if so, how many? An answer to that question would offer clues as to the importance of the issue. The more important the issue, the more appropriate it is to consider major reforms to deal with it. The less important, the less it is appropriate to undertake radical surgery to deal with it.

Unfortunately, in regard to cost and delay we are not very knowledgeable about the facts. Take costs. There have been remarkably few studies of the costs of litigation. The Report gives some preliminary figures from a study of 673 cases being conducted by Professor Hazel Genn in the Supreme Court Taxing Office. But, at least until that study is completed, we have few hard data even about the average cost of cases of different categories—other than the superficial information published in the annual report of the Legal Aid Board. But average figures are not enough. We want to know in what proportion of cases costs vary from the norm.

We also want to know about costs in cases that are not taxed or legally aided, which are far more numerous than taxed cases. But there is no information about costs in those cases. In personal injury cases the normal thing is for the insurance company to agree to pay the solicitors' bill in full—simply to avoid the trouble, delay and cost of the taxation process. (Sometimes it is done as a 'sweetener' to get the solicitor to persuade the client to settle.) One imagines that in settled cases involving the business or commercial world taxation is equally rare—that costs come in as part of the settlement deal.

The Report states (p. 3(c)) that procedure and costs should be proportionate to the nature of the issues involved and (p. 10, paras. 19–20) that 'disproportionate cost is most severe at the lower end of the scale'. Figures are cited from Hazel Genn's preliminary analysis in Annex 3 showing that where damages are low, costs are a very high proportion of the damages, and may even be higher than the damages, whilst where the damages are high, costs form a much lower proportion. This surely is hardly surprising.

To show (p. 10, para 20) that personal injury cases resulting in average damages of £694 on average cost £836, does not establish that the costs were disproportionate. They might be wholly proportionate to the amount of work involved. The suggestion that they should be proportionate to the amount of damages begs the question. Why is that thought to be the right test—unless one could say that there is (or should be) a correlation between the size of the claim and the work needing to be done, which is not so. What in a small case would be proportionate costs? 10%, 25%, 50%, 75%, 100%? The question is, proportionate from what point of view?

For most people that question probably suggests the further question as to who is paying the costs. When we consider whether the costs are disproportionate it makes a good deal of difference if they are being borne by a private individual or by an institution such as an insurance company or trade union or the legal aid fund. So, for instance, in the overwhelming majority of personal injury cases the plaintiff succeeds—usually in a pre-trial settlement. He gets his damages and his costs. Providing he does not pay the costs, whether they are higher or lower is a matter of little concern to him. Professor Hazell Genn's recent study of damages, conducted for the Law Commission[4], showed that this is the norm. In interviews with victims of accidents who got damages, about three in four of respondents overall 'said that their costs had been completely covered by legal aid or by the defendant, or by a trade union'. (In cases involving damages of over £20,000 the figure was nearly four out of five.) Only one quarter of the sample reported that they had to pay something toward their legal costs. I doubt if many of these successful claimants would suggest that the costs in their cases were disproportionate. If there were studies of unsuccessful claimants, we might find that many of them, too, did not in fact have to pay either their own or the other side's costs.

Lord Woolf speaks of disproportionate costs as if what that means is obvious, when it is far from obvious.

The same is true in regard to delay. The Report (p. 13, para 35) states that in 1994, High Court cases on average took 163 weeks in London and 189 weeks elsewhere to progress from issue to trial and that in the county courts the figure was 80 weeks. Most of the time was between issue and set-

[4] H. Genn, *Personal Injury Compensation: How Much is Enough?* (Law Com. No.225), pp. 149–50.

ting down. The Report says 'These figures are unacceptable in relation to the great generality of cases'. (*ibid*)

But how can one know that the figures are unacceptable unless one has some idea as to the reasons for the delay? No such information exists. The Report states, 'In the majority of cases the reasons for delay arise from failure to progress the case efficiently, wasting time on peripheral issues or procedural skirmishing to wear down an opponent or to excuse failure to get on with the case'. No evidence is given for this savage critique of the practices of litigation lawyers and their clients. So far as I know, none exists. Of course, any of these are factors in some cases, but the statement that it explains delay in the majority of cases is, I believe, wholly unfounded—and in my view, is very unlikely to be true.

Moreover, those figures relate only to the tiny proportion of cases that go to trial, whereas most cases do not go to trial. The Cantley Committee in 1979[5] made the point very graphically. Taking personal injury cases in London in 1977, there were 9,001 writs issued, 2,345 cases set down for trial and a mere 317 (3% of the 9,000) judgments after trial. Are the cases that settle without a trial also taking too long? We do not know because in most cases that settle we have no figures for delay—let alone figures for excessive delay.

Cantley's assessment of the problem of delay was very different from that offered by Lord Woolf. Looking at High Court personal injury cases it concluded (p. 2, para 2):

(1) 'In most cases the writ is issued within a reasonable time after the cause of action (75% within 24 months).'
(2) 'Most cases are set down within a reasonable time after the issue of the writ (45–50% within 12 months and 80% within 24 months).'
(3) 'There is a small proportion of cases which appears to be unduly delayed.'

It added (para 2(4) ):

> Observation and experience, but not verifiable by figures . . . indicate that there are some cases, a very small proportion of the total which pass through the interlocutory process and which from time to time reach trial, where the delay is clearly due to slackness or incompetence or has been deliberately prolonged in the hope that a virtually hopeless case can be brought to some kind of settlement.

Cantley suggested that the problem of delay could be addressed by a simple new rule. Where a case had not been set down for trial eighteen months after issue of the proceedings, the plaintiff's solicitor should be required to report on the progress of the case. If appropriate, a summons could then be issued and the court could give directions. This proposal had the great

[5] *Report of the Personal Injuries Litigation Procedure Working Party*, Cmnd. 7476, 1979.

merit of being aimed solely at cases that showed *prima facie* evidence of delay. Unfortunately, it was not implemented.

Today we are little further forward in understanding the basic facts about civil litigation. We have a great deal of hunch, anecdote and assertion but little in the way of relevant fact. In particular, we still do not know whether the problem is major or minor; we do not understand the causes of the increase in the cost of litigation; nor do we know how much of the delay in litigation is matter for criticism and, if so, of whom or what.

But Lord Woolf's Report is clear that 'something needs to be done' and it sets out its solution in chapter 5 entitled 'The Need for Case Management by the Courts'. This states that to achieve the objectives of reducing cost, delay and complexity 'there is no alternative to a fundamental shift in the responsibility for the management of civil litigation from litigants and their legal advisers to the courts'(p. 26, para 2).

There are several reasons why I believe that this is a cure that is likely to be considerably worse than the disease:

1. *Most cases do not need any intervention by the courts because they settle.* The point was made by the Cantley Committee[6]: 'Any solution which concentrates on speeding cases to trial, but which makes settlement less likely or more expensive, might be bought at an unduly high price.' If most cases would settle anyway without the intervention of the court, it is not a good idea to transform the system by involving the court and generating costs for the system and the parties when to do so will increase the costs for both in those cases—which are far more numerous than the cases that do reach the court. This is front-loading of costs on cases that almost certainly do not need it. (The issue as to the front-loading of costs in cases that do go the distance to trial, or to the door of the court, or at least a good way toward the court is a separate matter to which I return below.)

Of the 4,420 actions disposed of in 1994 in the Queen's Bench Division, 13% were determined after trial, 35% were settled with a court order and 52% were 'settled without court order, struck out or withdrawn before hearing'.[7] The category mainly in issue here is the last. Since they are lumped together, one does not know the breakdown as between 'settled without court order', 'struck out' and 'withdrawn before hearing', but it is doubtful whether many of these cases would benefit from any part of the Woolf plan for case management. Yet I suspect that a considerable proportion of that 52% of cases would be included in the Woolf net. Even if the settlement, striking out or withdrawal were achieved more speedily, the

[6] *Report of the Personal Injuries Litigation Procedure Working Party*, Cmnd. 7476, 1979 para 9.

[7] *Judicial Statistics*, 1994, p. 30, Table 3.4. The figure of 35% is an aggregate of cols.C, D, E, F; the figure of 52% is col. G.

benefit of such earlier disposal is unlikely to be greater than the detriment of the extra costs for both the system and litigants.

I believe that the same would also be true for some of the 35% of cases that were settled with a court order. The breakdown in the *Judicial Statistics* here is 'settled during trial' (5% of the 4,420), 'approval of prior settlement given' (8%), 'settled without notice'(7%), and 'settled with consent order before hearing' (15%). The categories are baffling but I imagine that in a fair proportion of these cases even the most ardent supporter of court management would accept that application of the proposed new system would not add anything of value.

The Report (p. 32,para 23) does acknowledge the argument made by 'a minority of commentators'[8] that 'since the majority of cases settle in any event (95–97 per cent of personal injury cases), it is unnecessary to introduce an expensive new system purely for the benefit of the cases that do not settle'. Lord Woolf responded, 'My recommendations will not, however prevent settlement; in fact they are designed to encourage earlier and fairer settlements which not only avoid the expense and inconvenience of settling at the door of the court, but also more accurately reflect the merits of the case'.

But this misses the point made. It is not suggested that the Woolf plan will prevent settlement. It is quite possible that in some cases it may even speed it up and, in particular, may reduce the number of settlements at the door of the court. The worry is rather that implementation of the Woolf plan risks increasing costs uselessly in a very large number of cases where it has no such beneficial effect.

The balance of net additional cost as against net additional savings is of course also posed in regard to the small minority of cases that go all the way to trial or that settle at or near to the hearing. Those are the main target of the Woolf reforms. I believe (and argue below) that even there the case for intervention by court management is not made out.

2. *It is most unlikely that giving the courts a management role will increase the efficiency of the system.* First, judges are not expert in management. Neither in practice before they became judges nor on the bench will most of them have had any opportunity to develop management skills. The Report admits as much but suggests that the deficiency could be remedied by special training. Such training will itself be a new cost for the system—starting with training in IT skills. Whether it will 'take' will depend on the quality of the training and the appetite of the judges for this new role. I would incline to be sceptical on both counts.

[8] The writer, for instance, expressed these concerns at one of the seminars organised by the Woolf inquiry and subsequently published an edited version of the remarks—'Are there any clothes for the Emperor to wear? *New L.J.*, 3 February 1995, p. 131.

But even if the training were good and the judges showed enthusiasm for the role, it by no means follows that net efficiency gains would follow. The evidence from other jurisdictions, and especially the United States, is not encouraging. The Report (p. 32, para 21(c)) refers to the suggestion that 'there is a lack of reliable research evidence on the effectiveness of case management by the courts'. It asserts (p. 33, para 25) that 'attempts to monitor the introduction of case management systems in the United States suggest that they have been effective in reducing delay, although the results are less conclusive as regards the saving of costs'.[9]

What I have seen of the literature regarding court management suggests, to the contrary, that the cupboard is pretty bare.[10] It is not that there is no evidence, but rather that there is a good deal of evidence and that basically it is negative or at most inconclusive.

Summarising the results of such research, one report concluded:

> The speed with which cases move does not seem to be influenced by court workload, trial rates, case mix, procedural rules or judicial involvement in settlement conferences. Indeed, the injection of additional resources intended to accelerate litigation—judges, courtrooms, support staff—has often ended in embarrassing failure.[11]

In response, the Woolf Report (p. 32, para 23) refers merely to a 1994 research project in Toronto which 'demonstrated that managed cases are disposed of in the system at twice the rate of non-managed cases'. It is doubtful whether the study actually stands for the proposition for which it is cited.[12] But be that is it may, Lord Woolf seems not to have acknowledged that there is a significant volume of respectable research that does not support his main recommendation. This research cannot just be brushed aside or wished away. (This treatment of the research literature also somewhat undermines the credibility of the otherwise very welcome calls in the Report for pilot studies, monitoring and research.)

[9] The Report at that point refers to Annex 2 on Research but inspection of Annex 2 gives no further clue as to what studies were relied on for the view expressed in the text. The general inadaquacy of the referencing in the Report is a matter for comment. In too many instances there are citations of statistics or quotations with no indication of source.

[10] And see in this volume, Richard Marcus, 'Déjà vu all over again? An American Reaction to the Woolf Report', pp. 232–35 below, especially p. 234.

[11] R. Dingwall, T. Durkin, W. L. Felstiner, 'Delay in Tort Cases: Critical Reflections on the Civil Justice Review', *Civil J.Qtrly.*,October 1990, p. 356.

[12] A report by Professor Carl Baar to the Civil Litigation Task Force of the Advocates Society: 'The Reduction and Control of Civil Case Backlog in Ontario', June 1994 'One of the primary purposes of case management is to expedite the pace of litigation, and in fact, Ontario's case management pilot projects (in Windsor and Sault Ste. Marie since September 1990, and in Toronto since December 1991) have all resulted in a more expeditious pace of litigation than would have been the case under existing rules and procedures.' (pp. 20–21).This sentence does not justify the statement in the text of the Woolf Report.

Even if there were *no* such negative research evidence from overseas, the basic concept proposed by Lord Woolf is clearly problematic. There is first the need for a 'radical change of culture for all concerned' (p. 18, para 4). Changes of culture are extremely difficult to achieve; radical changes are even more difficult. I would not put money on this having much success.

Most of the judges are former barristers, likely to be strongly wedded to the traditional attitudes of the adversary system. The more 'hands on' the case management required, the greater the culture change. The extent of the culture change required is evident from the lengthy quotation in the Report (p. 31, para 20) from the statement of the Federal Judicial Council as to what is meant by case management: 'It is active' with the judge anticipating problems before they arise; 'it is substantive'- the judge's involvement is not limited to procedural matters; 'it is continuing'—the judge periodically monitors the progress of the litigation to see that schedules are being followed, to consider modifications to the litigation plan and may call for interim reports. This does not sound like a programme that ordinary English High Court and circuit judges could easily be persuaded to embrace.

Even if they can be achieved, radical changes in culture need a great deal of justification. The legal culture of a country is not something to be tossed aside as if it was a matter of little account. There is a long history to the development of our model of the adversary system, a model that is deep in the unconscious psyche of every English lawyer and judge. To propose that it should be radically altered is to propose a major jolt to that collective unconscious. I would be the last to say that we should hang on to the existing system for sentimental reasons. I am only suggesting that it would wise not to jump too quickly. Once important traditions are jettisoned it is often impossible to recreate them. It is also sensible to bear in mind that reforms usually produce unexpected results. The more radical the reform, the greater the danger that they will prove unwelcome.

Court management has now been tried over more than twenty years in the United States. I do not believe that *in terms of the legal culture* the results have been especially good. An example is what it does to the role of the judge. To give the judge responsibility for the throughput of the caseload means that he is naturally tempted to step outside his judicial role into a very different role. The Report proposes that in multi-track cases (the most important and heaviest) there should be a preparatory hearing conducted by the trial judge. The American experience is that the court-management system often results in the judge at the pre-trial conference leaning on the parties in the hope of pushing them ('in their own best interests') toward settlement. The judge's concern to judge the case is subverted by his new concern to achieve a settlement.[13] I doubt whether many English judges (or for that matter, practitioners) would regard that as desirable. But it is a predictable and probably unavoidable outcome of making the judge accountable for the progressing of cases and then putting him in charge of the pre-trial hearings.

Also, will the judge who has taken a managing, controlling role pre-trial be seen to be as impartial as now when it comes to his role in the trial?

Moreover, implementation of the Woolf proposals would involve huge costs for the system that Lord Woolf has not sufficiently appreciated (or at least acknowledged). To get a sense of this it is useful to consider what the Report actually proposes in the name of greater efficiency and reduction in cost. The list that follows deals only with recommendations that have significant cost implications for the LCD. Some also affect the parties. (The numbers refer to the list of recommendations on pp. 223–233):

- All cases where a defence is received to be examined by a procedural judge who would allocate the case to its appropriate track. (No. 4)
- Parties to be allowed to apply for the case to be re-allocated to a different track. (p. 42, paras.7–8)
- The court to have a power to summon parties of its own motion with a view to summary disposal of the matter—even before a defence has been issued. (p. 38, para 18)
- In fast-track cases, after receipt of a defence, the judge to consider whether to vary standard directions in regard to expert witness reports, date of delivery of witness summaries, setting the time-table for pre-trial stages and setting the week of trial. (p. 44, para 12)
- In fast-track cases district judges to play a pro-active role—communicating with the parties or their advisers by phone, fax or letter, holding conference calls, etc. (p. 44, para 14)
- District judge to monitor the checklist filled out by the parties and the documentation. (p. 45, para 15)
- For multi-track cases, the procedural judge to decide whether the case requires full hands-on judicial control, more limited judicial management or simply standard directions.(p. 38, para 22)
- On the multi-track, two interlocutory hearings—the case management conference and the pre-trial review. (No. 7)
- Senior judges to oversee the system. (Nos. 12–15)
- The Court Service to appoint corresponding officials to act in partnership with the new supervising judges. (No. 16)
- Teams of judges and Masters (or district judges) to manage cases. (No. 18)

[13] On this issue see especially the writings of Professor Judith Resnick, *viz* 'Managerial Judges', 96 *Harvard L.Rev.*, 1982, p. 374; 'Failing Faith: Adjudicatory Procedure in Decline', 53 *Univ.Chicago L.Rev.*, 1986, p. 494.

- Training and monitoring of judges in relation to case management. (No. 23)
- Judges engaged in small claims cases to be trained with a view to achieving greater consistency of approach. (p. 110, para 35)
- Personal computers for judges powerful enough to support all the proposals in the report. (No. 31)
- Video and telephone conferencing facilities for all judges and especially the procedural judges in regard to case management. (No. 33)
- Video recording and viewing facilities at appropriate centres. (No. 34)
- The court to ensure that the pleadings follow the new rule to 'plainly state the factual ingredients of their case so that the true nature and scope of the dispute can be identified'. (No. 76)
- If the issues cannot be identified from the pleadings, the procedural judge to seek clarification by written request or phone and, if needed, a management conference. (p. 156, paras.10–11) and can give directions (No. 78).
- Extra discovery in multi-track cases to be determined by procedural judge after considering the issues in the case, the resources and circumstances of the parties, likely costs and likely benefits. (No .92)
- The court to have complete control of the calling of expert evidence. (Nos. 101–105, 113)
- The court to direct the attention of the parties to alternative dispute resolution. (p. 37, para. 16)

The aggregate cost of these add-on features of the proposed scheme would be very considerable. Moreover there would be the further cost (not to speak of annoyance) of chasing and enforcing compliance with all the new rules—which could be quite troublesome. Whatever savings or reductions in cost may result for the parties in some cases from implementation of the Report, there is little likelihood of compensating financial gains for the LCD. Lord Woolf has I think considerably understated the extent to which implementation of his proposals will increase the burden on the taxpayer (as well litigants) in terms of more judges, more facilities and above all more process. The Treasury should ask some rather pointed questions before agreeing to implementation of this package in today's straitened circumstances where public expenditure is supposed to be under severe restraint.

Many of the additional duties and functions proposed for the courts involve more work for the lawyers. This is most obvious for multi-track cases where the two new pre-trial hearings and other proposed pre-trial activity will unquestionably generate a great deal of new work and cost not only before and during the new hearings but afterwards as the lawyers carry out the tasks prescribed for them by the court. But I suspect that even in fast-track cases the new regime will not cut costs as often as Lord Woolf believes. There will be more front-loading of costs, more written submissions and written evidence of ordinary and expert witnesses in lieu of oral evidence and the like. The Report proposes fixed costs assessed as a percentage of the value of the claim. Whether that reduces costs depends on the percentage. Moreover, if lawyers find the work does not pay, they will not do it.

*3. Case management by teams of judges and Masters will be inefficient* In the United States cases are assigned to judges who have a docket for which they are responsible. Lord Woolf rightly concluded that in our system, which relies so heavily on part-timers, this would not work. Instead, he proposes judicial teams. The focal point of the team would be the Master or district judge who would act as the manager of the team and the procedural judge. He would have the key responsibility for the management of cases handled by the team (p. 67, para 21). Composition of the team would vary. 'The aim will be to include judges at appropriate levels and with sufficient expertise to ensure flexibility and the efficient disposal of more specialist cases which do not in themselves merit a separate list' (*ibid.*, para 22).

This may be the only solution to the problem created by part-time judges, but it may be so poor a solution as to call into question the whole idea. If case management does not produce satisfactory results in the U.S. where at least a single judge has his docket, is it going to work where responsibility for the through-put of cases would be diffused amongst members of a team? It seems unlikely that the team approach could provide the same 'grip' as a single judge.

The team system would also significantly reduce the flexibility of the system of judicial allocation. If the judge is assigned to a team, he is less available to be deployed elsewhere. This reduction in flexibility of judicial deployment will be a serious effect of the Woolf proposals. It applies most notably to the concept, crucial to the Woolf scheme, of assigning judges to the multi-track cases that require hands-on management from a very early stage. Any gain in those cases has to be balanced against the loss to the efficiency of the system as a whole. The more that judges are tied into particular cases, the greater the problem of allocation—until the point would be reached where the only way to square the circle would be to appoint more judges. Lord Woolf's Report makes no acknowledgement of this regrettable fact of life.

It is also predictable that the organisation of the teams, of allocation of judges and the whole business of court management of cases will tend to exacerbate the already not invariably harmonious relations between judges and court administrators. It will provide a new, major and continuing source of tension and difficulty.

4. *If the judge at the pre-trial review has to be the trial judge, overall efficiency of the system declines* The same is true of the proposal (p. 48, para 4) that in multi-track cases the pre-trial review should be before the same judge as takes the trial. From the point of view of the case that may be desirable. From the point of view of the availability of judges generally it is very undesirable. Those charged with the task of allocating judges to cases will always want the maximum number of 'free' judges. Implementation of the Woolf scheme would greatly increase the number of pre-trial reviews and the number of judges unavailable generally because, having conducted the pre-trial review they would then be required to do the trial as well. That would be the opposite of an improvement in the efficiency of the system.[14]

5. *If counsel at the pre-trial review is supposed to be counsel at the trial, again the efficiency of the system is diminished* The same is true of the proposal that in these same cases counsel at the pre-trial review should be counsel at the trial (p. 49, para 8). Again, from the point of view of the individual case that may be desirable. From the point of view of the system it is not. It would mean that the unavailability of counsel for the trial would result in an adjournment—and another adjournment and another. There would be no end to it. The English rule that an adjournment is generally not granted when counsel of choice is unavailable sometimes deprives the client of the representative the case needs. But it has the great advantage that it keeps the flow of cases moving forward. Lord Woolf's proposal would significantly slow things down and, as a result, delays would lengthen. There is no recognition of this in the Report which simply states (p. 49, para 8): 'the counsel or solicitor instructed to attend the trial must appear at the pre-trial review'.

This proposal is not only counter-productive in terms of efficiency of the system. It is also unrealistic. In the heavier type of case justifying significant 'hands on' court management counsel at the trial will tend to be a leader or senior junior who is most unlikely to be willing or able to appear at the pre-trial review. In fact in all but very minor cases, pre-trial matters will (for understandable reasons) tend to be left, as they now are[15], to advocates

[14] The extent of the *increase* can be judged from the fact that it is now very rare for the judge at a pre-trial review to be the same as the judge at trial. The *Crown Court Study* done for the Royal Commission on Criminal Justice showed, for instance, that it was a different judge in over 80 per cent of cases—see note 17 below, at para. 2.8.4. Professor Michael Levi's study for the Royal Commission showed that the same was true equally in serious fraud cases—see note 18 below.

[15] In the recent experiment with Plea and Directions Hearings (PDHs) it was found that in only 8.5% of cases during the pilot did the initially briefed prosecution counsel attend both the POH and the substantive hearing. For defence counsel the figure was 27%. (Report of the National Steering Group, *Pilot Study of Recommendation 92*, Lord Chancellor's Department, Feb. 1994, p. 41, para. 120). Recommendation 92 was made by the Pre-Trial Issues Working Group in its Report in November, 1990.

junior to those who conduct the trial. To say that it should not be so achieves precisely nothing.

The proposal that clashes should be avoided by not having trials of multi-track cases on Fridays would cause further rigidities and waste in the system. Though aimed at solving one problem it would create other even greater problems.

6. *The proposed two (or more) interlocutory management hearings in multi-track cases will not prove cost-effective* The Report (p. 48, para. 4) places great emphasis on pre-trial hearings for multi-track cases. The first of these would be the case management conference called shortly after the defence is received, normally taken by the procedural judge. The second would be the pre-trial review about eight to ten weeks prior to the date of trial taken by the trial judge. At the case management conference the court would consider the questionnaire filled out by the parties, plus the claim, the defence and preliminary information as to the witnesses and documentary evidence on which the parties intend to rely. The court would give directions regarding the steps to be taken by each party prior to the pre-trial review, the dates by which such steps would have to be taken and the target date for the trial. Directions would cover a programme for discovery. (p. 49, paras. 9–10)

The later pre-trial review, it is said, would provide an opportunity 'to reconsider the key issues of the case and whether these can be narrowed further before the trial' (p. 50, para 12). The witnesses who need to give oral evidence would be identified. The management of documentary evidence would be agreed. The form of expert evidence would be determined.

These proposals are presented as if they were unproblematic. In fact however they raise the question whether such pre-trial hearings are on balance worthwhile. In the cases that settle later, would the pre-trial hearings on average contribute in a significant way to the achievement of the settlement? In the cases that go to trial, would the pre-trial hearings make a significant contribution in terms of reducing cost by shortening the trial? The contribution must of course be sufficient to outweigh the cost of the new pre-trial hearings. Common sense may suggest that a pre-trial hearing, at least for heavy cases, would be a good idea. But common sense is sometimes wrong.

There is now a body of empirical evidence about various kinds of pre-trial hearings. The results tend to be the opposite of what common sense suggests. Instead of simplifying trials or saving costs, such hearings tend to do the opposite. They seem generally to increase costs and lengthen trials.[16]:

[16] I referred to these studies in my Note of Dissent to the *Report of the Royal Commission on Criminal Justice*, 1993, Cm 2263, HMSO, pp. 228–229—where the same issue arose. On this issue see now also the Government's Consultation Document, 'Improving the Effectiveness of Pre-Trial Hearings in the Crown Court', Cm 2924, July 1955, pp. 10–15.

- In the *Crown Court Study* done for the Royal Commission on Criminal Justice, judges in cases where there was a pre-trial review were asked whether they thought that it had saved much time and money. As many as two-thirds (66%) said No. A quarter (24%) said that a little time and money had been saved. In only 8% a fair amount of time and money had been saved. A 'great deal' had been saved in only 1%.[17]
- Professor Michael Levi's study of serious fraud cases stated in regard to ordinary pre-trial reviews: 'none of the defence lawyers I interviewed argued that pre-trial reviews had any significant effect on the development of the case. . .'[18]
- The fate of the more formal preparatory hearings under the Serious Fraud regime is equally discouraging. The Roskill Committee said that a full day should be set aside for preparatory hearings.[19] In fact, however, in many of the cases brought by the Serious Fraud Office, preparatory hearings have taken weeks or even months. (In the case known as Guiness I, the preparatory hearing took three months.)
- The only proper study of the impact of pre-trial conferences, using matched samples, conducted in 3,000 personal injury cases in New Jersey, concluded that although they improved preparation, they did not shorten trials.[20] The researchers concluded that they therefore lowered rather than raised the efficiency of the system by absorbing a great deal of court and judge time without any compensating saving in the time required for trials.
- The experiment with Plea and Directions Hearings in three Crown Courts showed that a brief PDH (average length ten minutes) reduced trial times from an average of 4 hrs.41 minutes in the pre-pilot to 4 hrs. 12 minutes in the pilot. If the length of the PDH is added into the equation, there was therefore a reduction in court time of about 20 minutes per case.[21] This net gain would however have been wiped out if the length of the PDH had been much longer than ten minutes.

In light of the evidence of these various studies, one can hardly have much confidence that pre-trial hearings will promote the objectives envisaged for them in the Woolf Report. If anything, rather the contrary. The

17 M. Zander and P. Henderson, *The Crown Court Study*, Royal Commission on Criminal Justice, Research Study No. 19, (HMSO, 1993), sect. 2.8.9.

18 Michael Levi, *The Investigation, Prosecution and Trial of Serious Fraud*, Royal Commission on Criminal Justice Research Study No. 14 (HMSO, 1993), p. 105. Levi suggested, 'The problem is that the judge in the pre-trial reviews is seldom the trial judge, has seldom read the papers, and therefore understandably does not wish to become embroiled in complex matters.' That may or may not be the problem but, as has already been seen, having the pre-trial judge be the trial judge also creates considerable problems.

19 *Fraud Trials Committee Report*, 1986, HMSO, para. 6.52.

20 M. Rosenberg, *The Pre-Trial Conference and Effective Justice*, 1964, Columbia University Press, p. 68.

21 *op.cit.*, note 15 above, p. 20, para. 57.

Report proposes (p. 48, para 4) that they should normally be used in multi-track cases—on the hypothesis that hands-on case management is fundamentally a Good Thing because either it promotes settlement or it knocks the case into shape for the trial and thereby reduces its length and cost. My position would be the precise opposite. They should be used very sparingly on the ground that pre-trial hearings are fundamentally a Bad Thing because they tend to increase cost both in cases that settle and those that do not, and in cases that do not settle they tend also to lengthen trials.

7. *Do litigants want the courts to take over?* The Report is based on the unstated premise that litigants will benefit from judicial management of cases. I believe that this is a fundamental misapprehension. In pre-trial court management proceedings the judges will give directions and make a variety of decisions usually on the basis of insufficient information. There will be pressure to move things along regardless. The court will always know less about the particular circumstances of the case than the parties and their advisers. In my view, the progressing of cases is in general better left to the parties and their advisers who know about their case, at least until such time as there is evidence that they have not behaved as they should—as proposed by the Cantley Committee.

A study by the Rand Corporation suggests that what litigants want most is due process and fair handling of their cases. It seems that they are not primarily concerned about cost or delay or even,surprisingly, the result.[22] The idea that they will (or should) welcome a judicial take-over of the process of litigation is to be viewed with considerable scepticism.

By the same token I also doubt whether litigants will necessarily welcome the idea for fast-track cases of fixed costs and strict time-tables, both of which could have the effect of cutting lawyers' preparation, or of a trial restricted to three hours to be shared between the two sides. What they will want above all, one suspects, is that the case be prepared and presented properly. The same is true of the idea of the court-appointed expert which is unlikely to sit any better with the parties than with their advisers. Often, rightly or wrongly, they will feel the need to employ their own expert in addition and there will therefore have been an overall increase rather than a decrease in cost. But apart from the cost issue, I think it will be difficult to persuade the community of litigators and their clients that court-appointed experts are an improvement in terms of the quality of justice.

My conclusion therefore is that for all these reasons Lord Woolf has got it fundamentally wrong. Putting civil cases under judicial management is neither necessary nor desirable. Contrary to general opinion, there is no

[22] See E. Allan Lind *et al*, *The Perception of Justice: Tort Litigants' Views of Trial, Court Annexed Arbitration and Judicial Settlement Conferences*, (Rand Institute for Civil Justice, 1989). The study was the subject of an article by the writer in *New L.J.*, 20 October 1989, p. 1422.

solid evidence that there is a problem justifying so radical a solution. The case simply is not made out. If there were such evidence, the proposed solution would not cure the problem. It would be very costly and, worse, it would do more harm than good to the quality of justice.

Lord Woolf has asked whether his general approach is accepted. The answer must be No.

# 5

# *Making Tracks*

NICK ARMSTRONG*[1]

## INTRODUCTION

The Woolf inquiry into civil justice has brought in its wake a number of buzzwords and phrases. The Interim Report,[2] published in June, is littered with references to 'increased court management', the need for a change in litigation 'culture', and the concept of 'proportionality' between the costs of litigation and the amount at stake. The notion of 'tracking', however, is the theme around which all the others revolve.

Tracking is based on the idea that different cases should be treated differently. The argument seems incontrovertible. As Adrian Zuckerman has said, 'when procedural resources are finite, we should ration their employment'.[3] Put more simply, 'Cadillac-style procedures are not needed to process bicycle-size lawsuits'.[4] Civil process, it is said, must be tailored to the needs of the individual case.

But determining exactly how this ought to be done has proved problematic. We already have a crude tracking system in this country, in the form of the differences between the High Court, with its three divisions and the specialist jurisdictions of the Official Referees Court and the Commercial Court; the county courts; and the small claims jurisdiction. The boundaries between these jurisdictions have often been criticised. Consider for example the controversies that have arisen with regard to small claims, where it has been argued that the amount at stake should not be the only factor determining whether or not a case should be referred. The complexity of the legal and factual issues, the existence of a public interest, and the

* Irwin Mitchell Research Fellow, The Centre of Advanced Litigation, Nottingham Law School.

1 The author would like to thank Tony Jolowicz and Peter Jones for their comments on an earlier draft of this essay.

2 The Rt Hon the Lord Woolf, *Access to Justice*, Interim Report to the Lord Chancellor on the Civil Justice System in England and Wales (June 1995).

3 A. A. S. Zuckerman, 'A Reform of Civil Procedure—Rationing Procedure Rather Than Access to Justice' (1995) 22(2) J Law & Soc 155, 158.

4 M. Rosenberg, 'The Federal Rules After Half A Century' (1984) 36 Maine L Rev 243, 247.

procedural right to make full representations, have all been cited as other matters to be considered.[5]

Even where tracking systems become more sophisticated, similar problems arise. Many US state courts have experimented with different varieties of tracking systems, usually involving two to four tracks, distinguished by their respective timetables, the amount of judicial supervision and so on. Again, however, such systems have been criticised as being inflexible, and incapable of serving the full range of interests in the resolution of civil disputes.[6]

These issues do not only arise in the context of what might be called 'litigation tracks', though that is what is usually meant by tracking. Alternative dispute resolution (ADR) should also properly be regarded as one more process, or track, to which a dispute may be referred. Accordingly, the various disputes that have arisen in that context, including the suitability of disputes to ADR if there is an inequality of bargaining power,[7] if there is a possibility of coercion in the referral,[8] or if there is a discernible public interest which would be prejudiced were the dispute resolved privately,[9] may be seen as part and parcel of the same debate: how to devise track selection criteria for allocating procedural resources.

These questions have now been focused by Lord Woolf's proposed system of small claims, a fast-track, a multi-track and an increased emphasis on ADR. The effect of these proposals is to move the tracking debate on. We are no longer concerned with whether or not we should construct a new tracking system; we are about to get one. Our concern now is how to assess whether the incoming system operates more effectively than the one it will replace, and how, within the basic structure set out by Lord Woolf, it might be moulded as we learn more about it.

The purpose of this essay is to assist in that process by establishing the

[5] See P. Allen, 'Small Personal Injury Claims', [1994] JPIL 57, with regard to small claims; and generally, *Civil Justice: The Way Ahead. The Law Society's First Submission to Lord Woolf's Review of Civil Justice* (Civil Litigation and Courts and Legal Services Committees, March 1994), Chap. 6.

[6] See H. Bakke & M. Solomon, 'Case Differentiation: An Approach to Individualized Case Management' (1989) 73(1) Judicature 17; and M. L. Goodman, 'Effective Case Monitoring and Timely Dispositions: The Experience of One California Court' (1993) 76(5) Judicature 254.

[7] See e.g. H. Brown & A. Marriott, *ADR Principles and Practice* (London: Sweet & Maxwell, 1993) p. 399.

[8] See e.g. R. Ingleby, 'Court Sponsored Mediation: The Case Against Mandatory Participation' (1993) 56(3) MLR 441; and A. Nelle, 'Making Mediation Mandatory: A Proposed Framework' (1992) 7 Ohio St J Disp Res 187.

[9] See e.g. O. Fiss, 'Against Settlement' (1984) 93 Yale LJ 1073; L. Macklin, 'Promoting Settlement, Foregoing the Facts' (1986) 14 Rev Law & Soc Change 575; H. T. Edwards, 'Alternative Dispute Resolution: Panacea or Anathema?' (1986) 99 Harv L Rev 668; K. Karelis, 'Private Justice: How Civil Litigation is Becoming a Private Institution—The Rise of Private Dispute Centers' (1994) 23 Southwestern U L Rev 621; and N. Armstrong, 'ADR and the Public Interest in Personal Injury' [1994] JPIL 178.

principles upon which a tracking system ought properly to be designed. It takes as its premise the fact that it is impossible to determine the success of a civil justice system without an understanding of what that system should be trying to achieve. Only by carrying out such an analysis can we identify what are the problems to be overcome, and then establish how to do so. It is shown how such an analysis supports the concept of tracking through providing a series of choices where the needs of a particular case cannot readily be determined, but identifies further issues which need to be addressed in order to ensure that these choices are made properly. It argues that at the heart of everything Lord Woolf is trying to do there lies one simple question which has not yet been articulated: how much are we prepared to pay for civil justice? This essay suggests that there are implications inherent to that question deserving of our immediate attention if we are to succeed in providing a civil justice system which serves our sense of procedural values, but functions within the constraints of limited resources.

## MODELS OF CIVIL PROCESS: MANAGING AN ESSENTIAL TENSION

The debate over the function of a civil justice system revolves around a tension between two different models of civil process: the 'dispute resolution' model and the 'policy implementation' model.[10] Under the former, adjudication is understood simply as a method for peacefully resolving a conflict between private parties. The private interests are sovereign, and the state or public interest is limited to maximising the satisfaction of those interests in order to avoid forcible self-help. In other words, the interests of the parties must be realised, and the civil justice system must preserve its reputation of being capable of realising those interests, in order to create the incentives for disputants to use the court system: 'the rules of procedure should contain some carrots as well as sticks'.[11] The provision of courts and legal services, or 'access to justice', may therefore be explained as 'civilisation's substitute for vengeance'.[12]

The policy implementation model, by contrast, recognises a wider public interest. As well as observing the need to resolve the immediate dispute, this model also takes account of its potential effect on the future conduct of others.[13] The existence of the private conflict becomes an opportunity to

[10] See generally, O. Fiss, 'Two Models of Adjudication', in Goldwin & Schambra (eds), *How Does the Constitution Secure Rights?* (American Enterprise for Public Policy Research, 1985), p. 36; also published as 'The Social and Political Foundations of Adjudication' (1982) 6 Law & Human Behaviour 121; and K. E. Scott, 'Two Models of the Civil Process' (1975) 27 Stan L Rev 937.

[11] J. A. Jolowicz, 'On the Nature and Purposes of Civil Procedural Law', in I. R. Scott (ed.), *International Perspectives on Civil Justice* (London: Sweet & Maxwell, 1990), pp. 27, 45.

[12] E. J. Couture, 'The Nature of Judicial Process' (1950) 25 Tulane L Rev pp. 1, 7.

[13] See Scott, 'Two Models of Civil Process', *op. cit.*

clarify and determine the standards by which society governs itself. Those standards include the Rule of Law, the maintenance of which transcends the interests of the private parties in order to achieve justice for those who are never involved in actual proceedings.[14]

The difference between the two models, therefore, is one of emphasis between private and public interests. Under the dispute resolution model, the private interests of the parties take precedence; under the policy implementation model, they must sometimes yield to the wider public interest.

## Outcome and non-outcome related interests

There is an increasing amount of research which assists us in identifying the nature of these public and private interests. With regard to the private interests, the work of E. Allan Lind, Tom Tyler and others[15] has established that although as a general statement disputants want to win, 'winning' is made up of a number of different factors, all of which bear upon the perception of procedural fairness. These include the need to participate in the process, to be treated politely and with respect, and for neutrality and honesty on the part of the decision-maker.

It may be observed that not all of these factors necessarily bear upon the declared objective of the dispute resolution model; namely, to encourage the disputants to accept the result. Some of the interests, such as the need to be treated politely and with respect—an interest which includes the need to avoid unnecessary time and expense in resolving the dispute—are important in themselves, irrespective of the impact they may have on the outcome. This is a point made by Summers, who has argued that a system which possesses certain 'process values', as he calls them, might be described as 'good', irrespective of whether it produces 'correct' results.[16]

Nevertheless, it is clear that many of the interests identified do derive their importance from their relationship with the outcome, whether that effect is real or perceived. For example, the need to participate in the decision-making process is important, not because it guarantees a result which is correct in any objective sense, but because a procedure which allows the parties the opportunity to participate is perceived by them as more likely

[14] Jolowicz, 'On the Nature and Purposes of Civil Procedural Law', *op. cit.* at p. 45.

[15] See e.g. J. Thibaut & L. Walker, *Procedural Justice: A Psychological Analysis* (Erlbaum Associates, 1975); L. Walker, E. A. Lind 7 J. Thibaut, 'The Relation Between Procedural and Distributive Justice', (1979) 65 Virg L Rev 1401; E. A. Lind & T. R. Tyler, *The Social Psychology of Procedural Justice* (Plenum Press, 1988); and T. R. Tyler, 'A Psychological Perspective on the Settlement of Mass Tort Claims', (1990) 53 Law & Contemp Probs 199. For a useful abridged account of the work done in this area, see T. R. Tyler, 'Procedure or Result: What Do Disputants Want From Legal Authorities?', in K. Mackie (ed.), *A Handbook of Dispute Resolution: ADR in Action* (London: Routledge, 1991), p. 19.

[16] R. S. Summers, 'Evaluating and Improving Legal Processes—A Plea for "Process Values" ', (1974) 60 Cornell L Rev 1.

to produce a result which is subjectively correct, i.e. consistent with their view of the matter in dispute. As Redish and Marshall,[17] and Bayles[18] all point out, the value of participation is that it allows a party to express his or her point of view. It is based on a desire to influence: to bring about 'substantive change in the state agent's action or attitude.'[19] The same is true of the desire for neutrality on the part of the decision maker and, in some ways, interpersonal respect. The former requires a decision maker who will not take into account irrelevant considerations, which would reduce the influence of the parties' representations; the latter suggests that the decision maker is listening, and is taking the parties' representations seriously.

This suggests that a distinction exists between interests which are outcome-related, and interests which are not. Such a proposition is not controversial: it equates with the more commonly made distinction between procedural quality, and procedural efficiency. Both of these are process values which are important because of their impact on the perceptions of the parties, which in turn is important because of its effect on the likelihood of the parties accepting the result.

Expressing the distinction in this way permits us to begin to understand how conflicts between quality and efficiency related interests ought to be resolved. The most obvious example of such a conflict is between the need for preparation on the one hand—serving the interests of the parties in making full and proper representations—and the need to keep costs to a minimum on the other. The question now becomes a matter of disputant psychology.

A number of recent research projects suggest that given a conflict between quality and efficiency, the quality interests should prevail. Work carried out by the RAND corporation in 1989 found that litigant satisfaction with civil process strongly correlated with their perceptions of neutrality, the dignity of the procedure, and perceived control over case events and outcomes. There was a significantly lower correlation between litigant satisfaction and the time and expense associated with the procedure.[20] These findings reflect a similar study by Norman Poythress, conducted in 1993, which created a hypothetical case study in order to measure participants' reactions to a variety of alternative processes. Again, it was found that 'only outcome control, defined as the 'best chance of winning the case', significantly predicted preferences'.[21]

17 M. H. Redish & L. C. Marshall, 'Adjudicatory Independence and the Values of Procedural Due Process' (1986) 95 Yale LJ 455, 487.

18 M. Bayles, 'Principles for Legal Procedure', (1986) 5 Law & Phil 33, 51.

19 Redish & Marshall, *op cit.*

20 E. A. Lind *et al*, *The Perception of Justice: Tort Litigants' Views of trial, Court-Annexed Arbitration, and Judicial Settlement Conferences,* (RAND, 1989).

21 N. G. Poythress, 'Procedural Preferences, Perceptions of Fairness, and Compliance With Outcomes', (1994) 18(4) Law & Human Behaviour, 361, 373.

Most of the research conducted in this area has considered only the views of individual litigants, not corporate entities, and a substantial proportion of it has tended to concentrate on tort plaintiffs.[22] As such, it is subject to the criticism that these kind of litigants are not always representative: their priorities may be slightly different. Tort plaintiffs are usually 'one-shot', as opposed to 'repeat' players, in that they are probably using the civil justice system for the only time in their lives, and the personal nature of tort claims may lead them to emphasise outcome over non-outcome related interests where a corporate client may not. As Hedley has observed, personal injury plaintiffs 'often seem to be pursuing truth *simpliciter*, or public recognition, or punishment of the defendant',[23] and questionnaires addressed to the victims of medical accidents also reveal that these kind of plaintiffs tend to attach a greater importance to getting an explanation for what has happened, an appreciation of what they have suffered, or concerns about accountability and standards of care in the medical profession, than they do the desire for compensation.[24] All of these concerns predicate a level of procedural quality, defined in terms of its impact on outcomes.

It may be argued that in the commercial world, where 'time is money', and where the interests of litigants are often not personal to any one individual, there may be less importance attached to the quality of outcomes than there is in re-establishing a working relationship, freeing company employees from the pressures of litigation, or otherwise 'returning things to normal'. However, this suggestion is belied by recent research conducted by the London firm of Simmons & Simmons, which found that corporate litigants also tended to emphasise more qualitative interests. Only a minority considered that 'the courts should be far more commercial and businesslike, even if this did mean sacrificing to some extent the delivery of "perfect" justice'. The majority took the view that efficiency gains were only desirable 'without a significant sacrifice to the quality of justice'.[25]

The implication, therefore, is that outcome-related interests should be regarded as more important, so far as the private interests are concerned, than the non-outcome related interests. Quality is more important than efficiency. However, variations within this general rule are likely to remain. Though the opportunity to put their side of the story in the fullest and most persuasive way possible will remain a disputant's priority, there will be lim-

[22] Both the RAND and Poythress studies considered only individual litigants, though neither was exclusively plaintiff or defendant-orientated.

[23] S. Hedley, 'Group Personal Injury Litigation and Public Opinion' (1994) 14 LS 70, 76.

[24] C. Vincent, m. Young & A. Phillips, 'Why Do People Sue Doctors? A Study of Patients and Relatives Taking Legal Action', (1994) 343 *The Lancet* 1609.

[25] *A Paper on Lord Woolf's Proposals for the Reform of the Civil Justice System* (Simmons & Simmons, March 1995); published as P. Mitchard, 'Corporate Clients and Civil Justice' [1995] *The Litigator* 279.

its to what they are prepared to pay for the privilege of doing so. As Adrian Zuckerman has observed, 'even justice may be bought at too high a price'.[26]

## The public interest

In making this observation, Zuckerman was also concerned with the impact that striving for perfect justice in every case would have on the civil justice system as a whole. This is a public interest, and may transcend the interests of the parties. Indeed, just as the private interests in civil dispute resolution may be reduced to the categories of outcome and non-outcome interests, so may the public interest.

As described above, the policy implementation model seeks codes for future conduct. These amount to legal and factual precedents, and depend for their legitimacy on being objectively correct. To meet the needs of the policy implementation model, such codes must conform to the standards set by the Rule of Law, and to standards of factual accuracy. For example, if the value of a precedent is its provision of a judicially tested source of information, such as information about whether a drug produces the side-effects alleged, then that value derives from the assumption that the information is objectively true. The need for legal and factual precedents is an outcome-related public interest.

But this is not the public interest referred to by Zuckerman. That public interest is based on the public purse. It acknowledges that there is a finite amount of money available for the running of the civil justice system, and that those resources must be distributed equitably:

> It is axiomatic that the object of procedure is to render litigants their due; namely, to return judgments which correctly apply the law to the true facts. But this does not mean that the state has an obligation to provide the most accurate civil procedure regardless of cost. It would be absurd to say that we are entitled to the best possible legal procedure, however expensive, when we cannot lay a credible claim to the best possible health service or to the best possible transport system.[27]

There is, in other words, a limit to what the public is prepared to pay for. In the same way as justice for private litigants—full participation and so on—may be bought at too high a price—so the public benefits deriving from the outcome of a dispute, which range from the narrower goal of securing the satisfaction of the parties to the wider goal of securing precedents, may sometimes not be worth the costs burdens of securing such benefits. Thus, we have public outcome and non-outcome related interests and there is a potential for conflict between them.

[26] A. S. S. Zuckerman, 'Quality and Economy in Civil Procedure: The Case for Commuting Correct Judgments for Timely judgments', (1994) 14(3) OJLS 353, 361.

[27] 'A Reform of Civil Procedure—Rationing Procedure Rather Than Access to Justice', *op cit* at p. 160.

Unlike the conflicts between private outcome and non-outcome related interests, the question of exactly what it is that the public is prepared to pay for has never properly been addressed. There are, however, some indications, for example deriving from the rules on wasted costs under Order 62 rule 11 of the Rules of the Supreme Court. The leading authority in that area, *Ridehalgh* v. *Horsefield*,[28] holds that whilst 'clients are free to reject advice and insist that cases be litigated', and the legal representative's duty stops at advising the client of the likelihood of failure, there is a distinction between cases which are 'bound to fail' and cases which amount to an abuse of process[29]. In other words, the public is not prepared to subsidise the vexatious and oppressive[30] use of its court system.

The idea that there is no right to make unbridled use of public resources has been rapidly gaining ground over recent years. The 1993 report of the Heilbron Committee reflected such sentiments where it stated that '[i]n principle we believe that once a citizen has invoked the process of the court, it is incumbent upon him, either personally or through his legal representatives, to prosecute the suit with diligence.'[31] Cyril Glasser has also detected traces of this philosophy in the trend towards increased case management by the court:

> The need to limit the cost of court services and the provision of legal aid has become a major preoccupation of the government department involved. In this context the neutrality of the court is replaced, not by a desire to play an inquisitorial role in the substance of the dispute itself, but by an active need to ensure that litigants are closely supervised in their use of public resources.[32]

Support for this view is found in a number of recent decisions, including those related to striking out for want of prosecution, where reference has been made to 'the power of the courts to regulate the progress of actions in the public interest';[33] and those concerned with increased openness in pre-trial civil procedure: 'the overriding duty of the court [is] to uphold justice and save public funds.'[34]

## The conflict between public and private interests

Just as outcome and non-outcome related interests may conflict, so may the public and private interests. The best example of this is with the increased

[28] [1994] 3 WLR 462.

[29] *id.* at pp. 479–80.

[30] This definition of 'abuse of process' is Sir Jack Jacob's: see 'The Inherent Jurisdiction of the Court' in *The Reform of Civil Procedural Law and Other Essays* (1982) pp. 221, 234.

[31] *Civil Justice on Trial—The Case for Change* (Independent Working Party of the Bar and the Law Society, June 1993), para. 4.27.

[32] C. Glasser, 'Civil Procedure and the Lawyers—The Adversary System and the Decline of the Orality Principle', [1993] 56(3) MLR 307, 308.

[33] *Harwood v. Courtalds Ltd., The Times*, 2 Feb. 1993, *per* Steyn LJ.

[34] *Buchanan v. Abba Warehouses, Current Law*, Nov. 1993, para. 243.

use of ADR, which gives rise to two such potential conflicts: first, are the parties to a dispute entitled to settle that dispute privately, through ADR or otherwise, in the face of the public interest in obtaining a precedent; and second, are the parties to a dispute entitled to utilise the public resource of the courts where there is no such public interest, or where to do so would be contrary to the public interest in the proper use of public resources?

The last of these is the situation described above: there is no right to make unbridled use of the courts if to do so amounts to an abuse of process. The potential for the outcome-related public interest to conflict with the private interests, on the other hand, gives rise to more problems. It depends upon the relative weight we attach to the public and private interests arising out of a dispute, or, in other words, whether we embrace the dispute resolution or policy implementation philosophy of civil process.

It is often assumed that in this country, the dispute resolution model of civil process prevails. The courts are there, it is said, to resolve private disputes. They are, as Damaska puts it, purely 'reactive', in that they respond to an existing situation and seek to resolve it, rather than seeking to use disputants as a vehicle for achieving some wider society goal.[35] Evidence of this approach is found in the idea, currently in vogue,[36] that courts provide a service, with litigants as their consumers. They respond to the needs of those consumers, whose needs are sovereign: the civil justice version of the adage 'the customer is always right'. It may be seen that this is the same idea as that underlying the dispute resolution philosophy: the maximisation of the private interests is all.

Further support is found in the traditional acceptance in this country of an adversarial system of civil procedure. The principal distinction between adversarial and inquisitorial styles of procedure is that with the former, the parties retain control over the conduct of proceedings.[37] They determine the subject-matter of the dispute by way of framing the issues in pleadings and other documents, they control the form and content of the evidence and argument presented to the court, and they determine the speed with which the proceedings develop. Under an inquisitorial system, by contrast, this all remains within the control of the court. Such distinctions mean that the adversarial style of procedure lies most easily with the dispute resolution model of civil process. The private interests are sovereign, and the

[35] M. Damaska, *The Faces of Justice and State Authority*, (Yale UP, 1986).

[36] See e.g. the Civil Justice Review 1988, introduced by Lord Hailsham with a lay majority in order to 'stimulate interest in the report by the clients and potential consumers of the system' (cited by R. Thomas, 'Civil Justice Review—Treating Litigants As Consumers', (1990) 9 CJQ 51); and Saville J., *Discussion Paper on the Commercial Court*, (Oct. 1992), where the approach of the Commercial Court was described as seeking to provide 'a dispute resolution service for the international and commercial community.'

[37] See generally, J. Jacob, *The Fabric of English Civil Justice* (London: Stevens, 1987), pp. 5–32.

persons best able to determine those interests are the private parties, so the conduct of proceedings is left to them. Equally, where the public interest is sovereign, the entity best placed to serve that interest is the court, so the proceedings become inquisitorial.

Thus, as Damaska has observed, different styles of proceedings should not be regarded as different means to a shared end, where '[j]ustice—imagined as the instrument of a group dominating the socioeconomic formation—retains its identity, even as the shape of the instrument changes', but rather as reflecting different concepts of 'justice'.[38] These different concepts are the maximisation of the private interests or the realisation of the wider public interest.

So understood, the English tradition of adversarialism implies a preference for private over public interests in civil dispute resolution. Indeed, in this country, where parties choose to take their dispute to an alternative forum, they are entitled to do so. In other words, given a conflict between private and public interests, the private interests prevail.

However, as William Twining has observed, 'it is a truism of procedural scholarship that it is misleading to equate Anglo-American procedure with "adversary" proceedings or systems influenced by Roman Law with "inquisitorial" proceedings. . . . Most procedural arrangements, let alone most "systems" of arrangements, are hybrids.'[39] German civil procedure, for example, which is usually classified as 'inquisitorial', has been lauded for its 'adroit balance between nonadversarial and adversarial values'.[40] In this country, the development of court management of pre-trial civil procedure also marks a trend towards a more inquisitorial style of procedure.[41] Court control over the speed with which proceedings develop, by way of timetabling, is one example. Lord Taylor's practice direction,[42] which requires courts to exercise their discretion to limit the issues on which they wish to be addressed, effectively gives the court power over subject matter. In requiring courts to exercise control over discovery, the length of oral submissions and examination, and to make use of skeleton arguments, it is giving power over the form and content of evidence and argument. These are all the characteristics of an inquisitorial style of proceeding.

The development of court management may be explained in terms of the failure of adversarial civil procedure to always serve the goals of the dis-

[38] *Op cit* at p. 7.

[39] W. Twining, 'Alternative to What? Theories of Litigation, Procedure and Dispute Settlement in Anglo-American Jurisprudence: Some Neglected Classics', (1993) 56 MLR 380, 390.

[40] J. Langbein, 'The German Advantage in Civil Procedure' (1985) 52 U Chi L Rev 823, 840.

[41] See generally N. Armstrong, 'Court Management: From Perception to Reality' [1995] *The Litigator* 116; and *id*, 'Perspectives on Court Management' (1994) 144(6633) NLJ 131.

[42] Practice Direction (Civil Litigation: Case Management) [1995] 1 WLR 508.

pute resolution model of civil process. It was observed above that the adversarial system rests on the assumption that the parties are best placed to act in their own interests. This, it may be said, ignores the fact that the parties are represented by lawyers, who may not always be acting in their client's interests due to incompetence, a desire to inflate fees, or due to factors inherent to the lawyer-client relationship.[43] Court management, which is rooted in part in the rationale that lawyers are an obstacle to efficient litigation management—'In an ideal world there should be no need for court control, competent solicitors would ensure that actions were brought on for trial at an early stage and that the actions were ready for trial'[44]—may therefore be seen as an ad hoc response to a fundamental flaw in the adversarial system's design. In casting themselves in a more pro-active role, judicial case managers are seeking to bring lawyers' activities more into line with the interests of their clients, as required by the dispute resolution model.

However, an alternative explanation for this hybridism of procedural types is that the values behind them are hybrid. In addition to the evidence of the dispute resolution philosophy, cited above, there are also examples in English civil process of where the language of the policy implementation model has been adopted. This is the essence of the tension between the two models mentioned above, and is understandable in view of the fact that the difference between the models often turns on unrealistic distinctions between individuals and groups (or societies) made up of individuals. Fiss writes:

> Dispute resolution depicts a sociological impoverished universe, one that does not account for social groups and bureaucratic institutions. There is no room in the story for sociological entities that are so familiar to contemporary litigation. Social groups like the inmates of a prison or patients in a hospital have no place in the story. Nor is there recognition of the existence of groups that transcend institutions, like racial minorities or the handicapped, groups whose social identity and reality are as secure in our society as the individual in the state of nature. Furthermore, there is no room in the story for the public school system, the prison, the mental hospital, or the housing authority. The world is composed exclusively of individuals.[45]

[43] See e.g. D. E. Rosenthal, *Lawyer and Client: Who's In Charge?* (Russell Sage Foundation, 1974); and M. Strauss, 'Toward a Revised Model of the Attorney–Client Relationship: The Argument for autonomy' (1987) 65 N Cal L Rev 315.

[44] D. Greenslade, 'Access to Justice—A View From the County Court' [1995] *The Litigator* 108, 111. There are numerous examples of this rhetoric, including the Civil Justice Review, *op cit*, para. 205; the KPMG Peat Marwick *Study on Causes of Delay in the High Court and County Courts* (Lord Chancellor's Department, Jan. 1994); and in cases: see e.g. *Harwood v. Courtaulds, op cit*; *Ketteman v. Hansel Properties Ltd*, [1988] 1 All ER 38; and *Lonrho plc. v. Fayed, The Independent*, 23 June 1993.

[45] 'The Social land Political Foundations of Adjudication', *op cit* at pp. 122–3.

Consider our reliance on precedents as a source of law, mentioned above. As Jolowics points out, were a strict dispute resolution philosophy to be applied, the only reason for resolving disputes consistently and in accordance with the substantive law would be if that were more likely to improve the chances of the parties accepting the outcome and avoiding self-help.[46] This is quite obviously not the case. Precedents are a by-product of the resolution of a private dispute, but their value derives from their capacity to aid in the resolution of future disputes.[47] That is consistent with the aims of the dispute resolution model, but necessitates the recognition of the plurality of disputes or, in other words, the fact that the private dispute has occurred concomitantly with other private disputes: a practical consequence of the reality that individuals live in a society comprised of other individuals. This is the stuff of politics, and it may be noted that analogies are sometimes drawn between the dispute resolution model—Damaska's 'reactive' state which yields to the sovereignty of the private rights—and laissez-faire capitalism. Subjecting the parties to an imposition of the wider public interest, on the other hand, is analogous to socialism.[48] It is beyond the scope of this essay to pursue this analogy too far, but it demonstrates that, as Cappelletti has written, '[p]rocedure is *not* pure form. It is the meeting of conflicts, of policies, of ideas.'[49] Far from being just a technical study of local practices and rules, he observes, those who concern themselves with procedural change are investigating 'the great waves of history: the socioeconomic as well as the intellectual changes, revolutions, and stagnations of history.'[50] As such, it is unsurprising that there is a hybridism of models of civil process in a world where improved international awareness and cooperation has led to a hybridism of social groups, cultures and political ideologies.

Another example of this overlap between the models is the assumption that our civil justice system seeks to establish objective truth. One of the primary advantages of the adversarial approach is held to be that it is better able than inquisitorial process to get at the truth. Kötz, for example,

[46] M. Cappelletti & J. A. Jolowicz, *Public Interest Parties and the Active Role of the Court in Civil Litigation* (1975), p. 168.

[47] This value is not, of course, confined to precedents. The resolution of private disputes sends a number of 'signals' which bear upon future disputes, including information about delays, costs, publicity and the anguish of litigation. See M. Galanter, 'Justice in Many Rooms', in M. Cappelletti (ed.), *Access to Justice and the Welfare State* (European University Institute, 1981).

[48] See Cappelletti & Jolowicz, *id*; and P. T. Wangerin, 'The Political and Economic Roots of the "Adversary System" of Justice and "Alternative Dispute Resolution" ' (1994) 9(2) Ohio St J. Disp Res 203, who argues that procedural systems are not so much founded on different socio-political ideologies as different conceptions of the nature of human beings.

[49] M. Cappelletti, 'Social and Political Aspects of Civil Procedure—Reforms and Trends in Western and Eastern Europe' (1971) 69 Mich L Rev 847, 886.

[50] *Id.* at p. 885.

concedes that some features of the inquisitorial style of proceeding can have 'disadvantages [in] that fine factual distinctions may get lost in the process and that the colour of the testimony is also lost.'[51] The reason is that an adversarial system creates the incentives for every avenue of inquiry to be investigated, because each side has such a strong stake in the court's rejection of his opponent's assertions.[52] Some may disagree with this claim,[53] and it is notable that in this country, where the parties agree a fact as true the court has no power to look behind that agreement. Contrast the situation in Germany, where section 138 of the *Zivilprozessordnung* gives the court the power to go outside an admission of fact by the parties 'if the contrary appears to be true'.[54] Nevertheless, it seems to have been assumed that because of the incentives peculiar to the adversarial system, the parties' version of the truth will rarely, if ever, be inconsistent with that which is objectively true, and that this has to be a goal of any civil justice system. As Summers writes:

> If truth (in light of relevant rules) were not the primary object of the trial, the public would probably lose confidence in the process. If the objective of seeking truth turned out to be pretense, or to be quite secondary, the public would discover this and would almost certainly want to devise trials that were primarily truth-orientated, for the public would readily see that there cannot be a rule of law without rule over fact.[55]

There are other instances of where the policy implementation philosophy has infiltrated the English civil justice system. The relator action, judicial review, and the representative action are all procedural mechanisms designed to further the interests of persons other than the named parties to the proceedings. Indeed, they are sometimes described as 'public law'

51 'Civil Litigation and the Public Interest' (1982) 1 CJQ 237, 241.

52 M. P. Golding, 'On the Adversary System and Justice', in R. Bronaugh (ed.), *Philosophical Law* (Westport, Conn: Greenwood Press, 1978), pp. 98, 108. See also L. Fuller, 'The Adversary System', in Berman (ed.), *Talks on American Law* (Voice of America Forum Lectures, 1972), pp. 35, 45.

53 See e.g. M. E. Frankel, 'The Search for Truth: An Umpireal View' (1975) 123 U Penn L Rev 1031.

54 See Cappelletti & Jolowicz, *id*; E. J. Cohn, *Manual of German Law* (2nd edn. 1971); B. Kaplan, A. T. von Mehren & R. Schaefer, 'Phases of German Civil Procedure I' (1958) 71 Harv L Rev 1193; H. Kötz, 'Civil Litigation and the Public Interest' *op cit*; J. Langbein, 'The German Advantage in Civil Procedure', *op cit*; and J. Ratliff, 'Civil Procedure in Germany' (1983) 2 CJQ 237.

55 R. S. Summers, 'Comment: On the Adversary System and Justice', in Bronaugh, *op cit*, at pp. 122, 124. *Cf. Air Canada v. Secretary of State for Trade* [1983] 1 All ER 910, 919, *per* Lord Wilberforce: 'There is no . . . duty to ascertain some independent truth. It often happens . . . that an adjudication has to be made which is not, and is known to be, the whole truth of the matter; yet, if the decision has been in accordance with the available evidence and with the law, justice will have been fairly done.' This quote underlines the difficulty in drawing comparisons between systems and further demonstrates the extent to which lines are necessarily blurred.

mechanisms,[56] derived from the old Chancery jurisdiction; a jurisdiction expressly concerned with the implementation of Royal policy,[57] not the resolution of private disputes.

Can it be said, then, that the move towards increased court management in this country is indicative of a new sympathy for the goals of the policy implementation model of civil process? This was the situation during the early development of managerial judging in the United States. Recognising that trend as early as 1971, Cappelletti wrote:

> [T]he movement toward a more active involvement of the judge in controlling litigation reflects the growing pressure for public intervention in private life which is a feature of our epoch. Indeed, this renewed clash between the adversarial and the inquisitorial approaches to litigation is but one aspect of the major challenge of our time: to reconcile private freedom with social justice.[58]

This is a view also held by Abram Chayes[59] and Donald Horowitz,[60] both of who describe a changing role of the judiciary throughout the 1960s and 1970s in judicial review and other 'public law' cases. According to Horowitz, these developments were based on social changes; properly understood as changes in the way society at that time was prioritising the interests of the individual as against the interests of the state. He refers to the 'restlessness of that important decade' which 'affected judges, as it affected elites throughout the society'.[61]

This trend, however, proved short-lived. Even at the time Horowitz was writing, the pendulum was beginning to swing back towards the dispute resolution philosophy with the advent of the 1980s, arguably due to that decade's emphasis on individualism. Having acknowledged the development throughout the 1960s and 1970s of what he calls 'structural reform litigation'—meaning actions which transcend the private ends of the parties by, for example, bringing public service providers or manufacturers of consumer goods into line with public values such as equality, due process, or public safety regulations—Fiss observed:

> Today we feel increasing doubts about the existence of public values, all is individ-

[56] See Jolowicz's discussion of representative and class actions together with what he calls 'public interest' actions, in 'Some Twentieth-Century Developments in Anglo-American Civil Procedure', in *Studi in Onore de Enrico Tullio Liebman I* (1979), pp. 217, 271–2; and generally, J. Winter, 'Acting for Classes: Strategies for Representing Group Interests' (1993) 44 NILQ 276, 284; and N. Armstrong, 'ADR and the Public Interest in Personal Injury', *op cit*.

[57] See e.g. H. P. Glenn, 'The Dilemma of Class Action Reform' (1986) 6 OJLS 262.

[58] 'Social and Political Aspects of Civil Procedure', *op cit* at p. 884.

[59] A. Chayes, 'The Role of the Judge in Public Law Litigation' (1976) 89 Harv L Rev 1281, 1290.

[60] D. L. Horowitz, 'Decreeing Organizational Change Change: Judicial Supervision of Public Institutions' [1983] Duke LJ 1265; and *id*, 'The Courts As Guardians of the Public Interest' (1977) 37 Pub Admin Rev 148.

[61] 'Decreeing Organizational Change', *id* at p. 1283.

ual interests or at least individual morality, and the dispute resolution model of adjudication, like the night-watchman state, accommodates those doubts. Both afford an easy haven for all those who would deny or minimize the role of public values in our social life and the need for governmental power to realize those values.[62]

This demonstrates the fluid nature of the way in which society can prioritise its interests as against the interests of individuals. In the US, it has caused a number of commentators to explore the question why the rights of individuals should prevail over the interests of the state. One idea which has come to the fore as part of this debate is the concept of 'subsidisation'. This can be taken to support both sides of the argument: the private interests should prevail because the parties are, in the main, paying for the resolution of the dispute; or, as commentators such as Fiss[63] and Alschuler[64] have it, there is a right of public access to outcomes because the public subsidises the resolution of disputes by way of providing courts as a public resource. Other commentators, such as Marcus (writing in the context of public access to materials obtained on discovery), have taken issue with what they see as this 'broader contention that litigants who use the courts should make a public disclosure of pertinent information as a sort of price tag for admittance',[65] and have also questioned whether 'public interest' can be accurately defined.[66]

The English debate over civil justice reform has not yet progressed so far as the consideration of these issues. The available material provides no evidence that English court management has been founded on an increased awareness of society goals, nor that those who espouse the 'courts as a service' argument have also taken into account the effect that might have on the competing objectives of civil process. Horowitz cites England as an example of where the legal institutions are too 'hidebound' and 'formalistic' to take account of changes in procedural forms or doctrine.[67] That may be being a little unfair. Francis Miller has recently described how the adversarial system is a comparatively recent development in this country; born

62 'The Social and Political Foundations of Adjudication', *op cit* at p. 128. This was written in 1982, and repeated in largely the same terms in 1985: see 'Two Models of Adjudication', *op cit* at p. 48. For further evidence of this switch back away from the policy implementation goals, see R. L. Carter, 'The Federal Rules of Civil Procedure as a Vindicator of Civil Rights' (1989) 137 U Penn L Rev 2179, 2183, on civil rights litigation; and R. L. Marcus, 'Public Law Litigation and Legal Scholarship' (1988) 21 U Mich JL Ref 647, 648, discussing the impact of Chayes' work.

63 'Against Settlement', *op cit* at p. 1085.

64 A. W. Alschuler, 'Mediation With A Mugger: The Shortage of Adjudicative Services and the Need for a Two-Tier Trial System in Civil Cases' (1986) 99 Harv L Rev 1808, 1816.

65 R. L. Marcus, 'The Discovery Confidentiality Controversy' [1991] U Ill L Rev 457, 473.

66 *id.* at p. 479. A similar point is made by Judith Resnik, 'Due Process: A public Dimension' [1987] U Fla L Rev 405, 420.

67 'Decreeing Organizational Change', *op cit* at p. 1289.

out of judges' realisation that with the advance of technology they could no longer expect to be sufficiently well-informed to conduct inquiries themselves. Accordingly, they began to rely more and more on representations from the parties until this party-controlled civil process evolved into the adversarial process as we know it today.[68] Taken together with other recent developments, such as the present controversy over increased judicial activism in regulating decisions of government ministers[69]—a trend reminiscent of that described by Chayes and Horowitz—this all tends to suggest that the shape of English civil justice is capable of being altered by external influences, and that judges are sometimes prepared to adopt a more policy-shaping role in decision making. It seems reasonable to suppose, therefore, particularly in the current climate of procedural reform, that our system at least possesses the potential for change.

But the real lesson to be learned from the foregoing is this. Given that we do not know whether we embrace either the dispute resolution or the policy implementation model of civil process, we must assume that potentially, we embrace both. There is a great deal that is unknown, and will remain unknown, about the functions of a civil justice system. The interface between the private outcome and non-outcome related interests is a question of disputant psychology, and to some extent yields to empirical research. Within certain basic parameters, however, it is susceptible to change. The interface between public and private interests, on the other hand, and the question to what extent the public is prepared to subsidise the civil justice system, is largely a matter of socio-political culture. As such, this too possesses an inherent unknowability. All we can say with certainty is that any civil dispute potentially gives rise to a wide range of interests, that these interests may be categorised according to whether they are public or private, outcome or non-outcome related, and that the make-up of our civil justice system is determined by how we prioritise these interests. This sense of priorities is impossible to predict, because it will vary from individual to individual, dispute to dispute, and with time.

## TRACKING SYSTEMS

It is this essential unknowability about the weight we assign the various interests in civil justice that makes tracking such an attractive concept. Rather than seeking the impossible, which is to design a unitary system that can cater for all these unknowns, we should seek only to isolate broad categories of interests and design a system of alternatives which can accommodate them.

[68] F. miller, 'The Adversarial Myth' (1995) NLJ 734, 735 (19 May).

[69] See e.g. B. Johnson, 'The Long Arm of the Law', *The Spectator*, 17 June 1995, p. 8.

This requires a knowledge of how different processes are capable of furthering our sense of priorities. Unfortunately, it is well established that this kind of information is sadly lacking from the study of English civil procedure. Instead of conducting extensive empirical research into the actual effects in terms of costs and delay of reforms such as exchange of witness statements, the impact of court management or the burdens of discovery, our procedural reformers tend instead to rely on what has been called 'lawyers' anecdotes, war stories and bar room chatter.'[70] The result is that we have very little idea as to what the impact of civil process on the interests we have identified.

Lord Woolf has acknowledged this lack of information, and has catered for it in his report. As one commentator with experience of the 1988 Civil Justice Review observed recently, our lack of knowledge means that 'the worth of detailed recommendations matters less than the machinery for securing the will for change'.[71] Lord Woolf has therefore opted to provide us with a 'provisional agenda', or basic structure, for changes he intends to fill in later, rather than a set of reforms ready for immediate incorporation into the rule books. His call for the monitoring of developments abroad in ADR,[72] for pilot projects to provide information on the costs and appropriateness of certain cases to his fast-track,[73] and for the establishment of a Civil Justice Council with responsibility for overseeing and co-ordinating the implementation of his proposals,[74] are all part of a general plea for more information and continued research.

Thus, the tracking system which Lord Woolf has outlined should properly be regarded as an interim response forged on the basis of incomplete material. Nevertheless, he and his team have assiduously striven to make it representative of what we do know about the workings of our own and foreign civil justice systems. For example, his recommendation that ADR remain voluntary and within the private sector[75] reflects research which demonstrates that proximity between conciliation services and judicial processes tends to reduce the effectiveness of conciliation.[76] It also acknowledges the dangers in using data showing the effectiveness of voluntary ADR as a justification for introducing compulsory ADR.[77] Further,

[70] C. Glasser, 'Civil Procedure—A Time for Change', in R. Smith (ed.), *Shaping the Future* (Legal Action Group, 1995), pp. 209, 212. See also M. Zander, 'Are There Any Clothes For The Emperor to Wear?', NLJ 3 Feb. 1995, p. 154; and N. Armstrong, 'Standards of Judgment', (1995) 92(24) Gazette 10, 21 June.

[71] R. Thomas, 'Will the Woolf Proposals Work?' *The Times*, 27 June 1995.

[72] *Access to Justice*, *op cit* at p. 146.

[73] *Id.* at pp. 45–6.

[74] *id.* at pp. 220–1.

[75] *id.* at p. 143.

[76] S. Roberts, 'Mediation in the Lawyers' Embrace' (1992) 55 MLR 258, 262.

[77] See R. Ingleby, 'Court Sponsored Mediation: The Case Against Mandatory participation' (1993) 56 MLR 441, 442; and *id*, 'Why Not Toss A Coin? Issues of Quality and Efficiency in the Evaluation of Alternative Dispute Resolution', in *Papers from the 9th Annual Conference of the Australian Institute of Judicial Administration* (1991), p. 51.

voluntary ADR, promoted only through improved awareness and judicial suggestions, avoids the problems associated with assuming all disputes to be suitable to conciliatory processes, and the threat of coercion in compulsory referral.[78]

Similarly, Lord Woolf's distinction between the fast-track and the multi-track reflects the experience of US judicial case management, which suggests that 'intensive' judicial prodding tends only to produce efficiency gains in more complex cases. Contrary to widespread perceptions about the impact of court management, research conducted by Rosenberg,[79] Flanders,[80] Kritzer[81] and others[82] suggests that the more 'hands-on' judicial intervention becomes (meaning the involvement of the judge in a management conference with a view to narrowing issues and encouraging settlement, as opposed to largely automatic case management by timetables and other prompts), the less effective it becomes in terms of improving the case disposition rate or the rate of settlement.[83] Lord Woolf caters for this in minimising direct judicial involvement in the fast-track, and seeking to tailor the amount of judicial involvement to the needs of the case in the multi-track. He is also careful to observe that the change in judicial role must be accompanied by an expanded system of judicial training if judges are to feel equipped to intervene, and if abuses of the system by judicial heavy-handedness are to be avoided.[84]

[78] The exception to this approach being Lord Woolf's trailing of the idea in para. 34 of his chapter on ADR that an unreasonable refusal to resort to ADR be taken into account when deciding issues as to costs. The potential impact of such a sanction on the ideal type of negotiated settlement warrants discussion outside the scope of this essay, but see R. Ingleby, 'Court Sponsored Mediation', *op cit*; and P. Schuck, 'The Role of Judges in Settling Complex Cases: The Agent Orange Example' (1986) 53 U Chi L Rev 337.

[79] M. Rosenberg, *The Pretrial Conference and Effective Justice* (New York: Columbia University Press, 1964).

[80] S. Flanders, *Case Management and Court Management in United States District Courts* (Federal Judicial Center, 1977).

[81] H. M. Kritzer, 'The Judge's Role in Pretrial Case Processing: Assessing the Need for Change' (1982) 66 Judicature 28.

[82] See e.g. L. Walker & J. Thibaut, 'An Experimental Examination of Pretrial Conference Techniques' (1971) 55 Minn L Rev 1113; and generally, M. Provine, 'Managing Negotiated Justice: Settlement Procedures in the Courts' (1987) 12 Justice Sys J 91, 101–2.

[83] Though *cf.* Stevenson, Watson & Weissman, 'The Impact of Pretrial Conferences: An Interim Report of the Ontario Pretrial Conference Experiment' (1977) 15 Osgoode Hall LJ 591, for a study which produced favourable findings for judicial case management. Lord Woolf also cites another favourable study, conducted in 1994 and again in Canada, at p. 32 of his report.

[84] *Access to Justice*, *op cit* at p. 70. As with his recommendation about sanctions for failure to resort to ADR, however, it is arguable that Lord Woolf has gone too far in trailing the idea about judicial involvement in settlement discussions (*id.* at p. 146). This is one area where even the most vocal of the pro-court management lobby tend to draw the line (see e.g. R. F. Peckham, 'A Judicial Response to the Cost of Litigation: Case Management, Two Stage Discovery and Alternative Dispute Resolution' (1985) 37 Rutgers L Rev 235, 263; and W. W. Rayner, 'Judicial Authority in the Settlement of Civil Cases' (1985) 42 Washington & Lee L Rev 171) and in a questionnaire survey conducted by the present author in 1993, 71% of

On the face of it, therefore, the Woolf proposals go a long way towards providing disputants with a set of alternatives capable of accommodating the interests identified above. If they feel that their interests lie more in reconciliation and informal processes designed to foster creative, non-partisan solutions, then they are free to choose ADR. Improved information as to the relative benefits of conciliation and adjudication should be available to enable them to make that choice properly. Equally, should the parties elect to use the courts, Lord Woolf envisages that the allocation of a dispute to a litigation track should in principle be a judicial decision, but that it should be taken with regard to the wishes of the parties.[85] This affords litigants the opportunity to represent the court the nature of their interests in procedural quality and efficiency. Providing lawyers are properly equipped to tease out where the interests of their clients lie before they select the appropriate track, then again, Lord Woolf's proposed system should be able to cater for them. To the extent that unforeseen problems may arise later, Lord Woolf has set the monitoring machinery in place and challenged others to prove that his system is not working. As we learn more about the interests of disputants and the way different processes are capable of realising those interests, in theory there will be a programme for allowing the system to be adjusted.

A difficulty arises, however, if we revisit our analysis of the functions of a civil justice system. Too little attention appears to have been paid to the enduring interests of society as a whole in the resolution of civil disputes. A reading of Lord Woolf's report reveals that his main concern is with the interests of the parties. In devising a system of choices, it is necessary first to determine what choices are likely to be made, and Lord Woolf has done this on the basis of the interests of the parties as he perceives them. Chief among these is his concept of 'proportionality', which is founded on the assumption that no-one would choose to commence proceedings if the costs of doing so were likely to equal or exceed the amount at stake. Hence he has created the fast-track, where costs are to be fixed at a percentage of the sum in dispute.[86]

This is the basic principle. In addition, however, there are references throughout the report to the public interests that we have discussed above. Chapter One talks of the social need to give full and effective value to the substantive rights of members of society, and Chapter Three refers to the cost to society of civil litigation. With regard to the fast-track, Lord Woolf

respondents were opposed to an expanded judicial role in settlement: see N. Armstrong, 'Perspectives on Court Management' (1994) 144(6633) NLJ 131, 132.

[85] *Access to Justice*, *op cit* at p. 39. The views of the parties should also be taken into account in determining the appropriate level at which the case ought to proceed in the multi-track: see p. 49.

[86] *Id.* at p. 45.

makes exception for those cases which are 'of modest value but which involve complex issues of fact or law, issues of public interest or importance or a significant degree of oral expert evidence or multiple parties'.[87] On the basis that without that exception a number of cases which it is in the interests of society to have before a court would not be brought, Lord Woolf states that cases displaying these types of characteristics would not normally be suited to the fast-track.

It is unclear whether the full implications of what Lord Woolf is saying here have been appreciated. If his analysis of what disputants are likely to choose is correct—and logic tells us that unless we are unusually affluent and possessed of a penchant for bringing risky cases that are not cost-effective, he is—then disputants are still unlikely to bring these kinds of cases, whether or not there is a wider interest in them doing so. Under the present system, they do because legal aid is demand-led and, whatever the merits test may claim, is not subject to the usual principles of costs/benefit. But we are told this has to stop. The question, therefore, is whether Lord Woolf is floating the idea of a special category of cases, falling broadly within the definition of 'public interest', which may attract public subsidy.

This interpretation of Lord Woolf's intentions has the air of pure speculation. Nevertheless, it is consistent with the analysis of this essay, which has shown that every dispute gives rise to a range of public and private interests, and the question is how we prioritise them against each other and against the conflicting interests of the private and public purses. We have seen how this sense of priorities has fluctuated in the US with court management. Is it possible that Lord Woolf's report also marks a new awareness of society goals, such that is about to be enshrined in the rules of court?

The reasoning is straightforward. There are a number of benefits to having a civil justice system. From the private disputant's point of view, they seek the opportunity to tell their side of the story, to obtain an apology or to clear their name, to be taken seriously, to obtain compensation or the cessation of an undesirable state of affairs and so on. As a society, we consider it desirable that these disputes should be resolved peaceably and without resort to forcible self-help, and we also use the existence of these private disputes as an opportunity to clarify and determine the standards by which we choose to be governed. The only question that remains is, how much are we prepared to pay for obtaining these benefits?

Lord Woolf's enterprise is largely an exercise in showing what we are not prepared to pay for. For example, we are not prepared to sink funds into inefficient processes. We could, in other words, get the same benefits for less money. Thus, we are not prepared to fund dilatory and incompetent prac-

[87] *Access to Justice*, *op cit* at p. 42.

titioners, nor pay for unnecessary complexity in our procedures. Similarly, we are not prepared to pay anything if the returns are unlikely to match the investment.

Viewed in this light, it does not seem unreasonable to suppose that Lord Woolf is prepared to let society pay for things where it is likely to receive a discernible benefit. Hence the public interest exception to the fast-track criteria. Early on in the course of his inquiry, he also stated that savings to public funds derived from his reforms may be re-distributed throughout the system. This has been described as unduly optimistic about the attitude of the Treasury,[88] but that does not negate the significance of the fact that he is raising the issue.

The real area of interest in all this is how far to take this line of thinking, and how to give it practical effect. We have a system of choices. There will be instances where the public takes an interest in how this choice is made. When are we prepared to allow that interest to override the interests of the parties? How is a public interest to be defined? Having identified one, how much are we prepared to pay to have it realised? Should we go to the extreme described by Glasser as 'not too fanciful to imagine', which is to reserve our courts for public interest cases only?[89] Finally, are we wrong to assume that judges are properly equipped to make this decision? However much training we may be able to provide, the question what is the public prepared to pay for is one which is critical to the make-up of our civil justice system. As cited above, judges have been known on occasion to regard themselves as guardians of the public purse, but are we happy to leave this within their competence, to be applied on a case-by-case basis with perhaps little regard to the approach of their fellows? In Germany, where there is a long established tradition of public subsidisation of civil litigation, the situations where it arises are prescribed by legislation.[90]

## CONCLUSION

These questions require answers. There is an essential unknowability about some of the workings of a civil justice system, and tracking is the beginning of an answer to these problems, if only because it allows for the existence of the unknowns. But that unknowability does not excuse us from setting our priorities. Just as tracking is a system of choices, so we have some choices to make in constructing our new system. How we make those choices will affect the whole fabric of our civil justice system for decades to come.

88 C. Glasser, 'Civil Procedure—A Time For Change', *op cit* at p. 215.

89 Glasser, *id* at p. 214.

90 See H. Kötz, 'Civil Litigation and the Public Interest' (1982) 1 CJQ 237.

The purpose of this essay has been to show what we are choosing between. It has shown that our traditional reliance on an adversarial system of procedure, and our preference for regarding courts as a service, tends to mask the complexities of what it is that we want from a civil justice system. Even this short analysis has shown that once we scratch the surface a little, our goals and expectations of civil justice amount to an intricate mixture of both dispute resolution and policy implementation models of civil process. Both are essential to the socio-political make-up of our system, and the effectiveness of that system must be judged accordingly.

This is the real challenge of the post-Woolf world. Whilst this essay aspires to identify the criteria against which Lord Woolf's tracking system may be assessed, it is the duty of others to carry out that analysis. Define what you want to do, then do it. The failure to take this initial step has been the stumbling block of so many previous efforts at fundamental reform. We now have the opportunity to rectify that failure.

# 6

# *A Fresh Approach: Uniform Rules of Court*

DICK GREENSLADE*

Lord Woolf's terms of reference required not only a review of the procedures for civil litigation but also the provision of a new uniform set of rules covering both High Court and county court. Clearly the two aspects are inextricably linked. New procedures require new rules. No new single code is possible until the of differing procedures in High Court and county court are merged.

Perhaps more significantly, procedural changes of the scale proposed by Lord Woolf require a fresh approach to the way in which rules are framed. New rules expressed in more modern form may assist in creating the new culture that is essential if the new approach to civil litigation is to succeed. As stated in the interim report 'in order to produce a new system with a new ethos, the rules have to be changed in a fundamental ways' (Chapter 26 para. 2). As a minor example, stress on 'statements of fact' rather than 'pleadings' is not merely a change of phraseology, it seeks to encourage a move away from the more formal and technical methods of pleading (strictly alien to the old rules as much as the new) towards a simpler fact basis for litigation.

## THE BACKGROUND

It will be helpful to consider what rules are for, what they can achieve, to whom they are to be addressed, the language that needs to be used and how they are to be applied.

### What Rules are for

Existing Rules of Court have mixed purposes, they prescribe, they empower, they make administrative provision, to some extent (albeit only indirectly) they describe. Above all they control, to a relatively limited but

* Dick Greenslade. A district judge in England and Wales, formerly member of the County Court Rule Committee, a Woolf assessor.

sometimes crucial extent, the way in which two (or more) adversaries approach the 'big bang' of their day in court.

The adversarial system leaves much of the control to the parties. They can choose to be slow or seek to be quick. They can choose when and whether to take a particular step, They can enforce or, largely, ignore the rules. If the parties agree the court has had, at least until recently, limited influence. 'Conduct pace and extent are left almost completely to the parties. There is no effective control of their worst excesses' (Chapter 3 para. 5)—'the rules are flouted on a vast scale. The timetables they contain are generally ignored and their other requirements are complied with when convenient to the interests of one or other party . . .' (Chapter 3 Para 6).

If they do not agree, there is enormous scope for tactical 'gamesmanship'. 'the litigation process is too often seen as a battlefield where no rules apply . . . questions of expense, delay, compromise and fairness may have only low priority (Chapter 3 para. 4). Attempts in the past to encourage the court to get hold of an action 'by the scruff of the neck', eg the pre trial review in the county court and the Summons for Directions in the High Court following the Evershed Report[1] have had relatively little impact. As the Editors of the Supreme Court Practice say 'the present practice does not always live up to the expectations of the Evershed Report. The court will indeed make sure that the pleadings are in order and that the case is fit for trial; but it has been found difficult to be 'robust' in directing the parties how to prepare their case.'[2]

Changes in the Rules have encouraged a movement towards 'cards on the table litigation' but only interstitially and by default rather than by setting a clear objective and providing a defined path towards that objective. One of the few relatively successful efforts to control the freedom of the parties (or, rather, their lawyers) to litigate as they choose is the much litigated provision for 'automatic striking out' in CCR Ord 17 r.11(9).

Rules of Court are prescriptive: should they also be descriptive? or is that the function of other publications, official or private? The rules provide information,eg, about what needs to be done to commence proceedings, where they can be commenced what happens to the proceedings when commenced, how the defendant is to be made aware of the proceedings and what he should do. However, in traditional form this information is not easily accessible except to the trained lawyer. Even when accessible many of the rules will have been the subject of judicial interpretation and practices will have become established to the extent that they are often regarded as rules of law. Judicial gloss has encouraged, if not necessitated, the publication of many practice books, primarily the Supreme Court Practice ('the White Book') and the County Court Practice ('the Green Book') 'enabling

[1] Final Report of the Committee on Supreme Court Practice 1953 (Cmd 8878)
[2] The Supreme Court Practice 1995, para 25.1.1.

[practitioners] to navigate through a sea of decisions and finely drawn distinctions'. Indeed much of the criticism of the sheer size of the existing rules relates (not unfairly) as much, if not more, to these Practices as to the rules themselves.

Rules as presently drafted do not provide a simple 'layman's guide' to court procedure—'the language and format of the rules act as a barrier to the use of the civil justice system by ordinary people' (Chapter 17, para. 7). Yet litigants in person will often take considerable trouble to acquaint themselves with the rules only to find that lawyers flaunt them with seeming impunity. The attitude of the courts only too often seems to be 'yes, but . . .'. 'The situation is made worse for [litigants in person] if they have tried to understand and comply with the rules only to find that they appear to be flouted by lawyers and that this is effectively condoned by the courts.' (Chapter 17 para. 7).

The interim report suggests that description is to be part of the functions of the new rules 'it is no doubt necessary for the rules to be fuller and more detailed, so that the parties can find all the guidance they need without resort to the court for instruction' (Chapter 26, para. 4). More positively, the aim of the rules is said to be 'an instruction manual to guide and assist the flow of litigation' (Chapter 26, para. 5).

However, the reference to an 'instruction manual' may of itself be ambiguous. Is the model to be the 'owner's handbook' supplied with the new car of the 'workshop manual' provided to the garage. They overlap but serve very different purposes. The 'workshop manual' designed for technicians may be represented by the Rules in their present form supplemented by the Practices, the owner's handbook more by leaflets (eg in the case of small claims and some routine aspects of county court litigation) or by private publications designed to guide lawyers and/or lay litigants through the 'litigation maze'. This is a subject which needs further consideration but at this stage I would suggest that the aim should be to provide in the rules all the essential material for the main stream of litigation in a way that will enable the lay litigant with or without professional or other advice to conduct litigation, if necessary, without resort to other publications.

### To whom are rules addressed?

In the traditional adversarial system they are primarily addressed to the lawyers for the litigants. However lawyers are not the only users. The main users are judges, the court administration, lawyers and litigants (primarily but not only those acting in person). In addition an increasingly important user will be the advice worker. The court system relies heavily on the work of advice agencies in assisting lay litigants. Such reliance is likely to increase substantially over the coming years. Lord Woolf's report recognises the vital role that agencies will be required to play and the general thrust of the Government's Green Paper on Legal Aid *Legal Aid—Targeting Need* (Cmd 2854) indicates a substantially increased role for advice agencies.

The needs of all should be taken into account by the draftsman of the rules. All have differing needs and different approaches to the way in which they use the Rules.

Judges look to the rules to see what is required of litigants (less often what is required of the courts). They look to see what sanctions are available in the case of breach. However they will frequently temper precise observance of the rules with the needs of 'justice' in the instant case. The effect may be justice in the particular case but repeated qualification or even overriding of the rules leads to non-observance and, arguably at least, an overall failure to provide justice within the system. Time limits become increasingly flexible, anything that can conceivably be compensated (usually at some stage in the dim and distant future) by a costs order can be remedied. The civil process becomes more and more a lottery with increasing scope for tactical manoeuvring.

The administration looks at rules to define its responsibility and to ensure that steps are taken in accordance with the requirements of the rules. On the whole they, and litigants in person, pay more attention to the literal wording of the rules than the other main players. Most frequently court staff will have regard to official guidance and 'job cards' in the bulk of their day to day work only looking at the rules to resolve particular problems.

The attitude of lawyers differs considerably. There are some who seek to obey both the letter and the spirit of the rules. More often rules tend to be ignored, time limits overlooked in the anticipation that it will all come right in the end, failings in procedure will not prevent the judge from 'doing justice'. While it could have been anticipated that the introduction of 'automatic striking out' by CCR Ord 17 r.11 would have caused some casualties, who could possibly have anticipated that 20,000 cases or more would be struck out primarily because of a failure (a) to diarise the 'automatic timetable' and (b) to make a simple application to extend the timetable to meet the particular needs of a case?

Far worse is the attitude of some, a minority but a significant and growing minority, of lawyers regarding the rules as scope for endless procedural manoeuvring avoiding the day when they will have to confess that they have no case and settle. Requests for the most detailed particulars, interrogatories of extraordinary length and complexity, applications for yet more discovery all have a significant part in the increasing cost and delay in litigation—'the Rules have been used as a tactical weapon to obstruct progress and inflate costs' (Chapter 26 para. 5).

Though more experienced than the average lay litigant the advice agencies need a 'litigation manual' prepared in such a way as to be easily understood and followed. Their needs are for simplicity and clarity in the rules not only so that advice workers can easily understand them but also so that they can equally easily explain procedural points to their clients.

The majority of litigants in person look to the Rules for what they cannot find—a simple and easily understood explanation/description of a procedure, perceived as fair which will be followed by all involved in the action. One particular need for lay litigants (and indeed advisors and many lawyers) is a means of finding their way from one rule to another. Few rules are or could be fully self contained, an understanding is required of other rules which relate to the subject but to which there is at present no direct reference. Many rules will to refer to 'service', to time limits, to the making of applications. The average lay litigant will have difficulty in understanding what is meant and in finding the relevant rules. Some form of cross referencing whether it be direct '(see rule x.oo)', by footnotes to a similar effect or by highlighting particular words and expressions so that they can be followed up through a glossary or index will be needed. Such tools are largely unknown to the draftsmen of Statutory Instruments but are going to be necessary if the new rules really are to provide an 'instruction manual' for lay litigants.

At a time when there is a rapid growth in the numbers of litigants in person—and not only in the 'small claims' arena—it must be wrong that individual rights may depend on relatively incomprehensible and inaccessible procedural rules.

Not only must the language and style be more user friendly but there will need to be a clear and logical structure to the rules. Issue of the claim, service, defence, default judgment, summary disposal, case management should follow in a logical sequence. In all cases the placing of a particular rule will need to be decided by reference to where a lay litigant is most likely to look. For example in the present High Court rules provisions as to service on a partnership are contained in the rules dealing with different aspects of partnership. In the county court the rule as to service on a partnership will be found among the rules relating to service—this, surely, will be the logical place to look.

The draftsman of any new code of rules will need to have regard to all these needs—and pitfalls—in deciding how to approach his task.

### The language of the rules

Traditionally the language of the Rules has required background knowledge in order to understand the particular rule and how it may be construed by the court. The user will also need a general working knowledge of the structure of the rules themselves and the way in which they interrelate to place the rule in its context. The language has become increasingly technical. Part of the reason for this has been the need to 'overrule' decisions of the courts affecting or limiting the application of the rules—hence the very substantial rewriting of RSC Ord 2 to meet the decision in *Re Pritchard* [1963] Ch 502 and to remove the distinction made in that case between nullity and mere irregularity. Already technical language becomes burdened with substantial accretions of judicial interpretation and semantic dissection complicating already complex concepts: complex for the lawyer, let alone the layman embarking on an action in the civil courts. '. . .The size and number of the rules is now such that . . . they are wholly inaccessible to those unfamiliar with them, and complex and daunting even to those who are familiar with them. It might even be said that the rules themselves have become an obstacle to access to justice' (Chapter 26 para. 6). Can language designed to be 'judge proof' succeed in avoiding the accretions of case law yet provide a simple guide for the non expert? Can the rules be all things to all men—is it desirable that they should?

Complexity, says the report, takes two obvious forms: too many ways of doing the same or similar things, the use of specialised terms and an over elaborate style of language (Chapter 26 para. 6). It also lies in the sheer length and the number of words used (Chapter 26, para. 17). Not less significant can be the general layout of the rules in long paragraphs and sentences, far from easy for the unskilled eye to follow.

Account needs to be taken by the draftsman of the new opportunities provided by, as well as the requirements of, Information Technology. Not only will rules be required to be 'on disc' but the use of information technology brings about new opportunities for indexing and cross referencing. Access to the rules may be by way of the 'Arizona' terminals (Chapter 13 para. 20) which will guide a litigant through the process and assist him in the production of forms required for the purpose of his litigation.

Rules should surely be couched in the simplest and most direct language. Propositions should be kept short. There is no need to 'write down' to the lowest level of litigant. Simple and direct language will speak to all.

## How rules are applied

Reference has already been made to the problems caused not primarily by the rules themselves but the way in which they are applied. Sufficient has been said to identify the culture of non-observance brought about by the courts failing to exercise discipline over non compliance with the rules and directions and timetables given by the court. Even when the rules are applied or directions enforced by the 'procedural judge', delay and expense are frequently caused by appeals whether or not they are successful. It is right to say that they may make Masters and district judges feel inhibited sometimes from enforcement of the rules or the giving of robust directions by the feeling that they will not be supported on appeal.

This problem cannot simply be resolved by the language or approach of the rules themselves. Part of the answer must lie in the 'team culture' among judges recommended in the interim report and part by a fresh approach to the question of appeal. Should procedural appeals effectively be a rehearing—a second chance for the appellant to get his 'tackle in order'? Could they be restricted to matters of principle? Is there some way of restricting the precedential effect of decisions of the Court of Appeal which turn on the facts of a particular case but are culled by text book editors in a seemingly endless attempt at 'semantic dissection' of the rules?

However, even if the rules themselves cannot solve the problem a fresh approach to the style and language of the rules may be of assistance in establishing a new culture.

### Relationship to Practice Directions and Guides

One confusing feature of present litigation is the profusion of Practice Directions issued by various officers of the High Court and by individual county courts frequently after inadequate consultation. The *vires* of some of these directions is at least suspect. Many Practice Directions appear out of date although never formally rescinded. Recently Practice Guides have been issued by the Commercial Court, the Official Referee and by the Chancery Division. The exact relationship between these directions and guides (and Practice Notes and Statements) and the rules is not altogether clear. Rules should make clear the authority of Practice Statements and Guides, their provenance, the relationship between them and the rules and the sanctions to be attached to non-observance. While there is much to be said for making the rules completely self sufficient there is an equally strong argument for a system of Directions having almost the force of rule and Guides which will expand and to some extent interpret the rules and provide a clear description of procedures and the way in which the rules interrelate. However care must be taken to limit Directions and Guides as much as is possible and to ensure that they are kept up to date.

## THE WOOLF APPROACH

### An overriding objective

The Woolf approach to procedural reform is not to discard entirely the adversarial approach but rather to institute a system of court controlled case management. The principle is that parties are free to negotiate at their own speed prior to the commencement of litigation. Once litigation has started control passes to the court. This immediately requires a substantial and not uncomplicated change to the rules. If 'hands on' judicial management were required in all cases the rules could be very much reduced in size as they would need only to provide the basic framework leaving the individual directions to be given by the procedural judges to suit the needs of each case. Unfortunately life is never so simple and the cost of such control would be disproportionate in the majority of cases—hence the proposals for a new system of 'tracking'. The rules will still have to provide fairly detailed structures for the smaller and medium size cases although in the larger cases directions given at Case Management Conferences and Pre Trial Reviews will replace the need for rules over significant areas of case preparation.

What is clear is that considerable powers are to be given to procedural judges whether in deciding on the appropriate track, in tailoring standard directions to meet the needs of the instant case or in using the full case management powers. An objective is required.

The Dworkinian distinction differentiates *rules*—which are applicable in an all or nothing fashion, ie rules dictate the outcome, from *principles*—standards which guide but do not determine and from *policy* which sets out a 'goal to be reached'. Rules of Court are typically rules in the narrow sense, eg the plaintiff may enter judgment on proving certain matters if no defence is filed/served. Others are principles, eg many rules empower the court to make orders—an order for security for costs—but do not require it to make such an order even if the 'threshold' conditions are met, the court is given a discretion whether or not and in what manner the power should be exercised. In reaching a decision the court will balance many factors not provided for in the rule.

Hitherto Rules of Court have not amounted to 'policy' in the narrow sense although it is possible to draw out threads of policy from individual rules and much judicial interpretation can be regarded as being designed to provide such policy. For example the judgment of the Court of Appeal in *Ridehalgh v Horsefield* [1994] Ch 205, [1994] 3 All ER 848, CA dealing with 'wasted costs orders' under RSC Ord 62 r.11 (which could be argued to have largely emasculated the rule, based as it was on statute!) or *Rastin v British Steel plc* [1994] 2 All ER 641, [1994] 1 WLR 732, CA dealing with the way in which courts should approach the exercise of its power to restore actions 'automatically struck out' under CCR Ord 19 r.11(9). It may be more correct to regard these cases as seeking to provide consistency in the application of principles rather than as establishing policy but the borderline is a thin one.

Lord Woolf in his general or (perhaps more aptly) overriding objective provides for the first time a rule embodying quite clearly a goal, or perhaps rather a series of goals, for the conduct of civil litigation and the manner in which the courts are to exercise their powers under the rules (in the more traditional sense).

This one rule is included in the interim report in what is presumably a draft form:

(1) the general objective of these rules is to enable the court to deal with cases justly
(2) the court shall apply these rules so as to further the general objective
(3) dealing with a case justly includes:
 (a) making allowances for any inequality between the parties
 (b) saving the parties expense
 (c) handling the case in ways which are proportionate
  (i) to the amount of money involved
  (ii) to the importance of the issues, and
  (iii) to the parties' financial position
 (d) ensuring that the case is handled and completed expeditiously; and
 (e) allotting an appropriate share of the court's resources to the case while taking into account the need to devote resources to other cases'

The novelty of this proposed rule lies in its generality and in the fact that it is addressed to the court, and addressed to the court not in terms of empowerment but as a requirement restricting and controlling the way in which the court exercises its discretion and powers under the rules. There are other models, the general rubric in the Matrimonial Causes Act 1973, s. 25(1) springs immediately to mind but the idea of an all controlling policy objective is novel in the history of English Codes of Rules.

While it may be somewhat of a semantic exercise the question needs to be asked whether the overriding objective deals solely with the application of the rules or in their construction. Frequently the practical difference will be slight but as presently drafted the overriding objective would appear to be restricted to questions of application.

The rule is also novel in terms of a procedural rule in that it is addressed to practical and, even perhaps, social matters rather than purely 'legal' issues. In the past Oscar Wilde's famous comment that the law, like the Ritz, is open to all has in litigation meant that the Rolls Royce system of procedure must apply, a single standard inaccessible to all but the very rich or the very poor. Now the finances of the parties are to be taken into account, if a party cannot afford expensive experts or massive discovery the court will have to find a way in which the case can be 'dealt with justly' without putting that party at a disadvantage.

Not only is the financial position of a party relevant but also the cost of any particular step in relationship to the benefit to be derived from it. This may not be clear from the first draft of the overriding objective but appears, eg, from recommendation 92

In determining whether to order extra discovery, the procedural judge should have regard to the issues in the case and the order in which they are likely to be resolved, the resources and circumstances of the parties,the likely cost of extra discovery and the likely benefit.

The judiciary is being put into the position when what previously would have been totally ignored will now come to the forefront of its thinking, proportionality both in terms of the resources of the parties and the cost effectiveness of particular steps will become all important.

It is at least arguable that when introducing such a novel concept the rule maker should be bold and ensure that the definition of 'deal justly' is spelt out clearly and definitively in the Rules and does not merely rely on an inclusive approach—how is it to be determined what other factors are to be taken into account, will rules of construction such as the *eiusdem generis* apply?. A bold statement that dealing justly 'means . . .' would seem preferable.

Paras (3)(a)–(d) seem self explanatory and reasonably easy to apply though the expressions 'make allowances' may be rather weak and even somewhat condescending. 'Take account of' or 'taking steps to redress' might be more effective expressions.

Sub para (e) is less so. The broad intention would appear to be that the principle of proportionality will apply to the use of court resources. This is admirable in principle but is only to a limited extent within the power of the procedural judge. A shorter trial will clearly make less demands on judicial and other resources and release time for others. The same may be said of any 'reference out' to some form of ADR (or 'down' to the small claims track). Use of a lower level of judiciary will reduce costs. However, it is difficult to see how such matters fall easily within the concept of 'dealing with a case justly'. It appears to be a separate issue which would be better addressed as such even within the ambit of the overriding objective. There seems to be no reason in principle why court resources should not be taken into account just as resources in the health service may be taken into account in deciding whether and how to treat a particular patient. It would be better to state this principle separately rather than to seek to bring it under the umbrella of 'dealing justly'.

A further aspect which is not mentioned but which may be of significance in ensuring effective case management. This arises out of the way in which courts only too frequently tend to look at the issue of 'fairness' solely in relation to the instant case without taking into account the cumulative effect of continual relaxation of rules on the culture of litigation. A further objective that the court should take into account the wider effect that any decision in the instant case may have could well make a valuable contribution to the narrower concept of dealing justly with the instant case. The reports says ' the defects . . . arise from the *repeated* failure of parties or lawyers to observe those rules *and of the courts to police them'* (Chapter 16 para.2—author's emphasis) It seems right that the demands on overall resources and the need to preserve reasonable discipline in compliance with the rules should be regarded as proper matters for the court to take account of in applying the rules.

## Construction and Application of the Rules

However well worded the rules may be it is the responsibility of the profession and the judiciary—and primarily the latter—to apply the rules appropriately. Most of the failings of the present procedure may be said with some truth to lie not at the door of the draftsman or even in the developing complexity and technicality of the rules but in the way in which they are applied—or not. Over technical application is to be avoided, the rules are to be read as a whole not 'dissected and viewed word by word under a microscope', the rules are to be 'deliberately framed so that the approach of those construing them can be more purposive and less technical. It will thus be the responsibility of the judiciary to make the new system work (Chapter 26, para. 26).

The purposive approach to the construction—as opposed to the application—of rules may be it has its dangers. Lord Woolf cites with approval words by Lord Denning in *James Buchanan & Co Ltd v Babco Forwarding and Shipping (UK) Ltd* [1977] QB 208, CA

> . . . judges do not go by the literal meaning of the words or by the grammatical structure of the sentence. They go by the design or purpose . . . behind it. When they come upon a situation which is to their minds within the spirit—but not the letter of the legislation, they solve the problem by looking at the design and purpose of the legislature—at the effect it was sought to achieve. They then interpret the legislation so as to produce the desired effect. This means that they fill in gaps, quite unashamedly, without hesitation. They ask simply: what is the sensible way of dealing with this situation so as to give effect to the presumed purpose of the legislation.

This was a decision dealing with the interpretation of European legislation and describes the practice of the judges of the Court of Justice at Luxembourg (though it seems consonant with recent decisions of the present Court of Appeal). It is hard to disagree with the sentiment behind this judgment and yet there are dangers. Over technicality is one extreme the other is such 'woolliness' in the application of the rules, the view that perceived 'fairness' requires a rule to be relaxed or, indeed, waived, that they no longer are regarded as controlling the process of litigation. However tempting and right this may appear to be in a single case the cumulative effect of such an approach to construction can be that the rules cease to bite and the objectives of proportionate speed and cost effectiveness are once again lost.

Present overtechnical and over verbose pleading clearly breaches both the letter and spirit of the present rules as to pleading (RSC Ord 18 r.7—'every pleading must contain, and contain only, a statement in a summary form of the material facts on which the party pleading relies . . .') yet decisions of the courts have tended, if anything, to encourage over technicality. On the other hand, for example, the present approach that amendment of pleadings can seldom be refused even at a very late stage in the proceedings both encourages over-technicality and increases delay, it is an encouragement to sloppiness in pleading—'it can be put right later'—'However negligent or careless may have been the first omission, and however late the proposed amendment, the amendment should be allowed if it can be made without injustice to the other side' per Brett MR in *Clarapede v Commercial Union Association* (1883) 32 WR 362, CA.

It is indeed a very fine line between perceived fairness in the instant case and such a generous approach to failure to comply with rules that the latter lack force. As has previously been suggested, much of the fault in the present system of civil litigation is to be laid not at the rules, over complex and technical as they may be, but at the continued eating away at their effectiveness by decisions of the courts. One might ask whether the provisions of RSC Ord 25 .r,8 (automatic directions in personal injury cases) have ever been observed or how many Summons for Directions have been issued within one month of the close of pleadings (RSC Ord 25 r.1(1)) and what steps have ever been taken by the courts to discipline parties so that the rules and their time limits are observed. It was for this reason that the Automatic Directions in the county court provided for an ultimate sanction of 'automatic striking out'.

This is not to ignore the need to do justice in the instant case—this is the function of the courts and is the stated overriding objective of the proposed new rules. A balance has to be sought. Perhaps the real failure of the present system is the difficulty of applying an appropriate sanction. Too often the only sanction applied is the crude one of 'striking out' an action or defence. The very crudeness of the sanction invites the making of exceptions. What seems to be required is a series of sanctions appropriate to the offence and, in many cases, applying automatically unless the defaulter seeks and obtains relief. The mere requirement to seek relief is some degree of sanction, the onus is on the defaulter, not as at present primarily on the 'innocent' party. The defaulter would have to show that it was reasonable to grant relief. It could well be that the two stage process suggested in *Rastin v British Steel* (above) firstly a threshold requirement that the defaulter should show that apart from the particular lapse he had conducted the case with reasonable diligence. If that test were met the court could grant belief if no prejudice would be suffered by the other party. Such an approach would provide a realistic method of providing discipline especially if accompanied by orders that the costs 'thrown away' should be paid forthwith. In addition the court could impose such conditions and make such directions as it thought appropriate to make sure that the claim proceeded without unnecessary delay or expense.

## General objectives for the New Rules

No further detailed indications are given at the style or content of any other rules but in Chapter 26 para. 25 Lord Woolf sets out his three objectives for the making of new rules:

(a) to identify the core propositions in the rules and to cut down the number of interconnecting provisions which are used
(b) to provide procedures which apply to the broadest possible range of cases and to reduce the number of instances in which a separate regime is provided for a special type of case, and
(c) to reduce the size of the rules and the number of propositions contained in them, to remove verbiage and to adopt a simpler and plainer style of drafting

Rules must be clear, perceived to be fair and reasonable and not disobeyed with impunity. This principle needs to stand alongside the principles of a purposive approach to construction and indeed alongside the overriding objective.

The task of removing technical language from the rules wherever possible is a difficult but highly important one. There are two main objectives. The first is simply to make the rules more understandable. The second is to try and cut away the burden of judicial interpretation where similar words in earlier rules have been endlessly dissected by the courts. Wherever possible normal English words bereft of technical meanings should be used. However the battle to avoid traditional technical expressions may well not always avail, such expressions as 'service', 'default' even 'judgment' are generally understood and the search for simple alternatives may well prove undesirable. To the extent that this proves to be the case the rules should include a simple Glossary explaining clearly what particular expressions mean.

Each rule will need to follow so far as practicable a single and consistent pattern

first, the purpose of the rule should be set out clearly and succinctly
it should state
  to whom, and
  in what circumstances
    the rule applies
  and who is entitled to act on it

the procedure needs to be clearly set out
when and how any appropriate application may be made
the courts powers and responsibilities in effecting the purpose stated
the parties should be directed to the next step even if by cross-reference or footnote.

A case has already been made for the rules to be so far as possible descriptive rather than merely prescriptive. How far can this approach go? The reference to an 'instruction manual' has been discussed above. Lord Woolf compares in paras 32 & 33 the use of leaflets to explain and the rules themselves—possibly the same distinction as between an owner's handbook and the workshop manual. There are clear difficulties in the use of what is commonly referred to as Plain English when the purpose is not simply descriptive but also prescriptive. However while it is clearly correct that 'guidance and rules have distinct functions', it is less obvious that 'this is bound to reflected in the language that they each use'. It may be truer to say that the language of the rules may need to vary in accordance with the type of concept that is being dealt with. Language that will be suitable for a simple procedural rule may be less so where the rule is more technical in nature.

Many rules in essence set out a sequence of events (description) which the players are to follow and provide a sanction of some form or other if they fail to do so (prescription). It is difficult to see any reason in principle why the two cannot be combined though there are undoubtedly practical difficulties.

Consider the common event of a default judgment. A claimant needs to know what can be done if the defendant does not file a defence. He needs to know

- what requirements there are for the defendant to file a defence
- within what time this needs to be done
- what are his rights in the absence of a defence
- how does he enforce those rights, what form of application he needs to make, to whom and when.

The court administration will need to know the same basic facts and also be placed under a duty to enter judgment if the claimant applies and the necessary conditions are met.

A rule on the following lines would be both descriptive and prescriptive

'DEFAULT JUDGMENT
Object:
To enable the court to give judgment without trial when a defendant does not file a defence

To what claims does the rule apply:
All except claims for possession of residential premises

Who may apply:
The Claimant
When may an application be made:
Once 28 days have passed from the date of service (see rule—)

How is an application to be made:
By completing Form x including a declaration

- giving the method of service (as to service see rule—)
- stating that to the best of the claimant's belief the claim form will have come to the defendants attention at least 28 days before the application is made
- stating what sum of money is still due from the defendant

The Application is to be filed at the court office.

What will the court do
The court shall enter judgment against the defendant if satisfied that he has been served, has had at least twenty eight days to file a defence and that no defence has been served.
The court shall serve a copy of the judgment on all parties

What form does such a judgment take.

(1) If the claim is for a specific sum of money—Form a
(2) If the claim is for an undefined sum of money—Form ab
(3) If the claim is for the return of goods—Form ac
(4) If the claim is for possession of land—Form ad
(5) Where the claim is for any other relief—Form ae

What is the effect on the defendant
Once judgment has been entered he will be unable to take any further step in the proceedings except

- to apply to set aside judgment (Rule—)
- to make application for time to pay (rule—)
- to apply to suspend enforcement (rule—)
- to be heard with regard to any application made by the claimant with regard to enforcement of the judgment

What are the claimants rights?
to take steps to enforce the judgment (see rules —) if payment is not made as ordered or the judgment not complied with.

While no doubt substantial improvements can be made to the drafting, the format shows the possibility of providing a relatively userfriendly rule which combines description and some degree of prescription.

An important issue is how a rule expressed in such a form is likely to be interpreted by the courts. It would be dangerous to express too firm an opinion but it may be that the approach to style and language would reduce the likelihood of detailed dissection of individual words, the thrust is towards describing a process as a whole. However, it must be said that this particular illustration may well not apply to more technical matters such as the provisions for amending pleadings to introduce a new party once a relevant time limit has expired (See the present RSC Ord 20 r.5.). It is unlikely that one single style will meet all the needs for rulemaking and it will be interesting to see how the draftsman approaches the task of providing a broadly common style and approach to rules of differing types, primarily those which do describe a process and those which define or limit rights of litigants.

Whatever the approach the first requirement is that the language should be simple and direct. The aim or object of each rule should be stated, the procedure set out and the court's powers listed. It is essential that the lay litigant can see the relationship of the rule to other relevant rules and for this reason some form of cross referencing will be necessary.

Practice Guides and explanatory leaflets will doubtless be used and of value but it is surely essential that the rules should so far as possible be self standing and, even more importantly, not only be understandable in themselves but also direct the lay litigant (and indeed the lawyer) to other interlinking or relevant rules.

## Size

The drive to reduce the size of the rules is important but not at the expense of clarity and comprehensibility. If the rules are to form a 'litigation handbook' for the lay litigant (and others)it will be necessary to allow a certain amount of repetition and/or introduce a system of cross referencing.

A substantial reduction can be achieved by the elimination of the rules which deal with what are primarily administrative procedures—see, for example, RSC Ords 63, 64, 65 and 68. These can be replaced by internal administrative directions to staff or by Practice Guides.

## Specialist Jurisdictions

A significant part of the second phase of Lord Woolf's inquiry will be to deal with the differing practices of the specialist divisions and courts and the specialist, primarily statutory jurisdiction of both High Court and county court. The Rules of the Supreme Court contain a number of Orders dealing solely with this specialist jurisdictions. There are a large number of rules dealing with specifically Chancery practice. However there is far less provision in the rules for the work of the Commercial Court and the Official Referee. In those instances the rules provide the bare bones but much of the day to day procedure is dealt with by Practice Guides. This may well be the way forward for other specialist jurisdictions.

The ability to limit the size of the rules—and to keep them easily comprehensible—will depend to some extent on the extent to which the specialist jurisdictions will be able to work within the general framework suggested by Lord Woolf in the Interim Report.

The main structure that is proposed is that of a single form of claim, statements of fact replacing pleadings, case management and dates for trial being fixed shortly after the filing of the defence. Within that broad structure there is room for considerable flexibility, particularly in more complex 'multi track' cases. The single form of originating process would have some impact on Chancery procedure, boasting as it does several different methods of commencing proceedings. It is difficult to see why a single form of Claim should not be used in Chancery work although there may well need to be some form of fixed date procedure (which will be needed in eg county court possession proceedings in any event). The single form of originating process would not appear to cause difficulty in the Commercial or the Official Referees Courts where proceedings will normally be commenced by Writ. There may be some difficulty in Admiralty work both because of the international nature of much of such work and also because of the distinction between writs *in rem* and writs *in personam* (though even that can find some echoes in possession proceedings in both High Court and county court).

Assuming that the specialist Divisions and courts will only deal with substantial multi-track matters in future the system of case management proposed by Woolf should deal effectively with their needs.

In the county court housing actions have led to unnecessarily complex rules and the opportunity needs to be taken to simplify these proceedings so far as possible, although, as recognised by Lord Woolf, many of the complexities arise from the complexities of the statute law to be applied. It is unlikely that this jurisdiction will justify extensive 'hands on' case management and it may be that a 'housing track' will prove desirable.

The growing importance of judicial review and of multi party actions will require a review of and indeed the provision of new procedures but the broad structure proposed in the report should be able to apply with some modifications.

It may be desirable that where are discrete areas needing their own procedures these procedures should be set out in a schedule to the general rules—or even in a Practice Guide—rather than complicating the main structure.

## CONCLUSION

The interim report and its discussion of the principles lying behind the drafting of new rules presents a real prospect of achieving a completely new approach to Rules of Court, not only unifying the procedures of High Court and county court, not only providing the formal structure for the radical changes that Lord Woolf proposes but, as importantly, providing a new sort of user friendly, easily followed and understood code of rules to meet the needs of all users of the civil process and their advisors whether professional or lay. We shall have to await the final report to see to what extent the various issues discussed in this paper are satisfactorily resolved.

# 7

# *Discovery in Commercial Litigation*

DAVID MACKIE*

## 1. INTRODUCTION

1.1. Commercial cases are in many ways less important than those involving crime, children or people's homes. The impact on the community of commercial cases is however wider than the benefit to the balance of payments. Commercial cases, tried not only in the Commercial Court but also elsewhere in the High Court and in the County Court, daily affect and blight the careers of ordinary people, determine whether or not businesses and sometimes whole industries are to survive, factories and oil fields to remain open and communities to flourish. One aspect of the unacceptable increase in the cost of commercial litigation has been the effect of discovery of documents.

1.2. There is a perception, widely held by litigation lawyers that discovery causes expense and delay out of proportion to the benefit it brings to the parties and the court. Does it? If so why? At first sight it might seem surprising that a mundane procedure which has developed quietly over a long period shaped by the requirements of the court, the lawyers, and clients, is a cause of waste and inefficiencies. Discussion about the role and effectiveness of discovery in civil litigation usually involves only generalisations drawn from personal experience. I therefore conducted a survey, by questionnaire, of the experiences of 45 solicitors in my firm's litigation department, drawn from all levels of age and experience (from newly qualified solicitors to partners), to produce a view of the value of discovery in commercial litigation. The results incorporate views that are necessarily subjective and, for reasons of confidentiality, details of the 86 current or recently completed cases considered cannot be disclosed. This survey does not, therefore, begin to enter the ranks of scholarship but it may be of some interest.

* Head of Litigation, Allen & Overy; a Recorder.

## 2. WHAT DOES DISCOVERY INVOLVE?

2.1. It is first helpful to recall what discovery involves. Order 24 of the Rules of the Supreme Court requires that after the close of pleadings, the parties to an action have to make a list of all documents which are or have been in their possession, custody or power relating to the matters in question. The test of relevance is wide.[1] At the heart of discovery is the obligation to disclose all relevant material, particularly that which advances or harms a party's own case.

2.2. The process involves the reading and listing of the relevant documents[2] and exchanging lists with the other side. Listing normally requires each document to be described. Privileged material has to be identified and described in general terms but not disclosed.[3] Each side then studies the other's documents and will often ask for more. Many requests for more documents are uncontroversial and cover relevant areas which had not occurred to the drafter of the list. Other requests are more contentious. A party's solicitor may ask for whole categories of documents, the relevance but not the existence of which is in dispute, for particular documents referred to or hinted at in those disclosed and/or for sets of documents which are known or suspected to exist.

2.3. Most clients will be disappointed if their solicitors do not seek further discovery. When solicitors urge their clients to make full discovery of all their documents, including the harmful ones, they wield the stick of the rules. They also dangle the carrot that it will be easier to attack their adversary's discovery if their clients have themselves complied fully. Where a request for documents is refused there will often be an application to the court. This leads to rounds of hearings preceded by exchanges of affidavits and often skeleton arguments about the points in issue.

2.4. Some time before the trial of an action the lawyers prepare and agree trial bundles containing the documents to be used at the hearing. In a large case these bundles will usually contain only a small proportion of the documents disclosed on discovery and there will often be only one or two 'core' bundles in regular use at trial.

[1] Compagnie Financiére du Pacifique v. Peruvian Guano Co. (1882) 11 QBD 55.

[2] 'document' is defined widely. It is not just paper but 'to anything upon which evidence or information is recorded in a manner intelligible to the sense or capable of being made intelligible by the use of equipment'. So tapes, films, discs and databases of all descriptions are included.

[3] Privileged documents are those protected by legal professional privilege, those which tend to criminate or expose to a penalty the party disclosing them and those privileged on the grounds of public policy. Order 24/5/5 to 24/5/18 Rules of the Supreme Court discusses.

## 3. SOME RESULTS OF THE SURVEY

3.1. **Was discovery useful?** In 17 of the 86 cases considered in our survey, the initial discovery process yielded significant documents which solicitors believed would not have otherwise come to light. These documents were significant in that they made a difference to the outcome or the way in which the case was put. In 69 cases discovery yielded nothing useful.

3.2. **In what ways did the 'significant' documents assist the case?** Here, unedited except for names, are the reasons given by individual solicitors as to why discovery was useful:

Discovery obligations meant that the client had to produce confidential documents to us which they would otherwise have with-held.

Some significant documents were produced by our opponents, which were helpful in explaining the fact that the true business had not been written down.

Our opponents' documents were significant as they showed that the defendants' work practices had not been followed.

An examination of our opponents' documents showed that they had tampered with them, using tippex. This went to the veracity of the claim as well as to individual witnesses.

Our opponent provided us with reports on controls and accounting which assisted in developing the area of contributory fault.

An examination of our clients' documents revealed comments made by our opponent (an ex-director) concerning a false loan.

An examination of our clients' documents forced us to reassess their case.

Documents disclosed by our clients revealed a damaging picture of the motives certain individuals had for entering into the transaction in issue.

Internal memoranda produced by our opponents enabled us to conclude that their pleaded defence on liability could not really be sustained.

Our opponent has produced potentially useful documents, and inspection is continuing.

Our case on contributory negligence could only be put together on the basis of the opponents' discovery.

An examination of our opponents' documents assisted in the calculation of quantum of damages.

Disclosure by our clients of an internal note caused our opponents to radically amend their defence.

Our opponents produced a letter which indicated that certain of their allegations could not be upheld.

An inspection of our opponents' documents revealed a forged invoice which supported the counterclaim.

Our clients' documents yielded memoranda which are relevant to state of mind. These may however be only marginally useful.

Our opponents' documents contained correspondence about the reasons for the decision to dismiss our client.

An examination of our opponents' documents was essential to proving our case, as it enabled us to analyse the product relevant to the case.

Without discovery our client would not have allowed us to review any of its documentation on the grounds of secrecy.

In this case significant documents were also revealed by the other side on discovery, although there is a suspicion that there may be further relevant documents that they are withholding.

3.3. It can be seen that in some cases the fact that such a wide-ranging obligation existed assisted solicitors in obtaining sight of the client's own documents. In other cases the advantage was seen to be access to material affecting the credit of a witness, not something for which discovery can directly be sought. These uses are of course incidental to the real aim of discovery.

3.4. **Was the cost of discovery justified?** The range of cases studied varied, in terms of amount in dispute, from very small sums to hundreds of millions of pounds. We found that, in cases where the amount at stake was less than £50,000, and the quantity of paper disclosed filled two or three lever arch files of documents, discovery seemed to be an effective way of eliciting the truth. On average the discovery process took up only 5–10% of the time spent on the case as a whole. In larger cases, discovery could take up as much as 20% of the time spent on the action. This is a great deal bearing in mind the other processes involved in litigation, such as drafting pleadings, conferences with counsel, interlocutory applications, seeking, obtaining and assessing expert evidence and taking and drafting witness statements. In one of the cases, 50% of the cost of the proceedings to date, some hundreds of thousands of pounds, was attributable to sorting, reading and listing the client's own documents.

3.5. Where cases reached trial, only a small proportion of the documents produced on discovery were relied upon. A typical case involves the disclosure of 2,000 files of documents, of which 120 would reach court in one form or another and 16 would be used reasonably extensively at the trial. This, to some extent, reflects the process of formulating any argument; of first identifying all the material that may be relevant, thinking things through, sifting and then using only what really matters. This work needs to be done regardless of the obligation to give discovery. Against that, it is very common at the end of a case when judge, counsel and clients have all gone home, for the solicitors on each side to look ruefully at each other and the mounds of unopened files over which they fought so hard in the pre-trial exchanges. Furthermore, the experience of solicitors is consistent with that of the judiciary, see for example the Foreword by Lord Justice Steyn (as he then was) to 'Discovery'[4] where he said:

> The discovery process often runs riot. It is the experience of Commercial judges that usually 95 per cent of the documents contained in the trial bundles are wholly irrelevant and never mentioned by either side. The discovery process adds greatly to the duration and cost of litigation, and helps a defendant (or plaintiff) to put off the day of financial reckoning. It contributes to the tyranny of modern civil litigation.

3.6. The use of a computer database system for discovery is now quite common but very expensive. Such a system was used in eight of the 86 cases surveyed. In the very largest cases, the computer was an invaluable aid in locating particular documents on request but this benefit was off-set (but only to some extent) by the cost of inputting the data and the time which this took. Obviously the value of the database depends absolutely on the quality of the input. Where, as in some cases, the majority of the material is already on a computer database the objection on ground of cost diminishes. When exchanging documents and examining one's opponents a computer may be virtually useless, either because the adversary has not used one or has used its own quite separate system. The impact of the development of technology on the burden of discovery merits study but advances are we feel unlikely to reduce the relative cost.

3.7. Simple chronological listing in accordance with Order 24 worked well in smaller cases perhaps because these are disputes of the size that the original draftsman may have had in mind when formulating the rule. These smaller cases with fewer documents probably resemble, in terms of quantity of paper, the large cases of forty years ago.

3.8. **How far do solicitors co-operate over discovery?** In practice, solicitors did not often reach agreement on a form of listing of bundles of documents. Solicitors tend to insist on individual listing and pagination as required by the rules. I refer at 4.2 below to the demanding nature of the rules. Solicitors felt that, in many cases, it would have been more useful to both parties for documentation to be listed by reference to particular transactions or by reference to the client's own files, rather than individually and chronologically.

3.9. In only a handful of the 86 cases surveyed were the parties prepared to agree a limited form of discovery. By 'limited' I mean agreeing that only certain specific classes of documents or those relevant to particular issues

[4] Matthews and Malek, Sweet & Maxwell 1992.

were to be disclosed or that documents within a particular time period only would be disclosed. I refer to possible reasons for this at 4.22 below.

3.10. **How useful are applications for further discovery?** In 32 cases some form of further discovery was sought by one side or the other. This resulted, in 14 cases, in the disclosure of further documents which were seen as significant.

3.11. Applications for further discovery and for verification tended to be used in two types of cases. The first was when a party was put on notice that a specific document might exist because it was referred to either in other documents or, in one case, in the other party's witness statement. The second type was where one party did not accept that the other had made full discovery, either because that party believed documents must exist which dealt with a particular issue or because he did not trust the other party. In many of the cases in which clients had adopted this latter approach, some fraud or conspiracy was being alleged.

3.12. **What happened in these 32 applications?** In two cases, orders were obtained from the court unopposed to protect a party from the risk of action abroad, or to guard against applications from a party's customers which might have followed voluntary disclosure. In 14 applications documents were yielded to one side or the other, which were felt to be 'significant'. A number of these were however documents which were 'embarrassing' rather than damaging. Others went to credibility of witnesses rather than the merits. Two applications were only necessary because the other side did not appear to be aware of basic discovery obligations. Some of these applications took only a few hours of lawyer's time but others were very substantial, taking the solicitors '50 hours', 'two weeks', 'a month' and often involved other lawyers in the firm and junior and leading counsel.

3.13. It will gratify the reader with fixed views about the attitude of City firms to know that it was felt by a number of solicitors that the Court would entertain and grant 'unreasonable' applications for further discovery where they were made by individuals against corporate entities. In one particular case, the costs of proceeding in the claim rose to one third of the many hundreds of thousands of pounds in issue, primarily as a result of repeated applications by the defendant, which were upheld by the Court, for documentation which the plaintiff felt was irrelevant and which did not ultimately assist the defendant's case.

3.14. **Conclusion.** In a few cases discovery was crucial to the outcome. Most of these were claims involving alleged fraud or dishonesty. A court examining these cases in their early stages, would in my judgment, have had little difficulty in identifying which ones required full discovery and which did not.

## 4. WHAT CAUSES THE INEFFICIENCY OF DISCOVERY?

4.1. This enormous waste of time and money is contributed to by a variety of factors, some of which are the following:

4.2. **Listing requirements.** The rules for preparing lists of documents are set out in RSC Order 24 rule 5. These provisions have generally been enforced literally by judges who temper the harsh practical consequences of their rulings with exhortations to solicitors to apply common sense and to co-operate over such matters.

4.3. Order 24 rule 5 provides—

> (1) A list of documents made in compliance with rule 2 or with an order under rule 3 must be in Form No. 26 in Appendix A, and must enumerate the documents in a convenient order and as shortly as possible but describing each of them or, in the case of bundles of documents of the same nature, each bundle, sufficiently to enable it to be identified.

4.4. When preparing discovery for cases it is obviously convenient, particularly in very large matters, to list documents by files provided by the client rather than by each individual document on the basis that these are 'of the same nature'. In practice this happens without objection in innumerable cases. Where the solicitors do not agree the courts have, in the past, been rigorous. Thus in *Sveriges Angfartygs Assurans Forening v. The 1976 Eagle Insurance Company SA and others*[5] the court considered a reinsurance broker's file which included telexes, faxes, notes of telephone calls, working papers, statements of account and invoices and various odds and ends. The court held that 'on any ordinary use of English' these were not documents 'of the same nature'. Different documents though dealing with the same subject matter or transaction and filed or bundled together originally have to be listed one by one. The court disapproved of 19th century authorities in the Supreme Court Practice which appeared to suggest a less literal approach.

4.5. When listing, one by one, the roughly 200 documents in the file the solicitors will, on the other hand, have to be careful not to describe them too fully. 'If the descriptions are prolix, the party giving them may be ordered to pay the costs occasioned by the prolixity'.[6]

4.6. It will be seen that such a task can quickly become time consuming and expensive. It is, however, unfair to let irritation at what may seem an over literal approach obscure a central problem of which the judges have been rightly conscious. If the party disclosing documents is not required to list them accurately the burden of discovery is shifted to the other side

[5] Unreported: Queens Bench Division (Commercial Court) 28 March 1990.

[6] Order 24/5/2 Rules of the Supreme Court.

which, faced with an unlisted warehouse full of documents then has to incur the expense of listing and analysing material with which it is likely to be unfamiliar. As put in *Sveriges*[7] the problem is this:

The dispute between the parties before me in truth arises from that situation. Who is to do the work? Is it the party giving the discovery or the party to whom the discovery is being given. Clearly circumstances may differ from one case to another, but one of the purposes of the Rules of Court, is to lay down what the ordinary division of responsibility shall be and what is the starting point both for the parties and the Court in considering who shall do what. The Rules of Court require the party giving the discovery to itemise the individual documents with some description, however brief, of the document. The obligation is qualified by a limited exception regarding documents of the same nature which may be disclosed by a bundle. Subject to that exception, the party giving the discovery must do the work.

As Henry J (as he then was) observed in *Minories Finance v. Arthur Young*:[8]

. . . It does not seem to me to be a proper solution simply to give to the defendants the task of rummaging through the documents and giving them the key of the warehouse in order to do so. The onus to make discovery is on the party whose documents they are.

4.7. In a very small case, inadequacies in a short list of a few documents cause no injustice. The aggrieved party can still read and appraise the documents in a few minutes, or hours. Where the discovery is very great in volume the need for particular description becomes more important. The greater the volume, the more crucial an accurate description becomes.

4.8. **Breadth of test.** The test for discovery is a very wide one[9] extending not just to material which would be evidence but also to any document which contains information which may either directly or indirectly enable a party to advance his own case or damage the case of his adversary. The test was laid down by Brett LJ (as he then was) in 1882 when life was less documented. Unsurprisingly no-one in 1882 addressed to the court a 'floodgates' argument about the effect that such a broad test would have upon a world where decisions are much more documented than they were and where technology has vastly increased the scope and scale of document reproduction and distribution.

4.9. **Logistics.** Often the documents are located on a number of sites. Sometimes they are so voluminous that they cannot be moved and the solicitors have to go to the sites to view the documents. This results in travel expenses and often there are no facilities on site for reorganisation of the documents or listing. It may be necessary to store vital documents, like title

[7] Unreported: Queens Bench Division (Commercial Court) 28 March 1990.
[8] Unreported: Queens Bench Division 31 March 1988.
[9] Compagnie Financiére du Pacifique v. Peruvian Guano Co. (1882) 11 QBD 55.

deeds, in a fire proof room, or if the documentation is commercially sensitive it may have to be kept under lock and key.

4.10. The fact that documents may be on a number of sites substantially increases the work. As one person alone cannot list all the documents, the list itself will have to be checked a number of times to prevent duplication and to standardise the descriptions used. Often different people describe the same document, albeit accurately, in different ways. In practice, a great amount of time is wasted in sorting and listing. It also inevitably leads to documents getting lost.

4.11. When different individuals within a client organisation have annotated the same document all versions of that document must be disclosed. It is time consuming to track down all the versions of a document and it is generally a pointless element of the discovery exercise providing no real benefit to anyone.

4.12. It can take an inordinate amount of time to review 'documents' for relevance, particularly tape recordings and computer disks with which lawyers are not always well equipped to deal.

4.13. **Professional pride.** Solicitors take a professional pride in giving full discovery and even in disclosing material that will assist their opponent. It is a part of the legal process where the office lawyer, not the advocate, takes the lead. Where there is doubt as to whether to disclose too little or too much the usual (and professionally commendable) choice is too much. This can often lead to requests for further discovery by the opposing party who latches on to the fact that a party has disclosed a document which may not really be relevant, but which refers to, say, 15 others. If it is argued that those 15 documents are not relevant the opposing party will say that they are mentioned in a document which is disclosed and this may lead to a relevant train of enquiry.

4.14. **Tactics.** There is a temptation to list and disclose a warehouse full of documents rather than a file. This may be because the reading of a warehouse full of documents imposes costs and inconvenience on the other side, perhaps helping to bring them to the negotiating table. It is also because some solicitors forced to disclose a damaging needle, will do so in a haystack rather than a small file. In most cases it is simply because it is easier, cheaper and safer to list and disclose a mass of material rather than to analyse it closely for its true relevance.

4.15. **Approach of judges.** Until very recently judges inclined instinctively to wider rather than narrower discovery because it could do no harm and might do good. It is commonplace for judges when making wide discovery orders to refer to the technical ability of solicitors to achieve this. The solicitors nod with pride and get on with it. Large firms of solicitors have the ability to list and distribute documents on a huge scale, 24 hours a day, seven days a week and smaller firms have access to bureaux which can do the same. The trend has created a whole new grade of legal workers, the name 'paralegal' borrowed from the US, who pass their generally short careers, sifting, collating and copying documents. In many firms the paralegals are young temporary staff often of great intellectual distinction including a good number of brilliant, but resting, actors singers and dancers.

4.16. A similarly principled but costly approach by judges, nowadays less common, is to impress upon solicitors the duty of personally supervising discovery particularly where their clients were based abroad. There are very good reasons for insisting on this given the extent of the obligation to make discovery. There are rightly severe consequences for solicitors and clients who fail to do so. Faced with the choice of taking a risk by disclosing only the three thin files of documents really bearing on the issues or avoiding all possible criticism by spending three weeks in January at the clients' offices in Barbados, solicitors were inclined to answer the safer call of duty. The result has often been the reading, listing and copying of unnecessary documents, which then have to be read (generally also in Barbados) by the other side.

4.17. Those who order discovery in the very largest cases are generally either High Court judges or Queen's Bench masters who, coming from the Bar, may understandably have little experience of the practical difficulties involved. The waste, but not the cost, is inadvertently concealed by firms of solicitors taking pride in producing, in an ordered way and apparently without effort, vast quantities of paper.

4.18. **Precedent and uncertainty.** There is a general view that the operation of precedent should not determine procedural matters where flexibility is crucial.[10] Despite this perception precedent has often been allowed to leave important issues of discovery unresolved for substantial periods.

4.19. A piece of paper (for example the minutes of a board meeting) may deal with a variety of matters, some of which are relevant for discovery and some of which concern something quite different. Common sense might suggest that the answer is to disclose what is relevant and cover up the rest. Thus until the decision of the Court of Appeal in *GE Capital Corporate*

[10] e.g. In *Sveriges* 'The citation of 19th century cases decided under different circumstances (the decision of disputes about privilege) and under different Rules of Court is not a correct approach to providing the answer to practical questions of procedure in the last decade of the 20th century under the present Rules of Court. Decisions on procedural matters are governed by the Rules of Court in force at the time and the practical considerations pertaining at the time. Such decisions are neither binding nor persuasive one hundred years later when different rules and considerations are applicable. Decisions of courts on purely procedural questions are not of permanent validity or authority. The procedure of the courts, subject to the framework of legislation and delegated legislation, has to develop and adapt and what may or may not have been an appropriate decision in the 19th century is not necessarily still appropriate in the 20th century. If not appropriate, it should not be followed even if it was the decision of an Appellate Court.'

*Finance Group Limited v. Bankers Trust Co*[11] a solicitor did not and could not know whether it was acceptable to cover up those parts of a discoverable document which were not relevant because they dealt with another subject. The difficulty is resolved in favour of common sense in a clear cut way by Hoffmann LJ (as he then was) with Dillon LJ pointing up past disagreements that 'The recent decisions on this topic of Saville J and Gatehouse J in the Commercial Court are to be preferred to the recent decisions in the Chancery Division'.

4.20. There is a similar and more worrying issue where part of a document contains material that should be disclosed but other bits consist of records of legal advice. For 14 years (since *Great Atlantic Insurance Co v. Home Insurance Co* [1981[ 1 WLR 529) it has been unclear whether disclosing the unprivileged part of a partly privileged document amounts to a waiver of privilege. The obvious good sense of permitting full disclosure but protecting legitimate privilege led to judges devising stratagems to help parties achieve this. As Hoffmann LJ put it in *GE Capital*, adding powerful support to the view that disclosure of the unprivileged part should not waive privilege in the remainder, 'I admire the ingenuity but games like this should not be necessary.'

4.21. Solicitors owe a duty to the court to give full discovery about which, in my experience, they are conscientious. Considerable care and thought are directed to the frequent marginal decisions as to whether or not a document is relevant or privileged. An error of judgment may attract severe criticism and sanctions from, depending on its nature, the court or the client. There is little room for second thoughts or for changing one's view. The right to claim privilege for protected material can easily be lost by waiver and the opportunities for retrieving a document disclosed in error are limited and complex.[12]

4.22. **Difficulty in reaching agreement.** We are frequently reminded that the rules of court permit the parties to agree to limit discovery and that solicitors rarely do so.[13] It is not because solicitors are ignorant of the rules. It is unrealistic to expect parties to bitterly fought out litigation to invoke this rule except on rare occasions. A client may agree to his solicitor's suggestion that his own discovery be restricted to save costs and time. When the client is asked to agree that the other side be spared the expense and inconvenience of disclosing documents to him which are, admittedly, relevant to the case but expensive or difficult for his opponent to provide, it is obvious what his answer will be. Few cases (particularly actions involving discovery as opposed to originating summonses) are seen by the parties as

[11] [1995] 1 WLR 172.

[12] See the summary in Discovery (Matthews & Malek, Sweet & Maxwell 1992) paragraphs 9.12 to 9.14.

[13] RSC order 24 rule 1(2)

a dispassionate request for judicial determination. Mistrust is at the heart of disputes which reach the courts. It would be odd for the victim of a large fraud, perhaps with his career at stake, to surrender the right to see relevant material. The cases where parties co-operate will tend to be the quickest and cheapest to determine.

4.23. It is easy to confuse those solicitors' exchanges which consist of ill-tempered and pointless point scoring with those which voice legitimate and deeply held concerns which clients are paying them to articulate. Co-operation between solicitors over procedural matters is routine, in most cases, but there is much less room for 'give and take' when one side seeks to save money by not disclosing what is conceded to be relevant material. Agreement is particularly difficult as discovery closely follows the close of pleadings when it is difficult to be certain that an apparently minor concession will not become a major error once the real issues are more clearly identified. Under the present system this often does not happen until shortly before trial. If solicitors were obliged, not just permitted, to agree to limit discovery then it would be easier for them to persuade each other and their clients to follow common sense.

## 5. POSTSCRIPT

5.1. This essay was prepared before the recent Practice Direction on Case Management[14] had been digested or applied. Experience suggests that some of the problems are being dealt with. For example the Chancery Guide[15] imposes helpful requirements which will often limit the burden of discovery. There is reason to hope, therefore, that these observations will, by the time of publication, be of historical interest only.

[14] Practice Direction (*Civil Litigation: Case Management*) [1995] 1 WLR 262.
[15] *Chancery Guide*. HMSO April 1995—Chapter 3.4.

# 8

# *The Woolf Report: Against the Public Interest?*

CONRAD DEHN, Q.C.*

## I. ACCESS TO JUSTICE: THE PUBLIC'S ACCESS

In the introduction to his Report Lord Woolf says the first aim of his review is to improve access to justice.

There are two aspects of access to justice, both important. One is the access of an individual claimant or respondent. The other is that of the public as such, including the press. Except incidentally, the Report deals only with the former, and the effect of what it proposes will be to reduce the latter.

Though Parliament has provided for certain exceptions concerning family law, it is a fundamental rule of the English legal system (overlapping with the maxim 'Justice must not only be done but be seen to be done') that justice has to be administered in open court.[1]

The importance of this rule is stressed by Lord Shaw in *Scott*: he cites Bentham, 'Only in proportion as publicity has any place can any of the checks against judicial injustice operate. Where there is no publicity there is no justice . . . It is the keenest spur to exertion and the surest of all guards against improbity. It keeps the judge himself when trying under trial'; and Hallam 'Civil liberty in this kingdom has two direct guarantees; the open administration of justice according to known laws truly interpreted, and fair constructions of evidence; and the right of Parliament without let or hindrance to inquire into and obtain redress of public grievances. Of these the first is by far the most indispensable.'

Lord Shaw goes on to say, prophetically, (pp. 477–8) 'There is no greater danger of usurpation than that which proceeds little by little, under cover of rules of procedure, and at the instance of judges themselves'.

In *Att-Gen v Leveller* (1979) AC 440, Lord Diplock at p. 450 says 'If the way that Courts behave can not be hidden from the public ear and eye this

* Conrad Dehn QC is a practising barrister, a Recorder of the Crown Court, a Deputy High Court Judge and a Bencher of Gray's Inn.

[1] *Scott v Scott* (1913) AC 417, 434, 437, 445, esp. 477 (except where a public hearing would defeat the ends of justice or the administration of justice would be rendered impracticable by the presence of the public: p. 439); *McPherson v McPherson* (1936) AC 177. The exceptions do not include the saving of time or money: see *McPherson* p. 202.

provides a safeguard against judicial arbitrariness or idiosyncrasy and maintains the public confidence in the administration of justice'; and in *Home Office v Harman* (1983) AC 280 Lord Diplock at p. 303 quotes from Lord Shaw in *Scott* and says 'the reason for the rule is to discipline the judiciary—to keep the judges themselves up to the mark'. Lord Diplock did not spell out, as he could have done, that this covered reducing the risk of corruption or even the suspicion of it.

The European Convention of Human Rights in Art 6(1) provides that 'in the determination of his civil rights and obligations . . . everyone is entitled to a fair and public hearing . . . by an independent and impartial tribunal established by law. Judgment shall be pronounced publicly but the press and public may be excluded from all or part of the trial in the interests of morals, public order or national security . . . or to the extent strictly necessary in the opinion of the court in special circumstances where publicity would prejudice the interests of justice'. It will be noted that the exceptions there do not include saving time or money.

It was therefore disturbing that the Practice Direction (Civil Litigation: Case Management) (1995) 1 W.L.R. 262 handed down on 24th January this year by two of the most senior judges, the Lord Chief Justice and the Vice-Chancellor, provided inter alia: '3. Unless otherwise ordered, every witness statement is to stand as the evidence-in-chief of the witness concerned' without providing for making witness statements available to the public. Practice Directions do not have to be approved by Parliament or follow consultations with the legal profession, let alone the public.

Except in those few cases decided on documentary evidence only, the evidence of witnesses is the most important part of any trial involving questions of fact. To provide that that part shall not in general be made public is inconsistent with the rule in *Scott* and greatly reduces its effectiveness. If the public do not know what that evidence is, they can not follow the case and can not assess whether the judge is doing his job properly. To be able to hear such cross-examination as there may be is not enough: in the first place, it is likely to be unintelligible without knowing the evidence in chief, and in the second it is likely to deal with only a limited number of the matters contained in such evidence.

The public's ability to follow a case in Court and so make the rule effective was further eroded by the provisions in the Practice Direction that the Court would 'exercise its discretion' (it was assumed that it had such a discretion) to limit the length of oral submissions, the time allowed for the examination and cross-examination of witnesses, the issues on which it wished to be addressed, and reading aloud from documents and authorities. These provisions made it likely that a Court would be deciding the case before it on argument as well as on evidence much of which was not heard in open court but contained only in documents read privately by the Judge.

The Report does not in terms support the Practice Direction (see pp. 175–9) but its proposals, if adopted, will make the position even worse from this point of view. Although these proposals would allow witness statements to be amplified orally but no new point introduced without leave (p. 177 paras. 11–12, p. 179 para. 17), they would allow no cross-examination except by leave (p. 179 para. 18) and the Report suggests leave should usually not be given. Further, the Report proposes in relation to the 'fast track' that:

(i) (p. 43 para. 8) a district judge's decision whether a case should be dealt with on the fast track should be taken not only in private but apparently on his own;
(ii) (p. 44 para. 10(e)) only limited oral evidence from witnesses of fact should be allowed, supplemented by written evidence;
(iii) (p. 44 para. 10(g)) the judge's reasons for decisions could be given in writing; and
(iv) (p. 45 paras. 12, 14) the judge would decide what directions to give not only in private but often on his own.

When dealing with the 'multi-track' the Report proposes that

(i) (p. 51 para. 16) procedural applications including those for injunctions should be heard in chambers (which they are not at present in the Chancery Division): although the Report goes on to say (para. 17) that the intention is not to exclude the public and that the judge can always adjourn into court or allow members of the public to attend the hearing, this is not sufficient. Bearing in mind the purpose of proceedings being in public, this should not be left to the judge's discretion or even to the wishes of the parties (as suggested on p. 145 para. 38), but should be obligatory; and
(ii) (p. 69 para. 31, p. 84 para. 9, p. 86 para. 15, p. 87 para. 17) a judge may hear applications by using video or telephone conference facilities, without any reference as to how this is to be reconciled with the rule.

The need to discipline the judiciary will, if anything, be still greater if the Report's proposals are adopted because, first, the powers and role of the judges will be substantially increased and, second, there will have to be a considerable increase in the numbers of the judiciary (p. 95 para. 3) so that some lawyers who would not now be regarded as the most suitable for appointment are likely to have to be appointed.

It is of course possible that the saving in time and money which the Practice Direction and the Report's proposals are hoped to bring about may be regarded as more important than maintaining the principle of open justice, but this is not a matter for the judiciary or the profession but for

Parliament to decide after having had the arguments put before it. It is disappointing that neither the Practice Direction nor the Report makes any reference to the rule in *Scott* or the effect of its respective provisions or proposals on that rule.

On the other hand it would be possible, by the introduction of suitable measures, to maintain the rule in substance if not altogether in form and to keep it effective whilst still adopting the Report's proposals. It is a matter for regret and surprise that no reference has so far been made to the desirability of such measures, especially as the need therefor was recognised in the Civil Justice Review, 1988, (paras. 298–302 & recommendation 33).

In the European Court of Justice the judge-rapporteur's 'rapport d'audience' setting out the facts of the case and summarising the respective arguments of the parties is made public on the day of the hearing by being placed on a table outside the court room for interested members of the public (Brown & Kennedy, Court of Justice of the European Communities, 4th Edn, p. 257).

The measures I have in mind are that in cases where the rule now applies:

(1) copies of witness statements, skeleton arguments and any judgments not delivered in open court should be made available to the press and any members of the public in Court: this would be in line with the Practice Direction (Court of Appeal: Handed Down Judgments) (1995) 1 W.L.R. 1055; the cost at any rate of the first two should fall upon the parties;
(2) the case management conferences proposed by the Report (p. 39 para. 25, p. 48 para. 4) should be held in open court: this would indeed facilitate and enhance the monitoring which it regards as so desirable (p. 71 paras. 38–40);
(3) the hearings by telephone and video-conferencing and expert evidence by video-link which the Report recommends (p. 84 para. 9,p. 86 para. 15, p. 87 para. 17, p. 191 para. 37) should be recorded and stored on disk or videocassette, and any member of the public interested should be able, for an appropriate fee, to listen to or watch the recording;
(4) all judgments should be recorded and stored on disk and any member of the public interested should be able, for an appropriate fee, to listen to the recording; and
(5) eventually all public documents relating to a case—pleadings, witness statements, skeleton arguments, transcripts of Court proceedings, documents put in evidence, judgments—should be stored on disk and be available to any member of the public for an appropriate fee. The Report indeed proposes (p. 82 para. 3) that such material should be

available to the judge through IT and (p. 82 para. 5) 'eventually' to the public (see also p. 92 para. 32).

For my own part I think every court or court complex should give one of its officers the job of facilitating public access by being available to answer queries from the public as to what cases were being tried on any day, what they were about, what stage they had reached, and who the judge and advocates were.

Apart from the principal purpose of publicity for Court proceedings, ie disciplining the judges, there are important secondary advantages of open justice which are also prejudiced by the Practice Direction and endangered by the proposals in the Report. These include enabling false or misleading evidence to be corrected as a result of someone with knowledge of particular facts hearing or reading about evidence relating thereto being given in Court and coming forward to correct it; enabling parties to cases where similar issues arise to see how they may be best addressed; enabling solicitors and public to watch, assess and compare advocates in action; and sometimes enabling the authorities to learn about unlawful practices being carried on. The importance of the last is not to be underestimated: the fact that the authorities may learn from a public hearing of unlawful practices which a party to a case has been carrying on may deter him from embarking on them in the first place or encourage him to be reasonable in negotiations in the second.

## II. THE PRINCIPLES UNDERLYING THE REPORT

The Report sets out a number of principles: I wish to deal here with only three of them.

The Report starts (p. 2 para. 1) by quoting with approval Sir Jack Jacob's statement

(1) that the administration of civil justice '. . . manifests the political will of the State that . . . civil wrongs . . . be made good, so far as practicable, by compensation and satisfaction . . .'.

The Report then goes on to say (p. 3 para. 3) inter alia

(2) that '(b) the system should be fair and be seen to be so by ensuring that litigants have an equal opportunity regardless of their resources to assert or defend their legal rights', and
(3) that '(c) . . . cost should be proportionate to the nature of the issues involved'.

I shall deal with (1)–(3) in turn.

(1) Sir Jack Jacobs' statement

In my view this goes too far. There are many civil wrongs which the State should not, and I would hope does not, want troubling its civil justice system or care whether they are made good or not. I refer to minor wrongs, eg acts of negligence causing minor injuries to property or person, minor nuisances, minor libels, breaches of contract causing minor damage, minor boundary disputes between neighbours.

A civilised society is, in my view, one where people put up with and do not seek to claim compensation for minor wrongs, and where those who suffer an injury or loss do not automatically look round to see if it can be said to result from some act or omission by someone else which can be characterised as a civil wrong for which they can sue to obtain compensation. The number of actions brought per head of the population is not a measure of civilisation.

The potential demand for litigation, like that for medicine, is probably almost limitless. Apart from the factors rightly stressed on p. 9 para. 14 of the Report, the most potent circumstance which may encourage such restraint and discourage such defendant-hunting is the expense of litigation. Where a would-be plaintiff is seeking legal aid he has to satisfy the Legal Aid Board that he has reasonable grounds for taking the proceedings under S. 15 (2) of the Legal Aid Act, 1988; but if litigation were free of cost, the prospect of getting damages out of someone else might become almost as attractive as the National Lottery.

The Report says that any (presumably would-be) litigant who can not afford to litigate is denied justice (p. 9 para. 13) and, whilst encouraging settlement and other forms of dispute resolution (see eg p. 49 para. 6, p. 149 para. 1 & cap. 18), appears to look with equanimity if not with enthusiasm on the prospect of increased litigation if its proposals are put into effect (p. 41 para. 2, p. 47 para. 24, p. 199 para. 1). It is right that on p. 203 para. 20 the Report does say 'a decision to conduct litigation . . . should not be totally free of financial risk. Because of the burdens which it imposes on society and on the court system and especially on the other parties to the litigation it should not be thought too easy an option'. This is a nod in the right direction, but it does not go far enough: it ignores the avarice which litigation thrives on and encourages and the bitterness and distress it usually causes in the end to one side or other or both. It is important to remember that litigation, claiming money from other people which they do not want to pay you or an order requiring them to do what they do not want to do, is a hostile activity, and a litigant is entitled to expect his lawyer to act as his champion and fight his corner. Litigation is not two disputing parties agreeing to take their problem to a court to decide it for them. To hope that it should be conducted in a non-combative environment (p. 8

para. 12, p. 30 para. 17(c), p. 151 paras. 7, 9, 10) like an application for judicial review (p. 152 para. 11) is over-optimistic. It is also important to remember that with few exceptions every case which fails is a case which should not have been brought and every case which succeeds should not have been contested.

*The expense of litigation*

The Report says that litigation is too expensive (p. 4 para. 1, p. 9 para. 13), presumably to manifest the appropriate political will described by Sir Jack Jacob. What is 'too expensive'?

The only basis for saying that something is too expensive is to show either

(A) that it is not being bought, or
(B) that someone who needs it and ought to have it can not afford it, and is therefore suffering unacceptably.

There is no evidence to either effect in the Report beyond the anecdotal evidence on p. 9 paras. 13 and 17 that a number of businesses told Lord Woolf it was often cheaper to pay up than defend an action, irrespective of the merits, and that many lawyers at his seminars told him they would not be able to afford their own services if they were caught up in legal proceedings. Particularly bearing in mind that such anecdotal evidence has been available at least since I began at the bar, and I daresay many decades before, this is not enough to justify the fundamental changes in our system which the Report proposes. Moreover it is right that it should sometimes be cheaper to pay up irrespective of the merits than to defend an action: any sensible person faced with a minor but awkward claim proceeds on that basis: the burdens on litigants referred to on p. 9 para. 14 of the Report will still exist if the Report's proposals are adopted.

The Report also refers to the possibility of foreigners ceasing to choose to litigate here because of the cost (p. 12 para. 28), but no figures are relied on as showing the number of cases over the years in which foreigners have chosen to sue each other here or that they are declining significantly.

It follows that I do not agree with the proposition expressed on p. 114 para. 50 of the Report as a general rule that 'a litigant should not have to make the undesirable choice between not being able to litigate at all and facing the risk of litigation at an uneconomic cost'. The consequence of that approach is inter alia the recommendation in the Report that a party's means should be taken into account by a procedural judge in deciding what court procedures are appropriate (p. 144 para. 34)—in other words that a plaintiff who claims to be impecunious and whose case the defendant believes is false can be put on a procedural 'track' by the court where the chance of its falsity being exposed by discovery and cross-examination is much reduced. That is not doing justice. It would moreover be liable also to involve considerable delay while the Court investigates the plaintiff's means: a defendant will sometimes reasonably wish to challenge that the plaintiff is as poor as he is claiming.

On p. 9 para. 15, pp. 27–28 para. 8, p. 116 para. 60 and p. 199 para. 2 of the Report, the argument is put forward that it is undesirable that even those who can afford them should have to pay high costs because this will lead to higher charges to their customers or reduced dividends for their shareholders, thereby damaging the economy in general. That is not a very good argument. If it were valid it would be an argument for keeping damages down too. The position is that from the point of view of the economy in general, of which lawyers are a part, costs received by lawyers go to increase the amount they can spend on employees and premises and other goods and services, and even shares in companies, and so are likely to benefit the economy generally to the like amount.

The real basis for the claim in the Report that litigation is too expensive is, I believe, that legal aid has become more expensive than the government is willing to bear, that as a result the government is reducing the eligibility limits for legal aid (p. 9 para. 16, p. 16 para. 45, p. 199 para. 1), and that as a result it is feared that some people who can now with state aid afford to litigate will in future decide they can not do so, so that the amount of litigation will decline. The Report's aim of making litigation quicker and cheaper may well be welcome to the profession if lawyers think the increase in the number of their cases will make up for the decline in their fees per case: this is indeed the bait held out in the Report (p. 47 para. 24).

Whether however the price to be paid in the reduced likelihood of the result being just may not be too high must be decided by Parliament and not by the profession.

I turn now to look at (A) and (B) above in more detail.

*(A) What is the evidence that litigation has become too expensive for people to embark upon it?*

In 1971 the population of England and Wales was 49,152 m and the number of proceedings begun in the Queens Bench Division of the High Court and in the County Court was 1,713,151.

In 1981 the population had risen to 49,634 m (a rise of 0.1%) and the number of such proceedings begun had risen to 2,274,887 (a rise of 32%).

In 1991 the population had risen to 51,099 m (a rise of 3%) and the number of such proceedings begun had risen to 4,057,100 (a rise of 78%).

These figures do not suggest that litigation is too expensive: if anything, they suggest that it may not be expensive enough. In 1991 the figure for claims per 100,000 of the population, 7,940, appears to be in line with if not greater than that in the USA.[2]

On p. 255 of his article on Litigation-Mania in England, Germany and the USA in the Cambridge Law Journal, 1990, Professor Markesinis describes the 1987/8 figure of civil actions in England as 'extraordinarily high given the absence of a contingency fee system and the unavailability of legal aid for victims with middle range earnings and above', and on p. 252 gives as the first reason for the then lower rate in England than in the USA the relative cheapness of access to the courts there.

It is right that between 1992 and 1994 there has been a fall in the number of such proceedings begun here to 2,815,869 (31% over three years) but the 1994 figure is still only lightly less than in 1989, the highest year before 1991, and equivalent to a rate of 5,474 claims per 100,000 of the population; and there is nothing in the Report to suggest that its view is based on this recent minor decline.[3]

It is also right that there has been between 1981 and 1993, despite a substantial increase in the number of writs issued in the Queens Bench Division, a steady decline in the number of cases set down for trial there each year (from 12,874 in 1981[4] to 10,862 in 1991[5] and 5,623 in 1993[6]) (p. 34 para. 3). This can only be due to more such cases settling or being otherwise determined without a trial, which is exactly what the Report desires (p. 14 para. 37, p. 19 para. 7(b), p. 22 para. 12, p. 29 para. 16, p. 30 para. 17(a), p. 32 para. 23, p. 116 para. 61, p. 194 para. 1).

It is not clear what proportion of these proceedings were financed by legal aid. According to graph 'Civil 1' on p. 41 and Table Civil 7 on p. 47 in the Legal Aid Board's Report for 1990–1 (HMSO), some 60,000 legal aid civil certificates were issued in 1981 for High Court, County Court and unspecified court proceedings (other than matrimonial) and some 160,000 in 1991. Assuming (which was not the case at any rate in 1991) that all the unspecified court proceedings were in the High Court or County Court, that none of the High Court proceedings were in the Chancery Division, and that none of the certificates were for defendants, it would appear that at most only some 3% of the proceedings started in the Queens Bench Division and the County Court in 1981 and 4% in 1991 were brought by legally aided plaintiffs. If that is so, it would seem that the overwhelming

[2] 14,800,000 civil actions for a population of 239,283,000, ie 6,185 actions per 100,000—figures taken from pp. 240 & 244 in Professor Markesinis' article on Litigation-Mania in England, Germany and the USA, Cambridge Law Journal, July 1990.

[3] The population figures come from Table 1.2 in Social Trends, 1995, (HMSO) and the figures for proceedings begun from the Civil Judicial Statistics for England and Wales (HMSO) ['J.S.'] (1971) Tables F and 21, (1982) Tables 3.1 and 7.1, and (1989)–(1994) Tables 3.1 and 4.1. Although many of the proceedings will have been brought by and against corporations, the population figures are still relevant.

[4] J.S. Table C.6(d).

[5] J.S. Table 3.5.

[6] J.S. Table 3.5.

majority of these proceedings are brought by people not at the state's but at their own expense. Though some of these will be corporations (p. 106 paras. 15, 16), some will be individuals who manage (contrary to the Report p. 16 para. 45) without legal aid.

However, those with legal aid do seem less willing to settle early: the proportion of legally aided parties to actions set down for trial in the Queens Bench Division was 25% in 1991 and 37% in 1993.[7]

*(B) Are there people who are suffering unacceptably because they can not afford to litigate?*

Steps should be taken, perhaps by means of an appropriate inquiry of a random sample of solicitors—there may be better ways—to seek to ascertain the extent to which it is the case that members of the public have or claim they have suffered material civil wrongs which have caused them material damage for which they have wanted to sue but could not afford to do so although advised they had reasonable prospects of success, and are as a result suffering unacceptably; and to assess the likely validity of a random sample of those claims and the possible compensation the claimants could expect.

(2) The Report's principle (b) '. . . litigants should have an equal opportunity regardless of their resources to assert or defend their legal rights'

This objective is impracticable of achievement. It could be achieved only by extending legal aid to all individuals and corporations whose own resources were not adequate for whatever litigation they might be involved in, by requiring lawyers to provide their services so cheaply that people with the necessary skills would not wish to be lawyers or to practise as such in this country, or by making all litigation so simple that anyone could undertake it on his own. None of these does the Report suggest. Even however the extension of legal aid would not meet the objective unless the state also paid the costs of defendants who defeated claims by legally aided plaintiffs, a proposal which the Report says should be considered (p. 202 para. 12(b), p. 205 paras. 26, 27).

(3) The Report's principle (c) 'cost should be proportionate to the nature of the issues involved'

Although this principle refers to cost being proportionate to the nature of the issues involved, the Report itself is particularly concerned with cases

[7] J.S. Tables 3.6.

where the costs exceed the value of a minor claim (p. 9 para. 18, p. 10 paras. 19, 20, p. 20 para. 7(c), p. 35 paras. 7, 9, p. 38 para. 23 (b), p. 41 para. 2). It appears to assume that in each of these cases the legal system and the lawyers are to blame (pp. 7–8 paras. 4–7, p. 8 paras. 7, 12, p. 11 para. 22(c), p. 13 para. 36, p. 18 para. 1, p. 27 paras. 5, 6, p. 29 para. 15). There is no more justification for that view than in thinking that when a garage advises that the cost of repairing a car will exceed its value there is something awry either with the garage's advice or with its charges. There is no reason why a case where the value of the claim is small should be simpler in fact or law than one where it is large. The position is that where the costs exceed the value of the claim a sensible person does not go to law, just as a sensible owner of such a car does not get it repaired. If one may be allowed anecdotal evidence oneself, one of the pieces of advice that I—and no doubt others—have given frequently in such cases as a barrister has been that in view of the difficulty or complexity of the matter the costs were likely to exceed the value of the claim so it would be unwise to sue or, as the case might be, to contest the claim; generally clients have accepted this advice, but sometimes they said that it was a matter of principle or that the other side must be taught a lesson, whatever the cost, and they went ahead; and if they did, the fact that the costs exceeded the amount of the claim was, in my view, no reflection on the legal system or the lawyers.

Annex III of the Report contains some Tables designed to illustrate the relationship between costs and the value of the claim which it relies on to support its argument that there are cases where the costs equal or exceed the value of the claim, that this is so particularly where the claim is minor, ie under £12,500 (p. 255 para. 15, Table 3.4), and that these cases (in fact cases where the claim is under £10,000) should go on the 'fast track'.

In its consideration of these cases, it is not however clear whether and, if so, to what extent the Report takes account of the fact that the reason for the costs being disproportionately high may be the complexity, in fact or law or both, of the case itself. It does in Table 3.6 and on pp. 257–8, paras. 18–19, take account of what the taxing masters call a case's 'weight', but it is not made clear what relationship that bears to the complexity of the issues. However, since on p. 41 para. 4 and p. 42 para. 5 the Report says that cases which involve complex issues of fact or law would not normally be suitable for the 'fast track', the inference is that 'weight' is distinct from complexity (see my comments in (iii) below on Table 3.6).

*The Tables*

(i) The Tables relate to only one year (1994–5) and do not therefore show whether the position in these cases is any different now from what it has been for years. It would be interesting also to see comparisons between increases over the same period in the cost of litigation and increases in eg auditors' and merchant bankers' fees and in the cost eg of medicine, education, and housing, private and public.

(ii) It is not wholly clear what the figures represent. They are said to be the costs allowed on taxation in 673 out of 2,000 cases submitted to the Supreme Court Taxing Office in 1994–5 (p. 251 paras. 4, 6), but the Tables do not state whether they were submitted pursuant to orders for legal aid taxation, or pursuant to orders that the loser should pay the winner's taxed costs, or because a client had required his own solicitor's costs to be taxed. It appears, however (p. 252 para. 2), that they include both legal aid and non legal aid cases, and it is possible therefore that in cases where both sides were legally aided both sides' costs were taxed. In view however of what is stated on p. 255 para. 15 I assume that in no case are both sides' costs included. Nor do the Tables show what proportion of the costs taxed are plaintiff's costs and what defendant's, and what borne by individuals and what by corporations. This would all be helpful information to have and which the Supreme Court Taxing Office should be able to provide. Further, except where there was a legal aid taxation one would imagine that these costs were taxed because the parties would not agree them, and that they would not agree them because they were disproportionately high; so it would be desirable to try to obtain some information about the relationship between the value of the claim and the costs in cases where the value of the claim was under £12,500 and the costs were agreed.

(iii) The Tables do not show why the costs exceeded the value of the claim or in particular whether there was some special difficulty or complexity about the claim and if so what it was; except that Table 3.6 showed that in each of the 28 'worst' cases the weight was in one of the three lightest of the five categories of weight. This, if weight does relate to the difficulty or complexity of the case, makes one wonder why the costs were allowed at such high figures, but, if it does not, suggests that it may well have been the difficulty or complexity of the case which led to the high cost.

(iv) In 226 of the cases (about one-third of the sample) no value was given—presumably because they were claims for damages—but it would have been helpful to know, where judgment was given for the plaintiff, how the amount thereof related to the costs allowed.

(v) Although the Tables refer (p. 251 para. 6) to a particular category called 'Breach of Copyright, Injunction/Declaration cases', it is not stated whether that category includes all cases where an injunction or declaration was claimed or only those where such relief was related to a claim for breach of copyright. If the latter, the Tables do not state in which of the other categories the claim was also for some such relief as an injunction or declaration, which might have been more important than the money value of the claim.

(vi) The Tables cover cases which settled before trial (p. 252 paras. 9–10) as well as cases which went to judgment, and it would be helpful to have Tables relating separately to each situation. One would hope and expect that where the case settled before trial the ratio of costs to the value of the claim was considerably lower.

Since in the ordinary way costs are not ordered against legally aided parties, it is probable that many of the figures in the Tables relate to costs which a non legally aided loser had been ordered to pay the winner, whether the latter was legally aided or not. It seems clear therefore from these Tables that a large number of people are willing even at their own expense to litigate minor claims where the costs exceed their value, which shows considerable enthusiasm for litigation. There is no evidence how the number compares with those who refused to litigate such claims for the same reason.

In these circumstances, without a good deal more data, it does not seem to me that a case is established for providing a special abbreviated form of procedure (the 'fast track') which all those pursuing minor claims would be obliged to follow (p. 42 para. 8); and before such a proposal was adopted a survey should be carried out of the successful parties in the cases which are the subject of these Tables to find out whether they would have preferred to have followed a procedure such as the 'fast track' which would have cost less but where the chance of their establishing their case would have been reduced. One can not presume that they would answer 'yes'.

Moreover, if the proposed new procedure is adopted and is effective it is likely, bearing in mind many people's apparent willingness already to spend disproportionate amounts on fighting minor claims, to encourage more people to bring and fight minor claims which they have hitherto not thought worth pursuing (pp. 203–4 paras. 19, 20). As a social desideratum this seems to me fairly low in the scale.

## III. THE 'FAST TRACK'

I turn now to the remedy ('the fast track') which the Report proposes for the defect it claims to have found in the legal system, but as to which (as will have appeared in (II (3) ) above) I am doubtful. It is that where a claim is under £10,000 there should be compulsory limits on the discovery which can be ordered (p. 43 para. 10(b), p. 169 para. 27, p. 171 para. 34, p. 172 para. 36), the evidence which can be given (p. 43 para. 10(d)–(e) ), the time the trial can take (p. 43 para. 10(c) ), and the amount the lawyer can charge (p. 45 para. 17, p. 117 para. 64), all in order to keep the costs proportionate to the value of the claim. Ex hypothesi, except on the assumption that at present lawyers in such cases are disclosing unnecessary documents, calling unnecessary evidence, challenging such evidence unnecessarily, arguing unnecessary points or arguing at unnecessary length, this means that such cases will not be tried as thoroughly as now, that relevant oral or documentary evidence will not be given, and relevant points not made.

In places the Report appears to be saying that lawyers in these cases are doing an unnecessary amount of work (see references in II (3) above), but, if that were so, then when their bills were taxed they would be taxed down accordingly. The Report does not say that this is so, and the costs in the Tables are the costs allowed on taxation.

*Getting at the truth*

The principal objective of the English civil justice system up to now has always been justice, to get at the truth as to what happened, who said and did what and why. Until now all proposals to reform the system have been designed to further this objective, by for example reducing the importance of technicalities and avoiding surprise. This Report is I think the first to recommend proposals calculated to make the achievement of this objective less likely.

The Report recognises the conflict between achieving this objective and the expenditure of time and money (p. 19 paras. 5–6) but in recommending that the achievement of this objective should no longer be put first, it does not in my view give sufficient weight to the fact that there are many parties and witnesses who give false evidence to serve their own interests, or because they are prejudiced, or because they are forgetful of matters inconsistent with their own interests, that it is intolerable and likely to be so regarded by the other party and possibly also by the public if such people can not be properly challenged and can therefore get away with their false evidence, and that it is only by the expenditure of time and money on the two instruments of discovery of documents and cross-examination, fashioned for that purpose, that they can be properly challenged.

It follows therefore that if these minor claims are to be determined in the manner suggested by the Report the chance of the truth being arrived at, of the result being one that accords with justice, must be materially reduced. It is of course reasonable that if the parties in such a case consent to such an abbreviated procedure they should be free to do so—just as they are free if they wish to decide liability by spinning a coin and taking any damages from certain digits in the National Lottery, a system as quick, cheap and fair as anyone could wish, but not just. They should not however be compelled to do so if either or both of them wish otherwise. The only rider to that that might possibly be acceptable is one that provided that legal aid should not be granted to a party to such a case unless he was willing to give his consent to such procedure. That might indeed be said to be merely an aspect of the question whether he had reasonable grounds for taking or defending the proceedings, within the meaning of S. 15 (2) of the Legal Aid Act 1988.

Further, the limits on costs and time (para p. 43 para. 10) are likely to give rise to problems in practice. The loser may well be in a position to complain that not all his points or all his evidence had been put before the Court, and that if they had been he would have won; his solicitor will presumably reply that he did his best in the limited time available and for the limited costs payable and deny causation. The client may then sue the solicitor for negligence, and another court will then have the task of deciding the difficult questions whether the solicitor did what a reasonably careful solicitor would have done in and for the time available and the costs payable and what difference the extra evidence or points might have made.

## IV. CRITICISM OF THE PRESENT SYSTEM

The Report says the process is too slow and too complex (p. 4 para. 1). These are not new criticisms; they are criticisms which are likely to be made of any legal system which goes beyond palm tree justice and tries to ascertain the truth of the facts in dispute and the correct application of the relevant law. Before we accept these criticisms of our system comparisons must be made not just with the costs of the very different system in Germany but with the effectiveness in achieving justice, the delays and the costs in several other countries, including in particular common law countries adopting the adversary system. No such comparisons are relied on in the Report, although research has been done on them by Professor Cranston (p. 33 para. 25, p. 248 para. 1), and on p. 11 paras. 25 and 26 and p. 12 para. 27 such a comparison as to costs is referred to.

As for complexity, the facts and the law in issue are in most cases far more complex than they were even a decade or two ago. One has only to consider the number and length of the statutes passed each year, the increased number of cases reported each year, the increase in the length of such reports, IT, the increase in the complexity of eg modern factories, medicine, and commercial transactions, to see why any lawsuit involving them is likely to be complex. It is remarkable that none of these matters is referred to as a cause of complexity in the list of causes given in the Report on pp. 15–16 para. 44, p. 18 para. 1(c).

## V. JUDICIAL MANAGEMENT

Apart from its proposal for a fast track procedure for claims under £10,000, the Report's principal proposal is for more judicial management of cases (p. 18 para. 2, p. 21 para. 8, p. 22 paras. 11, 12, cap. 5, cap. 6, cap. 8). This is based on its view, for which no hard evidence is cited, that as things are the lawyers on each side, for their own purposes, make cases last too long and cost too much (p. 7 paras. 5, 6). Although it is of course possible that this is the position and probable that it is sometimes so, I would have thought more reliable evidence should be required that it is a general problem before the probably irreversible changes to fundamental parts of our system which the Report proposes are made on that account (p. 18 paras. 2, 3, 4, p. 26 paras. 2, 3, p. 33 para. 24).

Information as to the extent to which lawyers' bills have been over past years and are being taxed down to exclude unreasonable expenditure might be helpful on this question.

*Problems*

Certain problems about judicial management within an adversarial system are in my view not adequately addressed in the Report, as follows :

(1) The judge should not decide what witnesses are to be called (p. 178 para. 15), and presumably by whom, bearing in mind that a particular potential witness may be of bad character or unfriendly to a particular party.

(2) The proposal that cross-examination should only be permitted if the judge gives leave (p. 179 para. 18) is unacceptable. In the first place, a party's witnesses should be given the opportunity to comment on the other side's version, and in the second place the Judge can not know and it may be undesirable for a party to tell him, and therefore also tell the other side and the witness in question, why he desires to cross-examine a particular witness to demonstrate the latter's unreliability, poor memory, prejudice, or dishonesty.

(3) The Report, in this case following the recommendation of the Civil Justice Review (para. 452; R. 61), is in favour of the Court having power of its own motion to order a split trial (p. 50 para. 11). I do not think it should where no party is in favour of this, as the parties are likely to be more alert to the disadvantages than the judge. There are cases where it is sensible to try issues separately but where that is so one or other or both parties generally want it. There are however many cases where the same witnesses have to give evidence on more than one issue and in those cases it is rarely sensible to try the issues separately:

(i) it will be annoying and expensive for the witness to have to come to court more than once

(ii) if the judge decides each issue as he goes along he will often have to express a view as to the credibility of the witness on that issue; if so there is a major problem if he changes his mind when dealing with a later issue; further, the opposite party must be able to cross-examine a witness on an early issue as to matters arising on later issues affecting his credibility, but, if it does, there is likely to be duplication and confusion. This problem is after all the reason why over the years the courts have generally been unwilling in this situation to try liability and damage separately.

Further, split trials can lead to the final decision coming later than otherwise because of the gaps between each section of the trial and the need for the parties to gear themselves up for each section in turn.

(4) If the judge makes an order that neither party has asked for (as eg on p. 42 para. 8) and either or both appeal successfully, who pays the costs? Unless it is the Lord Chancellor's Department, there is likely, rightly, to be great dissatisfaction. There is justice in making party A, who has persuaded the judge to make order X, to pay the costs if the Court of Appeal on party B's appeal take the view that order X was wrong; there is no justice in making either party pay the costs if the Judge has made order X against the arguments of both parties.

(5) If the judge imposes a time limit which a party's solicitor does not comply with it may not always be appropriate to strike out that party's claim or defence or order it to pay the other side's costs immediately as the Report proposes (eg p. 8 para. 7, p. 151 para. 9, p. 157 para. 13); in either case that party will generally have a claim against its solicitor for negligence; in the former case this will increase the amount of litigation, it will increase the staleness of actions being tried, and it is likely to increase the burden on the Legal Aid Fund; in the latter case it is likely to hold up the action whilst the costs are taxed, to give rise to problems of privilege during such taxation, and to lead to delay when the party seeks to change its solicitor.

It is for reasons such as these that the Courts rarely now use their powers to make such orders.

(6) The proposal (p. 52 para. 24) that 'unless there are circumstances which make this undesirable' an appeal to a judge should be dealt with by a member of the 'team' seems once more to put economy and speed before justice: a judge is going to be particularly unwilling to reverse a member of his own team with whom he knows he will be continuing to have to work on the case, and so may not be impartial.

(7) The proposal (p. 20 para. 7 (j)—(k)) that the parties should be held to the length of trial ordered is likely to give rise to problems in practice: what is to happen for example if the defendant has not concluded his case when time expires and contends that the reason is the time taken by the plaintiff or possibly the Judge?

(9) The proposal (p. 154 para. 5) that a party will not be allowed to amend to add a new point will lead to great problems since no court will be willing to see a case wrongly determined just because one side has discovered a crucial point late.

## VI. DISCOVERY

It is vital in my view if justice is to be done that each party should continue to be obliged to disclose all relevant documents including those adverse to his case: it is not in my view acceptable to substitute for this a rule that a party should be obliged to disclose only documents adverse to his case of which he is aware when the obligation to disclose arises (p. 69 para. 27, p. 171 para. 34, p. 172 para. 36). That would be unworkable with a corporation, would put a premium on forgetfulness, and would almost always be impracticable to challenge. It appears (p. 171 para. 33) that it is not proposed that the party and his solicitor will be under an obligation as now eg to look through his files, correspondence and diaries to see if there is anything there adverse to his case.

There is a problem now because in many cases there are a very large number of relevant documents. This is a feature of modern life and business and it is expensive and time-consuming to go through them all to decide which may be required at trial, and natural that a party will disclose all his relevant documents and leave it to the other side to look through them and find anything adverse to his case if they can. This is likely however to become much less expensive and time consuming in future, when it will be possible to 'scan' all documents onto disk and then to search quickly through the disks (pp. 85–6 paras. 13, 14).

## VII. CLASS ACTIONS

The Report does not deal with class actions. These are of great importance from the point of view of access to justice, though they give rise to formidable procedural problems. I hope that in his final Report Lord Woolf will deal comprehensively with them, with a view to extending their use.

## SUMMARY

There are many proposals in Lord Woolf's Report with which I agree. This paper has dealt with some of these with which I am not happy: as to those, I summarise my position as follows:

(1) Without the authority of Parliament no proposals to reform the legal system to save time or money should be introduced which depart from the rule that justice should be administered in open court; on the contrary, all such proposals should be designed to increase the effectiveness of that rule.

(2) No proposals as fundamental as those proposed in the Report, shift-

ing responsibility for the management of civil litigation from litigants and their advisers to the Court, and making the ascertainment of the truth and achieving justice no longer the overriding objective of the system, should be introduced

(a) without the authority of Parliament;
(b) without ensuring they do not encourage unreasonable litigation; and
(c) without taking full account of the various problems and disadvantages to which they give rise, some of which are referred to above.

# 9

# *The Adversarial Principle: Fairness and Efficiency: Reflections on the Recommendations of the Woolf Report*

NEIL ANDREWS*

## INTRODUCTION

### *(a) The Momentum for Change*

As Lord Woolf records[1,2], there have been sixty reports since 1851 dealing with small or large aspects of reform in the fields of English procedure, both civil and criminal. Against this background, when receiving a new report, it seems legitimate to pose two questions: are the proposals contained in the report truly significant; secondly, is the report likely to be implemented? It seems reasonable to say 'yes' to both these questions, although the second 'yes' is uttered not without regret, as will become clear.

Lord Woolf wishes to give large effect to an idea which the Civil Justice Review approved: that in pre-trial matters the court should take charge to ensure that the litigation is conducted with reasonable speed.[3] The parties, especially the plaintiff, cannot always be trusted to move the case forwards speedily enough, and both parties might take unreasonable advantage of the panoply of procedural institutions which add to the cost, delay and complexity of actions.

It is not surprising that Lord Woolf should be so strongly attracted to the interventionist model. The technology now exists to enable the courts to monitor the progress of litigation. In the county courts *automatic* striking out of slow litigation is already a harsh feature of the plaintiff

* M.A., B.C.L., Barrister, University Lecturer, University of Cambridge.

1 Lord Woolf, *Access to Justice* (Interim Report, June 1995) ch. 2, para.2 (hereafter '*Woolf*').

2 For a good list, J.A. Jolowicz, ' "General Ideas": the Reform of Civil Procedure', (1983) 3 L.S. 295, 296 n. 11.

3 Civil Justice Review (1988) Cm. 394, paras. 223-228; the technique has been applied in the U.S., but also vigorously criticised: Judith Resnik, 'Managerial Judges' (1982) 96 Harv. L.R. 376, 378, 427–430. See also Linda Silberman, 'Judicial Adjuncts revisited: Masters and Magistrates in the Federal Courts of the United States' in *International Perspectives on Civil Justice: Essays in Honour of Sir Jack Jacob*, ed. I.R. Scott, (London, 1990), 129, 164–165.

litigator's life.[4] The Lord Chief Justice and Vice Chancellor's *Practice Direction* of 1995 requires greater intervention by the court both during the earlier stages of litigation and at trial.[5] Perhaps Lord Griffiths' comment in *Ketteman* v. *Hansel Properties*[6] sums up the spirit of modern times: 'we can no longer afford to show the same indulgence towards the negligent conduct of litigation as was perhaps possible in a more leisured age.'

*(b) The Woolf Agenda*

Lord Woolf's main aims are: (a) to speed up civil justice, (b) to render civil procedure more accessible to ordinary people and to small businesses, (c) to eliminate the arcane language of civil procedure, (d) to promote swift settlement, (e) to simplify litigation and render it less costly by avoiding excessive (and disproportionate) resort to procedural devices, such as over-detailed pleadings, unreasonably expensive documentary discovery, the proliferation of unjustifiable interrogatories, over-lengthy witness statements, extravagant use of experts by private litigants, and unnecessary orality at trial. It should be added that the promotion of speedier settlement—see (d)—is another, indeed vital, source of procedural economy.

I believe Lord Woolf's commitment to (b) (access) and (c) (simplification of language) is important and beneficial. It is not possible to embrace so easily the other main aspects of his programme. (a) (acceleration) is a tough nut to crack and potentially an expensive one. Pushing cases through the various interlocutory stages and on to trial requires the court to be efficient, energetic and (in medium or large-scale cases) well-informed. It will demand a collective Herculean effort. Whether it can be achieved cheaply, fairly and constantly is the central question raised by the proposed new system. As for (e), (simplification of procedure in general), this reminds me of the question: are you in favour of tax cuts? No reasonable person would say 'no', but no reasonable person would unqualifiedly say 'yes' if he devoted five minutes thought to the consequences of drastic tax reductions. It is one thing to simplify aspects of procedure which are manifestly baroque and excessive, but it is another thing to scythe away at procedures which, properly applied, perform a valuable job. And so to this aspect of Lord Woolf's scheme the author feels compelled to give a nuanced response (see especially section 4(i) and (iii) below).

In section 2 I propose to set out the traditional pattern of English litigation (both pre-trial and at trial) which is conducted in accordance with the

[4] C.C.R. Ord. 17, r. 11 (3) (d), (9): *Rastin* v. *British Steel plc* [1994] 1 W.L.R. 732, C.A.; *Gardner* v. *Southwark L.B.C.* unreported, April 19, 1994, C.A.

[5] [1995] 1 W.L.R. 509; [1995] 1 W.L.R. 332 (Family Division); see also 'The Chancery Guide', 1995.

[6] [1987] A.C. 189, 220 G (comment made concerning proposed late amendment to add limitation defence towards end of trial: Neil Andrews, *Principles of Civil Procedure* (London, 1994) paras. 3-008 and 5-042).

adversarial principle. Section 3 is concerned with the impact of Lord Woolf's recommendations on the traditional institutions and values described in section 2. Section 4 is a discussion of both possible objections to Lord Woolf's recommendations and of their wider implications. The essay concludes with an alternative set of recommendations.

## 2. The Traditional Adversarial Principle[7]

Under an adversarial principle, it is the parties who dictate at all stages the form, content and pace of proceedings. In England the parties (in practice their lawyers) control the following matters:

(a) the initiation of the action;
(b) the framing of an action, especially the drawing up of pleadings;
(c) the decision whether to add additional parties to the action;[8]
(d) selection of material facts;
(e) the legal framework within which the cause of action is to be considered (for example, the framing of a cause of action in contract or tort, or both) as well as the selection of remedies[9];
(f) pre-trial progress of the litigation;
(g) the decision to apply for interim or summary (and final) relief;
(h) settlement or withdrawal of the action;
(i) the reception of evidence at trial (or in other hearings);
(j) submissions of law at trial;
(k) the decision to seek enforcement of a judgment;
(l) the decision to bring an appeal (sometimes subject to the court's permission).

Even before the Woolf report, it is notable that the courts have begun to intervene to ensure that the trial (at least in complex cases) is properly marshalled.[10] In complex commercial litigation, case management has already become a feature, especially in the Commercial Court. Although the striking out of an action for want of prosecution in accordance with the *Birkett*

[7] Para. 3-021 Andrews, *op.cit.*; M.R. Damaska, *The Faces of Justice and State Authority: A Comparative Approach to the Legal Process* (Yale U.P., 1986), pp. 104 *et seq.*; Cyril Glasser, 'Civil Procedure and the Lawyers—the Adversary Principle and the Decline of the Orality Principle' (1993) 56 M.L.R. 307; R. Eggleston, 'What's Wrong with the Adversary System?', (1975) 49 Aust. L.J. 428, 429, identifies these four strands: (i) pre-trial party control; (ii) limited or nil judicial involvement before continuous, oral trial; (iii) evidence elicited by parties by questions, judge merely clarifying occasionally; (iv) 'rules' of procedure policed only by opponent.

[8] For an exceptional case, *T.S.B. Private Bank S.A.* v. *Chabra* [1992] 1 W.L.R. 231, Mummery J., on which Andrews, *op.cit.*, para. 4-002; see also Damaska, *op.cit.* p. 117.

[9] Damaska, *op.cit.* pp. 117–118, esp. on U.S. conflicting material.

[10] *Ashmore* v. *Corporation of Lloyd's* [1992] 1 W.L.R. 446, H.L., on which Andrews, *op. cit.*, para. 3-014.

v. *James* principles[11] has become a broken reed, in county courts a more vigorous form of control is the new rule requiring the automatic striking out of protracted litigation.[12] The 1995 *Practice Direction*[13] states that the court will control or restrict discovery, oral submissions at trial, examination and cross-examination of witnesses, the issues to be considered at trial, reading aloud from documents or authorities. All of this judicial intervention is justified by 'the paramount importance of reducing the cost and delay of civil litigation.' The 1995 *Practice Direction* also provides that cases in which trial will last more than 10 days will be subject to pre-trial review by the court.

The adversarial system works reasonably well if the plaintiff is keen to pursue the action with utmost speed, does not allow the litigation to become bogged down in interlocutory skirmishes which are unreasonable or which merely offer distraction from the main issues, and if the defendant chooses not to sabotage the case's progress by unco-operative behaviour or by making applications which retard the case.

The same system also rests on a number of presuppositions[14]:

(i) that the parties are both legally represented;
(ii) that their lawyers are roughly of the same calibre[15];
(iii) that each of the party's lawyers will be predominantly concerned to advance his client's interest, so that the overall attainment of justice will be a by-product of the collision of adversaries[16];
(iv) that the court itself seldom needs to intervene to safeguard the public interest. In a sense the stereotype of English civil justice is a *private* dispute conducted before an official.[17]

It is clear that the Woolf report is a watershed in the history of this principle. If implemented in full, the report threatens to banish many aspects of the principle to the history books.[18] Lord Woolf does pay some scant respect to the traditional adversarial model of English civil justice, but his compliment (in the context of a 270 page report) is so fleeting that it is unclear what he thinks is admirable and worthy of preservation.[19]

[11] [1978] A.C. 297, Andrews, *op. cit.*, paras. 10-030 to 10-043.
[12] See n. 4 above. [13] [1995] 1 W.L.R. 508.
[14] Andrews, *op. cit.*, para. 3-002.
[15] See *Woolf* at p. 3 on the need for both parties to enjoy an 'equal opportunity, regardless of their resources, to assert or defend their legal right'. See also Damaska, *op.cit.* pp. 103–104; John H. Langbein, 'The German Advantage in Civil Procedure' (1985) 52 U.Chi.L.R. 823, 843.
[16] See J.A. Jolowicz, (1988) 8 L.S. 1, 4–5, quoting Lord Wilberforce in *Air Canada* v. *Secretary of State for Trade* [1983] 2 A.C. 394, 438.
[17] *The Fabric of English Civil Justice* (London, 1987) p. 8.
[18] For the extent of this, see text at p. 175 below.
[19] *Woolf*, pp. 18–19 and 29, para. 15.

## 3. The Woolf Recommendations and their Impact upon the Adversarial Principle

### *(a) Lord Woolf's Guiding Principles and Goals*

His first recommendation, a clarion blast, is central to his overall strategy

> There should be a fundamental transfer in the responsibility for the management of civil litigation from litigants and their legal advisers to the courts.[20]

It is clear that Lord Woolf does not aim merely to tinker[21] with the English process of civil justice. Rather he wishes to shake up the present system so that it can deliver justice more cheaply and quickly. At the same time Lord Woolf acknowledges the constraints of procedural fairness, which he lists as follows[22]:

(i) '[the system] should be just[23] in the results it delivers';
(ii) 'it should be fair and seen to be so by (a) ensuring that litigants have an equal opportunity, regardless of their resources, to assert or defend their legal rights; and (b) [by] providing every litigant with an adequate opportunity to state his own case and answer his opponent's; and (c) [by] treating like cases alike.'[24]

These central principles are then juxtaposed with other *desiderata*, or goals, which can be contrasted with the preceding principles because they are precepts of efficiency and sound-management:

(i) procedure and the cost of litigation should be 'proportionate to the nature of the issues involved';
(ii) actions should be conducted 'with reasonable speed';
(iii) procedure should be 'effective: adequately resourced and organised so as to give effect to the [preceding principles and goals].'

The major problems of the present system of civil procedure identified by Lord Woolf are substantially those already described in the Civil Justice Review[25]: the high cost of litigation[26], delay[27] and complexity[28]. He adds to these[29] the problem of the present adversarial 'culture', which he summarises in this way: 'the adversarial process [viz. the absence of judicial control] is likely to . . . degenerate into an environment in which the litigation process is too often seen as a battle field where no rules apply.'

[20] See also *ibid.*, ch.4, p.18, para. 2.
[21] Procedural tinkering was Roscoe Pound's *bête noire*: J.A. Jolowicz, (1988) 8 L.S. 1, 13.
[22] *Woolf*, ch. 1, para. 3.
[23] Although not necessarily accurate in its decisions: *ibid.*, p. 19, paras. 5–6.
[24] He adds three more principles: that procedure should be *comprehensible* to those who use it, *responsive* to their needs, and it should promote '*certainty*'.
[25] *Woolf*, p. 7, sentence 1; and cp. *Civil Justice Review* (1988) Cm. 394, para. 48.
[26] *Ibid.*, ch. 3, paras. 12–28.
[27] *Ibid.* paras. 29–43.
[28] *Ibid.* para. 4.
[29] *Ibid.* paras. 3–11.

Lord Woolf is also concerned about 'the forgotten classes'. It is well known that middle income individuals[30], who are ineligible for legal aid, and small or medium-sized businesses, are denied effective access to the court because of the high cost of English litigation. In a procedural sense, therefore, such individuals can be defamed with impunity. If, however, they suffer a small consumer misfortune, or they claim to have been unfairly dismissed from employment, they can proceed in person before a small claims court or an Industrial Tribunal. Lord Woolf admits[31] that, outside the small claims jurisdiction, parties will still have a practical need to be legally represented even after his reforms are implemented.

Lord Woolf also refers[32] to the wasteful present system which leads to 'every aspect of the case [being] fully investigated [by the parties]. This encourages excessive work and cost on issues which are often recognised from an early stage to be peripheral.'

He also complains that the administration of civil justice enjoys only a 'low priority' compared with criminal justice.[33] Finally, he is fearful that, unless the luxuriant system of English procedure is curbed by judicial control, foreign litigants might cease to use London as a forum and instead turn to, for example, New York, Germany, Holland and other places.[34]

## 4. Assessment

### *Questions of Fairness*

(i) *Accuracy of Decision-Making and Public Faith in the Civil Justice System*
According to one school of thought, trial is an extravagance to be discouraged. The full-blown apparatus of preparation for trial (elaborate pleadings, extensive discovery, interrogatories, expert reports and witness statements) has been criticised as excessive and disproportionate when applied to many disputes. However, according to another school of thought[35], it is sound that justice is so inaccessible: 'the most basic effect of inefficiency [viz., the expense and consequent inaccessibility of trial] is that it deters litigation.'

Lord Woolf takes a pragmatic middle way between these two schools. He is keen to encourage settlement and sees it as the primary means of disposing of cases. But at the same time he wants to make litigation more eco-

[30] *Woolf*, p. 7, sentence 1; and cp. *Civil Justice Review* (1988) Cm. 394, p.9, para 17; see also p. 39, para. 9.

[31] *Ibid.* ch. 15, para. 3.

[32] *Ibid.*, ch. 3, para. 22(c); see also Langbein, *op.cit.* n. 15 above, p. 831.

[33] *Woolf*, ch. 3, paras. 48–50.

[34] *Ibid.*, p. 12, para. 28; p. 28, para 9.

[35] E.g., Samuel Gross, 'The American Advantage: the Value of Inefficient Adjudication', (1987) 85 Mich. L.Rev. 734, 752.

nomical, efficient and, consequently, more accessible in minor or middling cases. To increase access to justice, he is prepared to introduce a less grand style of litigation, especially on the fast-track[36]:

> the achievement of the right result needs to be balanced against the expenditure of the time and money needed to achieve that result.

The question is by no means novel: should we be prepared to sacrifice some degree of forensic accuracy in order to render justice more accessible? Consider how Lord Brougham in 1830 argued that the introduction of poor men's courts (introduced in 1846) should be supported, even though the quality of justice might be inferior to that dispensed by the Royal courts: 'better something of justice than nothing—it may be slovenly justice, but . . . I should rather even slovenly justice than the absolute, peremptory and inflexible denial of all justice.'[37] Certainly one can agree that when a claim is for a few thousand pounds in respect of a luxury holiday, it makes no sense to expose both parties to the cost and delay of traditional litigation in the county courts or, certainly, the High Court.

But in the name of efficiency Lord Woolf wishes to ration discovery, interrogatories, use of expert witnesses, cross-examination, and even allow the court to control the definition of the issues for *all* litigation, even that in excess of £10,000. Each of these procedural tools is expensive to use, but each offers a litigant a greater chance of uncovering material which will defeat the other party. If access to these tools is denied or restricted, it follows that the chance of arriving at an accurate decision is reduced. Does this matter? The author thinks it does matter a great deal and that care must be taken not to dilute the quality of fact-finding, procedural fairness and the correct application of the law to the facts of a case. Lord Woolf might discover that the value attached to accuracy in adjudication is the very kernel of our system of civil justice. Parties do not mind the risk of inaccuracy if they freely enter a settlement arrangement so that the risk of error is consciously or impliedly assumed by each party.[38] Nor do they particularly mind the same danger if they have freely entered upon a cost-cutting exercise and are happy to abide by an arbitrator's decision or even a judge's provisional view based upon affidavit material. Speaking of litigants' use of interlocutory injunctions in the period before *American Cyanamid*, Peter Prescott said[39]:

> . . . the practical effect of the [doctrine that a plaintiff needed to show a *prima facie* case *on the merits*] was that interlocutory motions for an injunction became a cheap

[36] *Woolf* ch. 4, para. 6.

[37] 1830: col. 259, H.C.Deb. xxiv, quoted C. J. Whelan, *Small Claims: A Comparative Study*, Oxford, 1990.

[38] N.H. Andrews, [1989] L.M.C.L.Q. 421, 'Mistaken Settlement of Disputed Claims'.

[39] (1975) 91 L.Q.R. 168 at 169.

and speedy means of testing the strength of the parties' respective cases. That the standard of justice done on motion was high is demonstrated by the fact that in only a very few cases was the result at the trial different from that arrived at on motion. Indeed, in practice the parties usually elected to settle on the basis of the interlocutory finding without going to trial at all. It is understood that the cost of such truncated proceedings was often less than that of an opinion on the merits by a fashionable leader; the same could be said of the delay involved. Understandably, the procedure proved popular with litigants; so that, for example, of the thousand or so passing-off cases there have been in the last decade, all (or virtually all) of them were 'decided' on motion.

But one must contrast this happy account of litigants' access to cheap justice with the position of a losing litigant who feels that the system, through cutting corners, has let him down. Once such a litigant has had his 'day in court' and has received, therefore, the only public form of adjudication available to him, it will come as scant consolation to be told that the possible inaccuracy of the result is something that must be tolerated in the interest of efficiency.

Lord Woolf might respond to this by saying that for too long English Civil justice has been predicated on the basis that everyone has a chance to travel by Rolls-Royce if only he had the money, and that such élitism can no longer be justified. He would object that it is inefficient to allow litigants to run amok by excessive use of the procedural armoury and that it is also unfair to allow them to do so because, by increasing the cost and difficulty of litigation, this will deny justice to many potential plaintiffs and expose defendants to an unreasonable pressure to capitulate. Furthermore, he might say that lay people would settle for travel by Mini-Metro and access to a less grand style of litigation.

To this the author would retort that a good deal of the populist sting is taken out of the debate once the small claims jurisdiction is increased to £3,000, as Lord Woolf proposes, and once the fast-track for cases less than £10,000 is introduced. Claims in excess of that amount, which would normally proceed to the multi-track, might be dealt with more cheaply if the parties elect to proceed by the fast-track or even opt for arbitration. The English system needs to be preserved against the corrosive effect of excessive zeal for cost-cutting. Not all adjudication should be effected on the cheap. To use Lord Devlin's metaphor, there must be some tribute to the Minotaur.[40] This is the price which is to be paid for good quality fact-finding, meticulous development of case-law doctrine and the support of a system which offers access to specialised and expert lawyers.

[40] Patrick Devlin, *The Judge*, (Oxford, 1981) p. 106.

(ii) *Beyond the Golden Age of Judicial Passivity at Trial*

The author has discussed elsewhere the attractive English tradition that a trial judge should remain passive when dealing with the submission of evidence[41]:

> The principle of party control ensures that the court remains detached and passive. This is considered to be beneficial in two main ways. First, the court can preserve its impartiality. Secondly, detachment during a hearing will save the court from falling into error.

Sir Jack Jacob's view[42] is this:

> the passive role of the English court greatly enhances the standing, the influence and authority of the judiciary at all levels and may well account for the high respect and esteem in which they are held, as well as their comparatively small numbers.

But Lord Woolf wishes to abandon this passivity. He proposes that the judge should exercise very substantial control both before and during trial, not merely to marshall the case (an approach which has already received the approval of the House of Lords[43]) but, it seems, to control both the quality and quantity of evidence which is received by the court. This will imperil the court's appearance of impartiality.[44]

(iii) *Judicial Case-Management and Litigation Lawyers*

How will Lord Woolf's new interventionist style of litigation be received by litigants and lawyers? The pessimistic view is that they will resent being pushed around by over-zealous, fussy or even ill-motivated and tyrannical judges, especially during the pre-trial stages of the case. There are numerous opportunities for discord: formulation of the case, control of discovery, rationing or prohibiting the use of experts, appointment of independent witnesses, timetabling of the litigation, the decision whether to allow amplification at trial of witness statements, as well as control of cross-examination, and the draconian use of costs awards, including wasted costs orders against lawyers. Not only is such drastic judicial intervention likely to antagonise one (or perhaps both) of the parties, it is inevitable that seasoned litigation lawyers will soon grow cynical and communicate this to their clients. One can well imagine that, for example, Boswell Q.C. will tell his client that last week, before a different High Court judge, a much more generous discovery order was made, or that a more lenient approach was adopted towards cross-examination of witnesses. In such circumstances, it

[41] Andrews, *Principles of Civil Procedure*, para. 3–002.

[42] *The Fabric of English Civil Justice* (1987), p.12; the argument is supported in the U.S.A. by S. Gross, *op.cit.*, at p. 746, n. 39, citing S. Landsman, *The Adversary System: A Description and Defense* (1984) p. 50 and J. Merryman, *The Civil Law Tradition* (1969) pp. 130–131.

[43] See n. 10 above.

[44] Damaska, *op.cit.* n. 7 above, pp. 120–121.

will soon become a forensic game, much more so than at present, to try to avoid certain judges and gain access, for tactical reasons, to particular judges. This is the consequence of allowing judges greater discretion in the control of litigation.[45]

Lord Woolf perhaps would concede that his proposals do raise this danger, but he might respond sanguinely that it will be avoided because judges under his new system will display exemplary professionalism, efficiency and fairness. But is this hope a realistic one? Could it not go horribly wrong?[46]

(iv) *The Adversarial Tradition and English Cultural Values*

Sir Jack Jacob[47] has said of the adversarial principle:

> it reflects and responds to English cultural values, and conforms more closely with the English character of independent and 'fair play' . . .

Damaska has fortified this, arguing that the adversarial principle reflects a deep tenet of liberal political theory. According to that theory, it is not the role of the state to engage in 'coercive paternalism' but instead to facilitate private endeavour and to set minimalist rules of fair-dealing.[48]

Of course, an extreme policy of laissez-faire in litigation would be likely to offend notions of fairness and efficiency. For this reason there can be no quarrel with Lord Woolf's recommendation that the courts should intervene to correct manifest procedural inequality between the parties. Thus the court will try to assist the unrepresented party, notably in small claims litigation, even though this will imperil the court's impartiality. Another qualification upon Damaska's laissez-faire idea must be the problem of excessive delay. The author would concede that it is appropriate to adjust the adversarial principle to ensure that litigation does not meander or become dormant.[49] But, beyond this, there seems no convincing reason to mutilate it. In particular, Lord Woolf is creating an unjustified danger of judicial meddling and the appearance of bias when he proposes that in general the court should seek to 'formulate the real issues of questions between the parties'. Let this extraordinary power be reserved for cases where the litigant has made a nonsense of his 'statement of case' or 'defence', because he has received no legal advice. To intervene more generally than this creates an obvious danger that the court's appearance of impartiality will be destroyed, a theme developed by Damaska.[50] There is also a practical prob-

[45] For an argument against conferring such discretion, see section (ii) in Conclusion below.

[46] Langbein, *op.cit.* n. 15 above, at pp. 848, 861 (citing Resnik).

[47] *The Fabric of English Civil Justice* (London, 1987) p. 15; J.A. Jolowicz (1988) 8 L.S. 1, 7 quotes Hamson, writing in *The Times* in a similar vein.

[48] *Op.cit.* n. 7 above, pp. 104 *et seq.*

[49] The author also accepts that discovery should be limited to avoid abuse: see the author's recommendations in Conclusion section (ii).

[50] *Op.cit.* n. 7 above, pp. 114 *et seq.*; and see Resnik's convincing criticism of U.S. case-management, *op.cit.* n. 3 above, at pp. 427–430.

lem. Judicial comprehension of the legal issues presupposes knowledge of the facts. But such knowledge is acquired slowly and expensively. One wonders, therefore, what Lord Woolf has in mind when he envisages judges even at the outset grappling with the case's formulation.

(v) *Should Settlement be the Primary Aim of the System?*

Lord Woolf, agreeing with the Heilbron-Hodge report, says[51]: 'the philosophy of litigation should be primarily to encourage early settlement of disputes'.[52]

Settlement which occurs in the face of a proper understanding of the merits of both sides' position is clearly the desirable aim of any rational system. Even so, there are important qualifications. First, the court should not be seen to foster settlement by coercion or persuasion, especially since settlement can be the product of gross social and economic inequality.[53] The point is sharply made: 'The court itself should not be seen to be active in persuading parties. . .to accept less than the law provides lest the values inherent in our law become still more depreciated in our society.'[54] Secondly, a settlement which brushes under the carpet a point of public interest is not an unqualified good. In the United States Owen Fiss, in an important polemic 'Against Settlement'[55], has argued that there is a value in holding up a mirror at trial to matters of wide public importance, especially disputes concerning civil rights or alleged misconduct by powerful organisations.

Personnel Problems

(i) *Litigation's Reduced Status as a Career?*

If Lord Woolf's recommendations are adopted, the role of a litigator and of an advocate in civil cases will be diminished. The court will have greater involvement in the case and, consequently, a good deal of the individual lawyer's responsibility will have been taken away from him or her. Of course, exceptional cases will remain which involve great complexity or matters of public interest. For such work the large litigation firm and the small team of experienced barristers will remain indispensable. But under Lord Woolf's new regime, one wonders what will be the fate of litigators engaged in ordinary or even medium-sized actions. If, as the author fears,

51 *Woolf* ch. 2, para. 7(a).

52 *Naylor* v. *Preston A.H.A.* [1987] 1 W.L.R. 958, 967-968, C.A.

53 '. . . settlements can be fair and prudent arrangements; but that can also be squalid scenes of bullying acted out in the law's back-alleys', Andrews, *Principles of Civil Procedure*, para. 2-011; similarly, Glasser *op.cit.* n. 7 above p. 309.

54 J.A. Jolowicz (1988) 8 L.S. 111, 119.

55 (1984) 93 Yale L.J. 1073–1090, reprinted ch. 16, *Procedure* (Aldershot, 1992) ed. D. Galligan.

there might be a gradual down-grading of such lawyers' jobs, it will become difficult to attract the better lawyers into this side of practice.

Another worry is that this will diminish the pool of talented litigation lawyers from which judicial appointments can be made.

### (ii) *An Over-Burdened Judiciary?*

Is it not likely that the increase in judicial work which will be necessitated by Lord Woolf's proposals might well place the judiciary at all levels under increasing pressure?[56] One must also wonder whether the significant involvement of judges in pre-trial preparation will confer the same job satisfaction as adjudication under the present adversarial system. Might it not be suggested, therefore, that Lord Woolf is unduly sanguine in stating that there will be no problem in attracting good quality people to the new civil bench?

## CONCLUSION

### (i) *Taking Stock of Lord Woolf's Main Proposals*

The recommendations concerned with increasing access to justice in minor or middling cases are attractive. But the core of his report concerns 'case-management' and the overthrowing of many aspects of the adversarial principle. In England we have been slow to require judges to intervene substantially in a case before it proceeds to trial, other than in the specialised contexts of group litigation and other types of complex cases. Instead the traditional assumption has been that the parties' lawyers will prepare the case thoroughly and that the plaintiff will maintain a reasonable momentum in the quest for its resolution. If that assumption is sound, it would merely aggravate cost and delay to impose on the parties a system of pre-trial official paternalism.

The key to Lord Woolf's assault on this tradition is that he no longer trusts the parties' lawyers to prepare the case sensibly, carefully and with reasonable speed. So the judges must assume control of both preparation for trial and trial itself. In the author's opinion, there is a reasonable case for imposing an official check against unreasonable delay (probably using a series of provisional deadlines), abuse of discovery and excessive orality at trial (see my recommendations below). In complex cases too, there is a need for case-management (although this is already available for large commercial cases and group actions). But it is deeply controversial whether it is right to inflict on litigants and their lawyers a system of judicial case-

[56] Glasser *op.cit* n. 7 above, p. 317 rightly sees *American Cyanamid* as a response to potential overload of interim injunctions; similarly see Andrews, *op.cit.*, paras. 9-024–9-025 for defensive case law relating to R.S.C. Ord. 14 (summary judgment).

management which is wider and more intrusive than this. To summarise the objections made already, it can be said that Lord Woolf's report has implications for (i) the perceived fairness and accuracy of the civil process, especially trial; (ii) the relationship of co-operation between lawyers and the bench; (iii) the efficiency and status of the judiciary; and (iv) the allure of litigation as a career for practitioners and prospective judges.

(ii) *An Alternative Set of Recommendations*

It is suggested that Lord Woolf should offer a more modest set of proposals for the modification of the adversarial principle. The following alternative recommendations are suggested:

(a) The court should abandon its passive position at hearings where there is one or more unrepresented litigant; it is believed that this will reflect 'best practice' already observed by English judges.

(b) Except where one party is unrepresented, the court should not take the initiative to define the case (that is the pleadings or 'statement of case'), but this task should be left to the parties and their legal advisors.

(c) There should be provisional guidelines which prescribe the *quantity* of documentary discovery. These guidelines will not be uniform, but will be divided into bands according to the value or importance of the case. In heavy cases, excessive discovery might be curbed by placing the onus on a party to show that this provisional allotment should be waived by the court because of the special features of the case, notably its complexity and value, taking into account also the timetable for completing the pre-trial stages of the litigation.

(d) There should be similar provisional guidelines, once more divided into bands to reflect the case's value or importance, which prescribe the time within which preparation for trial is to be completed (or perhaps different stages of complex litigation). Where these periods are exceeded, the plaintiff's solicitor and counsel should be required to send a sealed explanation to the court. The plaintiff should also be asked to send a sealed report in which he comments on the lawyer's competence, and this report should be made quite independently of the lawyers. Once the case is concluded, and if the plaintiff wishes, the court shall have power to decide (a) whether there has been unjustified delay caused by the plaintiff's lawyers or lawyer, (b) if so, whether this is the consequence of 'undue' or 'excessive' dereliction of professional responsibility; (c) if the default is 'undue', whether to impose a reduction in the fee recoverable (or recovered already) by the lawyer in respect of the litigation; (d) if the default is 'excessive', whether to impose a still more severe reduction of the lawyer's fee. The court would also be required to take into account whether there has been any contributory delay caused by the defendant. It might also be necessary to introduce a parallel set of provisions to deal with delay caused by a defendant's lawyer. But it is believed that the main need for protection is against delay attributable to a plaintiff's own lawyers. The present recommendation is to be understood as a modification and perhaps stiffening of the existing procedure governing 'wasted costs' orders.[57]

(e) The court should not seek to control on an *ad hoc* basis the process of cross-examination. Nor should there be *ad hoc* control, before or at trial, of the number of witnesses or experts to be called by a party. Instead there should be a set of provisional guidelines prescribing the time available to each party for the presentation and development of his case at trial. These guidelines will fix different periods for cases according to their value, complexity or importance. It will be the responsibility of the parties before the case comes on for trial to petition the court to allow an increase upon this allowance. That application should be decided by an official other than the nominated trial judge.

The author's recommendations (c), (d) and (e) indicate that he agrees with some parts of Lord Woolf's diagnosis of the present system's ills, namely that there is a need to adjust the adversarial principle to tackle, respectively, the problems of unbridled discovery, undue pre-trial delay and excessive orality at trial. But my measures are based on the superiority of rules (guidelines, directions, call them what you will) over *ad hoc* exercises of subjective, antagonistic and potentially prejudicial judicial discretion to meet the perceived exigencies of individual cases. Thus the Cantley Committee noted:

> The basic principle which can be discovered in the changes in our procedure over the years is a change from order to rule. Until 1919 the parties were not allowed to plead except by order: until 1965 discovery was by order only. The Rules have been gradually extended in their operation and more and more matters which originally were allowed or required only by order in any given case are now provided for by rule applicable to all cases.[58]

Discretion cannot be eliminated but it should enter only if exceptions to these rules are sought by one or more of the parties. Most of the time, therefore, disgruntled litigants and lawyers, chafing against these constraints, will have only the rules to blame and not a human target. In all

[57] R.S.C. Ord. 62, r. 11; Andrews, *Principles of Civil Procedure*, para.'s 10-053–10-063.

[58] 'Report of the Personal Injuries Litigation Procedure Working Party' (1979: Cmnd. 7476), p. 13.

these cases, even those governed by recommendation (e), the discretion will be exercised before trial by someone other than the trial judge.

It is submitted that a system of rules or guidelines is a much less dangerous means of achieving Lord Woolf's goals. It is also more likely to be acceptable to lawyers. One should not take for granted their willingness to co-operate with a new system, nor should they have a veto on necessary change. Rather, care must be taken to achieve conditions where a spirit of co-operation is likely to be fostered. One cannot expect all litigation lawyers to accept even these diluted recommendations. But it seems to the author that the recommendations just presented are a means of tackling the most pressing problems of modern litigation, at the same time preserving more than Lord Woolf's bare husk of the adversarial principle.

# 10

# *Raising the Small Claims Limit*

JOHN BALDWIN*

## INTRODUCTION

In his interim report on the reform of civil justice, Lord Woolf recommends a number of changes to the small claims jurisdiction in this country, by far the most important of which is a very substantial rise in the small claims limit. This move represents the principal means suggested in the report for increasing access to the courts for the ordinary citizen. In this paper, an attempt will be made to anticipate some of the main effects of this change and to assess the difficulties likely to arise when it is implemented. On the basis of his own research on small claims procedures in England and Wales, the writer will argue that Lord Woolf's proposals do not satisfactorily address the serious practical and empirical problems raised over many years in the small claims literature and may not in consequence provide the enhanced access to justice that is anticipated.

## THE SMALL CLAIMS PROPOSALS

It is no real surprise that Lord Woolf looks to a massive raising of the small claims limit (from its present level of £1,000 to £3,000[1]) as a main way of easing the crisis in civil justice. Other commentators have in the past recommended the same course as a convenient expedient in coping with the alarming rise in the costs of civil litigation, though few have suggested a rise of the magnitude proposed by Lord Woolf. The move is in line with an underlying theme in the Inquiry that 'proceedings should be conducted and disposed of in a manner, at a cost and within a timescale which is appropriate, taking into account the nature of the issues involved and the means of the parties' (p. 20), and the increased small claims jurisdiction forms the first tier of a three tier system which will seek to give effect to these principles. The three-fold increase in the small claims limit will be by far the

* Director, Institute of Judicial Administration, University of Birmingham.

[1] Lord Woolf recommends that the effects of this increase be monitored with a view to a possible further rise to £5,000.

largest single rise ever introduced in this country. The idea was so enthusiastically received at the Lord Chancellor's Department that, on the very day the interim report was published, a Press Release was issued by the Lord Chancellor announcing that he would take immediate action to raise the limit as had been recommended.

It emerges clearly in Lord Woolf's report that he is thoroughly content with the operation of the existing small claims regime, asserting (though with little supporting evidence) that it is 'a forum which is fair and appropriate to litigants in person' (p. 104).[2] Beyond proposing the raising of the small claims limit, he recommends only minor changes to present arrangements for dealing with small claims. These modifications include widening the discretion exercised by district judges to transfer cases into (and out of) the small claims procedure; somewhat greater use of a paper arbitration option so as to improve access for businesses and the self-employed, and the provision of early evening and Saturday hearings. He also floats some imaginative ideas about the use of mobile courts in smaller country towns.

The main weakness that Lord Woolf identifies in the present operation of small claims is the wide diversity in the approach that district judges adopt in dealing with them—a finding that was very evident in the author's own research on small claims procedures.[3] This research is cited in the interim report (on p. 111) to show that little, if any, training in handling small claims has been available to district judges. Lord Woolf argues that much more extensive guidance and training should be provided for judges in playing the interventionist role so as to achieve greater consistency in procedure and in applying the substantive law. It is significant that he envisages that judges at all levels will in the future play a more interventionist role at hearings, 'to hold the ring', as he puts it, 'and ensure the adequate presentation of the litigant's case' (p. 23). This will have serious implications for the kind of judicial training that will be required. Although he does not go into detail, he makes the very important point that there is also 'a need for guidance as to best practice' (p. 110). It is not clear exactly what he has in mind here, but if it is a code of practice for district judges, it would be more likely in this writer's view to reduce inconsistencies amongst judges (and at lower cost) than would enhanced training programmes.

The vexed question whether or not personal injury claims should be dealt with inside the expanded small claims regime is examined in some detail in this interim report. Lord Woolf favours the line taken by the powerful P.I.

[2] In the *Report of the Review Body on Civil Justice* (Cm 394, 1988), the Civil Justice Review had also concluded, with similar wording, that the small claims procedure had 'fulfilled its aim of providing a suitable forum for use by the general public' (para. 505).

[3] This research, which has been funded by the Lord Chancellor's Department, the Office of Fair Trading and the Economic and Social Research Council, has been in progress for the past two years.

lobby which has for years vociferously argued that personal injury claims are qualitatively different from other claims and therefore unsuitable for a procedure operating largely without legal representation. (He describes the Association of Personal Injury Lawyers as 'particularly emphatic as to the inappropriateness of the small claims procedure for personal injury cases' p. 46). He proposes that, instead of personal injury cases being dealt with under the small claims procedure, they should be placed on the 'fast track', unless one of the parties wishes to invoke the small claims jurisdiction and the court agrees. In following this course, Lord Woolf has probably succeeded in avoiding confrontation with these (and other) interest groups who might well have sought to scupper his small claims proposals had he dealt differently with this sensitive question.

Instead of this happening, Lord Woolf's recommendations relating to small claims have, at least in the weeks immediately following publication, received the almost universal approbation of practising lawyers and widespread endorsement from other quarters as well.[4] The assumption is made by virtually all commentators that there will in the future be a very substantial increase in the number of cases handled under the small claims jurisdiction. (An editorial in the *New Law Journal*, 23 June 1995, stated that the extended small claims jurisdiction 'will provide a simple procedure for hundreds of thousands more cases each year' p. 913). It is after all the expansion of the scope of the scheme that Lord Woolf regards as 'the primary way of increasing access to justice for ordinary people' (p. 100).

But will these proposals work? Much of what Lord Woolf says about small claims is eminently sensible, occasionally radical, and (unlike much earlier discussion) set within an elaborately constructed organising framework. Small claims occupy a discrete—and central—position in the proposed new order. If, however, they are to have any real chance of success, a first requirement must be that Lord Woolf's concern that the rise in the limit be 'accompanied by better training for district judges, a more consistent judicial approach and better information, advice and support for litigants' (p. 118) be satisfactorily addressed.

On these questions, as on many others raised in the Inquiry, Lord Woolf emerges as a man who is to quite a remarkable degree optimistic and self-confident. But one wonders whether his optimism might be misplaced. It must be conceded that the prospects of the Inquiry producing the fundamental and radical re-thinking that is now required are distinctly unpropitious, not least because, as is acknowledged on page 4 of this interim report, no fewer than sixty reports on aspects of civil procedure and

[4] An editorial in the *New Law Journal* (23 June 1995) noted that 'the report received almost universal praise from consumer groups to City law firms' (p. 913), and, in the same issue of the journal, A. Gusskurth, 'Plaudits with Provisos', refers to the 'unrestrained enthusiasm' amongst solicitors for the proposals (p. 935).

the organisation of the courts in this country have preceded this one by Lord Woolf. And he anticipates on page 97 that only 'modest additional expense' will be required to carry out his programme of reform in a complex implementation programme that he envisages will be completed over a period of years. This is a quite extraordinary claim, and one's scepticism about its validity is not by any means allayed by the vagueness and generality of all discussions of the resource implications of the measures proposed in this interim report.

Perhaps the greatest strength of the report lies in its determination to address the problems that presently confront potential litigants in person, and one might reasonably expect a great acceleration in many forms of 'do-it-yourself' justice, particularly in the small claims arena, as a direct result of what is proposed. In this writer's view, the basic limitation of this brand of justice is that lay litigants cannot be expected to view their disputes in a strict legal context or even to know how they should go about proving their case. This problem emerged clearly in the author's own study of the operation of small claim procedures.[5] It was apparent in hearing after hearing that, left to their own devices, many lay litigants turn up empty-handed, without relevant documents or witnesses. It was interesting to note in the study how the district judges responded in that situation: they adopted a fundamentally pragmatic approach in seeking to reach decisions. Their natural inclination (and it is one strongly endorsed by Lord Woolf) was to avoid adjourning hearings unless there was no alternative. The writer's observations of small claims hearings revealed clearly that district judges dealing with small claims tried in most circumstances to reach a decision with whatever evidence was available to them on the day.

A determination to reach a decision masks, however, the important point about the operation of small claims procedures where litigants in person are involved. Notwithstanding the idiosyncrasies of individual judges, some of whom may reach decisions that owe more to common sense than to the law,[6] lay litigants will be obliged in most situations to prove their case within a legal framework. Even though the author's observations of small claims hearings showed that most lay people are capable of functioning effectively enough at hearings and are able to put over their grievances to district judges competently and concisely, they frequently fail fully to appreciate that it is not enough to feel an acute sense of injustice about their

[5] In this study, small claims hearings have been observed, litigants and district judges interviewed, and court records extensively studied in many county courts throughout England and Wales.

[6] The disinclination of certain district judges to apply the principles of English law in making decisions in small claims was raised by the writer and is discussed at pp. 107–109 in the interim report. Lord Woolf expresses himself unreservedly out of sympathy with those judges who have assumed, because of the fluidity of small claims procedures, that they should be free to apply their own notions of justice and fairness rather than the substantive law.

case: they must still establish that it has legal validity. This requirement is not by any means a straightforward task or one that can be conveniently conveyed to lay people in a few simple leaflets.[7]

Lord Woolf has many interesting ideas about how the difficulties that confront lay litigants might be tackled. Some of these ideas struck this writer as somewhat vague and tentative,[8] however, and Lord Woolf is certainly at his most enthusiastic and expansive when discussing the benefits, both for litigants and for judges, to be derived from I.T. He deals in curiously disproportionate detail with ways that information might be conveyed to litigants by means of self-service legal 'kiosks', the use of interactive videos and legal information systems. However, if Lord Woolf's recommendations relating to the public funding of duty advice schemes (at courts handling housing and debt cases) were to be taken seriously and to be implemented in such a way that preliminary advice about the legal validity of claims were readily and systematically available to litigants, then they would go a long way in meeting what the present writer views as the fundamental flaw with D.I.Y. justice.

## DIFFICULTIES IN IMPLEMENTATION

Small claims represent the cheap and cheerful end of the judicial market, and, as noted above, the approach adopted in dealing with them tends to be determinedly pragmatic. Although most district judges, in this writer's experience, listen to lay litigants with considerable patience and sensitivity, no one could pretend that small claims hearings provide more than a swift and relatively crude mechanism by which to resolve these kinds of dispute. It seems that litigants are by and large content if they are offered a final decision following a procedure they accept as fair. The writer conducted interviews with 262 small claims plaintiffs and defendants, most of whom expressed general satisfaction with the procedures they encountered and said that their claims had been dealt with expeditiously and fairly. But small claims hearings do not provide (as district judges were fond of telling the

[7] Indeed, the leaflets are bound to be almost totally useless for this purpose. In their examination of fifteen American small claims courts, S Weller, J. C. Ruhnka and J. A. Martin, 'American Small Claims Courts' pp. 5–23 in (ed.) C. J. Whelan, *Small Claims Courts: A Comparative Study* (Oxford: Clarendon Press, 1990), noted that 'even the most elaborate booklet . . . contained nothing which would assist a litigant in determining whether he had a case worth filing or what evidence he should bring to trial' (p. 13).

[8] For instance, his proposals with regard to the courts taking a more pro-active role in providing information to litigants are dealt with only briefly. He foresees the possibility that, as court staff are liberated by the new technology from time-consuming and repetitive work, they will be able to 'undertake the higher quality and more demanding work of assisting litigants and providing support to judges on cases management' (p. 122).

writer) Rolls Royce justice: rather justice inevitably takes the form of a quick decision based upon what is very often inadequate evidence.

This approach is more easily defended in relation to small sums, and there is no evidence to suggest that many litigants in person want their disputes resolved by elaborate or formal legal procedures.[9] However, one must seriously doubt that the rough-and-ready approach adopted by district judges—which they commonly described to the writer as doing the best they could with the little relevant evidence available to them—will prove appropriate or even acceptable where more sensitive issues and much larger sums are at stake. 'How far can we go in relying on common-sense to get us through?' is how one district judge put it in an interview with the author. The danger is that expanding the small claims limit may serve further to encourage the development of separate tiers of justice for those who can afford legal representation and those who cannot. Lord Woolf's proposals will inevitably mean that unrefined legal procedures, based upon simple and admittedly crude forms of D.I.Y. case preparation and presentation, will be stretched to apply to an ever-growing range of disputes.

In Lord Woolf's discussion of small claims, one sees in sharp focus an underlying uncertainty (even contradiction) that runs through much of this interim report. It is not clear whether the expansion of the small claims jurisdiction is intended merely to mop up the present overflow of cases from other parts of the civil justice system or whether it represents a genuine effort to enhance access to justice by inducing many people who are at present put off from using the courts to activate the small claims procedure in the future. If the objective is the latter (and there are many indications in the report that Lord Woolf is genuinely concerned about limited access), it is difficult to see how it is to be achieved without substantial corresponding increases in resources—something that Lord Woolf explicitly states in his report will not be needed to implement his proposals in their entirety.

It is in truth difficult to predict the effects of a massive increase in the small claims limit, since in the history of small claims in this country there has never been anything like the £2,000 increase in the limit that is recommended. It is perhaps odd that, despite the popular appeal that the procedure undoubtedly enjoys,[10] the small claims limit has been raised only four

[9] A recent survey, entitled *Civil Law and the Public*, jointly conducted by the B.B.C. and the National Consumer Council and based upon over 8,000 adults in England and Wales, showed that most lay people prefer their legal problems to be dealt with by informal means—particularly if they produce a mediated settlement in which they can actively participate—rather than formal court adjudication. (The writer is indebted to Mr Simon Coates of the B.B.C.'s Law in Action for making the draft report of this interesting survey available to him).

[10] The Civil Justice Review (1988) *op cit*, for instance, concluded that the small claims procedure was 'substantially sound in that it is able to produce results, without major delay and cost, which satisfy a large number of those who use it' (para. 507). The writer's own research adds a measure of support to this sanguine conclusion.

times since the procedure was introduced in 1973.[11] Once changes in the Retail Price index are taken into account, it is apparent that the present limit of £1,000 is in real terms only marginally higher than it was fifteen years ago.[12] It is, furthermore, low compared to the limit set in many other jurisdictions. (In many parts of the United States, for instance, the limit is $5,000 or higher, and comparable figures apply commonly in Australia and Canada). Seen in this light, the course recommended by Lord Woolf is not perhaps as bold as it might at first appear.

Although one can do no more than speculate at this stage about what the effects of raising the small claims limit to £3,000 might be, it is nonetheless evident that it is a move that will reinforce the tendency, already strong, for small claims hearings to dominate proceedings in the county courts, a phenomenon that is not much discussed in the interim report. It is worth pausing to consider the official figures on the growth of numbers of small claims hearings in the past twenty years because they are so remarkable. Year after year, small claims have formed an increasing proportion of county court business. Annual publication of the *Judicial Statistics* has shown how the proportion of cases disposed of by the small claims procedure has risen in virtually every year since it was introduced. In 1973, well over ten times as many judgments in the county courts were entered after trial (involving a full hearing in court) as by arbitration (ie by the small claims procedure). Five years later, that figure was reduced to three times as many. By 1982, rather more judgments were being entered following arbitration than by trial, a trend that has accelerated ever since. Nowadays about 80 per cent of cases of all defended actions in the county courts are being dealt with under the small claims procedure.[13]

In numerical terms, the increase has been no less dramatic, and the last few years have seen something of an explosion in the numbers of small claims hearings. A ten-fold rise occurred between 1978 and 1993 in England and Wales. The number doubled between 1990 and 1993, when almost 106,000 such hearings were held. The small claims regime is already, therefore, the predominant mode of disposal of defended actions in the county courts. The periodic raising of the small claims limit (with consequent automatic referral of claims within that limit to the small claims procedure) has markedly reinforced the trend for more and more claims to be dealt with under the procedure and has had the effect of reducing the numbers of traditional trials in the county courts. It is evident that proposals in the report will themselves reinforce this trend in the future.

[11] In 1973, the small claims limit was fixed at £75. This was raised to £100 in October 1974, to £200 in July 1978, to £500 in October 1981 and to £1,000 in July 1991.

[12] The writer is grateful to Ms Melissa Morse of the Civil Policy Branch of the Lord Chancellor's Department for making this information available to him.

[13] See Table 4.6 in *Judicial Statistics Annual Report 1993* and Table 4.7 in *Judicial Statistics Annual Report 1994*.

As already noted, Lord Woolf takes a refreshingly sanguine view of the small claims procedure. The broad principles enunciated in his Inquiry—equality of access to the courts regardless of resources to assert or defend legal rights, just delivery of results, a system seen to be fair, costs proportionate to the nature of issues, speed, devising procedures that are understandable, responsive, certain and effective—reveal a sincere determination to shift the focus of the civil justice system to meet the needs of litigants rather than court professionals. As Lord Woolf readily acknowledges, this shift will require nothing short of a change in the culture and the thinking about how civil justice processes should operate, and, if past experience is any guide, the difficulties in bringing about a change of culture should not be under-estimated. But he is surely right to regard the acid test of legal processes as being what the litigants themselves make of them.[14] In addition to being frequently portrayed as too expensive, slow, complex and intimidating to ordinary people, the courts have been criticised for their tendency to operate for the convenience of court personnel, especially judges, instead of the convenience of the parties.[15]

Yet there are reasons to be sceptical about the prospects of the proposed changes to small claims securing the much greater access to justice for ordinary people that Lord Woolf anticipates will follow implementation. It is for a start curious that, at the very time that a massive increase in the small claims limit is being implemented, the figures cited by Lord Woolf show a substantial reduction in numbers of small claims hearings. (The figures given on page 102 of the interim report indicate that 87,885 cases were disposed of under the small claims procedure in 1994, a fall of no less than 17 per cent on the 1993 figure of 105,843[16]). This is the first year in the history of small claims in this country that there has not been an increase in the number of hearings, and a reduction of this magnitude would appear to be more than a little disconcerting. Yet the paradox is not mentioned, still less explored, in the interim report. The capacity of the county courts

[14] There are increasing signs that the litigant's perspective is being taken seriously in the courts. For example, the Lord Chancellor's Department now conducts national surveys of court users. In some small claims courts in the United States, the parties are asked to complete a users' questionnaire (of the kind commonly found in hotel rooms) and invited to comment on the standard of service they have received.

[15] As T. W. Church, *A Consumer's Perspective on the Courts* (Melbourne: Australian Institute of Judicial Administration Incorporated, 1990) argued:

> Most courts . . . are organized for the convenience of judges, of court staff, and of lawyers; usually in that order. If the convenience of the public is considered at all, it comes well behind these courthouse 'regulars' . . . Yet no consumer-oriented establishment could set its priorities in this way . . . With the exception of the prison service and perhaps a few unrepentant social welfare organizations, I know of no organizations . . which appear to be quite as cavalier about their clientele as are the courts of the English speaking world (p. 7).

[16] These figures were confirmed in July 1995 in the subsequent publication of the *Judicial Statistics Annual Report 1994*.

to hold small claims hearings is finite, and one wonders, on the basis of these statistics, whether district judges, after years of rapid and sustained expansion, have now have reached saturation point in the numbers of small claims hearings they are able, or indeed prepared, to conduct.

Findings from the writer's own research are somewhat disquieting on this score. In interviews conducted with 33 district judges in 1994 at eighteen county courts throughout England and Wales, it was readily apparent that the popular appeal of small claims did not extend to the district judges themselves. 'Arbitration day is not the most popular day in the judge's calendar' is how a district judge on the Northern Circuit put it to the author when discussing the probability that the small claims limit would be increased, and few of his colleagues in other parts of the country expressed a more enthusiastic view. Almost a half of the 33 judges said that they would be opposed to any increase at all, and a further fifth wanted no more than expansion in line with rates of inflation. Only just over a quarter could be described as sympathetic to an increase in the small claims limit of the magnitude recommended by Lord Woolf.

It is a mistake, therefore, to assume that simply because most district judges now play the interventionist role at small claims hearings with some relish they want to do much more of it. On the contrary: dealing with small claims is regarded by most district judges as difficult and unsatisfying judicial work which is tolerable only in relatively small doses. District judges will inevitably bear the brunt of the expansion in the small claims workload, but there is no indication in the interim report that their views were systematically canvassed about how far the limit should be extended. One consequence might be that the delays already experienced at some county courts in dealing with small claims (about which Lord Woolf himself expresses concern) will become much more common. In the writer's own research, it was apparent that long delays were experienced at certain courts, and in four of the twelve county courts he examined, over ten per cent of small claims had not been concluded within a year.[17] It might be reasonably anticipated that delays will become a growing problem in the longer term, and, if this happens, it will defeat one of the main purposes of dealing with more cases under the simplified small claims procedure.

As Lord Woolf himself acknowledges, conducting hearings where the judge has to compensate for the lack of legal representation is taxing for the judges concerned, and it is surely a mistake to assume that district judges will be able to perform just as competently when they are obliged to

[17] In this part of the writer's research, based on an examination of 1,800 files drawn from a dozen county courts around the country, it was apparent that, though most small claims were dealt with reasonably expeditiously (almost two thirds were concluded within six months from the time the summons was issued), there were nevertheless wide variations from court to court.

take on growing numbers of more complex small claims where higher sums of money are at stake. Although district judges are very much the work-horses of the civil justice system,[18] there are limits to what they can do, particularly since they are to assume under the new order much greater responsibility than hitherto for case management.[19] It is striking how vague is the discussion in the interim report about whether many new judicial appointments, especially at district judge level, will be needed to give effect to the added responsibilities that judges will have to assume in relation to the expansion of the small claims jurisdiction and the judicial case management role. While it is conceded that 'there may need to be some increase in the number of judges' (p. 70), no indication whatever is given anywhere in the report as to the numbers of extra judges who might be required. However, without large numbers of new judicial appointments—something that Lord Woolf does not apparently see as necessary[20]—serious doubts must be expressed about the capacity of district judges to cope with the additional burdens that will be placed upon them.

## THE EXISTING RESEARCH ON SMALL CLAIMS

The approach adopted in the Inquiry so far is resolutely intuitive, and the report contains no detailed consideration of the relevant research and writing on any subject. In reaching his recommendations, it seems that Lord Woolf has relied largely upon own long professional experience, tempered and supported by the views expressed by contributors in the extensive soundings taken in the series of regional seminars he held, and the evidence that was submitted to his Inquiry. There is, no doubt, much to be said in favour of trusting the intuition and judgement of a seasoned and respected observer, and, as happened in the case of Lord Woolf's inquiry into prison disturbances,[21] the result is much more likely to be a report that is bolder in conception and more direct in purpose than a committee, commission or working party would produce.

But this approach has certain limitations, and in this case one conse-

[18] One district judge told the writer that he had kept a record of the number of judicial decisions he had made in the course of a single calendar month, and he had found that the total was no fewer than 486.

[19] The proposals relating to the need for case management are discussed in Section II of the interim report.

[20] Instead of judicial appointments, Lord Woolf places emphasis upon providing judges with additional assistance from the court administration, team working, the greater use of technology, and the attachment of law clerks to management teams. He makes a few tentative references to compensatory savings that might be achieved by these means in the two page chapter on resources

[21] See the Rt Hon Lord Justice Woolf and His Honour Judge Stephen Tumim, *Prison Disturbances April 1990: Report of an Inquiry*, Cm 1456 (London: H.M.S.O., 1991).

quence is that limited account is taken of the existing research and writing. While it would have been unrealistic to have expected that a sustained programme of research would have been conducted to inform the work of the Inquiry, it is nevertheless somewhat disappointing that only a handful of straightforward fact-gathering exercises (mainly small-scale surveys of the costs of civil litigation), albeit undertaken by some distinguished personnel, were carried out specifically for the Inquiry.[22] No real effort was made, it seems, to get to grips with the existing research evidence, and little of the published research on small claims is cited in the report. The interim report contains discussion of some findings of research,[23] but these receive prominence, it seems, mainly because of the fortuitous circumstance that their authors happened to submit their findings to the Inquiry. Since the questions surrounding small claims and the civil justice system generally have been largely overlooked by researchers and other commentators in this country (a point acknowledged by Lord Woolf on page 33), it is a pity that the little that has been written on the subject is so much neglected in this interim report. It would be an exaggeration—but only a slight one—to say that the Inquiry has to date been conducted in an empirical and information vacuum.

It is unfortunate, therefore, that many of the issues that have preoccupied commentators who have written about small claims in the past are dealt with only superficially in the report. Some of the key questions are indeed side-stepped or ignored altogether. Although it might be argued that many of these issues are merely academic concerns that have slight relevance in an interim report which is mainly concerned establishing broad principles and framing new directions for policy, there are nevertheless some matters which need to be addressed if one is to have confidence that a substantial raising of the small claims limit will succeed in enhancing access to justice for the ordinary citizen. The questions that this writer thinks worthy of consideration include the appropriate role of legal and other forms of representation; the subjugation of the interests of individuals to those business and commercial concerns; the forbidding image of the county courts, and the enforcement of judgments.

It is interesting to consider what light some of the mainstream academic literature might shed on the consequences of the substantial raising of the small claims limit. On the basis of much earlier writing, one immediate fear is that expanding the small claims jurisdiction will be just as likely to promote and reinforce dominance of the procedure by commercial interests as to increase access to justice for the ordinary citizen. Indeed, there is much

[22] Details of the work that was undertaken as part of the Inquiry or submitted to it are given at pages 248–66.

[23] The present writer's research on small claims procedures is, for instance, cited in several places in chapter 16 of the interim report.

evidence to suggest that expanding the limit may well be at the expense of the ordinary litigant. Some writers have identified serious dangers in the proliferation of informal and simplified legal procedures, like small claims, arguing that expanding their scope is more likely to weaken the lay litigant's position than strengthen it.[24] This consideration would seem to be all the more important when (as is constantly reiterated in the interim report) the over-riding goal is to achieve early settlement[25].

The findings of research on the prospects of court reform producing real change are not particularly encouraging. Enough is already known about the ineffectiveness of court reform recommendations to feel unease at radical commonsense proposals. Research (mainly conducted in the United States) has shown, for instance, that fundamental court reform is extremely difficult to effect, and the bolder the proposals for change, the more likely they are to backfire or to have unanticipated consequences.[26] While one could not have reasonably expected a detailed examination of these questions in the interim report, some discussion of the paradoxes and contradictions that inhere in the small claims jurisdiction would nevertheless have been valuable if only to satisfy sceptics that these issues had been acknowledged and confronted.

The treatment of comparative materials is similarly cursory with little more than occasional respectful nods in that direction.[27] This again is to be regretted since such materials could have shed light on the likely effects of some of the proposals. It would have been useful, for example, to have drawn on such materials in discussing the role that might be played by non-

[24] These writers have viewed the development and expansion of informal mechanisms as extending the coercive arm of the state rather than as enhancing citizens' rights: see in particular R. L. Abel 'The Contradictions of Informal Justice' pp. 267–320 in (ed.) R. L. Abel, *The Politics of Informal Justice* (New York: Academic Press, 1982) who writes, 'Coercion serves to 'persuade' parties to submit to informal justice, 'to 'agree' to the outcome, and to comply with it' (p. 271). The way that law operates so as to buttress the position of the powerful rather than to protect the rights of the weak has become a main focus in what has become known as the 'critical legal studies movement': see, for instance, S. E. Merry, *Getting Justice and Getting Even* (Chicago: University of Chicago Press, 1990) at p. 7–11.

[25] One problem with seeking early settlement of issues is highlighted in research carried out by Hazel Genn, *Hard Bargaining: Out of Court Settlements in Personal Injury Actions* (Oxford: Clarendon Press, 1987). In that study, Genn draws attention to the importance of the relative bargaining strength of the parties in the determining settlement outcomes. See also M. Galanter, 'Why the Haves Come Out Ahead: Speculations on the Limits of Legal Change' 9 *Law and Society Review* (1974) 95–160.

[26] See in particular M. M. Feeley, *Court Reform on Trial: Why Simple Solutions Fail* (New York: Basic Books, 1983); F. Feeney, 'Evaluating Trial Court Performance' 12 *The Justice System Journal* (1987) 148–69; C. Menkel-Meadow, 'Pursuing Settlement in an Adversary Culture: A Tale of Innovation Co-opted or "The Law of ADR" ' 19 *Florida State University Law Review* (1991) 1–46, and R. Matthews, 'Reassessing informal Justice' pp. 3–23 in (ed.) R Matthews, *Informal Justice?* (London: Sage, 1988).

[27] Some comparative materials are cited in the section of the report dealing with case management, and an overview of the comparative research on this subject was prepared for the Inquiry by Lord Woolf's academic consultant, Professor Ross Cranston.

judicial adjudicators in dealing with small claims. Lord Woolf puts forward imaginative ideas about the development of forms of A.D.R. and the use of solicitors, surveyors, engineers, patent agents and other professionals (particularly those who have taken early retirement) to play the part-time role of 'civil magistrates'.[28] The way that such personnel would be accommodated within an essentially legal regime is not explored. Although Lord Woolf sees the opportunity for such people playing a significant role in the expanded small claims scheme, no attempt is made to examine the experiences of those jurisdictions where such personnel are already in place. The use of non-lawyer referees in the Small Claims Tribunals in New Zealand and in some parts of Australia would have provided particularly instructive models, and there are readily accessible materials in the standard academic literature that might have been used to bolster these ideas.[29] In that context, some discussion of the prominent part-time role that deputy district judges currently play in small claims at many county courts in this country might also have been illuminating.

The more general literature on 'access to justice' would have been of considerable relevance to the Inquiry. This body of writing, which dates back to the late 1960s, demonstrates how difficult it is for ordinary people to surmount the formidable barriers that impede access to justice. It shows that lay litigants who make it as far as the courts, having overcome these barriers, are likely to represent the tip of a very large iceberg of 'unmet legal need'.[30] There are, therefore, many other members of the public with serious grievances who fall by the wayside and fail to pursue matters as far as the courts. The evidence suggests that, no matter how informal legal procedures might be and no matter how sympathetic or interventionist judges might be, most lay litigants shy away from the prospect of a court appearance. It is easy for the academic observer—and perhaps for the judicial observer too—who is familiar with the relaxed approach adopted by most district judges, to overlook the simple point that the courts remain for large

[28] These proposals are discussed at page 145 of the interim report.

[29] See on this C. N. Yin and R. Cranston, 'Small Claims Tribunals in Australia' pp. 49–71 in (ed.) C. J. Whelan *op cit* and A. Frame, 'Fundamental Elements of the Small Claims Tribunal System in New Zealand' pp. 73–98 in (ed.) C. J. Whelan *op cit*.

[30] A substantial literature has built up over the years around the question of 'unmet legal need' and 'barriers to justice'. Studies measuring 'unmet legal need' are now somewhat out of fashion, and most of the research which sheds light on the scale of the problem in this country was carried out in the 1970s: see, for example, P. Morris, R. White and P. Lewis, *Social Needs and Legal Action* (London: Martin Robertson, 1972); B. Abel-Smith, M. Zander and R. Brooke, *Legal Problems and the Citizen* (London: Heinemann, 1973), and A. Byles and P. Morris, *Unmet Need* (London: Routledge, 1977). An important study of accident cases, conducted more recently by members of the Oxford Centre for Socio-Legal Studies, examined why so many potential plaintiffs fail to pursue actions: see in particular H. Genn, (1984) 'Who Claims Compensation: Factors Associated with Claiming and Obtaining Damages' pp. 45–78 in (eds) D. Harris, M. Maclean, H. Genn, S. Lloyd-Bostock, P. Fenn, P. Corfield and Y. Brittan, *Compensation and Support for Illness and Injury* (Oxford: Clarendon Press, 1994).

sections of the population uninviting institutions, to be visited only in extreme circumstances. And, in the eyes of many defendants, even those with a strong case, 'being taken to court' is abhorrent and carries a social stigma which use of the term 'defendant' reinforces. Furthermore, the fear of 'not being believed' by the judge is sometimes perceived even as carrying quasi-criminal connotations. 'I've never been in trouble before in my life' is how one middle-aged defendant expressed his thoughts in an interview with the author.

Rather than face a court appearance (which may well be viewed as inconvenient, disagreeable, and the outcome highly uncertain), the temptation is either to forget the whole thing or simply to pay up whatever sum is claimed. This temptation exists whatever the rights and wrongs of the litigant's case. For many litigants, it is an uphill struggle to set legal processes in motion, and only those who are experienced or determined are likely to overcome the many obstacles that such a course inevitably involves. This applies regardless of the level of the informality of procedures or the amount of money that is at stake. All the available research evidence indicates that it is common for people who are not accustomed to speaking in a public place to anticipate the court appearance with considerable trepidation.[31] Despite the reassuring tone and clarity of the leaflets about small claims procedures that are nowadays put out by the Lord Chancellor's Department, it is apparent that few plaintiffs or defendants have much idea about what lies in store when their cases reach the court. A typically grim appraisal of this prospect was made by a defendant in the writer's research who said that 'the layman is undoubtedly going to feel nervous, whether he has something to fear or not'.

The obvious implication of these observations as far as Lord Woolf's Inquiry is concerned is that, to enhance citizens' access to justice, it is not enough merely to provide improved facilities or to expand the scope of informal procedures or to encourage judges to become pro-active: the greater difficulty is to persuade people, even those involved in serious legal disputes, to make use of the procedures. As already noted, it is unclear in Lord Woolf's report whether the aim is to attract new business to the county courts—in other words, to make a genuine effort to increase access to justice—or whether it is rather to deal with the present volume of cases by procedures that are simpler and more congenial for the participants than those presently in operation.

[31] The experiences of one litigant appearing at a small claims hearing are given in J. Price, 'Small Claims—Major Challenge' *Legal Action* (September 1993 p. 8). She refers to 'a ball and chain of ignorance' that she felt she was dragging.

## CONCLUSION

It has not been the intention in this paper to raise criticisms of Lord Woolf's proposals to expand the jurisdiction of small claims procedures—a move with which the writer is very much in sympathy. Many of the objectives in the Inquiry to facilitate access to justice and to assist litigants in person to present their cases are wholly laudable, yet they may prove elusive. There is always a danger that, in seeking to widen access to the courts, lay litigants may become the victims, not the beneficiaries, of simplified legal procedures. All the evidence shows that the image of the civil courts is off-putting as far as ordinary people are concerned. There is little public knowledge of small claims procedures (or of other alternative methods of resolving disputes), and public attitudes to the courts remain stubbornly antipathetical.

A main problem confronting legal reformers is that, whatever the rhetoric, the civil courts are not commonly viewed as the arena in which rights might be asserted or in which wrongs might be remedied. Indeed, the public perception is frequently the very opposite. 'The courts have to overcome their image as the place where ordinary people are taken, commonly by creditors, rather than as one to which they resort on their own initiative to resolve a dispute' is how the point was made in a report prepared by the Office of Fair Trading.[32] 'Access to Justice' is a powerful and evocative rallying cry, but to large sectors of the populace it still seems to carry little meaning or relevance. Worse, there is a danger that it may become no more than a mere catch-phrase, devoid of substance. In the view of this writer, there is little in Lord Woolf's interim report that will help to overcome this underlying problem.

[32] Office of Fair Trading, *Consumer Redress Mechanisms* (London: Office of Fair Trading, 1991) at p. 46.

# 11

# *Why Public Law is Private Law: An Invitation to Lord Woolf*

CAROL HARLOW*

## 1. WHY THE DIVIDE?

The Civil Justice Review of 1988 made two assumptions about public law proceedings, the first being that public law cases would continue to be dealt with by the High Court, the second that public law (Order 53) procedures fell outside its remit.[1] In arriving at this conclusion—agreed, we are told, 'on consultation', though no further reasons are given—the Review left untouched some very real deficiencies in judicial review procedure. To quote Professor Wade, the defects of Order 53 procedure were (and remain) 'mainly those of an elaborate legal system—procedural complexity, cost and delay of litigation and the strain on limited judicial resources'.[2] Since that date, judicial review procedures have been subjected to a separate review by the Law Commission[3] which did not simply assume that public law proceedings should remain with the High Court but explored alternative options. At the end of the day, however, the decision was made that the status quo should remain. The arrival of the interim Woolf Report[4] allows this fundamental question to be re-opened and Lord Woolf, in a public lecture delivered late last year, has hinted at the possibility of so doing.[5]

It is not my intention to take issue with Lord Woolf's wider proposition that 'the distinction between public and private law issues goes far beyond the correctness of the procedure by which a challenge to an activity should

* Professor of Law, Department of Law, London School of Economics.

I am grateful to Nicholas Bamforth, Lee Bridges, Ross Cranston, Cyril Glasser, Richard Rawlings and Adrian Zuckerman for comments and helpful suggestions.

1 *Civil Justice Review*, Cm 394 (1988), paras 5 (iii), 120 (i) and 2 (i).

2 H. W. R. Wade and Christopher Forsyth, *Administrative Law*, (Oxford: University Press) 7th. edn. 1994, p. v.

3 *Administrative Law: Judicial Review and Statutory Appeals*, Law Com Nos 126 (1993) (consultation paper) and 226 (1994) (final report) (herafter referred to by their numbers).

4 *Access to Justice*, Interim Report to the Lord Chancellor on the civil justice system in England and Wales, June 1995 (hereafter Woolf).

5 Lord Woolf 'Droit Public—English Style' [1995] PL 57, 62.

be brought[6]'. I have already expressed my views on this issue and remain unconverted.[7] Nor is this essay merely an excuse to fight the 'exclusivity' rule, whose utility I am not alone in deploring[8] despite the skilful defence mounted by Lord Woolf. My case is that the Law Commission, which largely addressed itself to procedure, followed the contours of the existing model of judicial review far too closely. Woolf promotes a new approach to the problems besetting civil justice, which forms a new context and comparator for judicial review proceedings. Lord Woolf has greater freedom to manoeuvre than the Law Commission, which saw certain essential matters as outside its remit; for example, the use of Crown List judges, although a matter of concern to the Law Commission, was taken to be an operational question for the Lord Chief Justice to settle.[9] Organisational matters fall clearly within Lord Woolf's remit. I shall argue that judicial review procedure can slot easily into the new proposals for reform of civil procedure, leaving us with a single set of coherent procedures to cover the whole area of civil justice. A two-way learning process in which judicial review proceedings form a useful prototype for accelerated procedure should now begin.

Lord Woolf's objective for good civil procedure is a lofty one, borrowed from the doyen of English civil procedure, Sir Jack Jacob, who says of the civil justice system that it 'responds to the social need to give full and effective value to the substantive rights of members of society which would otherwise be diminished or denuded of worth or even reality'.[10] If this aphorism is true of civil justice generally, how much greater is its applicability to proceedings against or involving the state. Many of Woolf's priorities—for example, the need for speed and fairness, together with a perceived need for effectiveness[11]—echo those of the Law Commission. At the top of its own list of priorities,[12] however, the Law Commission rightly placed 'the importance of vindicating the rule of law, so that public bodies take lawful decisions and are prevented from relying on invalid decisions'. There is nothing here to prevent the arrangements for judicial review from being, in common with civil justice generally, speedy, accessible and user-

[6] Lord Woolf 'Droit Public—English Style' [1995] PL 57, 62.

[7] C. Harlow, ' "Public" and "Private" Law: Definition Without Distinction' (1980) 43 *Modern Law Review* 241 and 'Changing the Mindset: The Place of Theory in English Administrative Law', (1994) 14 OJLS 419.

[8] e.g., John Alder 'Hunting the Chimera—the End of O'Reilly v Mackman' (1989) 13 *Legal Studies* 183; Wade, op. cit., pp. 684-5. And see, JUSTICE/All Souls Review *Administrative Justice—Some Necessary Reforms*, Report of the Committee of the JUSTICE/All Souls Review of Administrative Law in the United Kingdom (Oxford: Clarendon) 1988, p. 166, recommendations 1 and 2.

[9] Talk by Sir Henry Brooke to Sweet and Maxwell conference, 'Judicial Review in Question', December 1993 (hereafter Brooke). I am grateful to Sir Henry for a copy of this unpublished paper.

[10] Woolf, Ch 1, para 1, p.2.

[11] ibid, para 3.

[12] Law Com No 126, para 2.3 (a), p.4.

friendly; indeed, only when citizens can obtain speedy remedies for their grievances will substantive rights receive full and effective value, in itself an important vindication of the rule of law. In moving towards these goals, however, we must not leave out of account the special objectives of public law proceedings. Pragmatic procedural performance indicators must on occasion give way to the need for powerful remedies backed by the authority of a respected and authoritative court. Metaphorically speaking, we do not always want to find mice under the throne.[13]

Assuming then that Lord Woolf incorporates consideration of public law proceedings into the second stage of his review, what should be his approach? I am inviting him to wipe the slate clean and explore the case for broad structural reform. The time has come, I suggest, to take a number of radical suggestions for reform and consider their merits. Lord Woolf will have his own ideas for an agenda. He has been personally active over a long period in promoting reform of judicial review procedure.[14] He participated energetically in the discussions surrounding the Law Commission Consultation Paper[15] and it would be surprising if he were omitted from the 'consultation' list mentioned by the Civil Justive Review. There are many radical ideas on his personal shopping list, including a proposal for a Director of Civil Proceedings, an idea which certainly warrants further consideration. But while I hope that Lord Woolf will take out his shopping list, this essay also contains a warning. Woolf's second stage needs to be firmly under-pinned by empirical research of the kind pioneered by Sunkin and Bridges.[16]

## 2. ENDING EXCLUSIVITY

### (a) Waste

Likening the exclusivity rule to the medieval forms of action, Professor Wade sees it as causing meritorious cases to fail merely because of choice of the wrong form of action. This he rightly adjudges 'a serious setback for administrative law'.[17] It was, incidentally, precisely the problem which the Law Commission believed it had resolved in 1969.[18] Even Lord Woolf, a

[13] The metaphor is borrowed from Allan Hutchinson, 'Mice under a chair: Democracy, courts and the administrative state' 40 Univ of Toronto LJ 374 (1990).

[14] *Protection of the Public—A New Challenge*, op. cit.

[15] 'Judicial Review: A Possible Programme for Reform', [1992] PL 221.

[16] Maurice Sunkin, 'What is happening to judicial review?' (1987) 50 MLR 432; Maurice Sunkin, Lee Bridges, George Meszaros, *Judicial Review in Perspective, An Investigation of Trends in the Use and Operation of the Judicial Review procedure in England and Wales*, Public Law Project, London, June 1993 (hereafter PLPa). I am grateful to Lee Bridges for allowing me to see the forthcoming revised edition (herafter PLPc).

[17] *Administrative Law*, p. 682.

recent convert to exclusivity,[19] describes the growing list of cases fought solely on jurisdictional points, often as far as the House of Lords, as 'unedifying disputes', advancing the unconvincing defence that 'cases which appear to involve a barren dispute as to procedure can involve a battle over a substantive issue of importance'. Substitution of procedural argument for argument on the merits was another problem the Law Commission hoped to resolve. The 1993 Law Commission Consultation Paper referred to the need to avoid 'further sterile procedural argument in the higher courts'.[20]

Each landmark case on exclusivity is hailed as a final solution, though it would be more honest to admit that the costly litigation will last just as long as the supply of wealthy defendants willing to avail themselves of procedural advantages[21]; thus *Roy v Kensington and Chelsea and Westminster Family Practitioner Committee*, in which the House of Lords authorised a more flexible approach, was nonetheless soon followed by *Mercury v British Telecom*[22]*, again fought to the highest level on a purely procedural point. The pecuniary cost and wasted judge-hours are inestimable, while the fact that so many public law proceedings are ultimately resolved by the unitary appellate jurisdiction, having arrived there by a diversity of routes, cuts the ground from under the exclusivity argument.[23] I am not arguing that the principles applicable in such cases will always be the same as those in which no element of public interest is involved but the removal of the exclusivity rule will, on the one hand, allow more flexibility in applying the substantive rules[24] and, on the other, remove the incentive for this type of 'lawgame'.

### (b) Caseload

A second argument against exclusivity lies in the burgeoning Crown Office list and the consequential backlog. The relative speed of judicial review pro-

[18] See, *Remedies in Administrative Law*, Law Com Working Paper No 40, 1971 and Final Report, Law Com No 73 (1976).

[19] See, 'Public Law—Private Law: Why the Divide? A Personal View [1986] PL 220. But in *Protection of the Public—A New Challenge*, The Hamlyn Lectures (London: Stevens) 1990, pp. 30–31, he describes himself as divided and in a state of confusion over exclusivity. In 'Droit Public—English Style' [1995] *Public Law* 57, 60–62, he expresses himself in favour of the rule, yet at p. 61 uses the phrase cited in the text.

[20] Law Com No 126, para. 3.20.

[21] For the reasons, see R. W. Rawlings, 'The Euro-law Game: Some Deductions from a Saga' (1993) 20 *J. of Law and Society* 309; C. Harlow, *Compensation and Government Torts* (London: Sweet and Maxwell) 1982, pp. 111–3.

[22] Reported respectively at [1992] 1 AC 624 and *The Times* 10 February 1995.

[23] For example, the Asylum Act 1993 in an attempt to curtail the number of immigration cases brought under Order 53, created an appeal from the Immigration Appeals Tribunal directly to the Court of Appeal. On an unsuccessful attempt to standardise the confusing appellate machinery, see Law Com Nos 126 and 226.

[24] For a fuller discussion, see Martin Loughlin, 'Courts and Governance' in P. B. H. Birks (ed.), *The Frontiers of Liability*, vol. 1, (Oxford University Press) 1994.

ceedings, a factor in the perceived effectiveness of the remedies obtainable, has always been a matter of justifiable pride for English lawyers. Delay impedes the administrative process, undercuts the mandatory character of relief, and may necessitate applications for interim relief or even compensation.[25] At the date of the Law Commission Consultation Paper, there was apparently 'very great public concern' about delays.[26] The Public Law Project had shown considerable slippage in the time taken to get 'leave to apply' (the first stage of all judicial review applications[27]) between 1987 and 1991.[28] This finding was influential in persuading the Law Commission that 'leave' should normally be by paper application. In the same period, the total time between first lodging of an application and final determination had slipped still further.[29] Without awaiting the final report, the judiciary took immediate action. Better deployment of the available judiciary, a measure of delegation (for example, deputy judges now hear housing cases) and an increase in the number of judges assigned to the Crown Office list, helped to bring delays under control: waiting time in the Divisional Court has been reduced from 10.2 to 7.3 months and before a single judge from 21.3 to 12 months.[30] It is noteworthy that the report on steps taken bears the stamp of the interim Woolf proposals, redolent of the terminology of caseload management, targets and performance indicators. But we need to take care before accepting the common assumption that delays are necessarily litigant-induced and spring from bad case-management by the parties.[31] An equally plausible suggestion is that delay represents time taken by the parties in trying to negotiate settlements. The truth is that reasons for delay have never been fully explored by a consumer survey.

Whatever the reasons for delay, savings are unlikely to be achieved in the long-term through a down-turn in applications. The caseload continues to rise; from 2129 in 1990 to 2886 in 1993.[32] Lord Woolf has himself used the analogy of a motorway whose tailback had become more and more

[25] *Kirklees BC v Wickes Building Supplies* [1990] 1 WLR 1237 is suggestive.

[26] Law Com No 226, p. 163.

[27] See, Grahame Aldous and John Alder, *Applications for Judicial Review, Law and Practice of the Crown Office* (London: Butterworths) 2nd edn 1993, pp. 139–150. The Law Commission (No 226, para 5.8) recommends that the term 'preliminary consideration' be substituted for 'leave', retained here as more convenient.

[28] In 1991 only 21.2% of table applications took more than 30 days, although 42.8% of oral applications took longer; in 1987, 66.75% of the 386 oral applications had been completed in under 20 days: PLPa Table 4.4.

[29] In 1987, when a sharp increase in applications was recorded, 20.7% were complete in under 90 days while 30% took more than 360 days, of which 9% took over 540 days. In 1991, 18.9% were complete in 90 days while 60% remained incomplete after 360 days of which 50% had exceeded 540 days: PLPa Table 4.4 and pp. 57–9.

[30] Law Com No 226, Appendix C, pp. 163–173, where the statistics and steps taken to reduce delay are fully recorded.

[31] B. C. Cairns, 'Managing Civil Litigation: An Australian Adaption of American Experience' (1994) ? *Civil Justice Quarterly* 50.

[32] Law Com No 226, p. 166.

disturbing;[33] between 1981 and 1992, applications increased fourfold from 558 to 2439, a figure which continues to rise. The final total for 1994 is 3208. Perhaps the most disturbing feature of the rising caseload is that it replicates an international trend. In neighbouring France, exponential growth has necessitated a total restructuring of the administrative law system, with the introduction in 1987 of a new tier of appellate tribunals to relieve pressure on the Council of State.[34] A similar growth pattern can be observed at the European Court of Justice, where applications rose from 314 in 1988 to 486 in 1993 and 341 in 1994 despite the creation of a Court of First Instance to relieve pressure on the ECJ, whose own caseload continued to rise from 169 in 1989, the first year of operation, to 397 in 1994. An average of 613 cases is pending before the Court of Justice,[35] leading to the prediction that the Court, which already sits in Chambers, may need to be more selective.[36] Similarly, the number of applications referred to the European Court of Human Rights has leaped from 16 in 1983 to 93 in 1991, despite the stringent filter of the Commission, itself overwhelmed by a growing backlog (a jump of 2,332 in 1991 to 2,465 a year later) which has necessitated a total overhaul of the adjudicative machinery.[37] The lesson is very clear: courts in western society must anticipate the continuation of heavy caseloads. They must introduce appropriate procedures while there is still time.[38]

### (c) Access

Yet viewed as a system of rights and remedies, English judicial review remains relatively inaccessible, with a narrow outreach. The reasons include access to legal advice, cost and legal aid. Some findings from the Public

[33] [1992] *Public Law* 221.

[34] The caseload of the Conseil d'Etat diminished from 10,927 registrations in 1993 to 9,197 in 1994 and this has been accompanied by an increase in the clear up rate from 10,698 to 12,844 per annum, causing a reduction in backlog from 23,456 to 19,693 cases. The improvement is partly due to an internal reform of working methods but largely to the increased load of the Cours administratives d'appel whose caseload grew from of 4,271 in 1990 to 9,435 in 1994, with a rise in backlog from 7,242 to 10,963. In the same period the total of complaints registered in first instance administrative tribunals rose from 6,9853 to 9,4744 (gross figures), showing a small but steady annual rise. See, Etudes et Documents No 46, Rapport public du Conseil d'Etat, 1994 (Paris: La Documentation francaise) 1995.

[35] See (1993) 18 *European Law Review* 177. The figures used are averaged over the years 1988–1992.

[36] Tom Kennedy, 'First steps towards a European certiorari?' (1992) 18 *European Law Review* 121.

[37] See further, *Survey of Activities and Statistics* (Strasbourg: European Commission on Human Rights) annually; Alistair Mowbray [1991] *Public Law* 353 and [1993] *Public Law* 419.

[38] This is the theme of M. Galanter, 'Law Abounding: Legalisation around the North Atlantic' (1996) 55 *Modern Law Review* 1. See also, Jean-Paul Jacque and Joseph Weiler, 'On the Road to European Union—A New Judicial Architecture. An Agenda for the Intergovernmental Conference', (1990) 27 *Common Market Law Review* 185.

Law Project survey are suggestive. Applications both for judicial review and for legal aid are geographically distributed disproportionately, clustered around London, with Wales, the North and East Anglia particularly poorly represented.[39] This necessarily raises the question whether centralisation is limiting access. Again, the uncertain operation of the legal aid rules turn access to judicial review into 'a lottery'.[40] Law centres and CABx use judicial review rarely, handling a mere 6–7.5% of represented cases in the PLP sample.[41] This must make access highly problematic for the most disadvantaged sectors of the community. A limited in-depth study of housing cases by Forbes and Wright[42] showed that many potential judicial review cases are never recognised. It would seem probable that these groups lack information about judical review procedures, which remain technical and inaccessible. In many parts of the country, the same ignorance seems to afflict private practitioners. Should we deduce that someone living in mid-Wales has a small chance that his potential judicial review application will be recognised? Or do groups form part of a network, centred in London on specialist solicitors like Winstanley Burgess? The plain truth is that we do not know how to interpret these scraps of information.

### (d) Centralisation

The Law Commission Consultation Paper devoted 10 pages to consideration of the exclusivity principle, setting out 3 options for reform.[43] Studiously neutral, the Paper merely noted 'continuing doubts as to whether the principle of exclusivity is the correct one to protect . . . issues of public policy'.[44] No trace of doubt is allowed to remain in the Final Report, where the Law Commission complacently declares itself satisfied with the existing position,[45] with a passing mention of 'strong support' for a centralised, High Court jurisdiction and 'strong feelings' in favour of hearing applications against the Crown in London.[46] Yet for those prepared to read between the lines, the Commission records that the unavailability of judicial review outside London was 'one of two main themes

[39] PLPa, p. 21 and Table 2.2 shows that 55.4% of applications originated in London, 1.6% from Yorkshire, 1.4% from the North East and 2% from Wales. PLPc (forthcoming), Chapter 4, shows a comparable picture for legal aid.

[40] PLPc, Ch 4.

[41] PLPa p. 38 and Table 3.4.

[42] D. Forbes and S. Wright, *Housing Cases in Nine CABx*, cited PLPi p. 15. Their point receives some support from Ian Loveland's study of homelessness decisions, *Housing Homeless Persons, Administrative Law and Process* (Oxford: Clarendon Press) 1995, pp. 319–20, where he points to the need for access to independent advice.

[43] Law Com. No. 126, para. 3.19.

[44] Law Com No 126, para. 3.20.

[45] para. 3.15.

[46] At present, it is always open to the Crown to select a London venue for trial, a position which requires legislative change: see, sections 19, 20(2) Crown Proceedings Act, 1947 and RSC, Order 77, r.2. See also *Civil Justice Review*, Cm. 394 (1988), paras. 120, 124.

which cropped up again and again'. It was heavily criticised by users, especially local authorities situated more than 75 miles from London. And although centralisation in London was favoured (as one might expect) by practitioners and government departments, 27 of 36 respondents supported some degree of decentralisation.[47] Was this difference because, on this important aspect of access, nobody troubled to consult the consumers?

## 3. TWO FLEXIBLE FRIENDS

To create a more effective and integrated system of administrative justice, two procedural changes are necessary. Their introduction would allow the problems of outreach to be addressed while retaining the advantages of a powerful administrative division.

### 1. Transfers

RSC Order 53 r 9 (5) provides that the court may, where the remedy sought is a declaration, injunction or damages, allow an application for judicial review to proceed as though begun by writ. It has long been accepted that this power is both one-sided and too narrow.[48] The Law Commission has already recommended amendment to allow transfer into, as well as out of, Order 53.[49] In practice, there is already flexibility. Indeed, proponents of exclusivity are apt to overlook the number of 'public law' issues decided by the Chancery Division.[50] A rational case can be made too for transferring some tax cases (including appeals) direct to the Chancery Division.[51] This might might be of additional benefit in the light of Woolf's finding that 'the sense of team spirit among the Chancery judges and their relationship with the Chancery Bar results in a more effective and efficient disposal of work'.[52] Similar considerations apply to family matters (1–2% of the caseload), given the rising number of cases querying the use of local authority powers already familiar in the lists of the Family Division.[53] Cases involv-

[47] Law Com No. 226, App C, paras 1.2 and 4.1–6.3, particularly 4.2. Local authorities also pointed to 'the public perception of the authority of the High Court, as opposed to the local county court, over the decisions of local authorities' (App. C, para. 6.1).

[48] For the manner in which it operates, see, Aldous and Alder, p. 158.

[49] Law Com No 226, para 3.21 and Draft Order 53, rule 11(2)(3).

[50] Notably, in recent years, the 'Spycatcher' litigation and other cases concerning confidential information in the possession of public bodies. See, e.g., *Attorney General v Guardian Newspapers and others* [1987] 1 WLR 1248 (Sir Nicholas Browne-Wilkinson VC) and *Attorney General v Guardian Newspapers and others (No 2)* [1988] 2 WLR 805.

[51] Unpublished submission of Mr. A. Moses QC at seminar of 12 May 1994, Institute of Advanced Legal Studies.

[52] Section III, p. 27.

[53] See, e.g, *R v Birmingham Juvenile Court ex p G (Minors)* [1988] 1 WLR 950 (Sir Stephen Brown); *R v North Yorkshire CC ex p M* [1989] QB 411, *R v Wandsworth LBC ex p P* (1988)

ing the Child Support Agency have also been listed in the Family Division. Both allocations are justified by the need to ensure the paramountcy of the overriding principle of 'the welfare of the child' in all family cases.

Reform here would permit cases which raise points of law of constitutional or general importance or are otherwise controversial to be sent for hearing by a nominated judge. There are strong arguments also for High Court jurisdiction in cases of urgency and in applications for mandatory remedies against the Crown. But it should not be hard to persuade Lord Woolf, a keen advocate of collaboration with Ombudsmen,[54] that transfer between the High Court and local courts is also necessary. Once we abandon the assumption that every application for judicial review is 'special' in the sense of containing difficult points of law, cases which seem to possess no particularly difficult features can be allocated to the fast track and remitted to local courts. Indeed, such a development may already be anticipated in Woolf's comment that 'many cases suitable for the fast track may not be financially quantifiable'.[55] Judicial review would then be both a specialist list[56] and a branch of the multi-track.[57]

A prime example is that of the housing and homelessness cases aimed at local government, which head the list of judicial review and legal aid applications.[58] Before 1983, some of these cases found their way to county courts as damages claims; after the ultimatum in *Cocks v Thanet* this ceased to be possible.[59] Partly in consequence, partly no doubt through the absence of a proper appeal system, the number of applications multiplied. This provoked a second ultimatum from the House of Lords,[60] persuaded that the 'prolific use of judicial review to contest homelessness decisions' needed to be stemmed. A more stringent test of justiciablity brought an immediate reduction, halving the homelessness caseload in the next year; significantly, however, the drop was temporary and numbers rose steadily thereafter.[61]

87 LGR 370 (Ewbank J). 'Right to life' cases are also public law cases heard by the Family Division: see, e.g., *In Re T (Adult Refusal of Treatment)* [1993] Fam 95.

54 *Protection of the Public,* pp. 87–91; Woolf, Section IV, paras 18–20.

55 Woolf, Section II, para. 6.

56 Woolf, Section III, para 25.

57 Section II, Ch 8.

58 Immigration and housing accounted for approximately 40% of all reviews between 1987 and 1991. Housing cases rose from 141 (9.3%) in 1987 to 108 (23.8%) in the first quarter of 1991: PLPa Table 1.1. Between 1987 and 1991, homelessness accounted for between 50% and 75% of the housing cases: PLPi Table 1.1. and Table 1.5. 62.5% of legal aid applications were aimed at local authorities in the last quarter of 1991, a total of 553 cases made up of 300 homelessness and 155 housing cases: PLPc Table 4.2.

59 *Thornton v Kirklees Metropolitan Borough Council* [1979] QB 626, which permitted an action for damages, was reversed by *Cocks v Thanet DC* [1983] 2 AC 286. On the continuing complexities of the boundary in this area, see *R v Northavon Council ex p Palmer* (CA, 13 July 1995, unreported; Roger Toulson QC (1994) 26 HLR 572).

60 *R v Hillingdon BC ex p Puhlhofer* [1986] AC 484.

61 See, Maurice Sunkin, 'Trends in the Use of Judicial Review Before and After Swati and Puhlhofer' (1987) 137 *New Law Journal* 731. The caseload fell from 66 in 1985 to 32 in 1986, rising again to 84 in 1987; 105 in 1988, 176 in 1989.

When we remember that the quantity of housing cases involving similar issues, such as repossession, rent arrears or repairs,[62] which fall to be decided by county courts, the case for the multi-track approach in this area is irrefutable. Indeed, many would argue that this does not go far enough; it is the case for a special Housing Court or tribunal which is irrefutable.

A more flexible procedure suggested by Sir William Wade[63] to make the prerogative orders available in writ actions was rejected by the Law Commission but could be reconsidered. And why should written, 'Divisional Court' procedures not be available, at least where no serious dispute of fact arises and by agreement with the parties, in other courts?

### 2. Reference Procedure

After the decision in *Wandsworth LBC v Winder*,[64] difficult points of public law, including the validity of secondary legislation or complex claims to public interest immunity, may in practice crop up before County Courts, Crown Courts and Magistrates' Courts. One way to resolve this problem would be to allow difficult points of law to be argued before the High Court before transfer to a county court. This would depend on their being identified by a judge at an early stage in the proceedings, however. A more flexible alternative is to put a reference procedure at the disposal of the High Court. The rejection of this idea by the Law Commission on the unproven grounds that it would result in 'a multiplicity of proceedings, increased cost and further delay',[65] should be re-considered. There is no concrete evidence that this will be so, indeed rather the contrary.[66] The French Conseil d'Etat has been given a new power of reference[67] which it uses in a handful of cases annually. Reference procedure is typically less time-consuming than a full hearing.[68]

Reference procedure serves several functions. It can be used like a 'case stated' during the course of a trial to settle a point of law on which an authoritative ruling is desirable.[69] The choice is left to the tribunal—I will

[62] e.g, *Smith v Cardiff Corporation* [1954] 1 QB 210 *Wandsworth LBC v Winder* [1984] 3 WLR 1254. And see, C. Harlow and R. Rawlings, *Pressure Through Law* (London: Routledge) 1992, pp. 137–141.

[63] 'Procedure and Prerogative in Public Law' (1985) 101 LQR 180.

[64] [1985] AC 461.

[65] Law Com No 226, para 3.22.

[66] Stephen Shute, 'Prosecution Appeals Against Sentence: The First Five Years' (1994) 57 *Modern Law Review* 745 shows that 140 references were made by the Attorney-General in the first five years: see, Table I.

[67] Art 12 of the Law of 31 December 1987. On the origins, see Bernard Pacteau, 'La longue marche de la nouvelle reforme du contentieux administratif' (1988) 4 *Rev. fr. Droit adm.* 168, 178.

[68] e.g., preliminary references under Article 177 EEC to the ECJ take an average of 17.8 months compared to 24.3 months for direct actions. The increasing number of these references is one factor adding to delay in domestic cases.

[69] See, eg, *Foster v Chief Adjudication Officer* [1993] 2 WLR 292 (validity of delegated legislation).

not diverge to consider from which tribunals reference would be possible—which can either resolve the point subject to appeal or refer it immediately to the High Court for a ruling.[70] It could also be used as a civil law equivalent of Attorney-General's reference procedure, introduced by s 36 of the Criminal Justice Act 1988 as a method of appealing against sentence, to settle points of law which arise in a number of courts simultaneously and which are in danger of being decided differently.[71] It might also serve as the basis for a formal procedure for advisory opinions, a development advocated both by Lord Woolf and Sir John Laws but insufficiently scrutinised by the Law Commission.[72]

For reference procedure to work, every aspect of the reference, including the question whether to refer to the High Court or, in appropriate cases, to the European Court of Justice, must rest entirely within the judge's discretion and be non-appealable, subject only to suggestions from the parties. It should not, of course, be wholly discretionary; the parameters for reference could be laid down in a Practice Statement by the High Court itself or, as Emery has suggested,[73] the last word could be left with the High Court on a paper application for leave to refer.

## 4. LEAVE

### Stage 1: Preliminary Consideration

Concluding their 1992 study of leave proceedings, Sunkin and LeSueur predicted not only that the leave requirement would remain a feature of public law procedure for the foreseeable future but also that it might become a feature of other proceedings.[74] This prophesy seems likely to be fulfilled. They also showed that the leave requirement at present serves inconsistent objectives, interpreted by different judges along a spectrum ranging from

[70] Carl Emery, 'Collateral Attack—Attacking *Ultra Vires* Action Indirectly in Courts and Tribunals' (1993) 56 *Modern Law Review* 643, 667–8.

[71] For the so-called 'vires' defence, see, *R v Reading Crown ex p Hutchinson* [1988] QB 384, *R v Oxford Crown Court ex p Smith* [1988] QB 384, *DPP v Hutchinson and Smith* [1990] 2 AC 783; and see, Carl Emery, 'The Vires Defence—"Ultra Vires" as a Defence to Criminal or Civil Proceedings' (1992) 51 Cam LJ 308, especially 344–8. For the so-called 'Euro-defence', see, the 'Sunday Trading' cases, C145/88 *Torfaen v B and Q* [1990] 1 CMLR 337, *Kirklees BC v Wickes Building Supplies* [1990] 1 WLR 1237, [1990] 2 CMLR 501; and see, R. Rawlings, 'The Euro-law Game' (above).

[72] *Protection of the Public*, pp. 47, 109–113; Sir John Laws, 'Judicial Remedies and the Constitution' (1994) 57 *Modern Law Review* 213, 214-9; Law Com No 226, paras 8.9–8.14.

[73] Carl Emery, 'Judicial review and statutory appeals—options for reform' [1993] *Public Law* 262, 265, where he argues also that a well-designed procedure would help solve the case-load crisis.

[74] 'Applications for Judicial Review: The Requirement of Leave' [1993] PL 102, 127.

Lord Diplock's 'quick perusal'[75] to the so-called 'hard look' test.[76] The Public Law Project confirmed its use as 'a means of limiting caseload pressures on the system'[77] and called for greater transparency, while the Law Commission described the procedure as a 'filter' and advised modifying Rule 3 (5) to provide that leave would only be granted where the application disclosed 'a serious issue'. This test was later criticised for 'ratcheting up' the leave requirement to the 'very hard look' of *Puhlhofer*,[78] a move which Gordon attributes to 'a case load management philosophy'.[79] If leave is indeed to be used as part of a coherent case load management strategy, then this should be openly stated, either in a re-drafted Order 53 or—perhaps more acceptable to the nominated judges—through a Practice Direction.

Woolf creates space, however, for a more radical restructuring. Leave should probably become the point when essential procedural choices are made to shape the progress of a judicial review. Standard form pre-litigation questionnaires would be introduced,[80] requiring the applicant to state: whether alternative recourse existed and, if so, why judicial review was more appropriate; whether an ouster clause governed the application; whether the time limit had been exceeded and, if so, why; whether the applicant was personally and directly aggrieved or sought to bring himself within the criteria of a public interest applicant. As Bridges has suggested, standard form questionnaires should be issued to the respondent, as they are in discrimination cases, inviting a short statement of the defence and setting a (short) time limit within which to respond to these preliminary issues.[81] The existence of the application would then be published in an official Crown Office list with a brief outline of the subject-matter to protect the rights of third parties (discussed below).

### *(a) Standing*

The first matter to be resolved at the leave stage[82] should be that of standing. An important objective for the present judiciary has been to produce a 'public interest' model of judicial review, flexible enough to allow important points of law to be tested before a court even where no individual is sufficntly affected.[83] This has led to a gradual relaxation of standing rules

[75] *R v Inland Revenue Commissioners ex p National Federation of Self-Employed and Small Businesses Ltd* [1982] AC 617, 644.

[76] PLPa, Ch 6 and Table 6.3. And see, *R v Home Secretary ex p Doorga* [1990] Crown Office Digest 109.

[77] PLPa p. 95.

[78] Above, note 60.

[79] See, Richard Gordon QC, 'The Law Commission and Judicial Review: Managing the tensions between case management and public interest challenges' [1995] PL 11, 14.

[80] See, PLPb, paras 6.14–6.21.

[81] PLPb, paras 6.1–6.21.

[82] See, PLPb, para. 7.11.

[83] As in *R v Secretary of State for the Environment ex p Rose Theatre Trust Co* [1990] 2 WLR 186.

to the benefit of public interest groups,[84] a development approved by the Law Commission, which recommended a two-track system of standing. While individual applicants would continue to show that they 'have been personally adversely affected by the decision which is the subject of the complaint',[85] s 31(4)(b) of the Supreme Court Act 1981 would be amended to allow an application to go forward where 'the High Court considers that it is in the public interest for the applicant to make the application'. The court would possess a 'broad discretion', subject only to considerations listed by the Law Commision.[86] These include (i) the importance of the legal point, (ii) the chances of the issue being raised in any other proceedings and (iii) concern that the courts should have the benefit of 'the conflicting points of view of those most directly affected'. These considerations are perfectly proper, if inadequate, as guidance; however, the Law Commission listed amongst relevant criteria, 'the allocation of scarce judicial resources'. This is surely an indicator of too great a preoccupation with case load management?

It is suggested that Guidelines which draw on the present caselaw relating to public interest standing should be published, probably as a Practice Direction. These might entail showing (1) that the applicant is a group which acts at the request of a person or class of persons who would have standing to apply for judicial review or of persons who might otherwise not be able to apply for judicial review (a formulation covering the *CPAG* cases); or (2) that it represents the views (though not the legal interests) of its members (the *Federation* test); or (3) that the applicant is a statutory body and the subject matter falls within its statutory remit (the *EOC* test); or (4) that the matter is one of public interest and properly the subject of an application for judicial review and that the group possesses expertise in the subject-matter of the application (the *Greenpeace* test). In addition, the applicant should show that the application is one in which there is a good chance of success (the hard look test) and either that the statutory time limit has been complied with or that there are good reasons why this is not the case.

### *(b) Timeliness*

The second point to be resolved is the question of limitation, considered a primary reason for retention of the exclusivity rule. Considerable unfairness is in practice caused by the interaction of Ord 53 r 4 as amended in 1980 to require promptness by the applicant *within* an overall time limit of three

[84] *R v Inland Revenue Commissioners ex p Federation of Self-Employed and Small Businesses* [1982] AC 617; *R v Foreign and Commonwealth Secretary ex p World Development Movement* [1995] 1 All ER 611; *R v Employment Secretary ex p EOC* [1994] 2 WLR 409; *R v Social Services Secretary ex p CPAG* [1990] 1 QB 540; *R v Inspectorate of Pollution ex p Greenpeace (No 2)* [1994] 4 All ER 329. And see, P. Cane, 'Standing up for the Public' [1995] PL 270.

[85] Law Com No 226, para 5.20.

[86] Law Com No 226, para. 5.22.

months, and s 31(6) Supreme Court Act 1981, which grants a general discretion to refuse relief where it would be 'detrimental to good administration' so to do.[87] Time limits are justifiable in terms of the principle of administrative speed and certainty prioritised by the Law Commission,[88] although the present time limit may be too short, as administrative errors do not always come to light immediately. Discretion *within* a statutory time limit must always be unacceptable, though some flexibility with remedies may be appropriate.[89] Gordon has also argued[90] that disciplinary time limits are inappropriate for public interest challenges. The Law Commission in 1973 thought that relief should never be refused solely on grounds of delay, preferring flexibility[91] and certainly a number of jurisdictions manage successfully without fixed time limits.[92] Arguably there are more appropriate ways to deal with untimeliness, including refusal of legal aid, described by the Public Law Project 'as an early filter of unmeritorious cases',[93] discretion with respect to remedies, or an appropriate costs order. And even if promptness *outside* the limitation period is the only thing left to discretion, it should be structured. Guidelines are once again necessary in the interests of transparency and consistency.

### Stage 2: Directions

At a resumed leave application, final decisions would be made on these preliminary matters and directions given on the further matters of discovery, exchange of affidavits and evidence.

#### *(a) Discovery*

Despite the fact that only one-third of respondents to the Law Commission saw the present regime as satisfactory,[94] the Law Commission recom-

[87] For the history, see, Aldous and Alder, pp. 133–8; *R v Dairy Produce Quotas Tribunal ex p Caswell* [1989] 1 WLR 1089; *R v Stratford-on-Avon DC ex p Jackson* [1985] 3 All ER 769. *R v ITC ex p TV NI, The Times*, 30 December 1991 and *R v Swale Council ex p RSPB* [1991] JPL 39 are particularly hard decisions.

[88] Law Com No 126, para 2.3(b).

[89] See, Sir Thomas Bingham, 'Should Public Law Remedies be Discretionary?' [1991] PL 64. But see A. Lindsay, 'Delay in Judicial Review Cases: A Conundrum Solved?' [1995] PL 417.

[90] [1995] PL at 16.

[91] JUSTICE/All Souls, para 6.29.

[92] See Law Com No 126, paras 4.16–4.22, which show that Scotland, much of Canada, New Zealand and some Australian states rely largely on judicial discretion to strike out stale actions. See also *Administrative Justice—Some Necessary Reforms*, Report of the Committee of the JUSTICE/All Souls Review of Administrative Law in the United Kingdom (Oxford: Clarendon) 1988 pp. 165–7, where the English time limit is criticised as too short.

[93] PLPc, Ch 4, discussing the interlock between the 'actual arguablity' test of legal aid established by *R v Legal Aid Board ex p Hughes* (1992) 142 *New Law Journal* 1304, and the criteria for leave in judicial review set out in *ex p Boorga* (above).

[94] Law Com No 226, para 7.8.

mended no change. It is worth repeating the arguments for a more expansive regime. Zuckerman has likened[95] procedural questions to a balance, in which speed and cost may have to be weighed against accuracy and the quality of justice. He has argued too in favour of rationing procedure rather than access to justice.[96] But he has also issued a powerful warning of the peculiar dangers for public law inherent in such an approach. Stressing the public interest dimension in 'the disclosure of the *whole* truth' (emphasis mine), he goes on to query both the desirability of 'judicial assumption of responsibility for the public interest' and whether this trust has been wisely exercised. Under the rubric of full disclosure and public interest, he argues, the judges have condoned official secrecy and the suppression of evidence which was by any standard both relevant and important to the determination of the truth.[97] In similar vein, Gordon accuses 'a succession of bemused judges' of adopting the 'Catch 22' position that 'if a decision was *Wednesbury* irrational no discovery was necessary, and that if it was not self-evidently irrational discovery must be irrelevant'.[98] To sum up, discovery in public law cases goes some way towards rectifying the absence of freedom of information legislation and acts as a balance against obsessive official secrecy[99] and special criteria therefore apply. It is essential to bear this in mind when the generally restrictive Woolf proposals on discovery come to be implemented.[100]

### *(b) Intervention*

Finally, Woolf provides an occasion to make appropriate provision for interventions, a popular and inexpensive way for courts (in the Law Commission's phrase) to 'have the benefit of 'the conflicting points of view of those most directly affected' or, indeed, of the public more generally. This gap in judicial review procedure was left untouched by the Law

[95] A. A. S. Zuckerman, 'Quality and Economy in Civil Procedure—The Case for Commuting Correct Judgements for Timely Judgements' (1994) 14 *Oxford Journal of Legal Studies* 354.

[96] 'A Reform of Civil Procedure—Rationing Procedure rather than Access to Justice' (1995) 22 *J. of Law and Society* 155.

[97] A. A. S. Zuckerman, 'Public Interest Immunity—A Matter of Prime Judicial Responsibility' (1994) 57 *Modern Law Review* 703, 704–5. See also, *Makanjuola v Commissioner of Police for the Metropolis* [1992] 3 All ER 617. The issues are well discussed in G. Ganz, '*Matrix Churchill* and Public Interest Immunity' (1993) 56 *Modern Law Review* 630; Adam Tomkins, 'Public Interest Immunity after Matrix Churchill' [1993] PL 650.

[98] [1995] *Public Law* at 18, citing *R v Environment Secretary ex p Doncaster BC* [1990] COD 441.C. Harlow, and R. W. Rawlings, *Pressure Through Law*, op. cit., pp. 172–5.

[99] C. Harlow, 'Public Interest Litigation: the State of the Art' in J. Cooper and R. Dhavan (eds) *Public Interest Law* (Oxford: Basil Blackwell) 1986; Gordon [1995] PL at 16. The Public Law Project (PLPc) cites *R v Norfolk CC ex p M* [1989] QB 619 as a case in which critical information was unavailable to the applicant before the substantive hearing. See also S. Grosz 'Pergau be damned' (1994) 144 NLJ 1708, discussing *R* v. *Secretary of State for Foreign Affairs ex The World Development Movement* [1995] 1 WLR 386.

[100] Woolf, section V, Ch 21.

Commission. Ord 53 r 9 (1) permits the court to hear a non-party, but only in opposition to the application, a provision buttressed by r 5(3), which requires the application to be served on all persons directly affected; curiously, there is no provision to hear third parties who wish to be heard *in support of* the plaintiff. Furthermore—a sharp contrast with North American procedure, where amicus intervention by public interest groups is commonplace[101]—there is no provision in Order 53 for a third party wishing to intervene in proceedings on 'public interest' grounds to be heard by the court, the tacit assumption being that this function can be assumed by an official *amicus curiae*, an appointment lying wholly within the court's discretion. Yet requests to be heard in the role of amicus are becoming commoner and, although so far official or quasi-official bodies are favoured,[102] the fortifications were recently breached in the *Phoenix Aviation* case,[103] where Compassion in World Farming, a public interest group previously granted standing to sue,[104] was joined under r 9(1) and was heard in support of the respondent airport authority. The position of intervenors needs to be regularised, which requires amendment to the Rules. Guidelines, probably comparable to those already suggested for standing, are also necessary. Timely publication of the application at the first stage of leave would allow interventions to be presented in writing at the second stage of leave. It may be that here, some consideration of the intervenor's capacity to meet costs is relevant. As it is my view, however, that intervention procedure should be largely written and that only exceptionally should intervenors be allowed to make an oral presentation at trial, costs of intervention would be limited.

## 5. AN INVITATION AND A WARNING

At the start of this essay, I extended an invitation to Lord Woolf to take public law proceedings into the second stage of his review and treat its pro-

[101] G. Caldeira and J. Wright 'Organised Interests and Agenda-Setting in the US Supreme Court 82 *American Political Science Review* 1109 (1988) and 'Amici Curiae before the Supreme Court: Who Participates, When and How Much?' 52 *Journal of Politics* 782 (1990) (United States); P. Bryden, 'Public Interest Litigation in the Courts' (1987) 66 *Canadian Bar Review* 490 (Canada); Harlow and Rawlings, *Pressure Through Law*, pp. 90–92.

[102] Most commonly the Attorney General or Official Solicitor. But see, *Shields v E. Coomes (Holdings) Ltd* [1978] 1 WLR 1408 (EOC); *Science Research Council v Nasse, Leyland Cars v Vyas* [1979] 3 WLR 762 (CRE and EOC); *R v Home Secretary ex p Sivakumaran* [1988] AC 958 ( (UN Commissioner for Refugees).

[103] *R v Coventry Airport and City Council ex p Phoenix Aviation* [unreported at time of going to press]. And see, *Phoenix General Insurance Company of Greece v Halvinon Insurance* [1988] QB 216 (insurer). Contrast *Gillick v W Norfolk and Wisbech AHA* [1986] AC 112, where the Children's Legal Centre was refused leave to become a party or to present a written amicus brief.

[104] *R v Ministry of Agriculture and Fisheries ex p Roberts* [1991] 1 CMLR 555.

cedures as capable of incorporation. I have followed his example[105] by sketching only the broad outlines of a joint programme. Many crucial questions remain unasked. There is nothing in this essay about costs, a question of fundamental importance unthinkably brushed aside by the Law Commission.[106] Woolf has costs under review with much needed empirical studies;[107] it is surely not too late to add data on judicial review proceedings.

There is nothing about legal aid, problematic in that it is based on the model of an individual litigant pursuing a personal interest,[108] unsuitable to judicial review and public interest litigation. These are grave problems which may be reflected in the rising number of litigants in person, a phenomenon which has sounded alarm bells in the Royal Courts of Justice and brought a temporary package of emergency measures from the Judges' Council.[109] Although the Law Commission referred constantly to 'consumers', there were few traces of consumer input into their report;[110] this compares very unfavourably with work in the field of tribunals.[111] A start could at least be made by questioning litigants in person and systematically consulting the Crown Office Users' Association.

Again, we know little about the fashionable notion of negotiation or settlement[112] and whether it is a mark of success or failure. Here again, the public interest element may need special consideration. We have all heard stories of applicants 'bought off' at the door of the court by government departments eager to avoid review; these stories need to be carefully investigated.[113]

[105] Woolf, Introduction.

[106] Law Com 226, paras. 10.2–10.10. The Report recommends formalising the power for the applicant in a public interest challenge to have costs paid from public funds, whether it wins or loses (10.5, 10.6).

[107] Woolf, Annexes 3, 4, 5.

[108] Lee Bridges, 'Judicial review and legal aid' *Legal Action*, November 1994, p. 16 and PLPc (forthcoming).

[109] *New Law Journal*, 14 July 1995, p. 1023. In judicial review, there was a percentage rise from 7.9% to 13.7% between 1987 and 1991: PLPa, Table 3.5. in the court of Appeal, litigants in person have risen from 1 in 10 to 1 in 3 in three years (1989/90 to 1993/4).

[110] Evidence was received from the National Consumer Council, the Law Centres Federation, Public Law Project, the local ombudsman (David Yardley) and one or two firms of legal aid practitioners: Law Com No 226, pp.185–8.

[111] H. Genn and Y. Genn, *The Effectiveness of Representation at Tribunals*, Lord Chancellor's Department (London: HMSO) 1989; J. Baldwin, N. Wikeley and R. Young, *Judging Social Security: The Adjudication of Claims for Benefit in Britain* (Oxford University Press) 1992; Roy Sainsbury, 'Internal Reviews and the Weakening of Social Security Claimants' Rights of Appeal', in G. Richardson and H. Genn, *Administrative Law and Government Action* (Oxford: Clarendon) 1994. For a general survey of the literature, see, R. W. Rawlings, *Grievance Procedure and Administrative Justice, A Review of Socio-Legal Research*, (London: Economic and Social Research Council) 1987.

[112] Though see, H. Genn, 'Tribunals and Informal Justice'(1993) 56 *Modern Law Review* 393 and compare the same author's *Hard Bargaining: Out of Court Settlement in personal Injury Actions* (Oxford: Clarendon) 1987.

[113] A major ESRC research project directed by M. Sunkin and L. Bridges into 'The Dynamics of Public Law Litigation', is likely to provide some of the answers.

For Dennis Galligan,[114] there is a clear relationship between procedures and outcomes. Novelty is not *per se* a ground for procedural reform. In returning judicial review to its right place as part of the 'ordinary' civil law system, we do need to bear its 'special' quality in mind. Given the role of judicial review in vindication of the Rule of Law, we cannot be too careful to get the relationship between procedures and outcomes right.

[114] *Discretionary Powers, A Legal Study of Official Discretion* (Oxford: Clarendon) 1990, p. 336.

# 12

# 'Déjà Vu *All Over Again'?*

## *An American Reaction to the Woolf Report*

RICHARD L. MARCUS*

Lord Woolf's Interim Report is a remarkable accomplishment. Appearing some fifteen months after his appointment, it examines the whole of the English civil justice apparatus and makes a detailed proposal for a 'fundamental shift in the responsibility for the management of civil litigation,'[1] for which the basic tool is to be case management. His proposed revolution in judicial operation would seek to alter the adversary culture of the UK as well. To those ends, the Report proposes what appears to be a quite substantial restructuring of the English court system. Overall it is both highly creative and extremely thought-provoking.

To American eyes, much that is in the Report calls to mind a famous remark attributed to American baseball player Yogi Berra—'*Deja vu* all over again.'[2] Cross-cultural comparisons are often risky, even when they are between two systems with a common origin and tradition,[3] but they can sometimes yield insights of both a descriptive and a prescriptive variety. This paper attempts to provide both. It offers a descriptive comparison showing the many correlations, and some differences, between problems in the UK and in the US. It then chronicles the emergence of case management in the US over the past 30 years and, based on that experience, offers some cautions about Lord Woolf's prescription for the UK, in part stressing the differences between the two legal systems.

* Professor of Law, University of California, Hastings College of the Law.

[1] Report at 18.

[2] See J. Bartlett, *Familiar Quotations*, 16th edn. 1992, 754. Although this is one of Berra's most popular lines, he insisted that he didn't actually say it. See P. Dickson, *Baseball's Greatest Quotations*, 1991, 44.

[3] Lord Woolf recognizes these difficulties. See Report at 136 (cautioning that US experience with ADR might not be replicated in UK).

## A COMPARISON OF THE PROBLEMS

People preoccupied with their own problems often assume those problems are unique. For an American, one striking insight to be gleaned from the Report is the similarity of the problems that receive attention in both countries, although with some notable exceptions. This probably should not be a surprise, given the common origin of our legal systems. But at least in this country it has in recent years become extremely popular to deride our system of civil justice as uniquely debilitated. Moreover, in at least some particulars American lawyers are urged to envy, and perhaps to emulate, the practices of the UK.[4] Hence, to find out that the very same sorts of rhetoric exist on both sides of the Atlantic is important. It is almost refreshing to find somebody else bemoaning a 'Litigation Crisis,'[5] for instance. In addition, it is instructive to find that many of the components of that crisis bear close resemblance to the concerns that many here believe to be uniquely American.

*Litigation cost*: It is frankly astonishing to find that a 'typical' comment received by Lord Woolf from users of the English courts is that the risk and cost of civil litigation are 'higher in the UK . . . than in any other country in which we operate in the world, except, possibly, the State of California.'[6] The example of a company that was thinking of relocating its litigation from London to New York[7] to reduce civil litigation risks and costs would likely astound New Yorkers and many members of the US Congress. In this country we have repeatedly been reminded of a study by the Rand Corporation showing that in American asbestos litigation only about 39% of defense expenditures found their way into plaintiffs' pockets in cases in which plaintiffs obtained a settlement or won a judgment.[8] But the figures for the asbestos cases may be something of an aberration in US litigation.[9]

[4] A notable example is the routine shifting of costs including attorneys' fees in the UK. As demonstrated by Professor Issacharoff's paper in this collection, the English rule is a mixed blessing. Thoughtful Americans appreciate these problems. See *Report of the Federal Courts Study Committee*, 1990, 105 (opposing adoption of 'loser pays' rule in US).

[5] See Report at 5.

[6] *Id.* at 11–12.

[7] *Id.* at 12; 28.

[8] J. Kakalik, P. Ebener, W. Felsteiner, G. Haggstrom & M. Shanley, *Variation in Asbestos Litigation Compensation and Expenses*, 1984, 72–91. These researchers examined a random sample of 513 cases drawn from among some 4,000 closed asbestos cases through the end of 1982 and determined the amounts paid for litigation costs by both defendants and plaintiffs in cases where plaintiffs received a judgment.

[9] Thus, these researchers found that defense litigation expenses were high in asbestos litigation compared to other types of tort litigation, and explained that difference on the ground that typically an asbestos case involves a large cast of defendants which contribute only a small sum toward settlement of the case but still have to foot the cost of defending a case. Defense costs declined as a proportion of defense expenditures as the size of the claim increased. The percentage of defense expenditures actually received by the plaintiff ranged from less than 20% in cases with low compensation to 49% for those with compensation over $500,000. See J. Kakalik, P. Ebener, W. Felsteiner, G. Haggstrom & M. Shanley, *supra* note 8, at 91.

The detailed cost figures in Annex III of the Report suggest (assuming the losing litigant's costs roughly equal the winner's) that this is commonplace in the UK. Indeed, in more than one quarter of the cases profiled in Table 3.5 the costs were more than the claim. Without in any way suggesting that concern about the cost of litigation in the US is unjustified, it is fair to conclude that the Woolf Report shows that it is hardly unique.

*Discovery*: Another common assumption in America is that discovery is uniquely American and that abuse of discovery is of concern only here. We are routinely 'reminded' that no other system in the world permits discovery on the scale authorized in our courts, and that in fact almost all of the rest of the world is so appalled by US discovery that other countries have implemented blocking devices to hamper or prevent discovery there in connection with American litigation.[10] Yet studies of American civil litigation that carefully reviewed case files showed that extensive discovery was a rare thing, and indeed that formal discovery was limited to a minority of cases.[11] The Report reveals that discovery is similarly at the heart of the cost problem in the UK, and for much the same reason. Particularly in large commercial cases, as in the US, it can consume enormous resources.

*Delay*: Besides cost and discovery, the other prime popular criticism of American civil litigation is that it is slow. In 1990, the American Congress enacted the Civil Justice Reform Act principally to pressure the judiciary to remedy problems of cost and delay in federal courts.[12] It had available

In contrast, a study of air crash litigation (in which there are large settlements and fewer defendants) found that 71% of defense payout in those cases was net compensation to plaintiffs. J. Kakalik, E. King, M. Traynor, P. Ebener & L. Picus, *Costs and Compensation Paid in Aviation Accident Litigation*, 1988, 86–96. In "average" tort cases, approximately 50% of defense payouts went to litigation expense. See J. Kakalik & N. Pace, *Costs and Compensation Paid in Tort Litigation*, 1986.

[10] See generally G. Born & D. Westin, *International Civil Litigation in United States Courts*, 2d ed. 1992, 345–50 (contrasting attitude toward party-controlled discovery in the US with much stricter view in most other countries).

[11] A 1978 study by the Federal Judicial Center of over 3,000 civil cases in six federal district courts showed that in 52% of the cases there was no formal discovery at all, and that only 5% of the cases had more than ten discovery requests. P. Connolly, E. Holleman & M. Kuhlman, 1978, *Judicial Control and the Civil Litigation Process: Discovery*. A 1992 study of five state courts by the National Center for State Courts found that formal discovery was conducted relatively infrequently in cases in those courts, but that certain types of cases seemed to generate more discovery. Keilitz, Hanson & Daley, 'Is Civil Discovery Out of Control?' (1993) 17 *St. Ct. J.* 8; Keilitz, Hanson & Semiatin, 'Attorneys' Views of the Civil Discovery Process in the State Trial Courts' (1993) 32 *Judges' J.* 2. See also Weinstein, 'What Discovery Abuse?' (1989) 69 *B.U.L. Rev.* 649, 653–54 (questioning whether there actually is discovery abuse in US courts).

There is competing evidence. A 1988 survey of federal district judges and attorneys who practice in federal court showed widespread belief that abuse of the discovery process was the single greatest contributor to the high cost of litigation. Louis Harris & Assoc., *Procedural Reform of the Civil Justice System*, 1989; see also Brazil, 'Views from the Front Lines: Observations by Chicago Lawyers About the System of Civil Discovery' (1980) 1980 *Amer. Bar Found. Res. J.* 217 (reporting that in at least 50% of more complicated cases one party believes that it has avoiding revealing something important despite discovery).

[12] See 28 U.S.C. § 471 *et seq.*

to it, but did not evidently credit, a detailed examination by the Rand Corporation of case durations in federal courts from 1971 to 1989 showing that the median time from filing to disposition of cases was nine months and had not fluctuated significantly during the period.[13] Notwithstanding, Congress directed the federal courts to undertake an extensive nationwide effort to ensure that trial dates be set within eighteen months of filing.[14] It is therefore quite informative for an American to read that delay ranks as a serious problem in the UK as well, and even more so to learn[15] that most cases take between four and six *years* to settle.

*Excessive adversarialness*: For the last 15 years American litigators have been reminded with increasing frequency that 'Rambo litigation' is on the rise in this country, and that the profession had lost its previous gentility. These discouraging developments in large measure have paralleled the rise of lawyering as a business; as clients became more and more willing to shop for legal talent many of them seemingly opted for lawyers who displayed a killer instinct. Fearful that they might lose out in the battle for clients, other lawyers felt they had to follow suit, and things reached such a pass that local bar associations felt obliged to promulgate guides to manners for lawyers. Perhaps similar economic forces have been at work in the UK, but one suspects that there is still a significant difference of degree between the two countries; the very concept of intentionally spilling coffee on opposing counsel's papers would probably not occur to the English practitioner.

*Experts*: Yet another bane of American civil litigation is the proliferation of expert witnesses. A study of cases tried in the state courts in California in the mid-1980's showed that experts testified in 86% of trials, with an average of 3.8 experts per case.[16] Another found that the number of regularly-testifying experts in the Chicago area increased 1500% from 1974 to 1989.[17] It is therefore interesting to learn from the Report[18] that similar overuse of experts has become a serious problem in the UK. But there is no reference to problems of 'junk science'—claims of personal injury based on 'scientific' theories that purport to connect up a variety of modern cir-

[13] T. Dungworth & N. Pace, *Statistical Overview of Civil Litigation in the Federal Courts*, 1990, 19–20. The mean time was longer, as some cases took a good deal more than the median time. Yet even this was relatively constant at 14 months. *Id.* Fewer than 10% of cases took over three years. *Id.* at 20. These overall figures varied according to case type, however. See *id.* at 21–5.

[14] 28 U.S.C. § 473(a)(2)(B).

[15] Report at 14.

[16] Gross, 'Expert Evidence' (1991) 1991 *Wisconsin L. Rev.* 1113, 1119.

[17] Green, 'Expert Witnesses and Sufficiency of Evidence in Toxic Substances Litigation' (1992) 86 *Nw. L. Rev.* 643, 669.

[18] Report at 181.

[19] For a tirade on this subject, see P. Huber, *Galileo's Revenge: Junk Science in the Courtroom*, 1991. In Daubert v. Merrell Dow Pharmaceuticals, Inc., 113 S.Ct. 2786 (1993), the Supreme Court refined the proper approach courts should use in deciding whether to allow such expert scientific testimony.

cumstances to serious ailments.[19] This is probably due to the absence of product liability claims in the UK. So worse expert witness headaches could exist than the ones that plague the UK.

*Mass torts*: Particularly in the US federal court system, a prime concern over the last decade has been the emergence and growth of 'mass tort' cases such as suits for personal injuries due to asbestos, Dalkon Shield, silicone gel breast implants, etc. In some parts of the country, the abundance of such cases is said to threaten the ability of the civil courts to function at all, and overall they are said to threaten the ability of the courts to cope with other demands. There is no mention of anything remotely similar in the Report, presumably due to the absence of American-style product liability doctrine in the UK.

*Caseload crunch*: The most striking omission from the Report to an American, however, is concern with spiralling case filings. Certainly there have in the past been periods of rapid caseload growth in England,[20] but the Report places no emphasis on present concerns about increased filings of civil cases.[21] That is not surprising since the delay and cost problems would be expected to deter filings.[22] But on the American scene caseload increases tend to be heavily featured in crisis rhetoric about the court system.[23] Although these numbers have been invoked to support a variety of changes in American civil litigation designed to impede the filing of suits, empirical research has deflated many of the claims about the significance of rising caseloads.[24]

[20] See Brooks, 'Litigants and Attorneys in the King's Bench and Common Pleas, 1560–1640' in *Legal Records and the Historian*, J. Baker ed. 1978, at 41 (reporting litigation boom in England in the 16th and 17th centuries).

[21] Indeed, at one point it appears to distinguish the US from the UK on this ground. See Report at 136 (stating that the UK, unlike the US, does not suffer from lack of court resources for civil trials).

[22] As Professor Zuckerman has recently pointed out, the reality seems to be that cost keeps down the number of filings in the UK, but by the somewhat-dubious route of excluding those who lack the wherewithal to support litigation. See Zuckerman, 'A Reform of Civil Procedure—Rationing Procedure Rather than Access to Justice' (1995) 22 *J. Law & Soc'y* 155.

[23] An example is provided by the Report of the President's Council on Competitiveness, issued in 1991, which featured bar graphs showing increases in filings. See *Agenda for Civil Justice Reform in America*, 1991, 4–5. A related point often made in America, but not mentioned in the Report concerning the UK, is that in some quarters the outcomes in decided cases seem to be out of hand. Indeed, the President's Council on Competitiveness, chaired by the Vice President (himself a lawyer) even cited a finance professor's estimate that 'the average lawyer takes $1 million a year from the country's output of goods and services.' *Id.* at 1. These concerns lie behind legislation in the US Congress to curtail product liability litigation and otherwise to alter the legal system. The Report indicates no concern that litigation outcomes (as opposed to expenses) endanger UK business.

[24] For example, see the work of Professor Galanter. E.g., Galanter, 'The Life and Times of the Big Six: or, The Federal Courts Since the Good Old Days' (1988) 1988 *Wis. L. Rev.* 921 (explaining that caseload increase can be connected to explicit governmental policies that fuel increases in filings); Galanter, 'The Day After the Litigation Explosion' (1986) 46 *Md. L. Rev.* 3. For counterarguments, see Marvell, 'Caseload Growth—Past and Future Trends' (1987) 71

*Empirical base*: The caseload growth experience in America suggests a final concern from the American perspective—the empirical basis for the far-reaching prescription in the Report. As the foregoing discussion suggests, in the US the discussion of problems of civil litigation has become extremely politicized. With disturbing frequency, it seems that important policy issues concerning civil litigation are being decided on the basis of the 'cosmic anecdote.' Crisis rhetoric has become prevalent, and has seemingly been invoked to further hidden agendas.[25]

Serious social science work here has combatted that tendency, but the anecdotal approach does not go away. As a consequence, the Report's talk of crisis based on reports from businesses concerning alleged nuisance settlements,[26] and the repeated invocation of the company that supposedly was considering relocating its litigation in New York,[27] raise hackles about whether radical reforms are being based on anecdotes rather than solid empirical work. Without a doubt Annex III contains what appears to be solid data, but it would probably be desirable to obtain or reveal more. For in the American experience, as illustrated by the Rand study that showed no increase in delay in federal courts, hard empirical data may shatter, or at least undermine, broadly shared empirical assumptions.

## THE AMERICAN RESPONSE TO THESE PROBLEMS

It is obvious that American input influenced the Woolf Report. Indeed, it should be apparent to readers of the Report that its central recommendation—inaugurating a system of case management—is essentially based on the experience of the American federal courts.[28] It is therefore useful to elaborate on that experience with a brief canvas of the development of American responses to problems in civil litigation. As this review shows, the current state of case management in the American federal courts is the product of a gradual and protracted evolution, and that period has displayed other features that a cross-cultural borrower should note.

The current epoch in American civil litigation can be traced to the adoption of the Federal Rules of Civil Procedure in 1938. These rules adopted changes in practice and effected changes in attitude and orientation somewhat like the English Judiciary Acts of the late 19th century. At their heart, they sought to diminish the importance of pleading and substitute a fairly

*Judicature* 151 (arguing that Galanter has failed to account for the effect of the overall economy on filing rates, and that increases are indeed growing).

[25] See Marcus, 'Of Babies and Bathwater: The Prospects of Procedural Progress' (1993) 59 *Brooklyn L. Rev.* 761, 762–67 (describing crisis mentality and suggesting that it can invite radical and hasty solutions); Robel, 'The Politics of Crisis in the Federal Courts' (1991) 7 *Ohio St. J. Disp. Res.* 115.

[26] Report at 9.

[27] *Id.* at 12; 28.

[28] See *Id.* at 31.

revolutionary system of pretrial discovery (modeled somewhat on equity) that was largely free of judicial control.[29] There ensued some conflict within the federal judiciary about tightening up pleading requirements, particularly in more complex cases, but by and large the first three decades after adoption of the Federal Rules passed placidly.[30]

The notable exception was a growing uneasiness about protracted cases. By the late 1940's these had emerged as a sufficient concern to prompt the appointment of a high-level commission to investigate improved ways of handling them. Its 1951 report largely focused on refined trial methods, but it also identified the prime problems as delay, over-discovery and expense.[31] It suggested that the solution to these problems in protracted cases would be increased involvement of the judge, especially to stimulate definition of the issues. In 1955, the Chief Justice appointed a special panel of federal judges to study the pretrial organization and trial of complicated cases. After holding seminars on such cases,[32] it issued a booklet entitled the *Handbook of Recommended Procedures for the Trial of Protracted Cases* in 1960.[33]

The problems presented by protracted or complex litigation soon escalated. After successful prosection of manufacturers of electrical equipment for price-fixing, some 2,000 private treble damage antitrust actions, involving over 25,000 claims, were filed in federal courts across the nation. Confronted with unprecedented problems of administering duplicative discovery in those cases, the Chief Justice appointed a special ad hoc committee of judges to oversee their pretrial preparation.[34] The experiment was such a success that in 1968 Congress created a Judicial Panel on Multidistrict Litigation with authority to transfer related cases for combined pretrial preparation under the supervision of a single judge.[35] The Panel, in turn, published a *Manual for Complex Litigation* in 1969.[36] The principal thrust of the *Manual* was to encourage more active pretrial involvement by the trial judge in the development of the case.

29 See Subrin, 'How Equity Conquered Common Law: The Federal Rules of Civil Procedure in Historical Perspective' (1987) 135 *U.Pa. L. Rev.* 909.

30 For chronicles of these developments, see Marcus, 'The Revival of Fact Pleading Under the Federal Rules of Civil Procedure' (1986) 86 *Colum. L. Rev.* 433; Resnik, 'Failing Faith: Adjudicatory Procedure in Decline' (1986) 53 *U. Chi. L. Rev.* 494.

31 'Procedure in Anti-Trust and Other Protracted Cases' (1951) 13 F.R.D. 62.

32 'Proceedings of the Seminar on Protracted Cases, Aug. 26–30, 1957, at N.Y.U. Law School' (1957) 21 F.R.D. 395; 'Proceedings of the Seminar on Protracted Cases, Aug. 25–30, 1958, at Stanford Law School (1958) 23 F.R.D. 319.

33 25 F.R.D. 351.

34 Note, 'The Judicial Panel and the Conduct of Multidistrict Litigation' (1974) 87 *Harv. L. Rev.* 1001, 1001 n.1.

35 28 U.S.C. § 1407.

36 *Manual for Complex Litigation* (1969). This was succeeded by the *Manual for Complex Litigation (Second)* in 1985 and the *Manual for Complex Litigation (Third)* in 1995. Lord Woolf quotes from the *Manual (Third)* on p. 31 of the Report.

The American case management movement originated in this attention to complex litigation.[37] A 1958 judicial seminar on complex cases thus resolved that the judge should 'take actual control of the case and rigorously exercise such control throughout the proceedings.'[38] In the 1970's individual federal judges in large cities such as San Francisco and New York began using these innovative methods of handling complex cases for their ordinary cases as well. These innovations had been spurred in 1969 by the general adoption in metropolitan district courts of the single assignment system.[39] Under this system a case was assigned to a specific judge on filing and remained the responsibility of that judge until it was tried or otherwise resolved. Activist judges began summoning the lawyers to appear before them shortly after the case was filed. At these status or pretrial conferences, the judges would question the lawyers about the needs of their cases and try to provide direction for the pretrial development. They would also stress their insistence on cooperation in pretrial development and seek to curb the actions of unduly combative attorneys. Depending on the complexity of the cases, these judges might schedule repeated status conferences to check up on the evolution of the cases. Thus was born the case management movement among American federal judges.[40] By 1974, a study of six metropolitan districts found that most courts visited were characterized by 'strong case management' in one form or another.[41]

Somewhat as a byproduct of the case management movement, judicial involvement in settlement promotion began to grow.[42] Judges who inquired about the needs of a case also found it desirable to raise the possibility of settlement with the lawyers early. Should there appear to be a reasonable prospect of settlement, they would offer to mediate or to assign the case to another judge for a settlement conference. These sessions would focus on the merits of the cases, but might display a somewhat guarded enthusiasm for merits resolution. Thus, a federal judge describing this process at a sem-

[37] Pretrial conferences to plan the trial—events that occur much later in the case than the case management proposed by the Report—go back to the state courts in the 1920's. See Friesen, 'The Trial Management Conference,' 1990, 29 *Judges' J.* 4, 4; Sunderland, 'The Theory and Practice of Pre-trial Procedure,' 1937, 36 Mich. L. Rev. 215, 225.

[38] 'Resolutions at the Seminar on Protracted Cases' (1958) 23 F.R.D. 319, 614–15; for another such early endorsement, see Ryan, 'Effect of Calendar Control on the Disposition of Litigation' (1960) 28 F.R.D. 66, 67.

[39] Peckham, 'A Judicial Response to the Cost of Litigation: Case Management, Two-Stage Discovery Planning and Alternative Dispute Resolution,' 1985, 37 *Rutgers L. Rev.* 253, 257.

[40] For a description of this activity, see Peckham, 'The Federal Judge as Case Manager: The New Role in Guiding a Case From Filing to Disposition' (1981) 69 *Calif. L. Rev.* 770; see also W. Schwarzer, *Managing Antitrust and Other Complex Litigation: A Handbook for Lawyers and Judges*, 1982.

[41] S. Flanders, *Case Management and Court Management in United States District Courts*, 1977, x.

[42] For a description of the integral role of settlement conferences in case management currently in the US, see In re Novak, 932 F.2d 1397, 1404 (11th Cir. 1991).

inar for newly-appointed judges in 1975 confided that '[o]ptimal justice is usually found somewhere between the polar positions of the litigants. Trial is likely to produce a polar solution, and often the jury or the judge has no choice except all or nothing. Settlement is usually the avenue that allows a more just result.'[43]

Seeking such 'just results,' judges could emphasize litigation cost as a reason for settling. This same judge instructed his newly-appointed colleagues that '[y]ou can usually recognize readily the candidates for settlement. . . . They are the cases in which the amount involved is small in relation to the anticipated costs of litigation.'[44] In some instances, it was thought that judges would also play on uncertainty about the legal merits as levers to encourage settlement.[45] In any event, settlement became a prime objective of case management and some judges seemingly came to regard having to hold a trial as evidence of a failure of case management.[46]

The judges who pioneered case management also proselytized. As the speech quoted above from a seminar for new judges suggests, they tried to persuade their colleagues to follow the path they had blazed. Due in large measure to concern about over-discovery, the makers of the national rules also began to heed their message and to write case management into the rules. In 1980 and 1983 the Federal Rules of Civil Procedure were revised to curtail litigation and encourage judges to intervene sooner and more vigorously. No longer did they invite litigants to use discovery with abandon; instead they directed the judge to curtail discovery that was disproportionate.[47] In addition, they required the judge to hold a conference in every case within 120 days of filing to establish deadlines for completion of various pretrial tasks and otherwise to consider appropriate judicial restrictions on the litigating latitude accorded the parties.[48]

These rule changes coincided with growing enthusiasm for sanctions in American federal courts. Whether this impulse connects with case management is unclear. The 1983 amendment to Rule 11 of the Federal Rules of Civil Procedure—imposing on lawyers an affirmative duty to investigate the

[43] Tone, 'The Role of the Judge in the Settlement Process' in *Seminars for Newly Appointed United States District Judges*, 1975, 57, 60.

[44] Id. at 62.

[45] See Schuck, 'The Role of Judges in Settling Complex Cases: The Agent Orange Example' (1986) 53 *U. Chi. L. Rev.* 337, 358 (describing ways in which judge can play on legal uncertainty to foster settlement); Marcus, 'Apocalypse Now?' (1987) 85 *Mich. L. Rev.* 1267, 1291–95.

[46] See Brunet, 'Questioning the Quality of Alternative Dispute Resolution' (1987) 62 *Tulane L. Rev.* 1, 50 (referring to 'an attitude that a trial represents judicial failure').

[47] These provisions regarding disproportionate discovery are now contained in Fed. R. Civ. P. 26(b)(2). They have been largely ineffective. See 8 C. Wright, A. Miller & R. Marcus, *Federal Practice & Procedure*, 2d ed. 1994, § 2008.1.

[48] Fed. R. Civ. P. 16(b) directed the court, within 120 days of the service of the defendant, to limit the time to join other parties, amend the pleadings, file motions or complete discovery.

basis for their filings in court and requiring the court to impose sanctions on them should they violate the rule—led to a sharp increase in the number of sanctions motions, which became a cottage industry of sorts. Besides poisoning relations among lawyers and providing a further incentive toward extreme adversarial behavior, Rule 11 was said to have given vent to an anti-plaintiff bias among judges, particularly in civil rights cases. Solid empirical evaluation of these claims proved difficult, but eventually showed the actual circumstances to be much less extreme than strident critics claimed.[49] The rules related to case management were also increasingly encrusted with sanctions provisions,[50] but no comparable outburst of sanctioning occurred under these rules.

More subtly over the past 20 years, federal judges' willingness to decide cases short of trial has seemed to be growing. This challenged the popular conception during the first quarter century after adoption of the Federal Rules that neither pleadings motions nor motions for summary judgment stood a significant chance of success, and that if they were granted they would almost certainly be reversed on appeal.[51] Concerned about growth in litigation, some judges began insisting on enhanced fact pleading to survive pleading motions.[52] In 1986, the Supreme Court rejected the perceived

[49] See Burbank, 'The Transformation of American Civil Procedure: The Example of Rule 11' (1989) 137 *U. Pa. L. Rev.* 1925; T. Willging, *The Rule 11 Sanctioning Process*, 1988; Wiggins, Willging & Steinstra, 'The Federal Judicial Center's Study of Rule 11' (Nov. 1991) *FJC Directions* 3.

[50] E.g., Fed. R. Civ. P. 16(f) (failure to participate in pretrial conferences or to obey pretrial orders); 26(g)(3) (signing of discovery requests or responses that are unreasonable, unduly burdensome or expensive, or interposed for an improper purpose); 30(d) (conduct of a deposition so as to harass a party, or conduct to impede a deposition); 37(c)(1) (failure to disclose without formal discovery matters subject to an obligation to disclose).

[51] Regarding summary judgment, it was reported in 1991 that '[s]tatistical analysis indicates that the rate of affirmance of summary judgments is similar to the overall rate of affirmance in civil cases.' W. Schwarzer, A. Hirsch & D. Barrans, *The Analysis and Decision of Summary Judgment Motions*, 1991, 4 n.13; see also Pierce, 'Summary Judgment: A Favored Means of Summarily Resolving Disputes' (1987) 53 *Brooklyn L. Rev.* 279, 281–84 (Second Circuit usually affirms grants of summary judgment). It has even been suggested that the appellate courts' reputed aversion to summary judgment is another 'cosmic anecdote.' Stempel, 'A Distorted Mirror: The Supreme Court's Shimmering View of Summary Judgment, Directed Verdict, and the Adjudication Process' (1988) 49 *Ohio St. L.J.* 95, 160.

Regarding pleadings motions, the conventional wisdom was that they could not succeed under the 'notice' pleading regime of the Federal Rules. Thus, a prominent American professor referred to their poor 'batting average' and opined that they were 'last effectively used during the McKinley Administration' at the turn of the century. A. Miller, *The August 1983 Amendments to the Federal Rules of Civil Procedure*, 1984, 7–8. In some kinds of cases, the courts have seemed more exacting. See Marcus, *supra* note 30. But empirical inquiry raised questions about whether this shift has occurred. See T. Willging, *Use of Rule 12(b)(6) in Two Federal District Courts*, 1989 (finding that motions under Rule 12(b)(6)—which deals with dismissal on the pleadings—appeared to be less frequent in 1988 than in 1975 and proposing methods for further empirical examination of 'the Marcus thesis').

[52] For a review of this development, see Judge Keeton's scholarly opinion in Cash Energy, Inc. v. Weiner, 768 F. Supp. 892 (D. Mass. 1991). As pointed out in the previous footnote, the extent of this activity is unclear. The Supreme Court's decision in Leatherman v. Tarrant

bias against summary judgment, declaring that it 'is properly regarded not as a disfavored procedural shortcut, but rather as an integral part of the Federal Rules as a whole.'[53]

Yet another theme of the 1980's in American litigation was increased interest in cost-shifting as a tool for controlling litigation. Despite the American rule that each side bears its own attorneys' fees, enthusiasm began to develop in many quarters for what we call the 'English rule' that the costs should abide the event and include attorneys fees. Rule 11 sanctions were often used as cost-shifting measures, with attorneys' fees customarily forming the principal ingredient of those costs.[54] And repeated, though unsuccessful, efforts were made to expand the application of Rule 68 of the Federal Rules, which allows a defendant to make a settlement offer and recover its costs if plaintiff rebuffs the offer but does not do better than it at trial.[55]

Throughout the period, the alternative dispute resolution movement also grew as a result of concern about difficulties with civil litigation. There was a time when American judges felt that they could not even enforce contractual commitments to arbitrate because litigants have a right to their day in court despite such agreements. That time has long passed. In 1925 Congress passed a federal Arbitration Act that directed courts to order parties who had included agreements to arbitrate in contracts 'affecting commerce' to present their disputes to arbitrators.[56] As the American conception of what 'affects commerce' grew, the application of this statute grew also, and the Supreme Court undertook in the 1980's to remove obstacles to arbitration of a variety of federal claims previously thought immune to such treatment.[57] Many states had similar provisions directing enforcement of arbitration agreements.[58]

In part fueled by the case management movement, alternative dispute resolution moved far beyond this contractual basis by the 1980's. Already in the 1970's some federal district courts, such as the one in San Francisco, had begun requiring all litigants with certain types of claims under a

County Narcotics Intell. & Coord. Unit, 113 S.Ct. 1160 (1993), may have curtailed latitude to tighten up pleading requirements through judicial action.

[53] Celotex Corp. v. Catrett, 477 U.S. 317, 327 (1986).

[54] In 1993, Rule 11 was amended to eliminate the use of Rule 11 as a device to shift attorneys' fees.

[55] See Simon, 'The Riddle of Rule 68' (1985) 54 *Geo. Wash. L. Rev.* 1; Burbank, 'Proposals to Amend Rule 68—Time to Abandon Ship' (1986) 19 *U. Mich. J. L. Ref.* 425. The English practice, and Lord Woolf's proposals for changing it, are contained in chapter 24 of the Report.

[56] 9 U.S.C. §§ 1 *et seq.*

[57] E.g., Shearson/American Express, Inc. v. McMahon, 482 U.S. 220 (1987) (securities fraud claims); Gilmer v. Interstate/Johnson Lane Corp., 500 U.S. 20 (1991) (employment contracts).

[58] See Cal. Code Civ. Proc §§ 1280–94.2.

certain dollar limit to submit them to nonbinding arbitration before proceeding with litigation in court. Court-annexed alternatives to formal litigation greatly expanded in the 1980's; by the end of the decade the federal court in San Francisco had several other options for litigants besides nonbinding arbitration.[59] Meanwhile state courts in many areas began the practice of 'settlement weeks,' during which the judges would not try cases but only attempt to settle them. An industry of private dispute resolution came into being to provide alternative and often expedited court-like services for those who could pay for them. Often these providers offered lucrative employment to formerly public judges who had retired.

Many of these developments should ring bells for readers of the Woolf Report. Besides providing that insight, they are recounted here to underscore another point made in the initial section of this paper—they did not produce a feeling that the 'problem' of civil litigation had been 'solved.' To the contrary, the sense that civil litigation was out of control in the US continued to escalate as the 1990's arrived, and the solutions proposed became more aggressive.

Under the influence of a prominent US Senator, a study report was prepared in 1989 that chronicled a variety of deficiencies in American civil litigation and proposed a number of principles—largely more case management and curtailing discovery—to solve these problems.[60] Congress reacted in 1990 by passing the Civil Justice Reform Act,[61] in which it found that cost and delay are serious problems in the federal courts and prescribed increased case management as the cure to these ills. The Act required all federal district courts to adopt Cost and Delay Reduction Plans designed with the input of local advisory groups. These plans incorporated a smorgasbord of remedies, generally promoting case management and simplified discovery.[62] Their effectiveness is currently being studied.[63] The

[59] See *Dispute Resolution Procedures in the Northern District of California* (1995) (describing the court's ADR Multi-Option Program including court-annexed arbitration, early neutral evaluation, mediation and judicial settlement conferences). For a further description, see Brazil, 'A Close Look at Three Court-sponsored ADR Programs: Why They Exist, How They Operate, What They Deliver, and Whether They Threaten Important Values,' 1990, 1990 *U. Chi. L. Forum* 303.

[60] Brookings Institution, *Justice for All, Reducing Costs and Delay in Civil Litigation*, 1989.

[61] 28 U.S.C. §§ 471 *et seq.*

[62] These plans could involve very specific calendars for action to expedite proceedings. For example, in July, 1992, the Northern District of California adopted the following time line for its pilot case management program:

| DAY | ACTIVITY |
|---|---|
| 0 | Complaint filed, case assigned to pilot judge |
| 40 | Last day to serve all defendants |
| 45 | Last day to file proof(s) of service |
| 46 | Court issues Order to Show Cause why the complaint should not be dismissed if plaintiff has not filed proof that at least one defendant has been served |
| 90 | Last day to complete required disclosures |
| 100 | Last day to complete meet and confer re case management |

Act also prompted the promulgation of a *Manual for Litigation Management and Cost and Delay Reduction*, published in 1992.[64]

Responding to similar concerns, and to perceived political pressure, the framers of the Federal Rules brought forth a package of amendments in 1993. Some of these were so controversial that Congress almost deleted them from the package.[65] Clearly the most controversial was an initial disclosure requirement that directs litigants early in the case to volunteer to the other side the identities of every known witness and a list of all documents with information relevant to disputed facts 'pleaded with particularity' in the pleadings.[66] At least some judges suggested that such disclosure might soon supersede formal discovery.[67] The amendments also place numerical limits on the unilateral use of certain types of discovery.[68]

Probably the key impact of the 1993 amendments, however, was to further the push toward case management. Thus, Rule 26(f) now directs the parties to meet and confer about a wide range of subjects and to develop a discovery plan within approximately 90 days of the filing of the case,[69] and then to prepare a joint report to the court describing the discovery plan and

| DAY | ACTIVITY |
|---|---|
| 110 | Last day to file and serve Case Management Statement and Proposed Order |
| 120 | Judge conducts initial Case Management Conference |
| 130 | Judge issues initial Case Management Order |

General Order No. 34, N.D. Cal., Appendix C. This basic format has been incorporated into the Court's new local rules. See N.D. Cal. Local Rule 16–2(a).

[63] The legislation directed that ten 'pilot districts' designated by the federal Judicial Conference implement plans including specified elements by a certain date. See Pub. L. 101–650 §105. The experience of these ten districts is being studied by the Institute of Civil Justice of the Rand Corporation, and its report is expected in 1997. The legislation also created three 'demonstration districts.' See Pub. L. 101–650 §104. Two of these—the Northern District of Ohio and the Western District of Michigan—were to experiment with 'differential case management,' and the third, the Northern District of California, was to experiment with court-annexed alternative dispute resolution. These experiments are being studied by the Federal Judicial Center.

[64] This pamphlet includes a fairly extensive bibliography on case management. See *Manual for Litigation Management and Cost and Delay Reduction*, 1992, 339–51.

[65] See H.R. 2814, 103rd Cong., 1st Sess. (deleting mandatory initial disclosure provision from 1993 amendments). This measure was passed by the House of Representatives but not by the Senate.

[66] See Fed. R. Civ. P. 26(a)(1). An earlier version of this provision was more demanding, and did not limit the duty to disclose to claims pleaded with particularity. For a review of these controversies, see Marcus, *supra* note 25, at 805–12. It is unclear to this reader whether Lord Woolf contemplates broader disclosure without formal discovery. See Report at 168–70 (describing disclosure of 'adverse documents').

[67] One district judge opined, while the controversy was boiling, that '[s]ome observers of civil litigation believe that discovery rights will be taken from lawyers within the next decade or two, to be replaced by a system of standard disclosures.' Wauchop v. Domino's Pizza Inc., 143 F.R.D. 199, 200 (N.D. Ind. 1992).

[68] See Fed. R. Civ. P. 30(a)(2)(A) (ten depositions per side); 33(a) (25 interrogatories per party).

[69] For discussion of this provision, see 8 C. Wright, A. Miller & R. Marcus, *Federal Practice & Procedure*, 2d ed. 1994, § 2051.1.

addressing a wide range of other issues. The judge uses the report at the initial pretrial conference, and then issues an order setting deadlines for the completion of tasks and to control and focus the litigation. Thus, on both the legislative and rule-making fronts the cure of the 1990's for civil litigation ills in the US has been more case management.

## AMERICAN PERSPECTIVES ON LORD WOOLF'S PROPOSALS

A reading of the Woolf Report suggests that, although many problems in the UK look like the problems in the US, the English judicial system's reaction to them has to date been quite different. Most significantly, there appears to have been no comparable experience with case management. Drawing on the American experience leads to a number of reactions to the Report's prescription.

*Effectiveness of judicial management*: As the Report recognizes,[70] there are legitimate questions about whether judicial management will work. Of course, there may be different views on what it means for case management to 'work.' One reaction to the American experience of the past twenty years is that case management has not worked because things have not, from all reports, gotten better. Thus, the Rand study in 1990 showed that case durations were constant over the period 1971–89.[71] Another is that case management has worked, for things are not gotten worse despite the increase in filings.[72] Thus, the strongest American judicial proponent of case management extolled it in 1981 by citing statistics on increases in caseload and reduced time to disposition, concluding that 'it is the judge's new role as case manager that has made this impressive productivity record possible.'[73]

There is much to cheer in the American experience. Case management unquestionably has won wide support in the American judiciary. In 1990, the Federal Courts Study Committee endorsed it strongly.[74] Judicial support has grown pervasive among federal judges, and a comparison of litigation duration in the US and the UK (in the face of rising caseloads in America) provides substantial support for this confidence. It has also been highly successful in attracting support from lawyers, and the American Bar

[70] See Report at 32–33.

[71] T. Dungworth & N. Pace, *supra* note 13.

[72] On this score, another parallel between the US and the UK deserves mention. The Report refers to the low priority attached to civil litigation as compared with criminal cases. See Report at 16. In the US, the Speedy Trial Act, 18 U.S.C. §§ 3161 *et seq.* mandates prompt trial in criminal cases. Recently, fighting crime has become big political business in this country, and there have been significant increases in the number of criminal trials. As a consequence, some American courts face a risk that they may have no time to try civil cases. Hopefully the UK can avoid this problem.

[73] Peckham, *supra* note 40, at 770.

[74] See *Report of the Federal Courts Study Committee*, 1990, at 99–100.

Association has endorsed the idea.[75] Congress itself embraced case management in 1990 in passing the CJRA. The notion that judges should take responsibility for the progress of cases before them is intuitively attractive as well. Hence many academics, including this writer, strongly support case management as practiced in the US.

Nevertheless, there are gaps in the proof that case management does work. The initial empirical support was a study in the mid-1970's that examined six metropolitan district courts and showed an apparent relationship between certain case management practices and the duration of cases in those courts.[76] It concluded that courts could and should routinely enforce time limits to force lawyers to complete tasks promptly in order to speed litigation up. When Rule 16 was fortified in 1983 to require scheduling of time limits in all cases, this study was cited as showing that cost and delay were reduced by such judicial intervention.[77] Given that delays appear to have remained relatively constant during the 1971–89 period despite growing caseloads, case management may have produced good results. At least in terms of fostering settlement, however, a 1987 study by the Federal Judicial Center reported that 'the traditional scheduling of a firm trial date, coupled with benign neglect until the day of trial, also works.'[78] The case for delay reduction is not airtight, particularly with regard to vigorous intrusion by the judge into the details of the case.

There seems to be little doubt that energetic case management does do something—it causes lawyers to do more work under judicial scrutiny, with the judges pressing the lawyers to get the job done faster. Whether this actually reduces litigation cost is uncertain. The 1977 American study relayed the assumptions of pro-management judges that it does,[79] and that intuition seems reasonable, particularly in a system like ours where many lawyers are paid by the hour. But there are also some intuitive reasons to question the assumption, at least as it applies to the question whether

[75] See Peckham, *supra* note 39, at 259–60 (describing support for case management among the bar).

[76] S. Flanders, *supra* note 41. Earlier studies of American courts had focused on cases that went to trial and the value of judicial involvement shortly before trial rather than judicial intervention from the outset. See M. Rosenberg, *The Pretrial Conference and Effective Justice*, 1964; H. Zeisel, H. Kalven, Jr. & B. Bucholz, *Delay in the Court*, 1959.

[77] See Rule 16 Advisory Committee Note.

[78] T. Willging, *Trends in Asbestos Litigation*, 1987, 73.

[79] Flanders, *supra* note 41, at 71:

The first section of this chapter proposed, following suggestions from Judge J. Lawrence King, Judge Alvin B. Rubin, and others, that litigation cost may be proportionate to litigation time. Setting schedules is an indirect way to control cost; judges also control cost directly by limiting the case preparation to be undertaken. Perhaps there is no one but the judge, in an adversary system, who can prevent lawyers from imposing unacceptable costs and other burdens on each other, to their mutual detriment and that of their clients.

See also *id.* at 70 ('Judge J. Lawrence King of the Southern District of Florida feels that litigation cost is generally proportionate to litigation time.').

judges will reduce litigation costs by pressing lawyers to do things sooner than they otherwise would. A prime thrust of the Report appears to be forcing lawyers to adhere to time limits proposed in the rules.[80] At least in this country, those time limits are often quite brief, and it is uncertain whether rigid adherence to them would reduce costs. Requiring lawyers to act with greater alacrity will not always save money, a point partly acknowledged in the Report.[81] Indeed, lawyers in this country tend to charge extra when required to work on an emergency basis, and it is a commonplace that tasks can actually take longer when done in haste. Certainly having to go to court to seek relief from court-imposed time deadlines is not likely to reduce litigation expense. Accordingly, it could be that even if things are done more rapidly they are not done more cheaply.

One is left to rely on intuition because there are really no data to prove or disprove the effect of case management on costs.[82] Unlike the UK, the US does not regularly monitor the amounts expended on litigation, so that it is very difficult to relate such expenditures to case management. Moreover, on at least one point, the 1977 study made a finding that calls the assumption into question by finding that more discovery is recorded in fast courts than in slow ones.[83] Similarly, a report prepared for the American Bar Association indicated that case management did not lead to settlement in a greater percentage of cases.[84]

Under these circumstances, it is not possible to state unequivocally that case management successfully reduces litigation cost and delay even though it probably does make a positive contribution. Conceivably the ongoing study of implementation of the Civil Justice Reform Act will provide some firmer proof, but for now one is left only with the satisfied reports of the judicial participants. Of course, one need not necessarily have statistically-validated evidence to adopt a reform experiment.[85] But the absence of such proof from America could validly bear on the attractiveness of Lord

[80] See Report at 3, 13; 27. This was also a theme raised in the 1977 American study. See S. Flanders, *supra* note 41, at 17 (describing view of leading judge that problems would be solved if lawyers were made to 'practice law according to the rules' regarding time limits).

[81] See Report at 161 (noting importance of avoiding frontloading of smaller cases that may not be defended).

[82] The Report does cite an unidentified publication of the National Center for State Courts affirming the intuition that reducing delay cuts litigation cost. See Report at 13. But there is no indication that this conclusion is based on a study of case management, which is largely restricted to the federal courts.

[83] Flanders, *supra* note 41, at 25.

[84] ABA Action Commission to Reduce Court Costs and Delay, *Attacking Litigation Costs and Delay*, 1984, 12, cited in Peckham, *supra* note 39, at 259.

[85] See Report at 33 (acknowledging lack of research but recommending that proposals be implemented in stages and carefully monitored); see also Marcus, *supra* note 25, at 770 (arguing that requiring empirical proof that procedural reforms will be effective equal to that required to establish effectiveness of new drugs seeking approval by the Food and Drug Administration would immobilize procedural reform).

Woolf's recommendation for the English judicial system. Moreover, it is important to realize as well that there are differences between the two legal systems that could frustrate case management in England even in the face of unequivocal American evidence.

*The need for a single firm hand*: The starting point for case management in the US was the single assignment system; only when a single judge was responsible for a case from start from finish, and able to accumulate and implement knowledge about it, was this approach possible.[86] The strongest proponent of case management among American judges found this arrangement crucial:

> Under such a system, a judge is more motivated to monitor and expedite his cases because he feels a greater individual responsibility for those cases than under the master calendar system. He becomes aware that a judge's lack of diligence and organization will soon be reflected in the increase in his pending case load. The judge's familiarity with the case enables him to deal more efficiently with any pretrial motions, discovery disputes, and trial scheduling.[87]

Case management must be much more difficult in a system where different judges preside at different points in the case. Moreover, having anyone but the ultimate decisionmaker superintending the earlier development of the case may rob that supervision of much of its value. Thus, in America the idea of assigning case management tasks to magistrate judges was criticized because ultimately district judges would try the case and therefore their personal involvement from the outset was crucial.[88] Probably experience with use of magistrate judges has softened this objection in the US, but that is largely because district judges rely on them and litigants have learned that.[89]

The Report recognizes the desirability of a single assignment system,[90] but says that it is impossible to reproduce in the UK. It does propose the interesting alternative of a 'procedural team' for collaborative case management.[91] This may preserve some of the advantages of the single assignment system, but seems still to divorce the pretrial management from the conduct of the trial, which was thought unduly to dilute management in

86 Resnik, *supra* note 30, at 523 & n. 127.

87 Peckham, *supra* note 39, at 257.

88 The Report of the National Commission for the Review of the Antitrust Laws and Procedures (1979) 80 F.R.D. 509 opined that 'While talented individual masters or magistrates may help in expediting some complex cases, their general use does not appear to offer any substantial hope of expediting pretrial procedures. Unless masters and magistrates are used in close consultation and virtual partnership with judges, their presence in a case may actually add to its complexity and hinder direct supervision by the district judge.' *Id.* at 530.

89 See Seron, 'The Professional Project of Parajudges: The Case of U.S. Magistrates' (1988) 22 *Law & Soc'y Rev.* 557 (finding that role assigned to magistrate judges varied from district to district, and that they were most effective where treated as co-equal judicial officers with district judges).

90 See Report at 63; see also *id.* at 40; 48.

91 See Report at 66–68. This resembles the sort of cooperation thought necessary to make case management by a magistrate effective in the US. See *supra* note 88.

this country. Perhaps there is some saving grace to this shared power arrangement simply because it dilutes the potential authority of the case manager. In the US there is concern that case management, with its frequent and somewhat unstructured interaction between the judge and the lawyers, will vastly expand the judge's power because the lawyers will recognize that it is necessary to curry favor with the judge since many critically important decisions are treated as discretionary and therefore not subject to careful review on appeal.[92] Having a shared management scheme may provide an antidote to this tendency. But this is a very slender silver lining to a dark cloud; overall, this circumstance bodes ill for the success of case management in the UK.

*Challenging new tasks for judges*: As compared to more formal conventional interaction judges have with the parties, case management challenges judges to make quick decisions based on limited information. Another strong American judicial proponent of management reports 'sobering experiences' in which he reversed his original decision on learning that the problem was more complex than he initially appreciated.[93] Although unconvinced that most discovery disputes require formal briefing and argument, he has become more sensitive to 'the dangers inherent in speedy and wholly oral proceedings.'[94] Perhaps English judges are more accustomed to ruling entirely on the basis of oral submissions, but they should recognize the educational challenge that entails.

In short, case management is hard. In America, case management is designed to produce a discovery plan that can be extremely specific, perhaps identifying all witnesses by name and detailing the duration of all depositions. But as a prominent judge said in the early 1980's when the case management provisions were first put into the Federal Rules, '[i]t's very difficult for the judge to ask, "Well, you're spending too much time with John Jones, Sales Vice-President of the company. Why are you spending so much time with a salesman?" He can't know why you're spending so much time with him; he can't know that much about your case.'[95] The process of issue focusing and delineation proposed by the Report carries equal difficulties, and some of the contemplated judicial tasks (such as picking experts and apportioning fee shifting) look harder than what American judges do. The Report acknowledges these challenges.[96] The point needs to be emphasized.

[92] E.g., Resnik, 'Managerial Judges' (1982) 96 *Harv. L. Rev.* 376, 424–31.

[93] Brazil, 'Special Masters in Complex Cases: Extending the Judiciary or Reshaping Adjudication?' (1986) 53 *U. Chi. L. Rev.* 394, 420.

[94] *Id.*

[95] Higginbotham, 'Discovery Management Considerations in Antitrust Cases' (1982) 51 *Antitr. L.J.* 231, 236.

[96] See Report at 70 ('This will place new demands on all judges. It will require training and the acquisition of new skills.'); see also *id.* at 64 (need for specialized judges); 67 (need for teams of procedural judges to 'include judges at appropriate levels and with sufficient experience').

*The risk of micro-management or cookie cutter treatment*: One of the points about the difficulty of this task is to appreciate how many details the Report may wish the judge to resolve, or at least address. From the outset, a judge is supposed to 'take responsibility for ensuring that claimants and defendants plainly state the factual ingredients of their case.'[97] Similarly, judges are to specify what expert is to be used[98] and inquire for specifics on costs accrued and anticipated,[99] perhaps making the cost-shifting vary according to the issue involved.[100]

Not only is this demanding for judges, it can be unduly intrusive on lawyers. Moreover, because it is demanding for judges they may turn to a 'one size fits all' approach. As an American observer reported in 1989, '[c]ase-by-case management developed because the transaction costs of procedural rules with broad attorney latitude were too high. . . . [T]he judiciary has already demonstrated that it thinks the transaction costs of ad hoc case-by-case management are also too high. Judges are already turning to formal limitations and definitions in order to reduce transaction costs.'[101] In the state court system in California, a 'fast track' system has been introduced that carries such patterned requirements system-wide; lawyers report regularly being peppered by the court's computers with reminders that they have missed deadlines.[102] Particularly under the Report's fast track proposal, and potentially with its multi-track proposal,[103] both the undue intrusiveness problem and the rigidity problem pose worries.

*The relationship between case management and settlement promotion*: The American experience suggests that settlement promotion can be one of the most important byproducts of case management. Indeed, some judges in this country seem to treat it as the principal purpose of management, and there are suggestions that they mold their case management orders with a view to inducing settlement. It does not seem that this was the objective proposed for case management twenty years ago.[104] Rather, it was a pragmatic response to coping with the problems of cost and delay that came to occupy center stage because case managers wanted their work to be effective and saw settlement as a very important effect. Thus, while acknowledging that 'some people consider case management and alternative dispute resolution to be two separate and unrelated approaches,' the leading

97 Report at 155.

98 *Id.* at 185.

99 *Id.* at 200.

100 *Id.* at 204.

101 Subrin, 'Federal Rules, Local Rules and State Rules: Uniformity, Divergence, and Emerging Procedural Patterns (1989) 137 *U. Pa. L. Rev.* 1999, 2049.

102 Freeman, 'On the San Diego Fast Track' (1989) 9 *Calif. Lawyer* 43.

103 Thus, in the multi-track proposal the Report recommends a 'fixed timetable' that could be changed only for 'good reason,' with another date 'immediately substituted.'

104 Thus, the 1977 Federal Judicial Center study endorsing case management was distinctly unenthusiastic about settlement promotion. See S. Flanders, *supra* note 41, at 37 ('Judicial participation in settlement produces mixed results. A limited role may be valuable, but data suggest that a large expenditure of judicial time is fruitless.').

American exponent of case management explained that in his view 'they are complementary and interrelated.'[105]

The judicial role in settlement promotion poses many problems. It may be justified by what Professor Galanter has called the 'cool' theme or the 'warm' theme.[106] The former emphasizes the efficacy of settlement as a way of clearing dockets. Of course, that raises the somewhat uncertain question whether judicial promotion actually promotes settlements, one on which the US experience is ambiguous.[107] More significantly, the notion of the judge as a vigorous pursuer of a deal, any deal, that will end the case is hardly attractive. Indeed, given the supposed role of cost and delay as stimuli for settlements, the judge could theoretically have an incentive to manipulate those factors in a way that prods the parties into settling. The 'warm' theme stresses compromise as more likely to lead to a satisfactory solution of a dispute than resolution in strict adherence to the pertinent rules of law. Much as this may reflect human nature, there comes a point at which the job of the court is to apply the law, not to assist and prod the parties in working their way around it.[108] Beyond these sorts of basic questions lie important specifics about the nature of settlement promotion techniques used by or in connection with the court that have received much attention in America, where there is a vast literature on the subject.[109]

The Report is curiously ambivalent about the relation between case management and ADR. It treats ADR as a separate topic far removed from the basic coverage of case management,[110] and some comments there suggest a distinct separation between case management and ADR.[111] But elsewhere, the Report seems to contemplate an intimate relationship between the two. Thus, it recommends that the parties be required to report their discussions

[105] See Peckham, *supra* note 39, at 268.

[106] See Galanter, 'The Emergence of the Judge as a Mediator in Civil Cases' (1986) 69 *Judicature* 256.

[107] A decade ago, Judge Posner challenged the assumption that settlement promotion led to more settlements. See Posner, 'The Summary Jury Trial and Other Methods of Alternative Dispute Resolution: Some Cautionary Observations' (1986) 53 *U. Chi. L. Rev.* 366. An empirical study at about the same time concluded that in asbestos litigation some settlement promotion activities did seem to work, but that '[e]fforts to produce earlier settlements appear justifiable only on grounds of improving the quality of settlements.' T. Willging, *supra* note 78, at 70–76.

[108] That a judge might be tempted to do so is suggested by the comment by an American judge, quoted *supra* at text accompanying note 43, that settlement yields 'optimal justice' compared to the 'polar solution' produced by a trial. Some nonlegal participants in the ADR community go well beyond this view and reject law altogether. See Marlow, 'The Rule of Law in Divorce Mediation' (1985) 9 *Mediation Q.* 5, 5–6 (reporting that divorce mediation rejects the idea that legal rules embody any necessary wisdom or logic, viewing them instead as 'arbitrary principles').

[109] See D. Stienstra & T. Willging, *Alternatives to Litigation: Do They Have a Place in Federal District Courts?*, 1995; Brazil, *supra* note 59. The most forceful attack on ADR is Fiss, 'Against Settlement' (1984), 93 *Yale L.J.* 1073.

[110] ADR is covered in chapter 18, which is included in a section entitled 'Assisting the Litigant.' Case management is a section unto itself, containing chapters 5–8.

of ADR at every case management conference and that the judge should be able to take account of a litigant's 'unreasonable refusal to attempt ADR' in determining the future conduct of the litigation and, perhaps, in assessing costs.[112] Not only does this suggestion seem to verge on mandatory ADR, it also may go beyond what American courts will allow as a part of case management.[113] Further attention to this relationship is necessary.

*The value of the adversary system*: The advent of managerial judging and the growing emphasis on settlement promotion among American judges have reminded us that the adversary system did not emerge entirely by accident. One need not embrace a *laissez faire* attitude toward the conduct of litigation[114] to recognize that there are values to an adversary presentation that need to be preserved even as the excesses of adversarial conduct are curtailed.

The notion that adversarial presentations promote accurate decisions by providing incentives for presentation of favorable evidence is hackneyed but still has force. More significantly, a case manager may too easily be persuaded to embrace the first impression of the case. As noted above, judges will have to operate on somewhat sparse and impressionistic information in making their managerial decisions. But those impressions tend to harden; 'what starts as a preliminary diagnosis designed to direct the inquiry tends, quickly and imperceptibly, to become a fixed conclusion . . . . An

[111] See Report at 136 (rejecting compulsory ADR as improper in principle); 143 (stating that adding a system of court-annexed ADR would not currently be appropriate given the variety of other changes being proposed).

[112] *Id.* at 144.

[113] American courts continue to struggle with the limits on judicial power to promote settlements. In Newton v. A.C. & S., Inc., 918 F.2d 1121 (3d Cir. 1990), the court overturned a fine of $1,000 for failure to settle by a certain date, finding that sanctioned party had right to be heard before being fined. It affirmed that there is power to sanction for 'unjustified failure to comply with the court's schedule for settlement.' In Kothe v. Smith, 771 F.2d 667 (2d Cir. 1985), the judge recommended settlement at between $20,000 and $30,000 during a pretrial conference and warned that if the parties settled for a comparable figure during trial he would sanction the 'dilatory party.' When the parties settled for $20,000 after one day of trial, the judge imposed over $2,000 in costs on defendant. Stressing that there was no showing that defendant had acted wrongfully, the appellate court reversed. It noted that 'pressure tactics to coerce settlement simply are not permissible.' *Id.* at 669. Compare White v. Raymark Indus., Inc., 783 F.2d 1175 (4th Cir. 1986), in which the court imposed jurors' costs of $2,000 on defendant because it violated a local rule requiring that parties who settle cases give the clerk's office notice of the settlement. The appellate court upheld the order, noting that plaintiff had tried valiantly to reach a settlement but had been frustrated until too late by the failure of defendant's insurer to respond to settlement inquiries.

[114] See Report at 30 (describing Australian shift from *laissez faire* approach); Peckham, *supra* note 39, at 266 (criticizing Professor Resnik, an opponent of case management, for taking an *laissez faire* attitude toward the conduct of litigation). Professor Resnik believes case management inherently creates a variety of serious risks of compromising impartiality and thereby conflicts with the proper judicial role. See Resnik, *supra* note 92. Although these are serious concerns, they are also manageable and do not warrant wholesale rejection of case management.

adversarial presentation seems the only effective means for combatting this natural human tendency to judge too swiftly in terms of the familiar that which is not yet fully known.'[115] In pursuit of a cooperative atmosphere, the managerial judge may be tempted to overlook this potentially disruptive yet important value of our adversary tradition.

*Restraining The sanctions impulse*: Notably absent from the Report is emphasis on sanctions, although the idea does surface.[116] Recent American experience is quite different. As noted above, the 1983 amendment to Rule 11 made sanctions the most prominent procedural issue of the following decade. Several large and still-growing books were written about that rule alone, and sanctions provisions were placed and amplified in other rules, as well as the codes of many states. The Supreme Court went beyond these to embrace a concept of inherent power to sanction.[117] Perhaps because of the historical coincidence that these developments occurred in the US at the same time as the growth of case management, it has seemed that they might be intrinsically connected. Perhaps the judge who becomes actively involved is prone to become impatient and vindictive. Perhaps the impulse to punish is simply more prevalent in this country than in England.

Whatever the explanation, the Report's apparent decision that sanctions are not the way to solve modern litigation problems seems sensible.[119] Should it prove in the future that there some intrinsic tendency toward sanctions in case management, this tendency should be resisted. In the US the tumult over the 1983 version of Rule 11 eventually led to an unprecedented 'call' for commentary and study of Rule 11, and this led in time to 1993 amendments that soften its operation. No longer are sanctions mandatory if there is an infraction, and ordinarily sanctions do not consist of cost shifting and, if monetary, are paid into court and not to the 'victim.'[119]

*Reform from the top down or the bottom up*: The Report recognizes the need for an educational program to accomplish the cultural change in litigation that it hopes will occur. But in terms of actually effecting a change in procedure, it is clear that this program will come from the center and be accomplished from on high. This contrasts strikingly with the US experience and reality.

[115] Fuller, 'The Forms and Limits of Adjudication' (1978) 92 *Harv. L. Rev.* 353, 383.

[116] Thus, regarding pleadings issues the Report says '[t]hese problems are compounded by what is seen as a widespread failure of courts to apply meaningful sanctions.' Report at 154; see also *id.* at 38 (recommending imposition of sanctions for delay in making dispositive motions).

[117] Chambers v. NASCO, Inc., 501 U.S. 32 (1991).

[118] It should be noted that a good deal of this American sanctioning may represent efforts by judges to accomplish fee-shifting in a legal system that does not authorize it.

[119] Elements in the US Congress, however, have spoken in favor of returning to more-frequent imposition of stiff sanctions.

The US experience with regard to case management is largely the reverse. The innovation came at the local level; judges in San Francisco, Chicago, New York and other places thought up and tried out new ways of handling litigation. Satisfied that these were superior, they then embarked on a course of gentle persuasion to get other judges to do the same. Only well into the development did national rules begin to address case management issues, and as these rules became more directive they still left much latitude to the judge to determine how far to go. Always there was as much a note of exhortation as command. Even the intervention by Congress in the Civil Justice Reform Act in 1990 largely operated on the local level.

From many perspectives, the apparent English reality of control from the center looks enviable to American eyes. Today many decry the balkanization of procedure in American federal courts.[120] In the 1980's the federal Judicial Conference woke up to the existence of local rules, finding that thousands of these existed in federal courts across the land and that many of them seemed beyond the local courts' authority, sometimes directly (and impermissibly) contradicting national rules.[121] Moreover, many judges added standing orders announcing their own personal rules. In a dispersed judicial operation with cases assigned to a single judge for all purposes, each judge can become something of an independent lord. The comparative orderliness of the English approach is refreshing.

But there are some counter-arguments. In America case management was developed by judges 'in the trenches' and spread by persuasion. In a sense it was born and grew organically; judges who did not feel comfortable with it did not have to do it. As the Report implicitly recognizes, for case management to work the judges have to believe in it. Whether this commitment can be imposed from above is at least open to question. Moreover, the American element of experiment, of trial and error, seems missing from the thorough prescription proffered in the Report. Local innovation and deviation carry with them the promise of evolution. Will the Report's prescription, assuming it can be imposed from above, face a risk of calcifying? True, the creation of a Civil Justice Council[122] should reduce this risk. Nevertheless, a centrally managed and controlled scheme of case management appears much more difficult to impose than the home-grown American variety.

*Inviting a caseload crunch*: Finally, assuming the Report's proposal is successfully implemented, that may even lead to further problems. If cost and delay have deterred prospective litigants from using the courts in the UK,

[120] Tobias, 'Civil Justice Reform and the Balkanization of Federal Civil Procedure,' 1992, 24 Az. St. L.J. 1393.

[121] Committee on Rules of Practice and Procedure, Judicial Conference of the United States, *Local Rules Project*, 1989.

[122] Report, ch. 27.

what will happen when these problems are abated? One possibility is that caseloads will increase, which could make the English experience resemble the American one even more closely.

## CONCLUSION

Two generations ago a leading American judge noted that 'judicial reform is no sport for the short-winded.'[123] Perhaps his remarks had particular application to the dispersed American judicial arrangement, but the basic point is likely true in most countries. Legal institutions change slowly; getting them to adopt significantly different methods of operation requires persistent effort. In the words of the author of the American Federal Rules, 'reformers must follow their dream and leave compromise to others.'[124]

Sobering though this must be, even more sobering is the fate of the successful reformer, for the success will likely more often be limited to getting the new procedure implemented than also eliminating the problem it was designed to solve. Whether or not legal reform tends, as some suggest, to focus on undoing the consequences of the previous generation's reforms, the history of procedural reform has reached a point to leave one somewhat jaded with it. As the Report notes,[125] since 1851 there have been some 60 reports on procedure and the organization of the English courts. These have presumably led to many changes, and yet problems persist. In 1906 Roscoe Pound argued that dissatisfaction with civil litigation was unavoidable.[126] Perhaps that is why reforms in procedure rarely deliver all that is hoped.

An American's *deja vu* reaction to the Woolf Report could be a very positive sign, given the favorable reaction to case management in this country. Indeed, it is worth noting that something like case management was supposedly endorsed in England more than a century ago.[127] But there are strong reasons for caution. The American 'success' story is played out against a background of mounting caseloads that evidently don't trouble the UK. Our experience does not offer hard proof that the types of cost

[123] Vanderbilt, 'Introduction to Minimum Standards of Judicial Administration,' in 2 *Selected Writings of Arthur Vanderbilt*, 1967, 43.

[124] Clark, 'The Federal Rules of Civil Procedure: 1938–58, Two Decades of the Federal Civil Rules' (1958) 58 *Colum. L. Rev.* 435, 448.

[125] Report at 4.

[126] Pound, 'The Causes of Popular Dissatisfaction with the Administration of Justice (1906) 29 *Reports of the ABA* 395.

[127] See S. Rosenbaum, *The Rule-Making Authority in the English Supreme Court*, 1917, 75 (describing an 1881 report from the Lord Chancellor endorsing 'a change in procedure which would enable the court, at an early stage of the litigation, to obtain control over the suit, and exercise a close supervision over the proceedings in the action').

and delay problems profiled in the Report would be solved by case management. Moreover, differences between the two systems—most notably the single assignment system in the US and the attendant 'bottom up' flexibility of reform here—present real problems for borrowing the method. In addition, American practices such as aggressive settlement promotion and increased sanctioning that have accompanied the development of case management might prove unpalatable in the UK. Like the proverbial greener grass on the other side of the fence, civil litigation reforms from the other side of the Atlantic may prove disappointing.

# 13

# *Too Much Lawyering, Too Little Law*

SAMUEL ISSACHAROFF*[1]

Sometimes it appears, Tolstoy to the contrary, that unhappy families are indeed alike. From the vantage point of an American academic lawyer, what is most striking in first reading the admirable Report produced by Lord Woolf is its uncanny familiarity. Despite contact with the British civil justice system that is best described as episodic and anecdotal, I am nonetheless struck by the ready comprehensibility of the Report's depiction of the malaise of a common law system afflicted by an escalation of legal costs and a growing sense that justice is inaccessible to the bulk of the population. There is nothing foreign or remote in the idea of a legal system administered by an overburdened and understaffed judiciary, nor by the inability of law to provide security and redress in those daily affairs that Hobbes described as giving the essential incentives to industry in civilized societies.[2]

No better case for reform can be made than the statistical evidence of the wholly unacceptable level of costs that currently afflict the system. According to a sample of cases from the Supreme Court Taxing Office, the *average* costs allowed in cases worth £12,500 or less were £12,044.[3] Assuming a comparable level of expenditures on the losing side in these cases, then the transaction costs associated with the legal system exceed the merits of the dispute by a factor of two to one. This absolutely extraordinary level of expenditures means that the legal system is simply too expensive, too inefficient, and too sclerotic to provide a meaningful forum for

* Charles Tilford McCormick Professor of Law, University of Texas School of Law.

[1] I gratefully acknowledge the helpful comments of Douglas Laycock, Richard Marcus, and Adrian Zuckerman on this paper. I am also grateful for the reseach assistance of Bret Tate.

[2] Thomas Hobbes, *Leviathan* 71 (Everyman, 1994) ('. . . wherein men live without other security, than what their own strength, and the own invention shall furnish them withall. In such condition, there is no place for Industry; because the fruit thereof is uncertain . . .'). In defining the need for 'an accessible and effective system of civil litigation,' the Report quotes from Lord Diplock to the effect that, 'Every civilized system of government requires that the state should make available to all its citizens a means for the just and peaceful settlement of disputes between them as to their respective legal rights.' Report at 2.

[3] Report at 35.

dispute resolution in the commonplace social interactions that fall within the confines of tort, contract and property.

The greatest strength of the Woolf Report is its candid willingness to confront a legal system that by its generous insistence on providing the fullest protection of the law to all disputes, effectively denies any legal recourse to large numbers of disputants. The picture of the legal system that emerges from the Report is one that produces too much lawyering in the relatively few litigated disputes, and too little law in the resolution of the everyday conflicts of life. In echoing Lord Devlin, the Report stresses the need to discipline the legal system, to recognize that indeed 'half a loaf is better than no bread.'[4] This, in turn, requires mechanisms for calibrating the level of justice available to disputants according to the stakes in the controversy. What emerges is an attempt to recast the legal system as less global, less party-controlled, less of a free market—in short, as managed justice.

The impetus for managerial judging bridges the shores of the Atlantic.[5] Since the adoption of the Federal Rules of Civil Procedure in 1938, and intensifying since 1983, as chronicled more fully by Professor Richard Marcus,[6] American federal civil procedure has undergone a series of reforms aimed at increasing the power of judges to manage litigation. Some highlights include having scheduled pretrial and discovery conferences, together with increased judicial power to sanction wayward attorney conduct, increased use of summary judgment powers, increased capacity to experiment with streamlined discovery procedures, increased use of court-annexed alternative dispute resolution procedures, and the increased capacity of local courts to create local rules of procedure to deal with particular case specific problems.[7] While these reforms are specific to the American legal culture, and particularly to the nettlesome role of the jury in civil cases as the ultimate trier of fact, the overall objectives are congruent to those found in the Woolf Report.

The Report's conception of managerial judging rests on a tripartite foundation. The first is the use of managerial prerogatives to channel litigation

[4] *Report* at 19 (*quoting* Lord Devlin, *What's Wrong With The Law* (BBC 1970) ).

[5] *See, e.g.*, A. Miller, *The August 1983 Amendments to the Federal Rules of Civil Procedure: Promoting Effective Case Management and Lawyer Responsibility* 2 (1983 amendments to the American Federal Rules of Civil Procedure 'represent an integrated package' granting greater managerial discretion to federal courts).

[6] *See* Richard Marcus, *An American Reaction to the Woolf Report*, that is included in this volume.

[7] As with all such reform efforts, there are bound to be mixed results. *See* Samuel Issacharoff & George Loewenstein, *Second Thoughts About Summary Judgment*, 100 Yale L. J. 73 (1990); Samuel Issacharoff & George Loewenstein, *Unintended Consequences of Mandatory Disclosure*, 73 Tex. L. Rev. 753 (1995); Linda S. Mullenix, *The Counter-Reformation in Procedural Justice*, 77 Minn. L. Rev. 375 (1992); Owen M. Fiss, *Against Settlements*, 93 Yale L. J. 1073 (1984); Richard L. Marcus and Edward F. Sherman, *Complex Litigation* 814–840 (1985).

in such a way as to streamline the process and reduce aggregate costs. The second is to increase the resources of the judiciary to play this more interventionist role. The third is to reform some of the rules of procedure to facilitate more economical administration of civil justice. As a general matter, I found the report more successful in the first two matters, and weaker in the scope of its conception of procedural reform. This weakness becomes clear when one considers the effect that procedure has on strategic considerations at almost every point in a legal dispute. The Report itself provides a strong example of how procedural changes can sometimes have unintended, negative effects in the cae of the English experience with witness statements. When modifying or changing procedure, there must be thought to how those changes will effect areas such as discovery, offers to settle and summary judgments.

While there is little that an outsider can contribute to the discussion of resource allocation within the court system, other than to note the obvious need for law clerks and researchers if the more interventionist goals for the judiciary are to be carried out, there is quite a bit that can be said about judging and procedure, even by a foreign observer. It is to these matters that I now turn.

## II. MANAGERIAL JUDGING

If the problem with the civil justice system in Britain today is excessive lawyering in those cases that are litigated and insufficient access to the courts in those cases that are not, then the Report's proposals must be assessed in terms of how they address these problems. Consistent with the critical role of pretrial procedure in defining litigation and its attendant costs, the Report directs its prime managerial focus on taking the direction of litigation out of the hands of the parties and placing it more firmly under the aegis of the courts. The most critical of the proposed reforms concern the discovery process, and I shall address these at some length. I shall then turn more briefly to the role of 'rough justice' and the issue of costs in litigation.

### A. Discovery and Information

The key to the Report's expansion of access to the courts is the limitation on the potential escalation of litigation costs. The first piece in this puzzle concerns the restriction on potential pretrial costs. In both Britain and the U.S., well upwards of 90 percent of filed cases are resolved prior to trial, either through settlement, abandonment of the claim, or dispositive legal resolution. This means that the bulk of the concern with costs regards the pretrial process, and the pretrial phase of litigation is in turn consumed in the arduous process of discovery. If costs are to be minimized then parties have to be able to restrict the amount of discovery they may undertake, and restrict the amount of discovery the opposing side may take—for which costs they may subsequently be taxed.

The Report seeks to limit costs by dividing cases into three classes. The first is a continuation of small claims court, with an expansion of the jurisdictional amount to £3,000. This is an area in which parties are presumptively representing themselves and in which formal discovery threatens to overwhelm the process. This is also an area in which costs are not taxed against the losing party, so that parties may realistically enter the process with a predetermined litigation 'budget.' The Report provides some evidence of general satisfaction with the mechanisms of small claims courts, but calls for additional access through information kiosks, plainer language in the proceedings, and a better staffed court system able to assist litigants in the presentation of their claims. Nonetheless, the Report acknowledges that the present system serves primarily as a clearinghouse for commercial debts, and that institutional repeat actors are the heaviest users of these facilities.

The second category is the fast-track for disputes ranging in value from £3,000–£10,000. This category also includes all personal injury claims under £10,000. The key to this category is a fixed time for going to trial and a rejection of party-controlled discovery under the century-old relevance standard.[8] Discovery in these cases would be limited to the production of the documents that the party intends to rely upon in support of her trial contention and those documents of which a party is aware that either support the adversary's case or undermine her own.

The same limitation on discovery would apply in the multi-track, which is the remaining category in which larger scale disputes would be found. Only upon completion of this limited form of discovery could the parties petition the court for further discovery into documents themselves relevant to the litigation or likely to lead litigants onto a relevant 'train of inquiry.' The objective is 'to limit the work to be done whenever possible,'[9] and to assist in fostering a 'co-operative, constructive' attitude to litigation.[10]

The division of litigation into three spheres depending on the stakes of the controversy is a useful, if somewhat schematic, starting point. In the U.S., beginning with the landmark constitutional due process case of *Matthews v. Eldridge*,[11] the overriding concern of procedural fairness has

[8] *See Compagnie Financiere du Pacifique* v. *Peruvian Guano Company* 11 L.T.R. 55 (QBD 1882) (defining the permissible scope of discovery as that which may fairly lead a litigant to information that may advance his own case or damage that of his opponent).

[9] Report at 170.

[10] *Id.* at 168.

[11] 424 U.S. 319 (1976). Since *Matthews*, the U.S. Supreme Court has increasingly abandoned attempts at setting categorical rules of constitutional procedure in favor of fact-based

been subject to a balancing test that depends critically on the rights at stake. Calibrating the amount of legal process to the actual scope of the controversy not only limits the exposure of the parties to potentially escalating legal costs, but it rations justice in a world in which legal resources are an unfortunately finite commodity.[12] With the increasing complexity of matters now brought before the national judiciaries and the expanded arsenals now available in litigation, it may be that, as Adrian Zuckerman notes, the search for global process regardless of the nature of the dispute, is a romantic notion that is simply unaffordable.[13]

Nonetheless, the law is replete with cases of small stakes that establish major principles of rights. The process of the common law is one in which the private interest in resolving disputes produces public goods in the form of developing legal principles. Without the capacity to develop fully breakthrough claims, even of modest stakes, not only will the law ossify, but there will be no basis for parties to 'bargain in the shadow of the law' through either alternative dispute resolution mechanisms, or through private settlement.[14] Accordingly, there must be procedures for petitioning for an expansion of the scope of discovery, even in disputes of limited financial stakes.

The Report seems to anticipate some mechanism of this sort by the early recourse of all litigants to a procedural judge. This is useful not just for the fast-track case, but more critically for the multi-track as well. Given the enormous array of cases that fall within this catch-all last category, it is by no means clear why the Report attempts to specify the exact discovery procedures to be in place in the multi-track. The large divergence in size and complexity of the cases that will fall within this broad category makes the attempt at *ex ante* determination of optimal procedure difficult. Particularly since the Report anticipates a broader degree of managerial intervention by the judiciary, there seems little reason to disable these

balances between competing private interests, the interest of the state, and the systemic risk of error from inadequate process. *See, e.g., Connecticut* v. *Doehr*, 501 U.S. 1 (1991) (balancing the rights at stake in prejudgment liens); *U.S.* v. *James Daniel Good Real Property*, 114 S.Ct. 492 (1993) (limiting civil forfeiture based on balancing of competing interests).

[12] I leave for others the potential conflict between managerial justice and the pledge of the Magna Carta that, 'To none will we sell, to none will we deny, to none will we delay, right or justice.' *Magna Carta*, Clause 40 (1215).

[13] A. A. S. Zuckerman, *Quality and Economy in Civil Procedure: The Case for Commuting Correct Judgments for Timely Judgments*, 14 Oxford J. of Leg. Studies 353 (1994).

[14] *See generally* Edward Brunet, *Questioning the Quality of Alternative Dispute Resolution*, 62 Tulane L. Rev. 1, 33–34, 54 (1987) (alternative dispute resolution systems often lead to limited discovery and the creation of rules that lack a structure for the normal exchange of information. With the limited breath of discovery, the quality of the resolution may lack, as may the development of the legal principles underlying the dispute's resolution).

judges from tailoring the rules of engagement to the particular circumstances of each case.[15]

It is at this point that one may look to the innovations of Judge Robert Parker, one of the most able trial judges in the U.S., recently appointed to the Court of Appeals. Based on his extensive trial court experience, most notably his role in attempting procedural innovations for aggregated handling of thousands of asbestos tort cases, Judge Parker fashioned a case-specific 'menu' approach to pretrial procedure in the Eastern District of Texas. The menu consisted of the following six preferred tracks for party-initiated discovery and pre-ordained disclosure of basic documents and witness information:

| | |
|---|---|
| Track One: | No discovery |
| Track Two: | Disclosure Only |
| Track Three: | Disclosure plus 15 interrogatories, 15 request for admission, depositions of the parties, and deposition on written questions of custodians of business records for third parties. |
| Track Four: | Disclosure plus 15 interrogatories, 15 requests for admissions, depositions of the parties, depositions on written questions of custodians of business records for third parties, and three other depositions per side (i.e., per party or per group of parties with a common interest.) |
| Track Five: | A discovery plan tailored by the judicial officer to fit the special management needs of the case. |

[15] This ties into a broader discussion of the distinction between procedural rules and looser standards to govern case-by-case evaluations. This is the classic division in procedure, well identified by Professor H. L. A. Hart as the need for

> compromise between two social needs: the need for certain rules which can, over great areas of conduct, safely be applied by private individuals to themselves without fresh official guidance or weighing up of social issues, and the need to leave open, for later settlement by an informed, official choice, issues which can only be properly appreciated and settled when they arise in a concrete case.

H. L. A. Hart, *The Concept of Law* 127 (1993). Professor Fred Schauer elaborates upon this as follows:

> [T]he choice of rule-based decision-making ordinarily entails disabling wise and sensitive decision-makers from making the best decisions in order to disable incompetent or simply wicked decision-makers from making worse decisions. Conversely, a decision procedure that avoids or diminishes the constraints of rules empowers the best decision-makers to make the best decisions, and accepts as a consequence that the same procedure also empowers less than the best decision-makers to make some number of less than the best decisions. A 'best case' perspective is necessarily averse to rules, for rule-based decision-making cannot produce the best result in every case. But a 'worst case' perspective is likely to embrace rules, recognizing that guarding against the worst case may in some circumstances be the best we can do.

Frederick Schauer, *Playing by the Rules: A Philosophical Examination of Rule-Based Decision-Making in Law and Life* 153 (1991).

Track Six: Specialized treatment and program as determined by the judicial officers.[16]

This approach is consistent with the preference for managed 'waves of discovery' that the American Federal Judicial Center has recommended for complex and multiparty cases.[17] These approaches share with the Woolf Report a critical understanding that litigation needs to be disciplined lest it overtake the rational bounds of the stakes in any particular controversy. They depart from the Report in their willingness to entrust greater discretionary oversight to the reviewing judge. This approach seems consistent with the general tenor of the Report and leads one to question whether the determination how to proceed should be left more centrally to the procedural judge overseeing any particular matter.

## B. Rough Justice

### *1. Real-World Trade-offs: Limitations on Discovery*

Rough justice is exactly that. There is every reason to believe that with less resources devoted to any particular case, with less discovery in particular and lawyering in general, the outcomes of cases are more likely to be erroneous, there is less likelihood for the law to develop to meet new societal demands, and there will be inevitably a certain sense of dispatch to the resolution of disputes. The Report, perhaps for reasons of diplomacy, or perhaps for reasons of limited desire to invoke the wrath of litigants, pretends that the alternatives to full process are equally good. The reality is unfortunately that no amount of court assistance, no amount of good will can overcome the lack of counsel and the lack of discovery.

The lack of discovery is particularly critical since the limitation on discovery is key to the cost reductions envisioned by the Report. In place of party-initiated discovery, the Report envisions a regime of self-discovery through the disclosure process for use in the fast track, and for presumptive use in the multi-track. This proposal is similar to the recent American reform in federal civil procedure which created categories of mandatory disclosure that stand independent of party-initiated requests for the production of information.[18] The one critical difference is that in the Report's

[16] *See* Order Amending Civil Justice Expense and Delay Reduction Plan, General Order No. 93–13, E.D. Tex., Sept. 2, 1993.

[17] For an overview of phased discovery, and the specific use of 'tracks' to tailor discovery to particular cases, *see* Edward F. Sherman, *A Process Model and Agenda for Civil Justice Reforms in the States*, 46 Stan. L. Rev. 1553, 1566–70 (1994). In addition, the Manual for Complex Litigation recommends the use of 'phased, sequence or targeted' discovery in order to bring discipline and contain costs in large-scale litigation. *See* Manual for Complex Litigation § 21.422 (3d ed. 1995).

[18] For my critical assessments of the American rule, *see* Issacharoff & Loewenstein, *Unintended Consequences*, *supra* note 7.

scenario, the required disclosure concludes the production of information.

On what basis then does the Report suggest that this disclosure is likely to provide all the information necessary to litigate disputes on their merits? The only suggestion is that the disclosure process will augur in a new era of cooperative endeavors in litigation such that the adversarially-tinged discovery practices of old will no longer be necessary. It may be that my experience as a litigator leaves me quite jaded to the millenarianism of the new cooperative ethos of dispute resolution. But every instinct is that self-disclosure is unlikely to reveal much that is damaging if there is no capacity to check on the adequacy of the disclosure. The exhortations to a new cooperative spirit are likely to be unavailing when the incentives all run to non-production by the attorneys (or by sophisticated parties) who know that there is no effective means of reviewing their production.

The absence of discovery is also likely to have most pronounced adverse effects upon individual private plaintiffs, who are most likely to be in a position or relying on the adversary's production of information through which they will make their case. The absence of discovery is a real-world trade-off that should be assessed and debated on its own terms. Indeed, there is good reason to debate the value generated by many expensive forms of information gathering in the litigatin process.

On the one hand, there are numerous substantive legal rules in which the elements of liability include specific proof of the state of mind of the defendant. While there are means of arriving at such proof inferentially, it remains the case that the best sources of such information, either direct or inferential, rest with the defendant. Limitations on discovery in such circumstances may well be thought likely to diminish the capacity of plaintiffs to prevail relative to what would occur in the absence of cost as a constraint to justice.

On the other hand, there is an expanding social science literature on behavioral and psychological impediments to decision-making that call into question the perceived wisdom that additional information should bring parties closer to agreement. One study conducted in an experimental setting with graduate business students found no difficulty in the negotiation of the sale of a piece of land when the student subjects were told only the value of the land for the purchasers and the cost of the land for the sellers. When asked to renegotiate after being told the value or cost to their counterpart, however, different conceptions of a 'fair' price emerged and a significant number of were unable to negotiate an exchange.[19] Other experimental studies confirm the difficulty of controlling for self-serving bias in

[19] *See* Colin F. Camerer & George Loewenstein, *Information, Fairness, and Efficiency in Bargaining*, in Justice (Barbara A. Mellers, ed., 1993).

the incorporation of information by parties with vested stakes in disputes.[20] In addition, there are grounds to question whether the quality of adjudication is on balance greater in countries with more ample discovery, such as England or the United States, or in countries with more controlled litigation processes, such as Germany.[21]

What can be concluded is that in exchange for limited access to information, the various tracks proposed by the Woolf Report offer certainty as to costs of pretrial practice. In my view this is a trade-off. Limited procedure is a device which forgoes more the allure of more perfect justice in favor of the actuality of economy and affordability. This must be evaluated against the development of the British system of procedure from the arcane pleading rules of the common law, to fact pleading after the Judicature Acts of 1873–75, to flirtations with American-style notice pleading. From the American perspective, the foreclosure of discovery appears to compromise at least in some cases the capacity to 'effectuate a well-founded claim,' in the manner advocated by Bentham.[22] If further liberalization of pleading is indeed 'necessary in order to extend the reach of justice and to improve its quality,'[23] then the Woolf Report fails to confront fully the real-world consequences of 'half-loaf' or simply rough justice. On the other hand, if the allure of perfect information is indeed chimerical , then directly confronting the nature of the trade-off allows for an informed assessment of the merits of the proposal *ex ante* and an evaluation of its workings *ex post*.

### 2. *Paradoxes of Procedural Shortcuts*

#### a) *The Experience of Witness Statements*

The Report does not fully assess the likely consequences of its endorsement of rough justice in a number of settings. In part, this is the result of excessive confidence in the capacity of a more user-friendly managerial court system to develop truth in a manner closer to the inquisitorial courts found in the continental civil law systems. In part also, as I shall discuss more fully in the next section on litigation costs, the failure to examine some likely consequences of the suggested reforms emerges from an excessive commitment to a promised deliverance to a newer and brighter day of cooperative endeavors in litigation.

Certainly, the Report is not without acknowledgment of the capacity for procedural reforms to produce paradoxical results. For example, the Report discusses the mixed history of witness statements in anticipation of

[20] *See, e.g.*, George Loewenstein, Samuel Issacharoff, Colin Camerer, & Linda Babcock, *Self-Serving Assessments of Fairness and Pretrial Bargaining*, 22 J. of Legal Studies 135 (1993).

[21] *See* A.A.S. Zuckerman, *A Reform of Civil Procedure—Rationing Procedure Rather Than Access to Justice*, 22 J. of Law & Society 155 (1995).

[22] Quoted in Sir Jack I. H. Jacob, *The Fabric of English Civil Justice* 100 (1987).

[23] *Id.* at 100.

trial.[24] Witness statements were originally intended to streamline trials by removing an element of litigation by ambush. They were also designed to produce a cheap and reliable form of information about the merits of the case that in turn should have streamlined the litigation process. Unfortunately, formal witness statements quickly turned into an independently significant step in the litigation process. Litigants feared foreclosure of claims or areas of testimony if the witness statements were incomplete, or if the court were to limit the trial testimony to the statement alone, or some brief elaboration on the witness statement. The result has been a significant escalation of pretrial costs as a consequence of tremendous lawyer efforts in finely honing the witness statement.[25]

While the unfortunate experience with witness statements is well chronicled in the Report, the Report suffers for its failure to generalize from the paradoxical results produced by the experiment with witness statements. Every procedural reform in litigation alters the incentives operating on the parties in such a way as to potentially compromise the intended effect. The key is not to abjure reform, but to try to comprehend it as part of an overall design operating on disputants.

*b) Offers to Settle*

An example of the underappreciation of the strategic implications of procedural reforms can be found in the Report's discussion of offers to settle. There is no obvious reason why such offers should be limited to circumstances in which the defendant physically deposits the amount of the judgment with the clerk of the court. This is a cumbersome process and one that imposes significant administrative strain on the court. The Report sensibly advocates abolishing this requirement and proposes an expansive use of offers of judgment by either side to facilitate the settlement process. But will this have the desired consequences? Perhaps, but perhaps not.

There are strategic concerns that make formal offers to settle problematic, even in cases that are likely to be resolved short of trial. First, the size of the offer communicates vital information about the perceived strength of a party's position. Once combined with restrictions on discovery, this becomes a critical piece of information that affects the litigation posture of the parties. Hence, there is an inescapable incentive to use offers to settle strategically, in much the way that poker players selectively convey information by their betting. The Report omits discussion of the strategic considerations in litigation to the detriment of the overall project.[26] Similarly,

[24] Report at 176.

[25] *See, e.g.,* Report at 176.

[26] This is an area where some of the tools of law and economics as well as game theory might be of assistance. For example, Professor Geoffrey Miller of New York University School of Law has recently proposed a mechanism in which litigants could make offers of settlement into a settlement clerk—without divulging the information to the other side. At any point at which the offers of the plaintiff and defendant converged, the clerk would

although the Report wants to allow plaintiffs to make compelling offers to settle, the stick of compulsion is an enhancement of the normal costs allowed by a factor of at most 10 percent.[27] Here a comparison with the relative disutility of Rule 68 of the American Federal Rules of Civil Procedure might properly raise the question whether such a modest enhancement is likely to give any real teeth to a plaintiff's offer.[28]

*c) Summary Disposition*

More disturbing is the Report's treatment of summary disposal, a practice that can be traced to the Bills of Exchange Act of 1855 in England[29] which developed a rudimentary procedure for summary judgment in a narrow category of contract cases involving liquidated claims met with only spurious defenses.[30] The Report envisions an expansive realm for summary disposal of cases, at any time in the proceeding, and even by the court *sua sponte* without prompting of the parties. Summary judgment would be proper whenever the court determines that one party 'has no realistic prospect of success' on part or all of her case.[31]

This proposal combines an unrealistic sense of court omniscience with an inattentiveness to the invitation that expanded summary judgment lends to strategic behavior. The key to summary judgment is a proper development of a fact record from which to concluded that a party 'has no realistic prospect of success.' Except in cases involving extravagant claims of law ('I believe that I am entitled to confiscate every second green automobile

administratively enter a judgment in the agreed upon amount. *See* Robert H. Gertner and Geoffrey P. Miller, *Settlement Escrow*, 24 J. of Legal Studies 87 (1995).

27 Report at p. 196. This proposal is similar to a recent development in state civil procedure in Wisconsin. Under Wis. Stat. §§ 807.01(3) & (4), if a plaintiff makes an offer of judgment that is rejected and the plaintiff then goes on to recover a judgment larger than the offer, the plaintiff is entitled to twice the normal taxable costs, as well as interest at 12 percent from the date of the demand to the date when the judgment is paid. Note that under the American rule, attorneys' fees are not normally recoverable as a part of costs.

28 Under Rule 68, a defendant may make an offer of judgment at any time until 10 days before trial. The plaintiff then has 10 days to accept or else the offer is deemed withdrawn. If the plaintiff does not exceed the offer at trial, then the plaintiff is liable for all of defendant's administrative costs after the date of the offer—costs which do not include attorneys' fees. Because the total amount of taxable costs (such as court fees, photocopying and postage) is relatively small, the rule has had little effect on American litigation. The Supreme Court tried to give the Rule some greater power by ruling that in those cases where by statute a prevailing plaintiff is entitled to recover attorneys' fees from the other side, an offer of judgment that is not exceeded at trial would terminate the recovery of fees from the time of the offer forward. *Marek* v. *Chesny*, 473 U.S. 1 (1985).

29 The Summary Procedure on Bills of Exchange Act, 18 & 19 Vict. c. 67 (1855). *See also* Martin B. Louis, *Federal Summary Judgment Doctrine: A Critical Analysis*, 83 Yale L.J. 745, 745 (1974); Charles E. Clark & Charles U. Samenow, *The Summary Judgment*, 38 Yale L.J. 423, 424 (1929).

30 *See generally* 10 Charles A. Wright, Arthur B. Miller, and May Kay Kane, *Federal Practice & Procedure*, §2711 (1983).

31 Report at 37.

on odd-numbered Tuesdays'), the ability of a court to sift out prospects of success will turn on an appraisal of fact. Where this knowledge of facts comes from is left unclear, unless the Report means to invite summary adjudication on the pleadings—which we could in turn anticipate would increase the costs associated with pleadings in much the same fashion as resulted in an increase in costs associated with witness statements.

This is compounded by an inattention to the strategic consequences of liberal summary judgment. The Report predicts that 'applications will generally be made soon after a defence is filed and I anticipate that defendants who seek summary disposal would file their application at the same time as their defence.'[32] This appears to be an invitation to what in the U.S. are termed 'out-of-the-box' summary judgment motions by which defendants demand a factual accounting of plaintiffs' claims before any discovery or exchange of information. At least under the Federal Rules in the U.S., a plaintiff may forestall a summary judgment motion by filing an affidavit under Rule 56(f)[33] documenting the inability to respond to the summary judgment motion without additional information. Absent this protection, liberalized summary judgment threatens to be a mechanism for forestalling potentially legitimate claims where the defendant has privileged access to vital information. I found no similar protection in the Report's recommendations.

I have written extensively on the complicated strategic considerations unleashed by liberalized summary judgment in the U.S., and even on some of its potentially disruptive effects on settlement.[34] I do not pretend to any conclusive position on the consequences of expanding summary judgment in the context of English legal practice, and in particular under the English rule of cost shifting. My experience is simply that a significant redirection in favour of summary disposition of cases is a tricky enterprise that requires greater attention to its strategic and equitable implications.

## C. The Cost of Legal Services

### *1. Underregulation*

One of the overrding concerns identified by the Report is the 'excessive and unaffordable cost' of litigation.[35] While the problem is clearly identified, the

[32] Report at 38.

[33] Rule 56(f) of the Federal Rules of Civil Procedure reads:

> Should it appear from the affidavits of a party opposing the motion that the party cannot for reasons stated present by affidavit facts essential to justify the party's opposition, the court may refuse the application for the judgment or may order a continuance to permit affidavits to be obtained or depositions to be taken or discovery to be had or may make such other order as is just.

[34] *See* Samuel Issacharoff and George Loewenstein, *Second Thoughts About Summary Judgment*, 100 Yale L. J. 73 (1990).

[35] Report at 9.

root sources cited in the Report are more problematic. The Report falls back on what in the U.S. has become a familiar refrain of lawyer bashing, including the common charge that the root of the problem is the 'unrestrained adversarial culture of the present system.'[36] Lawyers are repeatedly indicted in the Report for overly aggressive representation of their clients' interests, often to the detriment of the whole legal system. Thus, as an example, the Report early on targets lawyer conduct: 'The problem of cost is fuelled by the excessively combative environment in which so much litigation is now conducted.'[37]

The focus on lawyers is, in my view, largely misplaced for it casts attention away from the critical inquiry into what incentives are at work in the litigation process that promote an escalating spiral of costs. Indeed, the Report itself effectively addresses one of the problems by its imposition of managerial caps on what litigants in small cases may do—and by extension, on the standard of care to which their attorneys may be held. Thus, the Report wisely follows the counsel of the London Solicitors' Litigation Association, which directly tied the problem of litigation costs to the established responsibility of attorneys to their clients: 'Costs can only be effectively controlled by limiting the requirement for work to be carried out in discharge of the lawyers' duty to the client.'[38]

The Report's focus on the 'adversarial culture' is also misplaced because it detracts from the real insights of Lord Woolf's recommendations. Legal systems must accept that there are real disputes in civil society, and that real disputes generate heat and passion. Rather than carrying on with plaintive cries for a new cooperative millennium, a careful analysis of the incentives at work in litigation reveals the importance of managerial judges in limiting costs.

Why then do costs escalate in discovery? First, there is the possibility of harassment, which would be consistent with some form of misconduct. In discovery, each party may seek information from the opposing side pursuant to a variety of approved mechanisms. Because the cost of complying with requests for information generally substantially exceeds that of making the request, there is a significant risk of using discovery as a strategic ploy to impose burdens and costs on the opposing side. This is a classic form of what economists term a 'moral hazard' in which parties are not forced to internalize the full costs of their conduct.[39]

While the risks of strategic misuse of discovery are exaggerated under the American rule, they would apply as well under the British rule of cost-

[36] Report at 18. [37] Report at 8. [38] Report at 11.

[39] The classic moral hazard occurs whenever a party is able to obtain insurance that will relieve it of the consequences of conduct, particularly risk seeking conduct. *See generally, The New Palgrave: A Dictionary of Economics* 549 (John Eatwell et al. eds. 1987) (defining 'moral hazard' in economic terms); Richard Posner, *Economic Analysis of Law* 376–77 (3d edn. 1986) (discussing moral hazards involved in bankruptcy).

shifting to the losing side. Even under the British rule, once parties are in litigation, they are responsible for their costs only if they lose. If a party has a fifty percent chance of prevailing, for instance, then the discounted expected cost of each additional amount spent on discovery is only half the actual amount. In other words, if a party has a 50–50 chance of prevailing, then that party has only a one-in-two chance of paying for its own costs. While the moral hazard is not as great as under the American rule, it exists nonetheless.

But the moral hazard exists independent of its capacity for strategic misuse. So long as the costs of engaging in discovery are not internalized, there is no disincentive toward pursuing further investigation. This is compounded by two additional factors. First, as the London Solicitors' Litigation Association rightly identified, exhaustive investigation is seen as the lawyers' responsibility to the client. Consequently, the failure to engage in discovery is by definition a form of malpractice.

Second, and perhaps more critical, is the unknown potential for incremental costs to ward off a disastrous loss and the attendant cost shifting. If we think of additional discovery expenses as an insurance policy against the potential of not only assuming all the costs a party has already expended, but all the costs of the other side, then the impetus toward greater expenditures becomes clear. This is the reason that the emerging consensus on comparisons of British and American cost rules is that under the British system, parties are less likely to enter into litigation, but once there are more likely to expend greater resources.[40] Thus, the costs escalate in the first instance because of the tremendous financial blow that a trial loss would impose.[41] Second, because there is no way to monitor the other side's expenditures until a bill for costs is taxed, there is no means of mutual assurance that the other side is not unleashing all potential resources, and thereby presumably expanding its prospects of prevailing.

[40] For a recent overview of the economic literature on the English and American cost shifting rules, *see* James W. Hughes & Edward A. Snyder, *Litigation and Settlement under the English and American Rules: Theory and Evidence*, 38 J. of Law and Econ. 225 (1995). The work of Professors Hughes and Snyder is particularly illuminative since it contains an empirical comparison of medical malpractice claims in Florida before and after the state adopted an English cost shifting rule.

[41] I recently presented a similar thesis to a group of European law students in Holland. When challenged on the assertion that costs should rise more dramatically under a cost-shifting regime, I used the following auction illustration. I held up a 50 guilder note and asked two students how much they would be willing to bid for it. The rule of the auction is the same as in litigation under the British rule: the students could bid as little as they wished, but the loser was responsible for the 'costs,' which I defined as the losing bid. (An even closer parallel would have been to force the losing bidder to cover both the winning and losing bid.) The first student bid one guilder, followed by a two guilder bid from the other student. At this point, the bidders were locked in a series of infinite escalations since each incrementally higher bid would rationally forestall the acceptance of a devastating payout. (Needless to say, I did not attempt to collect on the bids.)

It is at this point that the lawyers play a significant role in the escalation of costs. Considering the impetus for clients to associate the amount of time spent on the case with the prospect of success, a lawyer billing by the hour has absolutely no incentive to curtail the time spent on discovery and pre-trial wrangling. Since the attorney not only does not internalize the costs but rather profits from them. The attorney has every incentive to bill more hours in the name of the good of the client.

The Report's proposals deal with both the prisoners' dilemma aspect of discovery and the incentives for esclation of lawyer's costs in two distinct ways. First, the managerial role of the procedural judge takes much of the power of escalation out of the hands of the litigants and their attorneys. This is done either by fixing the total amount of discovery in the small claims and fast track disputes, or by imposing a strong overseer in the multitrack. Second, the proposals give each side critical assurance that the adversary has not, in effect, launched its nuclear arsenal. Not only must each side obtain permission of the court before engaging in discovery from the other side, but each side must present periodic accountings for costs, thereby informing both the court and the other side of the scale of the controversy. Together, these reforms give every indication of creating systemic brakes on the costs of litigation. I would put my money on these sorts of structural protections over any exhortations to a new culture of adversarial communitarianism.

## 2. Overregulation

Market inefficiencies may result from markets that are overregulated as well as underregulated. While the Report focuses its reform efforts on greater regulation of fee arrangements, there is surprisingly little attention paid to possible deregulation of the legal services market, and to the potential salutary effect that competition might bring. The Report does single out this issue:

> It is, however, the case that market forces, which in other contexts have acted as a restraint on prices, operate rather weakly in relation to the supply of professional legal services. Factors associated with high charging are to be found in this field; notably, the restrictions on access to the market and the regulatory controls over practice considered necessary to maintain proper professional standards and the integrity of the legal system.[42]

What then, of the potential for deregulation of the legal market, consistent with the overriding objectives of insuring integrity and professionalism? The Report mentions in passing the recent innovation of conditional fees, an apparently restricted variant of the contingency fee that is

42 Report at 200.

commonplace in the U.S.[43] It is of course unobjectionable to pressure lawyers to disclose the nature of anticipated legal costs, as the Report forcefully does. But this innovation alone is unlikely to radically alter the unavailability of legal services to those who are neither wealthy nor eligible for legal aid. The fact that large numbers of people avoid recourse to the legal system for fear of high costs indicates not absence of knowledge about the prevailing fee structure, but exquisite sensitivity to it.

The Report is evasive on a critical issue of whether parties should be able to contract more broadly with attorneys. Would legal services be more broadly available if conditional fees were allowed? Would consumer welfare be enhanced? Would the possibility of unscrupulous attorney conduct overwhelm unsophisticated one-time purchasers of legal services? The Report's passing, and apparently positive, reference to conditional fees whets the appetite for a more comprehensive review of the legal services market.

If this is indeed Lord Woolf's view, then the Report entails a rather significant alteration of the way in which legal services are provided in Britain. As recently as 1987, a leading treatise on English procedure in commenting on the rejection of contingency fees in shareholder derivative actions confidently proclaimed, 'thus the contingency fee in England may be said to have been finally laid to rest.'[44] To the extent that contingency fees are working beneficially in the limited experience, one would hope for a greater discussion of their costs and benefits,[45] and their interaction with exposure of the presumably penurient litigant for costs should the opposing party prevail.

The discussion of fee arrangements leads also to the question of cost shifting. Conditional fees are but one of a series of potential reforms that

[43] Under the Courts and Legal Services Act 1990, §58, the Lord Chancellor was given authority to permit conditional fee agreements. As of 1994, the proposed conditional fees were to allow a 100 percent contingency enhancement of normal hourly fees in a specified range of cases, such as insolvency and personal injury. Neil Andrews, Principles of Civil Procedure 451 n.15a (1994).

[44] Sir Jack I. H. Jacob, *The Fabric of English Civil Justice* 289 (1987). The same hostility to contingency fees is expressed in a more recent treatise on English procedure. According to Neil Andrews, the contingency fee operates to inflate damage awards in the U.S., warps the conduct of lawyers who will 'fall victim to the temptation to act unprofessionally in order to win their contingency fee, and induces the public to litigate more freely.' Andrews, *supra* note 40 at 451. The rather facile attack on fees is most notable for its claim that contingency fees as opposed to hourly charges induce a divergence between the interests of lawyers and their clients. While there are problems inherent in any principal-agent relationship, the inducement to expend ever greater time on litigation seems most apparent when an attorney bills a client by the hour.

[45] The recent limited adoption of conditional fees has already generated a storm of controversy in Britain. *See* Sharon Wallach, *No win, no fee. But will justice be the loser with 'no win, no fee'? Opponents fear that conditional fees could lead to US-style litigation bonanzas, The Independent*, July 5, 1995, at 14. The limited adoption of conditional fees provides a wonderful arena for an empirical assessment of the effects of this reform.

are left relatively unexplored. For example, the Report is quite positive in describing the elimination of cost shifting against the losing party in small claims court. Yet the Report presents a rather formalistic account of the arguments for and against cost shifting, and concludes without much reasoning or argumentation that the present system should be retained.[46]

There are two distinct arguments for a relaxation of the English rule of cost shifting that may be gleaned from the Report. The first is that such a relaxation would allow broader access to the courts and would allow parties a more fixed exposure for legal costs if they do seek to assert a claim. The second is that there are externalities in the sense of public goods produced by broader access to the legal process. The first is a more realistic level of insurance for market actors who currently find the threat of potential litigation financially ruinous. The second is an expansion of law as society evolves.

If these gains are truly to be associated with the elimination of cost-shifting in small claims litigation, are there other areas where the harsh consequences of the British rule should be relaxed? Should citizens be relieved of cost-shifting in asserting claims against the State, or shareholders in challenging corporate conduct, or claimants in defamation actions, or claimants in cases of insurance non-payment? Each of these potentially involves parties with radical asymmetries of power and information. Each produces a certain measure of public benefit in litigation. Should the rule that inhibits these actions be modified for all such causes of action, or might it be subject to waiver or abridgment by a procedural judge at the threshold stages of litigation?[47] Insofar as the Report goes, these are questions for another day.

## III. OTHER ELEMENTS OF PROCEDURAL REFORM

Lord Woolf envisions a more engaged judiciary overseeing a leaner civil litigation system. The consumer of legal services would encounter a more streamlined retail mart where price information would be readily available, where more shopping assistance would be encountered in the form of consumer-friendly kiosks and subordinate court officials, and where the sale racks of price-limited dispute resolution would be clearly visible.

If I may be indulged this shopping metaphor one more step, why not proceed to reforms at the wholesale level. What about the impediments to

[46] Report at 204.

[47] One of the most 'extensive fee provision[s], authorizing partial fees in all cases unless the court otherwise directs' appears in Rule 82 of the Alaska Rules of Civil Procedure. Douglas Laycock, *Modern American Remedies* 846 (1994). The court has some discretion in this matter and may limit the fee award to avoid deterring other potential litigants.

aggregate resolution of disputes, to removing the costs associated with duplication of product services? I wish to raise two points of inquiry whose complexity necessarily goes beyond the scope of this commentary. Nonetheless, these potential areas of reform do raise significant questions about the dispensation of justice in mass society.

For example, one useful starting point may be the potential for a broader conception of estoppel. English law restricts estoppel of either the cause of action or issue variety to the parties to the original action, their successors in interest, or their privities.[48] Much economy may be gained by recognizing finality in factual determinations between similarly situated litigants. Thus, for example, should a lorry swerve out of control on a congested street, why should the issue of the driver's negligence be subject to repeat judicial inquiry? If the negligence is established in the first case to proceed to trial, where the driver has a full and fair opportunity to defend the merits of the claim, should not the driver be bound by that determination in all subsequent litigation emerging from the original road accident?

Broader estoppel can have two consequences. On the one hand, there are clearly tremendous efficiency gains to be had in dispute resolution by eliminating the incentive to repeat litigation over common factual issues. On the other hand, broader estoppel raises the stakes in any particular controversy, especially for repeat litigants. Whether the benefits of more broad-scale resolution of disputed issues outweigh the risk of greater incentives to litigate any particular controversy again seems an appropriate area for inquiry in refashioning English procedure.

The limitation on estoppel ties in to the absence of the most critical aggregative devices: joinder or claims and representative or class actions. The simple fact of the matter is that we live in mass society. The common tort scenario of centuries past is today much more likely to involve a multiplicity of actors. The horse bolting on the roadways of yesteryear is today more likely to be an accident on a common carrier. The claims made, the parties involved, and the attendant demands on the legal system will all expand in turn.

How then should the British legal system manage claims arising from a jet blown up over Lockerbie, the collapse of the Maxwell empire, or the mushrooming litigation over Lloyds? The Report to date has not addressed these matters. Hopefully, additional attention will be given to engaging the ongoing discussions of representative or class actions in English law.[49]

[48] Neil Andrews, *Principles of Civil Procedure* 511–13 (1994).

[49] Group litigation has evolved from the Middle Ages concept of representation of an entity, such as a guild or a village, to the modern efforts to meld together a group of individuals who each have control of their own lawsuit into a single cohesive unit. During this evolution, Britain has seen group representation change from a more generalized representation to a narrow representation focused on a particular problem. Along with this development, Britain has seen a dramatic change in the quantity of group litigation. In the Middle Ages,

British courts have allowed aggregate claims to go forward on a more-or-less ad hoc basis in settings as diverse as the Hillsborough Stadium football tragedy[50] to the common losses resulting from the sinking of a cargo ship.[51] Once again, the invitation to a systematic overview of English procedure would seemingly extend to the frontiers of procedural developments in the courts.

## CONCLUSION

These comments are self-consciously the product of an outsider to the British legal system. My objective is not to resolve the question of how best to proceed, but to respond from the vantage point of the American legal and academic experience. If there is one insight that can be garnered from the study of procedure in the U.S., it is an appreciation of the complex incentives that operate on parties to real-world disputes. If there is one overall criticism of the Woolf Report, it is a failure to systematically assess how the strategic incentives that drive litigants and their attorneys will play out in the altered procedural climate envisioned by the Report.

At the same time, no reader can walk away from the Woolf Report without recognizing that a functioning, centuries-old civil justice system is a daunting multi-headed beast. Lord Woolf's *Access to Justice* is a truly admirable effort to tame the beast. Its clear advocacy of a managerial regime and its wise attentiveness to the inefficiencies and inequities of a poorly functioning market are the critical starting points for any systemic reform. As the lawyers long ago learned, however, the devil is in the details.

group litigation flourished. This type of litigation continued to be a prominent force in Britain until the late 19th Century. However, it has slowly become almost 'extinct' in Britain in recent years. *See generally,* Stephen C. Yeazell, *From Medieval Group Litigation to the Modern Class Action* (1987).

50 *Chapman* v. *Chief Constable of South Yorkshire, The Times*, March 20, 1990 (allowing for the aggregate treatment of 900 claims).

51 *Monarch S.S. Co. Ltd.* v. *Greystoke Castle (Cargo Owners)*, [1947] A.C. 265 (H.L.).

# 14

# *Limiting Costs for Better Access to Justice: The German Approach*

DIETER LEIPOLD*[1]

## I. GENERAL REMARKS

The Woolf Report is, form a German point of view, very impressive and interesting. Generally German lawyers and scholars of jurisprudence admire the English System of Courts and Justice. One reason is the great English tradition, the other the observation that the number of judges, compared with the population, is so much lower than in Germany. The German system of civil procedure is not regarded to be ideal in any way. On the contrary there is a permanent effort to reform and improve the German civil procedure. To shorten up and to simplify the procedure have been the main aims of such reforms. At present the greatest problem is the increasing number of civil (and other) lawsuits in Germany. Whereas in the seventies the problem of access to justice was broadly discussed in Germany (and also almost worldwide), nowadays this question is not mentioned as frequently. By means of the reform of legal aid and the introduction of legal advice aid before the beginning of a lawsuit in 1980 the possibility for less wealthy people to go to court has been improved essentially (which doesn't mean that all problems on this field are really solved). Today, German people are said to go to the courts in too many cases, and the efforts to find alternative solutions (for example ways of alternative dispute resolution outside of the courts) have not been very successful until now.

It is not the purpose of the present essay to make proposals for the reform of English civil procedure. Each nation has its own legal culture and tradition and a reform must always be an organic evolution on the basis of this historical background. But there are a lot of statements and recommendations in the Woolf Report in regard to which a comparison with German regulations and experiences could be very interesting. This is especially the case in the field of the role of the judge. The idea of introducing

* Professor of Law, University of Freiburg im Breisgau.

[1] I owe special thanks to Winfried Holtermüller and Rufus Pichler for their helpful contributions to this essay.

a managerial judge finds many parallels in the German system. But comparing the multitude of situations where more activity of the judge could be introduced in English civil procedure with similar questions in the German system would require a broader and more intensive look on both legal systems than it is possible to provide here. For the moment I only want to emphasize that the German civil procedure is in the hand of the judge (or the panel of judges) from the very beginning. Probably in England some scholars are afraid to move from the adversary system to an inquisitorial system of court management is introduced in a broad manner. But it is not true (and in this point foreign descriptions of continental, especially German civil procedure are not always correct) that the German civil procedure is an inquisitorial system. We also call our system a party system, which means that the objective of the litigation, the issues and also the evidence are first and foremost determined by the parties. But the judge has to help the parties if necessary and he has to take evidence whereas the duty of the parties is to bring forward the evidence (to name the witnesses and so on). This is also important for the question of the costs involved in the taking of evidence and therefore the point is discussed below.

My purpose in this essay is to try to give an impression of the German cost system which is based on the principle of fixed costs. The Woolf Report refers to cost problems in many passages. I think that this practical emphasis of economic factors operating in civil procedure is an enormous merit of the report. The influence of cost regulations must not be underestimated and if you want to influence the reality of the procedure, you have to think about the degree to which the behaviour of the parties and especially of their representatives is influenced by economic factors. This influence cannot be denied, though in Germany lawyers and their official organisations use to emphasize that their decision of undertaking a lawsuit, recommending appeal and so on is only determined by legal aspects regardless of their personal income.

## II. RULE OF COSTS IN GERMAN CIVIL PROCEDURE

### 1. Basic rule

The basic rule in German civil procedure is that the costs follow the result of litigation: the losing party has to bear all the costs of the procedure, § 91 Abs. 1 ZPO. This means that the winner has the right to recover his costs from the loser (especially the fees for his lawyer) and that the court fees and expenses have to be paid by the loser (and have to be refunded to the winner as far as he paid to the court in advance). In case of an appeal or other remedies the unsuccessful party has to bear the costs of the process, § 97 ZPO.

Although the cost shifting rule does not always produce just results, there is no debate about this rule at present. In the seventies there was a broad discussion about access to justice and in those days various solutions were suggested; for example litigation without costs or an obligatory insurance system. But none of these suggestions was realized. To improve access to justice there was an important reform of legal aid, and legal advice aid in the forefield of litigation was introduced. To me it seems that the cost shifting rule has proven its merits. At present in Germany the biggest problem is seen in the continuously increasing number of actions. But it must be supposed that without the cost shifting rule and the risk of having to pay the full costs the trend of people going to court would grow even more.

The American no-costs rule is often criticized in Germany. Some commentators go so far as to suggest that American judgments should not be recognized and enforced in Germany because the American rule violates the German principle of public order (ordre public). The courts have not accepted this opinion, which indeed goes too far. But there is at least a potential inequality of treatment in American procedure. For a plaintiff may sometimes receive an award of damages which is larger than his loss (e.g. through exemplary or punitive damages) and thus recover his litigation expenses indirectly. The defendant, however, has no comparable chance of recouping his legal expenses.

Lord Woolf recommends that the cost shifting rule in its pure form should be confined, for example by increasing the small claims jurisdiction where the standard rule is 'no costs'. In German law on the contrary the cost shifting rule is applicable in all civil procedures. There is no special rule for small claims. But as legal fees are not calculated on an hourly basis but are fixed by statute the problem is not the same as in England. Nevertheless the German position has been criticized because in relation to the value of the claim the costs are higher in small claims than they are in claims of higher values. On the other hand one cannot reduce the lawyers' fees for small claims below a certain level. So this problem must be solved by financial aid for people with low wealth and income.

In German law there are also certain exceptions to the basic rule. Usually the loser has to pay the costs of the opponent's lawyer also in small claims. It doesn't matter if the party was obliged to be represented by law or if he would have been able to litigate for himself. But there is a different rule in labour courts. In the first instance there is no recovery of the expenses for a lawyer or other representatives, § 12 a ArbGG. The purpose of this rule is to facilitate the litigation for the employee by reducing the risk of costs if he loses the lawsuit. In practice he is often represented by a secretary of the trade union and does not have to pay costs for this service. On the other hand the employer is seen to be in a better economic status so that he can pay his lawyer anyway.

As in Germany the costs—court fees and lawyers' fees—depend on the value of the claim, the method of defining this value determines the amount of costs to be paid. Thus, another way to reduce the burden of costs is by confining the value of the claim. In some fields of German law you can find such rules. As an example one might mention § 23 b UWG (law against unfair competition), by which the value of the claim is reduced according to the financial capacity of the party. Parallels to this regulation can be found in § 144 Patentgesetz (patent law), § 26 Gebrauchsmustergesetz (law about utility patents) and § 31 a Warenzeichengesetz (law about trade marks). § 12 Abs. 1 S. 2 Gerichtskostengesetz (law about court fees) limits the value of claims dealing with general terms and conditions of trade to a maximum amount of 500,000 DM, but does not reduce the value of claims lying beyond this limit. Another regulation, § 16 Gerichtskostengesetz, reduces the value of the claim to a maximum of one year's rent in claims concerning rent and leasing affairs.

In effect the basic rule is made more tolerable for a less wealthy party, especially for a consumer. But as this system restricts the fees of the lawyer (and the court) and not only the sum to be refunded to the winner, it is not very popular among lawyers and has not been extended.

### 2. Modifications of the basic rule

There are several rules which modify the burden of costs.

The costs are proportionally divided if the plaintiff succeeds only to a certain degree (§ 92 ZPO). For example if he demands a sum of 100,000 DM as a recovery of damages and the court only gives judgment for 60,000 DM, the plaintiff has to pay two fifths and the defendant three fifths of the costs.

The defendant can avoid the costs if he accepts the claim in the early stage of the process and if he didn't give reason for the lawsuit by his previous behaviour. In this case the plaintiff has to bear all costs, § 93 ZPO.

In cases of divorce the costs are not distributed according to the basic rule. Here every party has to pay his own costs and half of the court fees, § 93 a ZPO. The court can render another cost order if this appears to be just.

## III. COSTS TO BE PAID

### 1. General remarks

The principle is that the party who has to pay the costs has to bear the court's costs and the opponent's costs.

The court's costs consist of court fees and court expenses. Court expenses are in particular the costs for witnesses and experts.

The costs of the opponent are to be compensated as far as they have been necessary and reasonable in the proceeding. These costs include recovery for loss of time and travel expenses for the party attending the trial. But the most important point is that the lawyers' fees have to be refunded in any case. It does not matter whether it was necessary by legal or practical standards to be represented by a lawyer. The costs that have to be refunded are always limited to the fees and expenses set down in the statute about lawyers' fees (Bundesrechtsanwalts-Gebührenordnung). If the winning party has agreed to pay more to his lawyer (see below), he cannot recover this additional sum.

### 2. The costs of adducing evidence

The costs of evidence form a part of the court's expenses which finally have to be paid by the party who bears the costs.

Witnesses and experts are not paid by the parties themselves but by the court. The party who wants a witness to be heard or an expert to be asked for his opinion, however, has to pay a sufficient sum of money to the court in advance. Otherwise the witness will not be summoned or the expert opinion will not be ordered.

The amounts to be paid are regulated by law (Gesetz über die Entschädigung von Zeugen und Sachverständigen, law about indemnification of witnesses and experts). For experts there are also legally restricted amounts per hour spent for the claim.

The parties can influence the costs of evidence by their requests for evidence. But this influence is limited because it is the duty of the court to examine the relevance of the evidence before giving an order to take evidence.

In German civil procedure there is nothing similar to pre-trial discovery. From its beginning the lawsuit is managed by the court. To be exact, it is managed by the same judge who has to sit in trial and who will render judgment if the case is not settled before. So there are no possibilities for a party to increase costs by demanding documents from the opponent.

A party may be forced by the circumstances of the case to spend money in gathering evidence. He can procure investigations or experts' opinions on his own. But these costs don't form part of the costs which the loser has to bear.

The witnesses and experts are heard by the court, usually at the trial, and, under certain circumstances, in a written form. The parties don't have to present the statements of witnesses in advance. As there are no depositions, no costs can be generated in this way. In this context it must be emphasized that German lawyers generally shrink from interviewing witnesses before trial. The reasons for this behaviour can be related to the professional duties of the lawyers. § 6 Abs. 5 of the 'Standesrichtlinien' (rules of lawyers' professional duties) contained a rule according to which even the impression of influencing the statement of a witness in an unobjective way had to be avoided. It must be mentioned that those 'Standesrichtlinien' are no longer considered to be directly effective norms because of constitutional reasons. In a formal sense, the legal power of those rules could not be compared with the one of statute or law. So a new legal basis has to be found to regulate the professional duties of German lawyers, but it is expected to correspond with the former rule in § 6 Abs. 5 of the 'Standesrichtlinien'. This means that direct contacts between a party's lawyer and a witness are not strictly prohibited but should generally be avoided.

## IV. COURT FEE SYSTEM

The court fees are regulated by the Gerichtskostengesetz. The latest reform of this law took place in 1994, when the system was simplified to make its application easier and at the same time the fees were raised.

The court fees are payable in a very schematic way not following the features of the concrete lawsuit but being determined by the stages that the litigation reaches. In every instance the fees are payable anew.

In the court of first instance three fee units are payable if the procedure is concluded by a judgment, but only one fee unit has to be paid if the claim is brought to an end by withdrawal of the action, judgment on the basis of an acknowledgement or by settlement.

In the second instance (appeal) there are different rules. Four and a half fee units must be paid if there is a judgment with written grounds. If the judgment does not have written reasons (which means waiver, acknowledgement, judgment by default or the parties' declaration that they consider grounds unnecessary) only three fee units arise.

In the third instance (called revision, which means appeal on a question of law to the Federal Court), up to five fee units can arise. This is the case if the Federal Court renders a judgment with written grounds.

The amount of the fee unit depends on the value of the claim, and is, in this sense, a basic sum which has to be multiplied by the factors mentioned above.

The amounts can be derived from the following table. The column 'three fee units' gives an impression of the costs of a full lawsuit in the first

| Value of the claim | One fee unit | Three fee units |
|---|---|---|
| up to 600 DM | 50 DM | 150 DM |
| 1,200 DM | 70 DM | 210 DM |
| 1,800 DM | 90 DM | 270 DM |
| 3,000 DM | 130 DM | 390 DM |
| 5,000 DM | 160 DM | 480 DM |
| 8,000 DM | 205 DM | 615 DM |
| 10,000 DM | 235 DM | 705 DM |
| 14,000 DM | 295 DM | 885 DM |
| 20,000 DM | 385 DM | 1,155 DM |
| 50,000 DM | 655 DM | 1,965 DM |
| 80,000 DM | 835 DM | 2,505 DM |
| 100,000 DM | 955 DM | 2,865 DM |
| 160,000 DM | 1,355 DM | 4,065 DM |
| 250,000 DM | 1,955 DM | 5,865 DM |
| 400,000 DM | 2,955 DM | 8,865 DM |
| 700,000 DM | 4,430 DM | 13,290 DM |
| 1 Mio DM | 5,905 DM | 17,715 DM |
| 3 Mio DM | 11,905 DM | 35,715 DM |
| 5 Mio DM | 17,905 DM | 53,715 DM |
| 10 Mio DM | 32,905 DM | 98,715 DM |
| 25 Mio DM | 77,905 DM | 233,715 DM |
| 50 Mio DM | 152,905 DM | 458,715 DM |
| 75 Mio DM | 227,905 DM | 683,715 DM |
| 100 Mio DM | 302,905 DM | 908,715 DM |

instance (including a judgment). But the expenses for witnesses, experts and so on are not included.

As may be seen from this table, there is no linear increase of the court fees in relation to the value of the claim. The percentage of costs is decreasing considerably with the value of the claim. A value of 100 Mio DM produces court fees (three fee units) of less than 1% of the value, whereas a value of the claim amounting to only 3,000 DM will lead to court fees of 13%.

*Lawyers' fee system*

The lawyers' fees are regulated by the Bundesrechtsanwaltsgebührenordnung (BRAGO, federal statute about lawyers' fees), recently reformed in 1994. For the conduct of a civil case the lawyer is not paid according to the working hours spent in the process. On the contrary the fees are—in a similar way as the court fees—fixed in a very schematic manner. The basic unit of a fee is charged at least once, but can go up to four times. This depends on the stage the procedure reaches. Thus the total amount of fees is increasing if the litigation is not brought to an end in an early stage. Typically the work done by the lawyer is also growing if the procedure goes on, and this is compensated by the duplication or triplication of the basic fee unit. But it does not matter how long the procedure actually lasts. So if once the three fee units are earned, there is no economic interest for a lawyer to lengthen the procedure in the same instance. But he can earn one more fee unit if a settlement between the parties is reached.

The first fee unit (procedure fee) is charged for the court proceeding in general. It is already earned with the commencement of the lawsuit.

The second fee unit (hearing fee) is earned if there is an oral hearing. It doesn't matter if this hearing is only preliminary or if it forms the basis for the final judgment (similar to the trial in English procedure). If there is more than one hearing or trial nevertheless the hearing fee may be charged only once.

The third fee unit (evidence fee) can be charged if the lawyer represents his party while evidence is taken. For example if the court hears witnesses and in this hearing the lawyer acts for his party, he earns the evidence fee. The evidence fee can also only be earned once in the same instance. So the lawyer doesn't get more money where ten witnesses and three expert witnesses are heard than he gains if there is only one witness. The lawyer has an economic interest that the procedure reaches the stage of taking evidence by the court, but he has no economic interest in expanding the evidence.

If the litigation is finished by court settlement, the lawyer also receives one fee unit as a settlement fee. To make it more lucrative for a lawyer to settle a case without litigation, the fee for an out-of-court settlement is now one unit and a half.

Similar to the court fees, the amount of every fee unit the lawyer can charge depends on the value of the claim. Very much like the court fees, the percentage of the fee unit compared to the value of the claim is higher at low values. But nevertheless the amount of the fee need not cover the working hours of the lawyer at a case with low value. It does not follow that the time spent by the lawyer is short because the value of the claim is not high. Such a claim may raise very difficult questions of fact and of law as well. The system is sometimes criticized because the fees for claims of lower value do not cover the expenditure of time. But the philosophy of the system is that there is usually a mixture of claims with quite different values in the practice of a lawyer, the higher fees from procedures with considerable values being destined to compensate the insufficient fees for small claims.

If the lawsuit is very complicated and the lawyer is not willing to conduct it by charging the fees provided in the fee statute, he can come to an agreement with the client about a higher fee than legally provided. But such an agreement is only valid if a declaration by the party is made in written form. To ensure that the client recognizes the nature of the declaration, it must not be contained within the paper giving authority to the lawyer nor within any other printed form containing other declarations. It is important to remember that such higher fees by agreement cannot be recovered from the opponent. Therefore a party will agree upon such a contract of costs only under specific circumstances.

Principally it is not allowed to stipulate fees which are lower than those provided by law, § 49 b BRAO (federal statute about lawyers). According to the intention of the law, competition of lawyers by offering lower prices is not desirable because in such a case the quality of the work of lawyers might decrease.

On the other hand, in German law it is forbidden to stipulate contingent fees, especially in the form that a part of the received sum has to be paid to the lawyer (quota litis). Recently this was regulated expressis verbis by statute law, the above mentioned § 49 b BRAO. But also in former times such a contract was invalid because it was seen as a violation of boni mores. The contrast to American practice is striking, but in Germany a contingent fee is considered to be not compatible with the principle of independence of the lawyer.

In the second instance (appeal) the system of the fee units is similar, but the units are raised to 130 per cent of the basic unit. And in the third instance (revision) the unit amounts to 200 per cent. So the cost risk is much higher in the further instances and each party thinking about going to appeal must take this into consideration. But for the lawyers it is of economic interest to go to the upper instances and therefore some people suppose that lawyers' advice about going to appeal is not always unselfish. Naturally the organisations of lawyers deny such a suspicion. The number of appeals is very high and, as a result, there is a debate about limiting the right to appeal.

The amount of the fee units can be seen from the following table. The column 'three fee units' shows the lawyer's fees in a first instance procedure reaching oral hearing and taking evidence. You must, however, be aware that the lawyer will additionally charge value-added tax (German 'Umsatzsteuer' amounting to 15% of the lawyer's fees) and a lump-sum amount of up to 40 DM for mail expenses.

| Value of the claim | one fee unit | three fee units |
|---|---|---|
| up to 600 DM | 50 DM | 150 DM |
| 1,200 DM | 90 DM | 270 DM |

| Value of the claim | one fee unit | three fee units |
|---:|---:|---:|
| 1,800 DM | 130 DM | 390 DM |
| 3,000 DM | 210 DM | 630 DM |
| 5,000 DM | 320 DM | 960 DM |
| 8,000 DM | 485 DM | 1,455 DM |
| 10,000 DM | 595 DM | 1,785 DM |
| 14,000 DM | 735 DM | 2,205 DM |
| 20,000 DM | 945 DM | 2,835 DM |
| 50,000 DM | 1,425 DM | 4,275 DM |
| 80,000 DM | 1,845 DM | 5,535 DM |
| 100,000 DM | 2,125 DM | 6,375 DM |
| 160,000 DM | 2,445 DM | 7,335 DM |
| 250,000 DM | 2,925 DM | 8,775 DM |
| 400,000 DM | 3,725 DM | 11,175 DM |
| 700,000 DM | 4,975 DM | 14,925 DM |
| 1 Mio DM | 6,225 DM | 18,675 DM |
| 3 Mio DM | 12,225 DM | 36,675 DM |
| 5 Mio DM | 18,225 DM | 54,675 DM |
| 10 Mio DM | 33,225 DM | 99,675 DM |
| 25 Mio DM | 79,225 DM | 234,675 DM |
| 50 Mio DM | 153,225 DM | 459,675 DM |
| 75 Mio DM | 228,225 DM | 684,675 DM |
| 100 Mio DM | 303,225 DM | 909,675 DM |

## VI. THE RISK OF COSTS IN TOTAL

Following the cost shifting rule the unsuccessful party has to pay the court fees and the fees of the opponent's lawyer. Moreover, he cannot recover the fees of his own lawyer. The addition of both lawyers' fees and the court fees shows the total amount of the cost risk. But also here it must be mentioned that costs for witnesses, experts, taxes etc. have to be added.

| Value of the claim | Total risk of costs if both parties are represented by lawyers |
|---:|---:|
| up to 600 DM | 450 DM |
| 1,200 DM | 750 DM |
| 1,800 DM | 1,050 DM |
| 3,000 DM | 1,650 DM |
| 5,000 DM | 2,400 DM |

| Value of the claim | Total risk of costs if both parties are represented by lawyers |
|---|---|
| 8,000 DM | 3,525 DM |
| 10,000 DM | 4,275 DM |
| 14,000 DM | 5,295 DM |
| 20,000 DM | 6,825 DM |
| 50,000 DM | 10,515 DM |
| 80,000 DM | 13,575 DM |
| 100,000 DM | 15,615 DM |
| 160,000 DM | 18,735 DM |
| 250,000 DM | 23,415 DM |
| 400,000 DM | 31,215 DM |
| 700,000 DM | 43,140 DM |
| 1 Mio DM | 55,065 DM |
| 3 Mio DM | 109,065 DM |
| 5 Mio DM | 163,065 DM |
| 10 Mio DM | 298,065 DM |
| 25 Mio DM | 703,065 DM |
| 50 Mio DM | 1,378,065 DM |
| 75 Mio DM | 2,053,065 DM |
| 100 Mio DM | 2,728,065 DM |

## VII. ACCESS TO JUSTICE AND LEGAL AID

### 1. Legal aid

The German system of legal aid (§§ 114 ff. ZPO) was fundamentally reformed in 1980, the latest minor reform taking place in autumn 1994.

The intention of legal aid is that the enforcement of a person's civil rights shall not depend on financial circumstances. Since access to justice must not be denied to people who normally couldn't afford the costs of litigation, legal aid helps them to either pursue their rights as a plaintiff in court or to properly defend themselves against claims brought against them.

Thus, the applicant's personal economic status determines whether legal aid will be granted or not. Basically, everybody must fully make use of his financial means to cover the costs of a lawsuit; not only his income (including receipts of rent and interest etc.) but also his property must be staked for a lawsuit.

Determining whether a person's financial power is sufficient to litigate without external support requires some arithmetical operations. A basic amount of momentarily 643 DM monthly for the applicant himself, a further sum of 643 DM for her husband or his wife and an additional amount of 452 DM for every person receiving maintenance from the applicant is deducted from the income or property. Furthermore, taxes, contributions to the legal social insurance system, the rent to be paid every month, and even the banks' lending rates for housing accommodations are deductions from income and property. The income remaining decides whether legal aid is granted in a non-repayable way (in case of minor incomes or property) or on the basis of repayable instalments. Considering the fact that rents and further costs of living are usually quite high especially in the larger German cities, even an income of more than 2,000 DM monthly need not be an obstacle for receiving legal aid even in the form of non-repayable grants, though repayable instalments appear to be the regular case. In effect, the appropriation of legal aid is a question of the applicant's individual economic situation, as it is regularly the case with social security benefits in Germany.

The introduction of repayable instalments was one of the main issues of the reform taking place in 1980, ending up a controversial debate.

Legal aid being granted in repayable instalments does not mean that the costs and fees arising from the lawsuit have to be paid off completely, as in these cases the applicant also does not have to stake all his income or property but only the appropriate part of it and the maximum number of monthly instalments is restricted to 48.

The applicant has to render an account of his economic situation using an official form before the court can decide. Legal aid being granted to an applicant means that no court fees and no fees for the applicant's lawyer have to be paid. The applicant's lawyer—who can be chosen deliberately—will only receive lower fees payable not by his client but by the state. § 123 Bundesrechtsanwalts-Gebührenordnung (federal statute about lawyers' fees) orders that from a value of the claim of 7,000 DM onwards the lawyer can only charge reduced fees, and in case the value of the claim exceeds 50,000 DM the amount of 'one fee' (in the above mentioned sense) is fixed at 765 DM without any further increase. In claims of higher value this, of course, means an economic sacrifice for the lawyer and must be considered as a compensation for bearing no risk of non-payment (the state having to pay instead of his poor client), but also as the lawyers' contribution to the German system of social welfare. The lawyer cannot avoid this result because he is obliged to act for every client to whom legal aid is being granted (§ 48 Bundesrechtsanwaltsordnung, federal statute about lawyers).

In case the party gaining legal aid is successful, his lawyer is allowed to charge the normal (higher) fees to be paid by the losing opponent. In effect, the poor party's lawyer is naturally interested in winning the claim in order to charge non-reduced fees. Although this will hardly have been intended by the legislator, the result comes very close to a contingent fee.

The opponent's costs of litigation, especially his lawyer's fees, are not covered by legal aid (§ 123 ZPO). To me this seems to be the main deficiency of the German system of legal aid. The successful opponent often has no realistic chance of getting his costs refunded. In these cases legal aid has created the possibility of poor parties starting claims in order to harass their opponents.

Thus, to prevent such a result in as many cases as possible, legal aid is only granted if the applicant has a sufficient chance of winning the claim and, moreover, the pursuit of rights is not wanton. 'Wanton' behaviour of the party in this sense means that a reasonably acting person would not go to court, for example because the opponent has always paid and is expected to pay in the future, too.

In every further instance legal aid must be applied for anew, any change in the applicant's income being one of the factors for the court's decision.

According to official statistics (Statistisches Bundesamt—federal board of statistics—Arbeitsunterlage Zivilgerichte, 1990) in less than 5% of all claims legal aid was granted to at least one of the two parties in the first instance in the year 1990 (figures related to the years after are not available yet). In the higher instances the figures are almost identical. The Eastern German districts are not mentioned in these statistics yet, but you can suppose that—due to lower average incomes in the Eastern parts of Germany—the quota of parties gaining legal aid is slightly higher there.

### 2. Legal advice aid

Legal aid is not available before a claim is brought to court. In many cases the question whether to go to court or not, whether a person has a claim or not, cannot be answered by a layman without consulting a legal expert. This legal advice costs money (the lawyer can charge fees according to §§ 118; 20 Bundesrechtsanwalts-Gebührenordnung, federal statute about lawyers' fees) and might not be affordable by poorer people. Thus, the same reasons which led to the introduction of legal aid were decisive for the German legislator to create legal advice aid (in German: Beratungshilfe) in 1980 (Beratungshilfegesetz, law about legal advice aid).

Legal advice aid, however, is also desirable to avoid unnecessary litigation or to explain a person's different possibilities of resolving a legal problem without going to court. This subject is also addressed in the Woolf Report (Ch. 17). In effect, the German system of legal aid is complemented by the system of legal advice aid.

Legal advice aid is defined as an assistance or advice for the safeguarding of rights other than in court proceedings (§ 1 Abs. 1 Beratungshilfegesetz). It is available on application for people who, because of their economic conditions, cannot find the necessary means for regular legal advice by a lawyer. Applicants have to meet the same conditions which must be met to receive legal aid in the form of non-repayable grants (see above). Additionally, the applicant must not have other comparable means of getting support (especially from an insurance for legal costs) nor must the safeguarding of his rights be wanton.

The application is made at the Amtsgericht, the applicant having to state why he wishes legal advice aid and having to expose his financial circumstances. He can also directly contact a lawyer and make the application subsequently. If all the conditions are met by the applicant, the Amtsgericht issues a certificate stating that he is entitled to legal advice aid in this particular case (§ 6 Beratungshilfegesetz).

With this certificate the applicant can consult a lawyer of his choice. Similar to legal aid, the lawyer is obliged to give the legal advice and assistance (§ 49 a Bundesrechtsanwaltsordnung, federal statute about lawyers).

The lawyer may charge the person seeking legal advice aid only an amount of 20 DM, getting another 45 to 200 DM from the state (depending on what he actually did in this case, § 132 Bundesrechtsanwalts-Gebührenordnung, federal statute on lawyers' fees). As is the case with legal aid, these fees are lower than the regular fee units.

If the party receiving legal advice aid is entitled to recover the costs for safeguarding his rights from the opponent (e.g. as a part of the damages to be recovered), the opponent has to pay the normal (higher) fees as laid down in the Bundesrechtsanwalts-Gebührenordnung. Apart from this, the German system of legal advice aid does indeed not appear lucrative for lawyers.

# 15

# *Regulating the Market for Civil Justice*

HUGH GRAVELLE*

## 1. INTRODUCTION

*Access to Justice* is the latest in a long line of reports and investigations prompted by concerns about the cost, complexity and delay in the civil justice process. The purpose of this chapter is to provide a non-technical economic analysis of the market for civil justice and to show that its peculiarities have significant implications for policy.

I need first to remove a possible barrier to understanding. In what follows I will use 'justice' as a handy portmanteau term for the services provided to individuals seeking to establish, define and enforce what they believe to be their civil legal rights. I hope that use of an economically orientated definition of justice as services whose production requires the use of scarce resources will prevent a common initial reaction based on an alternative definition of 'justice' as a welfare criterion. Interpreting justice as a value often leads to the view is that 'justice is priceless' and to the assertion that policy should always aim at improving access to 'justice'.

This assertion is based on a conflation of the two senses of justice and is mistaken. It is not true that increasing access to justice services is always welfare increasing. First, producing justice, in the sense of the services of the courts and the legal system has a cost. Increasing the provision of legal services uses inputs which could produce other goods and services. The benefits from improving access to justice services must be compared with the benefits forgone from a smaller output of other commodities.

Second, justice services are peculiar commodities. In many cases individuals use them to define and enforce their legal rights against others. But once a legal dispute has arisen an enhancement of one person's rights is necessarily a diminution of another's. Justice services are different from other services, such as health care: one person's consumption of health care may

* Professor of Economics, Queen Mary and Westfield College, University of London. This paper is based on my inaugural lecture delivered on 13 December 1994. Like the lecture it is aimed at the non-specialist, indeed non-economist. A fuller and more technical version (Gravelle, 1995) is available on request. An earlier version of the paper was given at a conference at the Institute for Advanced Legal Studies in June 1994.

make that person better off but it does not make anyone else directly worse off. Even if a costless increase in the supply of legal services is possible it would not necessarily be welfare enhancing.

I consider the peculiar nature of the justice services produced by the legal system in more detail in section 5. For the moment we need only note the first objection to the 'justice is priceless' assertion. 'Justice' as welfare may be priceless but justice as a service is costly.

My aims is to provide a framework to analyse proposals which have been put forward for improving access. I do so by outlining a positive model of the civil justice process. It is necessary to understand the way in which the demand for the services of the civil legal system is generated and the available supply is rationed in order to predict the effect of alternative policies. Once all the repercussions of a policy change have been accounted for the effects may be wider and different from those intended.

I first sketch out the civil justice process to emphasise the sequence of interdependent decisions, both before and after disputes arise, in the process and the fact that private and public services are required to assert one's civil rights. Section 3 incorporates the process into a simple model of the role of delay as the current rationing mechanism in the civil justice market. In section 4 I use the model to illustrate the usually complex and possibly perverse implications of different types of policy.

In section 5 I consider the welfare criteria to be used in assessing policy towards the civil justice process and the extent to which justice is a peculiar commodity justifying different rules from those normally applied to public sector services. I argue that policy should be guided primarily by efficiency considerations because legal rules and procedures are a highly imperfect means of pursuing distributional objectives. Given the prevalence of inefficiencies associated with the decisions at all stages in the civil justice process there appears to be ample justification for active policy intervention, whether by regulation of private legal services or by rationing and pricing of court procedures. However, we know very little about the direction, magnitude or policy responsiveness of inefficiencies at the pre-dispute stages of the civil justice process. We can make better informed guesses about the post-dispute stages and I argue that reforms should be primarily be guided by their effects on the inefficient decisions taken after a dispute arises.

In section 6 I switch attention from policy towards publicly supplied court services to the regulation of a privately supplied service required for access to justice: legal advice. I discuss contingent fees for lawyers and suggest that the arguments for restricting the contracts between lawyers and their clients are weak. Contingent fee contracts appear to have better risk sharing and incentive properties than hourly fee or the new mark up contracts and there seems no good reason why lawyers should be prevented from offering them.

## 2. THE CIVIL JUSTICE PROCESS

The civil justice process is a sequence of events and decisions by potential plaintiffs and defendants and their legal advisers which result in a trial only in very small proportion of cases.[1] Consider a negligence case in which an injured plaintiff sues a defendant for damages after an accident. The sequence of events and decisions necessary to generate a trial in such a case includes

(i) Both parties decide to participate in the risky activity (driving, having an operation . . .)
(ii) They both chose a level of care in the risky activity (speed, wearing seat belts . . .)
(iii) There is an accident.
(iv) The injured party (potential plaintiff) seeks legal advice from a lawyer.
(v) The plaintiff decides to bring suit.
(vi) The defendant seeks legal advice.
(vii) Both parties (and their lawyers) decide on bargaining and information gathering strategies.
(viii) The parties fail to reach an out of court settlement.
(ix) The case is put down on a waiting list and is eventually tried.

The costs, complexities and delays of the civil justice process influence decisions at all of these stages, not just those taken after a dispute arises. Decisions taken before the dispute are made in the light of the parties' expectations of the costs and benefits they will incur after the dispute (the accident) arises. For example, potential plaintiffs who feel they are unlikely to obtain satisfactory court remedies if injured may take out insurance, or decide not to participate in the risky activity, or exercise greater care in it. Potential defendants' care and participation will in part be affected by the expected costs (settlement or damage award and legal costs) incurred after an accident occurs. Bargaining strategies, and hence the settlement probability, will also depend on the parties' estimates of costs, delay, and the likely award.

The demand for trials in a case in which the parties have a pre-dispute contract is also generated by a sequence of decisions. For example, a house owner decides that she would like a new roof, she searches for builders, she

[1] In 1992 269,668 writs were issued in the High Court, Queens Bench Division. In 1993 5,623 cases were set down for trial and 650 were disposed after a trial (Lord Chancellor's Department, 1994, pp. 29–30). The Harvard Medical Malpractice Study reported that in New York State 4% of patients suffered a disabling medical injury, one quarter of which were the result of medical negligence. Only one in eight negligently injured patients filed suit (Welier, 1993).

negotiates a contract with a builder, then a dispute arises because she feels the work is poor quality, she consults a lawyer, she decides to bring suit, the parties bargain, they fail to agree and the plaintiff decides to put the case down on the list for trial and it is eventually tried.

Even this very sketchy account of the civil justice process brings out a number of important features which must be borne in mind when analysing policy proposals.

First, the importance of access to courts to enforce and define rights is much greater than indicated by the state's expenditure on providing courts services and individuals' expenditure on services of lawyers. Individuals make decisions in 'in the shadow' of the law. Changes in legal rights or in the ease of access to enforce rights influence the behaviour of individuals in all aspects of their lives.

Second, the production of justice requires inputs provided by the private sector (lawyers' services) and by the public sector (court services). Hence policy towards access to justice should address both the private and the public sectors and take account of the interactions between them.

Third, complaints about, and policies toward, the delay, cost and complexity of civil justice tend to be focused on the post-dispute events. But examining the impact of reforms on post-dispute decisions may be a misleading guide to the overall impact of policy. Once account is taken of the implications of policy for pre-dispute decisions the magnitude, or even the direction, of effects may be very different from than implied by the change in post-dispute behaviour. For example, a policy designed to reduce the number of trials by encouraging settlement could actually increase the number of trials if it also induces potential defendants in accident cases to take less care, thus increasing the number of accidents and disputes. Further, focusing policy solely on the cost, complexity and delay after a dispute has arisen ignores pre-dispute changes with significant welfare consequences, such as the number of accidents or the amount of contractually mediated exchange and production.

## 3. A SIMPLE MODEL OF THE MARKET FOR TRIALS

### 3.1. Demand for trials

The civil justice process sketched in the previous section generates demands by potential litigants for both privately supplied legal services and for publicly supplied court services, from procedural devices such as disclosure, to trials. These demands result from decisions or anticipation of decisions at all stages of the legal process. Since decisions at all stages are interdependent, factors which have a direct effect on one stage affect decisions and demands at all stages. In order to predict the effects of policies we need to understand the way in which the demand for services at each stage are brought into equality with the supply: the rationing mechanisms.

Privately supplied legal services are rationed by price. A reduction in the demand for lawyers' services will lead to a decrease in their price, simultaneously increasing the quantity demanded and reducing the quantity supplied to restore equilibrium.[2] By contrast the equilibrating mechanism in the market for services supplied by the courts to potential litigants is delay. Although prices are charged to potential litigants for many court services, they are not adjusted to keep demand in balance with supply. It is delay which adjusts to restore equilibrium.

Consider the demand for trials arising from, say, medical accidents. Let $D$ denote the number of trials demanded per period. $D$ is the product of the number ($N$) of potential accidents (episodes of treatment) multiplied by the probability that a treatment results in a trial. This probability is the product of the probability $A$ that treatment leads to an accident, the probability $B$ that the injured plaintiff brings suit and the probability ($F$) that the parties fail to settle the dispute before a trial. Thus the demand for trials is $D = NASF$.

Many factors influence the decisions which determine $N$, $A$, $B$ and $F$ but I restrict attention to those which can be influenced by policy. To keep the analysis simple and to focus on the peculiar rationing mechanism in the market for trials I make a number of plausible assumptions about the overall effects of policies[3] and write the demand for trials as

$$\begin{aligned} D &= NABF = N(t,k,f,\ c_p,\ c_d)A(t,k,f,c_p,c_d)B(t,k,f,c_p,c_d)F(t,k,f,c_p,c_d) \\ &= D(t,k,f,c_p,c_d), \end{aligned}$$

The probability $F$ that a dispute is not settled depends *inter alia* on the costs $c_p$, $c_d$ which the plaintiff and defendant expect to bear, on the fees $f$ charged for court services and on delay. $k$ is the time between the initial dispute (accident) and the case being set down on the waiting list for trials. $t$ is the length of time a case waits on the list before it is tried. Call $t$ the trial delay. The total delay is $k+t$. It is plausible that increases in anticipated litigation costs $(f,c_p,c_d)$ or delay increase the incentive for disputes to be settled.

The plaintiff's decision to bring suit if an accident occurs depends on his anticipated costs and benefits from the suit and thus on the likelihood of

[2] The reduced demand for conveyancing services provides one illustration.

[3] Cooter and Rubinfeld (1989) provide a survey of models of litigation. A fuller account of the delay model is in Gravelle (1990). For analyses of particular procedural topics using similar models and for further references see Gravelle (1989) [payment into court], Gravelle (1993) [cost shifting rules] and Gravelle and Waterson (1993) [contingent fees].

the case being settled, the size of the settlement and the costs and delay associated with a trial.

The probability of an accident $A$ varies with the care exercised by the defendant.[4] The defendant's care is influenced by the costs she expects to bear if an accident occurs. These depend on whether she expects an injured plaintiff to file suit and whether the dispute will be settled and if so at what level of compensation. Hence decisions on care and thus $A$ also depend on $t$, $k$, $f$, $c_p$, and $c_d$.

The number of potential accidents $N$ varies with the level of the risky activity in question. Potential plaintiffs' decisions to participate in the risky activity depend on the anticipated net benefits. These vary with the risk of an accident, the size of any anticipated compensation from the potential defendant and on the costs and delay associated with a legal dispute.

It is apparent that the effect of a policy on the number of trials depends on its effects on the decisions at all the stages in the civil justice process. Just considering one stage can be misleading. Suppose there is an increase in delay which reduces the plaintiff's bargaining strength[5] and make him more eager to settle: $F$ will fall. It will also reduce his incentive to bring suit: $B$ will also fall. But the defendant will realise that any injured potential plaintiff is less likely to file suit and more likely to settle for a smaller sum. Hence her expected post-accident costs are smaller and she has less incentive to take care: $A$ will increase. Finally, potential plaintiffs will realise that they run a greater accident risk and will be worse off if an accident occurs. Consequently $N$ will fall. Although it is plausible that the combined effect of changes in decisions at all stages reduces the demand for trials, the magnitude of the effect depend on what happens at all stages, not just the post-dispute stages.

### 3.2. Delay as a market clearing mechanism

The supply of trials is determined by the resources, such as judicial time and court buildings provided by the state. For the purposes of analysing policy I assume that supply is controlled by the policy maker so that no positive model of the supply side of the market is required.[6] If demand is not equal to

[4] In many accident cases, though less so with medical accidents, the plaintiff's care may also affect the accident probability.

[5] Trial damages may not be adjusted to compensate fully for delay. Damages may be smaller for injuries which result in death rather than disablement and the longer is the delay the greater the probability that the victim dies before the case is heard. The longer the delay the harder to prove the case.

[6] A full positive model of the market for trials would have to specify the supply function in more detail by considering the preferences of the politicians, judges etc. whose decisions determine the supply of trials. For example, if politicians respond to voters' concern about increases in delay by increasing the supply of trials the long run supply curve in (delay, trial) space in Figure 1 would not be vertical.

supply equilibrium must be established by changes in variables which influence demand. Neither the fees charged for court services nor the legal costs of litigants vary with the level of excess demand for trials. But increases in delay also reduce the demand for trials and the trial delay $t$ from setting down to trial does respond to excess demand and adjusts to clear the market.

The stage from setting down to trial differs fundamentally from the stages from incident to setting down. The time $k$ from incident to setting down is determined by the behaviour of the parties within constraints imposed by the rules of legal procedure. An increase in the time taken over the initial stages reduces the demand for trials but does not act as an equilibrating mechanism since it does not respond to the difference between the demand and supply of trials.

By contrast the time $t$ from setting down to trial does vary with the excess demand for trials. Most cases put down on the list settle and do not lead to trial but a proportion are eventually tried. If the number of cases added to the waiting list in a period generates more unsettled cases than can be tried each period the waiting list grows and the waiting time $t$ for a trial increases. The increase in $t$ reduces the number of cases added to the list, or increases the proportion settling once on the list, until the demand for trials equals the supply.

Figure 1 plots the demand curve and the supply curve for trials.[7] The vertical axis measures the trial delay $t$ from setting down to trial. Remember that trial delay is only part of the total delay and that even if trial delay is zero total delay could still be long.

The horizontal axis measures the number of trials per period. In keeping with the assumption that the short run supply of trials is fixed the supply curve $S$ is vertical: changes in delay have no effect on the number of trials supplied in each period. The demand curve $D^0$ is downward sloping to reflect the assumption that increase in $t$ reduce the number of trials demanded.[8] The equilibrium delay from setting down to trial is $t_0$. If t is less than $t_0$ the number of cases set down each period generates more unsettled cases than are tried each period and the waiting time $t$ increases. Conversely if $t$ exceeds $t_0$.

The figure shows the equilibrium stock $W_0$ of cases waiting in the list which will eventually result in a trial. When a new case which will result in a trial is added to the list it must wait until the $W_0$ cases already on the list have been tried. If cases are tried at the rate of $S$ per week and it takes $t_0$ weeks before a new case on the list is tried then the number of cases waiting is $W_0 = t_0S$.

[7] The fact that a large proportion of cases set down are settled without a trial is ignored in the diagrammatic analysis for simplicity. It would make no qualitative difference to the conclusions. See Gravelle (1995).

[8] Ignore $D^1$ until section 4.

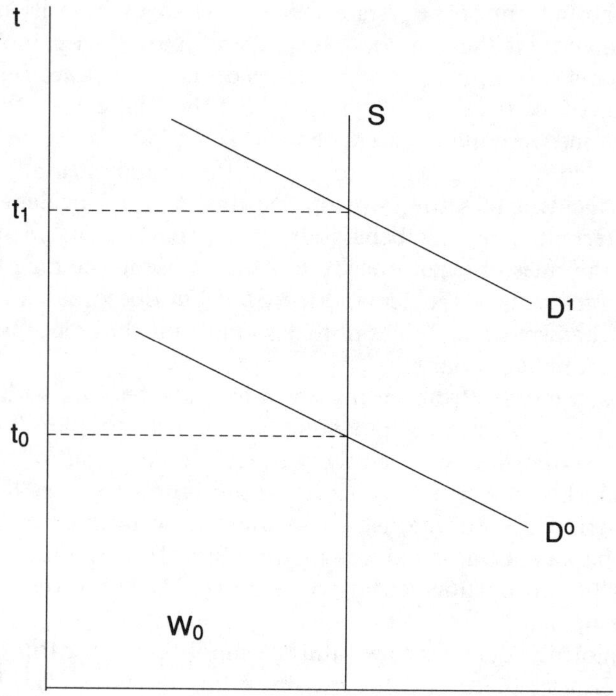


Fig. 1

Rationing trials by waiting list is similar to the NHS rationing of hospital treatment for non-life threatening conditions. Attention is often focused on the number of NHS patients waiting on the list for treatment, perhaps because it is a dramatically large number. With the legal system attention tends to be focused on the delay rather on the rather small stock of cases waiting on the waiting list for a trial.[9]

## 4. PREDICTING THE EFFECTS OF POLICIES

In this section I show how the model of the market for trials can be used to examine some of the implications of reforms suggested by Lord Woolf and others. Space limitations prevent a detailed examination of all the

[9] In the QBD in 1993 the median time from writ to setting down was 139 weeks and from setting down to disposal or trial was 38 weeks (Lord Chancellor's Department, 1994, Table 3.8). The number waiting for hospital treatment in England in March 1994 was 1,065,400 (Department of Health, 1994, Table 5.21).

implications of all the proposals in *Access to Justice* which are in any case dealt with in more detail in other chapters. Rather my intention is to examine the effects of reforms on delay in the civil justice process and to show that policies aimed at particular aspects of the civil justice process can have wider, and possibly perverse consequences.

Reforms can be roughly grouped into four types: supply increases, demand shifts, cost reductions, and procedure rationing. I also examine the consequences of charges for the use of court services. I concentrate on the delay implications of policies but it must be remembered that reforms affect decisions at all stages in the process and these must be taken into account of when reforms are evaluated. I defer a discussion of the evaluation of the policies to section 5.

### 4.1. Increases in the supply of trials

One obvious method of reducing delay is to increase the supply of trials by procedural and other means. It may be possible to produce more trials at little increase in public sector costs by greater reliance on written argument to reduce the time taken over each trial, more active list management and controls on the use of expert witnesses. Alternatively more judges could be appointed and courts built.

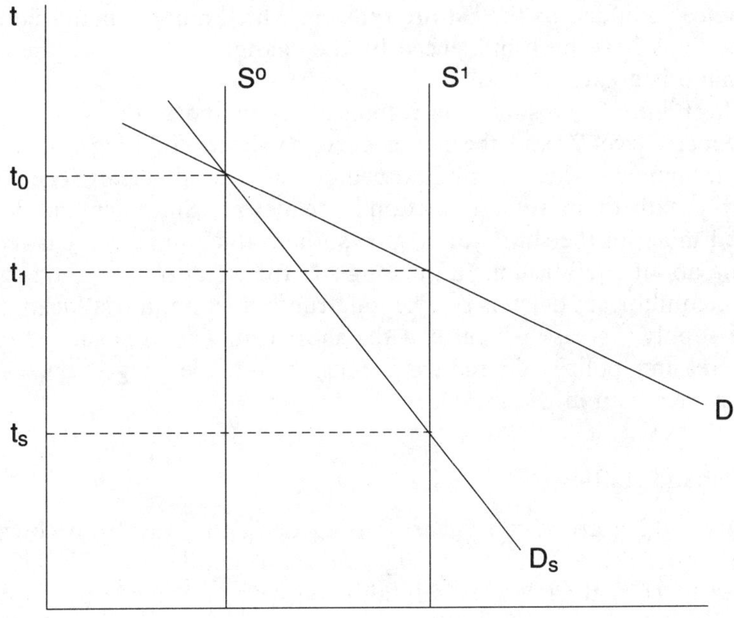


Fig. 2

The effect of an increase in supply is shown in Figure 2 where the capacity of the system is increased from $S^0$ to $S^1$ and, as a result, post-setting down delay falls from $t_0$ to $t_1$. The effect of an increase in supply on delay depends on the responses of litigants. Increases in supply achieve a smaller reduction in delay the more responsive is demand to delay since the increase in trials demanded necessary to restore equilibrium is then generated by a smaller reduction in delay.

As Lindsay and Feigenbaum (1984) point out in the context of waiting lists for hospital treatment, increasing the capacity of the system will not necessarily reduce the number of cases awaiting trial in equilibrium. The number of cases on the waiting list is the product of the trial delay $t$ and the number of cases tried each period $S : W = tS$. An increase in $S$ reduces delay and so it is possible for $tS$ to fall or increase when supply increase. An increase in the numbers waiting could be accompanied by a reduced waiting time.

Figure 2 can also be used to illustrate the difference between the long and short run effects of a supply increase. The change in demand for trials induced by a given reduction in delay is greater in the long run than in the short run. The initial demand effect of a reduction in $t$ is on the cases which are about to be added to the waiting list in the next period. Most of the decisions in these cases have been made and the reduction in delay affects the demand only by altering their bargaining behaviour. In subsequent periods the cases added to the list are those in which more demand determining decisions have been influenced by the change in delay and the change in demand is greater.

In the Figure 2 the short run response of demand to delay is shown by the steeper curve $D_s$ and the flatter curve $D$ shows the long run response after the change in delay has influenced decisions at all stages. The increase in supply leads to an initial reduction in delay to $t_s$. Since demand does not respond much in the short run a substantial reduction in delay is required to bring about equilibrium. In the long run the effect on demand is greater and the equilibrium delay is $t_1$. The long run reduction in trial delay caused by the supply increase is less than the short run. Thus the success of supply increasing policies in reducing delay should be judged over several years, rather than in the short run.

### 4.2. Demand shifting

Measures which are successful in shifting demand away from courts will clearly reduce delay. In terms of Figure 1 the demand curve will shift down from $D^1$ to $D^0$ and trial delay will fall from $t_1$ to $t_0$. Providing information about alternative dispute resolution or encouraging settlement offers by permitting plaintiffs as well as defendants to make offers which can affect the award of costs in the event of a trial can increase the proportion of cases which settle before a trial.

The main criteria for allocating cases between the High Court and the County Courts is the amount claimed. Increasing the threshold switches demand from the High Court to the County Courts, reducing the delay in the High Court and increasing the delay in the County Courts.

Such jurisdiction changes may also influence the effectiveness of other measures to reduce delay. Suppose, for example, that the responsiveness (elasticity) of demand for trials with respect to delay is greater the smaller the amount at stake. Raising the threshold for High Court cases transfers cases which have a value lower than the average High Court case but greater than the average County Court case. Hence the elasticity of demand for trials will fall in both the High Court (because lower valued cases have been transferred away) and in the County Courts (because the cases transferred in have higher than average value). Such a policy is a useful complement to supply increasing measures designed to reduce delay since the reduction in delay after a supply increase is greater the less elastic the demand.

### 4.3. Reductions in litigation costs

Many reforms would have the effect of reducing the cost of legal services for potential litigants or, equivalently, of improving quality for a given cost. The effect of such reforms can be represented as reducing the litigation costs of plaintiffs and defendants ($c_p$ and $c_d$). But reductions in litigation costs increase the demand for trials and lead to increases in trial delay to restore equilibrium in the market for trials. In Figure 1 the demand curve $D^0$ is generated by a high initial level of litigation costs $c_p$ and $d_d$. Reductions in $c_p$ and $d_d$ increase the demand for trials at any given level of delay. Hence the demand curve shifts upward to $D^1$ and the excess demand stimulated by the reduction in litigation costs drives up the equilibrium trial delay from $t_0$ to $t_1$.

With a given supply of trials the aims of reducing the delay and costs of the legal process are contradictory since any reduction in litigants's costs stimulates demand and increases delay.

### 4.4. Rationing of procedure

The stages between the plaintiff issuing a writ and the case being set down for trial are regulated by procedural rules which fix time limits within which certain stages are to be completed and the circumstances in which procedures can be used. As Zuckerman (1995) puts it, the use of procedural devices is rationed. Many of the proposals in *Access to Justice* would have the effect of tightening the rationing of procedure to further restrict litigants' freedom of action during the course of the dispute. The aim of the proposals is to reduce both litigation costs and delay.

Total delay from incident to trial is the time from incident to setting down plus the delay from setting down on the waiting list until trial: $k + t$. Rationing of procedure reduces the delay $k$ from incident to setting down but the effect on the demand for trials, and hence on the equilibrium delay from setting down to trial, must be taken into account in assessing the effect on total delay.

Figure 1 illustrates. Suppose that tighter rationing of procedure reduces the delay from incident to setting down from $k_0$ to $k_1$. With a shorter pre-setting down delay more trials are demanded for any given trial delay $t$. In the Figure the demand curve shifts to the right from $D_0$ to $D^1$ and increases the delay from setting down to trial from $t_0$ to $t_1$. The reduction in total delay is smaller than the original reduction in the delay from incident to setting down. The change in total delay resulting from the reduction in $k$ depends on the relative elasticity of demand to $k$ and $t$. If demand is more responsive to pre-setting down procedural delay than to trial delay then total delay will actually increase since a large increase in $t$ is required to choke off the additional demand generated by a small reduction in $k$. Total delay may be increased by a reform designed to reduce it!

### 4.5. Charging for court services

The structure and rationale of the fees charged for the services of the courts has received little attention. There are 25 categories of fees levied by the High Court at various stages of the judicial process. The services charged for range from photocopying (25p per page) to writs of execution (£10 per writ) to applications to a Judge in Chambers (£25). To an economist the most obvious policy for reducing delay is to increase the prices charged for the use of court services. In terms of Figure 1, increasing the fees for court services shifts the demand curve from $D^1$ to $D^0$, reducing delay from $t_1$ to $t_0$. By increasing the fees sufficiently it would be possible to shift the demand curve down until the trial delay was zero: cases could be heard as soon as they were set down.

## 5. EVALUATING REFORMS

I have suggested that it can be helpful to analyse the civil justice process as part of a market, albeit somewhat peculiar, for private and public legal services. The state currently regulates this market by controlling the types of services provided by civil courts, by setting prices for these services and by restricting their use. In the private sector the state intervenes by altering the price of services, for example by providing legal aid, and by regulating the relationship between lawyers and their clients.

In this section I want to show how economists' concepts of market failure can be used to evaluate interventions in the private sector of the market and to provide a criterion for the supply of public civil justice services. I first suggest that under certain assumptions policy towards legal service should consist of little or no regulation of private legal services and a simple pricing rule for public civil justice. I then provide a rationale for regulation and alternative pricing rules by recognising that the critical underlying assumptions may not be satisfied.

The allocation of resources is said to be Pareto efficient when it is impossible to change the allocation so as to make at least one individual better off and no one else worse off. The output of a commodity is efficient in this sense if the benefit from consumption of an additional unit is equal to the cost of producing that extra unit: marginal benefit equals marginal cost. Under certain circumstances unregulated markets result in an efficient allocation of resources. Each consumer takes the price of the commodity as given and adjusts consumption until the marginal benefit is equal to the cost to them of an additional unit which, on a market, is its price. Since competitive suppliers are forced to sell at a price equal to marginal cost, the price mechanism leads to efficiency where marginal benefits to consumers equals marginal cost of production. Hence, if markets are competitive and complete, in the sense that there are markets for all commodities, a market economy is efficient.

This result, known as the First Theorem of Welfare Economics, when coupled with the Second Theorem of Welfare Economics which deals with distributional issues, has powerful and simple implications for policy. The Second Theorem establishes that, provided certain conditions on technology and preferences are satisfied, the best way to deal with inequities in distribution is not to intervene directly in the working of markets but to make lump sum redistributions of initial endowments amongst individuals and then to leave individuals to operate in the markets with their redistributed endowments. Policy in a world where the conditions of the Theorems are satisfied would consist of redistribution by lump sum transfers and, if necessary, ensuring that markets are complete and competitive.

For commodities produced in the public sector the logic underlying the two Theorems implies that distributional considerations should have no influence on the price charged which should set equal to marginal cost, so that consumers equate marginal benefit to marginal cost. If the services provided by the courts are regarded as conventional commodities the parties to a dispute should at each stage in the legal process be charged a fee equal to the additional cost their decision to proceed to another stage imposes on the civil justice system.

The absence of any fee for a trial at present means that litigants do not have to take account of the value of the time of judges, court officials or the opportunity costs of court buildings when they reach the final stage of the legal process after setting down. At this stage they can still settle and avoid imposing the public sector costs of a trial on the taxpayers. If fees should reflect marginal costs the fee structure is clearly defective and a substantial daily fee should be charged for the trials.[10]

A second reason for the suggesting that the fee structure is inefficient is the existence of the delay from setting down to trial. Both time and money prices can act as rationing devices because both impose costs on consumers and both adjust automatically to equate demand and supply. Rationing by waiting is inefficient compared with rationing by price because the time cost imposed on the consumers is not offset by a corresponding benefit for suppliers. With rationing by price the costs to consumers are exactly offset by the revenue gained by the suppliers (Barzel, 1974; Cheung, 1974).

The efficient pricing policy for a service provided by the public sector is attractively simple: set the price to clear the market with a zero queue and in the longer term adjust the supply of the service until the market clearing price is equal to marginal cost.

If this prescription applied to court services it would imply that the charges for trials should be introduced and raised until the trial delay falls to zero. The charge $f$ should be set at the level which shifts the demand curve for trials in Figure 1 downward until it cuts the supply line at the horizontal axis.

### 5.1. Efficiency or equity as guide to policy

When the welfare Theorems hold a concern for equity leads to lump sum redistribution of endowments rather than to intervention in the markets for particular goods and services. Policies towards individual markets should be concerned only with efficiency. Unfortunately this simple result does not hold when we take account of what might be called the First Law of Public Finance: there are no feasible lump sum taxes or subsidies. All taxes and subsidies lead to inefficiency because they are not lump sum: by changing their decisions on outputs, input supply or consumption individuals can alter the amount of tax paid or subsidy received. This drives a wedge between the marginal benefits and costs of the decisions and creates inefficiency. The policy implication is that distributional considerations can justify regulation of particular markets or not pricing public sector services at marginal cost.

Changes in legal procedure and rules are, however, a highly imperfect

[10] The Court Services agency plans to align fees more closely with costs and to introduce daily hearing fees (Court Services, 1995, p. 8).

method of redistribution (Polinsky 1982). Legal rules are imprecise distributional instruments. Changes in legal procedure or the fees for court services have their initial effect on potential parties to disputes: plaintiffs and defendants. But distributional judgements are usually made on the basis of individuals' characteristics, such as income, which may be imperfectly correlated with their status as potential defendants or plaintiffs. Even if, on average, plaintiffs were poorer than defendants, a policy change which effectively transferred income from defendants to plaintiffs could, in a significant proportion of cases, transfer income from a poor to a rich litigant.

It may also be difficult to trace all the distributional consequences. The fact that the demand for court services reflects decisions taken before and after disputes arise means that one cannot evaluate the distributional consequences of procedural rules solely by reference to post-dispute effects such as the size of settlements made by defendants. Account must also be taken of the induced changes in pre-dispute decisions. Injured plaintiffs may be made better off, and defendants worse off, after an accident by rule changes which increase their bargaining power. But this may change the defendant's pre-accident levels of care and thus the accident rate which could reinforce or partially offset the post-accident effect.

Further, the ultimate incidence of legal rules may be very different from their initial incidence on litigants. Consider a class of cases in which plaintiffs are individuals and defendants are firms and the owners of firms are all richer than the plaintiffs. A policy change which initially favours plaintiffs over defendants apparently redistributes in the right direction (assuming we wish to reduce income inequality). But the response of the defendant firms may be to raise prices to cover their increased costs, making consumers worse off. The owners of firms will be worse off in the long run only if their firms were initially earning greater than supernormal returns. Thus the main redistributive effect may be from consumers to potential plaintiffs.

It can also be argued that there are more precise instruments than changes in fees for court services which can be used to redistribute in the desired direction (Kaplow and Shavell, 1984). Income taxes are a better method of making the poor better off since they are linked to the characteristic of individuals which is usually considered to be the most relevant for distributional considerations: their income. Even if it is accepted that redistribution should take the form of giving the poor greater access to justice services it is better to do so at the beginning of a legal dispute when redistribution can be more easily targeted by subsidised legal advice and representation. Concern for the poor's access to justice is likely to be better directed at the financing of their costs rather than at the method of rationing court services after their case has started.

It is sometime suggested that rationing by waiting is more equitable than rationing by price. Individuals with low wages, or with no job, have a smaller valuation of time spent queuing than those employed at high wages since the opportunity cost of their time is smaller. Thus reducing the money price and increasing the time price will shift consumption of the rationed commodity in favour of the poor.[11] In the case of commodities, such as court services or cold surgery, where rationing is by waiting list rather than waiting line, the argument does not apply. Increases in delay reduce demand because they increase the discounted value of the service being waited for. Thus we must consider how discount rates on the service vary across rich and poor to assess the distributional consequences of rationing by waiting list. In a dispute over damages the relevant interest rate is that applied to future sums of money. The poor are likely to face higher interest rates because they represent greater risks of default for lenders. In such cases rationing by waiting list redistributes against the poor. Distributional considerations do not seem a valid reason for not raising court fees to reduce delay.

It is therefore at least arguable that policy decisions affecting the civil justice process should be governed by efficiency considerations except possibly for the provision of state financed or subsidized legal expense insurance for the poor.[12]

### 5.2. Market failure and efficiency: are court services different?

Putting aside distributional considerations, I now consider whether there are features of court services which provide efficiency justifications for direct regulation and prices not equal to marginal cost.[13] The classification of the services provided by the civil courts shown in Figure 3 may be useful.[14] Civil courts provide three types of services

(a) *specification* of legal rules or property rights. (Do the auditors of a company owe a duty of care to purchasers of the company's shares? Can local authorities make legally binding contracts for derivative financial securities?)

[11] Even with commodities rationed by consumers physically waiting in line the argument is not always convincing since many high income individuals do not lose income whilst queuing.

[12] Subsidised access to legal services can be justified whether it was felt that individuals consume less than a desirable level of services because they are too poor, or because they are irrational or because it is felt that equity in the consumption of legal services is more important than equity in the distribution of income.

[13] There are many reasons why public services should not be priced at marginal cost (Brown and Sibley, 1986) but I wish to investigate those which are peculiar to court services.

[14] Since courts may also formulate rules for fact finding, such as 'proof of postage is proof of delivery', the boundary between rule making and fact finding services may not always be sharp. Some plaintiffs may also have a choice of pursuing a claim under contract or tort law.

| | Pre-dispute contract? | |
|---|---|---|
| | Yes | No |
| Rule making | Can local authorities make legally binding contracts for derivative securities? | Are landowners liable to users of public rights of of way for negligent non-feasance? |
| Fact finding | Were goods of satisfactory quality? | Was due care exercised? |
| Enforcement | Writs of execution against goods. Appointment of | Injunction against nuisance. Mandamus. |

Fig. 3

(b) *fact finding* so that the appropriate legal rules may be applied. (Were goods of satisfactory quality? Did the plaintiff's harm result from the defendant's action?)
(c) *Enforcement of legal rules or rights.* (Issuing warrants of execution against debtors or writs of delivery for specific goods.)

It is also important to distinguish between two types of litigation where the courts' services are supplied to litigants who have

(i) *pre-dispute contracts.* (The most common examples are debt contracts.)
(ii) *no pre-dispute contracts.* (Tort, judicial review, divorce.)

One of the crucial assumptions of the First Theorem of Welfare Economics is that markets are complete so that all decisions which affect other individuals are mediated through the market. There are several reasons why there is an incomplete set of markets associated with the civil justice process and hence why regulation and departures from marginal cost pricing may be efficient.

*Public goods.* The rules formulated as a consequence of one case influence subsequent behaviour in similar circumstances by other potential litigants. Since such rules affect all subsequent decision makers and no decision maker can avoid their effect, the precedents created by a case are non-optional, non-excludable public goods. Such goods are unlikely to be produced efficiently by voluntary market exchanges: those who 'consume' them (subsequent decision makers) cannot be made to compensate those who bear the cost of producing them (the litigants).

Other things being equal cases which are likely to generate precedents with desirable consequences for behaviour should face a lower price than other cases. Some law and economics scholars argue that the common law tends to produce efficiency enhancing precedents.[15] The argument is that inefficient legal rules generate more disputes and, even if judges decided cases at random (as far as their efficiency consequences were concerned) are thus more likely to be overturned. Even the supporters of this view acknowledge that convergence of this process is slow and uncertain. However, if on average, new precedents do improve the efficiency of resource allocation, the implication is that court services should be priced at less than marginal cost. Where it is appears that a case raises particularly important legal issues an especially reduced price could be set. Alternatively, as at present, procedural rules could allow it to proceed more rapidly to courts in the higher tiers.

*Externalities.* In tort and other cases where there is no pre-dispute contract between the litigants and in which the actions of litigants can affect the number of disputes there are likely to be externalities. Each party will take pre-dispute decisions in the light of the post-dispute payoffs they will receive. Neither will have any incentive to take account of the effect of these decisions on the other. For example, the post-accident expected cost falling on a potential injurer depends on the likelihood of settlement, the litigation cost sharing rules and the size of award made if there is a trial. If the defendant's expected post-accident cost does not equal the expected cost the accident imposes on the plaintiff the defendant will take an inefficient amount of care. The fees for the services of the courts and the procedural rules should be set to reduce the inefficiency of the defendant's care decision. Similarly for other inefficient decisions in the process generating the demand for trials.[16]

Legal disputes are contests in which each party makes decisions on procedures and expenditures to improve their expected proceeds. In many instances these decisions also generate externalities, not because each party ignores their effect on the other but precisely because each party uses them to inflict costs on the other. The procedures, such as discovery, may have a social value in that they improve the accuracy of adjudication or improve the accuracy of information available to parties and thus promote settlement, but they are chosen with regard to their private benefit to a litigant (Cooter and Rubinfeld, 1994). The use of procedures as weapons in a con-

[15] See the survey in (Aronson, 1986).

[16] I have shown that efficiency may require setting a price too low to clear the market for trials: it can be efficient to have a positive trial delay and to price below marginal cost (Gravelle, 1990). Unfortunately it is not difficult to construct plausible models in which these considerations could imply price above or below marginal cost and no trial delay. The policy conclusions turn out to depend on rather fine details of the model.

test is perhaps the most powerful argument for regulation of their use (Zuckerman, 1995).

*Incomplete contracts.* When the parties have a pre-dispute contract they can attempt to negotiate the terms of their contract to control their actions so that their individual incentives are aligned with their joint payoffs. If they are successful their contract is complete and there are no pre-dispute externalities to justify regulation of post-dispute behaviour or departure from marginal cost court fees. But if their contract is incomplete their actions before the dispute are not necessarily jointly efficient and there may be efficiency justifications for regulation.

For example, the parties may be able to affect the probability that one or other defaults on the contract. In the case of debt contracts the debtor may, by making greater efforts, be able to alter the probability that he can repay the loan. His effort will in part be determined by his expectation about the creditor's attempts to enforce the contract if he defaults. If the post-default level of enforcement is not controlled through the contract[17] the level of enforcement will be chosen after default by the creditor. At that stage the creditor is only concerned with her post-default recovery, not with the effect of enforcement on the debtor's pre-default actions.[18] The fees the courts charge for enforcing contracts can alter the creditor's enforcement decision to make it more nearly correspond to the level which would have been chosen with complete contracts. Adjusting the fees for court services or controls on their use can repair some of the holes in incomplete contracts and this leads to some departure from the marginal cost pricing rule for court services.

## 5.3. Second or third best policies?

It is apparent that court services are different and that there are efficiency arguments from departing from the 'first best' policy rules of pricing at marginal cost and not regulating the use of legal services. But it is also true that the appropriate 'second best' policies are complicated. Given that different types of case are associated with different types of inefficiency, different regulations would also be required for the litigants in different types of case. In each type of case, calculation of the second best policy would require very detailed information on preferences and technology and the correct positive model of decision making by potential litigants.

For many aspects of the civil justice process further research is required before we can even guess at the optimal second best policies. But in the

[17] Control could be explicit via a term in the contract, or implicit, if the creditor is willing to maintain a reputation for pursuing defaulting debtors.

[18] Gravelle (1986) has a fuller discussion of default and the pricing of court enforcement services.

meantime policy has to be made and the complexities and uncertainties make errors in policy likely. It may be that the second best price for a particular court service should be above or below marginal cost but we do not know which. In these circumstances the 'third best' policy may be to adopt the first best marginal cost pricing rule. Even though we know it is not optimal, the expected welfare cost of choosing the wrong second best rule (setting price above marginal cost when it should be below or vice versa) is greater the expected welfare loss from setting price equal to marginal cost (Ng, 1983). Similar 'third best' arguments apply to regulation of legal services.

Only if we are fairly certain about the direction of the inefficiencies in the decisions at a particular stage of the process and the effect of policies on the decisions should policies depart from the first best policies of marginal cost pricing and no regulation. I suspect that at the moment we know so little about the direction, magnitude and policy responsiveness of inefficiencies in most pre-dispute decisions that such inefficiencies should have little effect on policy towards civil justice. At the post-dispute stage the direction of inefficiencies is more apparent, for example in the use of discovery, and the use of second best rules to control these inefficiencies is more easily justified.

The extent to which regulation of procedure or pricing should be used to correct inefficiencies should also depend on their relative effectiveness compared with alternative policy instruments. In many instances inefficiencies are better corrected by policy instruments aimed directly at them rather than by controls on, or pricing of, post-dispute services. For example, direct regulation of safety or subsidies to safety enhancing measures seems a better method of reducing accidents than altering the fees or rules concerning legal services once an accident has occurred and a dispute has arisen. Increases in the number of valuable precedents could be more directly produced by allowing courts to seek US style *Brandeis briefs* in which the wider economic or social implications raised by a particular case are examined on behalf of the court by someone other than the litigants or their lawyers.

## 6. REGULATION OF LAWYER–CLIENT CONTRACTS: CONTINGENT FEES

In this section I consider the rationale for regulating the contract between potential litigants and their lawyers. Lawyers are paid at an hourly rate and it has been suggested that this is an incentive to increase the amount of work done and to increase costs and delay (*Access to Justice*, 1995, p. 11; Zuckerman, 1995). It is now possible for lawyers in some types of case to be paid on a conditional or *mark up* fee basis: they get nothing if the case is lost but their normal hourly fees plus a percentage mark up (not exceeding 100%) if the case is won. Other forms of conditional payment, such as the American style *share* contract under which the lawyer gets a proportion of the settlement or damage award, are not legally enforceable and contrary to the rules of the professional bodies.

I first describe the type of contract which economic theory[19] suggests would be chosen by lawyers and potential litigants in the absence of any regulation and compare it with the hourly fee, mark up and share contracts. I then discuss whether restricting the type of contract can be justified as being in the interests of potential litigants or on wider public interest (efficiency) grounds.

### 6.1. Privately efficient lawyer–client contracts

In what follows I assume that the lawyer's professional ethics, whilst leading her to consider some aspects of the client's welfare, do not mean that she is a complete altruist with respect to her client. In the absence of regulation the contract will be privately efficient in the sense that there is no other feasible contract which would make the lawyer or client better off without making the other worse off. Although the extent of competition in the market for lawyers' services influences the way in which the total gain from the contract is distributed between the lawyer and client it would not affect the basic structure of the contract.

The contract must address three main issues: hidden information, hidden action and risk sharing. The lawyer knows more about the law and legal procedure and provides advice, based on this superior information, to the client about whether to bring suit, whether to accept offers from the other side and which expert witnesses to engage.[20] The client may also possess information which can affect the outcome. For example he may know just how serous is his whiplash neck or back injury, or whether his conduct might have been partly to blame for the accident.

The lawyer's efforts affect the payoffs from the case through the costs and the time take over the case, the probability of winning and the level of the award. The client's behaviour may affect the outcome of the case, for example, by giving a convincing performance in the witness box or not indulging in strenuous activities prior to trial in a personal injury case. These actions, particularly the lawyer's, may be difficult or impossible to observe and so cannot be directly controlled by the contract.

A legal case can be thought of as a potentially profitable asset with risky

[19] There is a large body of literature on Principal-Agent or contract theory concerned with the nature of efficient contracts. See Rickman (1994) for references and an application to lawyer–client contracts.

[20] Lawyers are of differing inherent quality and the client may find it difficult to judge quality until after the case. This creates another role for contract terms: signalling the quality of the lawyer.

payoffs: the difference between the revenue (the settlement or award) and costs incurred (net of any cost shifting to the losing litigant). The contract between the client and lawyer will allocate the risks between them. When the client is an individual and the lawyer is a partnership with a well diversified portfolio of cases an efficient risk sharing arrangement would place most of the risk on the lawyer.

The privately efficient contract between lawyer and client must allocate risk between them appropriately and motivate them to take appropriate action and supply relevant information and advice. Given the multiple objectives and the limited number of relevant and observable variables to which the lawyer's remuneration could be linked the privately efficient contract is a trade off between risk sharing and incentives.

### 6.2. Actual contracts

Figure 4 compares the incentive and risk sharing properties of the current English hourly fee, the newly introduced mark up contract and the US contingent fee or share contract. The hourly fee contract seems to perform poorly on all criteria except probably the least important: motivating client effort. Under the mark up contract the lawyer's income is not contingent

| | Type of contract | | |
|---|---|---|---|
| | Hourly Fee | Mark Up | Contingent Fee |
| Client effort | Yes | Yes | Yes |
| Lawyer effort | | | |
| Winning | No | Yes | Yes |
| Award | No | No | Yes |
| Cost reduction | No | ? | Yes |
| Lawyer advice | | | |
| On suit | Bias for | ? | Bias against |
| On settlement | Bias for | ? | Bias for |
| Client risks | | | |
| Costs | High | Low* | None* |
| Revenue | High | High | Low |

* With insurance against cost shifting

Fig. 4

on the revenue or the costs but on whether the case is won or not. Increases in the settlement or award have no effect on the lawyer's reward. Hence she has an incentive to increase her efforts to win but not to increase the quantum. The implications for her cost reducing incentives are ambiguous: she gets a larger income if she wins if her billed costs are larger but if she loses she bears all these costs. Similarly the incentives for biased advice are unclear. However, the contract does shift cost risk in the right direction, particularly if coupled with insurance against bearing the opponent's costs if the case is lost.

US contingent fee contracts put all the cost risk on the lawyer, which is efficient for cost reducing incentives but leads to biased advice. Some of the revenue risk is also shifted to the lawyer who gets a proportion of the revenue from the case which varies from 20% to 50%. If my assumptions about the risk aversion of lawyers and clients and their relative influence on the case revenue are correct the US revenue share seems somewhat low for efficiency. The explanation is probably that US contracts are constrained by professional rules and statute so that the lawyer is not permitted to pay the client a fixed fee in exchange for a high revenue share. In order to achieve the same expected income for the client he must be given a larger share of the revenue and the lawyer a smaller one.

This restriction also prevents the lawyer buying the case outright from the client, as has been advocated (Shukatris, 1985). The possible disincentive effects on client effort do not suggest that permitting the lawyer to pay the client a fixed fee for the case would be efficient. However, lifting the restriction would enable the revenue share to be increased and the US scheme to move closer to a privately efficient trade off between incentives and risk sharing.

It appears that the hourly fee scheme is the worst of the three contracts. The mark up scheme is an improvement on the current scheme. For many types of case and litigants the contingent fee scheme appears to be better than either which presumably explains why it is commonly used in the US for civil disputes even though hourly and mark up contracts are permitted.

### 6.3. Why regulate lawyer–client contracts?

Justifications for regulation of lawyer–client contracts concern the effect of the contract on the client or the wider public interest implications of contracts for the sequence of decisions generating the demand for trials. None of these arguments seems convincing.

*Contractual imperfections*. It can be argued that clients are exploited by their lawyers because they are in a weak market position when they choose a lawyer. The costs of searching for other lawyers willing to take on their case may be significant and it is difficult to judge the advice and service they provide. Hidden action and hidden knowledge mean that the unregulated client–lawyer contract is a compromise between risk sharing and incentives. It is second best privately efficient: even if the contract is chosen by lawyer she will seek to be efficient in her exploitation of the client's potentially profitable asset: the legal dispute. Hence direct regulation of the terms of the contract is unlikely to produce a more privately efficient trade off. If it is desired to increase the client's payoffs from the case it would be better to increase competition in the market, thereby forcing lawyers to offer contracts which are still privately efficient but give more of the proceeds to the client. For example, restrictions on advertising should be further weakened and consumer groups could be subsidised to produce and publicise 'standard' form contingency contracts which have a more equitable division of the gains from the case.

*Regulation as commitment.* Suppose that a plaintiff can choose between two contracts with his lawyer. Contract 1 motivates his lawyer to drag out the case and imposes high post-dispute costs on both litigants. Contract 2 motives the lawyer to reduce litigation costs and delay. Both contracts yield the same expected settlement or damage award. The plaintiff will choose contract 2. Contract 1 imposes greater post-dispute costs on the defendant and would lead to greater care and a smaller dispute probability. If the plaintiff is sufficiently better off if no dispute occurs it is possible that *ex ante* he would be better off if the potential defendant believed that he would choose contract 1, rather than contract 2 which the defendant knows will actually be chosen if there is a dispute. Unfortunately the plaintiff cannot commit himself before a dispute to take an action (contract 1) which would be irrational once a dispute has occurred.

In these circumstances the plaintiff would be better of *ex ante* if contract 2 was not allowed. It is possible to construct examples in which the hourly fee contract is better *ex ante* but worse *ex post* than the mark up contract (Gravelle and Waterson, 1993). In these instances regulation in the form of banning mark up contracts is in the interests of clients. However, the examples are based on special assumptions and I do not believe that the argument for regulation as commitment is very strong.

*Public interest arguments.* Since the contract is chosen in the interests of client and lawyer they ignore the types of externalities and public good aspects of precedent production described in section 5. By regulating their choice of contract it may be possible to reduce inefficiencies elsewhere or to stimulate the production precedents. However, again, one would need very detailed information in order to calculate the optimal method of intervening in the client–lawyer contract and there seem to be better, more direct methods of reducing such inefficiencies or improving the quality of legal argument or encouraging cases which set valuable precedents.

## REFERENCES


Aranson, P. H. (1986). 'Economic efficiency and the common law: a critical survey', in *Law and Economics and the Economics of Legal Regulation*, G. Skogh and J. M. Schulenburg (eds.), Nijhoff, Amsterdam, 51–84.

Barzel, Y. (1974). 'A theory of rationing by waiting', *Journal of Law and Economics*, 17, 73–95.

Brown, S. J. and Sibley, D. S. (1986). *The Theory of Public Utility Price*, Cambridge University Press.

Cheung, S. C. (1974), 'A theory of price control', *Journal of Law and Economics*, 17, 53–71.

Cooter, R. D. and Rubinfeld, D. L. (1989). 'Economic analysis of legal disputes and their resolution', *Journal of Economic Literature*, 27, 1067–1097.

Cooter, R. D. and Rubinfeld, D. L. (1994). 'An economic model of legal discovery', *Journal of Legal Studies*, 23, 435–464.

Court Service. (1995). *The Court Service Business Plan*, Court Service, London.

Department of Health. (1994). *Health and Personal Social Service Statistics for England: 1994 Edition*, HMSO.

Gravelle, H. S. E. (1986). 'Default risks and optimal pricing of court enforcement services', in *Law and Economics and the Economics of Legal Regulation*, G. Skogh and J. M. Schulenburg (eds.), Nijhoff, Amsterdam, 85–112.

Gravelle, H. S. E. (1989). 'Accidents and the allocation of legal costs with an uninformed court', *Geneva Papers in Risk and Insurance*, 14, 11–26.

Gravelle, H. S. E. (1990). 'Rationing trials by waiting: welfare implications', *International Review of Law and Economics*, 10, 255–270.

Gravelle, H. S. E. (1993). 'The efficiency implications of cost shifting rules', *International Review of Law and Economics*, 13, 3–18.

Gravelle, H. S. E. (1995). 'The price of justice: regulating the market for civil justice', *QMW Discussion Paper*, No. 331, July.

Gravelle, H. S. E. and Waterson, M. (1993). 'No win, no fee: some economics of contingent legal fees', *Economic Journal*, 103, 1205–1220.

Kaplow, L. and Shavell, S. (1994). 'Why the legal system is less efficient than the income tax in redistributing income', *Journal of Legal Studies*, 23, 667–682.

Lindsay, C. M. and Feigenbaum, B. (1984). 'Rationing by waiting lists', *American Economic Review*, 74, 405–417.

Lord Chancellor's Department (1994). *Judicial Statistics 1994*, Cm 2623, HMSO.

Ng, Y. K. (1983). *Welfare Economics*, Macmillan.

Polinsky, A. M. (1982). *An Introduction to Law and Economics*, Little Brown.

Rickman, N. (1994). 'The economics of contingency fees in personal injury litigation', *Oxford Review of Economic Policy*, 10, 34–50.

Shukatris, M. J. (1987). 'A market in personal injury tort claims', *Journal of Legal Studies*, 16, 329–350.

Weiler, P. C. et al. (1993). *A Measure of Malpractice*, Harvard University Press.

Woolf, The Right Honourable The Lord (1995). *Access to Justice: Interim Report to the Lord Chancellor on the Civil Justice System in England and Wales*, June.

Zuckerman, A. A. S. (1995). 'A reform of civil procedure—rationing procedure rather than access to justice', *Journal of Law and Society*, 22, 155–188.

# 16

# *The Role of Legal Expenses Insurance in Securing Access to the Market tor Legal Services*[1]

NEIL RICKMAN AND ALASTAIR GRAY*

## 1. INTRODUCTION

Since the early 1980s, a desire to curtail public expenditure has encouraged the Government to promote private insurance in a diverse range of markets including pensions, health care, and income and mortgage protection. More recently, a rapid increase in state legal aid expenditure has prompted interest in whether individuals facing potentially large costs if they have to resort to the law might seek expanded protection from legal expenses insurance (LEI).

In early 1995 a Chief Secretary to the Treasury was quoted as describing legal expenses insurance as a 'neglected area' which could be extended.[2] However, other statements from senior members of the Government, including the Lord Chancellor, have been less enthusiastic about LEI. It has not figured greatly in recent proposals to reform the legal system or legal aid (Woolf 1995, LCD 1995), and appears to have been assigned a peripheral position for the foreseeable future as a mechanism for improving access to legal services.

The Lord Chancellor's Department has defined legal expenses insurance as 'payment of an annual premium to buy cover, in given categories of cases, for a claimant's legal costs (including any costs awarded against him), up to a limit of indemnity' (LCD, 1991, p. 29). Given the large number of

* Centre for Socio-legal Studies, Wolfson College, Oxford.

[1] An earlier version of this chapter was published by the Association of British Insurers as part of a report entitled Risk, Insurance and Welfare: the Changing Balance Between Public and Private Protection (ABI 1995), and we are grateful to the ABI for commissioning that work and allowing us to re-use parts of it here. The views expressed are purely those of the authors.

[2] Quoted in the Guardian 25/2./95, p. 32: Ian Wylie. Insurers draw up exclusion zones for legal cover as state aid is cut.

legal proceedings that take place each year, many at considerable cost, the scope for such coverage is potentially very substantial: in 1993, almost 3 million proceedings were commenced in the County Courts of England and Wales concerning the recovery of money or land; around 200,000 petitions were filed for dissolution of marriage; and a similar number of actions concerning mainly contract disputes or torts (civil wrongs) were commenced in the Queen's Bench Division of the High Court (LCD, 1994). At this higher level of the court system, cases typically involve disputes over goods or services sold, disputes over professional fees charged, and claims for personal injury arising from medical or employers negligence. All of these activities involved expenditure on legal services, the main item being advice from and representation by a solicitor. In 1991–92 the gross annual fee income of all solicitors in England and Wales was approximately £6.2 billion (Law Society, 1994). These costs, along with others like fees for expert witnesses, have been estimated to account for between 18% (Harris et al, 1984) and 84% (Civil Justice Review, 1986) of the damages recovered in personal injury cases, often paid by a private client.

Following on from this account of legal proceedings typically commenced, we can characterise the legal system as a mechanism which gives agents incentives to take account of the impact their actions may have on other parties: that is, to anticipate and pay attention to externalities associated with their actions. For example, a surgeon faced with the prospect of medical negligence claims may invest more resources in diagnostic equipment and more time in treatment. Or, a house-owner may as a result of the law take more care that a new home-extension does not infringe a neighbour's property rights. From this perspective, a legal system produces an efficient outcome when the costs to society of reducing further externalities are cancelled by the expected savings to society in terms of the lower prospects of accidents or disputes. In the instance of medical negligence, this point would be reached where the additional investments in diagnosis and treatment are equal to the expected reductions in the costs of settling claims. In the house-owner case, it would occur where further investments in plans, surveyors and communications with neighbours equal the savings to be made from avoiding complaints and possible legal action.

Of course in practice it is extremely difficult to quantify these externalities or incentive effects, and consequently very little is known about whether current levels of legal activity are too high, too low, or optimal. However, the framework of analysis allows us to predict that reaching the point of efficiency requires that individuals are able to commence or pursue compensation claims in order to guarantee that others face the full costs of their actions. If this is not possible, it follows that there may be some loss of efficiency (Posner, 1986). Therefore there are efficiency reasons for ensuring that individuals can bear the costs of using the law. There is also an equity argument, which states that justice is not like most goods and services, but is a fundamental right, so that rights would be infringed if individuals were excluded from the legal system solely because, for example, their income was insufficient to obtain access.

How can such efficiency losses and issues of equity be dealt with? In principle, there are a number of ways. First, an insurance market could facilitate access by allowing individuals to shift their risks of injury, loss, or legal costs. Second, a contingency fee system could allow the plaintiff to shift risk onto the lawyer, whose remuneration would be contingent upon the outcome of the case rather than the means of the client. Finally, there could be some form of income distribution or means-tested subsidy, subsidising access for plaintiffs or defendants with insufficient means.

The introduction of the legal aid scheme in 1950, and its subsequent expansion in scope and aggregate expenditure, indicates that UK public policy in the post-war period has emphasised the third option. The legal aid scheme is essentially a conditional financial contribution by the tax-payer towards the legal costs of individuals of limited means when defending or taking legal proceedings. The more fundamental objectives and purposes of the legal aid scheme are not easy to define, and contain several elements. First, legal aid can be seen as essentially a policy response to efficiency losses associated with a failure in the insurance market for legal expenses, for potential reasons discussed below. Secondly, but again related to efficiency, legal aid can be seen as a mechanism for redressing efficiency losses arising from the prevailing income distribution. Third, there is an equity argument—outlined above—that justice is a fundamental entitlement.

Despite these potential rationales for legal aid, the equity, efficiency, cost and general performance of the legal aid system have been subjected to close scrutiny in recent years, and some far-reaching reforms are in process of implementation. It therefore seems appropriate to examine the current state and future potential of the legal expenses insurance market, firstly as a response to difficulties besetting the legal aid system, but also more generally as a mechanism to help individuals afford the law.

This chapter describes the current role of legal expenses insurance in the market for legal services and speculates on ways in which that role might develop in the future. In doing so, it emphasises examination of the efficiency justifications for legal aid, in terms of private insurance markets failures, as opposed to the, perhaps more common, equity arguments. The chapter is structured as follow: Section 2 applies in simplified form the economic theory of insurance to legal expenses insurance, considering what problems might be encountered in a private market for such insurance but also asking what role the legal profession, capital markets and the state might usefully play. Section 3 looks at the current extent of legal expenses insurance cover in Britain, comparing this with eligibility for legal aid, and relating the observed patterns of coverage back to the discussion in Section 2. The section also considers the scope for expansion of LEI, in the context of a continuing legal aid system and other means of providing access to the legal system. In Section 4 a brief comparative study of legal expenses insurance in other jurisdictions is presented, providing an opportunity to consider what options are open to the market and whether LEI requires particular conditions to thrive. A concluding section assesses the way LEI has developed in Britain and its future development.

## 2. A THEORETICAL PERSPECTIVE ON LEGAL EXPENSES INSURANCE

It is possible to think of many circumstances in which individuals might resort to the law in pursuit of their objectives. In a disagreement with others, the law may be used as an arbitrator between conflicting points of view, for example if someone has been injured in an accident, or if a dispute arises over the division of property during a divorce. The law may also be used to confirm the legitimacy of cooperative arrangements, such as wilful property transfers through wills and conveyancing.

Despite their differences, all these circumstances have a common feature: they involve cost. The first type of cost involved is *financial*: the use of experts (lawyers, arbitrators, licensed conveyancers, witnesses) and, possibly, the legal system (courts, procedural devices) all involve paying for the resources used. However, to the extent that these expenses are predictable in their timing and amount, they should not constitute a barrier to use of the legal system, as long as capital markets are working efficiently. Indeed, legal expenses could be fully capitalised in the price of the transaction, as might happen in situations such as residential conveyancing. Given such predictability, one should be able to borrow against future recovery on the case, or against present and future income, in order to meet these expenses of using the law. For the insurance industry to have a role in helping individuals to meet these expenses, there must be some risk surrounding the timing and size of legal expenses. In turn, this causes risk averse individuals to suffer a *utility cost*, which insurance can help them to off-load onto organisations more able to bear the risks involved. The extent to which insurance might assist individuals in gaining access to the law therefore depends on the law-related risks they face and their attitudes towards them.

There are risks involved in both disagreements and cooperative agreements. In the latter case, these risks are simply to do with the potential cost of using the law; the extent to which there is uncertainty surrounding their timing being limited by the fact that the need for wilful acts can often be predicted in advance and, thus, planned for. It is difficult to generalise about whether these financial costs are hard to predict: in many cases they will not be, because the services involved will be of standard type and clearly required. Thus, though it would in principle be possible to insure against the costs of residential conveyancing or making a will, this is not the context in which legal expenses insurance could be expected to flourish. In the case of disagreements, however, costs are likely to be unpredictable in terms of their timing and amount. First, there will usually be uncertainty surrounding the timing of such circumstances: it is not usually possible to predict when (if at all) a road accident, or breach of contract, or acrimonious divorce, etc, will happen. Accordingly, the potential costs of such events are hard to plan for. Second, there is often much uncertainty attached to the costs involved here. This is because the variety of problems is much wider, the variety of inputs required is greater (lawyers, witnesses, legal procedure), because effort has to be expended in responding to the other side's claims as well as in making one's own, and—in Britain—because of the way in which legal costs are usually allocated (see below). As a result, the financial costs of resolving disputes by means of the law can be high (and may also have a high variance), and these conditions will, in principle, generate a demand from risk averse individuals for insurance against them.

In what circumstances, therefore, might the insurance market be expected to work efficiently? The answer to this question will help to explain perceived problems in the actual market for LEI, the appropriate policy responses, and consequently the future potential of this market.

Private insurance against legal expenses in contentious cases would require the following conditions for it to be successful:

(1) First, the probability of expenses being incurred would have to be predictable, independent across individuals and less than one.
(2) Second, a sufficient volume of business would have to be forthcoming to ensure that insurers were more risk neutral than most individuals and therefore more efficient risk bearers.
(3) Third, firms offering LEI must have knowledge of the law as it relates to claims made by policy-holders and knowledge of the policy-holders themselves.

Condition 1 is easily satisfied: the probability of being involved in a contentious legal case is certainly less than one, independent across individuals and, across a large enough number of cases, predictable (for most types of case). Conditions 2 and 3 are information requirements on the demand and supply sides of the market. On the demand side, individuals should have sufficient information about the legal expense risks they face to make them demand LEI policies (Condition (2)). Issues here are somewhat harder to fulfil. For example, as we shall argue in Section 3, most individuals have little idea of the probability that they may be involved in a legal case, and may underestimate this. This risk is objectively quite small: in 1989, for example, one-third of a million acts of litigation were initiated, equivalent to approximately 9 per 1000 adults,[3] or a risk of almost one in 10 over a 20 year period. Similarly, individuals may underestimate the legal expenses involved in a dispute; as indicated in Table 1, these can consume between one-fifth and four-fifths of any damages obtained, with most estimated falling in the range of one-third to one-half. The most recent survey, conducted by the Woolf Inquiry Team on a sample of cases submitted to the Supreme Court Taxing Office during 1994–95, found that the mean value of costs allowed was 61% of the value of the claim, (median = 25%), with no fewer than 16% of cases in which the bill was the equivalent of 100% or more of the claim value. Such costs are prohibitive to many people. Lord Pearson's Royal Commission (1978) and Harris et al. (1984) noted that only 10–15% of personal injury sufferers pursued their cases, with costs being an important influence on non-claimants and the overwhelming reason amongst those who abandoned their claim.

Moreover, the deterrence effect of such levels of costs to individuals when considering taking legal action is enhanced by the unpredictability of costs, which arises from the method for allocating legal costs between litigants commonly used in the UK. This allocates costs according to the 'indemnity rule' whereby the losing party pays the winner's costs as well as his/her own. The result is that parties' exposure to costs is increased and this will act as an extra deterrent to risk averse parties who might otherwise embark upon legal action.

Table 1: The Costs of Civil Litigation in England and Wales

| Study | Cost per pound of damages | |
|---|---|---|
| | Court | Mean percentage |
| Harris et al. (1984) | — | 18 |
| Civil Justice Review | County | 84 |
| | District | 32 |
| | High | 36 |
| Swanson (1988) | High | 52 |
| Woolf (1995) | Supreme | 61 |

Source: Swanson (1991), Table I.I; Woolf (1995).

[3] This figure is based on information supplied in LCD (1991), Annex A, Tables 3, 4, 5.

On the supply side, the principal-agent relationship that exists between insurers and the insured generates a number of information asymmetries, which may prevent suppliers from setting premiums sufficient to (at least) break even. Apart for the usual moral hazard and adverse selection problems associated with contracting and post-contract behaviour, information asymmetries also occur when claims on policies are made. These take several forms: (i) does the case have sufficient merit for the insurance company to avoid being exposed to unacceptable risk? (ii) what are the likely costs and how can they be controlled/monitored? (iii) which lawyers can be relied upon to provide accurate information on (i) and (ii)?[4] These difficulties are similar to those faced by American health insurance companies in the 1980s, where third party retrospective reimbursement schemes with fee-for-service payments provided neither physicians nor patients with sufficient incentives for cost control (see Culyer, 1993). Such problems are exacerbated for insurance companies by the British method of allocating costs, which increases the exposure to costs faced by insurers.

There are a number of ways in which insurance firms could overcome these problems. Perhaps the most important protection against incurring unnecessary cost is the choice of solicitor to confirm the merits of, and process, the case. In principle, a solicitor can be given correct incentives here through vertical integration (i.e., by creating an in-house legal team), fee contracts and/or the prospect of future business. A variety of these seems to be used: a recent survey for *Post Magazine* observed that '[o]pinion is split as to whether in-house handling or appointing solicitors is the most efficient method.' (p. 17). It appears that economies of scale can play a role here and the survey indicated that bulk-claims were often handled in-house, with more specialised ones being sent out to solicitors.

Companies will clearly want to play a role in the choice of lawyers for their policy-holders, whichever approach they adopt. This poses a problem: because lawyers act as agents for both the insured and the insurers, there is a chance that giving one of these principals the power to appoint will cause the other's interests to be relegated or neglected. Given this, it is significant that claimants' interests are now protected by the EC Directive 87/34 (implemented by the Insurance Companies (Legal Expenses Insurance) Regulations 1990, SI 1990/1159), which grants claimants a free choice of solicitor. It is interesting to note that most companies reserve the right to reject such nominations and may, indeed, nominate solicitors themselves who the client can reject. Another way of influencing clients in their

[4] The recently established Insurance Ombudsman reports that a significant number of policy complaints refer to (i) and (iii) here (NCC, 1994, p. 53). The NCC has also criticised LEI policies for the opaqueness of their wording and for failing to provide adequate arbitration procedures. There are also difficulties surrounding when a settlement is reasonable, who decides and what the insurer should do if the claimant does not wish to settle.

choice is to make policy terms dependent on it: for example, two companies offering policies reviewed in the *Which?* 1991 report reduced cover from £25,000 to £15,000 if clients chose their own solicitor. The extent to which companies retain control over solicitors is currently unclear, with the LCD noting in 1991 that the EC Directive had yet to be tested in court. Further, the extent to which such control assists them in minimising the effects of information asymmetries is also unknown. However, without this control it seems unlikely that they will be able to exert much effective influence.

Companies wishing to avoid making open-ended commitments to clients on the type and cost of cases they will fund may pursue other strategies, involving restrictions on cover (scope and extent—including an excess), case strength (policies tend only to fund those with 'reasonable prospects of success') and time limitation (most policies will not cover costs in cases started more than six months after the instigating event). The third restriction here is to ensure that fresh, recent evidence on the case is collected, before physical evidence is lost and memories have faded. The passage of time can have significant implications for case success, which, in turn, affects the prospect of shifting legal costs in Britain: Harris et al. (1984) noted that claims success dropped from over 70% to 45% for those who delayed consulting a lawyer for more than six months. Against this, however, is the fact that many claimants take time to make their claims. Insurance companies' six month limitations would have prevented 13.5% of Harris et al.'s sample from making a claims. In many cases, such delay may be unavoidable: for example in personal injury cases, the extent of damage may not be immediately apparent, or the need for medical treatment might prevent contact with a lawyer, so that short limitation periods penalise some potential claimants who cannot avoid making a delayed claim.

In practice, a number of these conditions for an efficient market in legal expenses to exist do not appear to be fulfilled, notably concerning the information requirements of both sides of the market. As a result, and as in other insurance markets, companies have introduced a variety of restrictions on the types of policy they will offer and the types of circumstance they will cover and have attempted to internalise some information problems through vertical integration into the market for lawyers.

## 3. THE UK LEGAL EXPENSES INSURANCE MARKET

Having placed LEI within a framework of economic theory, we now turn to a more detailed account of the actual market for LEI in the UK. It should be noted at the outset that information is limited by the relative newness of the market (the first policies were offered in Britain in 1974), and its reasonably small size (see below), exacerbated by incomplete reporting by firms to the Association of British Insurers and a recent increase in competition (and secrecy) in the market.[5] This heightened competition has come predominantly from direct line sales, which have begun to squeeze brokers' margins and encourage product differentiation within the market.

The UK market for LEI currently is dominated by two types of policy, which cover several main varieties of legal case: 'add-ons' to existing insurance policies (usually motor or home contents ones), or 'stand alone' policies which, as their name suggests, can be bought independently from other insurance cover and are designed to cover a wider range of legal expenses. Add-ons are most commonly provided in conjunction with motor insurance policies. A third type of assistance is 'advice only' cover, which provides telephone legal assistance to policy holders; it does not insulate them from legal costs, except to the extent that expert advice can enable them to make better informed decisions. Such advice is often provided in conjunction with house policies.

It is not possible to look at trends in the premium income derived from these different types of policies or in the relative use made of them by claimants, due to fluctuations over time in the number of firms reporting to the ABI. However, Table 2 provides some summary data from the ABI, averaged over the three years 1991–1993 to remove some of the fluctuations.

As the table shows, Family and Motor policies dominate the individual

Table 2: Legal expenses insurance policies, premiums and claims (annual average 1991-93)

| | Policy type: | | | |
|---|---|---|---|---|
| | All premiums | Family | Motor | Commercial |
| No. of policies (million) | n.a. | 6.1 | 6.5 | 0.2 |
| Gross premiums earned (£s million) | 68.3 | 15.2 | 37.0 | 17.3 |
| Average cost per premium (£s) | n.a. | 2.5 | 5.7 | 75.6 |
| Claim rate per 1000 policies | n.a. | 2 | 54 | 60 |
| Average amount per claim (£s) | 172 | 1457 | 85 | 1663 |

Source: ABI

[5] *Post Magazine* gives an interesting example of this secrecy. Responses to requests for telephone interviews included 'How do I know you're not a spy for the competition?' and 'We don't talk to the press any more.' (*Post Magazine*, 12/1/95, p. 17).

policies purchased in Britain, in terms of numbers. The size of the market, however, in terms of gross premiums is still quite small: the table indicates that gross premiums averaged almost £70m per annum between 1991 and 1993, but this is based on incomplete data and is an underestimate. This compares with total solicitor income of £6.2 billion and total gross expenditure of £1.4bn via the legal aid system. Commercial policies, which are small in number, still generate sizeable premium income. The reason for this can be seen from the particularly high average cost per premium of insured commercial cases (which, in turn might suggest that such cases are relatively more complicated than Motor or Family ones). The claim rates on Commercial and Motor policies are reasonably similar but those on Family ones are extremely low. Nevertheless, when claims are made on Family cases, they are much higher, on average, than for Motor cases and not much below Commercial ones. This might suggest that people are reluctant to use their insurance in Family matters unless a reasonably large amount is at stake. This is far less true of Motor cases, where many claims might be made as part of the process of claiming for vehicle damage.

Companies providing data to the ABI also reported gross premium income related to advice-only policies of £3.76 million per annum over the period 1991–93, with the number of calls for advice from policy holders averaging 171,000 per annum.

A joint Consumers' Association/Law Society report published in 1991 provides an alternative source of information on the current extent of legal expenses insurance in the UK. This was based on a survey which indicated that approximately 10 million people in Britain, or approximately one in four of the adult population, had some form of legal expenses cover. The survey demonstrated add-on policies to be by far the most common, but because they are a relatively small addition to an existing house, building, or car insurance policy, many individuals were not even aware they possessed cover; only 7% of respondents were aware that they did have some legal expenses insurance, or barely one in four of those who were covered.

In a summary of this survey in *Which?* magazine in 1991, details were published of 43 home policy add-ons offered by 30 major banks, building societies, insurance companies and brokers. The survey also looked at 9 stand-alone policies offered by 5 major providers. Considering add-on policies first, the survey indicated yearly premiums ranging from £3 to £50, with six offering the cover inclusive with the household policy. The range of cover was from £5,000 to £50,000 with £25,000 being the most common limit of cover. 12 policies had a nil excess, with the others ranging from £15 to £50, and with £30 being the most common excess. Turning to stand alone policies, the yearly premiums ranged from £15 to £162, and the limit of cover from £5,000 to £50,000, the latter figure being the most common. Seven of the nine policies had a nil excess, the other two having an excess of £50.

The areas most frequently excluded from coverage within these policies were claims reported more than six months after the event (27 add-on companies offered at least some polices with such a restriction, 3 stand-alone), construction, conversion and extension of buildings (25 add-on, 4 stand-alone) and planning claims against local authorities (24 add-on, 4 stand-alone). Virtually no policies covered fines or compensation, business contract disputes, community charge disputes, those with other insurers, or non-contentious cases' costs. Interestingly, only four add-on and three stand-alone policies covered criminal prosecution and only one stand-alone policy gave protection in matrimonial and custody cases. The largest provider of add-on policies, DAS, has emphasised that it is unrealistic to expect legal expenses insurers to cover all the areas currently covered by legal aid.[6] Thus, as was noted earlier, there are a number of supply-side imposed restrictions on its potential size.

Although there are clearly gaps in coverage which may be traced to the supply-side, in fact it is demand side failures which tend to be perceived as the chronic problem of LEI. As a Lord Chancellor's Department document noted in 1991: 'The major limitation of LEI . . . is that its relatively low volume puts it at risk from "adverse selection" . . .' (LCD, 1991, p. 30); in other words, the industry seems unable to attract enough customers to guarantee sufficient diversification of risk. This has led the NCC (1994, p. 52) to question the viability of the market: e.g., Care Assist (who offer stand-alone policies) expect a claim every two years and admit their business to be unprofitable. NCC also suggests there is recent evidence that some providers of stand-alone policies are pulling out of the market. It is not, however, clear that such exit from the market is due to insufficient demand or intensified competition.

The reasons for this apparently low volume of business are not well documented. Two obvious candidates arise: (i) that individuals believe their risk of incurring legal costs (and therefore their likely need for LEI) to be low, either through misperception or because the number is genuinely low, or (ii) that individuals believe themselves to be covered by other schemes such as Legal Aid or trade union ones. Regarding the first of these, there is little evidence on individuals' beliefs about their legal needs. Although the demand for legal services can be estimated from data on the use of solicitors and advice centres such as Citizens Advice Bureaux, this clearly does not capture the perceived risk of needing to use the law, which is prior to this need rather than conditional upon it. The same is true of figures on litigation rates within the population, though whether these are sufficiently low to justify a low expectation of becoming involved is not clear. Some evidence on the chances of being involved in a personal injury event which

[6] Ian Wylie: Insurers draw up exclusion zones for legal cover as state aid is cut. The Guardian 25/2./95, p32.

might potentially lead to use of the law can be found in Harris et al. (1984). There, information about 35,085 individuals was collected to find a sample who had been injured or ill for two weeks or more in the previous year (1975/6). Of these, 3,630 reported such circumstances (which translates into roughly 10% of the population), with 1,304 relating to road, work, home and leisure accidents and 2,226 relating to illness. Of course, these figures varied by observable characteristics such as age and type of work.

A second possible explanation for the apparently low volume of LEI business concerns the existence of legal aid: if individuals feel protected against legal expense by this scheme, they will not demand protection from the private market. Again, little evidence on the perceived substitutability (as opposed to complementarity) between legal aid and LEI is available. However, Lloyd-Bostock (1984) noted that '[k]nowledge of the legal aid and legal advice schemes was minimal among the accident victims in our sample.' (p. 67). This suggests that sufficient ignorance surrounds the existence and mechanics of legal aid to make perceived substitutability unlikely. Of course, the recent high profile given to rising legal aid expenditure, eligibility cuts and a small number of high cost legally aided cases has probably increased awareness of legal aid and the difficulty of obtaining it. Increased awareness of reduced eligibility might stimulate demand for LEI in future.

In summary, therefore, the market for LEI is apparently quite small at present, whether measured in terms of the premium income generated or in terms of the demand for policies. However, there is some evidence that the supply-side of the market is currently undergoing some structural change, with enhanced competition, brought about by alterations in the way that policies are marketed, generating lower prices and some product differentiation. It is too early to say whether this will inspire demand or, to the extent that coverage is offered at unrealistically competitive prices, tarnish the markets image, thereby further depressing demand. It also seems that both the profile and the structure of the legal aid system may significantly influence the LEI market. It therefore seems appropriate, at this point, to consider the nature of the current legal aid system.

## 3. THE UK LEGAL AID SYSTEM

The current prevalence of legal expenses insurance in the UK cannot be considered in isolation from the existence of the state legal aid scheme, which was introduced in 1950. Legal Aid has been defined as '. . . a form of conditional financial support, provided by the taxpayer, for individuals whose financial circumstances would prevent them from taking or defending proceedings without assistance with their legal costs.' (LCD, 1991, p. 5).

It is effectively a form of subsidised access to existing private legal practitioners, with availability subject to a means test and a merit test applied by legal practitioners. It has three main components: civil legal aid, criminal legal aid, and legal advice and assistance (the Green Form scheme). A range of smaller schemes have also been developed, notably assistance by way of representation (ABWOR), which enables a solicitor to represent a client in some tribunal proceedings; and two statutory duty solicitor schemes which provide immediate assistance and advice for people detained in police stations or for unrepresented defendants in magistrates courts.

Over time there have been a number of changes in the scope of legal aid. Since 1977 legal aid has not been available in uncontested divorce proceedings, and since 1989 (following the 1989 Children Act) it has been possible to award legal aid to children in their own right. In 1986 the Legal Aid Efficiency Scrutiny Committee proposed that most of the legal advice available under the legal aid Green Form scheme should be discontinued on the grounds that it primarily enabled citizens to arrange their private affairs in areas such as wills, conveyancing and probate, and should not be publicly subsidised (LCD 1986). These proposals engendered a hostile response, and were abandoned in the White Paper of March 1987 (HMSO, 1987).

When legal aid was first introduced in 1950, around 80% of the population were eligible for the scheme. But failures to uprate eligibility limits in line with growth of earnings, plus formal reductions in eligibility during the 1980s, have reduced the proportion of households eligible for legal aid to 57–61%, and of individuals from 51–66%, depending on which estimates are used (Murphy 1989; LCD 1991) Put another way, up to 16 million people in Great Britain have lost eligibility for legal aid in the last 15 years. Proposals to further reduce eligibility have met with strong criticism (Home Affairs Committee 1993; LCAC 1993), but it seems likely that eligibility will continue to be eroded.

In 1993/94 the legal aid system paid for a total of 3.4 million acts of legal assistance or service in England and Wales, at a net cost to the taxpayer of £1021m. The main areas of expenditure were civil non-matrimonial (£350m), civil matrimonial (£332m) and criminal (£291m). To place these figures in the context of the legal services industry as a whole, the proportion of solicitors' income derived from legal aid has been fairly stable at approximately 11% of the total throughout the 1980s. (LAG 1992). However, legal aid work is not evenly distributed across legal practices, with some law firms heavily dependent on it and others performing negligible amounts. In addition, there are regional differences, and outside London (with its large volumes of commercial law) legal aid accounts for about 17% of all solicitors income (Gray and Rickman 1994). The Bar is more heavily dependent on legal aid: the Bar Council in 1990 estimated that 27% of total barristers' fee income came from legal aid work.

There are few reliable comparative international data on legal aid systems, but most studies identify the British system as the most fully-developed: in 1989, one estimate of legal aid expenditure in eight European countries had the UK devoting 0.05% of Gross Domestic Product to legal aid, compared to 0.04% in the Netherlands, 0.025% in Sweden, 0.02% in Germany, 0.01% in Spain, 0.005% in France and Ireland, and 0.002% in Belgium (Cousins 1994).

Although the proportion of GDP devoted to legal aid varies between countries, most countries have experienced a rapid growth in legal aid expenditure in recent years. The UK is certainly no exception, and indeed rising legal aid costs have become a major UK policy issue in recent years: in the 10 years from 1983–84 to 1993–94 the net cost of the scheme rose at an average annual rate of over 18%, compared to a nominal GDP growth rate of 7.5%. The reasons for this growth rate are not clearly understood: it has been linked to supplier-induced demand impelled by a substantial growth rate in the numbers of practising solicitors, to a burgeoning volume of parliamentary legislation with major legal implications, to inefficiencies in the courts and other areas of the legal system, to procedural delays and complexities, and to changing social patterns such as increased poverty and inequality, high unemployment, and growing numbers of one-parent families.

The main areas in which growth has occurred and the essential nature of that growth are indicated in Table 3. The fastest growing area by far has been civil non-matrimonial law, where the number of legally aided cases has grown by around 12% annually for the last decade. This is three times the rate of growth experienced in other areas of legal aid. The real cost per case has also been growing steadily across all main areas of legal aid, at an annual rate of between 4% and 5%.

Table 3 : Decomposition of legal aid expenditure growth into price and volume increases, 1978–79 to 1992–93.

| | Nominal expenditure growth, 1978/79–1992–93 | Of which GDP deflator | Of which population growth | Of which volume growth | Of which expenditure growth per unit (case) |
|---|---|---|---|---|---|
| Civil: matrimonial | 16.53 | 7.48 | 0.24 | 3.83 | 4.17 |
| Civil: non-matrimonial | 26.46 | 7.48 | 0.24 | 11.72 | 5.06 |
| Criminal | 16.84 | 7.48 | 0.24 | 4.28 | 4.00 |

Source: Gray (1994)

As the cost of legal aid has escalated, so a number of responses have been forthcoming. Eligibility has been eroded substantially, and the Legal Aid Board and Lord Chancellor's Department have introduced a number of reforms intended to bring aggregate expenditure under control: for example, retrospective fee per item of service payment systems for solicitors have increasingly been replaced by prospectively negotiated standard fees, and a franchise contract system has been introduced, giving favourable treatment to firms meeting certain performance standards.

Most recently, a number of more far-reaching proposals have been made. A report by the Social Market Foundation in 1994 proposed reforms analogous to those introduced into the NHS: in particular, 'fundholders for justice' would be created, who would determine eligibility and merit, and then buy legal services from competing lawyers on behalf of the legally aided person (Bevan, Holland and Partington 1994). And in May 1995 the Lord Chancellor's Department issued a consultation paper, based on a system of block contracting, whereby each Legal Aid area office would receive a budget, would set its own priorities, and would then enter contracts with a range of suppliers to provide advice, assistance and representation in line with these priorities at an agreed cost, volume and quality and for an agreed period (LCD 1995). However, the Lord Chancellor has also made clear that some form of legal aid would continue to be the principle mechanism for increasing access to the law among the less well-off, and that legal expenses insurance does not have a major place in these reforms: 'I think legal expenses insurance . . . is a good thing and would like to see it develop, for example as part of the remuneration package of employees, but this is a matter for the commercial judgement of employers and the insurance industry, not for me, and I do not in any event see it as a likely to be of much more than marginal relevance in relation to legal aid in the foreseeable future.' (Mackay 1995, p. 9). Similarly, the LCD Consultation Paper noted that '. . . such [LEI] insurance is likely to have limited relevance to legal aid because it is unlikely that a system comprehensive enough to cover those most in need of legal aid would ever become commercially viable.' (LCD, 1995, para. 3.36).

## 4. INTERNATIONAL COMPARISONS OF LEGAL EXPENSES INSURANCE

A variety of group and individual LEI schemes are available in Europe, as in Britain, but Patterson (1992) notes that individual schemes tend to dominate, first appearing on the Continent in the 1920s, and gaining significance in the 1960s. The most common group policies in Europe are those provided by Italian and Swedish trade unions. In contrast to the European position, LEI in the United States tends to be dominated by group policies.

Germany

Legal expenses insurance is more extensive in Germany than in any other major industrialised country. In 1992 approximately 50% of German households held some form of legal expenses insurance policy. Around one-third of these policies relate exclusively to automobile-related legal risks, with the remainder providing general coverage. However, even general policies normally exclude important areas such as divorce and administrative law. Criminal actions are usually included in general policies, but only for actions arising through neglect: criminal deeds are excluded.

The high prevalence of legal expenses insurance in Germany is closely linked to the fact that legal fees are highly predictable; this in turn is because the remuneration of German lawyers is closely regulated, with standard fee scales to which all advocates are obliged to adhere, which are related to the estimated value of the issue in dispute, and which are applied across all courts.

In consequence of the well-developed market for legal expenses insurance, the proportion of cases assisted by the German legal aid scheme is in some areas very low. For example, a study in one region found that, in petty claims courts, legal aid was granted to only 3% of plaintiffs, 2% of defendants, and to both parties in less than 1% of cases (Hirte 1991 p. 116). In comparison, in areas such as most matrimonial disputes, which are beyond the scope of legal expenses insurance, over half of all cases are legally aided. As noted above, the share of national income devoted to legal aid in Germany is less than half the proportion in the UK.

Sweden

In Sweden, LEI is mandatory, principally because the otherwise extensive legal aid scheme does not cover liability for opponents' costs (Patterson, 1992). An estimated 80% of Swedish households have LEI. Again, it is noteworthy that the resources available to the Swedish legal aid scheme, as in Germany, are substantially less than in the UK.

United States

Private insurance for legal costs in the United States has grown 'exponentially' (Patterson, 1992, p. 169) in recent years. Part of the reason for this is the heavy use of advertising and incentives such as tax concessions to overcome any volume problem. The majority of group schemes emphasise preventive law, such as consultation as opposed to representation, in order to keep costs down and reap economies of scale.

One particularly different approach to those adopted in Europe is the legal clinic. These offer in-house legal services when required to a clientele which pays for membership on an instalment basis. Thus, they resemble the HMOs found in the American health care sector, using in-house practitioners to reduce information asymmetries. Costs are kept low through economies of scale gained by the extended use of para-legals and attracting a mass clientele, through substantial advertising campaigns. From their beginning in 1975, over 1,000 clinics existed in the US by 1990, with the two largest representing America's second and forty-second largest law firms (Abel, 1988, p. 217). In 1988, Abel reported that the largest, Hyatt Legal Services, spent over $5 million a year on advertising, attracting 18,000 new clients a month.

The efficacy of legal clinics has been disputed. Muris and McChesney (1979) argue that their advertising campaigns ensure widespread information amongst the public as well as guaranteeing quality. Coupling this with the low prices charged by clinics, the authors praise them. However, Abel (1988) observes that the clinics may simply divert custom from other legal practitioners, rather then generating new clientele. He thus questions the extent to which they have met the objective of servicing unmet legal need. Whether they are a more efficient mechanism for providing some of the same legal services currently provided by other legal practitioners remains an open question.

## 5. CONCLUSIONS: ACCESS TO JUSTICE AND THE FUTURE FOR LEGAL EXPENSES INSURANCE IN THE UK

In this chapter we have stressed the efficiency as well as the equity arguments which must be considered when examining policies to promote access to legal services. We have argued that an efficient legal system must be accessible in order that agents can expect to be confronted by the costs of their actions. Improved access (for instance through LEI, *inter alia*) might be an efficient outcome, but it is also possible that it might induce too much use of the legal system, thereby causing individuals to take more care in their actions than would be efficient. There is a perception of low demand for LEI in the UK, too low in all probability to sustain a flourishing market. But it is unclear whether, from an efficiency perspective, demand is 'too low' or is simply 'low'.

Bearing these initial points in mind, several observations can be made. The LEI market in Britain is currently quite small. This may not seem to be the case when considered in terms of the number of individuals holding some form of policy, but gross premium income is small both in absolute terms and in relation to the volume of legal aid or other privately funded legal work, while the coverage of many policies is quite limited.

One important issue which has not been seriously addressed concerns the interaction between legal expenses insurance and the existing system of legal aid. In some jurisdictions, such as Germany, legal expenses insurance coverage may render an individual ineligible for legal aid in areas covered by the insurance policy. This has not yet been proposed in the UK, and research evidence would be useful on the current and potential impact such a restriction would have on legal aid expenditure and on different sections of the population.

The legal aid scheme is currently undergoing extensive reform, with the stated aims of expanding eligibility through achieving cost effective service provision, and the Lord Chancellor has assessed legal expenses insurance as having 'marginal relevance in relation to legal aid in the foreseeable future', as noted earlier.[7] However, the ways in which the legal aid reforms take shape in practice, such as the necessity to prioritise certain types of service to stay within area block grant allocations, will inevitably mean some cases becoming less likely to receive legal aid, which could in turn increase demand for LEI in these areas. The ongoing reforms may also increase public awareness of the potentially costly nature of using the law, and of the tightness of legal aid eligibility, thereby increasing demand for LEI. LEI also provides coverage for some risks currently ignored by legal aid (prominent examples being much tribunal-related activity and the opponent's costs, within the indemnity limit). A related policy influence is the increased use of standard fees for legal practitioners performing legal aid work, and recent calls for legal costs to be capped. Assuming both of these become common practice, they would create a climate more favourable to LEI by making legal costs more predictable, as the German experience shows.

Another way to raise LEI volumes is to make the purchase of such policies compulsory (as with motoring insurance). To the extent that policies here were too expensive for low income groups, they could be subsidised, or legal aid could continue. Such a policy was considered, but rejected, by the LCD in its 1991 document, particularly on the grounds that it would merely shift the administrative burden of insurance from the public to the private sector.

However, while there does appear to be scope for growth in legal expenses insurance, it is clear that LEI will not provide a complete substitute for legal aid. One reason concerns the potential externalities which can be generated by bringing some cases, even if they are high risk ones—a 'public interest' argument. Here, the risk (and perhaps the size of the expected award) might lead the private benefits from bringing the case to be outweighed by the private costs: private insurance would not fund the

[7] This view is shared by the National Consumer Council (NCC, 1994, p. 51).

case. However, if there are social benefits to the case being heard (perhaps due to the legal precedent it would set), then the state would wish to step in and subsidise it. It interesting that the current merits test for legal aid effectively rules out such cases.

The legal profession could also have a role to play in helping to insure the public against legal costs. Lawyers are ideally placed to overcome a number of the information asymmetries inherent in legal cases. Accordingly, it seems certain that a flourishing LEI market would see increasing links between legal and insurance firms, or increased use of in-house legal advice. Of course, lawyers could actually insure clients against legal costs themselves by offering to work on a contingent fee basis. (Indeed, with capital market backing, they might also be suitable lenders.) In this case, as with American legal clinics, the roles of lawyer and insurer would be vertically integrated. Of course, such contingent fees are currently unenforceable in Britain, but the recent legalisation of a hybrid contingent fee (the 'conditional fee', where lawyers agree to waive their hourly fees if the case is lost in return for a mark-up on these if the case is successful) might be the first step in this direction. If this were to be the case, law firms might wish to insure themselves against lost cases. To the extent that this was done outside the Law Society's Indemnity Insurance Scheme (a compulsory insurance scheme to protect solicitors against professional negligence claims, introduced in 1976—see Bowles and Jones (1989) for a discussion), this might provide another role for the insurance industry to enter the market for legal services.

In summary, the development of a larger legal expenses insurance market in the UK has been hindered by the prevailing level of consumer demand, and supply-side restrictions on the types of policy available, often in response to important information asymmetries, including the adverse selection due to low volumes. Despite these difficulties, there is reason to suspect that, as in other areas where public expenditure currently plays an important role, private insurance arrangements will come to play an increasing role in funding legal services.

## REFERENCES

Abel, R. United States. In Abel & Lewis (eds), Lawyers in Society Vol 1: The Common Law World. UC Press, Berkeley Ca, 1988.

Association of British Insurers. Risk, Insurance and Welfare: The Changing Balance Between Public and Private Protection. London: ABI, 1995.

Bevan G, Holland T, Partington M. Organising cost-effective access to justice. Social Market Foundation memorandum No. 7. July 1994.

Bowles R and Jones P. Professional liability: an economic analysis. Aberdeen: Aberdeen University Press for the David Hume Institute. 1989.

Cousins, M. The politics of legal aid. Civil Justice Quarterly, 13, pp. 111–132, 1994.

Culyer A.Health care insurance and provision. In Barr & Whynes (eds), Current Issues in the Economics of Welfare, Macmillan, 1993.

Gray, A. The reform of legal aid. Oxford Review of Economic Policy, February, 1994.

Gray, A. & Rickman, N. Economic Modelling of Legal Aid Within the Legal Services Industry. Report to the LCD. August, 1994.

HMSO. Legal Aid in England and Wales: A New Framework. London HMSO, 1987.

Harris, D. et al. Compensation and Support for Illness and Injury. Clarendon Press, Oxford, 1984.

Hirte, H. Access to the courts for indigent persons: a comparative analysis of the legal framework in the UK, US and Germany. International and Comparative Law Quarterly, 1991.

Home Affairs Committee. Legal Aid: The Lord Chancellor's Proposals. Fifth Report from the Home Affairs Committee, HC517, Session 1992–3, London, HMSO.

Law Society. Annual Statistical Report 1994. London, The Law Society.

LAG. A Strategy for Justice: Publicly Funded Legal Services in the 1990s. Legal Action Group, 1992.

LCD (Lord Chancellor's Department). Legal Aid Efficiency Scrutiny (2 vols). London HMSO, 1986.

LCD. Review of the Financial Conditions for Legal Aid: Eligibility for Civil Legal Aid, A Consultation Paper. Lord Chancellor's Department, June 1991.

LCD. Judicial Statistics: Annual Report 1993. London: HMSO Cm2623, 1994.

LCD. Legal Aid—Targeting Need: The future of publicly funded help in solving legal problems and disputes in England and Wales. A Consultation Paper. London: HMSO Cm 2854, 1995.

LCAC. Lord Chancellor's Advisory Committee on Legal Aid, 40th Annual Report, London, HMSO, 1993.

Lloyd-Bostock, S. Fault and liability for accidents: the accident victim's perspective. In Harris et al. 1984.

Mackay, The Right Honourable The Lord Mackay of Clashfern, The Lord Chancellor. Text of a speech to the Social Market Foundation, as given, 11th January 1995. London, LCD 1995.

Muris, T, McChesney, F. Advertising and the price and quality of legal services: the case for legal clinics. American Bar Foundation Research Journal, 1979.

Murphy M. Legal Aid eligibility: calculations and interpretations of recent trends. London, Legal Action Group, 1989.

NCC. The Cost of Justice: The Lord Chancellor's Review of Spending on Legal Services. National Consumer Council, August, 1994.

Patterson A. Financing legal services: a comparative perspective. In Miller & Beaumont (eds), The Option of Litigating in Europe, 1992.

Pearson, Lord. Final Report of the Royal Commission on Civil Liability and Compensation for Personal Injury (I, II & III), Cmnd. 7054, London HMSO, 1978.

Swanson, T. The Importance of Contingent Fee Arrangements. Oxford Journal of Legal Studies, vol. 11, 1991.
Which? Magazine. Going to Law: One Law for the Rich? April, 1991, pp. 227–230.
Woolf, Lord. Access to Justice. Interim Report to the Lord Chancellor on the Civil Justice System in England and Wales. London: Woolf Inquiry Team, Room 438, Southside, 105 Victoria Street, London, SW1E 6QT, 1995.

# 17

# *The Economics of Cost-shifting Rules*

NEIL RICKMAN*

## 1. INTRODUCTION

It has long been recognised that cost, complexity and delay are significant features of the civil justice system in England and Wales. To some extent, these features can be viewed favourably: financial cost and delay can both act as valuable disincentives to prospective litigants whose cases would not justify the use of scarce legal resources, while complexity is perhaps an inevitable result of a system which seeks accuracy and fairness. Having said this, it seems likely that there is some level of cost and delay at which the disincentive effect is too great, leaving parties with legitimate claims without the legal means to pursue them. Similarly, as the complexity of procedure, judegments and statute increase, it seems reasonable that individuals will be deterred from using the legal system or be unable to monitor the quality of their lawyers' work. Such problems do not just prevent the redress of a particular wrong, they also blunt the deterrence effect of the law itself.

Unfortunately, it is extremely difficult to know what levels of cost, complexity and delay balance these costs and benefits, let alone whether a legal system has reached such levels. Instead, we are left with the need to judge on the basis of available evidence and of our views as to how the system would operate if it were reformed. Lord Woolf's interim report into enhancing access to justice takes the view that our civil justice system has reached the point where these features tip the balance against an efficient and effective legal system: he identifies them as 'the key problems facing civil justice today' (ch. 3, para. 1). There is some evidence for this. For instance, in the late seventies, both the Pearson Commission (1978) and the Centre for Socio-Legal Studies' research in Oxford (Harris et al., 1984) highlighted the high cost of personal injury litigation and estimated that approximately 15% of those dropping their cases did so due to reasons of

* Department of Economics, University of Surrey and Centre for Socio-Legal Studies, Wolfson College, Oxford. This paper is based on an earlier version written for Lord Woolf's committee, with Hugh Gravelle.

costs. What is more, this figure sheds no light on the number of cases which, for reasons of costs, were never initiated. Most recently, Lord Woolf's report quotes its own research into taxed Supreme Court cases (Annex III). This displays evidence of 'disproportionality' in the sense that many cases, small ones in particular, run up costs which constitute a significant percentage (sometimes over 100%) of the value of the claim in question. Lord Woolf's report also supports earlier findings of significant case delay in the civil justice system.[1]

Lord Woolf's solution is a series of procedural reforms, aimed at reducing cost, complexity and delay and thereby re-balancing the legal system in favour of access to justice and deterrence. The aim of this chapter is to consider one procedural reform, briefly discussed in chapter 25 of his report, and potentially at the centre of these 'key' problems: the way in which legal costs are allocated between litigants. Broadly speaking, the rule in England and Wales is that the financial costs of both parties will be borne by the losing litigant, a rule known variously as the 'indemnity rule', the 'cost-shifting rule' or that of 'costs following the event'. A variety of alternative rules exist, perhaps the most well known being that commonly used in America, which requires the two parties to bear their own costs, regardless of the case outcome. The question considered in the chapter is what effect these two rules have on litigation.

We seek to address this question by considering the financial incentives provided to litigants by English and American cost rules. For example, which rule makes a given case more likely to be filed? Which makes a filed case more likely to be dropped, or settled, or tried? How might the likely outcome of the case at these stages influence individuals' behaviour in their daily activities, thereby affecting the potential number of cases and the overall volume of litigation. To do this, we use the evidence which economists have compiled on the effects of cost allocation rules on the above issues. The intention is not to provide an extensive survey of the available literature, but rather to give an overview of its main results. The majority of these are from theoretical models because it is rare to find comparable data on cases from jurisdictions which have used both English or American cost rules. We do, however, summarise the small quantity of empirical evidence which is available.

The chapter is structured as follows. The next section gives a short account of the way in which economists have thought about the process of litigating a case and explains how they have attempted to analyse some of the linkages between the different stages mentioned above. This is followed by our survey of the theoretical hypotheses which economic models have generated about the way English and American cost rules will affect the

[1] For an excellent survey, see Swanson (1991).

behaviour of (prospective) litigants. This is split into two sections: the first looks at filing and settling a case and at the influence of cost rules on the parties' litigation expenditures; the second considers the cost rules' effects on the volume of cases filed and reaching trial. The fifth section then presents empirical evidence before a final section concludes.

## 2. THE LITIGATION PROCESS

Litigation can be thought of as a process involving a series of sequential decisions; we shall term this the 'litigation process'.[2] For economists, an important feature of this process is the way each of these decisions affect others taken at later stages in the case and how knowledge of events likely to happen later in the process might influence earlier actions (see Cooter and Rubinfeld, 1989; Rickman, 1995). Because these linkages will play an important role as the chapter progresses, we briefly discuss them now.

At the most general level, the litigation process involves the following:

1. the prospective plaintiff(s) and defendant(s) decide what levels of care to take when performing their activities;
2. if there is an accident, the prospective plaintiff(s) must then decide whether to take legal advice and, given that advice, whether to file a suit;
3. if a suit is filed, both parties must decide upon their negotiating strategies, on what settlement offers/demands to accept or reject and on what procedural devices to employ;
4. if settlement fails, whether to go to trial.

Of course, this simple list ignores many important features of litigation and includes a number of stages which would not be regarded as litigation by lawyers. Stages 1 and 2 are particular examples of the latter inclusions. The reason for this broad, and general, view is to emphasise the links which exist between different parts of the litigation process. These links mean that one should not introduce a particular policy reform without being aware of its potential effects elsewhere in the system: for instance, it may not be sensible to enhance settlements if this means that the parties adopt 'softer' bargaining strategies and that potential defendants can therefore expect to face a cost which is less than that imposed on others by their actions. This is particularly true if there is concern about how a change in procedure will affect the number of cases which the legal system is trying to handle (the 'volume of litigation'). The implication of this insight for our survey is that,

[2] We shall present our discussion of this process in terms of a personal injury dispute. As will be clear, the analysis can be modified to accomodate alternatives without significantly altering the final conclusions.

in order to assess the impact of altering cost rules, we must look at the effects of reform at each stage of the litigation process and its secondary effects elsewhere.

## 3. THEORETICAL ANALYSIS OF FILING AND SETTLING

The issue of how different cost allocation rules affect the litigation process is one of incentives: What incentives do the rules provide to litigants? One way to analyse this is with the aid of a theoretical model which looks at how changing between different cost rules affects litigants' decisions at different stages of the litigation process. Such theoretical analysis has the value of clarifying the different forces at work under these rules by developing a set of hypotheses (which, in turn, can be tested). It also provides the opportunity to run controlled 'thought' experiments given that jurisdictional differences seriously limit the opportunity for actual controlled experiments. In this section, we look at the different effects of English and American cost rules on the plaintiff's decision whether to file the case and on the prospects of settling the case if it has been filed. (We are thus assuming that an accident has occurred, something we shall alter in the next section: we are at Stage 3 of the litigation process.)

A number of factors will affect the way in which the parties react to the incentives provided by English and American cost rules. These will include their attitudes towards risk, the case information they possess and the extent to which they can influence the expenditures they make during the case. We begin by presenting results from a simple model where each of these is ignored. This provides the simplest environment for comparing the rules' effects. After having done this, we relax these assumptions to see what effects they have on the analysis.

### 3.1. A Simple Model[3]

Throughout the chapter, we shall assume that the plaintiff and the defendant view litigation as a purely financial matter. In the current section, we shall also employ the following assumptions:

1. both parties are 'risk neutral' (neither would pay extra to avoid the risk of going to trial);
2. both parties share the same information about the case;
3. neither party's expenditure on the case is affected by the type of cost allocation rule in place, i.e., they invest the same amounts in the case regardless of the cost rule.

[3] See Posner (1973) and Shavell (1982).

**Filing a Case:** We begin by asking which rule will lead to more cases being filed. given that an accident has occurred. Ignoring, for the moment, the possibility of a case being brought for its nuisance value, the plaintiff will generally file a case if the expected gains from doing so are positive. Therefore, to decide whether the English or American rule will lead to more cases being filed, we must ask which one brings the plaintiff the larger expected gains. Under the above assumptions, the English rule will lead to more cases being filed if the plaintiff is particularly optimistic about his chances of winning the case. The reason for this is that, if he is optimistic, he will expect to incur less legal costs under the English rule than under the American one because, in winning, he shifts liability for them onto the defendant. Under the American rule, he will be sure to pay his own costs, regardless of the case outcome. As a result, this makes pursuing the case more 'profitable' (in expectation) under the English rule so that more cases of any given type will be filed.

What if the plaintiff brings the case even though it has little chance of success? The hope is that the defendant will pay something to avoid the inconvenience of having to defend himself. Here, there is general agreement that the English rule is more likely to deter such 'nuisance suits' than its American counterpart (for example, see Rosenberg and Shavell, 1985). The reason is that a plaintiff with a weak case will expect to incur both parties' costs if the case is tested at trial. At the same time, if the defendant knows the case to be weak, he will also realise that defending the case will ultimately not cost him much. This makes him more likely to defend, making the plaintiff more likely to be taken to court. Of course, there may still be potential for nuisance suits to succeed under the English rule: perhaps the defendant does not want to spend a long time defending his case (his reputation may be at stake or time may be costly to him), or he may still expect to pay some fraction of his costs.[4] The point, however, is that this potential for success seems to be less likely than under the American rule, given our current assumptions.

**Case Selection:** Snyder and Hughes (1990) somewhat counter this view of nuisance suits. In particular, they predict that the English rule will cause more low valued cases to be filed (since the case does not have to be worth so much when there is a prospect of shifting costs to the other party) but, in contrast to nuisance suits, these low cases will have more merit (higher probabilities of winning), reflecting the need for optimism on the part of the plaintiff under the English rule. To the extent that the merit of a claim

[4] Lord Woolf's report, ch. 3, para. 13 confirms that nuisance suits can occur under the English rule. Interestingly, in the example he cites, the problem seems to be high legal costs. Given the results we cite below, concerning the English rule's impact on legal expenditure, this might suggest a reason to expect nuisance suits under this rule.

only becomes apparent as the case progresses, the authors therefore predict that the English rule will exhibit a higher drop-out rate than the American one, since the lower value claims will be less able to offset the higher expectation of costs if bad information emerges. Thus, they argue, it is not that the English rule will discourage small cases, but that, unlike with the American rule, they will have been brought for the 'right' reasons.

**Settling a Case:** Under either rule, a necessary condition for settlement to occur is that the amount which the defendant expects to pay by going to trial is larger than the amount which the plaintiff expects to win there. In this situation both can benefit from settling the case for an amount between these two expected values (we say there is a positive 'settlement range'). This position is illustrated in Figure 1, where the defendant expects to pay out £*x* at trial and the plaintiff expects to receive £*y*. The difference £$(x-y)$ is the settlement range and, provided this is positive, there are gains from settling. If we interpret the size of this settlement range as determining the likelihood of a case being settled, then we can decide whether the English rule leads to more settlement than the American one by asking whether it leads to a larger settlement range.

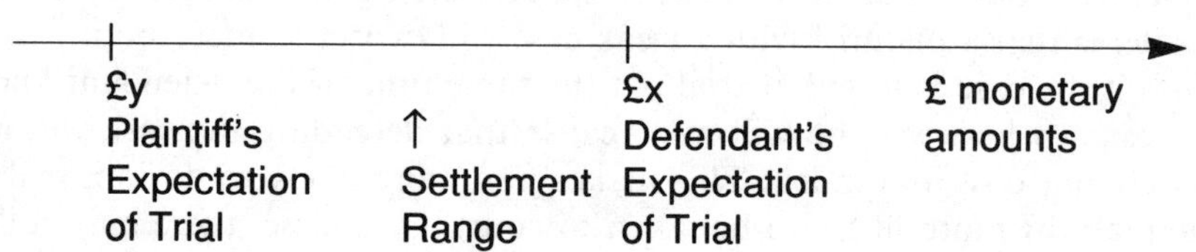


Fig. 1

It is easy to show that the English rule leads to a larger settlement range, and more settlement, than the American one when both parties are pessimistic about their chances at trial.[5] In this case, both believe they have a high chance of losing the case and that, therefore, they are likely to have to pay their opponent's costs. This makes the defendant expect to pay out a large amount at trial and the plaintiff expect to receive only a little. The result is a larger settlement range under the English rule and more settlement than under the American. On the other hand, if both parties are confident of their chances at trial, then they both expect to be able to shift their costs under the English rule, with the result that this rule makes settlement less likely than the American one.

[5] By 'pessimistic' we mean the following: if $p$ is the probability with which the plaintiff thinks he will win at trial and $q$ is the probability with which the defendant thinks the plaintiff will win at trial, then both sides being pessimistic means that $p < q$. Similarly, both sides would be 'optimistic' if $p > q$.

To summarise, we have the following hypotheses:

1. the English rule will lead to more case settlement, relative to the American rule, if the parties are both pessimistic about their chances at trial;
2. the English rule will lead to more cases being filed if the plaintiff is optimistic about his chances of winning;
3. it will lead to fewer nuisance suits but more low value claims which initially seem to have high merit.

Although, in principle, these results have interesting implications for the issues raised in the Introduction, they are derived from a simple model which ignores several important features of litigation. Thus, we now consider the effects of relaxing several of our simplifying assumptions.

### 3.2. Relaxing the Assumptions of the Simple Model

**Introducing Risk Aversion:** We have so far assumed that the litigants are unwilling to pay extra to avoid risk (they are 'risk neutral'). In fact, one can think of trial as being like a gamble where each party has a probability of winning and a complementary probability of losing. Given this, the parties may dislike the risk involved and be prepared to pay extra to avoid it (i.e., they may be 'risk averse'). This would obviously affect the maximum amounts they will offer/accept to avoid trial and will therefore alter the settlement range. In particular, we would expect the settlement range to be wider under both cost allocation rules if one or both of the parties is risk averse.[6] Again, we interpret this as implying that settlement is more likely than when the parties are risk neutral. We should recognise, however, that the amounts which parties will pay to avoid risk (their 'risk premia') will tend to vary with the extent of the risk, which in turn can be thought of as being related to the difference between what they receive from winning and losing. Since the English rule makes this difference larger than the American one, the English risk premia will be larger and the English settlement range will be correspondingly wider.

To summarise this reasoning, we can say that, relative to the situation when both parties are risk neutral, introducing risk aversion makes settlement more likely under both cost rules. We can also say that this effect will be greater under the English rule than under the American rule. When the parties are pessimistic about their chances at trial, so that they would be more willing to settle under the English rule anyway, we can go further and say that risk aversion makes them favour settlement even more strongly

[6] If the defendant is prepared to pay £$r$ to avoid risk and the plaintiff is prepared to pay £$s$, the settlement range becomes £$(x+r)$ –£$(y–s)$ > £$(x–y)$. In terms of Figure 1, the defendant's position moves to the right and plaintiff's moves to the left.

than the American one. Unfortunately, we cannot be so sure of this when the parties are optimistic about their chances: under these circumstances, the American rule would favour settlement amongst risk neutral parties but the effects of risk aversion work against this. Which effect dominates cannot be decided by theory. This is because we are not able to say how risk averse the parties are in general, and so we are unable to know the relative magnitudes of the effects of risk aversion under the two rules. Clearly, the more strongly averse to risk are the parties, the more chance there is that the English rule will lead to more settlement amongst risk averse parties than the American rule, even if both parties are optimistic.

We can also look at the effects of risk aversion on settlement filing. Now, the expected gains from filing are lower (by the amount of the risk premia under either scheme). Therefore, relatively less cases will be filed under both cost rules. Further, we know that the relative effect will be larger under the English rule than under the American one, As a result, still more optimism on the part of the plaintiff will be required for the English rule to continue to induce more filing.

Overall, the introduction of risk aversion moderates the effects of the cost rules on filing and settlement. This moderation is greater under the English rule than under the American one, but we cannot say whether it will offset the English rule's tendency to generate less settlement when the parties are risk neutral and optimistic about their chances at trial.

**Expenditures:** We have so far assumed that the parties cannot influence the costs of litigation. In fact, their expenditures here will tend to be the outcomes of their own choices and of the requirements placed upon them by their opponents. Thus we now ask how the different cost allocation rules might affect each party's expenditures and how these effects will influence their filing and settlement behaviour.

All of the theoretical work by economists in this area suggests that the English rule leads to higher expenditures on the case than the American rule. There are two reasons for this: (1) The English rule means that more is at stake at trial than the American rule does (the difference between winning and losing is greater). This means that both parties are willing to invest more under the English rule. (2) The English rule means that there is some chance of being able to shift all one's expenditures to the other side. This means that neither party *expects* to face the full cost of an increase in expenditure which, in turn, provides an incentive for such an increase to occur. Bringing these two together, both parties are effectively willing to 'work harder' (spend more) to generate a favourable probability of winning the case under the English rule than under the American one.

Turning to the implications of these results for settling, filing and case selection, Hause (1989) demonstrates that the higher trial expenditures under the English rule tend to increase the prospects of settlement. They do this by widening the settlement range relative to that under the American rule. We can extrapolate this back to say that the level of filing will also be reduced under the English rule because of the commensurate reduction in the net gain from trial.

**Private Information:** We have so far assumed that the litigants have the same information about the case. In fact, we might expect that each party will have some relevant information which the other does not possess: perhaps a defendant in a personal injury case knows how much care he was taking prior to the accident, or the plaintiff might know how badly he has been damaged. Although the process of discovery will tend to minimise these differences, it is still possible that they will exist right through the case. This is important because it means that we can no longer be sure that parties will settle when there is a positive settlement range: strategic behaviour by an informed party, or the inability to make accurate offers on the part of an uninformed one, might prevent the case from settling. Because of this, it is no longer enough for us to ask how English and American rules affect the settlement range. Instead, we must ask how they affect the parties' bargaining strategies, something we have been able to ignore until now.

Gravelle (1993) presents a comprehensive account of the effects of English and American rules in the context of private information. Given that the case has been filed, he assumes that the plaintiff has private information about his case and the defendant makes a settlement based only on his expectations about the plaintiff's information.[7] Both parties are risk neutral by assumption. Gravelle breaks down the probability of settlement occurring into its two components: the size of the defendant's offer and the probability of the plaintiff accepting it. The English and American cost rules are shown to have ambiguous effects on these two variables (we cannot say whether one or the other rules always raises the offer or probability). Some results are available, however. Thus, the plaintiff's probability of accepting any given offer from the defendant is lower, the more of his costs he expects the defendant to bear; as in the simple model, being able to shift costs tends to strengthen one's bargaining position. Further, the defendant's settlement offer will be higher under the English rule than the American one if both parties believe that the defendant will end up paying a positive fraction of the plaintiff's costs. In these circumstances, therefore, defendants will make higher offers under English rules but plaintiffs will be less willing to accept them.

It is interesting to ask what effects these two strategies have on the overall probability of settlement. Although they appear to operate in opposite

[7] Similar considerations to those discussed by Gravelle would enter the analysis if we made other informational assumptions: for example, the defendant can be given private information instead of the plaintiff, or, perhaps most likely, both parties might have private information.

directions, Gravelle establishes that the settlement result from our simple model carries over into this one: the English rule will bring about a higher probability of settlement than the American one if both parties are optimistic about their chances at trial, otherwise, the American rule will lead to the highest settlement probability.

### 3.3. Summary

In this section we have looked at the effects of the English and the American cost rule on the filing and settlement of cases and on the types of cases that might be filed. Although our original model was quite simple, it demonstrated that the effects in question can be quite subtle and difficult to predict. In particular, a move to the English rule enhances the role played by parties' expectations in litigation. As a result, we need to be able to determine what influences these expectations, and whether the different cost rules play a part here, before we can predict their effects on the quantity of cases filed and/or settled.

Matters are further complicated when we introduce more realism into the model. This is true in two senses. First, the added realism means that we have more factors to take into account when comparing the cost rules. For example, the introduction of risk aversion places added emphasis on the individual preferences of the parties'. Second, these extra factors often tend to offset the results from our simple model, thereby making it hard to arrive at unambiguous conclusions. Thus, both risk aversion and choice of expenditure levels have predictable qualitative effects but, in theoretical models, we are unable to quantify these effects in order to see whether they are more important than ones working in the other direction. The obvious example here occurs when the parties are optimistic about their prospects: in this case, risk aversion and choice of expenditure levels will work 'against' the effects of this optimism and enhance the prospects of settlement under the English rule relative to the American one. Without empirical evidence, however, we cannot tell which of these effects dominates and, therefore, which of the rules favours settlement. We shall say more about this in Section 5.

## 4. THE VOLUME OF LITIGATION

As we have seen, the costs of litigation need not only be the financial ones directly associated with the case. They can also involve those of delay. It seems reasonable that one cause of delay in cases is the volume of work which the legal system is trying to process at any given time; like all other systems, the legal one exhibits capacity constraints. We therefore turn now to ask what effects cost rules have on the volume of litigation. Here, the term 'volume of litigation' is used rather loosely to mean the number of accidents and the number of trials. We wish to know how the English and American rule affect each of these. Unfortunately, it is difficult to find unambiguous results here because, recalling Section 2, both the number of accidents and the number of cases are linked to each other via the settlement and filing behaviour we have already discussed.

### 4.1. The Number of Accidents

We begin with the number of accidents. This will, in part, be determined by the care individuals take in their daily business which will, in part, be influenced by the chances of a legal case being brought against them if they are involved in an accident. In general, we would expect individuals to take more care if they face a high chance of a suit being filed against them, of having to make a high settlement offer, or of having to go to trial. Thus, if the English rule leads to more case settlement than the American one and/or if it leads to lower settlement offers, and/or if it leads to less case filing, we would expect it to create more accidents.

From Section 3, we know how the cost rules affect settlement and filing behaviour. We also know, however, that these factors can offset each other when we are comparing the rules. Therefore, if the parties are risk neutral and if they cannot influence their case expenditures, we know that the English rule will cause less settlement if both parties are optimistic about their chances at trial. We also know that an optimistic plaintiff will be more likely to file a suit in such circumstances. Given this, we can say that there will be less accidents under the English rule than under the American one.

The outcome, when these assumptions are changed is less clear. For example, risk averse parties will be more likely to settle and file than risk neutral ones, under both rules. Yet these effects will be relatively larger under the English rule. It is therefore possible that the English rule will now lead to more accidents. This might be especially likely when the potential defendant is not risk averse but his expected opponent is likely to be.[8] Now, the potential defendant can exploit the other party's risk aversion under the English rule to a greater extent than under the American one. A similar observation can be made about the effects of cost rules on expenditure and the way this might influence pre-accident decisions. Finally, as we saw in

[8] For example, the potential defendant might be an employer deciding whether to invest in new safety equipment. His employees might be risk averse since they are afraid of losing their jobs through litigation, or they may not have used the legal system before, or they may not have trade union/legal aid support against costs. See Genn (1987) for some illuminating examples of why different parties might have different attitudes to risk in litigation. Interestingly, she finds, as we did in Section 3, that the English rule places more risk averse parties in weak bargaining positions.

Section 3, taking account of private information forces us to think about the size of the settlement amount as well as the prospects for settlement. We have seen that, in Gravelle's model, when the parties are optimistic and expect the defendant to pay a portion of the plaintiff's costs under English rules, the defendant's settlement offer is higher under the English rule than under the American one. This suggests that the defendant's expected costs following an accident will be higher under the English rule so that there will be fewer accidents under this rule in these circumstances.

### 4.2. The Number of Trials

Whether a case goes to trial will depend on all of the factors we have so far discussed: the number of accidents (potential cases), filing decisions and settlement behaviour. There is, however, an added complication. This arises from the fact that these influences will tend to work in opposite directions, thereby making it impossible to say, qualitatively, whether one rule will lead to more trials than another. To be precise, a rule which encourages filing and discourages settlement (as does the English rule in the simple model of Section 3.1 when the parties are optimistic and risk neutral) appears to make trial more likely. This is true, but *only conditional upon an accident having occurred.* In fact, as we have just seen, such settlement and filing behaviour will tend to reduce the number of accidents (other things equal) and this will have a negative effect on the number of trials.

## 5. EMPIRICAL EVIDENCE

The theoretical results described so far point to a number of qualitative effects which might be observed as we move from one cost rule to another. Of course, this says nothing about the magnitude of these effects, a point which is all the more important given that the effects often tend to work in opposite directions. We should, therefore, see theoretical results as assisting us in focusing our empirical analyses of these different cost rules. With this in mind, we now report the small amount of evidence on the quantitative effects of English and American cost rules.

There is very little evidence concerning the relative effects of the English and American rules on the decisions we have been focusing on (i.e., those to file, drop, settle and try a case). The main reason for this is that one clearly needs to be able to control for interjurisdictional differences when performing tests. Ideally, one needs a situation where a change in the law has led to the use of a different cost allocation rule for the same cases, within the same jurisdiction. There are occasional examples of this happening. For instance:

(i) Abere (1991) looks at the effects of a change in the cost allocation rules governing s. 16 of the Clayton Act (antitrust litigation in America) which occurred in 1976. Here the rules were changed from American to a 'proplaintiff' rule, where only a plaintiff has the opportunity to shift his costs.

(ii) Snyder and Hughes (1990) consider a medical negligence dataset from Florida. The Florida Medical Association (FMA) had argued for a change from American to English cost allocation rules, which finally took place in July 1980, lasting until September 1985.[9,10]

The other form of empirical evidence available to economists in testing their predictions about the effects of cost-shifting is experimental data. Because so much of what we wish to test is unobservable/unmeasurable/not measured, we can devise experiments to simulate the effects of the cost rules on participants' behaviour. In this way, we are able to control for some outside influences. A relevant paper here is Coursey and Stanley (1988).

We shall focus our survey on the work by Snyder and Hughes and by Coursey and Stanley, since Abere found no statistically significant differences between antitrust litigation behaviour under the American rule and the proplaintiff rule.

### 5.1. Snyder and Hughes (1990): Medical Negligence Data from Florida

These authors analyse a sample of 10,325 medical malpractice cases from the State of Florida, dating from the late 1970s, to the middle of the 1980s. Of the cases in the sample, 58% were litigated under the English rule. Although they do not have data on the decision to file a case, Snyder and Hughes have information on whether cases were dropped, settled or tried. They are therefore able to assess the impact of the cost rules on these decisions by comparing the sub-samples of cases using the English and American rules. They are not, however, able to say anything about how the rules affect the number of accidents and, therefore, the overall volume of litigation.

[9] The same authors have a second paper, analysing the effects of the English and American rules on case outcomes (plaintiff payoffs, etc.), using the same dataset. See Hughes and Snyder (1994).

[10] The reasons for the original change of rule are instructive: 'the FMA argued that fee shifting would discourage the pursuit of low merit claims.' (Snyder and Hughes, pp. 355–6). In fact, claim frequency actually rose by 25% between 1980 and 1985, although Snyder and Hughes note that, in retrospect, the data may have been misinterpreted. The FMA eventually lobbied for a return to the American rule because of other unexpected consequences of the English rule: (a) courts generally allowed costs to include the full contingent fee percentage, rather than 'value added' by the lawyer; (b) defendants (physicians) rarely benefited since insolvent parties were relieved from paying if they lost. This suggests that the courts' interpretations of how cost-shifting should work, as well as the incentives it creates, are important in determining its effects.

To begin with, the authors show that, amongst cases which were not dropped, the English rule raised the likelihood of going to trial. This suggests that the optimism effect identified in Section 3 above was offsetting others such as those from any litigant risk aversion or higher expenditures. They also show, however, that the English rule raised the probability of a case being dropped after filing. This is consistent with their view on the types of cases which are selected under the English rule in comparison to the American (see Section 3.1): in particular that, given low costs of filing a claim, the English rule encourages low value claims to be filed but that these are dropped as information about their chances becomes available. It is also possible that plaintiff risk aversion might have an affect here, again as information (and the greater prospect of trial) emerges.

Of course, these two results—on dropping and settling—work in opposite directions, so that we need some way of combining them in order to see their overall effect on the number of cases being dropped, settled and tried. To do this, the authors use their findings the predict how a hypothetical sample of cases would be treated under the English and American rule. the results are in Table 1.

Table 1: Predictions of Case Numbers Dropped, Settled and Tried from Snyder and Hughes (1990)

| | Stage reached | | | |
|---|---|---|---|---|
| | Number filed | Number dropped | Number settled | Number tried |
| American | 1,000 | 435 | 458 | 107 |
| English | 1,000 | 539 | 404 | 57 |

Source: Snyder and Hughes (1990), Figure 3, p. 365.

From this table we can see that, if 1,000 cases were filed under the American rule and under the English rule then Snyder and Hughes' sample predicts over 100 more would be dropped under the latter rule than the former (their 'case selection' prediction). Further, a smaller number of the cases (roughly half as many) would go to trial under the English rule. Therefore, although *ceteris paribus* the English rule makes trial more likely for a given case if it is not dropped, the fact that this rule also leads to more cases being dropped means that, overall, it causes fewer cases to reach trial. Thus, it appears that the English rule causes a more careful evaluation of the case's strengths to take place once it has been filed, thereby leading to more cases being dropped.

Table 2: Defendant Expenditure Predictions from Snyder and Hughes (1990), 1980 US Dollars

| | Defendant expenditure predictions |
|---|---|
| CASES AT TRIAL | |
| American Rule | $12,775 |
| English Rule | $20,775 |
| Percentage change due to English Rule | 61.3% |
| SETTLED CASES | |
| American Rule | $7,428 |
| English Rule | $10,890 |
| Percentage change due to English Rule | 46.6% |

Source: Snyder and Hughes (1990), Table 6, p. 375.

It will also be recalled from Section 3 that economic theory predicts parties' expenditures will be higher under the English rule than under the American one. Snyder and Hughes use their results to predict defendant expenditure on a representative case. Their results are in Table 2. The results confirm the theoretical predictions, for both settled and tried cases. Also, the margins concerned appear to be quite large.

The results from this paper are of some value in illuminating quantitative effects of English and American cost rules. Of particular interest is the empirical support they lend to the proposition that one should look at the whole litigation process before judging the overall effects of cost-shifting reform (or any others): it is only when Snyder and Hughes combine the overall effects of the English rule on cases dropped and settled that they are able to conclude that this rule will lead to less trial than its American counterpart. The paper is also interesting in that, to the extent that it confirms our expenditure predictions, it might give us confidence that our models capture some important aspects of the litigation process. Finally, the paper demonstrates the value of combining theoretical and empirical research in this area, suggesting that much fruitful data is contained in case files.

The overall message of the paper is that, for the sample in question, the English rule causes less cases to go to trial than the American rule, because it causes a larger number to be dropped. Amongst the cases which are not dropped, however, the parties' expenditure is significantly higher under the English rule (which, in turn, might help explain the high drop rate). Any policy recommendation on cost-shifting rules should weigh up these outcomes.

## 5.2. Coursey and Stanley (1988): Experimental Data

Coursey and Stanley respond to the lack of data in this area by setting up experiments to test for the existence of the incentive effects we have identified in Sections 3 and 4. In particular, they attempt to simulate litigation bargaining under alternative cost rules. Under the English and American cost rule, *inter alia*, four pairs of students were given 100 tokens to bargain over, each token being worth \$0.02 cents (so that \$2 were at stake in each game). If agreement was reached within five minutes, the parties kept their agreed shares; if not, a share was imposed upon them, randomly drawn from a commonly known distribution of outcomes. (This attempted to capture the uncertain nature of any trial which follows failure to settle a case.) Under the American rule, the cost to each party of having this random draw ('trial') occur was 20 tokens. Under the English rule, one party ('Person A') incurred costs of 40 tokens if their randomly assigned share was less than 50, otherwise the other party ('Person B') incurred these costs.

This process was repeated ten times, with students being randomly paired for each game. The bargaining involved anonymity and no vocal communication in order that particular students could not develop reputations over their bargaining strategies. Also, although the bargaining environment attempted to simulate settlement negotiations (with a settlement range of 100 and bargaining costs of 20 per side) the students were not informed of this. This was in case their behaviour was influenced by the way they felt plaintiffs or defendant *should* bargain, under the circumstances which might have reduced the precision with which the incentive effects of cost rules could be isolated. Finally, the experiments were conducted for two distributions of outcomes; the first a symmetric distribution around a mean of 50 (indicating that both parties would have a 50% chance of winning at 'trial'), and a second distribution with a mean of 30 and a higher chance of outcomes below 50 than above 50 (i.e., unfavourable to Person A).

Coursey and Stanley present results on settlement frequencies and settlement amounts. Looking at frequencies first, they found that, under both distributions of trial awards, the English rule generated more settlement than the American (87.5% and 72.% of cases settled under the English rule compared to 60% and 62.5% under the American). Given that neither party could be unduly optimistic or pessimistic in the experiments (they both know the random outcome distributions), and that neither could influence bargaining costs or had private information, this finding seems likely to be due to risk aversion on the parts of the players; i.e., the higher risk of paying the opponent's costs under the English rule encouraged settlement in the experiments.[11]

[11] Recall Section 3 and Genn (1987), discussed in note 8 above.

Moving to settlement amounts, both Persons received settlements around 50 under either cost rule when the random outcome distribution was symmetric. This is an intuitive outcome given that neither party had any extra bargaining power in this case. When the distribution was not symmetric, however, Person A (whose position was weakened in this case) received settlements below 50 under both cost rules. These were smaller under the English rule (averaging 32.2) than the American one (average 46.2). This suggests that the English rule allowed Person B to exploit the extra bargaining power implicit in the non-symmetric distribution, as our theory in Section 3 predicted.

Coursey and Stanley interpret their results as giving support to 'the premise that cost allocation rules in trial do affect the pretrial bargaining process' (p. 175). In particular, the results confirm that risk aversion can lead to the English rule generating more settlement than the American one and, also, that the English rule places relatively more bargaining power in the hands of a party with a strong case. As with Snyder and Hughes's results above, these results may or may not be desirable to policy makers.

## 6. CONCLUSION

The first conclusion to be drawn from the preceeding sections is that moving between English and American cost allocation rules can have an impact at all stages of the litigation process. The rule used will affect settlement behaviour, filing behaviour, pre-accident behaviour and, through all of these things, the number of cases going for trial. As a result, these rules will almost certainly influence the 'key problems' identified by Lord Woolf and referred in our Introduction. However, the impact of the rules has been shown to be quite subtle, with complications often arising from offsetting tendencies as we embellish a simple model of litigation. For this reason, we often rely on empirical work to determine which of these tendencies dominate.

Given this, it is useful to summarise the results we have found. We can make the following predictions about the effects of moving from the English to the American rule:

**Expenditures:** parties will spend less on the same case under the American rule as compared to the English rule. Snyder and Hughes found that tried cases were at least 61% more expensive and settled cases were 46% more expensive under the English rule.

**Filing:** An optimistic plaintiff will be less likely to file a given case under the American rule than under the English rule. Again, risk aversion and expenditure effects will tend to reduce the differences here.

**Case Selection:** The English rule can be predicted to cause more small value, high merit cases to be filed. Under the American rule, we would expect to see more small, low merit cases ('nuisance suits').

**Settlement:** Optimistic parties will be more likely to settle the same case under the American rule as compared to the English rule. This difference will, however, be smaller if the parties are risk averse or if they are allowed to determine their own expenditures. Both of these seem likely in the context of litigation between individuals. In Snyder and Hughes's sample, the optimism effect dominated the expenditure effect and meant that English rule cases were more likely to go to trial than American rule ones. Once, however, the case selection effect was taken into account, the higher number of cases dropped under the English rule meant that less cases in total went to trial. Thus, although the English rule made settlement less likely, it did so for a smaller number of cases reaching the settlement stage. The English rule seems to have a more extreme effect than the American one on risk averse parties' bargaining strategies (Coursey and Stanley).

**Accidents:** If the parties are optimistic, there will tend to be more accidents under the American rule than under the English rule. This is because the combination of higher settlement rates and lower filing rates under the American rule makes it unlikely that any given accident will end up at trial.

**Trials:** The effects of moving from the English rule to the American one are, in general, ambiguous. This is because the effects of the rules on settlement behaviour and the number of accidents work in opposite directions. As mentioned above, there is some evidence that the English rule reduces the number of cases going to trial overall.

Given our survey, it is hard to disagree with Gravelle that

> Cost-shifting rules do have . . . implications . . . for potential litigants, but their usefulness as policy instruments seems limited. The optimal cost-shifting rule is likely to vary depending on fine details of the objective circumstances of the parties . . . and their subjective probability beliefs. It seems more promising to pursue other, more direct, means of correcting the inefficient incentives . . . provided by a costly and imperfect legal system. (p. 18).

Whether the 'more direct' reforms proposed by Lord Woolf would achieve this goal remains to be seen, but his circumspect view of the value of altering the English cost allocation rule is, on balance, supported by this chapter. Perhaps, the simplest way to finally illustrate the complicated issues involved is to note that American litigation, appears to exhibit some similar 'key problems' as our own, even with a different cost rule. Apparently, if reformed cost rules are the answer to our difficulties, the appropriate package of reforms to accompany them needs considerably more research.

## REFERENCES

Abere, A. (1991): 'An Empirical Analysis of Alternative Rules for the Allocation of Legal Costs: Does Fee-Shifting Affect the Choice Between Settlement and Trial?', Working Paper No. 39, Centre for Law and Economic Studies, Columbia University School of Law, New York, USA.

Cooter, R. D. & Rubinfeld, D. L. (1989): 'Economic Analysis of Legal Disputes and Their Resolution', *Journal of Economic Literature*, vol. 27(3).

Coursey, D. L. & Stanley L. R. (1988): 'Pre-Trial Bargaining Behaviour Within the Shadow of the Law: Theory and Experimental Evidence', *International Review of Law and Economics*, vol. 8(2).

Genn, H. (1987): *Hard Bargaining: Out of Court Settlement in Personal Injury Actions*, Oxford.

Gravelle, H. S. E. (1993): 'The Efficiency Implications of Cost-Shifting Rules', *International Review of Law and Economics*, vol. 13(1).

Hause, J. C. (1989): 'Indemnity, Settlement and Litigation, or I'll Be Suing You', *Journal of Legal Studies*, vol. 18(1).

Hughes, J. W. & Snyder, E. A. (1995): 'Litigation and Settlement Under the English and American Rules: Theory and Evidence', *Journal of Law and Economics*, vol. 28(1).

Posner, R. A. (1973): 'An Economic Approach to Legal Procedure and Judicial Administration', *Journal of Legal Studies*, vol. 2(2).

Rickman, N. J. (1995): 'The Effects of Contingent and Hourly Fees on Litigation Outcomes', unpublished Ph.D. dissertation, McGill University, Montreal, Canada.

Rosenberg, D. & Shavell, S. (1985): 'A Model in Which Suits Are Brought for Their Nuisance Value', *International Review of Law and Economics*, vol. 5(1).

Shavell, S. (1982): 'Suit, Settlement and Trial: A Theoretical Analysis Under Alternative Methods for the Allocation of Legal Costs', *Journal of Legal Studies*, vol. 11(1).

Snyder, E. A. & Hughes, J. W. (1990): 'The English Rule for Allocating Legal Costs: Evidence Confronts Theory', *Journal of Law, Economics and Organization*, vol. 6(2).

# 18

# *The Government's Legal Aid Reforms*

TAMARA GORIELY*

Since the second world war, British governments have accepted that their responsibilities to provide access to justice do not end with the provision of courts. The state should also ensure that people have the advice and assistance they need to discover their legal rights and, if they choose, pursue legal solutions to their problems.[1] The Woolf report into civil procedure examines the warp of the access to justice debate. The weft is provided by legal services—by advice, information and assistance about legal rights and obligations from lawyers and others. Thus, whether citizens' access to justice will be improved over the next decade depends, in considerable measure, on the government's policy to legal aid. This chapter considers the green paper on reforming legal aid published in May 1995, *Legal Aid—Targeting Need.*[2] Here the government proposes to move from a demand-led legal aid scheme, paying lawyers on a case-by-case basis, to a cash-limited scheme based on block contracts with a limited number of solicitors and advice centres.

Most initial reactions to the proposals have been hostile.[3] Given the government's proclaimed desire to reduce public expenditure in general, and to control the legal aid budget in particular, it is inevitable that many commentators have viewed the green paper as a thinly veiled attempt to cut services. However, if the goverment's only desire was to save money, it would be simpler to continue to reduce eligibility and control pay. Instead, the

* Senior Lecturer in Law, University of East London. I would like to thank those who discussed the green paper with me, and who commented on earlier drafts of this chapter—including Alan Paterson, Marlene Winfield, Alison Macnair, Karen Mackay, and Richard Jenner. Responsibility for ignoring their best advice, and making mistakes anyhow, is of course mine.

[1] As the Hugues Commission put it, the need for legal services can be thought of in two stages: 'firstly enabling the client to identify, and if he judges it appropriate, to choose a legal solution; and, secondly, enabling the client to pursue a chosen legal solution': *Royal Commission on Legal Services in Scotland*, Cmnd 7846 (Edinburgh: HMSO, 1980), para. 2.9.

[2] Lord Chancellor's Department, *Legal Aid—Targeting Need*, Cm 2854 (London: HMSO, 1995).

[3] The Law Society, for example, declared that the 'proposal to impose crude cash limits' would 'turn civil legal aid into a lottery': *News Release*, 17 May 1995. See also Zander, M., 'Twelve Reasons for Rejecting the Legal Aid Green Paper', *New Law Journal*, 21 July 1995, p. 1098, and Abraham, A., 'Access with Strings', *Legal Action*, August 1995, p. 8.

green paper makes many welcome suggestions for improvement. It recognising the criticism made by Legal Action Group, the National Consumer Council and others that legal aid provides an unduly narrow range of services. It therefore proposes more help with social welfare law, more tribunal representation and more mediation. The hope is that these improvements can be paid for by a contractual system which incentivises lawyers to provide a more efficient, less litigious service. The green paper deserves careful and detailed examination to see how far these gains can be realised.

## ANALYSING THE EXISTING SCHEME: STRENGTHS AND WEAKNESSES

The standard analysis of state-funded legal aid schemes divides them between salaried schemes, which employ their own staff to provide legal help to the poor, and 'judicare' schemes, which pay private practitioners on a case-by-case basis.[4] The English legal aid scheme, conceived in 1945 in a bout of victory optimism, is the classic judicare scheme, and displays all the strengths and weaknesses of that model. On the plus side, it provides legal aid as of right to all those who qualify. People can choose and use their own solicitors in the traditional way. In theory, at least, the only difference comes in who pays the bill. The private profession is heavily committed to a scheme which accounts for around 12 per cent of solicitors' and 27 per cent of barristers' earnings.[5] Some 11,000 solicitors' offices take part in the scheme, providing wide geographic coverage.[6] Payment is demand-led in that the state is obliged to meet all the bills submitted to it which come within the rules. As demand for legal aid has grown, so has the service. It now provides more than three million acts of assistance to the general public each year, and, together with the Scottish scheme, is probably the best funded and most extensively used legal aid schemes in the world.[7]

Unfortunately, judicare schemes also display serious weaknesses. Legal Action Group (LAG) has criticised the legal aid scheme for the narrow range of services it offers, in which help is confined to advice, assistance and representation. These, LAG argues, should be supplemented by infor-

[4] For an analysis of the relative merits of each, see Paterson, A., 'Legal Aid at the Crossroads', (1991) 10 *Civil Justice Quarterly* 124.

[5] For figures of solicitors' income, see Law Society, *Trends in the Solicitors' Profession: Annual Statistical Report 1994*, p. 54 (although some reduction should be made to exclude VAT on legal aid payments). Figures for barristers are given in General Council of the Bar, *Strategies for the Future* (London, 1990).

[6] *Legal Aid Board Annual Report 1994–95*, HC 526 (London: HMSO, 1995), p. 97.

[7] In 1990, the French Conseil D'Etat calculated that while the Dutch spent around £6 per head on legal aid, the Germans spend £3 and the French spent 70p, the English spent around £9.80: *L'Aide juridique: pour un meillure accès au droit et à la justice* (Paris: Section du Rapport et des Etude, 1990).

mation, education and law reform.[8] Moreover, the casework provided is dominated by traditional areas of lawyers' practice—notably crime, matrimonial breakdown and personal injury work. As the National Consumer Council argued in 1989, the scheme:

> . . . does not give the poor and deprived accessible help in those fields of law which are of most concern to them, such as social security, housing, debt, employment and immigration. Although legal aid aims to overcome the cost barrier, it does not overcome any of the other barriers which people encounter in using lawyers. It does very little to inform people of their legal rights, and it does not prevent them from being intimidated by the idea of going into a solicitor's office. Few solicitors' offices are located in deprived areas where the poor have most need of them, and solicitors receive little training in social welfare law. The problem is circular—the poor do not thinking of using a lawyer for advice with their problems, hence lawyers do not develop skill and expertise in these areas, and a service is not available to those wishing to use it.[9]

In recent years, more solicitors have been concentrating on social welfare issues, and the number of bills submitted for these areas of work has increased rapidly—from 220,000 in 1990/91 to a peak of 467,000 in 1993/94.[10] However, the service is dependent on the efforts of a small number of firms, and tends to be concentrated in a few geographical areas, notably London and Merseyside.[11] With the reduction in green form eligibility, less work is being carried out, and in 1994/95, the number of bills fell to 443,000.[12] Moreover, the service provided under legal aid is rudimentary. With the exception of immigration, most help about social welfare under the green form scheme is limited to an hour or two of advice.[13] Legal aid covers only a very limited list of tribunals, despite clear evidence that those deprived of representation are more likely to lose their cases.[14] Furthermore, the scheme fails to use all the available skills. Only offices with a solicitor are able to receive legal aid money, although in the fields of debt and welfare benefits much more help is provided by advice agencies, who often possess greater expertise. Despite numerous calls that salaried staff within law and advice centres should play a greater role,[15] legal aid remains dominated by the private profession.

Government thinking, however, has focused not on the gaps in the

[8] Legal Action Group, *A Strategy for Justice* (London, 1992), p. 111.

[9] National Consumer Council, *Ordinary Justice* (London: HMSO, 1989), pp. 99–100.

[10] These figures include bills for immigration, welfare benefits, employment, debt and housing: see *Legal Aid Board Annual Report 1990–91*, HC 513 (London: HMSO, 1991) p. 70 and *Annual Report 1993–94*, HC 435 (London: HMSO, 1994), p. 92.

[11] Legal Aid Board Annual Report 1994–95, *op cit.*, n. 6, p. 106.

[12] *Ibid.*, p. 86.

[13] *Ibid.*, p. 88.

[14] Genn, H. and Genn, Y., *The Effectiveness of Representation at Tribunals* (London: Lord Chancellor's Department, 1989).

[15] See, for example, *Legal Aid Efficiency Scrutiny* (London: Lord Chancellor's Department, 1986); National Consumer Council, *op. cit.*, n. 9; Legal Action Group, *op. cit.*, n. 8.

scheme but on its growing expense. As the Legal Aid Board points out, over the last ten years, legal aid expenditure has been increasing at the rate of 17.5 per cent per annum—considerably more than either retail prices (4.9 per cent) or gross domestic product (7.4 per cent). While the number of cases dealt with under legal aid has shown a steady increase of almost 5 per cent per year, the greatest rise has been in the cost per case—increasing by an average of over 11 per cent per year.[16] Surprisingly little is know about why the cost per case should be increasing in this way. A report by the Social Market Foundation suggests that the major factor may be 'supplier-induced demand', in which lawyers deliberately over-supply clients on the grounds that someone else is paying.[17] In January 1995, the Lord Chancellor, Lord Mackay stated that he found such an analysis 'compelling'. The thesis, however, is based purely on economic theory, and little work has been carried out either to support or to disprove it with empirical evidence. An analysis carried out for LAG of the costs of legally-aided divorce between 1980 and 1989 suggests a mixed picture.[18] It found that there had been a real increase of 68 per cent over this period—accounted for mainly by a rise in the number of hours claimed, rather than in the hourly rate. Part of the reason was that divorce had become more complex. Domestic violence was taken more seriously, more couples had a house to fight over, and there was some evidence that men were more likely to challenge decisions over childcare. On the other hand, these reasons did not appear to account for the full increase: 'there seems to be some element in legal aid costs which is difficult to pin down and which so far has eluded the government and the legal aid authorities'.[19] As firms improved management systems, they were able to record their time better and claim for more hours; and as claims increased, so did notions of what was 'reasonable' in the circumstances.[20] As the Woolf report shows, increases in the time spent on litigation are by no means confined to legally aided cases. The dynamic of disputing means that where one side puts a greater effort into preparing a case, this must be matched if not bettered by the other party.

The government has not felt able to plan or control the increased budget. As the green paper admits, 'the measures open to the Government. . . to moderate the increase in cost have been crude'.[21] The Lord Chancellor's Department has three controls on expenditure: scope, remuneration, and eligibility. The reductions in the scope of the scheme have excluded matters

[16] *Legal Aid Board Annual Report 1994–95, op cit.*, n. 6, p. 5.

[17] Bevan, G., Holland, A. and Partington, M., *Organising Cost-Effective Access to Justice* (London: Social Market Foundation Memorandum, 1994).

[18] Goriely, T., *Legal Aid for Family and Care Work*, Background Paper 1, Nuffield Research Project, (London: Legal Action Group, 1991).

[19] *Ibid.*, p. 17. [20] *Ibid.*, *loc. cit.*

[21] *Legal Aid—Targeting Need*, para. 3.22.

for which the legal aid was hardly ever used, such as advice on wills and conveyancing. Predictably, this had little effect on expenditure. The government has made a number of attempts to curb lawyers' remuneration, by failing to increase hourly rates and attempting to introduce standard fees, most notably for criminal cases in magistrates' courts. This, however, involved a major political battle with the Law Society. Although magistrates' court standard fees were originally proposed in Spring 1989, they were not implemented until July 1993. It is still far from clear whether they will succeed in holding down costs or whether solicitors will learn to manipulate the rules to their advantage.[22]

In practice, the brunt of expenditure controls has been borne by reductions in eligibility. For many years, the easiest way of curbing expenditure was to fail to uprate the means test in line with inflation so that, according to one estimate, the proportion of households eligible for full civil legal aid declined form 81 per cent in 1979 to 54 per cent in 1989.[23] In 1986 the government introduced the first cut in cash terms by reducing dependants' allowances. Then in April 1993, the government reacted to a 35 per cent rise in the budget by implementing a major reduction. To widespread criticism,[24] the green form scheme was withdrawn from all those with a disposable income of more than £61 per week.[25] Meanwhile, people receiving civil legal aid for court proceedings were required to pay more. Not only were more people called on to make contributions, but their monthly contribution payments were increased and extended for the full length of the case. Legal Action Group provided an example of the effect: a single woman earning around £11,500 a year would previously have been assessed for the maximum contribution of £785, payable in 12 monthly instalments. After the changes, she would pay £1,500 per year, so that if the case lasted three years, her contributions would total £4,500.[26] The Rushcliffe Committee stressed that legal aid was not just for those 'normally classed as poor' but should extend to all those of moderate means who had difficulties paying for lawyers.[27] Since 1993, green form help has been available to the poor only, while full civil legal aid involves heavy contributions from those only just above the poverty line.

22 The rules, for example, allow both green form and standard fees to be claimed, and encourage solicitors to classify different defendants and offences as separate cases. For a full description of how solicitors can make the maximum use of standard fees, see Edwards, A., *Standard Fees in the Magistrates' Court: a Survival Guide* (London: Law Society, 1993).

23 M. Murphy, 'Civil Legal Aid Eligibility Estimates 1979–1990', appendix 1 in Legal Action Group, *op. cit.*, n. 8.

24 See Home Affairs Committee, *Legal Aid: the Lord Chancellor's Proposals*, HC 517 (London: HMSO, 1993).

25 This was raised to £72 in April 1995.

26 *Legal Action*, December 1992, p. 4.

27 *Report of the Committee on Legal Aid and Legal Advice in England and Wales*, Cmd 6641 (London: HMSO, 1945), para. 127(2),

### THE GREEN PAPER'S APPROACH: TARGETING, CASH-LIMITS AND CONTRACTS

The green paper accepts some of the analysis of legal aid's problems put forward by its critics. It agrees that to control costs by further cuts in eligibility 'would not be consistent with the objective of targeting those whose need is greatest',[28] even though it refuses to consider reversing previous reductions. It criticises the emphasis on divorce and personal injury at the expense of social welfare law,[29] the scheme's failure to provide representation at tribunals,[30] and the advice sector's lack of involvement.[31] The solution, it states, is to target funds 'on needs and priorities'.[32] The implicit promise is that provided lawyers' tendency to increase costs can be curtailed and savings made in matrimonial and personal injury litigation, more money will be available for social welfare law. Resources will be spent in those geographic areas where little is available at present. By including advice centres, help will be more accessible to those reluctant to visit solicitors, and the scheme will drawing on advice workers' specialist expertise. The green paper holds out a possibility of greater tribunal representation[33] and some help before inquests in 'exceptional cases'.[34] The hope is that by curbing 'litigation inflation', the proposals will bring costs per case under control and there will be no need for further reductions in eligibility.

There is much to welcome here. But serious questions remain. Do the potential benefits outweigh the obvious dangers of moving to a cash-limited scheme, where the overall resources available to legal aid could so easily be reduced? How far can the government's chosen mechanism—block contracts with a range of legal aid 'suppliers'—deliver the necessary cost reductions without unacceptable reductions in quality? The green paper's promises are muted. Without saving in the major areas of work, notably matrimonial legal aid, no funds will be available for improvements elsewhere.

Cash-limited legal aid schemes are not unusual. They are the normal means of provision in Australia and Canada, while the USA's Legal Services Corporation has always had its extremely limited budget fixed in advance. If well-planned and managed, limited funds can be used to make the maximum impact. Nevertheless, where money is tight—as it is within all developed welfare state—they inevitably involve making tough decisions over priorities. Thus New South Wales does not fund any matrimonial disputes which just involve property, while in 1990/91 Victoria's commission threatened not to fund any criminal case likely to cost more than

[28] *Legal Aid—Targeting Need*, para. 3.25.
[29] *Ibid.*, para. 3.8.
[30] *Ibid.*, para. 3.14.
[31] *Ibid.*, para. 3.15.
[32] *Ibid.*, para. 4.2.
[33] *Ibid.*, para. 8.15.
[34] *Ibid.*, para. 3.16.

$200,000.[35] As the Ontario scheme is discovering, it is particularly hard to move from the high expectations generated by a demand-led scheme to realities of a cash-limit.[36] Furthermore, almost all existing cash-limited schemes rely heavily on salaried lawyers employed by the Legal Aid Commissions themselves. The English, however, have tended to see salaried services as a threat to professional independence while the present government has its own ideological reasons for rejected extensions in state bureaucracy. Instead, in keeping with the prevailing ethos of market testing and privatisation, the emphasis is on 'contracts' with a number of competing private suppliers. It is necessary to examine the fine-print of the proposals with care to see whether such a scheme can deliver the government's promise that funds will be targeted to those in greatest need.

The following discussion examines the proposals under four headings. Section A starts with the decision-making processes. How will the budget be allocated and priorities set? Section B then looks at how the Board will secure sufficient access to legal aid providers. Section C considers the central principle of contracting with private practitioners. Will quality controls be adequate? Will firms be incentivised in the right way? Finally, section D looks at the involvement of the advice sector.

## A. Decision-making under the new scheme

*Legal Action* has described the green paper proposals as 'reminiscent of a Soviet command economy'.[37] A major feature of the English legal aid scheme is the extent to which decisions are taken centrally. In Canada and Australia, legal aid is run on a provincial or state basis. When the Dutch reorganised their scheme, they set up five regional Boards. In England and Wales, the scheme is, and will continue to be, run centrally. The green paper proposes that central government will establish priorities, set the budget for each area of work and for each region and lay down criteria for the grant of legal aid. In such a large and unwieldy scheme, it is all too easy for bureaucratic procedures to replace flexibility and creativity, and for decision-makers to lose touch with what is happening on the ground.

This problem is compounded by the fact that there is no national independent voice to comment on what the Department and Legal Aid Board are doing. During the expansion phase of legal aid in the 1960s and 70s, the Lord Chancellor's Legal Aid Advisory Committee played a major role in influencing legal aid policy. Since 1985, however, the legal aid debate has been dominated by the government's search for expenditure controls—and here the advisory committee was much less successful in influencing the

35 Legal Action Group, *op. cit.*, n. 8, p. 98.

36 See Smith, R., 'Managing in the Down Cycle', *Legal Action*, August 1995, p. 6.

37 Smith, R., 'Targeting Need: Budgeting Cost', *Legal Action*, June 1995, p. 9.

course of events. The department grew tired of the committee's predictable demands for more money to be spent, and finally, in January 1995, they abolished it. At the same time, the annual Legal Services Conferences, which brought different people together to comment on legal aid policy, were abandoned. The green paper's emphasis on planning gives rise to new needs for detailed, on-going consultation with a wide range of interested parties. Without some formal mechanism, there is a danger is that crucial decisions over priorities and contract specifications will be taken in private negotiations between the Board and the Law Society.

The most important decision, of course, will be to set the overall budget. Lord Mackay denies that the green paper is a cost-cutting measure and has no immediate plans to reduce the budget below 1995–96 levels.[38] He does intend, however, that the rate of growth should be curbed, and the proposals would make it much easier for future governments to introduce cuts. Legal aid will no longer depend on an assessment of need, but on 'judgements about what the country can afford to spend'.[39] As legal aid is hardly likely to feature prominently in either Conservative and Labour election manifestoes, the fear is that in times of economic stringency the budget will be arbitrarily reduced. Government itself is one of the main creators of legal needs, but it has been extremely poor at calculating the effects of new legislation on demand for advice and legal services. Although Bills are meant to be accompanied by financial memoranda showing all the costs which will result from them, legal aid estimates tend to be last minute guesses. Some, such as the suggestion that curtailing the right to silence will have no effect on legal aid costs, are highly questionable.[40] With a change to a planned economy, the department needs to improve radically the way it estimates such costs and negotiates with other departments for additional funding.

The green paper starts by suggesting that contracts might be administered by either the Legal Aid Board or local authorities, but in later chapters it fails to take the prospect of a transfer to local authorities seriously. In many areas of work (from housing and child care to pavement trips), local authorities are parties to the dispute, and it is difficult to see how they could be impartial in administering contracts with those challenging their decisions. Legal aid has always been seen as a national service, in which local authorities have no experience.

Here we assume that the contracting agents will be the Legal Aid Board's area offices, which are expected to metamorphose from their present paper-

[38] See, for example,'Control Not Cuts, Says Mackay Launching Legal Aid Paper', *New Law Journal*, 19 May 1995, p. 714.

[39] *Legal Aid—Targeting Need*, para. 4.28.

[40] *Legal Action* reports that in April and May 1995, following the changes of 10 April 1995, there was a 21% rise in requests for police station advice: August 1995, p. 4.

based role into experts on local needs. The green paper states that they will be advised by a 'network of Regional Committees' modelled on the North Western Legal Service Committee (NWLSC), to initiate consultation and generate public debate on fund allocation and local priorities.[41] NWLSC first began in 1977 as a pilot project in Greater Manchester, with representatives of the legal profession, advice centres, social and welfare services and the courts' administration. In 1982 it expanded its work to the whole of the North West and it has since initiated many practical projects to increase access to justice. Its work has been much admired, and there have been many calls for committees to be established in other areas.[42] Attempts to establish similar committees in the North East and South Wales failed, however, and NWLSC remains a brave and lonely example. Regional committees are clearly vital to the new arrangements, but the Board should not underestimate the difficulties of setting up twelve new organisations, especially as most potential members will be fighting amongst themselves for limited funds. Work to establish new committees should begin immediately: whatever proposals are introduced, they will be a useful improvement to the decision-making process, and they need to be securely in place before any move to contracting occurs. Moreover, if their views are to feed into the setting of national priorities, they need to meet before priorities are established.

### B. Managing Access

A feature of the present judicare scheme is that services are distributed highly unevenly. This is especially true of legal advice, and has been a feature of the scheme right from the beginning. In 1963, four years after the introduction of the first legal advice scheme, the Legal Aid Advisory Committee noted that London had the greatest use of the higher courts, while 'demand for legal advice in the North Western Area far exceeds that in any other area'. The Lord Chancellor's Department had 'no explanation of these figures'.[43] In 1995, regional differences remain: while London spent £4.77 per head of population on social welfare law and Merseyside spent £3.10, Eastern region spent a mere 60p.[44]

The green paper states that initially the allocation of legal aid for civil matters between areas will be based on historic expenditure patterns. However, in non-matrimonial civil matters 'the Department and Legal Aid Board will need to develop a system of allocation to the Areas based on

[41] *Legal Aid—Targeting Need*, para. 5.17.
[42] National Consumer Council, *op cit.*, n. 9, pp. 121–2.
[43] Public Records Office file LCO2 7502.
[44] Legal Aid Board Annual Report 1994–95, *op cit.*, n. 6, p. 106.

needs and priorities'.[45] This will build on the Board's work in using census data to predict need in social welfare areas.[46] Until now, it has been assumed that data to predict local need would be used to draw attention to under-provided areas, as part of a process of 'levelling-up'. The green paper, however, raises the prospect that the Lord Chancellor's Department will start to level-down. As with the health service, resources will be moved out of London and other 'over-provided' areas such as Merseyside. In the absence of any understanding of why some areas use more legal aid, this could be a dangerous course to take. The easy explanation is that it is just 'supplier-induced demand': more is provided in Merseyside because that is where solicitors chose to practice. But after such a long history of regional differences, it is likely that client attitudes have also been affected. Legal aid seems to be part of the disputing culture in Merseyside in a way that it is not in the Fens. Maybe Liverpudlians should become more like Fenlanders, but this is not the sort of change which can easily be introduced by Whitehall fiat.

Allocations between regions will be made in London: allocations within regions will be made by Area offices. Even here, hard political decisions will need to be made. The Board does not possess any data about the geographic distribution of legal aid within the English regions, but research in Scotland suggests that differences between districts are particularly pronounced: in 1992, while 22,000 Shetlanders received no housing advice at all, Wigtown in the rural south-west of Scotland generated one housing application for every 189 people.[47]

Inherent within the proposals is the intention to reduce the number of outlets from the present 11,000 solicitors' offices. The green paper does not commit itself to any particular number of suppliers, but it mentions that the Board expects to have franchised around 3,000 firms in the next two to three years. This, it states, will be 'a solid foundation on which to build block contacting'.[48] If one assumes that block contracts will distributed between 3,000 offices in the same proportions as under the current franchising scheme, there would be one matrimonial office for every 19,600 people, one personal injury office per 21,600 people and one crime office per 29,900 people. This may be just about acceptable in a London Borough of quarter of a million people (which on this basis would be allocated around 12 matrimonial and personal injury firms and eight criminal ones). It is unlikely to be acceptable, however, in rural areas, where, for example, there would be only 50 criminal firms for the whole of Devon and Cornwall. The

[45] *Legal Aid—Targeting Need*, para. 5.11.

[46] For a description of this work, see *Legal Aid Board Annual Report 1991–92*, HC 50, ch. 6. and *Legal Aid Board Annual Report 1994–95*, *op. cit.*, n. 6, pp. 30–1.

[47] Paterson, A., 'Access, Legal Aid and Rural Scotland', (1995) *Juridical Review* 266.

[48] *Legal Aid—Targeting Need*, para. 6.5.

government needs to be more specific as to how such a limited number of offices will be distributed between urban and rural areas, and how far it thinks it is reasonable for people to be expected to travel. Its assumptions need to be tested by research.

Geographic access is a particular problem for social welfare law. The evidence is that advice agencies serve extremely limited catchment areas: one study suggests that they draw half their users within half a mile of the centre, with only 10 per cent of users travelling more than two miles.[49] Even in rural areas, very few people travel more than five miles to visit an advice centre.[50] Legal aid area offices are unlikely to be sympathetic to claims that every village needs its own advice centre, and may question whether people who are unprepared to take the bus really want advice. It is dangerous, however, to ignore such empirical evidence as we have about how people actually use advice services without a much greater understanding of geographic barriers and how they operate on the poor and carless.

Finally, the green paper does not mention how the public will be informed about the new providers. Public awareness of the present scheme is low: in a 1990 Gallup poll, seven out of ten people said they did not understand how legal aid worked.[51] Under the new system, the information deficit will be even more serious, as people will only obtain help if they know which firm currently holds a contract to deal with their particular problem. Area offices will need to have a publicity budget and a carefully worked out strategy for providing information about contract-holders.

### C. Contracting with private practitioners

Central to the proposals is the use of 'block contracts' to deliver legal services. Usually 'block contracts' involve supplying a service to a given population, with the supplier taking the risk that the population may require either more or fewer services than the number predicted. In fact, the green paper uses the term in a different way, to cover what are normally described as 'price and volume' contracts—ie contracts to supply a given number of services (that is so many instances of advice and so many representations) at a given cost. It explains that:

> A block contract is a contract between an agent and a supplier for the provision of legal services to clients for an agreed period and cost. The contract would cover the type of service to be provided, the quality, volume and price. It would guarantee

[49] Kempson, E., *Good Advice for All* (London: National Consumer Council, 1986).

[50] See Blacksell, M., Economides, K. and Watkins, C., *Justice Outside the City* (Longmans, 1992). In research among the general population of Scotland, only 23 per cent said that they thought it reasonable to travel more than five miles to seek advice: MVA Consultancy, *Consumer Study of Knowledge and Use of Legal Services* (Edinburgh: Scottish Office, 1994).

[51] See Legal Action Group, *op. cit.*, n. 8, p. 26.

income to the supplier provided that the contract conditions were met. Payment would be in the form of regular predetermined sums rather than case by case.[52]

Each contract would cover only one area of work, so that a firm might have separate contracts in welfare benefits and personal injury work, or even in separate areas of personal injury work, such as road, work or medical negligence cases.

Legal aid area offices will have the formidable task of ensuring that its contractors provide sufficient and accessible services of the right quality to meet the needs of population. Unfortunately, there is little overseas experience to guide them. The United States have seen a highly fraught political debate over the future of the Legal Services Corporation, in which right-wing politician have advocated contracts with private suppliers. The context, however, is very different, with contracts seen as an alternative to politically committed salaried offices rather than to a judicare system.[53] Moreover, such monitoring exercises as have taken place have degenerated into rows about research methodology, and few conclusions can be drawn from them.[54] The greatest experience of contracting has been in the field of public defender systems, and here the results are not hopeful. In reviewing the experience of contracting such schemes, the Spangenberg Group concluded that 'in most cases, over time, the cost has gone up and the quality has gone down'.[55] There are two serious dangers. First is the tendency to weigh cost over quality. As discussed below, quality is extremely difficult to measure: it is much easier to rely on crude case counts than to quantify such intangibles as outcome and client satisfaction. The second problem is in finding sufficient suppliers to provide a competitive market. The first year is likely to see a good response but, over time, non-contracted firms lose interest. In the second round, there tend to be few competitive bidders, and their prices are much higher.[56] The more complex and bureaucratic the quality controls, the fewer the potential bidders.

*Deciding applications and managing the budget*

In most cash-limited legal aid schemes, decisions over who qualifies for legal aid are made by public authorities such as Legal Aid Commissions. The green paper proposals suggest instead that such decisions should be

[52] *Legal Aid—Targeting Need*, para. 4.6.

[53] See Singsen, G., 'The Role of Competition in Making Grants for the Provision of Legal Services to the Poor' (1991) 1 *Public Interest Law Journal* 57.

[54] For an analysis of the research in Orange County and San Antonio, see Meeker, J. W., Dombrink, J., and Quinn, E., 'Competitive Bidding and Legal Services for the Poor: an Analysis of the Scientific Evidence' (1990–91) 18 *Western State University Law Review* 611–3.

[55] *Findings Concering Contacting for the Delivery of Indigent Defense Services*, a memorandum prepared for the Center of Law and Social Policy by the Spangenberg Group, Newton, MA, 1989.

[56] This was particularly the case in Jacksonville, Florida: Address by Kent Spuhler, ABA 1989 Annual Pro Bono Conference (15 April 1989) cited in Singsen, *op. cit.*, n. 53.

made by private solicitor firms, who would balance government guidelines about priorities against the resources available under their contract.

The immediate fear is that the number of cases will exceed that budgeted for in some areas, so that at the end of the accounting period no assistance with divorces will be available in Darlington, and abandoned wives will need to move to Southampton in order to get help. According to the Law Society 'for the same type of case, legal aid might be available in Nuneaton, but not in Newcastle. In some parts of the country it would be available in June, but not in December. Variations of this sort will turn civil legal aid into a lottery.'[57] The Lord Chancellor, Lord Mackay, has dismissed such fears as 'pure fantasy'. He argues that 'individual contracts would be for different periods, so that while one local supplier was just beginning his or her contract, others would be in mid-term or coming to the end of theirs'. Funds could also be moved 'around the system' and a central reserve would cover unexpected circumstances.'[58]

Despite these assurances of flexibility, however, it is inherent in the proposals that some of those calling at a solicitor's office who would previously have qualified will no longer receive legal aid. One possible way of managing rejections it to accept cases until the money has been spent and then suspend services until the end of the financial year. The seriously underfunded Irish scheme, for example, was forced to suspend all services between November 1989 and July 1990.[59] There are other ways: solicitors might be encouraged to manage their budgets on a monthly or even a weekly basis. But *some* system for rejecting people is required, and the government is coy in explaining what it will be. For example, will rejected applicants be allowed to apply to other firms? Will they be able to apply again next month? Will they be placed on a waiting list? Or will firms simply even out work flow by booking in clients months ahead? Above all, will applicants have any right of appeal against the solicitor's decision? A strict one-rejection-and-you're-out system would prevent end-of-year crises, but has other snags. The waiting list approach, on the other hand, may lead to substantial delays, while allowing multiple applications may simply postpone the inevitable crisis.

Under the present scheme, solicitors are important gatekeepers to legal aid, in that in order to obtain legal aid one must find a lawyer willing to take up one's case. Until now, however, they have not made the formal decision on entitlement. The green paper states that solicitors will not be paid for this new task. It is one which they are not used to, which they will not like and where, inevitably, their judgements will be influenced by whether cases are profitable. Furthermore, a mass of independent solicitors,

[57] Law Society, *News Release*, 17 May 1995.

[58] 'Opening the Legal Aid Debate', *Legal Action*, June 1995, p. 4.

[59] Cousins, M., 'Neither Flesh nor Fowl' (1992) *Irish Law Times* 41.

with different ideological stances, operating in different areas under different budgetary pressures, are bound to produce inconsistent decisions. Serious questions arise about whether solicitors are the right people for the job. It would be quite possible, at least in large cities, for clients to apply to the area office for a decision, where they would be seen by an adviser, given initial help, a list of solicitors to choose from and a certificate for further work, in much the same way as suggested in the Rushcliffe report fifty years ago. Such applications may be easier than trailing around solicitors trying to find a firm with a relevant legal aid contract.

In any event, it is unacceptable to give solicitors the final say in whether someone should be granted legal aid. As the Citizen Charter stresses, public services should provide adequate redress. Even the social fund includes review by a semi-independent organisation, and a new review or appeals system will be needed for legal aid. Unlike the present appeals system, it should not assume that the litigant has legal help, but should provide an accessible second opinion from an independent source.

### *Quality Controls*

As the green paper points out, quality monitoring will be 'fundamental' to the new system.[60] Yet measuring the quality of legal services presents real problems, which the Board is very far from resolving. The green paper suggests, complacently, that the Board's franchising scheme already operates a viable quality assurance system, but this is far from the case.

Franchising has relied heavily on firms' compliance with practice management criteria, which measure the way a firm is managed, not the quality of the work itself. Firms applying for franchises after October 1994 have been required to comply with 'transaction criteria', which are detailed check-lists enabling an auditor to see what has been omitted from a solicitor's file.[61] Transaction criteria have been criticised for taking an overly mechanistic approach, concentrating on the file rather than on whether the lawyer understood the clients' concerns, communicated well or gave good advice.[62] Consumer representatives have argued that they should be combined with client surveys, but the Board failed to introduce clients' views

[60] *Legal Aid—Targeting Need*, para. 6.42.

[61] These were developed over the course of the Birmingham franchise scheme and are set out in volume 2 of Sherr, A., Moorhead, R. and Paterson, A., *Lawyers—the Quality Agenda*, Legal Aid Board (London: HMSO, 1994). They cover all the most common transactions carried out under legal aid and ask a series of 'yes/no' questions. Thus checklist for advising on the housing and financial difficulties of relationship breakdown, for example, asks 220 questions, ranging from whether the solicitor is aware of whether the client is receiving one parent benefit, to whether the solicitor advised the client of how long it might take and what the outcome was likely to be.

[62] Goriely, T. and Williams, T., *Measuring the Quality of Legal Aid Work* (London: Law Society, 1993). See also Smith, R., 'Transaction Criteria: the Face of the Future', *Legal Action*, February 1993, pp. 9–11.

into the franchising scheme, despite some initial pilots.[63] No information has been published about how transaction criteria are working in practice, and there continue to be question marks about how far compliance with the criteria correlates with peer assessment of what constitutes good work.[64]

The green paper treats transaction criteria as yesterday's news. It puts its main emphasis on outcome measures and suggests, with dubious optimism, that these 'will enable the Board Area Office to judge case result, time taken/delay and client satisfaction'.[65] The Lord Chancellor's Department, however, is wrong to give the impression that work on outcome measurements is well underway. In fact, after some piloting, the work was put on hold awaiting the publication of the green paper, and there is still a myriad of problems to be overcome. It is of course possible to collect information about whether the client won or lost, and if they won, how much they received. The problem lies in making sense of the results. To know that a head-injured client received a settlement of £100,000 tells one nothing unless one knows what the client should have received—and, so far, practical measures of what cases are objectively 'worth' have escaped researchers.[66] Of course, the law of averages helps—it might be more useful to know that firm A receives average compensation payments of £15,000 while firm B's average is £50,000. But it is only possible to make such comparisons if the case-profiles of firm A and firm B are similar. If firm A specialises in pavement trips while firm B specialises in medical negligence cases, then firm A may well be achieving the more impressive outcomes. Even categorising cases in this way may not be sufficient: suing over one local authority's pavements may be easier than suing over another's. One parent with a severely brain-injured baby may recommend a firm to other

[63] See Goriely, T., 'Quality of Legal Services: the Need for Consumer Research' (1993) 3 *Consumer Policy Review* 112.

[64] A small scale comparison between transaction criteria and peer assessment in nine personal injury and nine matrimonial files came to the unsettling conclusion that 'major differences of assessment of the personal injury cases between the auditors and the practitioners were mirrored by significant disagreement between the practitioners': Sherr et. al., *op. cit.*, n. 61, p. 59. No further work has been carried out since the Birmingham pilot.

[65] *Legal Aid—Targeting Need*, para. 6.44.

[66] Thus no measure of objective worth is included with the much respected National Compensation Survey: see Harris, D., et. al., *Compensation and Support for Illness and Injury* (Oxford: Clarendon Press, 1984). A study of 60 personal injury cases in New York asked a panel of five negligence experts to assess each cases and took a mean figure: Rosenthal, D., *Lawyer and Client: Who's in Charge?* (New York: Russell Sage, 1974). This, however, is feasible only with small samples. A study by G. W. Williams (*Legal Negotiations and Settlement*, West Publishing Co, St Paul 1983), reveals just how varied lawyers' achievements can be. Forty practicing lawyers in Iowa were divided into twenty pairs and asked to negotiate a settlement based on the same file. The settlement figures achieved ranged from $15,000 to $95,000. For a summary of the main literature on this subject, see Sherr et. al., *op. cit.*, n. 61 and Goriely, T., 'Debating the Quality of Legal Services: Differing Models of the Good Lawyer' (1994) 1 *International Journal of the Legal Profession* 159.

such parents so that, even among firms specialising in medical negligence cases, case profiles may be significantly different.

This is not to reject outcome measures, but simply to stress that their implementation will take a long time, involves assembling large amounts of data, and has uncertain results. For the first few years, the Board will need to collect a wide range of possible indicators which are not directly used for decision-making but which raise interesting questions to be pursued in other research. The hope is that, in time, the range of data can be reduced to a few key indicators which can be used as the basis of quality judgements. But outcome measures only start making sense when one is able to average them over a large number of cases. When the green paper states that quality assurance 'would not involve detailed monitoring of all cases' but would be confined to 'a thorough investigation of a sample of cases',[67] it is showing a certain economy with the truth. If contracting is sold to the profession on the basis of less case-related paperwork, onerous outcome reporting could well prove to be the final straw that breaks their willingness to tender. Nor will outcome measures prove popular with the Board, who will incur costs in processing data which have no immediate value. There is a real danger that in the first tough negotiations between Board and profession outcome measures will be jettisoned and burdensome quality controls replaced by simpler case counts.

Quality assurance depends on using proxies to measure underlying quality. It is vital to remember that the relationship between the proxy and underlying quality changes depending on how the proxy is used. To take one example given in the green paper: research may well show that good, combative personal injury litigators are willing to lose a few cases.[68] Thus the number of cases lost may, for research purposes, be a good proxy for measuring the robustness of the lawyer's approach. When one tells solicitors that they should be losing more cases, however, the relationship between the proxy (number of cases lost) and the underlying variable (robustness) alters. Some highly cautious lawyers may feel justified in becoming more careless over difficult cases, without becoming noticeably more combative. Finally, suppose one tells a firm that their continued existence depends on losing at least three cases before the end of the year. Without such losses, their contract will be withdrawn, the partners will go bankrupt and the staff be made redundant. Here the motivation to lose cases is utterly different, and the original research showing a high correlation between cases lost and a robust approach no longer applies. In academic jargon, this phenomenon is known as 'Goodhart's Law'. First developed in the field of economics, it states that any previously observed relationship between two variables disappears if one of the variables is tar-

[67] *Legal Aid—Targeting Need*, para. 6.42. [68] *Ibid.*, para. 6.45.

geted with a view to achieving a desired outcome for the other.[69] Its practical effect is that even the best researched quality assurance techniques can have unforeseen and unfortunate effects in practice. The greatest caution is required.

*Incentives*

The green paper talks a great deal about incentivising lawyers. Unfortunately, it was published a month before the Woolf report and was therefore not able to address the Woolf recommendations directly. There is no mention, for example, of the need to encourage greater use of information technology.[70] It does however suggest that one of the basic problems of the existing scheme is that solicitors have incentives to pursue court-based solutions, and hence to run up additional costs.[71] 'Essential' to the new scheme will be a new set of incentives for solicitors to act differently.[72] At this stage, however, the green paper tries to be all things to all people. As Table 1 shows, a long list of qualities is expected from the new suppliers. Although they are not necessarily incompatible, they do involve fine judgements between conflicting priorities.

The danger is that such a list is too subtle and multi-facetted to be achieved through contracting at arms-length. If one wants this degree of fine judgement, one needs to employ, educate and motivate one's own staff. The incentives introduced through contracting are likely to be much blunter than the green paper suggests, and will probably encourage a large number of quick cases. Provided the review procedure is adequate, the quality controls work and separate arrangements are made for important cases, there is something to be said for favouring initial advice over protracted litigation. But if the government is serious about travelling in this direction, it is vital to increase the green form means test so that initial advice is available to more of those who need it.

At a more fundamental level, it is dangerous to think that contractual incentives can substitute entirely for professional belief systems. Of course, lawyers, like everyone else in a market economy, work for the money. For years, the professions have denied this basic fact, and have rightly been pilloried for the fantasy that they are 'above' commercialism. But one should not swing to the opposite extreme and believe that everything can be achieved through the method of payment. In the end, lawyers will only do a good job if they believe in doing a good job. One must remember that:

> competitive pressure, like the Darwinian struggle for survival, selects between options, it does not itself generate them. It seems that in all spheres of production, from the factory that makes machines to the theatre that makes plays, the quality

[69] See Harden, I., *The Contracting State* (Buckingham: Open University Press, 1992), p. 65.

[70] Lord Woolf, *Access to Justice: Interim Report to the Lord Chancellor*, pp. 85–6.

[71] *Legal Aid—Targeting Need*, para. 3.29.

[72] *Ibid.*, para. 4.2.

Table 1: Incentives contained within the green paper

| **Suppliers should:** | | |
|---|---|---|
| provide the most effective service (para. 4.20(h)) | and | provide the most economical service (para. 4.20(h)) |
| seek out ways to resolve problems which do not involve the courts (para. 3.29) | and | not 'cherry pick' the easiest cases (para. 4.20(k)) |
| not pursue cases which do not have a reasonable chance of success (para. 6.40) | and | be prepared to lose cases in court (para. 6.45) |
| possess 'specific expertise' (para. 6.3(b)) | and | take a holistic approach to clients' problems (para. 4.15) |
| be able to decide for themselves when to buy in extra services (para. 6.29) | and | not disadvantage the Bar (para. 6.31) |
| provide a quality assured service according to established criteria (para. 4.20(b)) | and | find new ways of providing services (para. 4.20(i)) |
| be concentrated at certain centres on grounds of greater expertise and efficiency (para. 6.18) | and | provide reasonable access (para. 6.12) |
| constantly improve the quality of their service (para. 4.2) | and | not create virtual monopolies (para. 6.8) |
| provide the lowest price consistent with adequate quality (para. 6.24) | but | higher prices might be justified by better outcomes (para. 6.15) |

of outputs depends not only on the competition which selects between goods, but also on the existence of 'cultures of production' from which they are generated in the first place. Unless there are such cultures (which are found in family businesses, professions, and large corporations) where members become committed intrinsically to the nature and quality of what they produce, there will be few quality products which markets can select between.[73]

[73] Rustin, M., 'Flexibility in Higher Education', in Burrows, R. and Loader, B. (eds.), *Towards a Post-Fordist Welfare State?* (London: Routledge, 1994) at p. 198.

The government has yet to find a way in which it can work with solicitors' intrinsic commitment to legal aid rather than against it.

### D. Involving the Advice Sector

The green paper foresees that in areas of 'social welfare law' such as housing, employment, immigration, debt and welfare benefits, block contracts might be offered to advice agencies as well as solicitors. Advice agencies would give basic advice and assistance, and in some cases, may represent clients before tribunals. The government suggests that there is a need for further pilots to ensure that paying for more representatives does not simply make tribunals more elaborate and costly.[74] The recommendations follow on from the Legal Aid Board's 'Non-solicitor Agencies Franchising Pilot', in which 42 agencies have been given block grants on a highly flexible basis to see what they can achieve. The project is being monitored by the Policy Studies Institute which, at the time of writing, has not yet published its report.

There is a great deal to welcome here. It must be right to put more emphasis on social welfare law, and to use the great expertise that advice agencies have developed in these areas. The chance—however tentative—that legal aid might be used to improve tribunal representation should be seized. It must be remembered, though, that funding advice agencies is a wholly new role for the Legal Aid Board, and it has much to learn about what advice agencies can and cannot deliver.

There is no standardised product called 'advice'. The advice sector covers a wide range of Citizens' Advice Bureaux, independent generalist and specialist centres, each with its own traditions and approaches. The service ranges from short one-off enquires to specialist in-depth casework extending over many months. In some areas, most notably debt and welfare benefits, advice agencies often possess a greater level of expertise than the average solicitors' firm, and may provide a more sophisticated service. One study suggests that, on average, specialist debt advisers spend around 14 hours per case, spread over nine months,[75] compared with only 1.5 hours spent by solicitors under the average debt green form.[76] In the housing field, however, there is some evidence that citizens' advice bureaux lack the legal expertise and confidence they need to put the full range of options before their clients.[77] In the employment area, some specialist centres offer

[74] *Legal Aid—Targeting Need*, para. 8.15.

[75] Hinton, T. and Berthoud, R., *Money Advice Services* (London: Policy Studies Institute, 1988).

[76] *Legal Aid Board Annual Report 1994–95*, *op. cit.*, p. 88.

[77] Forbes, D. and Wright, S., *Housing Cases in Nine CABx*, prepared for the National Association of Citizens Advice Bureaux, 1990.

tribunal representation equal to any lawyer.[78] On the other hand, generalist Citizens Advice Bureaux may spend their time dealing with relatively simple queries about workplace conditions and attend tribunals only rarely.[79] When they do, volunteers may find themselves out of their depth in a highly legalistic environment.[80] If advice staff have an occupational fault, it is a tendency to believe they can perfom miracles. In pilot projects, a team of highly motivated but seriously underpaid staff may work wonders, but it would be wrong to use such pilots as a guide to what people need to be paid to provide a reliable, on-going nationwide service. Although the Citizens' Advice Bureaux movement has a long and honourable tradition of achieving a great deal with almost nothing, there are limits to what can be expected from underfunded voluntary agencies.

Furthermore, it would be wrong to tie advice agencies into the straightjacket of the present legal aid scheme. Many of the most innovative schemes—in-court advice, telephone advice, or test case litigation—do not fit comfortably within the existing legal aid regulations. It is particularly disappointing that the green paper says so little about court duty advice schemes. In 1988, the Civil Justice Review drew attention to the value of such schemes, especially for housing and debt work, and recommended that they should be eligible for legal aid funding.[81] The Legal Aid Board commissioned research which showed that the amounts of money involved were very modest: much could be achieved with under £1 million.[82] Despite this, nothing was done, and it was left to Lord Woolf to renew calls for funding.[83] Court advice schemes appear to be victims of the Lord Chancellor's Department's divisional structure, in which legal aid and court policy are dealt with by different sections, according to different time-tables and different spending priorities.

The existing green form eligibility limits are a major problem. Although advice centre clients are overwhelmingly poor,[84] the green form means test effectively excludes all those in work, and for debt and employment advice a significant proportion of those in need of help are over the limits. The green paper suggests that advice centres can continue to operate an 'open door' serving all comers only if they can find other sources of finance.[85] But there is no guarantee that other money can be found. If advice centres are

[78] Genn and Genn, *op cit.*, n. 14.

[79] See for example, Kempson, E., *Legal Advice and Assistance* (London: Policy Studies Institute, 1989), p. 44.

[80] Genn and Genn, *op. cit.*, n. 14.

[81] *Report of the Review Body on Civil Justice*, Cm 394 (London: HMSO, 1988) rec. 52.

[82] Bridges, L., *The Provision of Duty Advice Schemes in County Courts* (London: Legal Aid Board, 1991). See also National Consumer Council, *Court Without Advice* (London, 1992).

[83] Woolf, *op. cit.*, n. 70, pp. 126–9.

[84] See Childs, D., Hickey, A. and Winter, J., *Citizens' Advice* (London: Greater London Citizens Advice Bureau Service, 1985).

[85] *Legal Aid—Targeting Need*, para. 8.12.

forced to means-test their clients, they will no longer be seen as accessible services for all but as stigmatised services for the few.

In the family field, the alternative to private practice will be provided by mediation services, who will also be funded by block contracts. In dealing with crime, however, the government suggest no alternatives to the existing service provided by solicitors, despite the devastating criticisms of many private practitioners set out in *Standing Accused*.[86] Here McConville et al argue for new 'Community Legal Defence Centres' to operate alongside legal aid franchise holders, and combine criminal defence work with more general issues of community education and civil rights.[87] Such centres would fit in well with the new legal aid structure, and a few should be established on a pilot basis.

## CONCLUSION

The government is right to think that the present service provided by legal aid is too narrow and that a greater range of services should be brought within its remit. The green paper mentions the need to include mediation, advice on social welfare, tribunal representation and help with inquests. To this one might add information, county court duty advice services, community legal defence centres and national centres of excellence to pursue test cases. The question remains, however, about how these improvements are to be paid for. There appears to be some element of 'litigation inflation' driving up the costs of divorce and criminal trials. It would be attractive to think that by curbing this, one could not only avoid future reductions in eligibility but could find additional resources to fund new projects.

On the other hand, the proposals require a degree of trust in the intention of government which it is difficult to give. Not only the present administration but those of the future could all too easily use cash-limiting as a way of imposing arbitrary cuts on the legal aid budget. Moreover, only part of the increase in legal aid can be traced to supplier-induced demand. Much is a genuine response to social change and the benefits mentioned in the green paper cannot be paid for by efficiency savings alone. Intrinsic to the proposals is the notion that a proportion of those currently receiving legal aid will in future be turned away. The government needs to be more specific about who these people will be and how it will be done. Finally, there must be serious doubts about how far the government's chosen mechanisms—contracts with private practitioners—will be able to deliver the desired savings.

[86] McConville, M., Hodgson, J., Bridges, L. and Pavlovic, A., *Standing Accused* (Oxford: Clarendon Press, 1994).

[87] *Ibid.*, pp. 296–7.

Over the last few years, 'contracting' with the private sector has been elevated to the status of an ideology, and government departments have tended to gloss over the problems involved. On the most basic, administrative level, the Legal Aid Board will need to oversee thousands of contracts, each for different areas of work, with different quality mechanisms, at different prices, for different time periods, with different methods and timing of payments. The official line that this can all be paid for by less case-by-case reporting underestimates the amount of data needed to make outcome measurements work. Quality controls have not yet proved themselves, and there is a strong tendency to favour simple case counts over more subtle measurements of what has been achieved. Contractual incentives may turn out to be much blunter instruments that the green paper suggests, eroding existing professional belief systems while leaving little in their place. If solicitors feel that they no longer have any stake in the system, they could react cynically to any controls, providing the least they can get away with. Nor is it at all certain that firms will behave competitively in tendering for contracts. Experience from the United States suggests that after the first few years, the number of firms tendering for contracts will fall, causing prices to rise.

The overall verdict is that the government should proceed only with extreme caution. The green paper suggests that there should be pilot schemes to test the feasibility of tribunal representation and contracting (although primary legislation will be necessary to introduce exclusive schemes, even on a pilot basis). The need for research and development, however, goes wider than this. As a first step, the government will need to establish new national and regional consultative mechanisms. Research on quality standards is a priority: the transaction criteria should be checked to see how they correlate with peer assessment and client views, and outcome measures need to be developed. The Board also needs data on geographic access: where are the suppliers now? How large are the catchment areas served by advice centres and solicitors' offices? How many contracts will be needed? Only then can the department start to count the costs of administering—and publicising—the new system. Above all, the government should avoid a doctrinaire approach to contracting as the ideal method of delivering services. In a managed system, it is possible to run several different delivery methods alongside each other. Some services can be contracted: in others a grant to a voluntary body would provide greater flexibility. In rural areas, it may be simpler to continue to fund services on a case-by-case basis. In some cases—where, for example, insufficient solicitors are willing to tender—the Board could consider establishing its own salaried service.

The green paper shows that the Lord Chancellor's Department is prepared to think radically, even when treasury constraints impose severe limits on what can be done. They have still to demonstrate that they can listen, research, and refine their ideas into workable solutions. Unfortunately, there are no easy answers, and we still have a great deal to learn about using a limited amount of money to ensure the maximum access to law.

19

# *Time Management and Procedural Reform: Some Organizational Questions for Lord Woolf*

ROBERT DINGWALL* AND TOM DURKIN†

Many people seem to think that most contemporary legal systems are too slow in dealing with civil matters. The lethargy of the process is said to lead to expense which prevents people obtaining adequate redress for their grievances or resolution of their disputes. Ordinary men and women do not have the means to risk using the system. Even corporations and states are beginning to bridle at the outlays involved. One of the solutions endorsed by Lord Woolf and others is that the court should take control of the timetable of litigation rather than leaving this in the hands of the parties. A stable, predictable and strictly enforced schedule will concentrate everybody's minds, increase efficiency and reduce costs. The judiciary's active management of time is proposed as one of the necessary conditions for an accessible system of civil justice.

However, it is arguable that the 'problem of delay' is more complex than legal reformers have generally recognized and that the recurrent failure to solve it may result from a failure to address it in the correct terms. Barry Schwartz concluded his study of time with the argument that:

> Accordingly, an institutionalized willingness to wait . . . works in a more positive way by enabling the organization to accommodate some degree of autonomy on the part of its members . . . (T)olerance of delay may enhance rather than detract from efficiency when the object of autonomy is efficiency itself, in that a server may delay a client for the sake of highly important business whose completion would be systematically advantageous. A measure of permissiveness with respect to delay thus leads to the flexibility of an organization as well as the autonomy of its members. So when we take a sufficiently comprehensive (i.e., macroscopic) point of view, the manifestly negative aspects of waiting and congestion appear to serve quite positive ends.[1]

* Professor and Head of the School of Social Studies, University of Nottingham.

† Assistant Professor of Criminology and Sociology, University of Florida, Gainesville.

[1] B. Schwartz (1975) *Queuing and Waiting*, Chicago: University of Chicago, p. 194. Cited hereafter as 'Schwartz'.

Time management by the court may have perverse effects which aggravate rather than alleviate the related problems of cost and accessibility. This is particularly important if we understand that what matters to the parties is less likely to be the time spent in processing cases through the legal system than the total case processing time, that is the duration from a plaintiff first seeking legal advice to the resolution of the case. An acceleration of court processing need not affect the total processing time if it merely shifts work elsewhere and slows other parts of the system.

The perception of crisis in English civil justice is real enough. Lord Woolf's Inquiry[2] is the second attempt to promote reform in less than ten years, following the Civil Justice Review[3] of 1988. It is an interesting footnote to the study of the English policy process that the failure of the kind of management consultancy review favoured by Mrs. Thatcher's governments has been followed by what has been in all but name a Royal Commission, which has relied much more on the classic methods of written and oral evidence with a few commissioned inputs from academics. However, we should not accept the perception of crisis uncritically.

For one thing, there never seems to have been a Golden Age when civil justice was speedy and cheap. Charles Dickens's strictures on the Court of Chancery in *Bleak House* stand in a long line of criticism. Shakespeare was no great friend of the law: among the virtues of suicide contemplated by Hamlet is the avoidance of law's delay. Lord Woolf's report itself notes that there have been at least 60 reports since 1851 examining the procedure and organization of civil and criminal courts in England and Wales.[4] It is possible that we are seeing a similar phenomenon to that described by Geoffrey Pearson in his celebrated study of writings about juvenile delinquency, where he shows that the young were always better behaved about thirty years before the time at which an author was working, whether the account was published in 1860 or 1960.[5] As Pearson pointed out, the implication was that the study of the complaints about the young might tell us more about the complainers and about the nature of intergenerational relations than about the actual behaviour of young people. In the same way, it may be that the complaints about the justice system tell us more about the complainers than about the system itself. The problems are perceived by measuring the system against an ideal which is not itself subject to the same critical examination.[6]

[2] Woolf, LJ (1995) *Access to Justice: Interim Report to the Lord Chancellor on the Civil Justice system in England and Wales*, London, Lord Chancellor's Department. Cited hereafter as 'Woolf'.

[3] Civil Justice Review (1988) *Report of the Review Body on Civil Justice*, Cm. 394, London: HMSO.

[4] Woolf p. 2.

[5] G. Pearson (1983) *Hooligan: A History of Respectable Fears*, London: Macmillan

[6] This is a well-established line of argument in the sociology of social problems. Its source

Like beauty, time is in the eye of the beholder. We might also note that, relative to international comparisons, English civil justice does not seem to be particularly slow. There is no equivalent to the stasis of asbestos cases in the US, for example, where victims could find themselves waiting more than ten years to settle or try a case. Asbestos disease victims and lawyers in the U.K. reported that once a case was accepted by the legal system, it would generally be settled within a year or two. The delay in the U.K. was in moving a case to the point where the legal system would recognize it. A concern with time management by the courts would obscure the crucial time management roles of others actors in the social organization of law. Such diverse actors as unions, the DSS, the NHS, medical specialists, lawyers, and insurers are crucial to the success or failure of an asbestos claim. While not under the control of the court, these 'outside' actors control the pace of such litigation. Other than setting a trial date, judges have little influence on these proceedings. The court bent on time management might find that its wish is not the other's command.

If criticism is endemic, regardless of time, place or particular institutional arrangements, it is particularly important to avoid simply reiterating it. The special contribution of a sociologist may be to try to understand the civil justice process as an organization and why it works in the way that it does, before considering who the critics are and what motivates their analyses and proposals. Civil litigation is a complex social system, in which courts and trials play a rather small part and whose temporal rhythm may reflect the strategic behaviour of the principal actors more than their relative efficiency or inefficiency. As the economist Lester Thurow has observed, a long run failure to eliminate market imperfections may suggest that they are actually concealing efficiency gains.[7] The key is identifying the real goals. If we can understand the system in its own terms, we may be better able to make judgements about its performance and ways in which this might be improved. Could it be more effective to change the incentives for the existing actors than to impose a whole new game played by new rules with a dramatic increase in the powers of the referee? It is often seen as the mark of a good soccer match that the referee 'let the game flow' rather than penalizing every infringement. Might the same be true of civil litigation?

Unfortunately, legal research is not an easy task to accomplish in England. The Lord Chancellor's Department has not, historically, seen a

lies in the work of W. Waller (1936) 'Social Problems and the Mores' 1 *American Sociological Review* 922–33 and R. C. Fuller and R. Myers (1941) 'Some Aspects of a Theory of Social Problems' 6 *American Sociological Review* 24–32. Influential recent statements include M. Spector and J. Kitsuse (1973) 'Social Problems: A Re-formulation' 21 *Social Problems* 145–59 and A. F. Blum (1971) 'Methods for Recognizing, Formulating and Describing Social Problems' in E. O. Smigel, ed. *Handbook on the Study of Social Problems*, Chicago: Rand McNally.

[7] L. Thurow (1975) *Generating Inequality*, New York: Macmillan

role for itself as a customer for research and development activity in the administration of civil justice. The result is a lack of empirical work on the civil justice system, with the exception of those areas, especially family law, which touch on the concerns of other government departments with more active commissioning traditions. In effect, the only strategy for reform that the Department has had has been the *ad hoc*, one-off investigation of the kind represented by Lord Woolf's Inquiry or the Civil Justice Review. There is no tradition of continuing research which would feed into a constant process of quality and efficiency improvement and evaluation. It will, then, be necessary to rely partly on data collected in the course of studies for other purposes[8] and partly on the extensive body of work that has been produced in the USA, much of which has been usefully summarized by Malcolm Feeley.[9] Feeley initially proved that simple solutions to complex legal problems often fail. More recent work in law and legal delays has been moving the focus toward studying organizational and interorganizational networks.[10] Dixon's analysis of how courts work concluded that 'Future theoretical developments and research designs need to take seriously the organizational context perspective of sentencing'.[11] Galanter's review of reform efforts in the U.S. showed that 'reforms based on misreadings of the legal system may fail to accomplish the goals of their proponents'.[12] Haig and Stone predicted that the U.S. reforms aimed at ending 'civil justice expense and delay' would likely spawn 'expensive and protracted satellite litigation' as litigants attempted to figure out what the new rules meant and allowed.[13]

By focusing on the issue of time management within the Woolf Report, we can explore the issues which might arise in a more sociological approach to the problems of procedural reform and, in particular, the limitations of any solution which makes court control its centrepiece. In the present state of knowledge, it is hard to go beyond the sociologist's common role of

[8] The asbestos project was conducted by both the present authors in association with W. L. F. Felstiner and supported by the American Bar Foundation and the Economic and Social Research Council. The medical negligence research was conducted by RD with P Fenn and supported by the Nuffield Provincial Hospitals Trust, the Economic and Social Research Council and various District and Regional Health Authorities. The views and interpretations expressed here are ours alone.

[9] M. Feeley (1983) *Court Reform on Trial: Why Simple Solutions Fail*, New York: Basic Books.

[10] J. Martin and N. Maron (1994) 'Court Delays and Interorganizational Networks' 17 *Justice System Journal* 268–288); R. Dingwall, T. Durkin, W. L. F. Felstiner (1992) 'Delay in Tort Cases' 9 *Civil Justice Quarterly*; T. Durkin (1994) *Constructing Law* U. Chicago Ph.D. dissertation.

[11] J. Dixon (1995). 'The Organizational Context of Criminal Sentencing' 5 *American Journal of Sociology* 1198.

[12] Galanter, Marc (1993). 'The Tort Panic and After: A Commentary' 16 *Justice System Journal* 4.

[13] R. Haig and W. Stone (1993) 'Does all this litigation 'reform' really benefit the client?' in 67 *St. John's Law Review* 843–875.

demonstrating the complexity of what 'common sense' suggests are simple problems with obvious solutions. However, we hope to indicate that there are sufficient reasons to be cautious about radical changes and to encourage more systematic investment in both basic research and in the evaluation of innovations.

## THE WOOLF MODEL

How does Lord Woolf's analysis proceed? The main objectives of the reforms are summarized as being the encouragement of early settlement; the obligation to proceed with efficiency and despatch; and the simplification of procedure.[14] These are to be achieved by solving a set of fourteen problems described at length in Chapter 3, which can be grouped under the headings of adversarialism, cost, time, complexity, access and system priority.[15]

*Adversarialism*. This reflects the priority of party control in the English legal system, with the 'conduct, pace and extent of litigation left almost completely to the parties'. This allows them to use the procedure to harry each other at the expense of 'questions of expense, delay, compromise and fairness'. The powers of the courts have fallen behind the sophistication of the litigators.

*Cost*. Civil litigation is seen to be too expensive in both absolute and relative terms. It is a cost to business and to the taxpayer. In smaller cases, the costs of the action may exceed the value of the recovery. Conversely, sound defences may be more costly than paying off unmerited claims. Parties are also hampered by the unpredictability of costs, especially on the opposite side. The result is a possible loss of high-value business to other national jurisdictions.

*Delay*. Delay is said to compound the distress to plaintiffs by postponing remedies. It becomes more difficult to establish facts and may force settlements below the value of the claim by parties who do not have the emotional or material resources to continue. The only people who benefit from delay are legal advisers who can carry excessive caseloads by spreading action thinly over a long period of time. Since this is a pervasive phenomenon, lawyers are encouraged to be indulgent towards each others failings by not enforcing timetables. Cases are dragged out by excessive discovery and by late settlements. Since lawyers do the minimum work until a trial date prioritizes the case, negotiations come late in the day. In order to compensate for door-of-the-court settlements, courts overlist to avoid judicial downtime. If too few cases settle, others get knocked back.

[14] Woolf p. 5. [15] Woolf pp. 7–17.

Interlocutory hearings have grown as tactical weapons, introducing new sources of delay and demands on judicial time. Hearings are unpredictable in their duration and ineffectively planned.

*Complexity*. Civil procedure has grown in an incoherent and illogical fashion with different rules in different courts.

*Access*. The limitations on civil legal aid have excluded large sections of the population and led to an increase in litigants in person which is causing operational difficulties for the courts.

*System Priority*. Civil work ranks behind criminal and family business in the allocation of court resources.

The central philosophical shift recommended in the report is that the civil justice process should be reconstructed from its traditional basis of party control to a new foundation in judicial control. Essentially, judges will take over case management, assigning cases to different tracks according to their view of the value and complexity of the matters in issue. Once assigned to a track, the case will proceed according to the judge's view of the time and resources that should be allocated to it, whether by the court or by the parties. Each track will have a basic timetable from which departures will not normally be permitted. Around this core change, Lord Woolf makes a number of more detailed proposals about organizational and procedural reform, including the desirability of a single set of procedural rules, the allocation of business between different grades of judge, the possible extension of ADR and the strengthening of advice to litigants in person. He shows a particular enthusiasm for the use of information technology, with materials being moved or stored electronically and video-conferencing to discuss case management with parties and their advisers.

It should be stressed that a number of these analyses and remedies are clearly sensible and worth acting upon. The case for a single rule-book regardless of the court before which civil matters are being brought seems incontestable. The discussion of ADR and the debate about whether some types of disputes can best be settled outside the legal system, is also useful.[16] Some of the observations reflect Lord Woolf's incorporation of the social science commentary that was placed before the review: for instance, his appreciation of the inherent tendency of lawyers to overbook themselves.[17] If the remainder of this paper seems somewhat negative, it is because the issue of time management is one where the 'obvious' remedy is so seductive that its shortcomings need a particular dissection. At the end of the day, we may still decide that the balance of advantages and disad-

[16] Woolf p. 136.

[17] Woolf p. 12. Although it might be noted that he does not acknowledge that this tendency is inherent in the conditions of self-employment. For lawyers just as much as plumbers or builders, no work means no income. The self-employed are forced to overbook to insure against unemployment.

vantages favours change, but those disadvantages need to be clearly understood before a choice can be made. Our role is, perhaps, that of the devil's advocate. For this reason, we will not make too much of the obvious internal contradictions in Lord Woolf's statement of the background: on the one hand, we have a picture of a relentlessly adversarial system where parties harry each other; on the other, we have a cosy collusion to avoid the current rules and to allow everybody to overbook, dilute effort, and generally make more money. Can these both be true simultaneously? In fact they probably can, but each is a truth about part of the system and may not be a good basis for a reform of the whole.

## TIME AND THE EVALUATION OF HUMAN SERVICE ORGANIZATIONS

The sociology of time is a particularly esoteric and rather undeveloped field.[18] In essence, though, it starts from the observation that human society is as much an organization of time as of any other basic resource like space, energy, information or whatever. Society is one of the ways in which we solve the problems of our temporary existence. We are born, we live a while and then we die but society goes on. The specific incumbents of the judicial bench may change but the accumulated stock of precedents which bind them provides for the continuity and predictability of judgement across time.

Control of time is clearly a form of power.[19] Daily life involves constant decisions and contests over the allocation of time. When the Inland Revenue introduces self-assessment of personal taxation, for example, this is an expropriation of time, a declaration that the State now owns time that might previously have been devoted to other purposes. The taxpayer does not get a choice in the matter, except that whatever government savings may be transmitted through reductions in the rate of tax can be recycled into buying the time of a private tax adviser to avoid the commitment of one's own time. Time can be manipulated as a dimension of social organization. One of the nuances of the game of cricket, for instance, is the way in which teams can have a strategy for time, speeding up overs when things

[18] Some of the classic sources are: G. Gurvitch (1964) *The Spectrum of Social Time*, Dordrecht: D. Reidel; D. Maines (1987) 'The Significance of Temporality for the Development of Sociological Theory' 28 *Sociological Quarterly* 303–11; P. A. Sorokin and R. K. Merton (1937) 'Social Time: A Methodological and Functional Analysis' 42 *American Journal of Sociology* 615–29; E. Zerubavel (1985) *Hidden Rhythms*, Berkeley: University of California Press; J. Roth (1963) *Timetables*, Indianapolis: Bobbs Merrill; E. Zerubavel (1987) 'The Language of Time: Towards a Semiotics of Temporality' 28 *Sociological Quarterly* 343–56. A fuller account of our application of these ideas can be found in T. Durkin, R. Dingwall and W. L. F. Felstiner (1990) 'Plaited Cunning: Manipulating Time in Asbestos Litigation' *ABF Working Paper #9004*, Chicago: American Bar Foundation.

[19] Schwartz pp. 34–41.

are going well, and using time more intensively, or slowing down to obstruct a successful opponent. Commentators frequently note the way in which a team may be playing for time, preserving wickets in the hope of securing a draw when time expires rather than chasing a victory and risking a defeat.

Litigation is a process in time. As Lord Woolf recognizes, there is a temporal dimension to litigation strategy, just as there is in cricket. A party may seek to gain a strategic advantage from speeding up or slowing down a case. Equally, the parties may co-operate to play out the game for a draw which allows honour to be satisfied but makes a poor spectacle. However, time management in itself is neither positive nor negative. It is simply a fact of social life, which is accomplished in various ways. Delay is an evaluative label for the particular pace at which a party or parties move. It comes from a moral discourse which challenges the particular time management pattern that happens to be in force. But this evaluative language is itself the result of a choice by the observer. It implies an ideal world in which things would be done differently, importing a benchmark to the situation. To the extent that it is used to promote reform, it seeks to make the real world closer to the ideal. But this ideal is itself an expression of an interest, of a different distribution of value.

In the present context, the benchmark seems to be derived primarily from an ideal of efficiency, although Lord Woolf does make reference to other desirable goals which are likely to be promoted by greater efficiency. These correspond fairly well to the other classic dimensions of evaluation in human service organizations: effectiveness; equity; and humanity.[20] Here, effectiveness might be posed as the issue of whether the system produces the right result; equity as whether the system is perceived to be fair[21]; and humanity as whether it is responsive to individual circumstances. These dimensions are often in conflict. A quick solution may not be a just or fair solution and may involve an assembly line service rather than individual responsiveness. Think, for example, about the way that McDonalds train their staff in human relations to conceal the ferocious uniformity of the product and production. The objective is to encourage each customer to feel an individual despite the mass produced environment. This will clearly be a management problem for those involved in Lord Woolf's 'fast track' based upon the present small claims procedure. There are already complaints about the way in which a system designed to deal with individuals has been affected by its use for debt recovery by large corporations. People with legally arguable cases to resist repossessions by mortgage holders, for

[20] P. M. Strong and R. Dingwall (1989) 'Romantics and Stoics' in D. Silverman and J. Gubrium, eds., *The Politics of Field Research*, London: Sage.

[21] E. A. Lind and T. R. Tyler (1988) *The Social Psychology of Procedural Justice*, New York: Plenum.

example, are said to have lost the chance to defend these actions because of their limited access to advice and the low level of expertise on the plaintiffs' side. Small claims is typically work for trainees, executives and even unqualified clerks. Of course the tension between legal universals and particular cases has long been recognized by lawyers. There is a trade-off between equality and equity. Lord Woolf cites with approval an argument by Michael Zander suggesting that a slight increase in the error rate might be acceptable if it led to a significant cost saving.[22] This would be a shift in the trade-off between effectiveness and efficiency.[23] But the point is that the existing system embodies a trade-off between all of these dimensions which has its own measure of legitimacy. A shift in the current balance may produce dissatisfaction extending to sabotage as the people involved seek to preserve the balance which strikes them as proper.

The history of attempts at court reform in the US is littered with examples of local judges and lawyers colluding to maintain the status quo in the face of outside attempts at change. The courtroom work group of lawyers and judges have long been recognized as the enemy of victims and reformers alike.[24] If by chance the work group does not prevail, then it is likely that some latent or perverse effect will arise. The 'three strikes and you're out' criminal justice reforms[25] have shut down civil courts in California as more resources are shifted to the criminal courts. Courts and jails have become even more overcrowded as felons and judges resist 'taking a strike'. Felons have resisted plea bargains at the felony level, and judges have been willing to ignore or reclassify previous felony convictions as misdemeanors in order to gain a plea bargain for a pending case. Attempts to accelerate the preparation of cases for trial by 'fast tracking' serious felons have often led to more trials rather than more plea bargains and have simply shifted the congestion around without reducing the overall time to resolution.

Where time management by judges has been a success, it generally requires increased resources, and is followed by increased demands as plaintiff expectations of justice increase. Extra resources put into slow courts have encouraged lawyers to bring more cases. Successful management of time can also increase demands on the legal system. When one U.S. civil justice reform attempt, the Asbestos Claims Facility, was inaugurated

22 Woolf p. 19

23 There is, of course, no reason to suppose that a slight increase in the error rate *would* lead to a *significant* cost saving. It is equally plausible to suggest that a significant cost saving would be associated with a large increase in the error rate. There is no empirical evidence comparable to that in, say, health economics where studies of the change in the accuracy of X-ray interpretation against a given level of resource input allow fairly precise calculation of the savings associated with a shift from 98 to 95 per cent accuracy.

24 J. Dixon, note 10, pp. 1157–1198; R. Elias (1993) *Victims Still*. London: Sage; A. Karmen, (1990) *Crime Victims*. Belmont, Ca: Wadsworth.

25 These programs give people convicted of a third felony an additional sentence, usually from 25 years to life imprisonment.

to make claims handling faster and more efficient, it also lowered barriers to victim claiming. New claim filings went from 400 to 2,000 claims a month. The list of unexpected results can be multiplied.

Reform, then, needs careful handling if it is to have a real impact. In a highly decentralized organization, it is important to engineer a measure of consent in all quarters, especially if the intention is to achieve a high degree of standardization and centralization. The lessons of the Child Support Agency should be carefully studied by any policy maker in this area. An important element in fuelling the public protest seems to have been the loss of discretion in the system and the way in which this undermined the sense of legitimacy that had attached to the previous procedure. It should have been possible to move the benchmarks for support payments with much less public and professional hostility if some apparent consideration of individual circumstances had been maintained. Experience has taught us that simply announcing that a procedural reform is more efficient does not guarantee its acceptance if the people affected find that their sense of equity and humanity is affronted.

## TIME AND LITIGATION STRATEGY

When we consider the reform proposals, then, we need to begin by understanding how the present system works for the principal actors involved. For reasons of space, we cannot embrace all of the possible areas of civil litigation and we shall focus on personal injury matters. As Lord Woolf points out, there are special considerations about cases of this kind and they are not necessarily the best single model for civil procedure. On the other hand, there is probably more research evidence available about them than about other kinds of case and they are a paradigm of individuals encountering corporate actors, with all the issues about inequality in resources and bargaining skills that arise from this.[26] It is also arguable that commercial actors have a greater degree of flexibility and sophistication in forum-shopping for the resolution of their claims on each other and the system design issues may be rather different, except where there is a similar imbalance of power between, say, a small firm trying to recover a debt from a large corporation. If the state is concerned about commercial disputes moving offshore, then the answer may be to encourage the development of ADR or other private fora rather than changing the public courts into profit-seeking competitors in an international market. Is there a genuine

[26] M. Galanter (1975) 'Why the "Haves" Come Out Ahead: Speculations on the Limits of Legal Change' 9 *Law and Society Review* 95–160. See also J. Coleman (1982) *The Asymmetric Society*; Syracuse: Syracuse University Press.

state interest in many of the matters such that a public court system should be provided to meet them?

The first distinction that needs to be made is between idle (waiting) time and productive time.[27] These differ greatly in meaning and action. Idle time is time when nothing is happening. Idle time in law is easy to discover.[28] A case has been set down for trial and the parties are waiting for a date. The date finally arrives, and all parties wait in the hall at the start of the judge's day.[29] A plaintiff has made a first appointment to see the family solicitor after her return from a holiday. Productive time is the time that the actor controlling the litigation is managing to achieve some strategic outcome. Evidence is being collected, or expert opinions are being prepared. Legal time has different characters, but in Woolf all time is the same.

The asbestos litigation study was based on 220 interviews carried out between 1986 and 1991 with most of the kinds of people involved in PI cases: victims, insurance claim managers, solicitors, barristers, expert witnesses and union officials. In this area of litigation, most of the business was carried out by a few specialists in well-organized firms. Some of the firms were small niche practitioners, while others were large, multi-partner and often multi-branch operations working across a range of union or insurer matters. In their interviews, our informants made great play with their efficiency as a point of contrast between themselves and other members of their profession. They could conclude cases very quickly and sometimes did where the plaintiff had a terminal mesothelioma and there were no problems with diagnosis or liability. We were told that 100 of 100 cases settle at the door of the court. Defence lawyers generally did not introduce long delays once a claim reached the legal system, provided that the victim was represented by an expert lawyer *and* the DSS had formally recognized the presence of a disease. Both sides acknowledged, as Lord Woolf does[30] that the plaintiff lawyers could drive the pace if they chose to, although they usually did not. Why did they sometimes stretch out the processing (as opposed to idle) time? There are a number of reasons for this, but three seem to be particularly relevant here.

First, the case processing might be slowed because a medical condition was unclear or was expected to deteriorate. With asbestos cases, there is a decision about whether to claim a small amount of provisional damages for pleural plaques, which are evidence of lung damage but not disabling or life-threatening. This can establish liability in the event of subsequent asbestosis, mesothelioma or lung cancer. Limitation problems may also be

[27] B. Schwartz, note 1, 15.

[28] B. Schwartz, note 1, 26–7.

[29] Of course, one person's delay is another's productive time. Schwartz (1975) pointed out how a judge has power over litigants, and can maximize the productivity of his own time by imposing idle time on others.

[30] Woolf p. 7.

avoided, if it were argued, in the event of a serious condition developing, that the claim should have been brought on the first evidence of damage. On the other hand, the recoveries are small relative to the costs involved for both parties and the victims do not seem to regard them as proportionate to the impact of the diagnosis of asbestos damage, which is known to be a death sentence in the communities involved. In some cases, then, an intake interview might simply disappear into a drawer with a view to restarting at a time when the value of the claim had increased. Alternatively, if the plaintiff's death seemed to be imminent, the case might be held to avoid the extra cost of restarting it as a dependant's claim.

I hardly ever seal a writ before I've seen the main medical. I will in a mesothelioma case, if you've got 100 per cent assessment from the panel, if it's just been diagnosed, and I think I can get him damages within six to nine months, before he dies. If he's obviously on his last legs and about to peg out, and he's got a widow, I just stick the file in the cabinet anyway, because you're only going to have to amend it and start again for the widow. (*Plaintiff Solicitor*)

Delay increases efficiency here by saving the duplication of work in a provisional damages claim or of restarting a case. It may also be more humane in avoiding the stress of legal involvement at an inappropriate or difficult time. It does not necessarily compromise either effectiveness or equity.

Second, processing time may be extended because of the need to wait for access to a relevant expert, in this case a chest physician with a specialist knowledge of asbestos disease. A doctor who can write an authoritative report which the other party will treat as a basis for serious negotiation acquires that status from seeing a considerable number of cases. If these have to be fitted into a busy practice, then the patient will have to go into a queue. UK doctors are reluctant to become 'professional experts' and the lawyers are reluctant to encourage them because their independence is valued. Although doctors do now work mainly for one side or the other, there is a feeling that they should not be allowed to become hired guns. At the same time, each side reserves the right to shop for the expert who will write the most favourable report. Delay means that each side ends up with an expert report that defines its negotiating strength and which is respected by its adversary. This allows negotiation to proceed more quickly, since the authoritativeness of your expert is less likely to be challenged. This claims manager's response to a specific question about enlarging the pool of doctors used, implied by both the Civil Justice Review and Lord Woolf, makes the point:

I think it would in fact, at some stage, might actually cause the problems you're seeking to avoid. You've got two doctors, who are not terribly experienced, you're more likely to get an even more divergent opinion and the likelihood is you're going to end up in court more often, which of course doesn't help to get cases settled quickly. (*Claims Manager*)

A slow pace of gathering expert evidence is efficient if it accelerates later negotiations and avoids trials, since the parties have no temptation to put each other's experts in the box and see what they are worth. It may also be more humane if a victim is spared unnecessary, stressful and intrusive medical examinations by doctors inexperienced in looking for the sort of evidence that is required. It is likely to enhance the effectiveness of the system, since decisions are based on evidence of known quality and seems unlikely to affect the issue of equity in most personal injury cases. Medical negligence may be an exception to this, given the alleged difficulty of locating doctors who will accept commissions from plaintiffs to conduct examinations and express opinions. However, it has to be said that this complaint seems to be heard less frequently as a result of the activities of victim groups and an evolving notion of professional responsibility among the doctors.

The same arguments, broadly, apply to the selection of expert counsel and their opinions. Although legal rules require barristers to mimic a cab rank, plaintiff solicitors know an expert barrister is well worth waiting for. In other kinds of cases, it would not be difficult to envisage circumstances where extensive laboratory work was required to deal with issues of liability. We might suggest that the criminal justice system has thrown up enough examples of forensic science botched under organizational pressures for us to be cautious about increasing the demands in civil cases.

Third is the time taken to manage clients. Although this is becoming recognized in family business[31], its importance does not yet seem to have been fully acknowledged in other civil litigation. There is clearly a complex process involved in framing the client's complaint, developing their trust and managing their motivation to pursue the case to an appropriate outcome. Most clients will eventually have to settle for rather less than they really think is appropriate, whether because the defendants expect a discount for avoiding the uncertainty of a trial or because judicial calculations of the heads of damages fall short of actual losses.[32] The latter disappointment is inevitable, since the plaintiff's advisers will always have a duty to put forward the calculations most defensibly favourable to their client, while the judge is concerned to ensure that they accord with precedents and the 'going rate'.

This extract is from a barrister explaining to a plaintiff why he should settle for £75,000 when their figures added up to more than £100,000:

[31] E.g. A. Sarat and W. L. F. Felstiner (1986) 'Law and Strategy in the Divorce Lawyer's Office' 20 *Law and Society Review* 93–134

[32] H. Genn (1994) *Personal Injury Compensation: How Much is Enough?*, Law Com No.225.

On the best possible basis, you could have got about £90,000 in court so we're really discounting from that. I know our figures added up to more than £100,000 but I couldn't see any judge giving you more than £90,000. Our calculations all depend upon your having professional nursing. But your wife would be doing it and the judge would probably value her rather than a professional nurse. Even then, you're quite likely to get a judge who just assumes that's what wives are for and doesn't give you anything. Basically, you've taken a bit off the £90,000 for the uncertainty about the judge. You've taken off £15,000. It seems a sensible compromise. It gives you the certainty as opposed to the hope.

Over the history of this case, the plaintiff, an old and terminally ill man, had seen the expectations rise to over £100,000 as his advisers had done their calculations and then sought to dissuade him from accepting a defendant offer of £20,000. This had been a particularly difficult case because he was convinced that only wrongdoers appeared in court and saw the whole process as a terrible stigma. The management was a great challenge to the professionals to temper their rational analysis of litigation tactics with the sensitivity needed to ensure that their client could stay with the process. Efficiency was compromised in the interest of humanity. However, an effective and equitable result was still achieved. The processing time of a case may, then, reflect a compromise between efficiency, effectiveness, equity and humanity in ways which are not immediately obvious. Cases can take time for good reasons.

## TIME AND POWER

The previous section set out what were effectively factors *internal* to the civil justice system that affected the pace at which it moved. However, studies of organizations in general have increasingly pointed to the inadequacy of treating any institution as an hermetically sealed unit.[33] Organizations are constantly in interaction with their environments, which, of course, include other organizations or social institutions. The progress of cases in the civil justice system is, then, also affected by a set of *external* constraints. Time is one of these. The relations between civil justice and other institutions are, at least, in part shaped by a conflict about time management. More specifically, the pace at which a case moves is influenced by the priority that an issue receives within organizations for whom litigation is not a priority.

Two examples of this will have to suffice. The first relates to the availability of expert witnesses. We have already noted the processing time required to obtain a report from a preferred expert. In some areas, the

[33] See, for example, P. C. Nystrom and W. H. Starbuck (1981) *Handbook of Organizational Design* (2 volumes), Oxford: Oxford University Press; W. W. Powell and P. DiMaggio (1991) *The New Institutionalism in Organizational Analysis*, Chicago: University of Chicago Press.

expert may be a 'professional witness', in which case he or she is subject to the same structural constraints of self-employment that we have already seen in the case of lawyers' overbooking. Perhaps more interesting here, though, is the position of many of the medical experts who combine the provision of reports with a clinical practice within the NHS. The time of the legal work tends to be subordinated to the time of the clinical work. Although the doctors derive various benefits from their legal consultancy and may provide an important benefit to their patients, this is less important than treating sick people.

I have an asbestos clinic specifically in another building in (City) which I do weekly, where I see probably 10 or 15 people a week with asbestos induced diseases, not all new cases, but of those perhaps two new cases a week, and here I see perhaps 4 or 5 a week either for litigation or presenting with new asbestos induced diseases. (*Consultant Physician*)

The status of the doctor as an expert witness derives from the 500 or so consultations that he does each year but a relatively small proportion of these are for legal purposes and he is reluctant to increase this at the expense of clinical work. The specialist's authority derives from his or her experience of a flow of like cases: it cannot increase more rapidly than the doctor's rate of exposure to those cases, which, in turn, is a function of the time he or she is willing to make available, as well as of the incidence of the condition in the population. It may be possible to negotiate exceptional priority for an exceptional case but legal time must normally reach some accommodation with medical time. Lawyers and judges must respect these timetables, or lose valuable testimony. An expert chest physician in London is too busy to take lunch, and cannot work any harder. Plaintiff and defence lawyers know who the best physicians are, and recognize that an opinion from an inexperienced or outdated doctor will cause further delays when (and if) a claim ever reaches trial.

In the other example, however, the possibility of negotiation is virtually nil. This is when the legal system encounters government time. Asbestos litigation often involves an encounter with the records of two major bureaucracies: the Inland Revenue, whose records are the most reliable sources of employment history, and the Department of Social Security, whose agencies administer the state benefits for those injured by industrial accidents or subject to specified occupational diseases. Neither agency sees assisting victims to litigate as a central part of its mission and, as a result, devotes few resources to dealing with inquiries or requests for assistance.[34] The

[34] In fact, much like Miller's welfare bureaucrats in Milwaukee, observers charged that DSS employees sought to deny public recognition of social problems and victimizations. See G. Miller (1991) *Enforcing the Work Ethic*, Albany; University Press. See also R. Lewis (1987) *Compensation for Industrial Injury*, Abingdon: Professional Books; and N. Wikeley (1993) *Compensation for Industrial Disease* Aldershot: Dartmouth.

expectation that public bureaucracies will operate to treat all citizens in a formally equal fashion means that cases are supposed to be dealt with in a strict and impersonal order.[35]

During our asbestos research, the DSS was a major negative gatekeeper to the legal system (especially in occupational cases), and kept what Gurvitch[36] called bureaucratic and Schwartz[37] called organizational time. The DSS moved to its own schedule, and DSS deferred neither to legal or medical expert time.[38] Victims, lawyers, and courts found they had little influence over the timing and substance of DSS decisions even when they were patently wrong.[39] While the DSS has recently undergone changes, there is as yet little evidence that the new agencies are more responsive to legal time.

Similar problems are encountered in other contexts. One of the difficulties with medical negligence litigation is obviously the physical location of relevant records. Clearly, the priority of hospital records departments is with the support of current clinical needs rather than responding to queries which are not seen as having the same kind of impact on the subject. This forms an impediment to both plaintiffs and defendants in achieving a speedy disposition. On the other hand, a quicker response would mean diverting resources that might otherwise have been used for some enhancement to patient care, which is the principal organizational goal. If there is a choice between an extra pathology technician to process cancer biopsies more quickly or an extra records clerk to process lawyers' requests more quickly, it is not difficult to see why the former might be preferred. The time of the cancer patient is assigned priority over the time of the civil justice system.

Civil justice professionals are constantly dependent upon other people to provide them with material for a case, where the other person does not see this as a particularly important use of their time. Requests will be dealt with, but at a moment convenient to the recipient rather than the requester. A key constraint on case progress can easily be an organization which has little to do with the matter but which needs to be persuaded to supply some vital component. The organization will always be inclined to respond at its own pace, especially if it is under resource pressures which are influencing its ability to fulfil its main goals. Cases can only be processed more quickly if the legal system can find some way to interfere in the organization's views of its own priorities, whether by sanctions or incentives. Either way, it raises an issue about power, about the extent to which the legal system can impose its own timetables on others or must accommodate to them.

[35] M. Weber (1947) *The Theory of Social and Economic Organization*, New York: Free Press, pp. 329–41.

[36] G. Gurvitch, note 17, 101.

[37] Schwartz , note 1, pages 85, 99–100.

[38] Dingwall et al (1992), Durkin (1994), note 10.

[39] R. Lewis (1987).

## TIME AND WOOLF

The fundamental shift proposed by Lord Woolf is that the management of civil litigation should be shifted from the parties to the courts or, more specifically, to the teams of judges that he wishes to see created. A 'procedural judge' will decide which of three tracks a case should go down, all of which will have a fixed timetable. The 'fast track' will be completed in 20–30 weeks and the 'multi-track' for major cases will have a schedule set down that will become more precise as cases move towards trial. In more sociological language, time will become homogenous and unitary. In future, there will only be one time in litigation—court time—and this will pre-empt all other times, including those of other organizations outside the legal system. A major element of the multi-track procedure will be case management conferences and pre-trial reviews which lay clients or their authorized representatives will be required to attend. At these conferences, the lawyers will be obliged to produce statements of the costs incurred to date and the likely costs of proceeding to trial.

This shift is likely to have one important consequence for the civil justice system which does not seem to have been sufficiently recognized by Lord Woolf. If timetables are fixed, by statute or rule, then court and judge supply will have to be demand-led. As in Germany, judges will become more active supervisors, requiring more judges, which in turn will most probably bring more cases into the system.[40] At present, civil cases are matched to the resources made available by the state partly through listing delays. This is similar to the way in which we ration health care in this country (and Disney World rations entertainment) through waiting lists rather than by price. The Treasury is notoriously unhappy with demand-led areas of public expenditure: it has for years tried to find a way to cap GP prescription costs or social security expenditures. It is difficult to see the Treasury accepting this aspect of Lord Woolf's proposals unless the demand is covered by user charges. While it is part of the Courts Agency's objectives that court fees should, on balance, cover court costs, the removal of public subsidy will lead to price rises and a different basis of rationing. Lord Woolf's suggestions about case management may reduce some of the demands on some parts of the court system to compensate. But it is surely desirable that some further work is done on the economic aspects of these proposals if we are not to find that one barrier to access has been substituted for another.

In terms of the three examples we gave, it seems that the proposals are unlikely to have much effect on the first but would have a significant impact

[40] B. Markezinis (1990) 'Litigation Mania in England, Germany, and the USA' 49 *Cambridge Law Journal* 233–276.

on the second and third. If the new 'statements of case' which will replace pleadings do come to require more precise details, then it is likely that plaintiff lawyers will want to do more research before filing. At present, there can be incentives not to do much work on a case at all, if it is known that there will be long listing delays.

In London you waste time waiting for the court to take a case—about a year. But that can be minimized because well, it's very complicated. What we can do is to set the case down for trial which is what you have to do in the English legal system in order to get a trial date. But we can do that before we've completed all the interlocutory stages. And then use the dead year for preparation. (*Plaintiff Solicitor*)

If the case preparation time is shifted forward prior to serving the statements of case, then it is certainly possible that the net result will be to maintain the average duration of a case, from the day that a plaintiff walks into a lawyer's office to the date that a cheque is received, at about the present level. This incentive is strengthened by Lord Woolf's approach to the other issues.

The problem of expertise is to be solved almost by ignoring it. Lord Woolf asserts, for example, that the solution to the bottleneck caused by the limited supply of medical experts is to widen the range of doctors and to use more junior people.[41] While it may be true that a wider range of experts could be used, it is also arguable that lawyers are right to minimize the risks to their clients' cases by using doctors whose expertise and forensic skills command confidence. We have already noted the impact on settlement negotiations of using consultants whose expertise is uncertain or questioned by the other side. It is also puzzling that Lord Woolf should assume that the typical registrar would have any more time available than the typical consultant. Registrars are doctors in training who work under contracts which effectively require an exclusive commitment to the National Health Service. They are the workhorses of the hospital under the general guidance, advice and supervision of the consultant. The latter is normally employed on a sessional contract, with the possibility of limiting their NHS commitment in order to have time for private work, including litigation. Consultants also have more opportunities to focus their work, since registrars tend to move around within a specialty in order to develop their general competence.

In general, the courts would adopt a more interventionist approach to expert evidence. There would be a greater degree of pressure to settle differences before trial, to use court-appointed experts rather than each side recruiting their own and to underline the autonomy of the expert relative to the commissioning party. While these may have some effect, some scepticism is in order. Differences are not necessarily resolvable. In the asbestos

[41] Woolf p. 189; Schwartz p. 194.

study, different generations of doctors attached quite different significance to different sorts of evidence. Broadly speaking, older physicians relied on clinical judgement, where younger ones were more convinced by statistical and epidemiological data.[42] This is a clash of incommensurable paradigms. Lord Woolf acknowledges the problems of court-appointed experts including the risk of usurping the judicial role and the possible creation of a sinecure.[43] He does not regard these as compelling: others might disagree. Our evidence also suggests that the question of autonomy is a complex one. The lawyers we interviewed were clear that they did not want subservient experts. They wanted to be told if a case would not stand up before everybody wasted a lot of time and money on it. Having sorted this out, then certainly they expected the expert to become a team player and to help them present their case to its best advantage.

From a litigator's perspective, it is hard to resist the conclusion that the best strategy in a Woolf system is going to be to get your expert evidence in before the statement of case is prepared and to avoid as far as possible the regulatory control of the judiciary. This will be the way to continue to commission the experts of your choice and to prepare their evidence as you see fit. In doing so, of course, it is likely to magnify the advantages of plaintiffs in established types of claims, since the defence will be under much greater time pressure from the court compared with the present collusion between the lawyers in the interests of their notions of equity.[44]

It should be noted that the discussion of expertise is one of the few points where the impact of reform on other institutional actors is considered. Part of the benefit of the change is said to be the reduction in claims on the time of experts who have other priorities. On the other hand, it must also be recognized that experts are paid for making themselves available. If a doctor is not hanging around in court, there is no guarantee that he or she will actually be treating a clinic full of sick people rather than engaging in some other piece of private work like a batch of employment medicals. However, there should be further consideration of Lord Woolf's enthusiasm for new technology as a means of achieving this.[45] There is a growing body of evidence to suggest that video links are not simple substitutes for face-to-face interaction but introduce a new element of context which can have perverse results. This may be a particularly important area for further research and pilot projects.

Finally, we have the problem of the client. This, perhaps, is the most intractable. It is clear that an important element of Lord Woolf's

[42] A good example of this can be found in *Parkes v Port of London Authority* [1987] *Lexis*.

[43] Woolf p. 186–7.

[44] The 'British Rule' of shifting legal costs to the loser at trial is a negative gatekeeper to the legal system early in the natural history of claims types (i.e., asbestos diseases, thalidomide), but as cases become successful and numerous, the rule helps increase claims.

[45] Woolf pp. 86–7 and 191.

proposals is the use of case management and pre-trial reviews to put pressure on litigants to settle. The presentation of information on costs, for example, 'will enable the parties and the judge or Master conducting the hearing to make an informed decision as to the future of the proceedings in the light of their likely cost'. The lay client will normally have to be present to hear this discussion.[46] The difficulty arises when the client is a genuine lay person rather than a 'professional litigant' like an insurance company claims manager who can make a rational economic decision on the costs and merits of the case. With personal injury cases, we have little doubt that there is a significant group of litigants who would be so stressed by the nature of the occasion and so appalled by the bills that were being run up that they would be vulnerable to pressure to agree to settlements which did not reflect either the merits of their case or the scale of their losses. The 'have nots' might lose even more ground on the 'haves'.[47] Again, the answer from the plaintiff lawyers' perspective is to spend more time in preparing the client up front so that they can give a proper account of themselves before the judge. There should be some real concerns about the humanity of a system that may sweep in large numbers of people in poor health and circumstances to become the object of what they will undoubtedly perceive as professional intimidation.

While we recognize the persuasiveness of much of Lord Woolf's analysis, our suspicion must remain that it will not actually deliver compensation any more quickly to personal injury litigants and may not make much difference to the overall timetable of other kinds of civil case. What it does seem likely to do is to encourage plaintiff lawyers to do more research and case preparation before invoking the formal system and then to use the stricter timetable to force the pace on defendants in a way that has not previously occurred. The results may well disturb the parties' present understandings of equity and humanity.

## WHOSE INTERESTS DOES WOOLF SERVE?

Like any reform proposal, Lord Woolf's package seems likely to create both winners and losers. We have tried to give some idea of the possible pay-off matrix in our discussion and to encourage a sense of scepticism about some of the claims in the report. However, we should not conclude without underlining what is, in sociological terms, one of the most striking features of the report and that is its judge-centredness. The only clear winners from the reform are the judiciary. Judicial time *is* privileged.[48] If everything goes according to plan, judges will acquire a whole new raft of powers

[46] Woolf p. 49. [47] See note 17. [48] Woolf p. 223, Recommendation 1.

and authority to control parties rather than being at their beck and call. This will be particularly true for District Judges. All judges will get a more predictable working week with fewer of the frustrations of unstable and ever-changing lists as cases settle at the door of the court or are switched around at the last minute to fill up their time. More business is done on paper or through communication technology which also increases their ability to manage their time. Arguably, a more demand-led approach will also require some increase in judicial numbers, although this may come from a decline in family business if mediation takes a larger share there.[49]

This observation is not made in any spirit of malice or any imputation of conspiracy. If you ask a judge to write a report of this kind, there is a fair chance that the recommendations will be judge-centred. In the same way, if you commission an academic, they will usually call for more research! But it does present a problem for reforming a *system*. If this is going to succeed then it needs to take account of all of the interests involved. We have focused on personal injury cases. Victims want compensation as quickly as possible, but they also want procedural justice and respect. Insurance companies have a duty to their shareholders to test claims. There is an inherent conflict here. Victims will always claim that a civil justice system is too slow because no-one will write them a blank cheque on demand and punish the tortfeasor as a criminal. Insurers will always need to show their auditors that they have given proper time and consideration to the settlement or rejection of a claim. For victims, their injury is very personal, very important and an absolute priority. For insurers it is one of an array of cases to be dealt with as organizational time and resources permit and to be ranked in a way that gives some priority over others. Lawyers with their own agendas stand in the middle, trying to produce a reconciliation of these conflicting time management pressures. Plaintiff lawyers know that part of their role is to reflect their clients' complaints. At the same time, they recognize the dilemmas of their opponents and the need to give them 'reasonable space' to deal with their clients' concerns. Court control risks claiming more than it can deliver without fundamentally disrupting this equilibrium in a way that would undermine the legitimacy of the system.

This may not be too much of a problem unless it is believed that there are fundamental constitutional reasons why the state should be involved in civil disputes. There are other possibilities. In California, firms needing authoritative claim settlements have opted for a system of private judges. These fora take cases from the overburdened civil justice system, and are usually settled in a fraction of the time (and costs) of a public trial. In order

[49] Although there is no solid evidence that this will happen. It may be as plausible to propose that divorce mediation will extend intervention in cases that currently settle leaving those few that do get to trial essentially untouched.

to save time and money, many credit card companies require card holders to agree in advance to settle claims in a private mediation system.[50] Perhaps the insurance industry should set up its own private tribunal or arbitration scheme and bind claimants into that through the terms of the policies they write. However, Lord Woolf clearly rejects this view: 'A system of civil justice is essential to the maintenance of a civilised society'.[51] If this is the case, then it is important to acknowledge that the legitimacy of the system may be undermined just as much by perceived inequity or inhumanity as by perceived inefficiency. There is a small but definite risk that some aspects of these reforms will disrupt the crude balance of dissatisfactions on which the present arrangements rest.

We may need rather more creative thinking. The real lessons are to be found in the sociology of organizations rather than in the textbooks on legal procedures. Rule changes may have a symbolic function, both for the public and for those involved in the system. However, effective change is likely to require an understanding of why the system is organized as it is and the involvement of the various actors affected by its reconstruction. It is not the case that nothing can be done. However, we may make more progress by encouraging some local initiatives and studying them carefully than by going for a Big Bang across the whole country. We need to get the user community more closely linked to the reform project and driving it forward with their own ideas. At the very least, we need to pay very careful attention to the extensive, well-documented and generally dismal record of our US cousins in achieving court reform. This experience will not necessarily translate directly to the UK but it may help us to ask the right questions and to set the right level of expectations.

[50] Woolf explores this briefly in recommendations 62–65, pps 227–228.
[51] Woolf p. 2.

# 20

# *Access to Just Settlements: The Case of Medical Negligence*

HAZEL GENN*

## ACCESS TO JUSTICE AND THE INFORMATION BLACK HOLE

Debates about access to justice in the past have tended to focus on the extent to which citizens with 'legal problems' have been able to secure necessary legal advice and services in order to pursue or defend cases in the courts. The worry has been that many of those experiencing such 'legal problems' were failing to secure appropriate advice and representation and thus the opportunity of gaining the legal remedies to which they might be entitled. Empirical investigations into this phenomenon have identified the types of problems for which there was an unmet need, and attributed failure to secure legal advice—variously—to lack of legal sophistication, ignorance, lack of funds, social organization, and lack of legal advisers willing to deal with certain kinds of legal problems.[1] Interest in access to justice issues in the UK flourished during the 1960s and 1970s and after a period of relative quiet we now find academic and other researchers rediscovering the conundrums of civil justice. Perhaps for the first time, in recent history at least, there seems to be a publicly expressed congruence of concern among scholars, legal professionals, policy makers, consumers of legal services and their pressure groups about perceived deficiencies in the civil justice system.

Although arguments about what the civil justice system lacks and needs are frequently given an 'access to justice' label to lend greater weight to the various interests being promoted, the contentions are astonishingly contradictory and diverse. 'Access to justice', depending on what you are currently reading, requires unlimited legal aid; it requires cheaper legal costs; it requires opening up the market for legal services; it requires maintaining a monopoly over legal services; it requires the provision of alternative dispute

* Professor of Socio-Legal Studies, University College, London.

[1] See for example the research conducted by the *Royal Commission on Legal Services* 1979 London: HMSO, Cmnd 7648 and the study by B. Abel-Smith, M. Zander and R. Brook, 1973 *Legal Problems and the Citizen*, London:Heinemann.

resolution systems; it requires slick and streamlined expert courts where international business can resolve disagreements; it requires the provision of legitimate and authoritative judicial decision-making that operates under fair procedures; it requires simple adjudication systems that litigants can operate themselves; it requires a system in which an individual citizen can take on the might of the state in order to challenge decisions and assert legal rights; it requires a system offering the procedures and quality of decision-making that the tax-payer can afford. In the end it means everything and perhaps nothing.

'Access to justice' is an elusive concept. The ability or willingness to secure legal or para-legal advice in order to initiate or defend a claim in a court does not, of itself, ensure effective access to justice; it is only the beginning of the process. Effective access to *just outcomes* requires that litigants be able to make full use of the law and legal institutions; and that the outcome of disputes and claims should be determined by the merits of the arguments of the parties, and not by inequalities of wealth, power or experience. There are thus two important aspects to the concept of access to just outcomes—the ability to gain *entry* to the legal system, if that is what is desired, and the ability effectively to promote or defend a claim to the extent that the outcome reflects merits, rather than differential resources of the parties. A civil justice system which seeks to promote equal access to just outcomes requires procedures which maximise opportunities for entry to the system and offers procedures that minimise the effects of resource inequalities on outcomes.

Discussion about access to justice and the 'need' for legal advice and representation in the resolution of disputes has not often been supported by empirical information about the transformative processes by which citizens decide to pursue or eschew legal recourse for the issues and problems that face them; nor has it allowed itself to become bogged down in theoretical debate about the role of law in society. Arguments about why we embrace the concept of equal access to the courts are often framed in generalities relating to democratic or constitutional principles that citizens should be able to enforce their legal rights. Lord Woolf quotes with approval the statement by Lord Diplock in *Bremer v South India Shipping Corporation Ltd* (1981) AC 909, 917 that 'Every civilized system of government requires that the state should make available to all its citizens a means for the just and peaceful settlement of disputes between them as to their respective legal rights. The means provided are courts of justice to which every citizen has a constitutional right of access in the role of plaintiff'.[2] As a broad starting principle this is the sort of statement that is likely to invite little dissent, but more

[2] Lord Woolf (1995) *Access to Justice: Interim Report to the Lord Chancellor on the Civil Justice System in England and Wales*, London, Lord Chancellor's Department. Cited hereafter as 'Woolf'. Page 3.

searching fundamental questions about the nature of the civil justice system that we have constructed to achieve this aim are not routinely asked by the policy makers who determine the broad structure of the system; by the judges and lawyers who guard the minutiae of court activity; nor apparently by taxpayers who bank-roll the court system and legal aid. What is the civil justice system for? Who is the civil justice system for? Whose interests and values does it protect? There has been a dearth of discussion about these questions at a theoretical level, and equally importantly, there is a black hole where factual information that might inform such debate should be.

We have little reliable data about how the civil justice system operates from the perspective of users and potential users of courts and legal services. We have no large-scale information about variations in response to grievances and legal problems between individuals and groups or in relation to different types of legal problem or cause of action. There is an urgent need to understand the social, institutional, financial and psychological factors that lead individuals, businesses and institutions to litigate. What do litigants hope to achieve and to what extent does the process and outcome meet those objectives? We also know little about the kind of system that potential litigants might devise for themselves were they given the opportunity to visualise an ideal dispute resolution system. Some recent evidence suggests that the majority would favour almost any form of informal adjudication over court proceedings[3] and we know that, historically, commercial litigants with the resources to choose their dispute resolution forum have opted for less formal systems of arbitration rather than resolution through the ordinary courts.

Equally important and equally unasked are questions relating to what people do when they *do not* litigate. Why do some citizens just 'lump it' when they have a notionally 'legal' problem[4] and does it matter if they do? What kinds of solutions do consumers, businessmen, landlords, tenants, neighbours, or accident victims adopt when they cannot gain, or do not wish to gain access to the courts? What, if any, are the financial, social and psychic costs caused by denial of access to the courts? At what point does improving access to the courts elevate the social importance of lawyers and judges to an undesirable level? What causes the greater strain on social relationships and economic dynamism: denial of access to the courts or rampant litigiousness? If both are undesirable, how do we establish the optimum level of legal activity and how do we work towards that end?

These questions cannot be answered on the basis of anecdote or reflection, but require the collection and analysis of systematic empirical

[3] National Consumer Council Survey *Civil Law and the Public*. Based on questions asked of a nationally representative sample during an omnibus survey.

[4] See W. Felstiner, R. Abel, and A. Sarat, 'The Emergence and Transformation of Disputes: Naming, Blaming, Claiming . . .' 1980–81 *Law and Society Review* 15: 631–654.

data on a scale that has not so far been attempted in this country in the civil justice field.[5] All that we have to go on in considering these important questions are the 'war stories' of interested parties and fragments of information about particular corners of civil litigation, collected largely as a result of the idiosyncratic preoccupations of academic researchers.[6] Occasional flashes of interest in funding research into civil justice by the Lord Chancellor's Department[7] have fallen far short of a sustained programme of research although there is evidence of a renewed interest in gathering more systematic information.[8] Without a clearer understanding of litigants' objectives in using the formal legal system to seek remedies, to resolve disputes, or simply to gain acknowledgement of grievances, it is difficult to divine exactly what kinds of changes are desirable and likely to be effective in meeting these objectives. Further, without an understanding of how the current litigation system works, it is difficult to embark on piecemeal changes that are certain to improve its operation.

## COSTS, DELAY AND PROCEDURES

Despite this lack of knowledge about what exactly people want from the civil justice system there seems to be some degree of consensus about what

[5] The lack of information about the civil justice system, in comparison with the criminal justice system, is by no means a local problem. Writing in 1992 about the presumed litigation explosion in North America one commentator remarked: 'Data on the litigation system's behaviour are meager. Even the most complete data on federal and state court activity fall far short of answering the most pressing and fundamental questions about the performance of the litigation system . . . The lack of data on the civil justice system provides a striking contrast to the criminal justice system. . . . A lack of evidence, which might seem like an insuperable barrier, has barely slowed many policy-makers, scholars and other commentators. Their discussions about the behaviour of the tort liability system often have proceeded without even assembling the fragments that do exist, much less pausing to figure out how they fit together. The result is a picture of the litigation system built of little more than imagination.' Michael J. Saks 'Do We Really Know Anything About the Behaviour of the Tort Litigation System—and Why Not?' *University of Pennsylvania Law Review* Vol 140, No 4, April 1992, 1147–1292, p. 1154. In similar vein, Deborah Hensler concludes that 'Without a program of sustained research on litigation behaviour and outcomes, we will be forced to rely on reading the tea leaves to assess trends in the civil justice system.' 1993 'Reading the Tort Litigation Tea Leaves: What's Going on in the Civil Liability System?' *The Justice System Journal Special Issue, Torts: Understanding the Patterns in the Courts*, Vol 16/2 1993, 139–154.

[6] See the comments in the Economic and Social Research Council's *Review of Socio-Legal Studies* and the bibliography. ESRC May 1994.

[7] A series of projects were funded in the late 1980's. J. Baldwin and S. Hill (1988) *The Operation of the Green Form Scheme in England and Wales,* London: Lord Chancellor's Department; H. Genn and Y. Genn (1989) *The Effectiveness of Representation at Tribunals,* London: Lord Chancellor's Department; M. Jones-Lee and A. Ogus (1990) 'Evaluating Alternative Dispute Resolution: Measuring the Impact of Family Conciliation on Costs', 53, *Modern Law Review*, 57.

[8] See the speech by Michael Malone-Lee, Deputy Secretary LCD, Sheffield University January 1995.

they *do not* want. The analysis of the shortcomings of the civil justice system as expounded by the Woolf Report are familiar: civil litigation is too complicated, takes too long and costs too much. The result is that those who might want to litigate are prevented from doing so because they cannot afford to litigate and those who do litigate are frustrated by the length of cases and the cost in human and financial terms in relation to the amount at stake. The report acknowledges that these complaints are not new and that previous royal commissions, reports and reviews have failed to alleviate these problems. The Woolf Report attributes this to the fact that previous recommendations for reform have been only partially implemented. The report may be right, but it is likely that the inability to achieve even temporary, let alone lasting improvements, stems from an imperfect understanding of the way that the system *as a system* operates, its use by its various clients and guardians, the incentives built into the system, and the ways in which these incentives create an imperative for clients and guardians of the system to adapt creatively to changes in procedure.

The report isolates cost, delay and procedural complexity as the major complaints about the civil justice system but the interaction of these factors is likely to vary in different types of cases, with different configurations of parties having differential resources. While accepting the complaint that the cost of litigating is too high, in the absence of reliable information the report cannot analyse in any detailed why or how this occurs. The message conveyed is that costs are related, in unspecified ways, to procedures, to delay and more specifically, to the behaviour of the legal profession. *The nature and difficulty of the substantive law does not appear to have been considered.* The approach of the report to the activities of practitioners is interesting. Practitioners, are, according to the report, dilatory ('Litigants and their lawyers need to have imposed upon them an obligation to prosecute and defend their proceedings with efficiency and despatch'[9]); wantonly impervious to the higher principles of the legal system ('the litigation process is too often seen as a battlefield where no rules apply. In this environment, questions of expense, delay, compromise and fairness may have only low priority'[10]); uncontrollably aggressive ('the conduct, pace and extent of litigation are left almost completely to the parties. There is no effective control of their worst excesses. Indeed, the complexity of the present rules facilitates the use of adversarial tactics and is considered by many to require it'[11]); and bent on subversion of the rules of court ('The powers of the courts have fallen behind the more sophisticated and aggressive tactics of some litigators . . . the main procedural tools for conducting litigation efficiently have each become subverted from their proper purpose.'[12]).

[9] Woolf Report para. 7(b), page 5.

[10] Ibid. para. 4, page 7.

[11] Ibid. para. 6, page 7.

[12] Ibid. para. 7 page 8.

While these observations about the activities of lawyers may be justified, they do not, in themselves, constitute an explanation.

If litigation costs in general are unacceptably high, this has less to do with charging rates than with levels of activity. For run-of-the-mill litigation, the hourly rates of London suburban general practitioners are comparable with those of the average London suburban plumber. As the report notes, high absolute costs are the result of the *amount* of work that practitioners do for their clients. Litigation procedures determine what practitioners can or should legitimately do in pressing or defending a client's claim. Whether a practitioner is forced to engage in interlocutory skirmishes by the intransigence of an opponent, or whether he believes that adversarial tactics are the most likely route to a good outcome for his client, or whether the client himself wants an aggressive approach to be taken, the effect on costs will be similar. A question that requires sustained consideration but that is dodged by the report is at what point does a lawyer go beyond doing the best for his client and enter the zone of excessive adversarialism; and who is qualified to make that judgement? These issues are difficult and require closer attention from both a practical and ethical perspective than that given in Lord Woolf's report. Indeed, the report avoids direct engagement with these questions in favour of a running undercurrent of censure in relation to the activities of practitioners.

## LITIGATING SETTLEMENTS

The assumption of the proposed reforms is that through the twin principles of judicial case control and simplification of the procedures that facilitate adversarialism, problems of cost and delay will resolve themselves—settlements will occur earlier. One of the themes of the report is that 'the philosophy of litigation should be primarily to encourage early settlement of disputes.'[13] The problem, however, resides in the means of promoting settlements. Attacking parties and their lawyers for the legitimate use of adversarial litigation tactics highlights the difficulty of achieving *just* settlements by means of court procedures. The rules of litigation are geared toward preparation for win or lose adjudication. They have not been designed to facilitate an efficient and relatively bloodless compromise between diametrically opposed positions. Will the new litigation 'tracks' and judicial managers adopt radically different rules designed primarily to promote settlement through bureaucratic case processing? Or might the new system simply represent a cut-down and speeded-up adversarial process which may exacerbate resource inequalities between the parties to the settlement process?

[13] Woolf Report para. 7(a) page 5.

There is great variety in civil litigation: different types of disputes, different types of parties, and different configurations of parties. As a result it is not easy to generalise about the dynamics of litigation or to propose a litigation system appropriate to all. An instructive snippet of information which reinforces this point comes from a small survey of satisfaction with the civil justice system among corporate clients.[14] Somewhat buried among the reported data showing widespread criticism of the length and complexity of the litigation process, frustration at delays and its implications for management time, there is one statistic which reveals that 77% of insurance companies, who are most frequently brought into the litigation system as defendants, expressed satisfaction with the current litigation system. This, up to a point, speaks for itself. It suggests that the current system is operating to the satisfaction of at least some defendants with deep-pockets. What represents a problem or barrier to one party presents an opportunity for another.

In order to illustrate some of the difficulties of achieving just settlements be means of litigation procedures the following sections contribute further fragments of empirical information relating to personal injury and medical negligence claims and consider the likely impact of some of the proposed reforms on the propensity to litigate, and the settlement process. Personal injury and medical negligence cases are important areas of civil litigation in which private individuals characteristically proceed against institutional defendants in order to secure compensation for injuries. The imbalance of experience and resources differentiates personal injury litigation from many other types of litigation. Medical negligence cases have the same characteristic imbalance between the protagonists, and in addition display some of the difficulties more commonly associated with construction or building disputes when complicated expert evidence is crucial to the outcome of the claim. Although the Woolf report does not view either personal injury or medical negligence claims as 'typical' of civil claims, they represent a large and rising class of all litigation in the Queen's Bench Division and the county courts.

## COSTS AS A BARRIER TO ACCESS

References to the cost of civil litigation in the report indicate that it is a problem in several ways. First, the prospect of high costs may deter potential litigants from pursuing a meritorious claim because they are unable or unwilling to risk the possibility that if they fail in their claim they may be responsible not only for their own legal costs, but that they will also be

[14] *Litigation Reform: The Client's Perspective* Herbert Smith, January 1995.

responsible for the costs of their opponent. In this sense, the potential cost of a claim acts as a barrier to access to justice. 'For individual litigants the unaffordable cost of litigation constitutes a denial of access to justice.'[15] For those who can afford to pay their costs, there is another concern that the cost of resolving disputes is too high, either in absolute terms or in relation to the amount of money at stake in the claim. This is not a complaint about access but simply a complaint about the cost of legal services. A further effect of costs rules, together with the cost of legal services not addressed explicitly in the report, is its influence on the outcome of claims. This section considers the way in which fear of costs prevents entry into the legal system. The following section looks at the influence of differential resources on the outcome of claims.

The lack of up-to-date large-scale data concerning differential use of the legal system makes it impossible to quantify how many people with what kinds of problems are prevented from using the legal system on grounds of cost. Those who experience some problem or difficulty and who have theoretically good grounds for bringing an action must go through a number of processes in order to find their way into the civil justice system. Our understanding of this process is somewhat better for personal injury and medical negligence cases than for other areas of dispute or claim since some empirical research into responses to these matters has been carried out. Evidence suggests that despite increases in the number of personal injury claims commenced in the courts over recent years, only a minority of those who suffer accidental injury, and an even smaller minority of patients who have suffered medical accidents, attempt to initiate a claim for compensation. The most reliable national evidence about claiming behaviour among victims of accidental injury comes from two sources. The Pearson Commission[16] estimated that about 11% of accident victims took steps towards making a claim for damages and about 6½% of accident victims succeeded in obtaining compensation through the tort system.[17] The Oxford national survey[18] found that of a national sample of injury victims, three-quarters did not even consider the question of attempting to claim compensation. About 1 in 3 road accident victims, 1 in 4 work accident victims and 1 in 50 of other accident victims sought legal advice about claiming damages for their injuries. Of the total sample of accident victims only 12% succeeded in obtaining compensation. Among those who had considered claiming compensation but failed to take any advice, fear of legal costs

[15] Woolf Report page 9.

[16] *Report of the Royal Commission on Civil Liability and Compensation for Personal Injury*, Cmnd 7054, 1978.

[17] Ibid. Vol 2. Table 14.

[18] D. R. Harris, M. Maclean, H. Genn, S. Lloyd-Bostock, P Fenn, P. Corfield and Y. Brittan, *Compensation and Support for Illness and Injury*, Oxford: Clarendon Press, 1984.

was the third most common reason given. Fear of costs was also given as a reason for abandoning claims once advice had been taken.[19]

In recent years there has been a rise in the number of medical negligence actions being commenced,[20] although the success rate for medical negligence cases appears to remain low at around 25 to 30 per cent.[21] The Pearson Commission estimated that in 1973 about 40% of all medical negligence claimants were successful in obtaining compensation. More recent and somewhat tentative research on medical negligence litigation by the Law Society[22] found that of a sample of cases in which advice had been sought about bringing a claim, 10% of cases were abandoned at the first interview; 43% of cases were abandoned after perusal of experts reports; 25% of cases settled and 3% went to trial. The overall success rate was 40%. In almost one-fifth of cases that went to trial (18%) the plaintiff lost.

What we do know, therefore, is that in the field of personal injury and medical negligence litigation, only a minority of those who might be entitled to seek a remedy through the legal system take any positive steps to do so.[23] Of those who do take steps to bring a claim the chances of succeeding in obtaining some sort of settlement are quite high among road, work and other accidents (the Oxford study found that 80% of those who sought legal advice obtained some damages, albeit small amounts); however, among those attempting to secure damages for injuries caused by medical negligence cases the majority of cases commenced fail.

Some evidence concerning the significance of legal costs as a barrier to access for victims of medical accidents comes from recent research into medical negligence litigation[24]. In a postal questionnaire sent to specialist plaintiff and defence solicitors the following question was asked: 'What would you say are the three most important difficulties for plaintiffs in succeeding with medical negligence claims?' The question was left open and among the responses provided by *plaintiffs'* solicitors (table 1 below) the most frequently mentioned difficulty faced by plaintiffs was that of

[19] Ibid. Table 2.12 page 72, and page 113.

[20] See P. Fenn and C. Whelan 'Medical Litigation: trends, causes, consequences' in R. Dingwall ed *Socio-Legal Aspects of Medical Practice*, Royal College of Physicians of London, 1989.

[21] Ibid.

[22] The study was carried out by Bill Cole of the Law Society's Research and Planning Unit. The sample was based on cases drawn from 23 firms who are members of the Association for Victims of Medical Accidents (AVMA) solicitors panel.

[23] Some more recent evidence on this issue comes from the National Consumer Council Survey *Civil Law and the Public* which suggests that among respondents who claimed to have experienced a serious dispute within three years of their interview over three-quarters (78%) sought help with the dispute although it is unclear what proportion of those went any further.

[24] The research, funded by the Nuffield Foundation, focused on medical negligence claims. Data were collected by means of interviews carried out with doctors, health authority managers, solicitors and barristers; and postal questionnaires sent to samples of doctors and lawyers.

Table 1. Plaintiff solicitors' responses to the question: 'What would you say are the three most important difficulties for plaintiffs in succeeding with medical negligence claims?'

| Plaintiffs' Solicitors Perceptions of Greatest Difficulties for Plaintiffs | % |
|---|---|
| Financing the claim/Costs of action | 25 |
| Getting good experts to advise | 18 |
| Obtaining all medical records | 16 |
| Standard of care/Liability issues | 14 |
| Causation problems | 10 |
| Finding a specialist solicitor/barrister | 8 |
| Lack of co-operation from defence side | 4 |
| Stress on plaintiffs | 2 |
| Length of cases | 1 |
| Prejudice of judges | 1 |

financing the claim. Among the answers given by defence solicitors (table 2 below) finance was the second most frequently cited difficulty.

The problems relating to the funding of actions raised on the postal questionnaires were reinforced in interviews conducted with barristers and solicitors acting for plaintiffs and defendants. For example:

If the client is not eligible for legal aid I seldom issue and serve proceedings no matter how strong the case is . . . Something needs to be done quickly about the fund-

Table 2. Defence Solicitors' responses to the question: 'What would you say are the three most important difficulties for plaintiffs in succeeding with medical negligence claims?'

| Defence Solicitors' Perceptions of Greatest Difficulties for Plaintiffs | % |
|---|---|
| Finding a Specialist/competent solicitor | 25 |
| Financing the claim/Costs of action | 21 |
| Getting good experts to advise | 21 |
| Standard of care/Liability issues | 14 |
| Causation problems | 14 |
| Stress on plaintiffs | 4 |

ing of medical negligence actions. Justice and access to the law is only available to those that are poor and eligible for legal aid funding or minors. [Plaintiffs solicitor]

The serious concern about the risk of costs in medical negligence litigation is supported by the Woolf Inquiry's own preliminary analysis of taxed costs in civil cases which shows that medical negligence cases tend to attract costs that are high in absolute terms and relative to other types of cases, and the costs are also high in relation to sums recovered.[25] In the present research on medical negligence litigation, the cause of the high level of costs was attributed by specialist solicitors and barristers to a number of factors. A common view expressed by those whom we interviewed and those who completed postal questionnaires was that medical negligence cases are *inherently* complicated and that this leads to the inevitable expense of claims. Whether or not the defendant in a medical negligence case will be liable to pay compensation hinges on the ability of the injured patient to establish blameworthy conduct as the cause of his injuries. Success depends on whether the plaintiff can prove, on the basis of records of treatment and on the basis of the weight of opinion of medical experts, that the action of the doctor failed to be 'in accordance with the practice accepted by a responsible body of medical men skilled in that particular art' [the *Bolam* test[26]]. The plaintiff will *fail* to establish negligence if the court is unable to choose between two alternative approaches to treatment.

Almost without exception solicitors and barristers acting for plaintiffs and defendants stated that medical negligence claims are more difficult to pursue than other types of personal injury litigation. The most important factors given for the difficulty of cases were: the need for legal advisers to be able to comprehend medical issues; the difficulty of establishing a causal link between the doctor's actions and the physical damage complained of; the difficulty of collecting the necessary documentary evidence from records; the legal standard that must be met in order to establish liability; the absolute dependence on expert evidence in order to prove negligence; the scientific complexity of evidence.

One plaintiff's solicitor summed up the problem as follows:

Far more work has to be done and money spent before a solicitor can realistically advise a client as to liability. This means the initial financial risks are far greater and more likely to discourage plaintiffs. Expert evidence is essential for liability and causation. This is expensive, complex and requires far more thought and background reading than any other personal injury claim. Experts can be difficult to find—the wrong one can prove an expensive waste of time. The legal practitioner must have some experience or learn as much as he/she can in relation to the specific medical area before he/she can read the medical notes meaningfully and make a preliminary decision as to whether to proceed.

[25] See Annex III to the Report, pages 251–260.

[26] *Bolam v Friern Hospital Management Committee* [1957] 2 All ER 118, [1957] 1 WLR 582.

Another provided a vivid illustration of the way in which questions of liability must be approached in practical terms:

Liability investigations are fantastically paper-heavy. You have to get hold of notes which are often extremely bulky. You are usually only provided with photocopies. It is difficult to photocopy medical notes, because they are often done in blue ink, which photocopies very badly. They are on lots of different sizes of bits of paper. Some of the test investigation results are nightmare things to copy. They are tiny little see-through slips, or weeny little computer printouts that look like the things you get from Sainsbury's, with very faint ink. Even a solicitor, relatively experienced in medico-legal work who is very familiar with the general appearance and general purport of most types of medical notes, is going to be in real difficulties determining which of these tiny, tiny little computer printouts is going to be the one that is the key to the case . . . Almost always the edges will have been cut off in the photocopying process obscuring the dates or times which are normally done in the left-hand margin. You will almost certainly have to spend a great deal of time insisting that the defendant's solicitors get the originals, go to the defendant's solicitor's office, with your set of photocopies on one side and the originals on the other, check each and every page of the photocopies that you have been provided with against the originals..Inevitably some pages will have been missed out. [Plaintiff solicitor]

If these accounts of litigation given by specialist lawyers are accepted, we are forced to conclude that the complexity of cases, the amount of investigation, the need for experts, and the difficulties of establishing liability in all but the most blatant cases of negligence, render medical negligence a very expensive area of litigation. The uncertainties about the ability to prove that a doctor has been negligent, and that the negligent action was the cause of the damage suffered, make litigation a risky business for plaintiffs. Unless plaintiffs qualify for legal aid or are so wealthy that they can contemplate the risk of costs of several thousands of pounds with equanimity, the likelihood that a claim will go beyond very preliminary investigations is unlikely. The result, in the view of lawyers for both plaintiffs and defence is that claims *with merit* are abandoned because victims cannot afford to finance the claim (table 3 below).

The recent research by the Law Society provides some support for these views. In the study of 376 closed medical negligence files 78% of the cases had been funded by legal aid, and all of the cases that went to trial were legally-aided (3% of the 376). *No cases funded on a pro-bono basis or by private funding progressed beyond sending for experts reports.* The success rates among cases that proceeded beyond experts reports was 80%. This suggests that among those that fall out because of fear of costs a proportion would have a good chance of achieving a settlement and having all or most of their costs met by the defendant. The evidence, however, suggests that the risk of costs, together with the inevitable uncertainty over liability in this difficult field is too great to be borne.

Table 3.

| | Often true | | Sometimes true | |
|---|---|---|---|---|
| | Plaintiffs' solicitors | Defence solicitors | Plaintiffs' solicitors | Defence solicitors |
| Victims of medical negligence have to abandon good claims because they cannot afford to finance the claim themselves | 64% | 33% | 37% | 67% |

For potential plaintiffs this represents an example of denial of access to justice. For the defence, however, it represents something different. It provides the basis for an approach to the handling of litigation that is designed to increase the chances of abandonment. Defendants in personal injury and medical negligence actions are not required to disprove their negligence. It is for the plaintiff to establish that the defendant was negligent, and inertia is a positive and useful defence strategy that capitalizes on the unassisted plaintiff's fear of legal costs in order to maximize the possibility of abandonment. The use of delay is part of that strategy and is discussed further below.

How will the Woolf proposals improve the situation of plaintiffs in medical negligence and other types of litigation who are effectively denied the opportunity of seeking a remedy because the ability to establish liability can never be rendered certain, and the risk of losing, no matter how remote, is too frightening to contemplate? The court-focused nature of the Woolf report does not specify how the proposed changes in procedure will improve access in terms of entry to the system and thus fails to address directly the problem of those who wish to bring a claim but do not proceed beyond a first consultation and, perhaps, the first request from their solicitor for money on account. The assumption must be that the allocation of some cases to a fast-track with capped and certain costs will reduce the open-ended liability that is so threatening to potential litigants, thus increasing the chance that a proportion of those who are currently deterred from proceeding with meritorious claims will persevere and ultimately succeed—at which point their costs will be met by the other side. If costs can genuinely be contained this proposal has much to commend it. However, for cases like medical negligence, and the more difficult personal injury cases, the proposed fast track procedure is declared to be inappropriate and thus unlikely to offer a solution. So long as the legal principles and practical proof of liability remain unchanged, and so long as the litigation is geared toward preparation for trial adjudication it is difficult to see how these problems of access are to be significantly improved .[27]

## ACCESS TO FAIR SETTLEMENTS

The vast majority of civil claims are settled without trial and in personal injury and medical negligence cases settlement is clearly the norm. The Oxford study found that 97% of successful personal injury cases had settled out of court. In the recent Law Commission study of damages payments in personal injury (including medical negligence) cases it was found that 94% of plaintiffs receiving between £5,000 and £20,000 in damages had settled their claim out of court, and among those who received over £20,000, some 91% had settled their claims out of court.[28]

Settlement is so pervasive that it has been argued that in civil litigation those cases that result in contested hearings are to be considered as deviant.[29] Therefore, when we talk about refining litigation procedures we are considering the procedures by which the parties move toward settlement rather than trial. The conduct of negotiations and the path to settlement are largely dictated by court procedures. There is no separate settlement procedure. Settlement is achieved by preparing for trial—going through the ritualistic procedures determined appropriate for adversarial contest in open court. Parties who want peace and want it on good terms have no alternative, within the context of adversarial court procedures, but to prepare for war. 'There are not two distinct processes, negotiation and litigation; there is a single process of disputing in the vicinity of official tribunals that we might call litigotiation, that is, the strategic pursuit of a settlement through mobilizing the court process.'[30] Once the parties are committed to litigation, there are no procedures that might facilitate creative outcomes or that might minimise conflict. Negotiation within the litigation context is 'fundamentally different from the negotiations that might occur over the purchase of a house or in the context of developing a political agreement'.[31] Indeed, if one were to devise a system in which disputes could be rapidly negotiated to a compromise leaving both parties reasonably content with

[27] It is possible that the introduction of conditional fees may help to alleviate access difficulties but there is always the danger that unless procedural changes render cases less risky, lengthy and expensive, solicitors may be reluctant to act on this basis or if they do the damages will be largely consumed by a costs uplift.

[28] *Personal Injury Compensation: How Much is Enough?*, Law Commission Report No. 225. 1994.

[29] H. M. Kritzer, *Let's Make a Deal*, University of Wisconsin Press, 1991.

[30] M. Galanter, 'Worlds of Deals: Using Negotiation to Teach about Legal Process.' *Journal of Legal Education* 1984, 34:268–276. Page 268.

[31] Kritzer 1991 op cit. Page 136.

the outcome, one would be highly unlikely to start with anything resembling the rules of court.

Studies of the settlement process in civil cases[32] suggest that the imbalance of experience and resources between individual one-shotter plaintiffs and repeat-player institutional defendants can work to the disadvantage of the plaintiff to the extent that plaintiffs may abandon claims or agree to settle their claims at a considerable discount. How and why does this occur and is it an invariable rule? The course of litigation is influenced by the legal rules that determine liability for the specific case, and by the nature of the evidence required in order to prove liability and the extent of damage. The eventual outcome of a claim will not, however, simply reflect the plaintiffs factual situation in relation to the legal rules. Strong cases do not exist, they must be constructed. The outcome of settlement negotiations reflects the resources that the parties can bring to bear in order to construct the necessary evidence to prove or refute liability. Outcomes reflect the differential ability to risk payment of legal costs, the experience and skill of the parties' representatives, and the differential ability to withstand the strain of uncertainty about the outcome. Outcomes also reflect differential responses to, and use of, delay.

## DELAY

The effects of delay are important in civil litigation. Delay occurs at different stages in the process and for various reasons. In personal injury and medical negligence cases, delay occurs before a plaintiff seeks legal advice; delay occurs while solicitors collect information; delay occurs while waiting for information from the opposing side; delay occurs while solicitors try to negotiate a settlement before the issue of proceedings;[33] delay occurs while the parties wait for experts to investigate and produce their reports; delays occur while the parties wait for counsel to draft pleadings; delays occur

[32] See for example, M. Galanter, 'Why the "Haves" Come Out Ahead: Speculations on the Limits of Legal Change.' 1974, *Law and Society Review* 9:95–160; H. Genn, *Hard Bargaining: Out of Court Settlement in Personal Injury Actions*, Oxford: Clarendon Press, 1988; R. Mnookin and L. Kornhauser, 'Bargaining in the Shadow of the Law: The Case of Divorce.' 1979, *Yale Law Journal* 88:950–997; S. Wheeler, *Reservation of Title Clauses—Impact and Implications*, Oxford: OUP, 1991; R. Ingleby, *Solicitors and Divorce*, Oxford: Clarendon, 1992.

[33] The Pearson Commission found that the longest delay in the progress of actions occurred between the date of injury and issuing a writ, with an average delay of 26 months. Pearson Commission, op cit. Table 147 p. 181. A recent study carried out by the Scottish Office similarly found that the greatest cause of delay in the pursuit of compensation was found to be the period between incurring the injury and raising court proceedings. 'A clear tendency to raise actions at the time bar was observed in all procedures with the exception of optional cases in the Court of Session and summary cause in the sheriff courts.' *Personal Injury Litigation in the Scottish Courts: A Descriptive Analysis*. The Scottish Office Central Research Unit, 1995.

while the parties seek and exchange documentary evidence; delays occur while the parties wait for a trial date. Delay is endemic in the procedures and is used as a weapon. The recent Law Society study of a sample of closed medical negligence cases[34] revealed that on average cases took 33 months to conclude (median 26.5 months). Some 20% of the cases in the sample lasted 4¼ years with 10% lasting 5 years or longer.

Personal injury litigation is an area in which both plaintiffs and defendants firmly place responsibility for delay at the door of their opponent.[35] In ordinary personal injury cases insurance companies will argue that delay is caused by inexperienced solicitors failing to progress claims. Plaintiffs' solicitors argue that delay is caused by insurance companies failing to respond to correspondence and by blanket denials of liability. In the course of our research on medical negligence litigation we looked at the issue of delay as it was experienced primarily by plaintiffs. The responses to interviews and questionnaires highlighted some of the distinctive features of medical negligence cases in relation to delay. For example, hospitals control vital information about the treatment of patients and can use a strategy of passive adversarialism to make investigation difficult for the plaintiff and to increase the plaintiff's costs. This strategy was noted and castigated by many plaintiffs' solicitors. For example:

Sometimes they will try and hang on to things which they would rather you did not see right at the outset. And the number of times where cases have come within days of trial and then magically a set of notes which the health authority solicitors have sworn blind didn't ever exist or they couldn't find, magically appear. This is a nightmare if you have presented your case on the basis of one set of information, your expert opinion, on one set of information. [Plaintiffs solicitor]

The effect of this strategy is to contribute to delay and to force plaintiffs' solicitors to mobilize interlocutory procedures in order to secure the information that they need. The experience of some solicitors at least is that in the past the courts have not been willing, or have not felt themselves able to intervene. For example:

Why do defendants put so many obstacles in the way of plaintiffs?. They have to be forced to provide basic documentation. They delay. They don't comply with the law. They don't do things until they have to. They don't disclose all the documents they are obliged to. They don't answer all the questions they are obliged to. The plaintiff has to keep going back time, time and time again to force defendants to comply with their obligations under the law and then when we try and force the pace and go to the court and get district judges to force the defendant to do it, they give them a bit of time . . . the biggest single obstacle, the biggest factor that causes delay, is defendants. They have all the information. The guy who has used the wrong knife knows better than anybody else what was done. Not the poor victim

[34] Cole op cit. [35] See for example, H. Genn *Hard Bargaining*, op cit.

who was under the anaesthetic. . . . Because we have an adversarial system it is easier for them to say it is up to plaintiffs to prove it. But they have investigated the claim against them and they should hold their hands up if they know how it happened. They are relying on the fear factor. The plaintiffs don't really want to have to go to court . . . and they are worried about costs. (Plaintiff solicitor)

A recent analysis of health authority closed claims files showed wide variations between authorities in the average duration of medical negligence claims from the date of initiation to the date of their resolution. The study found some evidence to suggest that a policy operated by one authority of speedy disclosure of relevant information to claimants was associated with an increased willingness among claimants to abandon unjustifiable claims. The author attaches a note of caution for defendants by indicating that it is unclear whether such a policy 'also weakens the bargaining position of the Trusts in justifiable claims.'[36]

## EXPERTS AND DELAY

Views expressed by solicitors and barristers in interviews also emphasised the way in which dependence on expert evidence in medical negligence claims, which derives from the substantive law, creates special difficulties of access and delay for injured plaintiffs. Expert evidence is crucial to the success of medical negligence claims. It is the experts who establish appropriate standards and thus determine whether or not a doctor is to be held liable.

Medical negligence is more difficult in a sense that you don't have a purely objective standard. You don't have a standard which the judge can assess through his own experience. It is not like driving. Though the judge is a driver of motor cars, he is not an obstetrician. He is not a neurosurgeon. The judge is very dependent upon the witnesses. [Barrister]

During our research lawyers frequently referred both to the importance of securing good quality experts and the difficulties involved in so doing. The concern expressed about expert evidence within the Woolf report is justified, but some of the criticisms levelled at the use of experts[37] understate the significance of their evidence to questions of liability in medical negligence cases and the practical difficulties faced by plaintiffs in achieving a just settlement of their claim.

Experts are expensive, they introduce significant delay into litigation and may be more willing to act for the defence than for plaintiffs. Among

[36] Paul Fenn, 'Long Tail Liabilities and Risk Management in the NHS', Unpublished paper presented at the Hart Legal Workshop on Liability, *Regulation and Risk Management*, Institute of Advanced Legal Studies, London July 1995.

[37] Woolf Report, para. 11, page 8.

plaintiffs' solicitors responding to our questionnaire, a majority (63%) reported that it was difficult to find expert witnesses to act for plaintiffs; even among defence solicitors one-fifth agreed that it was difficult for plaintiffs to secure good expert witnesses (see table 4 below).

Table 4.

| | Agree | | Disagree | |
|---|---|---|---|---|
| | Plaintiffs solicitors | Defence solicitors | Plaintiffs solicitors | Defence solicitors |
| It is difficult to find expert witnesses to act for plaintiffs in medical negligence cases | 63% | 22% | 17% | 44% |

The reluctance of eminent experts to act for plaintiffs was frequently commented upon by plaintiffs' lawyers. The following extract is typical:

There is a large number of solicitors chasing a small number of experts who are prepared to do the work. Some have got waiting lists that extend years ahead..It is difficult. I have got a case on at the moment concerning genetic counselling. Two or three people we approached either were taught by this particular chap or had worked with him and I think it is a psychological thing. They can't turn round and start criticising this chap. They say 'I learned everything I know from him. I have trained with him.' There are those that just won't do it on principle. (Plaintiff Solicitor)

The contention among plaintiffs' solicitors about the difficulty of securing good quality experts to act for plaintiffs was supported by interviews that we conducted with doctors. The following quotations from interviews illustrate the problem from the perspective of doctors:

I have been asked to, but I haven't done so, because I didn't want to . I didn't want to seem to be disloyal to my fellow practitioners. I don't like the idea. I dislike the idea a lot . . . I think that one is always reticent to be critical of another person's judgement. I think that very few caring people enter into such a situation lightly because 'There but for the grace of God etc.' I have made mistakes too and I've not had any litigation. I hope that it will never happen. It would be a dreadful experience psychologically. [Consultant]

I don't think anybody likes to do it [for plaintiffs] because there is always this feeling that 'There but for the grace of God go I', and everybody has had a near miss inevitably. That's life. [Consultant]

There are quite a number of doctors who will have nothing to do with it. They think it is a dirty business and won't have anything to do with it. [Consultant]

This is an important issue. The Woolf report is committed to reducing delay caused by the use of experts. One solution is to encourage the use of a wider pool of doctors to provide expert evidence. While reasonable in principle, the likely effect on the plaintiff's ability to secure a quality of expert advice that is equal to that available to defendants must be considered if the objective of achieving just results is not to be compromised. The need for equality in the standing and experience of medical experts derives not from any procedural rule, but from the way in which the requirements of the substantive law in medical negligence are operationalized in court. The following extract from an interview with a barrister specialising in medical negligence clearly illustrates the problem:

Defendants, with their financial resources, can draw on professional expertise categorised on their databases. So they go to focus in on the right expert at the right time with regard to the right issue. Imagine you are running a medical negligence action and you run it on one expert's report. He reports as to liability, and on a simple exchange of medical reports, you find two strong experts from the other side. How are they arguing? There are saying there is no liability and if there is liability there is no causation. Now in those circumstances the plaintiff would have to throw his hand in. So I don't run a medical negligence action unless I have *two reports* on liability before I go any further at all.

This approach could be regarded as excessive and wasteful and likely to generate delay. In the experience of the legal representative it is a strategy that is likely to achieve an outcome for his client that reflects the merits of the case in relation to the law. It is also a strategy that can rarely be afforded without legal aid.

## THE EFFECT OF DELAY

The recent study of compensated accident victims conducted by the Law Commission (which included victims of medical negligence) reported that many of the settlements received by injured plaintiffs had, after several years, proved inadequate compensation for past and future loss of earnings. The study also exposed high levels of dissatisfaction with the amounts received in settlement of claims. Many respondents attributed the inadequacy of settlements to the pressure they had been under at the time they settled their claim. Solicitors whom we interviewed about medical negligence litigation supplied a similar picture of the effect of delay on plaintiffs and the critical impact that it may have on decisions about whether or not to accept a settlement. For example:

There is a tremendous burden on the plaintiff to get himself prepared for trial. Twice last year on the first day of the trial, there hadn't been an offer or even a sniff of settlement at all, and about half an hour before they were due to start, when the barristers were robed up and everyone was slightly on edge, counsel wafted over and said 'I think we ought to have a word about this one.' And in that sort of atmosphere, where they are completely keyed-up, they then have to start thinking about and listening to advice about whether x-thousand pounds or x-thousand pounds plus is or is not a good settlement. It is *not* the ideal environment for calm reflection, for thinking about an offer, trying to weigh up the risks, because the litigation is so uncertain. I think it is very bad. (Plaintiff's Solicitor)

Protracted proceedings also take a toll on the healthcare professionals who are the subject of negligence allegations. Evidence from our interviews with doctors suggests that the emotional impact of being involved in litigation is substantial, particularly in cases which result in serious injury, where the doctor acknowledges that something went wrong, but does not feel that his actions were in any way blameworthy. Interview transcripts provide graphic evidence of the strain imposed on doctors and reveal frequent utilisation of 'torture' metaphors in describing the experience of litigation over several years.

A very long time ago as an SHO allegations were made about my treatment at an inquest, and that was followed up by the beginning stages of litigation . . . it actually came to nothing but I reckon I had about five or six years of unhappiness over that in which I would occasionally wake up at night worried about it, in which I would dwell on it . . . so that actually affected me badly even though I wasn't sued, merely the faintest hint of it. So I think it is devastating to anybody, and it shouldn't be but it is . . . It is an appalling experience for the plaintiffs I agree, but I think it is an appalling experience for the defendants as well and one of the reasons why it is appalling is that the whole blasted thing takes so long and it hangs over you, year after year, without resolution, which I think is terrible for both sides. (Consultant—paediatrics)

The Woolf report makes a compelling argument for reducing delay in litigation and points to a number of causes of delay. It is necessary, however, to understand the causes and function of delay in the negotiating process in different *types* of litigation[38] before it is possible to assess, with any degree of certainty, how procedural changes may affect the dynamics of those negotiations and with what impact on different sides of a dispute. Moreover, concentrating on controlling delay once proceedings have been issued is likely to do little to reduce the long periods of delay that occur *before* proceedings are issued.

[38] See the chapter by Dingwall and Durkin on the significance of delay in asbestos cases.

# 21

# *Access to Justice: Lessons from Tribunals*

ROY SAINSBURY* AND HAZEL GENN†

In this chapter we wish to raise the profile of administrative tribunals in the debate about how to improve access to justice. It is often not appreciated that far more people have dealings with tribunals than ever come before the courts. Our aim therefore, is to examine whether there are lessons for the courts from our knowledge of how tribunals have developed over many years, and of their performance as bulk providers of justice. In setting ourselves this task we are able to draw on an eclectic array of tribunals, some of which have existed in one form or another since the early years of this century (such as social security tribunals) while others are very recent arrivals (such as the Special Educational Needs Tribunal, established in 1993). Tribunals are not only diverse in their subject matter (including, for example, immigration, tax, housing, child support, meat hygiene, betting levies, plant and seed varieties, and crofters), they also vary in their constitutions, procedures, practices and organisation. In this country, tribunals mainly hear appeals of individuals against decisions made by government officials or agencies acting on behalf of the state. For example, Social Security Appeal Tribunals (SSATs) hear appeals from benefit claimants against the decisions of Benefits Agency officials, and Mental Health Review Tribunals hear the appeals of people diagnosed as mentally ill who are compulsorily detained in hospital. However, some tribunals consider disputes between private individuals or organisations. Industrial Tribunals, for example, hear cases brought against employers for, among other things, unfair dismissal or racial discrimination. In all, there are over 60 different tribunals under the jurisdiction of the Council on Tribunals.[1] A number of other bodies perform the duties of tribunals although they may not be

* Social Policy Research Unit, the University of York.

† Professor of Socio-Legal Studies, University College, London.

[1] The Council on Tribunals was created by the Tribunals and Inquiries Act 1958, to oversee the operation and performance of tribunals within its jurisdiction. It has no executive powers but through publication of its Annual Reports and occasional Special Reports seeks to promote and improve the standards of tribunals. In recent years there have been calls for the Council's role to be strengthened and expanded (see, for example, JUSTICE-All souls, 1988; Williams, 1990, Bradley, 1991).

called by that name and are not within the Council's remit.[2] Such diversity allows us to identify not only what might commend the tribunal model but also the various weaknesses which should be avoided in any further expansion or development of tribunals.

Our inquiry begins by looking at what the Woolf Report itself has to say about tribunals. As will be seen, this is relatively little compared with other forms of alternative dispute resolution. Next, we will summarise the deficiencies of the courts identified by Woolf (with which we agree) that need addressing. In the next two sections we set out some reasons why tribunals not only offer lessons for the way in which courts run their business, but also why they are suitable bodies for hearing some cases currently dealt with in the courts. First, we summarise briefly their history from controversial court-substitutes to the main dispensers of administrative justice. We will then draw out, in a critical way, the positive and negative features of tribunals (including the principles on which they work, how appellants commence cases, tribunal structures and organisation, the practices and procedures of tribunal hearings, and the time taken to clear cases). We will conclude with a discussion of why we think tribunals have more to offer than suggested in the Woolf Report. In particular, it appears to us that the Report has missed an opportunity to consider the merits of tribunals as alternatives to the courts, that is, of transferring some of the work of the courts to established tribunals or creating new tribunals to hear specific cases. The remainder of the chapter argues the case for, at least, considering this policy option seriously.

## WOOLF ON TRIBUNALS

In Chapter Two of his report, Lord Woolf sets out the background for his review of the rules and procedures of the civil courts. He writes:

> Throughout the common law world there is acute concern over the many problems which exist in the resolution of disputes by the civil courts. The problems are basically the same. They concern the processes leading to the decisions made by the courts, rather than the decisions themselves. The process is too expensive, too slow and too complex. It places many litigants at a considerable disadvantage when compared to their opponents. The result is inadequate access to justice and an inefficient and ineffective system. (p. 4)

Given this rationale for Lord Woolf's inquiry, it is no surprise that the vast majority of his report and its 124 recommendations are concerned primarily with the civil courts. However, if we take as the overriding concern

[2] For example, Housing Benefit Review Boards which hear appeals against the decisions of local authorities on claims for housing benefit. which do not come within the Council on Tribunals' jurisdiction.

access to justice *per se*, and not access to justice *through the courts*, a range of alternatives to the courts suggest themselves. Lord Woolf does not ignore these. In Chapter 18, 'Alternative approaches to dispensing justice', the relative merits of various forms of alternative dispute resolution (ADR) are considered: arbitration, mediation, mini-trials and the services provided by the range of Ombudsmen. While offering a (cautiously) enthusiastic view of ADR, Lord Woolf sees their role as options, independent of the court system, that the parties to a dispute can choose before, or after, court proceedings have been initiated. He is not in favour of making the use of ADR compulsory in any way, for example before court proceedings can be taken. Sitting rather uncomfortably amidst the discussion of ADR are administrative tribunals. Woolf is right in classing tribunals differently to the more familiar forms of ADR:

> Administrative tribunals are ultimately subordinate to the courts, and are not a form of ADR in the sense of an additional option available to the parties since their jurisdiction normally excludes that of the courts. (p. 137)

Having made this observation, Woolf provides no detailed analysis of the relative merits of tribunals (as he does for arbitration and mini-trials, for example), but instead observes briefly:

> Some aspects of tribunal procedure might . . . provide a useful model for the courts, despite criticisms of tribunals for developing an increasingly legalistic approach. (p. 145)

Mentioned specifically are the 'hands-on case management' of Industrial Tribunal cases, which facilitates a conciliated settlement through the offices of ACAS, the interventionist approach to the conduct of hearings, and the role of presenting officers at SSATs who have a responsibility to aid unrepresented appellants.[3] Although there are no recommendations in the Report which flow from this brief analysis, the themes of greater control over the business of the courts, more interventionist judges, and support for litigants in person are reflected in many of the Report's proposals.

As we mentioned in the introduction, this treatment of tribunals is limited. In the next section we look at the problems with the courts as identified in the Woolf Report. The purpose of this is to show how Woolf's own analysis could have led him to consider in more depth how tribunals might address some of these problems.

[3] While it is true that tribunals are used to dealing with unrepresented appellants, the primary means of doing this is not through presenting officers (as the Woolf Report implies) but through the standard practice of tribunal members, particularly the Chair. It is worth noting that citing the role of presenting officers as a positive feature of tribunals that courts could usefully learn from, is at odds with some recent research evidence. Wikeley and Young (1991) show that although there is a powerful rhetoric which emphasises the *amicus curiae* role of the presenting officer, they found that this role was only practised in fewer than one in five of the 337 hearings they observed in their wide-ranging research on SSATs.

## THE PROBLEMS WITH COURTS

We have already noted Lord Woolf's criticism of the civil justice system in this country as being 'too expensive, too slow and too complex' (p. 4). The unacceptable result of this is that ordinary citizens are effectively denied access to justice. The problems stem partly from the tradition that the conduct of civil litigation is above all, adversarial, which in turn breeds a damaging adversarial culture. As Woolf writes:

> In this environment, questions of expense, delay, compromise and fairness may have only low priority. The consequence is that expense is often excessive, disproportionate and unpredictable; and delay is frequently unreasonable. (p. 7)

While some groups of litigants may be eligible for legal aid, the recent limits on the legal aid budget is resulting in a decreasing number of successful applications. The effect of this is to increase the number of people who are obliged to represent themselves in court, that is, litigants in person.

Delays are endemic in the court system. Woolf himself cites the following woeful catalogue of statistics:

> In 1994, High Court cases on average took 163 weeks in London and 189 weeks elsewhere to progress from issue to trial. The great majority of this time was between issue and setting down: 123 weeks in London and 148 weeks elsewhere. (p. 13)

The comment that 'These figures are unacceptable in relation to the great generality of cases' (p. 13) seems, if anything, to be a gross understatement. The distress and disadvantage that litigants suffer during lengthy delays are compounded by the difficulties faced by the court (such as failing memories and untraceable witnesses). Even at the end of the process litigants may not receive their just deserts:

> (Delay) . . . postpones settlement but may lead parties to settle for inadequate compensation because they are worn down by delay or cannot afford to continue. (p. 12)

The complexity of court procedures, according to Woolf, 'impedes access to the courts and imposes an unnecessary burden upon the parties' (p. 15). Particularly disadvantaged are litigants in person. Woolf traces the current complexity to no less than seven different sources including the rules of court, inconsistent procedures between different courts, the variety of ways of initiating proceedings, and the obscure and uncertain nature of much substantive law.

One response, that favoured by Woolf, is to tackle these problems by various means without major alterations to the existing court structure and its jurisdictions. In our view, there are convincing reasons for considering whether some of the duties of the courts could be allocated elsewhere.

### THE CASE FOR ADMINISTRATIVE TRIBUNALS I: THEIR HISTORY AS COURT-SUBSTITUTES

The debate about the proper place of tribunals in the judicial system, and their appropriate relationship with the courts is not new. The source of the controversy, at least in modern times, can be traced to the early years of this century. In designing the Old Age Pensions Act of 1908, the Liberal Government's disenchantment with the courts as an efficient and effective means of dealing with the large number of appeals arising out of the Workmen's Compensation Act of 1897 had convinced them that an alternative means of dealing with appeals was necessary. Their eventual choice of local authorities to hear appeals was logical since these were responsible for the overall administration of old age pensions on behalf of central government. In devising the national insurance scheme, eventually enacted in the National Insurance Act 1911, the Liberal Government of Lloyd George, and in particular Winston Churchill, drew extensively on the social insurance policies of Bismarck in Germany. Still convinced that the courts were inappropriate for hearing appeals of this kind, the British Government also adopted the Bismarckian idea of the tribunal. Hence, dissatisfied unemployment insurance claimants could appeal against the decision of an insurance officer to a 'court of referees'. Although labelled 'courts', courts of referees were nothing of the sort. They comprised three members, a Chair appointed by the Board of Trade, one member from a panel representing local employers, and the final member from a workmen's panel. The National Insurance Act also established separate arrangements, through friendly societies and industrial insurance companies, for hearing appeals about national health insurance.

Thus, before the First World War, there were four established means of hearing appeals: the courts, local authorities, tribunals and private organisations. In the years following the War, however, the tribunal model, unlike the others, was extended into more and more areas of public law. War pensions, industrial relations, widows' pensions, and (in Scotland) local authority rents all had their own specialised tribunals by the mid-1920s. This 'flight from the courts', as Wraith and Hutchesson (1973, p. 37) have described it, contributed to the attack on the 'new despotism' of state bureaucracy by Lord Hewart in 1929. As a response to Hewart, the Government appointed the Donoughmore Committee on Ministers' Powers which reported in 1932. Though lacking in firm recommendations about the future of tribunals, the Donoughmore Report (1932) provided sufficient endorsement to ensure their continued existence and expansion.

In the years that followed Donoughmore, particularly during and just after the Second World War, new tribunals were created in the wake of the expanding role of the state in regulating commercial and social relations and in providing the welfare services recommended in the Beveridge Report. Of particular interest was the legislation which put workmen's compensation on a new footing, no longer based on an adversarial contest between worker and employer, but now part of the National Insurance scheme. Entitlement to compensation, in the form of lump-sum payments and pensions, was now based on meeting eligibility conditions relating to the nature of the claimant's accident at work and not dependent on establishing fault. Appeals, previously heard by the courts, were now entrusted to new tribunals (depending on the substance of the appeal), the National Insurance Local Tribunal and the Medical Appeal Tribunal. This change in policy towards compensation for injury at work therefore led to the first example of the transfer of a jurisdiction from the courts to tribunals.

Although the Donoughmore Report was important to the continued use and development of tribunals, the next major review of tribunals (and still the most recent) guaranteed their place in the judicial system of Britain. The Franks Committee on Administrative Tribunals and Inquiries was established in 1956 and reported in 1957. Building on the analysis of Donoughmore, Franks reiterated the positive attributes of tribunals: 'cheapness, accessibility, freedom from technicality, expedition and expert knowledge of their particular subject'.[4] However, to be acceptable as alternatives to courts, tribunals had also to incorporate some of the principles associated with court proceedings—'openness, fairness and impartiality'. Importantly, the Franks Report also recommended the creation of the Council on Tribunals, mentioned earlier, which has been a continuing force for the improvement in the organisation and standards of tribunals. The overall importance of Franks is neatly summarised by Wraith and Hutchesson:

> . . . the Report represents a watershed between a recent past when tribunals were regarded as unavoidable expedients and a future when they are coming to be accepted for what they really are—an important part of the judicial system of the country. (p. 42)

Although written over twenty years ago, this assessment has only been reinforced by the increasing use of tribunals in a wide variety of policy settings, allowing Sayers and Webb to observe more recently:

> Tribunals have been described as the success story of post-war civil procedure. (Sayers and Webb, 1990, p. 36)

[4] Franks Report, para.38.

Most of the expansion of the tribunal system has been either through the creation of new tribunals (such as Special Educational Needs Tribunals, in 1993, and Disability Appeal Tribunals, in 1992) or by extending the jurisdiction of existing tribunals (such as Industrial Tribunals into the areas of race and sex discrimination). Examples of where the jurisdiction of the courts has been transferred to tribunals are comparatively rare. Apart from the example of workmen's compensation described earlier, only the policy area of maintenance and child support shares similarities.

In 1992, in a major break with the past, the Government removed the task of deciding the level of maintenance payments from the courts and placed it with a new administrative agency of the Department of Social Security, the Child Support Agency (CSA). In preparing the Child Support Bill consideration was given to placing appeals against the decisions of CSA officials with the existing Social Security Appeal Tribunals (though this was not eventually adopted). However, the debate about the proper location of appeals ranged further than a consideration of SSATs. Reflecting the history of the child support provisions, there was considerable backing for giving aggrieved parties the right of appeal directly to the courts. However, the eventual outcome was the establishment of another new tribunal, the Child Support Appeal Tribunal.[5]

The examples of workmen's compensation and child support are important because they show how tribunals were chosen in preference to courts even though the courts had extensive experience in both areas. However, both of these changes took place in the context of major changes in how initial decisions were to be made (in both cases by a government department). There are no precedents for transferring a jurisdiction to tribunals in the absence of changes to the basic structure of initial decision making.

In this section, we have tried to show the extent to which tribunals have become an integral and essential part of the judicial system of this country. The sheer volume of cases handled by tribunals is ample testament to the indispensable role they play. We now turn our attention to the role and record of tribunals in an attempt to assess whether they have lived up to the expectations placed upon them.

## THE CASE FOR TRIBUNALS II: LIVING UP TO EXPECTATIONS?

As we have mentioned earlier, there is a huge diversity in the organisation, structure and practices of the sixty or so different tribunals in this country. This is both a help and a hindrance in arguing for their extension into

[5] Interestingly, in what appears to be a sop to the family law lobby, the Child Support Act gives the Lord Chancellor the power at any future date of transferring appeals back to the courts.

jurisdictions associated with the courts. While we can point to the positive attributes of some tribunals, there will be others who perform less well. Our argument is not that all tribunals perform well (see Genn, 1994), but that there is a model of tribunal that performs better than others and which holds the promise of high standards of decision making, and therefore, increases the probability that substantive justice is delivered to the parties to a dispute or appeal. In this section it is useful to think about the model of tribunals under five distinct headings: structure and organisation, gaining access to tribunals, practices and procedures in the tribunal hearing, clearance times, and finally, the principles of judicial decision making. The reason for setting out the characteristics of tribunals in this way is to demonstrate that many of the features that Woolf wishes to see in courts already exist in tribunals.

### Tribunal structures and organisation

Tribunal organisation covers a wide range. For example, some tribunals exist as separate entities within each of the 450 local authorities in the country, without any central organisation. In contrast, many of the larger tribunals are organised under a 'presidential' system. The essence of the presidential system, which has been endorsed and encouraged by the Council on Tribunals, is that the operation of a particular tribunal is entrusted to a President (of High Court Judge status) independently of the government department responsible for making initial decisions. Management of the throughput of cases, the recruitment and selection of tribunal members, training, and monitoring performance are all handled by the President and his staff. Presidential systems are in place for many of the larger, long-standing tribunals, for example, Industrial Tribunals, Immigration Tribunals, the Lands Tribunal, VAT Tribunals, the London Rent Assessment Panel, and the Independent Tribunal Service (which covers the range of social security tribunals and Vaccine Damage Tribunals). The Special Educational Needs Tribunal, established in 1993, has one of the newest presidential organisations, testifying to the continuing success of this model of organisation.[6]

The presidential system of organisation has proved itself to be a major contributor to improving the standards of tribunal practice and decision making, and of case management. It has also succeeded in establishing the independence from government departments of many tribunals.

[6] In contrast to the expansion of Presidential systems, the Department of Health recently rejected the idea of a Presidential organisation for Mental Health Review Tribunals on the grounds that it did not justify the necessary resources. This decision was heavily criticised by the Council on Tribunals in their Annual Report for 1993–94.

### Gaining access to tribunals

The title of Lord Woolf's inquiry is ambiguous. *Access to Justice* is primarily concerned with improving people's chances of achieving substantive justice for themselves. However, before they can even have a chance of success they must gain access to the justice system itself. For many would-be litigants this is an insuperable obstacle. Ignorance, apprehension, anxiety, and the unknown costs of proceeding may all deter people at the outset from instigating proceedings.

In contrast, gaining access to the tribunal system is less fraught with problems. Whether or not some form of representation is eventually sought, the individual appellant can usually set the tribunal process in motion by the simple means of writing to the organisation responsible for the decision which is the subject of appeal. In some cases a self-completion form is available. There is, therefore, no need to incur expenses in seeking representation or hiring a lawyer. Furthermore, there are no associated court costs, for example, a fee for commencing an action.

Of course, it is also possible for litigants in person to commence court proceedings at little or no cost to themselves (a practice which we have already noted is on the increase) but this is still the exception rather than, as it is for tribunals, the norm.

### Practices and procedures in tribunal hearings

The diversity of tribunals, in the substance of the cases they hear and in the parties that come before them, is reflected in the practices and procedures that they adopt. This is part of their strength. They are not hidebound by a single set of rules and procedures but can adopt a *modus operandi* appropriate to their needs. Hence, we see in Industrial Tribunals, procedures and practices which are similar in some ways to the formality of court proceedings (with swearing in of witnesses, for example, and the cross-examination of witnesses). In contrast, social security tribunals have informal procedures which allow, for example, the parties themselves to decide the order in which cases will be presented, and a dialogue to develop between the parties and the tribunal rather than formal statements followed by examination of witnesses. Also, most tribunals are unencumbered by strict rules of evidence or standing.

The role of the tribunal members is, intentionally, proactive. Members are encouraged in their training to be interventionist, to elicit the evidence they require and establish the facts of each case. This role is even more important where the appellant is unrepresented (the tribunal equivalent of the litigant in person). The operation of tribunals is premised not on a passive role permitting the facts of a case to emerge from the adversarial process of argument and counter-argument, but on an *inquisitorial* pursuit of the truth. Hence tribunal members receive training in techniques of questioning appellants, representatives and presenting officers which do not intimidate or alienate them.

It cannot be claimed that, in the hearing room, all semblance of the adversarial conflict has been eradicated. Some tribunals hear cases which are inherently conflictual (such as those involving unfair dismissal heard by Industrial Tribunals), and in others involving representatives of government departments, outmoded adversarial attitudes sometimes persist (Baldwin *et al.,* 1992). However, it probably is fair to claim that in most types of tribunal the atmosphere that Chairs and members try to establish is informal and non-adversarial.

## Getting cases cleared

Long drawn-out court cases are, of course, nothing new. As we mentioned earlier, Lord Woolf cited delays as one of the major deficiencies of the courts. Crude statistics will show that on average most types of tribunal dispose of cases much more quickly than courts. However, such a simplistic comparison obscures the reasons for delays in both systems and therefore, does not help in the search for solutions to the problem. Delays may be caused by any number of circumstances, alone or in combination. One of the most undesirable reasons for delays identified by Lord Woolf, is the deliberate manipulation of the court system by lawyers in order to avoid a case reaching a conclusion in court. The recommendations for wresting control of the management of cases from lawyers to the courts are, therefore, sensible and welcome.

One of the major determinants of how long cases take to clear, in courts and tribunals, is the substance of the dispute or appeal itself. Difficult and complex cases, whether they are the responsibility of courts, tribunals or anybody else, need time. However, it does seem that even when tribunals have to grapple with complex questions of fact or law, they are able to deal with these relatively swiftly.

The impact on clearance times of the amount of resources available to courts or tribunals is poorly understood. Clearly, with more judges and more court premises, or more tribunals and more tribunal premises, more cases could be cleared relatively quickly. However, there are characteristics of the tribunal model of organisation and adjudication that tend to promote shorter clearance times. These include: ease of access to a tribunal hearing, the absence of pre-trial proceedings such as pleadings and discovery, the rare need for lawyers (or other representatives) to be involved, and the active role played by tribunal administrative staff in getting cases listed.

Having said all this, perhaps one of the most successful means of reducing clearance times is the removal of the adversarial nature of a case. In many tribunal hearings the task of the members is to decide an appeal on the evidence that is presented to them and that they have elicited themselves. Their role is not to referee a contest between adversarial parties. Where the adversarial element can be largely removed from a hearing, we might expect cases to be cleared more quickly. Although there is no evidence available at present to make a valid comparison, we might expect that disputes over maintenance and child support will be resolved more quickly by Child Support Appeal Tribunals than previously by the courts.[7]

## Principles of judicial decision making

The quality of justice is an elusive concept. Although courts and tribunals operate within different sets of rules and procedures, they are essentially aiming to achieve the same result: a just decision. The methods by which they attempt to reach just decisions are essentially the same, that is, through the process of judicial decision making. Hence, tribunals, as much as courts, have procedures to elicit evidence from which the facts of the case are decided. The appropriate law is then applied to those facts and a decision reached.

To be able to claim that tribunals actually operate within a model of judicial decision making has perhaps only been possible for some tribunals within the relatively recent past. It is certainly true that in the past some tribunals attracted unenviable reputations for poor and inconsistent standards of procedures and decision making (Supplementary Benefit Appeal Tribunals, the predecessors of Social Security Appeal Tribunals, are an example; see Adler and Bradley, 1976). However, the introduction of Presidential systems, more full-time tribunal members, and better training, have rendered these criticisms obsolete for many tribunals.[8]

Because the quality of justice is an elusive concept it is also difficult to measure empirically. Although the decisions of the higher courts may be an indicator of quality in individual cases, they cannot be taken as an adequate general measure of standards of decision making in the lower courts. Similarly, the decisions of appellate bodies which hear appeals against the decisions of tribunals cannot be used as a direct measure of the quality of tribunal decision making. In the absence of any published material on the quality of decision making (a gap that indicates a pressing need for further research), we must rely for confidence on the quality of the people charged

[7] Child Support Appeal Tribunals were established in 1992, but by the end of 1993 had heard only 38 cases (Council on Tribunals, Annual Report 1993–94).

[8] Having said that, there are still tribunals which fall a long way short of the standards attained by the best, for example, Housing Benefit Review Boards, which significantly fall outside the jurisdiction of the Council on Tribunals (see Sainsbury and Eardley, 1992).

with making decisions and with the procedures they employ. In this respect, tribunals that operate rigorous selection procedures and have training and monitoring programmes in place, can, in the absence of any counter-evidence, claim to offer high standards of decision making.

In this section we have reviewed, within the great diversity of tribunals in this country, the structure and organisation of tribunals, how people gain access to tribunals, the practices and procedures used in tribunal hearings, clearance times, and finally, how tribunals adopt the principles of judicial decision making. By doing so, we hope to have demonstrated the relevance of tribunals in a discussion of access to justice.

The next section draws together our analysis to propose that the tribunal model has more to offer than the Woolf Report suggests, and, in moving from the general to the particular, identifies specific areas of law where the tribunal option might be most appropriate.

## A NEW ROLE FOR TRIBUNALS?

Despite the numerous attempts to deal with the deficiencies of the civil courts in this country,[9] the Woolf Report delivers a severe indictment of their lack of success. The expensive, slow and complex system, he writes,

> . . . places many litigants at a considerable disadvantage when compared to their opponents. The result is inadequate access to justice and an inefficient and ineffective system. (p. 4)

Later he observes more bluntly:

> Serious flaws still remain within our system of civil justice. (p. 5)

In many ways, the Woolf Report is a bold and imaginative attempt to improve access to justice. However, most of its recommendations are for changes within the existing structures and jurisdictions of a court system which has proved itself somehow impervious to many of the efforts to improve it. It is for this reason that we feel that, alongside the proposals that Woolf suggests, there is scope for a more radical experiment in improving access to justice through greater use of the tribunal system.

In proposing that tribunals could undertake some of the current jurisdictions of the civil courts, we are not suggesting that they are invariably superior to courts nor that courts are fatally flawed. There is clearly a need for a variety of institutional forums in which to hear disputes and challenges between private citizens, and between citizens and the state. However, within our jurisprudence there are no principles which guide or

[9] Woolf himself notes 60 reports in the last 150 years on aspects of civil procedure and the organisation of the courts (p.4).

dictate the allocation of decision-making powers between the various arms of the executive and judiciary. Hence, divisions of labour between the courts and tribunals have essentially been *ad hoc* and pragmatic.

As we have seen, in the examples of workmen's compensation and child support, some jurisdictions have passed from the courts to tribunals. However, in both these cases, as we noted earlier, the change in appellate arrangements was a concomitant of wider changes in how first-order decisions were to be made. Our analysis of the developments in tribunals over recent years now leads us to suggest a more radical role for them, that is in assuming some decision-making responsibilities currently held by the courts. Our reasons for suggesting this are that many of the things that Woolf is trying to achieve through his recommendations are already present within the tribunal system, as we have shown in the previous section (such as routine case management, an inquisitorial and interventionist approach in hearings, easy access, and very low costs to the parties). Also, one of the themes running through much of Woolf's analysis and recommendations is that many of the problems with courts stem from the adversarial nature of their proceedings and that what the court system requires, therefore, is a *change of culture* among the judiciary and legal practitioners. An adversarial culture and a system which gives control of the progress of cases to the parties, breed delays, high costs and complexity. In the pursuit of a successful outcome to a case, little or no consideration is given to the use of scarce court resources. As Woolf writes:

> If 'time and money are no object' was the right approach in the past, then it certainly is not today. The achievement of the right result needs to be balanced against the expenditure of the time and money needed to achieve that result. (p. 19)

Changing the culture of any enterprise is difficult and often slow, if it can be achieved at all. People attracted to, and proficient within, an adversarial culture may well find it difficult to adapt to a new culture, even if they are minded to. It is puzzling, therefore, that Woolf does not consider more fully the form of dispute resolution that seems to offer exactly the kind of culture that he wishes to see, that is, the tribunal system. Although we recognise that there will always be a need for a variety of appropriate means of resolving disputes, including courts and tribunals, we also see scope for a new role for tribunals in specific areas based on pragmatism or their particular expertise.

There are a number of important reasons why tribunals are a credible alternative to the ordinary courts. In addition to the greater accessibility of tribunals in terms of cost, speed and simplicity of procedures, tribunals are also distinct from most courts in another crucial respect: specialist expertise. Tribunals benefit from specialist expertise in two ways. First, full-time legal Chairs of tribunals are specialists in the subject-matter of the tribunal simply because they hear only the cases within that jurisdiction. The second way in which tribunals benefit from specialist expertise comes from the inclusion in many three-person tribunals of a member with special professional knowledge of the field in question. For example, Mental Health Review Tribunals comprise a legal Chair, a psychiatrist who conducts his own examination of the patient prior to the hearing, and a lay member; Disability Appeal Tribunals responsible for evaluating medical evidence include a doctor and a lay person. Within existing tribunals there are many examples of expert and specialist adjudicative bodies which dispose of cases by means of accessible and affordable procedures. This can be contrasted with the advantages of generalist courts. Within most courts, judges are required to be generalists and there is so far no system by which the allocation of judges within courts is related to prior experience in practice. As a result, judges are experts on the law in general, but may boast no special expertise in the subject matter of a dispute upon which they are called to adjudicate. Hearings that involve technical matters, therefore, depend heavily on the expert evidence that parties marshall themselves, and the nature and quality of expert evidence presented may be crucial to the outcome of hearings.

Those who are unfamiliar with the work of tribunals sometimes wrongly assume that tribunals' decision making has more in common with routine administrative decision making than with individualistic judicial evaluations of fact and law. In fact tribunal decision making conforms to the traditional model involving hearing, evaluating and weighing evidence, assessing the credibility of witnesses, and reaching accurate decisions in accordance with the relevant body of law and regulations. Procedures must conform with principles of natural justice and tribunal decisions are subject to appeal.

In reaching accurate, reasoned and consistent decisions, many tribunals (for example Social Security Appeals Tribunals and Special Commissioners of Income Tax) have sometimes to grapple with fiendishly complex regulations. Other tribunals, such as Industrial Tribunals and hearings before Immigration Adjudicators, work within a large and expanding body of reported case law.

Industrial Tribunals provide an example of the way in which the tribunal system has been able to deal with private law issues of some complexity. They are expert, they are required to adjudicate on matters of considerable importance affecting people's livelihood and reputation, and they are responsible for quantifying damages. Although Industrial Tribunals are more adversarial than some other tribunals, the pre-hearing procedures are much more straightforward than in the courts and hearings are more flexible with the tribunal taking an interventionist role. It is also the case that the majority of Industrial Tribunal cases are settled before they reach a hearing. Since legal aid has never been available for representation at Industrial Tribunal hearings[10], the training of Chairs and the procedures within tribunals have been directed toward facilitating the presentation of cases by litigants in person.

Some of the matters currently before the courts pose particular problems of access for potential litigants. Lord Woolf himself singles out personal injury litigation and medical negligence litigation as being areas that have inherent difficulties and demand specialist expertise. One might also add, for example, building disputes which may involve relatively small sums of money but raise substantial legal questions. These kinds of disputes frequently concern complicated liability issues, may involve difficult causation problems and may require elaborate calculations in order quantify damages. Expert evidence is routinely relied upon by the courts to assist decision making on all of these matters. Litigating these kinds of cases in the county courts and High Court is complicated, lengthy and expensive. It is not something that potential plaintiffs can consider without legal representation. Private individuals who are not eligible for legal aid and are not backed by a trade union, risk a great deal in commencing an action against an insurance company or a hospital. Even where liability seems relatively straightforward the plaintiffs are always faced with the possibility that if they lose in court or are forced to abandon the case they will be responsible for substantial legal costs.

The Woolf Report envisages that the problems of access posed by these kinds of disputes will be alleviated by the general thrust of reform which stresses simplification of procedural rules, greater judicial control of timetables, and allocation of low and 'moderate' value claims to a 'fast track' which would have a 'very straightforward and limited procedure' enabling the introduction of 'standard fixed costs'.[11] One of the problems with this solution is that the Report accepts that 'exceptionally complex cases would not be appropriate for disposal on the fast track' and leaves open the question of the extent to which access to justice for victims of medical negligence or complicated personal injuries will be improved.

It is arguable that these types of matters might genuinely benefit from a more radical approach: rather than tinkering with existing procedures these cases could be diverted from the courts. Tribunals, whose members have specialist legal skills, or medical or other professional expertise and which adopt interventionist procedures, could dispose of cases more swiftly, with less expenditure on independent expert evidence, and with lower hearing costs.

[10] However, the recent Green Paper on Legal Aid (Lord Chancellor's Department, 1995) contains proposals that might lead to legal aid becoming available in limited circumstances for tribunal hearings.

[11] Woolf Report, para. 23, p. 47.

Interestingly, the Woolf Report itself appears to envisage the possibility of diverting personal injury cases away from the courts, although the suggestion is framed as a warning to those within the profession who might be opposed to the capping of legal costs on the fast track. As a postscript to the proposals for including personal injury cases in the new fast track procedure, the Report argues that 'the status quo cannot be retained'. Unless the legal profession is able to work within new cost budgets 'more fundamental measures, possibly involving the removal of at least moderate-sized injury claims from the litigation system, would have to be envisaged'. If, as we suspect, this means diverting cases to tribunal-type forums, why should this possibility be retained merely as a threat to the legal profession? Perhaps it should considered actively as a potentially beneficial and radical departure.

## CONCLUSION

The main thrust of Lord Woolf's inquiry is to improve access to justice by reviewing the current rules and procedures of the civil courts (Woolf Report, Introduction). It is welcome, therefore, that these terms of reference have been interpreted widely enough to include other means of improving people's access to justice through, for example, alternative dispute resolution methods. However, tribunals seem to be something of a blind spot for Lord Woolf. His considered enthusiasm for alternative dispute resolution does not extend to tribunals. Perhaps this should not surprise us. In the JUSTICE-All Souls report on administrative justice (1988) the following paragraph appears:

> It was suggested to us that the technique of entrusting any newly created statutory jurisdiction to a tribunal rather than to the courts has become too prevalent. In particular the Law Reform Committee of the Senate of the Inns of Court forwarded to us the comments of Lord Justice Woolf (as he then was) in which he cogently argued that more selectivity should be exercised before disputes were taken away from the courts and remitted to a tribunal for determination. (p. 216)

It would be hard to argue against a counsel of caution in devolving responsibilities from the courts to tribunals. But in the light of the crisis in the civil justice system, it appears to make sense to consider seriously any opportunity for reducing the pressures on hard-pressed courts. It might not have been the intention in the Woolf Report to foreclose debate about expanding the role of tribunals, but that could be the effect of failing to consider the advantages and disadvantages of such a course of action. The Woolf inquiry may not be the forum to pursue the debate further, but to anyone concerned with improving access to justice for ordinary citizens disadvantaged by lack of detailed knowledge of the courts and by limited resources, we suggest that the tribunal model could form part of a wider strategy in pursuit of that laudable objective.

## BIBLIOGRAPHY

Adler M. and Bradley A. W., *Justice, Discretion and Poverty*, (Abingdon,1976).

Baldwin J., Wikeley, N. and Young, R., *Judging Social Security,* (Oxford, 1992).

Bradley, A.W., 'The Council on Tribunals: Time for a Broader Role?', *Public Law*, Spring (1991), 6–10.

Donoughmore Committee, *Report of the Committee on Ministers' Powers*, Cmd. 4060, (London, 1932).

Franks Report, *Report of the Committee on Administrative Tribunals and Inquiries* Cmnd. 218, (London, 1957).

Genn, H., 'Tribunal Review of Administrative Decision-Making', in Richardson, G. and Genn, H., (eds.) *Administrative Law and Government Action*, (Oxford, 1994).

JUSTICE-All Souls, *Administrative Justice. Some Necessary Reforms,* (Oxford, 1988).

Lord Chancellor's Department, *Legal Aid—Targeting Need*, Cm 2854, (London, 1995).

Sainsbury R. and Eardley, T., *Housing Benefit Reviews*, (London, 1992).

Sayers, M. and Webb, A., 'Franks Revisited: A Model of the Ideal Tribunal', *Civil Justice Quarterly*, 9 (1990), 36–50.

Wikeley, N. and Young, R., 'Presenting Officers in Social Security Tribunals: The Theory and Practice of the Curious *Amici*', *Journal of Law and Society*, 18 (1991), 464–474.

Williams, D.G.T., 'The Tribunal System—Its Future Control and Supervision', *Public Law,* 9 (1990), 27–35.

Woolf, LJ, *Access to Justice*, (London, 1995).

Wraith, R.E. and Hutchesson, P.G., *Administrative Tribunals*, (London, 1973).

# 22

# *Legal Expenses Insurance*

VIVIEN PRAIS*

Lord Woolf has identified the present excessive and unpredictable cost of litigation as being 'one of the most fundamental problems confronting the civil justice system'. His Interim Report contains proposals for a new 'fast track' procedure which will include fixed costs based on the value of the claim. The Report predicts that the new procedure 'will improve access to justice for those who at present cannot afford to litigate'. It goes on, as something of an afterthought, to express the hope that 'it should encourage the development of . . . legal expenses insurance'. It is understandable that Lord Woolf should be cautious in his approach. Previous high hopes for the expansion of legal expenses insurance ('LEI') as a means of funding access to justice and, in some quarters, as a partial substitute for Legal Aid, have been disappointed. However, the industry is now in a better position than for some years to respond to the challenge. Its prospects could be much improved by reform of the current legal system based upon a thorough understanding of all aspects of this potential source of funding. By assuming LEI to be peripheral to the current reforms, a unique opportunity may be missed. It would be particularly ironic in the context of the major role played by LEI in the German system, which is referred to as offering 'swift and inexpensive civil litigation' and which is clearly an inspiration for some of the major proposals in the Report.

Legal expenses insurance has been defined as 'payment of an annual premium to buy cover, in given categories of cases, for a claimant's legal costs (including any costs awarded against him), up to a limit of indemnity'.[1] (While this definition accords with the traditional nature and function of LEI, it has been criticised by some sections of the LEI industry, who prefer the definition in the annual report of the Insurance Ombudsman of 1993 which says 'this type of insurance cover is designed, essentially to ease the financial pain of litigation'.) Broadly, the purpose of taking out legal

* Member of the Law Department, London School of Economics and Political Science. Acknowledgement is due to the Nuffield Foundation for a Small Grant which made the comparative research for this essay possible.

[1] Lord Chancellor's Department *Review of the Financial Conditions for Legal Aid. Eligibility for Civil Legal Aid, A Consultation Paper.*(1991).

expenses insurance is to obtain reimbursement for all legal costs and expenses incurred by the insured in relation to a legal dispute, including the legal costs of an opponent which the insured may be ordered to pay. It bears a close resemblance to medical expenses insurance and, in some jurisdictions, has suffered from similar problems of lack of control over the services provided and the fees charged. Unlike medical expenses insurance, it has not so far attracted any tax incentives in the UK. The prospect of additional 'private' funding for access to justice has been viewed with favour by the Government and legal authorities, but encouragement for the growth of LEI has been limited to hope and exhortation.

## The history of legal expenses insurance

The origins of legal expenses insurance lie in France in the 19th century. In 1885 a society was formed called 'Prévoyance Judiciaire' to meet future legal expenses of its members incurred either in bringing or defending legal proceedings. This initiative was short lived but was followed by a similar project in 1897 called 'Sou Médical'. A few details of the latter venture are worth recounting as an illustration of the essential purpose of LEI in its inception. The society was called 'Sou Médical' because the subscription amounted to a *sou* per day and because its purpose was to pay for legal advice and defence of its medical practitioner members if they were sued as a consequence of their professional activities. Its creation was inspired by the misfortune of one, Dr Laporte, who attended a confinement which ended in the death of both mother and child. Dr Laporte was a man of limited means and was apparently imprisoned as a result of not being able to pay the expenses of defending the resulting legal suit. His colleagues made a collection which raised enough money to obtain his release and were inspired to form 'Sou Médical' to protect themselves against a similar misfortune. The association was unfortunately no more successful than 'Prévoyance Judiciaire'.[2]

The early attempts at legal expenses insurance probably foundered on the difficulties of calculating risks, and therefore premiums, correctly. This particular problem was easier to overcome in relation to motoring risks and with the advent of popular motoring at the end of the First World War, the Society 'Défense Automobile et Sportive' (DAS) was founded at Mans in France and met with lasting success.[3] The concept, together with the acronym DAS ('Deutscher Automobil Schutz'), was adopted in Germany in 1928 and its performance quickly surpassed that of its forerunner in France. One explanation proffered for the greater success of LEI in Germany than in France has been the early development in Germany of specialist LEI

[2] Cerveau, B. and Tribondeau, D. *L'Assurance de Protection Juridique. Argus* (Argus 1991).
[3] Rials, A. *L'Acces a la Justice*. (Presses Universitaires de France 1993).

companies.[4] This specialisation was required by German legislation and was aimed at the conflict of interest which was assumed to arise if LEI were added to insurance policies principally intended to cover other risks. German insurance companies embarked upon a vigorous campaigns of marketing LEI policies in the early 1950s (at a time when the legal aid scheme had just been established in the UK and was at its most comprehensive!).

## Legal expenses insurance in England and Wales

Legal obstacles to the payment of legal expenses by a third party contributed to the relatively late development of LEI in England and Wales, but these were largely overcome during the 1960s.[5] We heard an echo of the early legal obstacles in the recent case of *Giles* v *Thompson* (Times Law Report of 1 June 1993). The case concerned the activities of organisations offering, to those involved in motor accidents, the 'free' hire of a replacement vehicle and funding of their claim against the other party to the accident, in circumstances where the claimant was very likely to succeed in his claim. The practice was to some extent in competition with LEI insurers. They were also concerned that the companies involved in such activities might not be soundly based and they approved a challenge to the practice in the Courts. The grounds of the action were that it was champertous and unlawful. The House of Lords held that such arrangements were lawful on the grounds that the funders were not wantonly or officiously interfering in the litigation, and made their profits from the hiring of the cars and not from the litigation.

Companies offering LEI began to operate in the UK in the early 1970s. They included DAS with its experience of success in France and particularly in Germany. The industry has had a very chequered history in this country. It has faced 'adverse-selection' (only those who are litigious take out policies) which is particularly damaging in a small market, an insurance industry organised in a way which did not favour the marketing of LEI, and unpredictable legal costs. A number of companies lost heavily and withdrew from the market but over the last two years there has been a return to profitability, and considerable growth. There are currently five main legal expenses specialists (compared with 33 in Germany). These are CareAssist, DAS, Hambro, Legal Protection Group (LPG) and Lawclub Legal Protection. They belong to the Legal Expenses Insurance Committee of the Association of British Insurers (ABI) which also includes Provident Insurance plc, GESA Assistance and Octavian Syndicate Management Ltd. In addition to those major players there are a number of companies providing an 'uninsured loss recovery' service. It is estimated that there are now some 70–80 small uninsured loss recovery companies active in the UK market.

[4] Ibid.

[5] Miller, J., 'Legal Expenses Insurance', *Solicitors Journal* (1988) vol. 32 No. 17.

LEI policies are categorised by the insurance industry for marketing and statistical purposes as either 'personal' or 'commercial'. Personal policies may also be effected as 'group' policies i.e. policies marketed to affinity or other groups. The LEI companies are finding group sales an increasingly attractive option as they provide a means of minimising adverse selection.

'Personal' policies are again sub-divided into either:

(1) 'stand-alones' i.e. policies for LEI unconnected with other insurance.

'Stand-alone' policies have proved difficult to market and unprofitable in this country and currently only LPG is offering the product. A typical personal 'stand-alone' policy (from LPG) costs £209.86p for indemnity cover of up to £25K per claim (£250K aggregate) with 10% co-insurance. The policy is expressed as covering 'all-risks' but there are a number of exclusions including matrimonial disputes and defamation.

(2) 'add-ons' i.e. LEI annexed to another form of insurance usually household or motor insurance.

A typical household 'add-on' with an indemnity limit of £25K and an excess of £50 costs £12 to purchase and cover would include consumer disputes and personal injury claims.

A typical motor 'add-on' with an indemnity limit of £50K costs £10 to purchase and covers disputes relating to death and personal injury arising from motor accidents and uninsured loss recovery.

Insurers have contended with the difficult marketing conditions which they found in the UK by adjusting cover offered in accordance with their claims experience. It is not currently possible to obtain cover for matrimonial disputes or defamation and only very limited cover for building disputes e.g. it may be possible to obtain cover for a dispute relating to a fitted kitchen but not an extension. Insurers have in some cases dealt with the worst aspects of adverse selection by excluding cover in respect of disputes of which the insured 'is already aware' and also by introducing a waiting period in respect of certain specified risks e.g. 30 days between the date when the policy is taken out and when cover takes effect.

'Commercial' policies are intended for businesses and the cover offered is relevant to their needs. Premiums will depend on the business turnover and the size of the payroll. Average premiums vary from one LEI company to another. They range from £500 for cover of £100K per claim and no aggregate claim limit, to £2000 for cover of £50K with a £1m aggregate claim limit. Risks covered will vary but may include disputes relating to business contracts, employees, inland revenue and customs and excise investigations, and disputed debt recovery.

In addition to the cover described, some companies offer a 24 hour telephone advice service. Use of this service is normally a 'bonus' of the insurance policy, although some policies may require the service to be consulted in the early stages of a dispute as a condition of cover. In some cases the use of the advice service is available for a subscription (unconnected with insurance) to affinity or other groups.

Central to a proper appreciation of the current role and future potential of LEI is an understanding of the dichotomy which has developed under the umbrella term of 'legal expenses insurance', between those companies offering 'pure' insurance and those who see themselves as providers of legal services with the insurance premium acting as a form of 'retainer'. Diversification into providing legal services has been prompted by a mixture of frustration with the quality and costs of independent lawyers, and a regulatory environment permitting such competition with traditional legal advisers. This development is reflected in the definition of legal expenses insurance in the European Community Directive of 1987 (87/344/EEC of 22 June 1987). It is described as undertaking , against the payment of a premium, 'to bear the costs of legal proceedings and to provide other services, directly linked to insurance cover, in particular with a view to securing compensation for the loss, damage or injury suffered by the insured person, by settlement out of court or through civil or criminal proceedings, defending or representing the insured person in civil, criminal, administrative or other proceedings or in respect of any claim made agains him'. The membership of the ABI Legal Expenses Committee includes companies from across the spectrum. LPG sees itself essentially as a provider of legal services, whereas Lawclub Legal Protection refers all claims to outside lawyers, albeit to its own 'panel' of around 60 firms. DAS carries out some 'in-house' claims processing and also has a 'panel' for referrals.

Some limitation upon the discretion of companies in the organisation of their services has been imposed by the Insurance Companies (Legal Expenses Insurance) Regulations 1990 implementing the 1987 European Directive. Regulation 6(1) provides that where recourse is had to a lawyer to defend, represent or serve the insured's interest, the insured is free to choose the lawyer. There was some doubt as to the full effect of this regulation but the Insurance Ombudsman ruled in 1993 that the insured could not object to the use of the insurer's own in-house lawyer before the use of a lawyer became mandatory i.e. in court proceedings.

There are no official figures for the number of people in the UK who currently have legal expenses insurance, but surveys and insurance industry estimates give reliable guidance on the extent and performance of LEI in recent years. In 1991 a joint Consumers' Association/Law Society Report indicated that approximately 10 million people in Britain had some form of legal expenses cover, but only 7 per cent of those responding to the survey were aware that they had such insurance.[6] Activity during the period 1991–93 is shown in Table 1 compiled from data provided by the ABI. This

[6] The Law Society, *Legal Expenses Insurance in the UK: A Report by Consumers' Association and the Law Society* (1991).

Table 1. Legal Expenses Insurance Policies and Premiums (Annual average 1991–3)

| Policy Type | Number of Policies (millions) | Gross Premiums £m |
|---|---|---|
| Family | 6.1 | 15.2 |
| Motor | 6.5 | 37 |
| Commercial | 0.2 | 17.3 |
| Total | 12.8 | 69.5 |

is almost certainly an under-estimate as not all members of the ABI Legal Expenses Committee submitted returns. Figures are not yet available for 1994 but a reliable industry estimate puts the UK gross premium income for 1994 at around £110m.

Although there has recently been consolidation and growth in the UK market it has been much less than had been expected and hoped for in the 1980s. In an article in the Solicitor's Journal of 1988 on 'Legal Expenses Insurance'[7] it was reported that 'top men in the insurance field for legal costs are already speculating that the 'boom market' can raise premium income by the mid 90's to as much as £1.2–£1.5 billion'. While, in comparison with actual figures achieved, this may appear to have been an unrealistic ambition, when put in the context of LEI among some other European countries, such expansion appears less fanciful. (It is perhaps ironic that in reality it was legal aid expenditure in the UK which came closer to those projected figures, rising to £1,021 billion for 1993/4!)

## Legal expenses insurance in Europe

While LEI plays only a minor role in the funding of access to justice in the UK, much more significant progress has been made in some other European countries.

The Comité Européen des Assurances ('CEA') based in Paris receives annual reports from the members of its Legal Expenses Insurance Committee. The members include insurance organisations in Austria, Belgium, Denmark, France, Germany, Greece, Italy, Luxembourg, the Netherlands, Portugal, Spain, Switzerland, and the United Kingdom. Most of the constituent members submit details of the annual premium income arising from the sale of legal expenses insurance. The returns from some of those countries which have significant LEI markets and which make a useful comparison with the UK are shown in Table 2. Since the CEA relies on

[7] Miller, J. 'Legal Expenses Insurance'.

Table 2

| Country | Population[1] | Total £m | Per Capita £ | Annual Premium[3] income as a percentage of GDP (1993) | Legal Aid as a[4] percentage of GDP (1989) |
|---|---|---|---|---|---|
| Austria | 7,761,706 | 139 | 18.05 | 0.12 | |
| France | 56,556,000 | 344[5] | 6.08 | 0.04 | 0.002 |
| Germany | 78,500,000 | 1,621 | 20.64 | 0.15 | 0.02 |
| Netherlands | 15,010,000 | 99 | 6.59 | 0.07 | 0.04 |
| Switzerland | 6,712,000 | 73 | 10.87 | 0.05 | |
| UK | 55,514,500 | 100[6] | 1.98 | 0.02 | 0.05 |

1 The Times Atlas of the World—1993 edn.
2 1993 National Reports of CEA—converted to sterling at average exchange rates for 1993.
3 OECD Main Economic Indicators—January 1995.
4 Cousins, M. (1994) 'The politics of legal aid'. Civil Justice Quarterly, 13 pp. 11–132.
5 CEA figures as qualified by French LEI industry.
6 LEI industry estimate.

individual members to make the returns and there are differences between the organisation of insurance markets in the various countries concerned, the figures may not be entirely reliable. However, even making allowance for substantial margins of error, the differences between the premium income generated by the LEI industry in the UK and the European countries listed are still very striking.

## The German experience

The most notable feature of the figures in Table 2 is that the annual premium income, both total and per capita is far higher for Germany than for any other country. Legal expenses insurance in Germany appears to have been a remarkable success story; for the insured, who thereby secure access to justice at a relatively modest cost, for their lawyers who have a reliable source of fees and for the insurance companies who have made healthy profits. Around 50 per cent of the population has LEI. Almost all policies are 'stand-alones' and a typical premium would be 374.80 DM (£162.73) with an excess of 200DM (£86.95), for comprehensive cover including consumer and property disputes (including landlord and tenant) and even matrimonial disputes. When the insured has a legal problem he goes straight to the lawyer of his own choice, whose fees are paid by the insurers. The insured's own lawyer decides on the merits of the case and the chances of the success of litigation (this may now be changing).

The very success of LEI in Germany gave rise to concern. It was generally believed that it was causing a flood of unmeritorious litigation. The concern was such that a 5 year research project was financed by the German Ministry of Justice and carried out under the auspices of the University of Giessen. The terms of reference were to consider the effect of LEI on the behaviour of insured people when faced with a dispute, on the way in which lawyers treat an 'insured' case and on the number of cases that go to court. The research is significant in relation to the Woolf report. It not only highlights the very different problems faced by the German and English legal systems—Woolf is primarily about 'inadequate access to justice' and the German investigation about a 'Prozesslawine' (avalanche of litigation)- but the results confirm that LEI is an important factor in obtaining access to justice, and not a means of indulging in unnecessary litigation. In a publication of 1994[8] based on the research, 'Rechtsschutzversicherung und Rechtsverfolgung', Professor W.Jagodzinski, Professor T. Raiser and Jurgen Riehl report on the results of the research project. In their introduction they refer to the concerns giving rise to the research project in the following terms: (translated from the German)

[8] Jogodzinski, H., Raiser, T. and Riehl, J. *Rechtschutzversicherung und Rechtsverfolgung*. (Bundesanzeiger, 1994).

If one asks the man on the street, or acquaintances and friends about the effect of legal expenses insurance, one usually receives the following answer: legal expenses insurance increases the willingness to consult lawyers and to initiate proceedings. This statement reflects a general experience; people use services which they receive free of charge without thinking very much about it. If one has paid an insurance premium one wishes to obtain some benefit from it. One goes more readily to the doctor and has expensive medicines prescribed without concern, if the costs are met by health insurance. The insurance companies also claim that they enable legal proceedings to be taken which would otherwise not be initiated.

The researchers go on to point out that the figures for insurance premium income of the insurance companies steadily increased between 1965 and 1991 from 200m DM (£90m) to over 3.5b. DM (£1.6b). At the same time the number of court cases increased until the middle of the Eighties. They add that it is therefore not surprising that judges and legal authorities claim that legal expenses insurance increases litigation, and that, 'Even lawyers, who should know best, are of the same view'.

The five year study included the analysis of 5,200 lawyers and court files and the questioning of around 800 lawyers. The results of that research confirmed the view that legal expenses insurance enabled the insured to issue proceedings more readily and to pursue those proceedings to judgment more tenaciously than if he did not have insurance. However, the influence of LEI as a negative element was found to have been overestimated. The increase in the numbers litigating as a result of being insured was shown to be only between 5 and 10 per cent. It was established that in civil law matters around 46 per cent of potential litigants who had insurance issued proceedings, whereas 33 per cent of those involved in similar disputes, but uninsured, did so. Between 5 and 8 per cent more litigants proceeded to judgment if they were insured than if they were not insured. Only 3 per cent more of those who were insured won their cases than those who were not insured.

The clearest differences between the insured and the uninsured were among those involved in motoring cases and small claims, but even in those areas the alleged increase in cases before the courts caused by legal expenses insurance was calculated to be no more than 6 per cent, The researchers suggested the following measures to counteract that proportion of the additional litigation attributable to legal expenses insurance:

1. Higher representation costs for lawyers and higher court fees.
2. Lower costs for initial advice from lawyers.
3. Stricter assessment of the chances of the success of an action before the insurers agree to pay.
4. An increase in the fees paid to lawyers for out of court settlements.
5. Greater care by the authorities in bringing charges for minor

motoring offences (where defendants were acquitted in about 30 per cent of those cases defended).

The insurers' associations have made some moves themselves as a result of the research report. They have recommended that their members should require a report from an independent lawyer upon the chances of success of cases financed by insurance funds (previously the insured's own lawyer made that decision). They also suggest that insurance cover should exclude very minor infringements of traffic regulations.

The reason for the outstanding success of LEI in Germany is composed of a combination of predisposing factors. Those most frequently quoted are:

1. The legal requirement that LEI could be provided only by specialist insurance companies
2. A vigorous marketing campaign in the 1950s and a channel of distribution favouring the development of LEI
3. Predictable legal costs fixed by scales and related to the amount of the claim

Legal expenses insurance has been a feature of the German legal system for so long that it is difficult to say with any certainty which features of the system favour the growth of LEI and which have been maintained because of the existence of LEI. The system of scale costs for litigation is cited as being an important factor in the predictability of costs and favourable to the growth of an LEI market. This is undoubtedly true, but it may equally be the case that the existence of a reliable source of funding for litigation makes the lawyers more amenable to scale costs and litigants less critical of those costs. Another feature of the German system favouring a profitable LEI market has been the tradition of 5 year insurance contracts (c.f. the usual annual contracts in the UK).

Less frequently cited, but perhaps even more important to the development of LEI, has been the environment of strict regulation of both the German insurance industry and the legal profession. The effect on insurance companies in promoting specialisation has already been noted; the position of the legal profession may have been even more significant. The scale costs referred to above are calculated as a percentage of the disputed amount; a lawyer is entitled to one fee for pre-trial work, a second fee for hearings, a third fee for assisting with evidence and a fourth fee for attempting a settlement. This system is thought to place emphasis on getting the business done as quickly as possible, since fees are not dependent on time spent, and encourages lawyers to reach a settlement, since this ensures a fourth fee.[9]

There are also restrictions upon the rights to practice and the establishment of firms. In general lawyers must be admitted to specific courts, and

[9] Skordaki, E. and Walker, D. *Regulating and Charging for Legal Services: An International Comparison* (1994) Research Study No.12 Law Society, London.

only a minority are admitted to state and higher state courts. In civil matters a '*Rechtsanwalt*' may only represent a party in the court in which he has been admitted to practise, is entitled to only one office and his office and home must be in the district of the appellate court. If a case is heard in a court in which the lawyer retained has not been admitted, then the party must also be represented by a lawyer admitted to that court, which results in two lawyers handling the same case. These territorial restrictions are known as 'localisation'. In recent years a number of firms have merged to work in trans-local partnerships across territorial boundaries. These were thought to be illegal but have been permitted by a ruling of the Federal Supreme Court provided that each partner in the 'trans-local' firm has only one place of practice.

Against this background of regulation and restriction, German lawyers enjoy monopolies and privileges which are a fading memory for English lawyers or which never existed in our jurisdiction! There are controls on who may give legal advice, and the principle of compulsory representation (*Prinzip des Anwaltszwang*) applies in many of the courts in Germany.

### The French experience

Legal expenses insurance has had a very different history in France from that in Germany and the current position is more comparable with that in the UK. As might be expected from the country which was the cradle of LEI, France has a more developed market than the UK, but growth has been relatively slow. Annual premium income is estimated to be around 3bn FF (£344m). A poll carried out in 1993 by the Louis Harris Institute indicated that 14 per cent of the French population had some form of LEI. The 1993 CEA report for France indicates that premiums for motor 'add-ons' vary from £4 to £48 per annum and household 'add-ons' from £2 to £53 per annum. The average premium for an 'all-risks' LEI policy is reported to be around £120.

The French legal system is experiencing problems which show interesting parallels with those in the UK. Andre Rials in his publication of 1993, 'L'Accès á la Justice',[10] points out that the fees of French lawyers are not fixed as in Germany. He refers to an article in the journal '50 Million de Consommateurs' of November 1991 on the unpredictability of the costs of an action which demonstrates that the fees of a lawyer for a case before the 'tribunal de grand instance' can vary from '2000 to 20,000 FF'. Traditionally the fees of the French Bar were not seen as compensation for work but 'a spontaneous testimony of the client's gratitude'.[11]

[10] Rials, *L'Acces a la Justice*.

[11] The Law Society, *Legal Expenses in the UK*.

At a time when the German Ministry of Justice was commissioning the Report on Legal Expenses Insurance referred to above, a Louis Harris Institute Poll was being carried out in France (1989) which showed that 89 per cent of French people thought that French justice was too slow, 83 per cent too complicated and 78 per cent too expensive. In the same year, the journal referred to above, '50 Millions de Consommateurs' found that 92 per cent thought French justice too slow, 56 per cent too expensive and 77 per cent too complicated. The Louis Harris Poll was commissioned by a leading Legal Expenses Insurance Company, 'L'Avenir', but is nonetheless an interesting indicator of the state of the French legal system. Its findings have an interesting echo in paragraph 1 of the Woolf Report which describes legal processes in England and Wales as 'too expensive, too slow and too complex'.

Hampered by the unpredictability of legal costs the development of LEI in France has been largely along the path of providing legal services linked to an insurance policy, at least up the point permitted by the 1987 Directive. This kind of legal expenses insurance has raised some apprehension among and opposition from lawyers, as is recognised by Cerveau and Tribondeau in their publication 'L'Assurance de Protection Juridique' (1991).[12] In a section entitled 'Lawyers and Legal Expenses Insurance' (p. 42) the authors write,

> Faced with the development of legal expenses insurance, lawyers have had certain reservations about the insurers fearing that legal expenses insurers would divert clients from their firms and limit their income through the imposition of scale costs.

In addition to experiencing problems with the cost, slowness and complexity of the legal system, the French have a less generous legal aid scheme than we have in England (see Table 2). The potential role of legal expenses insurance to facilitate access to justice for those too rich for legal aid, but too poor to litigate from their own resources has not escaped the attention of the public authorities. A report commissioned by the Prime Minister in December 1989 and entrusted to M. Bouchet, a member of the Conseil D'Etat recommended the use of insurance to facilitate access to justice, and particularly legal expenses insurance.[13] He wrote:

> Legal expenses insurance—with free choice of a lawyer paid directly by the insurers is particularly appropriate to litigation relating to property matters, particularly for building disputes and consumer goods, where the procedure is often long and expensive because of the high cost of technical expertise.

[12] Cerveau and Tribondeau, *L'Assurance de Protection Juridique.*

[13] Cerveau, B., 'Aide Juridique et Protection Juridique: L'Assurance au Secours de l'Etat. *Gazette du Palais* 13–15 September 1992.

He went on to suggest the possibility of fiscal incentives to facilitate the wider use of insurance. The proceedings of a 'Convention Justice' on 22 May 1991 under the auspices of the 'Etats generaux pour la France' included the following passage:[14]

> Parallel with legal aid, which must be restricted to the most needy, it would be desirable to promote a system of personal insurance permitting access to legal advice and assistance.

Apart from other similar expressions of encouragement, there have not been any concrete moves by the French authorities to assist the wider spread of legal expenses insurance. The greater role of LEI in France compared to the UK may be in part due to the early history of the industry in that country but more probably the result of the much less extensive legal aid scheme.

### Legal expenses insurance in the Netherlands

The legal expenses insurance industry in the Netherlands has had to compete with a very extensive legal aid scheme. Some 47 per cent of the population is eligible for legal aid (compared with some estimates for the UK of 38 per cent). It is estimated that around 9 per cent of the population have LEI. The figures in Table 2 show that per capita annual premium income is higher than in the UK. The reason for the difference is that 90 per cent of the Dutch LEI market is in 'stand-alone' policies whereas in the UK the position is reversed, with 90 per cent of the market consisting of the much cheaper 'add-ons'.

A personal family protection policy will cost around 310 NGL (£124) and will be expressed to be 'all-risks' but will have some exclusions e.g. matrimonial disputes. A motor 'add-on' costs around 85 NGL (£38). The Dutch LEI industry has developed along the lines of being providers of legal services. Most of the disputes covered by policies will be dealt with 'in-house' and the LEI companies are hopeful that the lawyers monopolies will be further reduced, enabling them to expand their legal services. The Dutch government is expected to seek to reduce the legal aid budget through reducing or holding down legal fees, rather than reducing eligibility. In the 1993 Netherlands CEA Report, it was said that Government discussions were expected on the possibilities of introducing compulsory legal expenses insurance as a substitute for or complement to legal aid. There have been no further developments in that direction, and the LEI industry is sceptical of its feasibility.

[14] Ibid.

Reasons for the slow development of LEI in the UK

In the light of an understanding of the developments of LEI in Germany and France, it is not difficult to identify the reasons for its slow and uncertain growth in the UK. There is little doubt that the establishment of a comprehensive legal aid system in the context of a general expansion of state benefits after the Second World War was a discouragement to self-help in the form of legal expenses insurance. (This adverse factor is rapidly diminishing in importance as attempts are made to keep the legal aid budget under control).

A significant contribution to the difficulties experienced by LEI companies in this country has been the uneven quality of service given by firms of solicitors and the unpredictability of costs. Over recent years the legal profession has been under a great deal of economic and political pressure to give up its traditional practices and privileges and to become commercial and competitive. Many of its monopolies and restrictive practices have been removed; advertising and 'touting' are tolerated if not positively encouraged. Whatever may have been the expected benefits of such changes, they have clearly not succeeded in increasing access to justice. They may have contributed to the problems with quality of service and costs experienced by LEI companies. It is particularly difficult to escape this conclusion when considering the very different position of the German legal profession, and its apparent contribution to the success of LEI. In the UK the LEI companies have imposed their own partial solution by using 'panels' of solicitors. In the absence of satisfactory statutory or professional regulation, they substitute agreements for rates of remuneration and exert quality control.

An additional disincentive to taking out LEI may be the traditional right of a litigant to appear personally in all courts in the land (c.f. Germany). This has been positively encouraged by the small claims procedure and tolerated, if sometimes ungraciously, at a higher level. In recent years DIY litigation has become something of a problem in the higher Courts where the procedure was not designed for the litigant in person.

Given the rather hostile environment outlined, the LEI industry in the UK has maintained a presence and achieved some limited growth by adapting to the circumstances. The result has been in the direction of providing legal services, and particularly telephone advice services, as described earlier. This development is to some extent in substitution for the services of independent lawyers. No criticism of the companies involved is intended; they are responding to market forces and providing a much needed service, particularly in newly expanding areas of need such as consumer disputes, which independent lawyers have often considered unprofitable. In different circumstances the insurers might have been able to perform their traditional role and to have left the giving of legal advice to the lawyers!

## The effect of the Woolf Report on the future of LEI

The implementation of the Woolf Report's proposals on the short term future of the LEI industry in the UK is likely to be favourable or at worst neutral. More predictable and moderate costs make insurance calculations easier and premiums more affordable. The 'fast-track' fixed costs for claims of £10,000 and under would therefore be welcomed. Most of the LEI policies currently issued in the UK are 'add-ons' to motor and household insurance policies and 90 per cent of the claims generated are below £10,000. It will be difficult for LEI in this country to make a serious contribution to access to justice without an expansion of 'stand-alone' policies and more extensive cover than is currently available. With the advent of wider coverage claims would be less concentrated in the '£10,000 or under' band. Early consideration of the possibility of extending 'fixed costs' to higher levels of claim should be a priority.

The proposal to raise the small claims limit from £1000 to £3000 is rather more controversial. While most LEI companies consider that they can absorb the additional costs, the change would marginally favour those companies who process their claims 'in-house' above those who are more 'traditional' insurers. The possibility envisaged in the Report of a raising of the limit to £5000 would have considerably more serious implications for all LEI insurers given the limited nature of their existing market.

Consideration of the long term implications of the Woolf Report on LEI require an appreciation of the very radical nature of the changes proposed. The thrust of the Report is undeniably to move the control of litigation from the legal professions to the judiciary and court staff. Complementary to those changes will be a positive encouragement to litigants to represent themselves in the small claims procedure and greater tolerance and assistance for litigants in person in the higher courts, Such a fundamental change has social and political implications which it is not the purpose of this essay to address. It is however, difficult to see, in the light of the comparisons with other jurisdictions made in this paper, that the fullest access to justice through LEI can be achieved with a legal profession, squeezed between a 'managing' judiciary and litigants in person. Delays in litigation undoubtedly cause hardship to some litigants and need to be addressed, but imposing more judicial control may not be the only or most effective method. The speed of litigation and the basis for charging fees are not unrelated. As was acknowledged in the Law Society's recent comparative study of legal fees, the German fee structure 'places emphasis on getting the business done as quickly as possible, since fees are not dependent on time spent'.

If the Woolf proposals are fully implemented and the introduction of conditional fees is also successful, the legal expenses insurance industry will be likely to follow the French pattern. Expansion will largely consist of providing services complementary to those of the legal profession. It is unlikely in those circumstances that it will ever play the role which it has in Germany, as a partner with the legal profession in providing access to 'swift and inexpensive litigation'.

## Conclusions

Lord Woolf has shown a refreshing willingness to look at other jurisdictions for inspiration in shaping his reforms. There are some particularly important lessons to be learned from this approach in the area of legal expenses insurance. Wholesale transplantation of the methods of other systems is neither practical nor desirable, but some comparison of the proposed changes with those features of other jurisdictions which foster the expansion growth of LEI is essential. The final shape of the reforms could have a significant effect on the future of the legal expenses insurance industry in this country. It may be a long time before another such opportunity presents itself to fashion our legal system in a way which will facilitate the development of a much needed source of alternative funding for access to justice.

# 23

# *Litigation and Settlement*

SIMON ROBERTS*

Over generations a particular culture of disputing has grown up in England, with parties resorting early, almost as a matter of course, to lawyers. So a single professional group has come to secure a virtual monopoly of control over dispute processes, managing them in accordance with their norms and understandings. At the same time, they have successfully projected a privileged association between their professional activities and the potent abstract conception of 'justice'. All this places formidable difficulties in the way of effective external criticism of 'the public justice system', and makes it seem normal and right for a fundamental review of the system to be conducted by a distinguished insider like Lord Woolf.

Lawyers have generally approached disputes in a distinctive way, setting out on the path towards the court at an early stage, hence conceptualising all of this part of their work as 'litigation'. They have nonetheless aimed to 'settle' disputes through bilateral exchanges with the other side ('lawyer negotiations'), typically a very long way down the avenue to trial, rather than allow them to go all the way to judgement. So a particular syndrome has developed under which 'late' settlement is achieved by using the procedural framework prescribed for bringing a dispute to trial and judgment: Litigation has come to be the chosen vehicle for settlement-directed negotiations. Thus in litigation two conceptually distinct goals have become entwined with each other—resolution through settlement and resolution through authoritative third-party determination—sharing a common procedural route. One result of this entanglement, of course, is that there is no mystery over the present growing interest in settlement and the concurrent increasing load upon the courts.

The 'duality' of litigation, this entrenched habit of approaching settlement by setting off towards the judge, has long been recognised, and been subject to extensive scholarly discussion, notably in North America.[1] But

* Professor of Law, London School of Economics and Political Science.

[1] See particularly Marc Galanter, 'World of deals: using negotiation to teach legal process' (1984) 34 Journal of Legal Education 268; Marc Galanter and Mia Cahill ' "Most Cases Settle": judicial promotion and regulation of settlements' (1994) 46 Stanford Law Review, 1339.

while aspects of this link have received critical examination, and the value of 'settlement' itself placed in question, the notion that the path to adjudication is an appropriate arena for negotiation has not been seriously challenged. Lord Woolf maintains this position. While radical changes in the management of litigation are proposed, its fundamental suitability as a vehicle for achieving settlement is taken for granted. I argue here that the failure to problematise this use of civil procedure represents a central weakness of Lord Woolf's report.

Lord Woolf's current commission takes place against a long history of uneasiness with the civil justice system. All over the common law world, civil justice arrangements had been under sustained critical examination for much of the period following the Second World War. A broad 'access to justice' movement had registered very general concern about the costs, delays and general inaccessibility of adjudication,[2] while a parallel discussion had problematised adjudication itself, pointing to the advantages of 'settlement'.[3] In the mid-1970's, a third discussion began to develop under the label of 'Alternative Dispute Resolution' and its universal acronym 'ADR'. This looked beyond the renovation of adjudication and arguments about the merit of settlement through lawyer negotiations to the possibilities of complementary and alternative forms. Under the stimulus of these conversations, civil justice became subject to sporadic official scrutiny, culminating in the protracted Civil Justice Review, concluded in 1988.

The Civil Justice Review resulted in some limited but important procedural revisions.[4] But during the 1980's more general changes became noticeable. Any attempt to categorise these changes must involve oversimplification, but in the broadest terms three things seem to have been happening at once in this jurisdiction. First, some new professional groups had begun to emerge, offering institutionalised mediatory support for party negotiations away from the surveillance of the legal profession. Second, in response to these developments, lawyers had initiated a counter-movement of recovery, becoming much more self-conscious about their negotiation procedures and re-modelling certain areas of litigation practice. Third, the courts were beginning to show increasing interest and involvement in preparations for trial, revealing a new determination to regulate the terms of access to judgment. Proponents of all these developments sought to co-opt the 'ADR' label.[5]

[2] M. Cappelletti & B. Garth (eds) *Access to Justice*, Vol.1 (1978).

[3] W. Burger, 'Agenda for 2000 AD: a need for systematic anticipation' (1976) 70 Federal Rules Decisions 83; D. Bok 'A flawed system of law and practice training' (1983) 33 *Journal of Legal Education* 530.

[4] See A. A. S. Zuckerman, 'A reform of civil procedure: rationing procedure rather than access to justice' (1995) 22 Journal of Law and Society 155.

[5] S. Roberts 'Re-Exploring the Pathways to Decision-making' (1994) 12 *Law in Context* 9.

ADR PRIOR TO WOOLF

So three distinct developments—the embryonic growth of a new cadre of professionals in dispute resolution in competition with lawyers; the responsive adjustments undertaken by the legal profession; and the growth of novel threshold procedures in front of the courts—have become identified with 'ADR'. ADR is thus a fugitive label, claimed by diverse interests rather than a coherent set of institutions and practices. Nor is it something growing up primarily outside the legal sphere. While one strand of ADR can be seen as a precarious movement of escape and resistance, ADR is centrally something which lawyers do, its scope increasingly carefully marked out in practitioners texts.[6] In England, lawyers may at first have been cautious, even uninterested, in ADR. But over the last five years they have moved rapidly to coopt it. The gracious but patronising tone of the Bar Council Report on Alternative Dispute Resolution, concluding 'that the case was made out for the courts themselves to embrace the systems of alternative dispute resolution'[7], perfectly captures the flavour of what has taken place.

The present, tentative steps towards the institutionalisation of 'mediation' and the emergence of a new professional grouping, the 'mediators', dependent as they are upon an apparently growing fashion for party negotiations remains precarious. This development is directly challenged by the counter-claim by lawyers that they are going to be mediators and that mediation is an established part of legal practice. If mediation is to develop in the context of established legal practice, it is hard to see it emerging as a narrow, facilitatory form of intervention concentrated around the support of communications between the parties. It will emerge as an 'evaluative' intervention—and lawyers are already using this term—not readily distinguishable from counselling, advisory and consultative processes. Similarly, it will only be through the survival of the 'mediator' as an autonomous professional that distinctive practice standards and institutions of quality assurance will crystallise.

The emergent 'professionals in dispute resolution' are threatened from another quarter. In a number of jurisdictions, mediators are being drawn into the public justice system, notably in the context of family disputes. This is already the case in Australia, and in England is directly proposed in the Government White Paper on divorce reform.[8] The offer of 'partnership'

[6] The arrival of ADR as part of the English lawyer's repertoire is confirmed by Sweet & Maxwell's publication of texts on the subject in successive years: A. Bevan, *Alternative Dispute Resolution* (1992); H. Brown & A. Marriott, *ADR Principles and Practice* (1993).

[7] *Report of the Committee on Alternative Dispute Resolution* (General Council of the Bar, October 1991).

[8] *Looking to the Future.*

poses a serious dilemma. Precarious independence is traded for economic security in any move closer to government and the courts. The potential consequences of such a move, in terms of co-option and regulation, are well documented.[9]

From the standpoint of the lawyer, the developments outlined above represent a dual threat to their previously unchallenged control of the conduct of dispute processes. This threat has prompted two principal reactions. First, the arrival of other professionals in dispute resolution and the entrenchment of new threshold procedures in the courts have converged, forcing lawyers to give much more attention to their practices in pursuit of settlement. The lawyer's control over client and settlement process is threatened at crucial moments, forcing reconsideration of the established habit of late-stage negotiations. One move to recover the situation lies in resort to the technical procedures of the mini-trial and early neutral evaluation, measures best understood as devices to head off consumer revolt by implicating the client in the settlement process and thus sharing control over it with him.

More generally this enforced concern with lawyer negotiations brings to the centre of attention a very important, hitherto largely uncharted area of legal practice. But while it would be going too far to say that both practitioners and academic lawyers have thought about negotiation only in the context of 'litigation', this is not far from the mark. The overriding presence of the court still informs the way in which lawyers write about negotiations. An immediately noticeable feature of this literature is its almost exclusive focus on 'strategic' issues; it is taken for granted that 'litigation' with its attendant procedures furnishes the overall processual framework. Even the most sophisticated work within this impoverished genre devotes marginal attention to larger questions about the nature and processual shape of negotiations.[10]

The second general reaction on the part of lawyers has been to present themselves in neutral advisory and consultancy roles and to attempt the co-option of 'mediation' as part of legal practice. The novel pretention to neutrality which these moves involve represents a step with far reaching and so far little considered consequences.[11]

Looking towards the court, the novel threshold procedures now in place and being advocated, represent an enormous shift when thought about in the context of existing understandings of what courts are and what they do. Reaching out as some of them do into the period before the trial, they con-

[9] R. Abel, *The Politics of Informal Justice* (1982); J. Auerbach, *Justice Without Law* (1983).

[10] See e.g. R. Fisher & W. Ury, *Getting to Yes* (1981); S. Goldberg, F. Sander & N. Rogers, *Dispute Resolution* (1992); J. Murray, A. Rau and E. Sherman, *Processes of Dispute Resolution: The Role of Lawyers* (1988); the *Negotiation Journal*, passim.

[11] S. Roberts, 'Alternative Dispute Resolution and Civil Justice: an unresolved relationship' (1993) 56 *The Modern Law Review* 452.

siderably extend the involvement of the court in a domain hitherto occupied by the parties and their professional representatives alone. So far it is uncertain how we should characterise these changes. Perhaps at present it is possible to view them simply as the beginnings of a new, relatively discrete procedural phase interposed between lawyer-negotiations and the trial, during which an institutionalised search for a settlement takes place. But the growing readiness among some members of the judiciary to themselves attempt 'mediation' takes these changes further than that, towards a fundamental transformation of the judicial role, as does the increased propensity of judges to assume a diagnostic function. If Sander's conception of the Multi-Door Courthouse, as 'a flexible and diverse panoply of dispute resolution processes', is realised in practice that transformation will have come about, forcing us to reconsider what a court 'is'.

## THE INTERIM REPORT AND ITS BACKGROUND

The disposition of the courts to intervene in the litigation process prior to trial developed far earlier in the United States than it did in this jurisdiction.[12] But in England it has now assumed a rapidly increasing momentum. In some areas this intervention has come to extend far beyond facilitating the excavation and exchange of information and ensuring that the landscape does not change too much before a court can act. It has come to involve the active sponsorship of settlement and the postponement of adjudication while that objective is pursued. This new managerialism became visible first in the Divorce County Courts, but is already recognisable across a much wider field. It is exemplified in the amendment of the Guide to Commercial Court Practice 'to ensure that legal advisers in all cases consider with their clients and the other parties concerned the possibility of attempting to resolve the particular dispute or particular issues by mediation, conciliation or otherwise.'[13] The present stance of the judiciary was confirmed in a general Practice Direction of 24 January, 1995, from the Lord Chief Justice and the Vice-Chancellor, setting out new requirements in the preparation and control of cases.[14] Announcing the Direction, the Lord Chief Justice said:

> The aim is to try and change the whole culture, the ethos, applying in the field of civil litigation. We have over the years been too ready to allow those who are litigating to dictate the pace at which cases proceed.

[12] The American history is discussed in Marc Galanter, 'The emergence of judge as mediator in civil cases' (1986) 69 *Judicature* 256.

[13] Practice Statement of 10 December 1993.

[14] (1995) 1 WLR 262.

Against this background, Lord Woolf has produced an Interim Report which shares Lord Taylor's perspective and ambitions, going on to make a diagnosis of surprising bluntness. Contemporary problems are attributed to the 'unrestrained adversarial culture of the present system' (I.4.1). Responsibility for this malaise, with its results in delay and excessive economic costs, is laid unequivocally at the door of the profession: 'The problem of cost is fuelled by the excessively combative environment in which so much litigation is now conducted' (I.3.12). With regard to delay: 'Judicial experience is that it is for the advisers' convenience that many adjournments are agreed' (I.3.31). Again: 'In the majority of cases the reasons for delay arise from failure to progress the case efficiently . . . wasting time on procedural skirmishing to wear down an opponent' (I.3.36). In the result, 'settlement too often occurs at too late a stage in the proceedings' . . . involving 'the parties in substantial additional costs' (I.3.37;38).

Overall, Lord Woolf sketches in with astonishing candour a picture of lawyers abusing the litigation process by using it as an arena for settlement strategies which suit them, but involve unnecessary costs and delays for their clients. Having identified the central problem in 'the uncontrolled nature of the litigation process' (I.3.1) under which 'the conduct, pace and extent of litigation are left almost completely to the parties' (I.3.5), the Report proposes one way to retrieve the situation: 'a fundamental shift in the responsibility for the management of civil litigation from litigants and their legal advisers to the courts' (I.4.2).

Case management is openly seen as having a dual objective:

> Its overall purpose is to encourage settlement of disputes at the earliest appropriate stage; and, where trial is unavoidable, to ensure that cases proceed as quickly as possible to a final hearing which is itself of strictly limited duration. (II.5.16)

In the jargon of post-modernism, there is something of a 'paradox' here. The judge, the archetype of authoritative third-party decision-making, is to assume responsibility for active supervision of the procedural path which, in the vast majority of cases, will lead to settlement—the antithesis of judgment. This proposal represents an enormous change in the historic role of the English judge, who has traditionally remained a potent but immobile backdrop to the preparations for trial. Even though Lord Woolf might argue that in instituting case management across the board of civil litigation he is doing no more than accelerate and rationalise a movement already in train, this radical shift in responsibility perhaps requires more careful justification than it receives in the Interim Report. If the primary objective is promoting 'settlement of disputes at the earliest appropriate stage', do we want to encourage lawyer negotiations for which the court assumes responsibility, in the immediate run up to the trial? On another level, might this new, wide-ranging involvement adversely affect the court's primary role of authoritative third-party decision-making?

The central difficulty with the Interim Report is that the procedural implications of the dual objectives of case management—trying to sponsor early settlement and getting appropriate cases speedily in front of the judge—are not fully thought through. He does not propose the establishment of a new, relatively discrete, procedural phase in which court sponsorship of 'settlement' is in temporal terms the primary objective, to be followed by a clear run through to judgment where settlement attempts fail. Rather, we are offered a 'mixed' process in which both objectives are taken forward concurrently within a single procedural framework. While a lot of thought has been given to delineating 'fast-track' and 'multi-track' routes to trial and judgment, the framework envisaged for settlement seeking remains hazy.

This problem is linked to one very conservative feature of the Interim Report. While case management can be seen as a radical prescription, Lord Woolf has perhaps been unimaginative in going along with the assumption that litigation must be the shared vehicle for lawyer negotiations and adjudication. In endorsing the position of the Heilbron/Hodge Working Party[15] Lord Woolf recognises that 'the philosophy of litigation should be primarily to encourage early settlement of disputes' (I.2.7), but at the same time in much of the language and assumptions of the Report clings to the idea that litigation is really about getting in front of the judge. The Report shrinks from the more radical solution of trying to disentangle settlement attempts from resort to adjudication.

At this point another structural weakness of the Report is highlighted. Given the central place accorded to the achievement of settlement, and the open recognition that litigation is a vehicle for this, it is puzzling that very little is said directly about lawyer negotiations. If we are to persist, as Woolf evidently concedes, in allowing civil procedure to provide the framework for lawyer negotiations, we need to theorise these representative negotiations in a way which reveals their processual shape, enabling a procedural environment to be developed appropriately around them.

## ADR IN THE WOOLF REPORT

A polite but cautious chapter on 'Alternative Approaches to Dispensing Justice' recognises that 'litigation is not the only means of achieving' . . . 'the fair, appropriate and effective resolution of civil disputes' (IV.18.1), and that it may under some circumstances be beneficial for parties 'to choose a

[15] *Civil Justice on Trial—The Case for Change* (1993).

form of dispute resolution that will enable them to work out a mutually acceptable solution rather than submit to legally correct adjudication' (IV.18.2). But Lord Woolf does not 'propose that ADR should be compulsory either as an alternative or as a preliminary to litigation' (IV.18.3) or consider the time right 'to introduce a new system of court-annexed ADR' (IV.18.30).

Instead, Woolf proposes that ADR should be brought into the frame in two ways, both building on the Practice Direction of 24 January 1995. First, responsibility for drawing ADR to the attention of disputants is laid upon lawyers in general terms: 'It is to be hoped that most lawyers will regard it as their responsibility to be able fully to acquaint their clients with the options . . .' (IV.18.32). Second, the Report proposes that judges should, as a matter of routine, discuss the use of ADR with the parties—rather than their legal representatives—at case management conferences and pre-trial reviews (IV.18.33). The outcome of this discussion would assist the judge to plan the future procedural route of the case, enabling him to take into account 'any unreasonable refusal to attempt ADR ' in doing so (IV.18.34).

While these proposals sound sensible at first sight, it is surely unrealistic to place upon lawyers the burden of publicising those parts of ADR which lie outside the scope of legal practice. We are already seeing, in the family sphere, a growing reluctance on the part of solicitors to refer disputes to voluntary sector mediators. Who is really going to risk placing valuable work in the hands of a threatening competitor? If there is a real intent to loosen the primary hold of lawyers over disputing, the pressure to do this will have to come from outside the profession—as the recent Government White Paper on the reform of divorce recognises.

So far as general judicial sponsorship of ADR is concerned, the proposed 'case management' procedures offer the obvious occasion for this. Careful use of this tool could become a significant means of bringing about earlier settlement. Woolf's strategy of insisting upon the lay parties' presence at case management conferences and the pre-trial reviews[16] and then discussing ADR directly with them, in effect co-opts the support of the client against the professional adviser. Judging by earlier experience—for example, the use of Directions Appointments in the Divorce County Courts under s.8 of the Children Act to discuss settlement—lawyers will react to this threat to their control over the client by seeking to bring forward their own settlement attempts to a time before the case management conference, ensuring discussion of 'settlement' on their terms.

Lord Woolf's way of handling ADR—as a discrete topic discussed in a separate chapter—in itself prevents him thinking about it in the most productive way. As the Report makes clear, 'ADR' is a label covering a wide

[16] 'The lay client, or someone fully authorised to act on his behalf, will be required to attend both hearings.' (II.8.8.).

variety of different interventions—from processes of third party determination (tribunals and arbitration) to specialised client-management devices developed by lawyers (the 'mini-trial') to facilitatory help with party negotiations (mediation). These interventions are potentially appropriate at very different moments in the life-cycle of disputes, and need to be related in different ways to the conventional path marked out by civil procedure. They cannot sensibly be discussed all of a piece in the way Woolf attempts.

Take the treatment of mediation. The Report states hesitantly, but accurately, that mediation 'is perhaps best described as a form of facilitated negotiation where a neutral third party guides the parties to their own solution' (IV.18.11). Two roles are identified for mediation: the first as an early stage procedure, 'preventing disputes entering the court system at all' (and here disputes between neighbours are singled out as being particularly appropriate); the second, as a means of facilitating settlement without the need for a trial at some stage 'after proceedings have been commenced' (IV.18.24–25). But all this is left very vague. While mediation has obvious applications in facilitating party negotiations, by providing a means of communication between them at a stage before a dispute has passed into the sphere of professional management, or where legal advisers refer the parties out to a mediator in preference to mandated negotiations by professional representatives, it is not clear how it might be used beyond that. The implication is that mediation might have a role as a bridging intervention between two legal teams. If there is such a role, it needs to be delineated much more precisely.

The Report also remains vague as to whether mediation is seen as an autonomous professional intervention, or as a novel facet of legal and other professional practices. At one point the idea is floated that distinguished retired professionals—solicitors, surveyors, engineers and patent agents are specified—might mediate in their retirement as 'civil magistrates' (IV.18.37). This bizarre montage, suggesting the same ignorance of the specialist nature of mediatory intervention as revealed in the earlier Beldham Report, can hardly represent Lord Woolf's considered view and deserves to be re-examined before the final report.

In the same way, the Interim Report offers enthusiastic support for 'mini-trials', which are 'presided over by a judicial figure or neutral adviser, and involve the abbreviated presentation of evidence by representatives of the parties who have authority to settle the dispute' (IV.18.9). But there is no serious effort to explore the nature of this institution, or the conditions under which it might appropriately be used. The device—otherwise known as the 'modified settlement conference' or 'executive tribunal' and closely related to 'early neutral evaluation' (ENE)—is one of a family of procedures developed in North America in the handling of complex commercial disputes. These were first used at a pre-trial stage, but have subsequently been adapted by the judiciary as tools for sponsoring settlement.

The mini-trial is essentially a predictive, forecasting device, invoked for the purposes of client management where legal teams find it difficult to bring clients round to the idea of settlement. The procedure followed is for the teams to present their respective cases to the lay parties themselves, who are assisted in evaluating their positions by a 'neutral adviser'. In this way clients gain directly their own understanding of the strengths and weaknesses of their respective cases and are provided with an indication of the likely outcome of adjudication.

Lawyers who advocate and use these devices say that one of the greatest obstacles to settlement is the stressed, impassioned corporate executive who will not listen to sensible professional advice in cases where a negotiated outcome is in the client's best interests. They claim that these procedures are often successful in bringing clients 'back to reality', making them agree to settle. It is hard to know what to make of these procedures, or of the justification for them offered by those who use them. They seem to imply a huge lack of confidence in traditional lawyering practises; and necessarily involve an unwelcome loss of control on the part of the lawyer. I have argued before[17] that these devices have their most immediate application as means of damping down unrealistic expectations which the legal teams may themselves have recklessly nourished, even created, at an earlier stage in the dispute process. They are the product of, and only made necessary in, a culture where the habit of late settlement—advantageous only to the profession—has left the client with insufficient information and advice in the early phases of a dispute. Arguably, their encouragement merely sustains existing habits which it is Lord Woolf's stated objective to get away from. More thought needs to be given to these procedures before they are endorsed in a final report.

## CONCLUSION

Woolf's recognition of, and concurrence in, a dual nature for litigation leaves the divergent objectives of settlement and judgment sadly entangled. His central project of judicial case management consequently implicates the courts in the management of negotiations as well as the achievement of adjudication. This is an inherently problematic approach which in the last resort leaves the very nature of 'the court' uncertain, as the early critics of 'informal justice' insisted. If fresh energy is to be directed towards early settlement—and that seems right—the path to judgment must be preserved uncluttered where that first objective fails.

[17] See source cited at footnote 11 above.

An alternative platform for modernisation would be to prize settlement and the pursuit of adjudication apart, providing one pathway for settlement-directed negotiation, and another leading to trial and judgment. Obviously, these two paths may sometimes have to be travelled sequentially, where settlement fails. But once disentangled, the path to settlement can be properly constructed around the natural processual phases of negotiation, and the one towards the trial around the imperatives of judgment. Once that blueprint is secure, the signposts indicating complementary and alternative forms will fall into place along the route. None of this is to deny that in a polity where adjudication is available, bilateral negotiations and third party determinations are inevitably to some extent entwined. Parties will negotiate with their own perceptions of 'what legal rules are' in mind, with an eye to what the judge might do in their case if they were subsequently to resort to adjudication. But it does not follow, as is presently the case in this culture, that negotiation must follow the route of civil process. Nor need there be active involvement of the court in sponsoring settlement. Careful thought should precede further progress along the latter route.